Information Systems Project Management

A Process Approach

Edition 2.0

Christoph Schneider
City University of Hong Kong

Mark A. Fuller
University of Massachusetts Amherst

Joseph S. Valacich
The University of Arizona

Joey F. George
Iowa State University

Founded in 2014, Prospect Press serves the academic discipline of Information Systems by publishing innovative textbooks across the curriculum including introductory, emerging, and upper level courses. Prospect Press offers reasonable prices by selling directly to students. Prospect Press provides tight relationships between authors, publisher, and adopters that many larger publishers are unable to offer. Based in Burlington, Vermont, Prospect Press distributes titles worldwide. We welcome new authors to send proposals or inquiries to Beth.Golub@ProspectPressVT.com.

Editor: Beth Lang Golub
Production Management: Rachel Paul
Cover Design: Annie Clark

eTextbook
- Edition 2.0
- ISBN: 978-1-943153-53-4
- Available from RedShelf.com and VitalSource.com

Printed Paperback
- Edition 2.0
- ISBN 978-1-943153-54-1
- Available from RedShelf.com

For more information, visit
http://prospectpressvt.com/titles/schneider-is-project-management/

Contents

Preface

Approach

Projects involving information systems (IS) are prevalent in virtually all organizations and are frequently a key determinant of an organization's competitiveness. The ability to manage these projects is thus a critical skill that can help drive organizational success. Projects in today's business environment are typically addressed by teams of skilled personnel whose activities are coordinated by a project manager. Further, these projects may involve significant global components, either in terms of the resultant system's intended users or in terms of the team members engaged in accomplishing the project itself.

Based on decades of combined teaching experience plus extensive experience in the high-technology and startup sectors, we seek to provide the knowledge and skills necessary to successfully manage information systems projects in the modern organization. This book takes an active learning approach to project management, with a focus on the process of project management rather than simply on a series of topical discussions about the components of project management. It operates on the assumption that project management in the modern organization is a complex, team-based process, which relies on systems that support both project management and collaboration activities. Further, this book assumes that, in many cases, project teams may be operating in a virtual context, where team members are at different locations—sometimes across the world. Our approach to project management thus tries to encompass the new working arrangements in our technology-driven global economy. Finally, the content of this book is firmly grounded on the *Project Management Body of Knowledge* (*PMBOK*; 6th edition), as provided by the Project Management Institute, which provides training and certifications to project managers worldwide. Our approach to learning project management thus emphasizes five key focal areas: process focus, team focus, technology focus, global focus, and *PMBOK* focus.

What's New in This Edition

Since our first edition was released more than a decade ago, the nature of projects, project management approaches, and technologies have all evolved considerably. In this extensively revised edition, we have taken care to reflect these changes, to facilitate teaching up-to-date project management skills and techniques. In particular, we have updated all content to be aligned with the sixth (and most recent) edition of *PMBOK*. Further, given that projects increasingly use agile approaches, we have included section appendices discussing approaches and techniques for managing projects in agile environments. Finally, we have updated the content to reflect the ever-evolving technological environment and its impact on project management.

Process Focus

Unlike the more common approach to learning project management that exposes you to a variety of project management subtopics, this book employs a *learning-by-doing* approach that actively engages you in *managing a real information systems project* as part of the class. After presenting foundational material in the first four chapters, we take you step-by-step through the stages of project management, with assignments corresponding to deliverables that typically would be required in an organization as employees tackle real information systems projects. While still covering the essential information associated with project management, this book also helps you actively learn project management by applying typical project management activities—such as the development of project charters, work breakdown structures, and project schedules—to an ongoing class project. This contextual treatment of information systems project management topics not only solidifies your understanding of various project management techniques but also creates an immediate understanding of why these techniques are essential components of effective project management.

Team Focus

Project management is largely a team sport, not an individual one. This book is unique in its focus on team-based project management. Although an individual working alone can gain some knowledge, the reality is that few organizational projects are done this way; thus knowledge acquired without consideration of the team is largely incomplete. This book covers the types of teams in organizations, the types of tasks those teams work on, the advantages gained by working in teams, and the problems (and solutions) that teams will encounter. Topics addressed include group processes, leadership, communication, team conflict, cross-cultural issues, and more.

Technology Focus

In order to successfully manage projects in today's complex business environments, project teams need to employ technologies such as project management software, group support technology, and knowledge management systems that capture project knowledge. The advantages of project management software are discussed, and you will be given hands-on experience using common project management software. You will then use this same project management software to support your course project. Group support technologies include the various communication and planning tools that project teams can use. In addition to discussing such tools throughout the text, we pay close attention to this topic in Chapter 4, with a focus on managing project communications. These collaborative technologies enable teams to communicate effectively across distance and time, reduce the losses associated with working in teams, and enhance decision-making. Likewise, knowledge management systems help project teams capture and recall knowledge accumulated from previous project teams and integrate such knowledge with current project experiences. Finally, few technological advances have changed society as much as mobile technologies and big data gathered from a variety of mobile devices, sensors, and users' online behaviors. More and more IS projects are now related to mobile technologies and big data, and both mobile devices and big data can help streamline project management processes.

Global Focus

This book illustrates the changing nature of projects in the modern world, particularly as it relates to global project management. Many of the chapters in this book—for example, those on teams, project communication, and outsourcing—focus on the changing face of project teams. Organizations involved in IS projects may span global boundaries either in the focus of the project itself or in the composition of its teams. Virtual teamwork, as an example, is commonplace as organizations put together resources to deliver IS projects. Outsourcing beyond one's home country is also commonplace. This book attempts to address these issues throughout its various chapters.

In addition to the inherent difficulties of working in teams, workers in today's organizations may no longer work in the same office, building, or even country as other project team members. The global virtual project team is a common organizational entity, and managing teams in this type of environment is even more complex. We address the unique advantages of virtual teams, the difficulties they encounter, and solutions to those difficulties. Project management is global in another sense as well: we live in a global economy, and outputs created by project teams may be intended for a global audience. As a result, project teams need to be sensitive to cultural differences when developing information systems applications.

Project Management Body of Knowledge Focus

One critical purpose of this textbook is to provide you with a high level of competency in all key areas of project management. As noted previously, the Project Management Institute (PMI)—a professional organization focused on meeting the needs of project managers—has encapsulated the key knowledge areas of project management into its *Project Management Body of Knowledge* (*PMBOK*). This text prepares you to master these knowledge areas and provides information consistent with PMI's professional project management certification exam. To further facilitate your use of this book as a study guide, the end of each chapter provides a table identifying the elements of *PMBOK* that each chapter has covered. By the conclusion of the textbook, you will have been exposed in detail to all the knowledge areas identified by *PMBOK* (6th edition). In addition to our alignment with *PMBOK*, we also provide other practical guidance gleaned from practicing project managers. Included in this book you'll find elements such as "Tips from the Pros," "Ethical Dilemmas," "Common Problems," and "Global Implications." These elements contain useful information that can be applied to future projects.

Audience

While *project management* is a general term and can be applied in many fields, this text is written specifically to focus on information systems projects. This textbook is targeted primarily at upper-division undergraduate students pursuing a management information systems or related degree. The treatment of project management material is also detailed enough for this book to be useful for graduate courses as well. Finally, this text, because of its close ties to *PMBOK*, can also serve as a useful study guide in preparation for PMI certification.

Common Chapter Elements

Each chapter has learning objectives and an opening case. Following this, an introduction provides an overview of what the current chapter covers. The main chapter contents are then presented, followed by an illustration of which *PMBOK* topics were covered, a running case illustrating the conversations and activities a typical project team might have during the relevant project management phase, a chapter summary, key terms, review questions, chapter exercises, an ongoing real business case (focused on the Sedona Management Group and the Seattle Seahawks) appropriate to the relevant chapter, and an ongoing information systems project that allows student teams to reinforce newly acquired project management techniques. This latter project is intended to give you hands-on experience managing all phases of the project life cycle.

Key Features

In addition to the standard elements, each chapter includes several pedagogical elements. The composition of each element reflects the current chapter content and helps you prepare for the intricacies of managing information systems projects.

Tips from the Pros

"Tips from the Pros" contain tips or information used by real project managers that describe what they do to make their projects successful and the pitfalls that experience has taught them to avoid.

Ethical Dilemmas

"Ethical Dilemmas" discuss some of the ethical questions faced by project managers or members of project teams as they try to achieve their goals.

Common Problems

"Common Problems" discuss barriers that project team members will frequently face and how to overcome them.

Global Implications

"Global Implications" address how project characteristics and management techniques vary as project teams cope with global outsourcing, offshoring, and international project teams.

Supplements

The following support materials are available at the Instructor Resources page at http://www.prospectpressvt.com/titles/fuller-project-management/instructor-resources:

- *Instructor's Manual.* The Instructor's Manual features not only answers to review, discussion, and case study questions, but also lecture outlines, teaching objectives, key terms, and teaching suggestions.
- *Test Item File.* The Test Item File is a collection of true-false, multiple-choice, and short essay questions.
- *PowerPoint Slides.* These slides build on key concepts in the text.

Organization

This book is divided into three major sections. Part I, "Project Management Foundations," includes chapters introducing the discipline of project management, the project life cycle, the management of project teams, and, finally, how to manage project communications with all project stakeholders. Part II, "Starting, Organizing, and Preparing the Project," includes chapters on managing various critical project activities, such as project scope, activity scheduling, resource assignment and project duration implications, project costs, project quality, project risk, and project procurement. Part III, "Executing, Controlling, and Ending the Project," includes chapters on managing project execution, as well as on managing project control and closure processes.

Table 2.2 Mapping Project Management Processes to Process Groups

	Process Groups				
	Initiating	Planning	Executing	Monitoring and Controlling	Closing
Project Integration Management	Develop Project Charter	Develop Project Management Plan	Direct and Manage Project Work Manage Project Knowledge	Monitor and Control Project Work Perform Integrated Change Control	Close Project or Phase
Project Scope Management		Plan Scope Management Collect Requirements Define Scope Create WBS		Validate Scope Control Scope	
Project Schedule Management		Plan Schedule Management Define Activities Sequence Activities Estimate Activity Durations Develop Schedule		Control Schedule	
Project Cost Management		Plan Cost Management Estimate Costs Determine Budget		Control Costs	
Project Quality Management		Plan Quality Management	Manage Quality	Control Quality	
Project Resource Management		Plan Resource Management Estimate Activity Resources	Acquire Resources Develop Team Manage Team	Control Resources	
Project Communications Management		Plan Communications Management	Manage Communications	Monitor Communications	
Project Risk Management		Plan Risk Management Identify Risks Perform Qualitative Risk Analysis Perform Quantitative Risk Analysis Plan Risk Responses	Implement Risk Responses	Monitor Risks	
Project Procurement Management		Plan Procurement Management	Conduct Procurements	Control Procurements	
Project Stakeholder Management	Identify Stakeholders	Plan Stakeholder Engagement	Manage Stakeholder Engagement	Monitor Stakeholder Engagement	

the organization include intangible aspects, such as organizational culture and organizational structure, but also more tangible aspects, such as resources, facilities, and infrastructure. External factors having an influence of a project outcome include the competitive situation, customer requirements, cultural norms, legal restrictions, and so on. As all these factors can have an impact on project outcomes, they should be used as inputs in various processes. In the following we will discuss different internal and external environmental factors.

Organizational Culture

Organizations develop their own unique cultures over time. An organization's culture reflects what those who work there hold to be most important. Some organizations are known for their aggressive cultures, such as brokerage firms and financial institutions that handle mergers and acquisitions. Other organizations have cultures that are relaxed, where rules are not as important as the quality of the final product. Some software development firms, especially during the internet boom, were known for being relatively relaxed. Still other organizations are like families, and many other types of cultures have emerged at different organizations. It is also important to note that cultures are not static—they change over time. For instance, the Ford Motor Company is different now than it was when it was founded more than a hundred years ago.

An organization's culture in its current manifestation often influences the projects it undertakes. For example, a software development project that originated in a brokerage firm in 1997 would be more likely to resemble the aggressive characteristics of a brokerage firm than to take on the relaxed characteristics of an internet company at the height of the internet boom.

The organizational culture also influences its governance. In other words, it influences aspects such as the rules, processes, and procedures, but also the way objectives are specified and achieved, the risk tolerance, and how the organization optimizes performance.

The Role of Key Decision Makers

Typically, projects are overseen by a steering committee, which can include senior managers who represent users and general management, as well as the director of the IT function or the CIO. This committee monitors the project's performance and ensures that the project deliverables are according to standards. Importantly, business managers play an important role as decision makers or members of the steering committee, as they can be crucial in driving the project toward success, such as by mobilizing support or resources. In IS projects that help generate revenue, support from business mangers is typically easy to obtain; in contrast, IS projects that are seen as cost centers often face difficulties in garnering the support of key business managers.

Organizational Structure

If you have taken a course on management or organizational design, or if you have worked for more than one company, you know that organizational structures can differ dramatically from one company to another. Organizational structure can also affect projects and how they are managed. One key area of a project that structure affects is the availability and allocation of resources.

Organizations may or may not be project based. Those that are not project based typically lack the management systems necessary for efficient and effective project management. Organizations that are project based typically are either those that get most of their revenue from projects, such as IT consulting firms, or those that have adopted a philosophy of management by projects. Project-based organizations have systems in place to support project management. There are many ways to categorize organizational structures. The Project Management Institute (2017) categorizes them as spanning a spectrum that ranges from functional to matrix to project-oriented.

Functional organization structure
A hierarchical organizational structure, sometimes thought of as resembling a pyramid, with top management at the fulcrum, direct workers at the bottom, and middle managers in between.

A **functional organization structure** is used in traditional hierarchical organizations; it is sometimes thought of as resembling a pyramid, with top management at the fulcrum, direct workers at the bottom, and middle managers in between (see Figure 2.9). Each employee has one clearly designated supervisor, and employees are grouped by specialization into accounting, marketing, information systems, manufacturing, and other functional groups. In such organizations, the scope of a project is limited to functional boundaries. People within different functional areas work separately on different parts of a project. For example, marketing determines what will sell, engineering designs the product based on what they learned from marketing, and engineering passes its specifications on to manufacturing, which separately determines how to build the product. Many times, engineering has to make product changes that marketing doesn't like, simply because they cannot develop a design that satisfies all of marketing's desires, and manufacturing has to make changes engineering doesn't like in order to build a working product based on the manufacturing technologies in place. This process is often called the "over the wall" problem—one group takes their part of the project and throws it "over the wall" to the next group. The result is often more work for everybody involved and a product that is less than what it could have been.

Project-oriented organization structure
A type of organization structure where people from different functional backgrounds work with each other throughout the lifetime of the project.

At the other extreme of the organizational structure spectrum is the **project-oriented organization structure** (see Figure 2.10). The project scope and team members cross organizational boundaries, with people from different functional backgrounds working with each other throughout the project's lifetime. Team members are all part of the same organizational unit instead of belonging to different functional areas. The organizational structure is designed to provide the necessary resources for project work. Project managers have the authority and independence necessary to carry the project through to successful completion because they report directly to the organization's chief executive.

Matrix organization structure
A type of organization structure that typically crosses functional design (on one axis) with some other design characteristic (on the other axis).

In the middle of the spectrum of organizational structures are **matrix organization structures**. Matrix organizations are so named because they typically cross functional design (on one axis) with some other design characteristic (on the other axis)—in this case, project management. There are several ways to organize matrix organizations. Figure 2.11 shows a strong matrix structure. A strong matrix has many of the characteristics of a project-oriented organization, with full-time project managers who have authority and full-time project administrative staff. Project staff report to project managers as well as to the heads of their functional areas. A weak matrix structure would more closely resemble a functional organization, with project managers acting more as coordinators than as independent managers.

Table 2.3 compares the features of functional, matrix, and project-oriented organizational structures. The table features three types of matrix designs: weak, balanced, and strong. It shows how different aspects of project management differ from one organizational structure to the next. It is especially revealing to look at how differences in organizational structure affect the project manager's role.

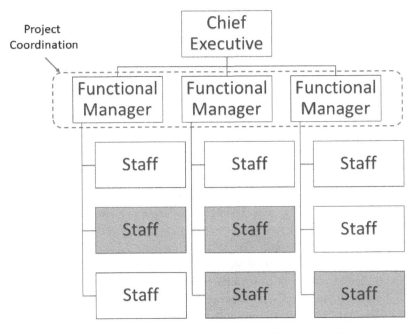

(Shaded boxes represent staff engaged in project activities)

Figure 2.9 A functional organization structure

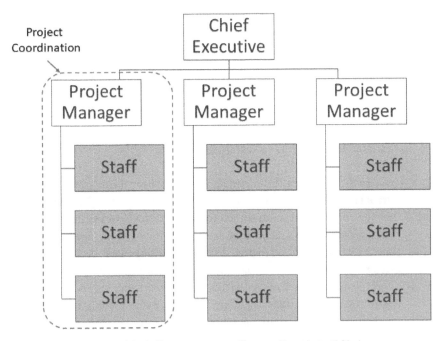

(Shaded boxes represent staff engaged in project activities)

Figure 2.10 A project-oriented organization structure

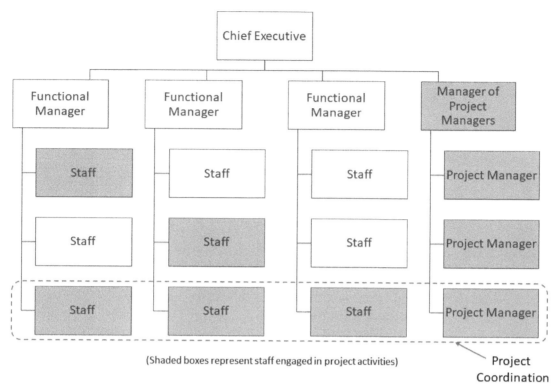

Figure 2.11 A strong matrix organization structure

Table 2.3 Comparing the Influences of Organizational Structure on Projects

| | Functional | Matrix | | | Project-Oriented |
		Weak	Balanced	Strong	
Project Manager's Authority	Little or none	Limited	Low to moderate	Moderate to high	High to almost total
Resource Availability	Little or none	Limited	Low to moderate	Moderate to high	High to almost total
Who Controls the Budget	Functional manager	Functional manager	Mixed	Project manager	Project manager
Project Manager's Role	Part-time	Part-time	Full-time	Full-time	Full-time
Project Management Administrative Staff	Part-time	Part-time	Part-time	Full-time	Full-time

Social, Economic, and Environmental Influences

Just as a project exists within a wider organizational context, it also exists within a context that extends beyond the organization. Elements of this still broader extraorganizational context can and will affect any given individual project. It has become something of a cliché, but business is increasingly dynamic and global, and these aspects of the larger business environment also affect individual projects. Although there are many different ways to think about the larger environment in which projects exist, here we will look at four areas of social, economic, and environmental influences:

1. Standards and regulations
2. Internationalization
3. Culture
4. Social-economic-environmental sustainability

These topics are important for the project managers' understanding of how trends in the business world may affect their projects.

Standards and Regulations

Standard
A document approved by a recognized body that provides, for common and repeated use, rules, guidelines, or characteristics for products, processes, or services with which compliance is not mandatory.

Regulation
A document that specifies product, process, or service characteristics, including the applicable administrative provisions, with which compliance is mandatory.

The International Organization for Standardization defines a **standard** as a "document approved by a recognized body, that provides, for common and repeated use, rules, guidelines, or characteristics for products, processes, or services with which compliance is not mandatory" (ISO, 1994). Similarly, a **regulation** is defined as a "document, which lays down product, process, or service characteristics, including the applicable administrative provisions, with which compliance is mandatory" (ISO, 1994). Standards may eventually become de facto regulations driven by market pressures or by habit. Compliance with standards and regulations can be mandated at different levels. The project manager may determine which standards need to be applied; the organization may have certain expectations for its projects or their products; the government, at whatever jurisdictional level, may impose regulations in the name of safety or other public goods.

Standards and regulations can have substantial impacts on a project. They may dictate the inclusion of additional design elements in a product, which increases project time and effort, or they may dictate the inclusion of additional processes in the project itself, such as safety testing. Sometimes these impacts are well known, sometimes not. Where the potential impacts are not well understood, the effects of standards and regulations need to be considered under project risk management. A regulatory law enacted in the United States in 2002 is the Sarbanes-Oxley Act (sometimes called SOX). The act was passed in the wake of several high-profile corporate fraud cases and bankruptcies, such as Enron and MCI. The focus of the act is to put more overt responsibility on executives to be aware of their companies' true financial situation. The outcomes of certain organizational projects, especially large multiyear projects, have impacts on corporate profitability and finances, so an accurate assessment of project status and the costs of completing them becomes doubly important under Sarbanes-Oxley reporting requirements.

Internationalization

Work in many industries today is becoming more and more global, with project and team members spread across many countries and time zones. This means that entire projects are global, too. For example, in software development, it is increasingly common for many project members to be located in South or Southeast Asia, where skill levels are high but pay is relatively low. Managers and team members for global projects need to take into account the effects of time zone differences, which affect the logistics of teleconferencing, as well as keep track of such things as national and regional holidays and political differences.

Cultural Influences

Where projects are global, cultural issues obviously exist that potentially can affect the project. However, even when a project exists entirely within national boundaries, culture can be an issue. In a heterogeneous population, such as exists in Europe or in the United States, project members may have very different backgrounds and views in such areas as politics, economics, ethnic origins, demographics, and religion. Project managers need to try to understand how these differences might affect project members and hence the project.

Social-Economic-Environmental Sustainability

All projects are planned and implemented within a larger social, economic, and environmental context that extends beyond the project, the organization, and even the nation where the project work was completed. As is the case with many human endeavors, projects have intended and unintended consequences. While one would hope that the intended consequences are all positive, the unintended consequences may be both positive and negative. Organizations are increasingly accountable for the project's results and its effects long after it has been completed, whether those effects were intended or not. Although it is, by definition, impossible to identify unintended consequences beforehand, thinking in terms of the project's larger social, economic, and environmental context may help alleviate some of the worst possible outcomes. Yet issues with social, economic, and environmental sustainability are increasingly considered when developing new projects. For example, organizations from Apple to Google are investing heavily in "green" data centers, trying to ensure that our growing data processing needs are fueled by renewable energy sources and trying to reduce the impact on the environment.

Organizational Process Assets

Organizational process assets
The processes, procedures, and knowledge bases relevant to the completion of a project.

Few projects exist in isolation, and most organizations have a portfolio of past, current, and future projects. **Organizational process assets** are the processes, procedures, and knowledge bases relevant to the completion of a project. Assets such as processes, guidelines, and templates guide how project processes are performed. Likewise, knowledge bases containing lessons learned and other historical information can inform current and future projects and are updated as the current project progresses. Content management systems and enterprise portals such as Microsoft SharePoint (see Figure 2.12), as well as project management software such as Easy Redmine 2018, enable storing both structured and unstructured data and are accessible to the relevant organizational members. In contrast to project management information systems used for a particular project, the focus of these knowledge bases is on long-term storage of historical information and on ease of retrieval for future projects. These knowledge bases are of particular importance, as when planning for future projects, it is important to know both what worked well and what did not. As a consequence, you will see different organizational process assets as inputs or outputs of various processes.

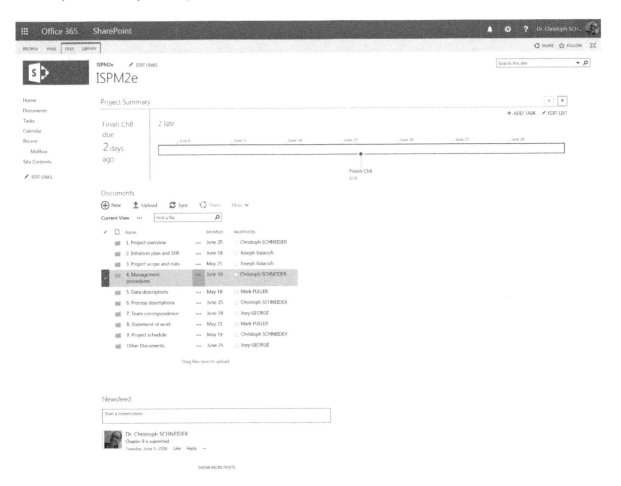

Figure 2.12 The Microsoft Office 365 SharePoint Enterprise Portal

Organizational Systems

In addition to the enterprise environmental factors and organizational process assets, a project manager needs to understand management elements and governance frameworks, so as to be able to obtain resources or influence project-related outcomes. In other words, the project manager needs to understand responsibilities, authorities, and chains of command within the organization, as well as the relevant processes and procedures to be followed. Another aspect having an influence on project outcomes is the project management office.

Project Management Office

Project management office (PMO)
An organizational unit created to centralize and coordinate the projects within an organization.

A **project management office (PMO)** is an organizational unit created to centralize and coordinate the projects within an organization. A project management office oversees the management of projects, programs, or both. Not all organizations have project management offices, but in larger organizations there are dedicated teams for managing a portfolio of projects. Matrix organizations often have a project management office, and organizations with project-oriented organizational structures will almost always have one. What a project management office does is not standard across organizations. In some organizations, the project management office may provide support for projects, whereas in others, the office may actually be responsible for all project results. In such cases, the project management office will delegate authority to the project manager and provide him or her with administrative support. Between these two extremes are many different sets of responsibilities and functions for the project management office. The existence of a project management office and its organizational role can have an impact on individual projects in a given organization.

Tips from the Pros: How to Avoid Wasting Time on Projects

Time is a crucial resource in project management, and it always seems to be in short supply. Many IS projects are late, despite recent advances in project management techniques and in software designed to improve the overall project management process; according to the Standish Group, in 2013, of those projects that were not completed on time, the average time overrun was over 100 percent. Here is a list of nine things known for wasting project time, along with suggestions from several project managers on how to deal with them:

1. *Rushing in.* There has always been a temptation in IS projects to skip analysis and design and go right to coding. If business requirements have not been adequately addressed upfront, however, there will be problems later, especially in testing, when it's discovered that business needs were not well defined. Good project managers resist this temptation, as following a basic rule of thumb, every hour of planning saves three hours of work.

2. *The life cycle rut.* Managers shouldn't use a life cycle just because it is familiar. As some traditional life cycles that are designed to yield fewer defects actually draw out project time, project managers should look for alternative life cycles that reduce defects but do not slow projects down.

3. *Poor communication.* Lack of communication is often the cause of project slowdowns. Video or telephone bridges that function like a conference call but are open all day can help maintain a communication channel and allow project members to find alternative solutions and keep the project going in case problems are encountered.

4. *Excessive research.* Project team members can waste weeks of time combing through industry white papers on products, and much of what they find is more hype than reality. Often, calling customer references to ask what their experiences have been with a product might provide quicker (and sometimes more reliable) background information.

5. *Untamed email.* Sometimes important email can get lost among spam and all the other email people receive. Project standards, such as an acronym for each project that is put in every email subject line, makes it easier to identify and file project-related email. Likewise, placing action items in the first couple of lines of an email allows them to be displayed in the email preview page.

6. *Indecision.* Business stakeholders waste project time when they cannot decide on issues such as technical standards that are key to the project. As a consequence, project managers should be assertive with stakeholders, explaining how their lack of a decision is affecting the project.

7. *Obsessing.* IT workers sometimes get so focused on a problem they lose track of time. Project rules dictating that if someone is stuck on a problem for a specified amount of time, the problem gets escalated and a buddy is assigned to help with it can help address this problem.

8. *Between-meeting paralysis.* If review meetings are held weekly, a problem that pops up just after a meeting may go a week without resolution, so short daily meetings should be held to make sure problems are addressed as soon as they are discovered. (Though meetings themselves can often be a huge time sink).

9. *Embellishment.* Many IT developers add features and embellish systems if they think they have the time to do so; thus project managers should use release criteria that define what "done" means so that developers know when to stop.

Based on: Haden (2017); Mearian (2004); Standish Group (2014).

Techniques and Technology to Support the Project Life Cycle

A project manager can utilize various techniques for documenting and visualizing project plans. Typically, a project manager can use graphical or textual reports, but graphical reports are often preferred due to their visual appeal and ease of understanding. The most commonly used are Gantt charts and network diagrams (recall that Gantt charts are now often referred to simply as bar charts). While both of these will be covered in greater detail later in the book, we will introduce them here. Gantt charts show when a task should begin and when it should end; as they are not intended to indicate how tasks must be ordered (precedence), they are often more useful for depicting relatively simple projects or subparts of a larger project, for showing the activities of a single worker, or for monitoring the progress of activities compared to the scheduled completion dates (see Figure 2.13). In modern project management software such as Microsoft Project, Gantt charts commonly also depict dependencies (see Figure 2.14a). In contrast, network diagrams illustrate how activities can be ordered by connecting a task to its predecessor and successor tasks (see Figure 2.14b). Sometimes a network diagram is preferable; other times a Gantt chart more clearly shows certain aspects of a project. The key differences between these two representations are as follows:

- A Gantt chart depicts the duration of tasks, whereas a network diagram depicts the sequence dependencies between tasks.

- A Gantt chart depicts the time overlap of tasks, whereas a network diagram does not show time overlap but does show which tasks can be done in parallel.

- Some forms of Gantt charts can depict the amount of time an activity can be delayed without negatively affecting the overall project schedule (slack time). A network diagram shows this by the data contained within activity rectangles.

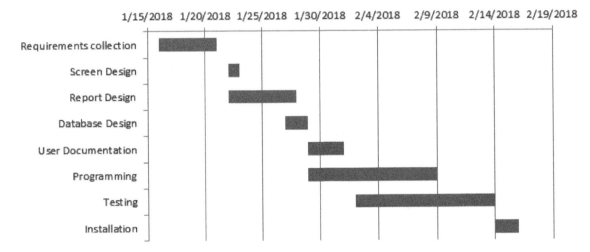

Figure 2.13   Gantt chart

(a)

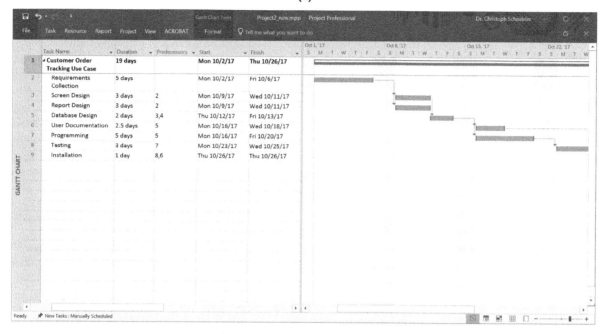

(b)

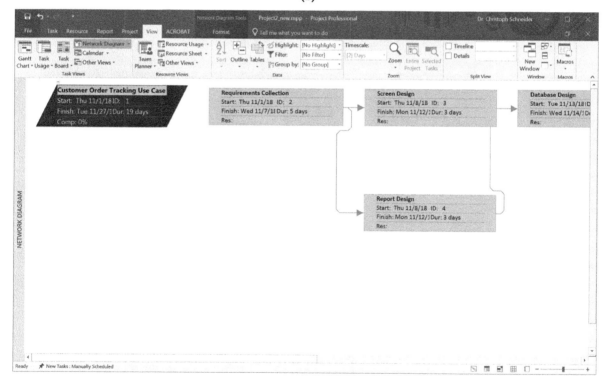

Figure 2.14 (a) Gantt chart and (b) network diagram in Microsoft Project 2016

Project managers also use textual reports that depict resource utilization by tasks, complexity of the project, and cost distributions to control activities. For example, Figure 2.15 shows a screen from Microsoft Project 2016 that summarizes all project activities, their durations in weeks, and their scheduled starting and ending dates.

Using project management software, the project manager can continuously monitor the status of all ongoing project activities. If any activity will be completed early or late, the project manager will update the duration of the activity. The software will then automatically adjust the scheduled start and finish times of all subsequent tasks. These changes will also be reflected in the updated Gantt chart or network diagram views presented by the software. In this way, the project manager can easily determine how the effects of changes in task duration will impact the overall completion date of a project. Likewise, the project manager can examine how adding or reducing resources for an activity might influence the duration of a task or the completion date of the project.

Network Diagrams and Project Life Cycles

Project scheduling and management is concerned with controlling time, costs, and resources. While the concepts of resources, critical path analysis, and slack will be covered in greater detail later in this text, we briefly introduce these concepts at this time to illustrate how information systems projects are managed, and how we get estimates regarding project durations. Resources are any person, group of people, piece of equipment, hardware, software, or material used in carrying out an activity. Network diagramming is a scheduling technique used for controlling resources. A network diagram is one of the most widely used and best-known scheduling methods. A major strength of network diagramming is its ability to show how changes to completion times impact the overall schedule. Because of this, it is sometimes used to manage IS projects, where

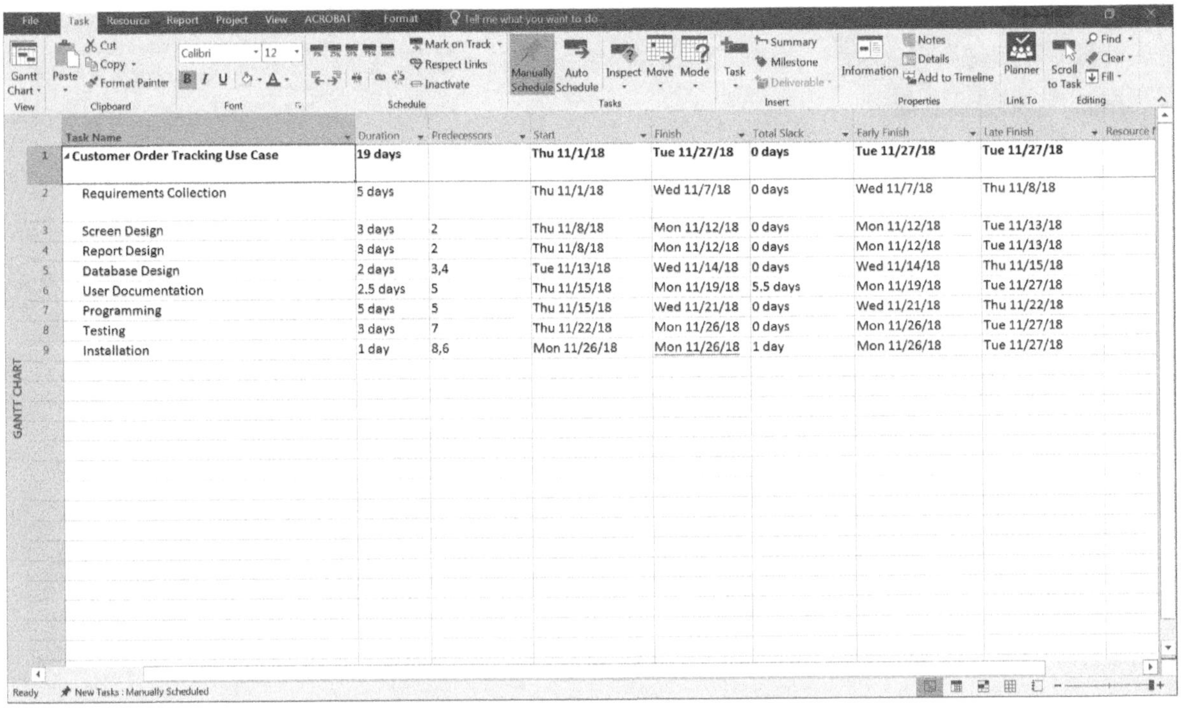

Task Name	Duration	Predecessors	Start	Finish	Total Slack	Early Finish	Late Finish	Resource
1 ◢ Customer Order Tracking Use Case	19 days		Thu 11/1/18	Tue 11/27/18	0 days	Tue 11/27/18	Tue 11/27/18	
2 Requirements Collection	5 days		Thu 11/1/18	Wed 11/7/18	0 days	Wed 11/7/18	Thu 11/8/18	
3 Screen Design	3 days	2	Thu 11/8/18	Mon 11/12/18	0 days	Mon 11/12/18	Tue 11/13/18	
4 Report Design	3 days	2	Thu 11/8/18	Mon 11/12/18	0 days	Mon 11/12/18	Tue 11/13/18	
5 Database Design	2 days	3,4	Tue 11/13/18	Wed 11/14/18	0 days	Wed 11/14/18	Thu 11/15/18	
6 User Documentation	2.5 days	5	Thu 11/15/18	Mon 11/19/18	5.5 days	Mon 11/19/18	Tue 11/27/18	
7 Programming	5 days	5	Thu 11/15/18	Wed 11/21/18	0 days	Wed 11/21/18	Thu 11/22/18	
8 Testing	3 days	7	Thu 11/22/18	Mon 11/26/18	0 days	Mon 11/26/18	Tue 11/27/18	
9 Installation	1 day	8,6	Mon 11/26/18	Mon 11/26/18	1 day	Mon 11/26/18	Tue 11/27/18	

Figure 2.15 A screen from Microsoft Project 2016 summarizing all project activities, their durations in weeks, and their scheduled starting and ending dates

variability in the duration of activities is the norm. A downside of using network diagrams is the added (sometimes unnecessary) work involved, so many practitioners prefer using Gantt charts. You would use a network diagram when tasks

- are well-defined and have a clear beginning and endpoint
- can be worked on independently of other tasks
- are ordered

To better understand project resource scheduling (again, covered more thoroughly in Chapter 7), we also need to briefly introduce the concept of a critical path. To illustrate this concept, assume that you have been assigned to work on a small project defining the major steps for a key feature within a larger system. We will call this the *Key Feature Project*. For this particular project, you identify seven major activities, and from your experience with similar projects, you make time estimates and order these activities as follows:

Activity	Time Estimate (In Days)	Preceding Activity
1. Collect Requirements	1	—
2. Design Screens	2	1
3. Design Database	2	1
4. Coding	3	2, 3
5. Documentation	2	4
6. Testing	3	4
7. Integration	1	5, 6

With this information, you are now able to draw a network diagram. Recall that network diagrams are composed of circles or rectangles (nodes) representing activities and connecting arrows showing required workflows (also referred to precedence diagramming method, see Chapter 6), as illustrated in Figure 2.16. The critical path of a network diagram is the sequence of connected activities that needs the longest overall time to complete. In other words, this is the shortest amount of time in which the project can be finished. Any activity that is part of this sequence is referred to as being "on" the **critical path**. If an activity that is on the on the critical path is delayed, the entire project will be delayed. Any node that is not on the critical path contains **slack time**—that is, it can be delayed (for some amount of time) without risking a delay in completing the project (addressed more thoroughly in Chapter 7). Thus nodes not on the critical path allow some flexibility in scheduling.

Critical path
The longest path through a network diagram illustrating the shortest amount of time in which a project can be completed.

Slack time
The amount of time that an activity can be delayed without delaying the project.

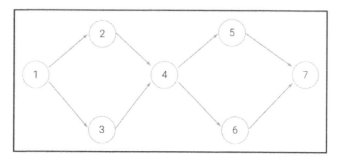

Figure 2.16   A network diagram for the Key Feature Project showing activities (represented by circles) and sequences of those activities (represented by arrows)

To determine the critical path and the expected completion time for the Key Feature Project, you must calculate the earliest and latest expected completion time for each activity by doing a forward pass through the network diagram (see Figure 2.17). First, you must first calculate the earliest expected completion time (T_E) for each activity; to do this, you have to add an activity's estimated time (ET) to the T_E of the preceding activity, working from the first activity toward the last. For example, to get T_E for Activity 2, take the T_E for Activity 1, which is 1 day (the T_E of the first activity equals its expected completion time), and add the ET for Activity 2, which is 2 days, giving a T_E of 3 days for Activity 2. In this case, TE for Activity 7 is equal to 10 days. If an activity is preceded by two or more activities, the highest T_E of the preceding activities is used to determine the following activity's expected completion time. In the Key Feature Project, Activity 7 is preceded by Activities 5 and 6; as the highest T_E of these activities is 9 days, the T_E for Activity 7 is 9 + 1 days, or 10 days. The T_E of the last activity of the project equals the amount of time the project should take to complete. However, note that we're using estimated times for each activity, so the overall projected completion time is also only an estimate, and the overall project may require more or less time. Figure 2.18 shows the network diagram for the Key Feature Project in Microsoft Project. As you can see, the critical path and activities on the critical path are highlighted in red.

The latest expected completion time (T_L) represents the latest time at which an activity must have been completed without having a negative effect on the project's completion time. To determine each activity's T_L, you will need to do a backward pass through the network diagram. The last activity's T_L equals its T_E, which represents the project's expected completion time. For the Key Feature Project, the T_E of Activity 7, and thus its T_L, is 10 days. Next, work from right to left toward Activity 1 and subtract the expected time for each activity. For example, this would give you a total T_L of 9 days for both Activities 5 and 6, because you subtract the ET of Activity 7, or 1 day, from its T_L of 10. If there is a difference between the latest and earliest expected completion times ($T_L - T_E$) of an activity, this represents the activity's slack time. The slack time calculations for all activities of the Key Feature Project are as follows:

Activity	T_E	T_L	Slack: $T_L - T_E$	On Critical Path?
1	1	1	0	Yes
2	3	3	0	Yes
3	3	3	0	Yes
4	6	6	0	Yes
5	8	9	1	No
6	9	9	0	Yes
7	10	10	0	Yes

As you can see, any activity that has a slack time of zero is on the critical path. For the Key Feature Project, all activities are on the critical path, except for Activity 5, which can be delayed by 1 day without affecting the completion date of the project. If two or more parallel activities have zero slack, there are multiple critical paths, as shown in Figures 2.17 and 2.18, where you can see two critical paths: 1–2–4 and 1–3–4. Further, project managers distinguish between *free slack* and *total slack*. If an activity can be delayed without having a negative effect on the immediately following activity, this is referred to as free slack. If an activity can be delayed without negatively affecting the overall completion time of the project, this is referred to as total slack. By examining

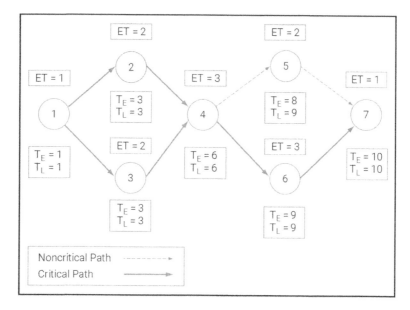

Figure 2.17 A network diagram for the Key Feature Project showing estimated times for each activity (in days) and the earliest and latest expected completion time for each activity

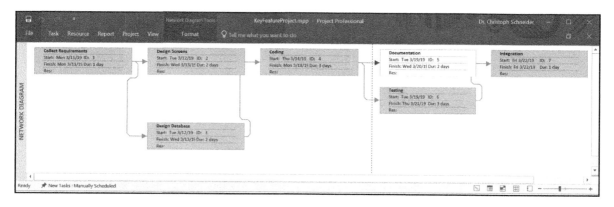

Figure 2.18 Network diagram for the Key Feature Project in Microsoft Project 2016

the free slack and total slack of each activity, the project manager can make tradeoffs or reassign resources if activities are delayed or the project schedule needs to be changed. We will revisit these concepts in greater detail in Chapter 7.

Estimating Project Times Using Three-Point Estimating

Another technique that can be used to support project scheduling is three-point estimating (see Chapter 1). While three-point estimating will be covered more comprehensively in Chapter 7, where we address managing project resources and duration, we introduce it here since it is another technique that helps us manage the project life cycle.

One of the most difficult and most error-prone activities in constructing a project schedule is the determination of each task's duration within a work breakdown structure (see Chapter 5 for more on work breakdown structures). It is particularly problematic to make these estimates when a task involves a high degree of complexity and uncertainty. Three-point estimating calculates a weighted average of optimistic, pessimistic, and realistic time estimates to estimate the *expected time* for a particular task. This technique helps you obtain a better estimate when there is some uncertainty as to how much time a task will require. It thus helps us understand the durations of tasks, which have implications on project life cycle times.

An Introduction to Microsoft Project

As discussed in Chapter 1, a wide variety of project management tools are available to help manage development projects. We will now illustrate the types of activities you would perform when using project management software using Microsoft Project 2016. While more information on Microsoft Project is covered in later chapters, we briefly illustrate the use of this software to show how it can be used to support IS projects. When using this software to manage a project, you need to perform at least the following activities:

- Establish a project starting or ending date.
- Enter tasks and assign task relationships.
- Select a scheduling method to review project reports.

Establishing a Project Starting Date

Assume you have been assigned to design, develop, and implement a new corporate intranet site for your company's personnel director. You have been given twelve weeks to complete this system, called *InfoNet*. The vision for InfoNet is to create a web portal for employees, providing information on corporate performance, news, benefits plans, training programs, job postings, corporate policies, and so on. The personnel director also would like InfoNet to be interactive so that employees could, for example, change insurance plans or register for training courses using an online interface.

A preliminary step in using Microsoft Project to represent a project schedule is to enter the project starting date into the system. Starting (or ending) dates are used to schedule future activities or backdate others based upon their duration and relationships to other activities. Figure 2.19 illustrates how to set a starting date of November 5, 2018, for the InfoNet project.

Entering Tasks and Assigning Task Relationships

The next step in defining a project is to establish project tasks, their duration, and sequence. Once you have done this, you can begin entering the tasks into Microsoft Project. The task entry screen, shown in Figure 2.20, is similar to a spreadsheet program. The user then enters a name, a duration for each activity, and task predecessors. Scheduled start and scheduled finish are automatically entered based upon the project start date and the durations entered. To set a task-precedent relationship, the task number (or numbers) that must be completed before the start of the current task is entered into the predecessors column. Based on this data, Microsoft Project (or other project management software) constructs the different types of charts, diagrams, or reports.

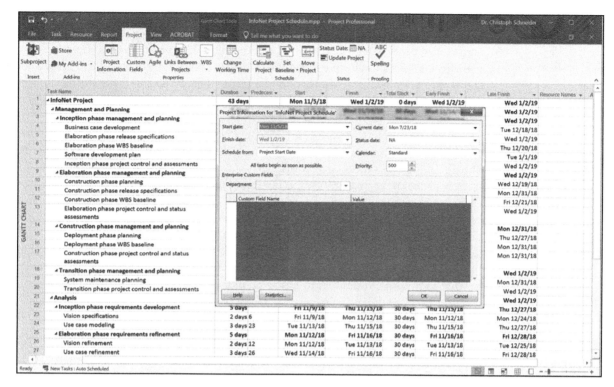

Figure 2.19 Establishing a project starting date in Microsoft Project 2016 for the InfoNet project

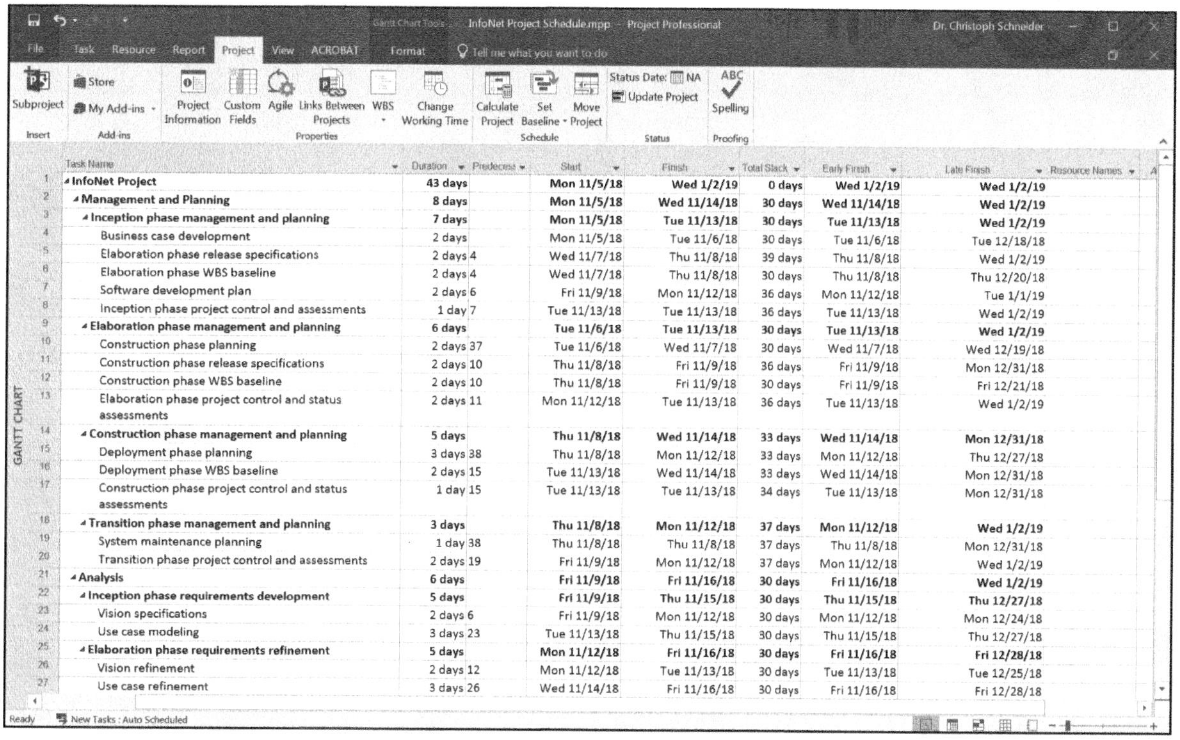

Figure 2.20 Entering tasks and assigning task relationships in Microsoft Project 2016 for the InfoNet project

Selecting a Scheduling Method to Review Project Reports

As you enter more and more task information into Microsoft Project, you can easily review the information by selecting different views or reports. For example, Figure 2.21 shows the current project information in a Gantt chart format, and Figure 2.22 shows a network diagram. You can easily change how you view the information by making a selection from the menu options.

This brief introduction to project management software only scratches the surface of these systems' power and features. In most projects, multiple types of resources are needed. In these instances, project management software allows managers to input and track resource usage and utilization. For example, a project manager can use resource calendars to define standard costing rates and daily availability for each resource, and set holidays, working hours, and vacations. In addition to being helpful for estimating durations, these features are also useful for estimating project costs and billing resources. Given that resources are often shared across multiple projects, it is useful to be able to record resource utilization to be aware of potential impacts on a project's schedule. Further, as assigning resources to tasks and billing resources are very time-consuming activities for most project managers, these tools can greatly facilitate a project manager's job. The tools provided in these powerful systems can greatly ease project planning and management and enhance the effective use of the resources committed to those jobs.

The Project Life Cycle and PMBOK

Throughout this chapter, we have discussed project life cycles, project management processes, the project management context, and technologies and techniques used to support the project life cycle. Specifically, we have talked about project phases and the

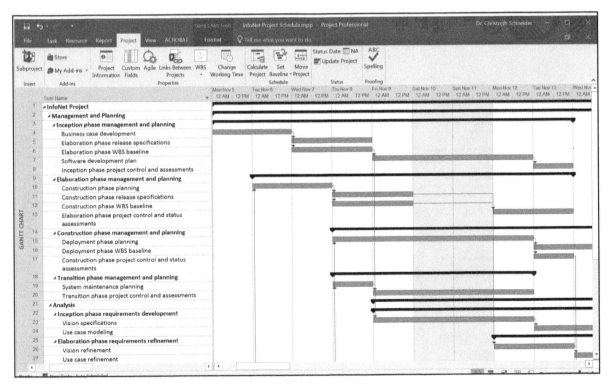

Figure 2.21 Gantt chart of the InfoNet project in Microsoft Project 2016

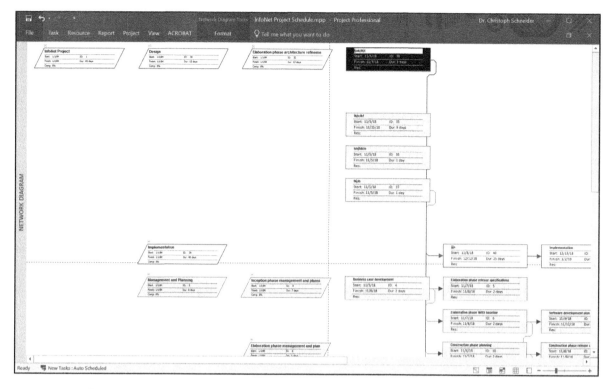

Figure 2.22   Network diagram of the InfoNet project in Microsoft Project 2016

project life cycle, the distinctions between project processes and process groups and how the processes interact with one another, enterprise environmental factors, and organizational process assets. In addition, we have briefly introduced fundamental techniques and highlighted how Microsoft Project is used for project management. Figure 2.23 identifies this coverage and illustrates the coverage of upcoming chapters as well.

Figure 2.23   Chapter 2 and *PMBOK* coverage

Key: ○ where the material is covered in the textbook; ● current chapter coverage

	Textbook Chapters ⟶	1	2	3	4	5	6	7	8	9	10	11	12
	PMBOK Knowledge Area												
1	Introduction												
1.2	Foundational Elements	○	●										
2	The Environment in Which Projects Operate												
2.2	Enterprise Environmental Factors		●										
2.2	Organizational Process Assets		●										
2.3	Organizational Systems		●										
3	The Role of the Project Manager												
3.2	Definition of a Project Manager	○											
3.3	The Project Manager's Sphere of Influence		●										

		1	2	3	4	5	6	7	8	9	10	11
3.4	Project Manager Competences	O	●	O								
3.5	Performing Integration		●									
4	**Project Integration Management**											
4.1	Develop Project Charter					O						
4.2	Develop Project Management Plan					O						
4.3	Direct and Manage Project Work										O	
4.4	Manage Project Knowledge										O	
4.5	Monitor and Control Project Work										O	O
4.6	Perform Integrated Change Control											O
4.7	Close Project or Phase									O		O
5	**Project Scope Management**											
5.1	Plan Scope Management					O						
5.2	Collect Requirements					O						
5.3	Define Scope					O						
5.4	Create WBS					O	O					
5.5	Validate Scope					O						
5.6	Control Scope					O						O
6	**Project Schedule Management**											
6.1	Plan Schedule Management						O					
6.2	Define Activities						O					
6.3	Sequence Activities						O					
6.4	Estimate Activity Durations							O				
6.5	Develop Schedule							O				
6.6	Control Schedule							O				O
7	**Project Cost Management**											
7.1	Plan Cost Management							O				
7.2	Estimate Costs							O				
7.3	Determine Budget							O				
7.4	Control Costs							O				O
8	**Project Quality Management**											
8.1	Plan Quality Management							O				
8.2	Manage Quality							O				
8.3	Control Quality							O				O
9	**Project Resource Management**											
9.1	Plan Resource Management							O				
9.2	Estimate Activity Resources						O	O				
9.3	Acquire Resources							O			O	
9.4	Develop Team			O								
9.5	Manage Team			O								
9.6	Control Resources							O				O

		1	2	3	4	5	6	7	8	9	10	11
10	**Project Communications Management**											
10.1	Plan Communications Management				O							
10.2	Manage Communications				O						O	
10.3	Monitor Communications				O							O
11	**Project Risk Management**											
11.1	Plan Risk Management								O			
11.2	Identify Risks								O		O	
11.3	Perform Qualitative Risk Analysis								O			
11.4	Perform Quantitative Risk Analysis								O			
11.5	Plan Risk Responses								O			
11.6	Implement Risk Responses								O		O	
11.7	Monitor Risks								O			O
12	**Project Procurement Management**											
12.1	Plan Procurement Management									O		
12.2	Conduct Procurements									O	O	
12.3	Control Procurements									O		O
13	**Project Stakeholder Management**											
12.1	Identify Stakeholders				O							
12.2	Plan Stakeholder Engagement				O							
12.3	Manage Stakeholder Engagement				O						O	
12.4	Monitor Stakeholder Engagement				O							O

Running Case: The Project Management Life Cycle

James Cheung looked around his new office. He couldn't believe that he was the assistant director of information technology at Jackie's Electronics, his favorite consumer electronics retail store. He always bought new Blu-Rays and video games for his Xbox at Jackie's. In fact, he had bought his Blu-Ray player and his Xbox at Jackie's, along with his surround-sound system and his forty-two-inch flat-screen 4K OLED. Now he worked there, too. The employee discount was a nice perk of his new job, but he was also glad that his technical and people skills were finally recognized by the people at Jackie's. He had worked for five years at Furniture Warehouse as a senior systems analyst, and it was clear that he was not going to be promoted there. He was really glad he had put his resume up on Monster.com and that now he had a higher salary and a great job with more responsibility at Jackie's.

Jackie's Electronics had started as a single electronics store in 2000 in San Francisco, California. The store was started by Anthony Chan in a strip mall. It was named after Jackie Chan, the martial arts artist and actor who was born in Anthony's hometown, Hong Kong. When he had grown the operation to a chain of thirteen stores in the Bay Area, it was too much for Anthony to handle. He sold his company in 2008, for a handsome profit, to the Kumamoto Corporation, a huge Japanese conglomerate that saw the chain of stores as a place to sell its many consumer electronics goods in the United States.

Kumamoto had aggressively expanded the chain to 218 stores nationwide by the time they sold it in 2015, for a handsome profit, to Andersons, a nationwide grocery store chain. Andersons was looking for a way to diversify and invest the considerable cash they had made in the grocery business. Andersons brought in professional management to run the chain and added fifteen more stores, including one in Mexico and three in Canada. Even though they originally wanted to move the headquarters to their base state of Delaware, Andersons decided to keep Jackie's headquartered in San Francisco.

The company had made some smart moves and had done well, James knew, but he also knew that competition was fierce. Jackie's competitors included big electronics retail chains like Best Buy, Circuit City, and CompUSA, as well as the electronics departments of huge chains like Walmart and

Target. In California, Fry's was a ferocious competitor. James knew that part of his job in IT was to help the company grow, prosper, and beat the competition—or at least survive.

Just then, as James was trying to decide if he needed a bigger TV, Sarah Codey, the chief operations officer at Jackie's, walked into his office. "How's it going, James? Frank keeping you busy?" Frank was Frank Miller, James's boss, the director of IT. He was away for the week, at a meeting in Tucson, Arizona. James quickly pulled his feet off his desk.

"Hi, Sarah. Oh, yeah, Frank keeps me busy. I've got to get through the entire corporate strategic IT plan before he gets back—he's going to quiz me—and then there's the new help desk training we are going to start next week."

"I didn't know we had a strategic IT plan," Sarah teased. "Anyway, what I came in here for is to give you some good news. I have decided to make you the project manager for a project that is crucial to our corporate survival."

"Me?" James said. "But I just got here."

"Who better than you? You have a different perspective, new ideas. You aren't chained down by the past and by the Jackie's way of doing things like the rest of us. Not that it matters, because you don't have a choice. Frank and I both agree that you are the best person for the job."

"So," James asked, "what's the project about?"

"Well," Sarah began, "the executive team has decided that the number-one priority we have right now is to not only survive but to thrive and to prosper, and the way to do that is to develop closer relationships with our customers. The other person on the executive team who is even more excited about this than me is Nick [Nick Baldwin, the head of marketing]. We want to attract new customers, like all our competitors. But also like our competitors, we want to keep our customers for life, kind of like a frequent flier program, but better. Better for us and for our loyal customers. And we want to provide incentives and rewards for the customers who spend the most. We are calling the project 'No Customer Escapes.'"

"I hope that's only an internal name," James joked. "Seriously, I can see how something like this would be good for Jackie's, and I can see how IT would play an important, no, crucial role in making something like this happen. OK, then, let's get started."

Adapted from: Valacich and George (2017).

Chapter Summary

Describe project life cycles. Life cycles can be classified as predictive life cycles, iterative life cycles, incremental life cycles, and agile life cycles. The choice of the life cycle largely depends on factors such as uncertainty and risk. Project life cycles differ in form and content from industry to industry and project to project, but the basic idea is the same: Projects are broken down into smaller pieces called phases. Output from one phase becomes input for the next. Phases end when they produce approved deliverables that were defined earlier in the project.

Explain the four parts of the information systems development life cycle. The information systems development life cycle has four phases: (1) systems planning, (2) systems analysis, (3) systems design, and (4) systems implementation. Planning involves identifying the need for a new system, analysis involves determining the requirements for the new system, design deals with creating the system's technical specifications, and implementation involves building and installing the system. Maintenance repeats the cycle and involves operating and improving the system during its lifetime.

Comprehend project management processes. The *Project Management Body of Knowledge* (*PMBOK*) lists forty-nine different project management processes that are categorized into five process groups: initiating, planning, executing, monitoring and controlling, and closing. As not all processes are equally important or applicable for every project, an experienced project manager uses tailoring to determine which processes to use, and how much emphasis to place on each, depending on the project's characteristics or constraints.

Understand the project management context. Projects exist within organizations, which exist within larger industrial, economic, and societal contexts. The success of a project is not only influenced by the project manager and the project team members, but also by a variety of factors internal and external to an organization, called *enterprise environmental factors*. Organizational process assets are the processes, procedures, and knowledge bases relevant to the completion of a project, and guide how project processes are performed. Understanding management elements and governance frameworks can help the project manager be able to obtain resources or influence project-related outcomes.

Understand techniques and technology to support the project life cycle. Gantt charts show when a task should begin and when it should end. As they are not intended to indicate how tasks must be ordered, Gantt charts are often more useful for depicting relatively simple projects or subparts of a larger project. Network diagrams illustrate how activities can be ordered by connecting a task to its predecessor and successor tasks. Software that supports project management allows a project manager to enter information about project activities, their start and end times, and their precedence relationships. The software can display project life cycles as Gantt charts or as network diagrams, and it can automatically calculate critical paths and slack times. Project management software also includes features for better managing human and material resources.

Key Terms Review

A. Agile life cycle
B. Critical path
C. Enterprise environmental factors
D. Functional organization structure
E. Incremental life cycle
F. Iterative life cycle
G. Logical design
H. Matrix organization structure
I. Organizational process assets
J. Phase
K. Phase gate
L. Physical design
M. Predictive life cycle
N. Process

O. Project management office (PMO)
P. Project-oriented organization structure
Q. Regulation
R. Slack time
S. Standard
T. Systems analysis
U. Systems design
V. Systems implementation
W. Systems maintenance
X. Systems planning
Y. Tailoring
Z. Work performance data
AA. Work performance information
BB. Work performance reports

Match each of the key terms with the definition that best fits it.

1. A document approved by a recognized body that provides, for common and repeated use, rules, guidelines, or characteristics for products, processes, or services with which compliance is not mandatory.

2. A document that specifies product, process, or service characteristics, including the applicable administrative provisions, with which compliance is mandatory.

3. A series of continuous actions that bring about a particular result, end, or condition.

4. A smaller part of a project.

5. A hierarchical organizational structure, sometimes thought of as resembling a pyramid, with top management at the fulcrum, direct workers at the bottom, and middle managers in between.

6. A type of organization structure that typically crosses functional design (on one axis) with some other design characteristic (on the other axis).

7. A type of organization structure where people from different functional backgrounds work with each other throughout the lifetime of the project.

8. An organizational unit created to centralize and coordinate the projects within an organization.

9. Analyzed and integrated work performance data.

10. Electronic or printed documents containing work performance information to be used for project-related decision-making.

11. Factors that are beyond the control of the project manager yet have an influence on the project outcome.

12. Iterations of the SDLC (after a system has been built), where programmers make the changes that users ask for, fix flaws, and modify the system to reflect changing business conditions.

13. Life cycle that allows for the use of prototypes to gain feedback.

14. Life cycle that combines the benefits of iterative and incremental life cycles by gaining rapid feedback and allowing for quickly delivering subsets of the final product.

15. Life cycle that focuses on speed of delivery by providing parts of the overall product as they are completed.

16. Life cycle—sometimes referred to as *waterfall model*—that is characterized as a sequential process.

17. Raw data about the outputs of activities or about the activities themselves.

18. Review of the deliverables at the end of a phase of the project.

19. Specifications that focus on the origin, flow, and processing of data in a system but are not tied to any specific hardware and systems software platform.

20. Structured systems design that can be broken down into smaller and smaller units for conversion into instructions written in a programming language.

21. The amount of time that an activity can be delayed without delaying the project.

22. The first phase of the SDLC, where the need for a new or enhanced system is identified and the proposed system's scope is determined.

23. The fourth phase in the SDLC, where system specifications are turned into a working system that is tested and then put into use.

24. The longest path through a network diagram illustrating the shortest amount of time in which a project can be completed.

25. The processes, procedures, and knowledge bases relevant to the completion of a project.

26. The second phase in the SDLC, where the systems requirements are determined, alternative solutions are developed, and one is chosen that best meets those requirements given the cost, labor, and technical resources the organization is willing to commit.

27. The selective use of processes to match the project's characteristics.

28. The third phase in the SDLC, where the descriptions of the recommended alternative are converted into a logical description and then into physical system specifications.

Review Questions

1. What is a project life cycle?
2. List and explain the four phases of the information systems development life cycle.
3. Are all project life cycles the same? Explain your answer.
4. What is a project management process?
5. Name and define the five project management process groups.
6. What is the difference between process groups and phases of the project life cycle?

7. How many project management processes are associated with planning? Why?

8. What are enterprise environmental factors? Why should project managers be aware of enterprise environmental factors?

9. Name three types of organizational structures and how they affect project management.

10. What are organizational process assets? How do organizational process assets influence a project?

11. What is the difference between a standard and a regulation?

12. What is the key difference between a Gantt chart and a network diagram? When should a Gantt chart be used? When should a network diagram be used?

13. What is a critical path on a network diagram?

14. What are the benefits of using project management software?

Chapter Exercises

1. A project has been defined to contain the following list of activities along with their required times for completion.

Activity No.	Activity	Time (Weeks)	Immediate Predecessors
1	Collect requirements	2	—
2	Analyze processes	3	1
3	Analyze data	3	2
4	Design processes	7	2
5	Design data	6	2
6	Design screens	1	3,4
7	Design reports	5	4,5
8	Program	4	6,7
9	Test and document	8	7
10	Install	2	8,9

a. Draw a network diagram for the activities.

b. Calculate the earliest expected completion time.

c. Show the critical path.

d. What would happen if activity 6 were revised to take 6 weeks instead of 1 week?

2. Construct a Gantt chart for the project defined in Problem 1.

3. Look again at the activities outlined in Problem 1. Assume that during the first week of the project your team discovers that the activity duration estimates were all wrong. Rather than 3 weeks, Activity 2 will take only two weeks to complete, whereas both Activities 4 and 7 will take three times longer than originally estimated. Further, all other activities will take twice as much time to complete. In addition, your team has noticed that additional training is needed. This new activity, number 11, will take one week to complete, and depends on the completion of Activities 10 and 9. Create a new network diagram representing the new earliest expected completion times.

4. Using the web, find one example each of a functional, matrix, and project-oriented organization. Prepare a five-minute presentation about the similarities and differences of these organizations.

5. You are the project manager for developing a fitness tracking app. Search the web for relevant standards and regulations for this project. Write a one-page report highlighting the most important standards and regulations, and how they influence the project or the final deliverable.

Chapter Case: Sedona Management Group and the Project Management Life Cycle

Sedona Management Group (SMG) is a small company situated in Bellevue, Washington. It specializes in developing custom software for websites, intranet, extranet, and electronic commerce applications using Windows 10, HTML5, CSS3, JavaScript, Ajax, SQL Server databases, and Adobe CC technologies. SMG's mission has been to develop high-quality and robust state-of-the-art internet-centric software, as well as commercial software products and components for clients. At the same time, the team at Sedona strives to achieve consumer satisfaction through the products and services they deliver to their clients.

The Sedona team has developed websites for many organizations, including the Seattle Seahawks, the Portland Trail Blazers, the Golden Baseball League, and Alliance Builder. These clients typically provide very good reviews of the products and services they receive from SMG. One positive review was from Mike Flood, vice president of community relations with the Seattle Seahawks. Flood not only praised SMG on the timely development of a high-quality website for the Seahawks but has also noted that since Sedona's development of an additional email-based permission marketing system, membership in the Hawk Mail Club has doubled and continues to grow. Other clients have indicated increases in revenues and improved customer service brought about by the improved quality and maintainability of their websites. How does the Sedona team achieve customer satisfaction? Tim Turnpaugh, the founder of SMG, attributes this achievement to the core competency of his team, which is great project management.

Turnpaugh stresses good project management at SMG, as project failure can result in business failure. He explains this relationship by making the important distinction between commercial and corporate software development. Turnpaugh defines commercial development as the development of software products for other commercial enterprises, where the software is the primary output from the organization, whereas in corporate development, software is developed in-house by an IT group that builds applications for the business as a whole. According to Turnpaugh, the risk associated with project failure in the commercial development market is simple to understand: do a bad job and you go out of business. In contrast, in corporate application development, the financial resources available to the IT group allow them to mitigate the risks associated with any one project running over time or over budget. Commercial development environments, such as SMG's, require very different project selection and management processes.

SMG spends a great deal of time ensuring that the right types of projects are selected. A primary characteristic of the projects that SMG chooses to pursue is based on project scope, both in terms of the initial size of the project and whether the group has experience and expertise in such projects. In terms of project management techniques associated with planning and execution, SMG follows a standardized life cycle, allowing it to approach every project in a very consistent manner. This maximizes Sedona's ability to anticipate and deal with problems they may encounter during the development process. As an example, after mapping out a project, one of the first execution processes SMG performs is to develop the back-end database associated with the website. They then turn to the administration aspect of the website, which involves updating its content, and defining security. In parallel with the development of the database, the team also develops the presentation layer, or the user interface, of the website. SMG strives to exploit high-quality project management techniques in all phases of the project management life cycle, which include initiating, planning, executing, monitoring and controlling, and closing. Further, SMG is very attentive to using the latest advances in technology, including the reuse of code if a project permits it, as well as using the latest in development environments. The team believes that leveraging technology has allowed them to double their work speed. All of these aspects help SMG ensure the timely and successful completion of the projects they undertake.

Chapter 2 Project Assignment

The Seattle Seahawks needed a website to allow fan discussion forums, the purchase of event tickets, and the provision of information on the team and players.

Similarly, an entertainer, whether a singer, a musician, or a comedian, needs a website that contains information about the artist, any forthcoming events, and any products fans can purchase online.

Moreover, from an entertainment standpoint, the internet is an invaluable tool to connect with fans and establish a fan base.

As part of this course, you will be managing the development of an entertainment website. At this point, the project involves uncertainty, and consequently it is a good practice to divide it into several phases. The project life cycle is a collection of these different phases. The assignment for this chapter requires you to develop a project life cycle for the website development project. For this assignment, provide responses to the following questions:

1. What are the four different phases of the information systems development life cycle?
2. Describe each of the phases briefly.

3. Provide a description of which activities you will perform in each individual phase of the website development project.
4. Compare your answers to those of your other team members.
5. Create a master document for the team that is a compilation of your individual work.

References

Association for Computing Machinery (1992). ACM Code of Ethics and Professional Conduct. *ACM*. Retrieved July 4, 2018, from https://www.acm.org/about-acm/code-of-ethics

Bergen, M. (2018, June 2). Google Won't Renew Pentagon AI Drone Deal after Staff Backlash. *Bloomberg.com*. Retrieved July 4, 2018, from https://www.bloomberg.com/news/articles/2018-06-01/google-won-t-renew-pentagon-ai-drone-deal-after-staff-backlash

Deutschman, A (2004, August 1). Inside the Mind of Jeff Bezos. *FastCompany*. Retrieved July 4, 2018, from https://www.fastcompany.com/50106/inside-mind-jeff-bezos-5

Evans, I. (2006). Agile Delivery at British Telecom. *Methods and Tools*. Retrieved July 4, 2018, from http://www.methodsandtools.com/archive/archive.php?id=43

George, J. F., Batra, D., Valacich, J. S., and Slater, J. (2007). *Object-Oriented Systems Analysis and Design* (2nd ed.). Upper Saddle River, NJ: Pearson Prentice Hall.

Grant, I. (2010, January 28). BT Switches to Agile Techniques to Create New Products. *Computer Weekly*. Retrieved July 4, 2018, from http://www.computerweekly.com/news/1280091969/BT-switches-to-agile-techniques-to-create-new-products

Haden, J. (2017, July 10). Why 99 Percent of All Meetings Are a Complete Waste of Money. *Inc.com*. Retrieved July 4, 2018, from https://www.inc.com/jeff-haden/why-99-percent-of-all-meetings-are-a-complete-waste.html

Hall, M. (2004, November 15). Offshoring Revives Man-Month Myth . . . *ComputerWorld*. Retrieved July 4, 2018, from https://www.computerworld.com/article/2568018/app-development/offshoring-revives-man-month-myth----.html

Hern, A. (2018, April 24). The Two-Pizza Rule and the Secret of Amazon's Success. *The Guardian*. Retrieved July 4, 2018, from https://www.theguardian.com/technology/2018/apr/24/the-two-pizza-rule-and-the-secret-of-amazons-success

International Organization for Standardization. (1994). *Code of Good Practice for Standardization (Draft International Standard)*. Geneva, Switzerland: ISO Press.

Mearian, L. (2004, May 31). Killing Time on IT Projects. *ComputerWorld*. Retrieved July 4, 2018, from http://www.computerworld.com/article/2564886/it-project-management/killing-time-on-it-projects.html

Nicholas, J. (2001). *Project Management for Business and Technology: Principles and Practice*. Upper Saddle River, NJ: Prentice Hall.

Project Management Institute (2017). *Agile Practice Guide*. Newton Square, PA: Author.

Project Management Institute (2017). *PMBOK: A Guide to the Project Management Body of Knowledge* (6th ed.). Newtown Square, PA: Author.

Standish Group (2014). CHAOS Report: 21st Anniversary Edition. *Standish Group*. Retrieved July 4, 2018, from https://www.standishgroup.com/sample_research_files/CHAOSReport2014.pdf

Valacich, J. S., and George, J. F. (2017). *Modern Systems Analysis and Design* (8th ed.). Boston: Pearson.

CHAPTER 3

Managing Project Teams

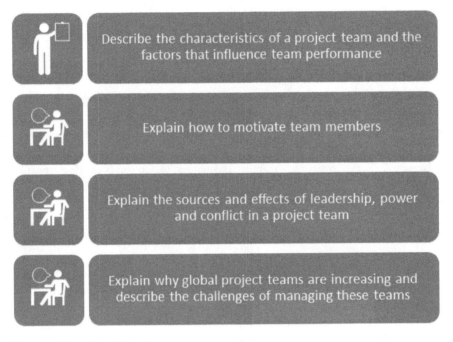

Describe the characteristics of a project team and the factors that influence team performance

Explain how to motivate team members

Explain the sources and effects of leadership, power and conflict in a project team

Explain why global project teams are increasing and describe the challenges of managing these teams

Figure 3.1   Chapter 3 learning objectives

Opening Case: Flexible Project Teams Deliver Project on Time

Consider the difficulty of a project undertaken by MD Robotics to develop a special purpose dexterous manipulator for the Canadian Space Agency. Given the risky nature of spacewalks, this specially developed robotic arm, called "Dextre," was to be developed to support the astronauts on the International Space Station (see Figure 3.2). To encourage freedom of communication as well as timely problem solving, the executive project team decided to co-locate project staff on a single floor of the MD Robotics facility. The Dextre project group was divided into smaller subproject teams, which in the spirit of true co-location and collaboration worked in an open office environment designed to promote communication. Project managers were able to freely interact with engineers, and project teams were able to communicate with each other under a "no-surprises rule" implemented by senior management. The no-surprises rule specified that project teams should communicate any needed design changes to other project teams as soon as they were identified. Although the senior

Figure 3.2 The International Space Station. *Source*: NASA.

management team was made aware of any design changes, it did not have to sign off before teams were allowed to implement the changes.

Using this team-based project structure, combined with the policy of allowing teams the autonomy to make developmental changes, MD Robotics was able to deliver Dextre to the Canadian Space Agency both on budget and on time. Designed for an active life of fifteen years, Dextre was launched in 2008 and continues to support the astronauts on the space station by allowing them to focus on scientific projects.

Based on: Canadian Space Agency (2016a, 2016b); Carey (2005).

Introduction

People are the most important and expensive part of an information systems project. Project time estimates for task completion and overall system quality are significantly influenced by the effectiveness of the project team. Unfortunately, good information systems personnel are in short supply. Not only does nearly every industry rely heavily on information systems professionals; an increase in cloud computing and big data analytics is creating even more demand for skilled technology workers.

The U.S. Bureau of Labor Statistics has reported that high demand for technology-related workers and escalating salaries could lead to inflation and lower corporate profits as companies scramble to offer competitive salaries to the best and brightest people in this industry. Given the competitiveness of this labor pool, retaining the best personnel is also a critical issue for many organizations. Therefore, finding ways not only to reward people adequately but also to create a positive work experience through well-managed projects, meaningful team assignments, and good interpersonal relationships can not only enhance project effectiveness but also help retain employees within the organization. Understanding the issues related to effectively managing project teams is the next step in gaining a comprehensive understanding of information systems project management.

In the next section, we begin by discussing what a project team is, how teams evolve, and the various factors that influence project team performance. This is followed by a discussion of several motivation theories that will help you better understand how team members can be influenced to achieve high work productivity and job satisfaction. Next, we discuss the roles of leadership, power, and conflict within project teams. Finally, we examine several issues related to the management of global project teams.

Developing and Managing the Project Team

Project team
Two or more people who share the same goals, are interdependent, have complementary skills, and are mutually accountable to the organization and to each member of the team.

In the context of organizational work, groups and teams are not necessarily the same thing. A group consists of two or more people who work together to achieve a common objective (Robbins and Judge, 2017). Yet a group may be formed for a temporary purpose, and its members may not necessarily share the same goals. A project team, however, is much more than a group. A **project team** is mutually accountable to the organization and to its own individual team members; the team members are also highly interdependent, having both shared goals and complementary skills (see Figure 3.3). When project teams are formed, the group of people typically takes some time to evolve into a high-performing project team, which is crucial to successful project completion.

Teams do not automatically become highly interdependent and productive. Researchers have found that teams develop and evolve through various stages as they work together over time (Robbins and Judge, 2017). During project team development, the project team moves through five stages—forming, storming, norming, performing, and adjourning—to reach optimal performance (Tuckman, 1965).

During *forming*, team members get to know each other and establish team goals and work assignments. This stage is completed when a majority of the members feel that they are part of the team. At this stage, leaders should coordinate team behaviors; picking the right team members and setting team goals can contribute to success at this stage. During *storming*, team members struggle to establish goals, power, and

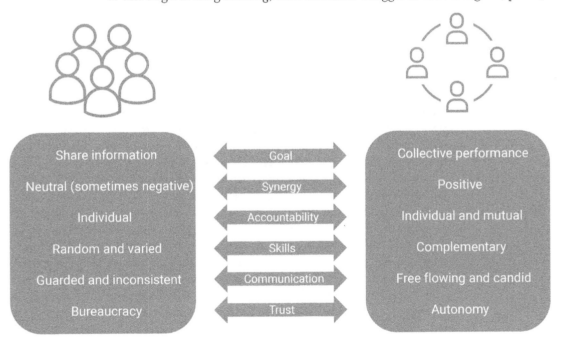

Figure 3.3   Comparing work groups and project teams. *Adapted from*: Robbins and Judge (2017).

leadership roles. At this stage, leaders should coach team members; developing mutual trust and acting as a resource to the team can contribute to success at this stage. This stage is completed when a majority of the members have a relatively clear understanding of each member's role within the team. During *norming*, teams develop a sense of common purpose and specify normal operating procedures. Additionally, during this stage, high levels of team collegiality are typically present, and close friendships are formed. This stage ends with members having a strong sense of proper team behavior. During *performing*, the team undertakes the actual project work. This stage ends with the completion of the project. During norming and performing, leaders should focus on empowering team members, obtain feedback from the team members, and engage with the team. For permanent, ongoing project teams, performing is the last stage in their evolution. For temporary teams established to complete a single project, there is also an adjourning stage. During *adjourning*, team members wrap up the project's final activities and engage in activities related to subsequent team assignments or jobs. During this stage, individuals often respond differently to adjournment—some members will delight in the team's accomplishments, whereas others will feel a sense of sadness or loss. Leaders should focus on supporting behaviors and facilitate the transition of high performing team members into future leadership roles. As a project manager, you need to understand where your team is in regard to its development, in order to better understand its challenges and its potential.

Recognizing the importance of project teams to project success, *PMBOK* includes two key processes related to project teams, both of which are part of the project execution process group: *Develop Team* and *Manage Team*.

One of the main goals of the *Develop Team* process is to transform the project team members into a functioning team. Often, this includes various team building activities and other social integration mechanisms (von Briel, Schneider, and Lowry, 2018) to develop trust and build a team spirit. In addition, it is during this stage that needed skills are developed using various forms of formal or informal training. Whereas collocating team members is very effective in developing teams, virtual teams can use communication technologies (discussed in Chapter 4) to compensate for spatial or temporal distance. To decide on the activities needed to bring the team from the forming to the performing stage, the project management plan, as well as various project documents (such as the project schedule, team assignments, or the team charter), are used to determine the needed roles and resources; likewise, enterprise environmental factors provide a background on team members' skills, performance, as well as geographic distribution, and organizational process assets provide information about teams and team performance on past projects. In addition to helping build a team, the activities conducted to develop the project team may affect the project schedule or team assignments, and team performance assessments can give guidance on areas for improvement, so as to maximize team performance.

The *Manage Team* process uses various conflict management, decision-making, and leadership techniques to maximize team performance during the execution of a project phase; in addition, the project management information system can help in optimizing the assignment of team members to tasks. Often, you will see project team members receiving team apparel to help keep up the team spirit, as well as certificates of appreciation to reward and recognize outstanding contributors to the team. In assessing the necessary activities during the *Manage Team* process, the project manager uses inputs such as the project management plan, the issue log, project team assignments, in addition to work performance reports, team performance assessments, and enterprise environmental factors and organizational process assets. Depending on the team's performance and necessary changes, various outputs result from the *Manage Team* process. For example, the departure of team members may impact the project schedule or budget, or may result in the need to outsource certain tasks. Thus outputs from the *Manage Team* process can range from change requests to team assignments to updates to the project management plan or other project documents, as well as enterprise environmental factors (such as performance assessments).

Contrary to popular views of teams and teamwork, teams are almost never static. Projects add people when needed. Similarly, they lose people when team members are relocated within the organization or quit to take new jobs or for some other reason. This ebb and flow of people on and off a project can be disruptive, and it is rarely anticipated in the project plan. Experienced project managers who have developed the management skills have learned how to deal with the disruptions caused by the flow of people in and out of projects. Less experienced project managers will develop these skills over time. In either case, it is important to recognize that project team membership is fluid and dynamic, and project managers should anticipate and plan for changes in personnel to whatever extent they can.

Factors That Influence Project Team Performance

Researchers have identified four primary factors that lead to effective teams: work design, composition, context, and process (see Figure 3.4). While the mere presence of these factors does not guarantee a productive project team, the presence makes higher performance much more likely. Numerous *work design* factors can be configured to

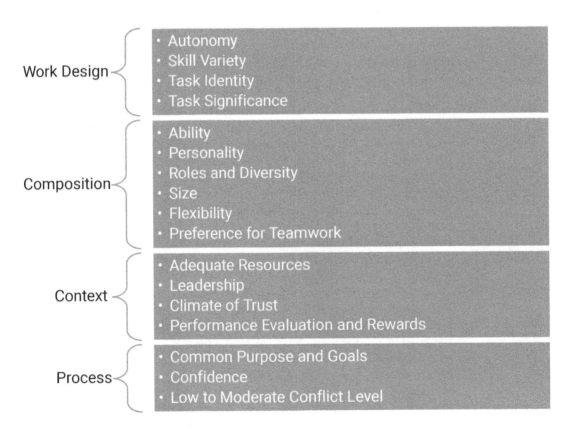

Work Design
- Autonomy
- Skill Variety
- Task Identity
- Task Significance

Composition
- Ability
- Personality
- Roles and Diversity
- Size
- Flexibility
- Preference for Teamwork

Context
- Adequate Resources
- Leadership
- Climate of Trust
- Performance Evaluation and Rewards

Process
- Common Purpose and Goals
- Confidence
- Low to Moderate Conflict Level

Figure 3.4 Project team performance factors. *Adapted from*: Robbins and Judge (2017).

influence team member performance. For instance, work design that provides team members with autonomy, skill variety, task identity, and significance has been found to be highly motivating. Likewise, *team composition* can also play a major role in project team performance. Factors that have been found to be important include member ability, personality, role diversity, size, flexibility, and preference for teamwork. Of these, personality and team size have been found to play a significant role in many project teams. For example, research has found that it can be very difficult to blend some personality types into an effective team. Because of this, many organizations give potential team members personality tests like the **Myers-Briggs Type Indicator (MBTI)** to more effectively match team members, identify leadership and interpersonal communication preferences, and help them learn more about each other.

Myers-Briggs Type Indicator (MBTI)
A widely used personality test.

Nonetheless, there is no universal agreement that such personality tests are accurate or even helpful. Likewise, team size can also significantly influence team performance. As the size of the team increases, it becomes increasingly difficult to effectively communicate and coordinate project activities. The rule of thumb is to use the fewest people possible; the most effective teams rarely have more than ten members (see Figure 3.5). If more than ten members are needed for a very large project, smaller subteams should be used to minimize communication and coordination problems. Getting the right people, and the right number of people, on your project team can make it easier for the group to perform.

All good sports teams have players with clearly defined roles and abilities. Likewise, a good project team needs members with a diversity of skills and abilities. It is also important to select members who are flexible—in regard to task activities and roles—and who clearly want to belong to the team. To be effective, project teams must

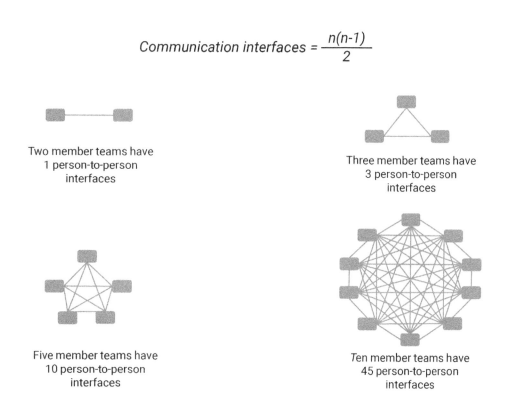

$$Communication\ interfaces = \frac{n(n-1)}{2}$$

Two member teams have
1 person-to-person
interfaces

Three member teams have
3 person-to-person
interfaces

Five member teams have
10 person-to-person
interfaces

Ten member teams have
45 person-to-person
interfaces

Figure 3.5 Team communication and management complexity increase rapidly with group size

agree on a broad range of member roles and must design work processes that ensure that all members contribute equally to the team's performance. An experienced project manager has a deep understanding of the variety of roles and skills needed to build a successful team. Researchers have found that people can also have different types of work personalities within software development teams, including the following (Howard, 2001; see Figure 3.6):

1. *Deliverer.* A person who is good at getting things done quickly and is good in emergency situations such as repairing a system failure.
2. *Prototyper.* A person who is useful for projects where the system requirements are initially unclear or in situations where building the right system is more important than building something quickly.
3. *Perfector.* A person whose work is meticulous and who is useful when everything must be done correctly, such as a system that could impact human safety.
4. *Producer.* A person who is good at getting a lot of work accomplished but may ignore standard conventions such as structured methods and documentation.
5. *Fixer.* A person who has a deep understanding of a system and can quickly examine a problem and make a needed repair.
6. *Finisher.* A person who is good at meeting deadlines but may ignore rules or procedures in order to do so.

Four *contextual factors*—adequate resources, leadership, trust, and performance evaluation and rewards—have also been found to be important for achieving high team performance. It is obvious that teams must have adequate resources or will feel it is impossible to succeed. High-performing project teams must also have clear leadership and structure so that members will know who is responsible for completing various tasks, as well as how schedules, tasks, and roles will be assigned. High-performing teams must also trust each other because doing so allows members to work independently and cooperatively. Lastly, a team-oriented performance evaluation and reward system is needed to achieve maximum team effort, commitment, and performance.

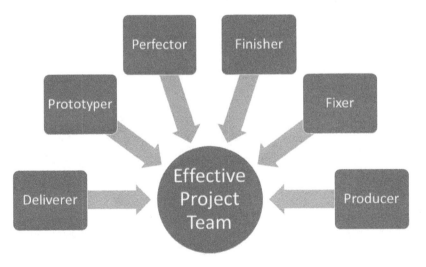

Figure 3.6 Information systems project teams need members with differing work personalities

Finally, three *process factors* also have been found to significantly shape the performance of project teams. Teams that share a common purpose and goals, have confidence in their ability to be successful, and have low-to-moderate levels of conflict typically perform better than teams that don't. In sum, many factors influence a team's performance. Understanding how various factors shape team performance will help you design a more effective team and achieve higher performance.

Tips from the Pros: How to Pick a Project Team

Experienced project managers become experts in how to best select the right members for a team. According to Bill Hagerup, a project management specialist at Ouellette & Associates Inc., a consulting firm in Bedford, New Hampshire, building a successful team takes the right mix of "soft" skills, personalities, and attitudes. Picking people exclusively for their technical skills is often a mistake. Some other tips include:

- *Keep teams small and manageable*. You often have to balance departmental representation with overall team effectiveness, but teams bigger than five members are typically difficult to manage.

- *Get the right personalities*. Look for people with strong work ethics and positive, upbeat personalities. One cynic can spoil the entire team's outlook, whereas positive upbeat personalities can lift the team's spirit.

- *Embrace diversity*. Because technology professions tend to attract similar types of people, work hard to build diversity on your teams so that they will not be as susceptible to groupthink and narrow solutions.

- *Reuse successful teams*. It takes a lot of work to build and nurture a successful team, so reuse successful teams whenever possible.

- *Plan ahead to get the right people*. The best people for a team are often very busy, so it is important to plan ahead to line up key people well in advance.

- *Use your network*. Getting the best people to join a team often requires that you convince their boss or others that it is in the organization's best interest for this person to be on your team. Use your friends and close colleagues to identify and recruit the right people.

When choosing project team members, there are a few other things to keep in mind. Given the importance of communication to project success, team members should be excellent communicators. Likewise, even though the project team members are often not involved in the project management aspects, they should still have a basic understanding of project management principles. Further, project team members should be highly organized, have an ability to "read" and motivate people, have accurate estimating skills, and be self-assured and willing to stand up for the project when needed.

Based on: Jones (2017); Melymuka (2004).

Motivating Team Members

Motivation
An individual's intensity, direction, and persistence of effort toward attaining a goal.

One of the keys to project success is having a project team with motivated members. **Motivation** refers to an individual's intensity, direction, and persistence of effort toward attaining a goal (Robbins and Judge, 2017). *Intensity* refers to how hard someone tries to attain the goal. However, intensity alone may not result in favorable results, unless the *Direction* of that intensity is channeled toward attaining the appropriate goal. Direction thus is focused on the quality of the effort. *Persistence* refers to how long someone maintains an effort toward the goal. To be ultimately successful, a person needs all three traits. For example, a person can work hard, but if this effort is not directed correctly or is not sustained, success may not be possible. Motivating team members is thus critical to reaching optimum team performance.

Over the years, a lot of research has been conducted to identify why and how people are motivated. From this research, it has been found that different people are motivated by different things and in different ways. For example, some people are primarily motivated by external factors such as financial rewards, whereas others are motivated by internal factors such as a sense of accomplishment. Also, different theories of motivation are useful for understanding work productivity as well as job satisfaction, absenteeism, and turnover. **Job satisfaction** refers to the general attitude a person has toward his or her job, **absenteeism** refers to the failure to report to work, and **turnover** refers to the rate at which people voluntarily or involuntarily leave an organization. Some theories have been good for understanding job satisfaction, whereas others have been useful for understanding work productivity. In sum, understanding why and how people are satisfied and how they are motivated to come to work, to stay with the organization, or to work hard is important for all project managers. Consequently, we briefly review various motivational theories to help you better understand motivation. More in-depth discussions of motivation can be found in Robbins and Judge (2017) or Verma (1996).

Need Theories of Motivation

For more than fifty years, researchers have examined various theories of how different personal factors can shape a person's motivation. Although support for these theories has been mixed when examined in controlled research settings, they are nonetheless widely used within organizations when designing work practices and reward systems. In this section, we briefly examine the most popular need theories of motivation.

Hierarchy of Needs

One of the most famous motivational theories is Maslow's **hierarchy of needs** (Maslow, 1954), which states that people have five basic needs, which differ in importance: physiological, safety, social, esteem, and self-actualization (see Figure 3.7). As each lower-level need is met (or substantially met), the next higher-level need becomes the individual's motivating focus. This means that if you want to motivate people, you need to understand where they are in this hierarchy and use mechanisms to help them satisfy needs at the next higher level. However, research has found that unsatisfied needs do not necessarily motivate, that satisfied needs do not always activate movement to higher levels in the hierarchy, and that more than one need from different levels may be desired simultaneously. As a result, researchers have continued to look for a more sophisticated understanding of motivation.

ERG Theory

A related theory, **ERG theory**, refined the hierarchy of needs theory, and argues that there are three core needs—existence, relatedness, and growth—of which more than one may be operating at the same time. Additionally, if the fulfillment of a higher-level need is unrealized, the desire to satisfy a lower-level need increases (Alderfer, 1969). Within ERG theory, existence focuses on satisfying our basic material needs and most closely relates to Maslow's physiological and safety needs. Relatedness focuses on maintaining interpersonal relationships and most closely relates to Maslow's social needs. Lastly, growth focuses on personal development and most closely relates to Maslow's esteem and self-actualization categories. Researchers have found ERG theory to be more valid than Maslow's hierarchy of needs because it more closely reflects our knowledge of how the importance of various factors can simultaneously motivate an individual.

Job satisfaction
The general attitude a person has toward his or her job.

Absenteeism
The failure to report to work.

Turnover
The rate at which people voluntarily or involuntarily leave an organization.

Hierarchy of needs
A hierarchy of needs—physiological, safety, social, esteem, and self-actualization—where as each need is met, the next higher level need becomes the motivating focus.

ERG theory
Three core needs—existence, relatedness, and growth—of which more than one may be operative at the same time; if the fulfillment of a higher-level need is unrealized, the desire to satisfy a lower-level need becomes the motivating focus.

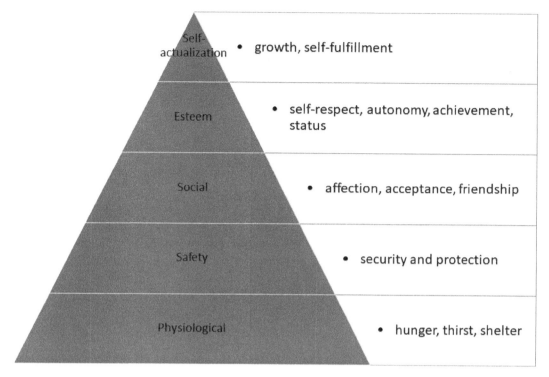

Figure 3.7 Maslow's hierarchy of needs

Two-Factor Theory

Two-factor theory
Intrinsic factors
(*motivational factors*)
are related to job
satisfaction, whereas
extrinsic factors
(*hygiene factors*) are
associated with job
dissatisfaction.

Another need theory, the motivational-hygiene theory, or simply the **two-factor theory** (Herzberg, Mausner, and Snyderman, 1959), predicts that the factors that lead to job satisfaction are separate and distinct from those that lead to dissatisfaction (see Figure 3.8). In particular, intrinsic factors (i.e., *motivational factors*), like achievement, recognition, advancement, and responsibility, are related to job satisfaction, while extrinsic factors (i.e., *hygiene factors*), like salary, relationships with colleagues, and work conditions, are associated with job dissatisfaction (see Table 3.1). In other words, people will not be dissatisfied if extrinsic factors are adequate, but they won't necessarily be satisfied either. For a person to be satisfied, intrinsic factors must also be adequately met. As with Maslow's hierarchy of needs, the two-factor theory is not universally accepted, but due to its intuitive appeal, many managers and organizations have embraced its concepts.

Theory of Needs

Theory of needs
Individuals' motivation
can be explained
by their need for
achievement, power,
and affiliation.

One last needs theory is the **theory of needs**, which proposes that individuals' motivation can be explained by their need for achievement, power, and affiliation (McClelland, 1961). The need for achievement refers to having a drive to excel beyond a set of standards. The need for power refers to having a drive to control the behavior of others. The need for affiliation refers to having the desire for close and friendly interpersonal relationships. Researchers have shown that high achievers are not necessarily good managers, but that good managers have a high need for power and a low need for affiliation. Of

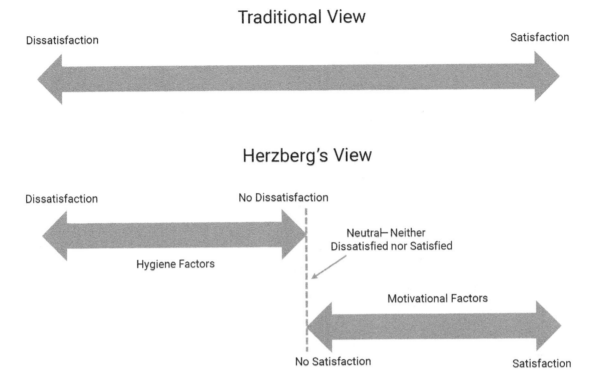

Figure 3.8 Contrasting views of job satisfaction in Herzberg's two-factor theory. *Adapted from*: Verma (1997).

Table 3.1 Common Hygiene and Motivational Factors

Hygiene Factors	Motivational Factors
• Company policies and administration • Relationship with supervisors, peers, and subordinates • Working conditions • Salary and benefits • Status • Security	• Opportunity for achievement • Opportunity for recognition • Challenges and variety of the work itself • Sense of responsibility • Opportunity for advancement • Opportunity for personal growth

all need theories, this theory has been found to best predict work productivity, whereas the others have had the most success in explaining a person's job satisfaction.

Process Theories of Motivation

Process theories attempt to understand a person's behavior based on intrinsic or personal factors used to motivate specific behavior. In general, this perspective on motivation suggests that project managers need to create a proper environment, work processes, and rewards to inspire the greatest motivation in people. Several of the most notable process theories of motivation are described next.

Theory X and Theory Y

Theory X and Theory Y reflect contrasting views of human behavior, management, and motivation (McGregor, 1960). Whereas **Theory X** assumes that people dislike work,

Theory X
Motivational theory that assumes people dislike work, are lazy, dislike responsibility, and must be coerced to work hard.

Theory Y
Motivational theory that assumes people like work, are creative, like autonomy, and seek responsibility.

Theory Z
Motivational theory reflecting the Japanese work philosophy that includes a belief in lifetime employment, strong company loyalty, and group consensus.

Goal-setting theory
Specific and difficult goals, with clear feedback on how well a person is meeting the goals, can enhance a person's work productivity.

Equity theory
Individuals compare their work inputs and outcomes with those of others and then respond to eliminate any inequities.

Reinforcement theory
A motivation theory that argues that both positive and negative feedback condition behavior.

Expectancy theory
People exert a high level of effort when they believe that (1) effort will lead to a good performance appraisal, (2) a good appraisal will lead to rewards, and (3) these rewards will satisfy their needs.

are lazy, dislike responsibility, and must be coerced to work hard, **Theory Y** assumes that people like work, are creative, like autonomy, and seek responsibility. A project manager who believes in Theory X will typically be autocratic, leave no doubt with others about who is in charge, and have little concern about the feelings of others. A Theory Y manager will be participative and encourage a high level of involvement by team members in their assignments, work processes, and decisions. Theory Y has been found to be a much better management philosophy for motivating professionals and highly educated individuals.

Theory Z

An extension to Theory X and Theory Y is **Theory Z** (Ouchi, 1981), which reflects the Japanese work philosophy that includes a belief in lifetime employment, strong company loyalty, and group consensus. A Theory Z management philosophy views workers as long-term partners who are capable of working without close supervision; decisions are made by the entire team with high levels of group consensus.

Goal-Setting Theory

Goal-setting theory offers another perspective on understanding a person's motivation (Locke, 1968) by suggesting that specific and difficult goals, with clear feedback on how well a person is meeting them, can enhance a person's work productivity. This means that telling someone to "do their best" will likely result in them *not* doing their best! However, giving people higher, specific job performance goals ("Please complete the new user interface by Friday noon") will most often lead to higher levels of performance, especially when clear feedback is given.

Equity Theory

Equity theory suggests that individuals compare their work inputs and outcomes with those of others and then respond to eliminate inequities (Adams, 1965). For example, if individuals feel they are not being treated fairly, they will work less, reduce their outputs, change their perceptions, or quit. In contrast, individuals who believe they are being treated fairly will remain relatively satisfied and motivated to perform. Although equity theory has demonstrated that making relative comparisons to others influences motivation, it is most powerful in predicting absenteeism and turnover, not levels of work productivity (Robbins and Judge, 2017).

Reinforcement Theory

Reinforcement theory argues that both positive and negative feedback, or reinforcement, conditions behavior (Komaki, Coombs, and Schepman, 1996). In other words, reinforcement theory proposes that if desirable behavior is rewarded—with pay increases, incentives, or other valued items—it will be repeated. Likewise, undesirable behavior can be discouraged by punishment. This theory has a very broad following and has become the basis of the reward systems within many modern organizations.

Expectancy Theory

Lastly, **expectancy theory**, one of the most widely accepted and supported motivational theories, predicts that people will be motivated to exert a high level of effort when they believe that effort will lead to a good performance appraisal, a good appraisal will lead to rewards, and these rewards will satisfy their needs (Vroom, 1964). Figure 3.9

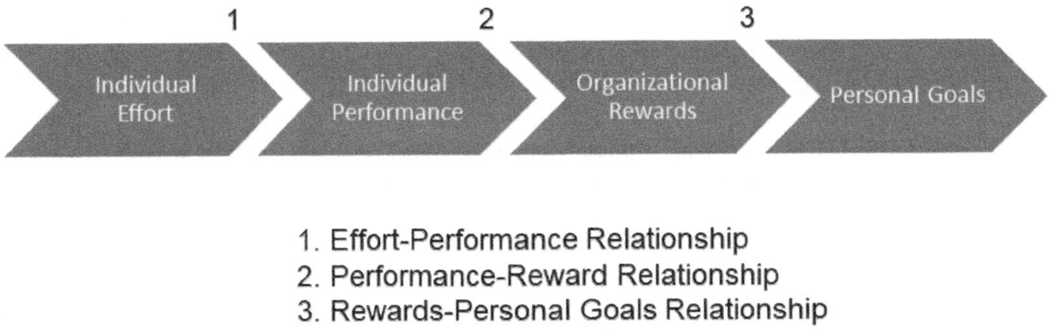

1. Effort-Performance Relationship
2. Performance-Reward Relationship
3. Rewards-Personal Goals Relationship

Figure 3.9 Expectancy theory links a person's effort to their performance, their performance to rewards, and their rewards to goals.

shows each of these three relationships. The effort-performance relationship reflects the belief that increased individual effort leads to higher work performance. The performance-rewards relationship reflects the belief that work performance at a particular level will lead to specific outcomes such as a bonus, a salary increase, or promotion. Finally, the rewards-personal goals relationship reflects the belief that organizational rewards will satisfy a person's goals or needs. Expectancy theory has been very useful for understanding why many workers are, or are not, motivated to do their jobs well. To adequately motivate employees to perform their best, the organization must design job evaluation and reward systems that accurately measure effort and performance, and it must design reward systems that meet each employee's specific needs. If employees believe that effort will lead to the rewards that meet their personal needs, then optimal work performance can be achieved.

General Guidelines for Motivating Team Members

As can be seen from this discussion of employee motivation, there is no single approach to optimally motivating people. Over the years, researchers have examined many approaches for enhancing motivation (see Table 3.2). From this work, several general recommendations can be made for managing your project team (Robbins and Judge, 2017):

1. *Recognize individual differences.* Because your team members will have different needs and goals, it is essential that you learn what is important to each person.
2. *Use specific goals and feedback.* Teams should set specific goals, with specific feedback on how each member is doing, in order to achieve optimal performance.
3. *Allow team members to participate in decisions that affect them.* Team members should be allowed to participate in most decisions that affect them in order to increase productivity, commitment, motivation, and job satisfaction.
4. *Link rewards to performance.* Rewards should be clearly tied to performance in order to optimally motivate team members.
5. *Check the system for equity.* Monitor team members for perceptions of inequality to make sure that any differences in experiences, skills, abilities, and effort lead to clear differences in pay, job assignments, and other rewards.

Table 3.2 Various Theories That Have Been Developed to Explain Motivation

Need Theories of Motivation	
Hierarchy of needs	A hierarchy of needs—physiological, safety, social, esteem, and self-actualization—in which as each need is met the next-higher-level need becomes the motivating focus
ERG theory	Three core needs—existence, relatedness, and growth—in which more than one need may be operative at the same time; if the fulfillment of a higher-level need is unrealized, the desire to satisfy a lower-level need becomes the motivating focus.
Two-factor theory	Intrinsic factors (motivational factors), such as achievement, recognition, advancement, and responsibility, are related to job satisfaction, whereas extrinsic factors (hygiene factors), such as salary, relationships with colleagues, and work conditions, are associated with dissatisfaction.
Theory of needs	Individuals' motivation can be explained by their need for achievement, power, and affiliation.
Process Theories of Motivation	
Theory X	Assumes that people dislike work, are lazy, dislike responsibilities, and must be coerced to work hard
Theory Y	Assumes that people like work, are creative, like autonomy, and seek responsibility.
Theory Z	Reflects the Japanese work philosophy that includes a belief in lifetime employment, strong company loyalty, and group consensus
Goal-setting theory	Specific and difficult goals, with clear feedback related to how well a person is meeting the goals, can be used to understand a person's work productivity.
Equity theory	Individuals compare their work inputs and outcomes with those of others and then respond to eliminate any inequities.
Reinforcement theory	Both positive and negative feedback condition behavior.
Expectancy theory	People's effort leads to their performance; their performance leads to rewards; and their rewards lead to the fulfillment of personal goals.

Understanding why and how people are motivated is an important skill for all project managers. Subtle changes in work processes, evaluation systems, and rewards can have a tremendous influence on a person's motivation. Next, we examine how leadership and power can also be used to influence the performance of project teams.

Common Problems: Managing Einsteins

An "Einstein"—sometimes called high-maintenance high-performance (or HMHP) employee—is an intelligent, curious, and technologically proficient knowledge worker who has the know-how to keep everything operating without costly delays, breakdowns, and crashes, and the ability to drive managers insane.

Information systems project teams often consist of extremely intelligent individuals who possess extraordinary skills but also sometimes abhor management authority. Researchers have identified six types of Einsteins that are common on technical project teams:

1. Arrogant Einsteins
2. Know-It-All Einsteins
3. Impatient Einsteins
4. Eccentric Einsteins
5. Disorganized Einsteins
6. Withdrawn Einsteins

Researchers point out how every type of Einstein can be troublesome to a project team in one way or another. However, with careful management, these team members can be nurtured to perform their best. To be successful, project managers must be skilled at profiling, recruiting, rewarding, leading, and even disciplining Einsteins.

Based on: Fisher (2012); Ivancevich and Duening (2002); Kerr (2014); Ryan (2018).

Leadership, Power, and Conflict in Project Teams

The exercise of leadership and power is a natural part of project teams. Over the life of a project, project managers and team members will interact with a broad range of people both from within the team and from outside. Some of these people may hold a higher rank within the organization, whereas others may be customers or contractors outside the organization. How you use your leadership abilities and power to influence the behavior of others can have a tremendous impact on the success or failure of a project.

Leadership and Project Team Effectiveness

Manager
A formal position of authority in an organization that is responsible for planning, organizing, directing, monitoring, and controlling the activities of others.

Leader
A person, who, by virtue of his or her personal attributes, can exert influence on others.

Leadership
The ability to influence people toward the achievement of goals.

The terms *management* and *leadership* are often used interchangeably but are really quite different. A **manager** is typically someone who has a formal position of authority and is responsible for planning, organizing, directing, monitoring, and controlling project activities. A **leader** is someone, who, by virtue of his or her personal attributes, can influence others. Therefore, **leadership** is defined as the ability to influence people toward the achievement of goals. Note that leaders may or may not be managers. Likewise, some managers may not be effective leaders. Effective project managers have the right mix of both management and leadership abilities (see Table 3.3). Experience has shown that successful project teams have great management and great leadership. Managers are essential for keeping the team on track. Leaders are critical for inspiring the team to define its vision and the steps needed to reach success. It has been said that good managers focus on "doing things right," whereas good leaders focus on "doing the right things." Successful projects need both!

Trait Theories of Leadership

As you might expect, there are different views on what makes a good leader and whether people are "born leaders" or can be "made" leaders through training and education. One body of research focused on identifying the traits, or personal attributes, of leaders.

Table 3.3 Characteristics of Managers versus Leaders

Managers Focus On:	Leaders Focus On:
Objectives	Vision
Telling how and when	Selling what and why
Shorter range	Longer range
Organization and structure	People
Autocracy	Democracy
Restraining	Enabling
Maintaining	Developing
Conforming	Challenging
Imitating	Originating
Administrating	Innovating
Controlling	Directing
Procedures	Policy
Consistency	Flexibility
Risk avoidance	Risk opportunity
Bottom line	Top line

Adapted from: Verma (1996).

These **trait theories of leadership** argue that personality, appearance, competency, and other personal characteristics differentiate leaders from nonleaders. This research has found that successful leaders often share some similar personal attributes, including:

Trait theories of leadership
A set of leadership theories that argue personality, appearance, competency, and other personal characteristics differentiate leaders from nonleaders.

- Intelligence and competency in task and organizational activities
- Maturity and a broad range of interests
- Considerate interpersonal skills and respect for the needs and differences of others
- Goal-oriented focus and a strong motivation to achieve success

Although trait-focused research has been useful for identifying characteristics of leaders, it has failed to determine why people become leaders or how people can be better leaders. Additionally, it has been found that people can possess the traits of leaders, but this alone does not guarantee success.

Behavioral Theories of Leadership

Behavioral theories of leadership
A set of leadership theories that suggest people's actions determine their potential to be successful leaders.

A second view of leadership can be found in the **behavioral theories of leadership**, which share the common view that people's actions, rather than personal traits, determine their potential to be successful leaders. In this work, two general types of leaders— task-oriented and relationship-oriented—have been identified. On the one hand, leaders who are relationship-oriented emphasize interpersonal relationships with team members in order to gain the greatest influence. For example, relationship-oriented leaders take a personal interest in team members and accept individual differences among them as being a positive team characteristic. In contrast, task-oriented leaders use their influence to get tasks completed as effectively as possible, with much less concern for the relationships among team members. There is no consensus on which type of leader is most effective. In some situations, task-oriented leaders have been most effective, whereas in others, relationship-oriented leaders have been most effective.

Contingency Theories of Leadership

Contingency theories of leadership
A set of leadership theories that suggest the situation is most critical for identifying leadership success.

A third and final general group of leadership theories, referred to as **contingency theories of leadership**, consider the *situation* the most critical element for identifying leadership success, and suggest that no particular leadership style or approach is always best. For example, the Fiedler Contingency Model examines the contexts in which task-oriented versus relationship-oriented leaders would be most successful (Fiedler, 1967), finding that the interplay of the leader-member relationships, the task structure, and the amount of power the leader possesses determines whether a task- or relationship-oriented leader would be most successful in a given situation (see Figure 3.10).

The Situational Leadership Model (SLM) focuses on characteristics of *followers* to determine the best leadership style (Blanchard, Fowler, and Hawkins, 2005). Specifically, followers can be competent (able) and committed (willing) to perform a task or can be incompetent and/or reluctant. Depending on a follower's competence and commitment, the leader should choose a different approach, focusing more on directive behavior (e.g., guiding a follower who lacks ability) or supportive behavior (e.g., coaching the unwilling; see Figure 3.11). Although the SLM is widely used in management training, research efforts to test its predictive power have been disappointing. Nevertheless, it remains a popular leadership approach for many organizations.

There are several other contingency-based models of leadership, each with its own strengths and weaknesses. Each variation attempts to refine certain aspects of the

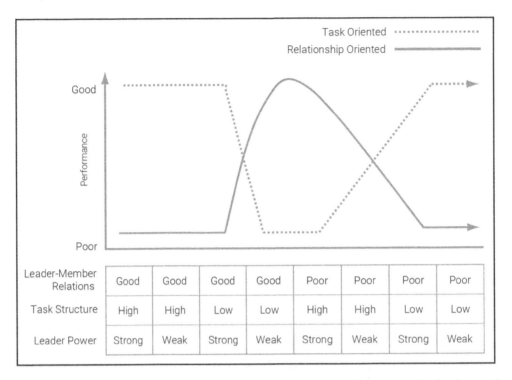

Figure 3.10 The influence of leader-member relations, task structure, and power on leadership performance. *Adapted from*: Robbins and Judge (2017).

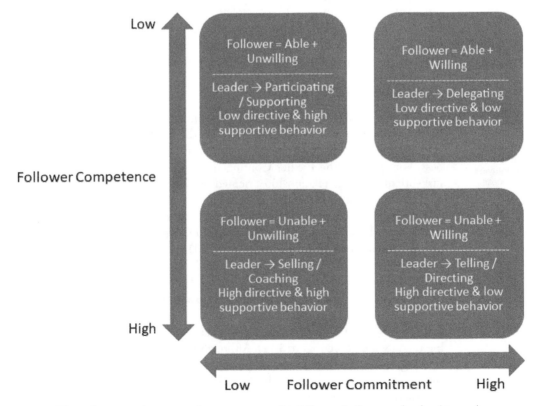

Figure 3.11 How the commitment and competency of a follower influences leadership style

context to better explain how leaders emerge and when they will be successful. Clearly, there is the potential for many types of successful leaders.

General Leadership Guidelines

Today, most leadership researchers believe that effective leadership can be taught and that the key to effective leadership can be summarized in five essential practices (Tucker, McCarthy, and Benton, 2002):

1. *Challenging the process.* Effective leaders search for opportunities to change the status quo and, by doing so, experiment and take risks.

2. *Inspiring a shared vision.* Effective leaders passionately believe they can make a difference and envision the future, enlisting other team members to see the same future.

3. *Enabling others to act.* Effective leaders cultivate collaboration and build spirited teams, strengthening others in the process by creating trust and fostering human dignity.

4. *Modeling the way.* Effective leaders create standards of excellence, set an example for others, and help others achieve success.

5. *Encouraging the heart.* Effective leaders recognize the contributions of others and celebrate their accomplishments, making team members feel like heroes.

With organizations becoming increasingly global and with the increasing use of global project teams within information systems projects, effective leadership has never been more important for achieving project team success. Achieving the right balance between being a manager and a leader is a significant challenge, but having the proper balance will help your project team reach its greatest potential.

Power within Project Teams

Power
The absolute capacity of a person to influence the behavior or attitudes of one or more target persons at a given point in time.

Closely related to leadership is power. **Power** refers to the absolute capacity of a person to influence the behavior or attitudes of one or more target persons at a given point in time (Yukl, 2006). Leaders use power to influence team members to achieve the team's goals. Power can be thought of as the ability to *force* people to do something they would not normally do. This makes power seem like a bad thing, but it isn't necessarily; the use of power to influence the behavior of others is a natural part of all project teams and organizations. Researchers have identified two different types of power: positional power (sometimes referred to as *formal power*) and personal power (French and Raven, 1959; Robbins and Judge, 2017). **Positional power** is based on an individual's position in an organization and can be one of five types:

Positional power
Power derived from an individual's position in an organization.

1. *Legitimate power.* Being able to influence people based on being in a position of authority

2. *Reward power.* Being able to influence people based on being in a position to distribute rewards

3. *Coercive power.* Being able to influence people based on being in a position to punish

4. *Information power.* Being able to influence people based on their dependency on controlled information

5. *Ecological power.* Being able to influence people based on controlling physical resources such as equipment and space

In contrast, **personal power** is an outcome of an individual's unique characteristics and can be one of three types:

1. *Expert power.* Being able to influence people based on having expertise, special skills, or knowledge (e.g., financial guru Warren Buffett)
2. *Referent power.* Being able to influence people based on their strong affection, admiration, or loyalty (e.g., former U.S. Secretary of State Colin Powell)
3. *Charismatic power.* Being able to influence people based on having a favorable personality and interpersonal style (e.g., entertainment mogul Oprah Winfrey)

In sum, each individual on a project team will possess different amounts of power, and this power will be derived from various sources, both positional and personal.

Understanding what power is, where it comes from, and why people possess it in differing amounts helps us to better understand various team roles and why and how some teams perform better than others. Of course, when power is exercised to influence people, it sometimes causes conflict. This topic is discussed next.

Managing and Resolving Project Team Conflict

Conflict is the opposition of people in an organization who have incompatible or opposing needs, drives, wishes, or external or internal demands (Verma, 1996). Like leadership and power, conflict is a natural part of project teams and organizations, and some *functional* conflict is necessary for a team to perform effectively. Whereas **functional conflict** helps support the goals of the team and improve its performance, **dysfunctional conflict** hinders group performance and interferes with team performance. So when we say that some conflict is good, we mean that some *functional* conflict is good (see Figure 3.12).

Among project teams, conflict can arise from tasks, work processes, or relationships (see Table 3.4). *Task conflict* relates to the content and goals of the work itself. *Relationship conflict* relates to interpersonal relationships among team members. *Process conflict* relates to how the work gets done within a team. Whereas low-to-moderate levels of task conflict, as well as low levels of process conflict, can help a team's performance, high levels of task conflict—not agreeing on what should be done and what the objective is—will never lead to enhanced performance. Likewise, moderate-to-high levels of process conflict—not agreeing on how work will be performed or who will do it—does not lead to enhanced performance. Further, relationship conflicts—personality conflicts and relationship problems—will always hinder team performance (Robbins and Judge, 2017). This means that functional conflict is always related to task and process issues, whereas dysfunctional conflict can be rooted in tasks, processes, or relationships. In sum, conflict can be thought of as varying in intensity from none to extreme (see Figure 3.13). Functional conflict is typically at the lower end of this continuum, whereas dysfunctional conflict can span its entire range.

Within project teams, researchers have identified the primary causes of conflict to be as follows (Thamhain and Wilemon, 1975):

1. *Schedule.* Disagreements on task duration and sequencing
2. *Project priorities.* Disagreements on project vision and scope

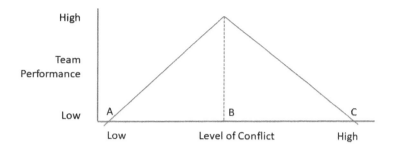

Situation	Level of Conflict	Type of Conflict	Team's Internal Characteristics	Level of Team Performance
A	Low to None	Dysfunctional	Apathetic, Stagnant, Nonresponsive to change, Lack of new ideas	Low
B	Optimal	Functional	Viable, Self-critical, Innovative	High
C	High	Dysfunctional	Disruptive, Chaotic, Uncooperative	Low

Figure 3.12 Conflict and team performance. *Adapted from*: Robbins and Judge (2017).

Table 3.4 Conditions That Can Lead to Project Conflict

Condition	Description
Ambiguous roles, work boundaries, responsibility, and authority	Project teams often have members with different reporting structures and overlapping or conflicting responsibilities that can lead to conflict.
Inconsistent or incompatible goals	Team members may perceive others to have different or conflicting goals that can lead to conflict.
Communication problems	Task, process, or relationship ambiguity can result in reduced or ineffective communication that can lead to conflict.
Dependence on another party	Team members depend on others to complete tasks or provide resources; delays or work quality issues can lead to conflict.
Specialization or differentiation	Team members from different professional backgrounds often have different viewpoints, languages, and goals that can lead to conflict.
Need for joint decision-making and consensus	Teams with a diverse mix of members may feel pressure to conform to the majority opinion, which can lead to conflict.
Behavior regulations	Project teams have norms for working together that may conflict with an individual's preferred work processes.
Unresolved prior conflicts	Past unresolved issues between team members can lead to conflict.

Adapted from: Verma (1995).

3. *Manpower.* Disagreements on the utilization of people, especially those simultaneously involved in multiple projects

4. *Technical.* Disagreements over system design elegance and resource limitations

5. *Administration.* Disagreements due to authority over key resources

6. *Personality.* Disagreements due to dysfunctional interpersonal interactions

7. *Cost.* Disagreements arising from increasing resource constraints as a project evolves

Figure 3.13 Conflict intensity can range from no conflict to extreme. *Adapted from*: Robbins and Judge (2017).

In most cases, effective project management can minimize these causes of conflict. For example, an incomplete work breakdown schedule can lead to conflict related to the project schedule, or a vague project scope statement can lead to conflict related to project priorities. Additionally, as a project evolves, different sources of conflict may be more likely (e.g., conflicts over project priorities will likely occur early within the project). In addition to effective project management techniques, many good conflict management approaches can be utilized. These are discussed next.

Although there is no single best way to manage all types of conflict, some approaches have been found to be better than others. Approaches for resolving conflict can range from completely autocratic to more cooperative. Situational factors, such as time pressure, the intensity of the conflict, the importance of the problem, and the level of cooperation among parties, can influence which approach is most appropriate. Likewise, because low-to-moderate levels of conflict have been found to benefit team performance, some techniques can be used to purposefully *stimulate* functional conflict within a team. **Conflict management**, the use of resolution and stimulation techniques to achieve a desired level of team conflict, is a valuable skill for all project managers. Table 3.5 summarizes many of the most widely used techniques. By using these techniques, you should be able to better sustain the desired level of conflict within your team.

Conflict management The use of resolution and stimulation techniques to achieve a desired level of team conflict.

Managing Project Politics

Politics are a natural part of all organizations and reflect the use of covert mechanisms to obtain power and control. Within the context of information systems projects, politics are the art of getting things done. Although some view politics as a somewhat evil or distasteful part of organizational life, they are not necessarily a bad thing or something to avoid. There are, of course, good and bad politicians; the good politicians look for win–win opportunities, while the bad look for opportunities to win at any cost. Being a successful project manager in modern organizations requires that you also become a savvy politician. Some advice for improving your political skills includes the following (Choo, 2003):

Table 3.5 Conflict Management Techniques for Resolving and Stimulating Team Conflict

Conflict Resolution Techniques	
Problem solving	Face-to-face meetings can be used to identify and resolve conflicts through open and candid discussions.
Shared goals	Create shared goals that can only be achieved through the cooperation of the conflicting parties
Resource expansion	When conflict is caused by resource scarcity—say, money, opportunities, space, equipment—additional resources can be used to resolve discrepancies.
Avoidance	Withdrawal from, or suppression of, the conflict
Smoothing	Playing down differences while emphasizing common interests between the conflicting parties
Compromise	Each party to the conflict gives up something of value.
Authoritative command	A person of power mandates an outcome and communicates it to the conflicting parties.
Altering team member behavior	Using some type of training or intervention to alter the attitudes or behaviors that are causing conflict
Altering the team structure	Changing the formal team structure so that conflicting members limit their interaction; a more extreme solution is to remove members from the team.
Conflict Stimulation Techniques	
Communication	Using ambiguous or threatening messages to increase conflict levels
Bringing in outsiders	Adding new members to the team who have different backgrounds, attitudes, values, or managerial styles
Restructuring the team	Realigning the tasks, work, or communication processes to disrupt the status quo
Appointing a devil's advocate	Having an assigned critic to argue against the team's majority position

Adapted from: Robbins and Judge (2017).

1. *Understand what your organization values.* To be a good organizational politician, you need to understand what the organization values (e.g., its mission, goals, and strategy) and align your personal goals and behavior to best help the organization achieve its objectives. By aligning your objectives with those of the organization, you are more likely to gain the support of powerful decision makers within the organization.

2. *Understand how decisions are made in your organization.* In most organizations, decisions are not necessarily made based on the formal organizational structure chart. Understanding how decisions are made and who truly has influence on those decisions is necessary for building successful alliances.

3. *Expand and strengthen your network.* To get complex development projects completed on time often requires that you are able to gain access to scarce resources and expertise. These valuable resources are often controlled by other managers who may or may not want to help you to be successful. Being a valued colleague to others by giving your time, expertise, and support is a great way to get a favor returned when one is critically needed.

4. *Develop a clear and easy-to-communicate story.* Being a successful politician requires having the right story, for the right audience, at the right time. Hearing the right story motivates team members, sponsors, and other critical stakeholders. Much like a successful coach, you must inspire confidence to get the most from you team.

5. *Lead by example.* If you are to be a great leader, your team must respect your values, judgment, work ethic, and competency to deliver a successful project. Successful

project managers understand that leading by example is a great way to inspire others to go beyond the call of duty to make the project a success.

In sum, project politics is not about winning at any cost. It is about finding common ground and building alliances to achieve organizational objectives. Being a successful project manager requires that you also be a skilled organizational politician.

Managing Global Project Teams

Global project team
A project team whose members are located throughout the world.

One important trend that most organizations are facing in the development of information systems is the increased use of **global project teams**, often referred to as *virtual teams*, with members located throughout the world. In this section, we first examine several catalysts for this trend. Next, we examine various challenges related to managing these teams. The section concludes with advice for developing stronger global information systems project teams.

Growing Numbers of Global Information Systems Projects

The use of global teams for information systems projects has become extremely popular. This growth can be attributed to three primary factors (see Figure 3.14):

1. Advances in telecommunications
2. Increased globalization
3. Increased outsourcing

All these factors are related. For example, advances in telecommunications have enabled organizations to more easily outsource part of their information systems operations, such as data entry, user support, or application programming, to locations that

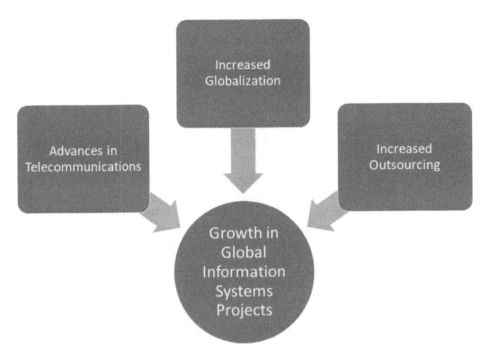

Figure 3.14   Factors that affected the growth in international information systems projects

offer cheaper labor. Yet without a high-quality network connection between sites, this would be much more difficult. In the remainder of this section, we briefly examine each of these factors.

Advances in Telecommunications

In the past decades, there have been tremendous advances in telecommunications. The proliferation of the internet and the web is the most significant example of how the connectivity across the globe has increased. Today more than 3.5 billion people have access to the internet. Advances in telecommunications—for example, twenty-four-hour global news, the internet, smartphones, instant messaging, and blogs—have led to vast increases in globalization and have also spurred the use of global project teams. A variety of communication technologies—ranging from mobile devices to electronic meeting systems—can enable teams located across the world to collaborate. (We will discuss communication and collaboration technologies in Chapter 4.)

Increased Globalization

Globalization
The integration of economies throughout the world, enabled by innovation and technological progress.

Globalization refers to the integration of economies throughout the world, enabled by innovation and technological progress (IMF, 2002). Today organizations are increasingly moving away from focusing exclusively on local markets. For example, Asian businesses such as Foxconn and Creative Technology are focusing on global markets by attempting to become serious competitors in the PC, telecommunications equipment, computer parts, and digital services industries. The Thai subsidiary of Texas Instruments is also increasing its global customer base, becoming one of the world's largest producers of microchips. PricewaterhouseCoopers is focusing on forming overseas partnerships to increase its client base and better serve regions away from its U.S. home. Today, more and more organizations are operating throughout the world; this, too, has led to an increased use of global project teams.

Changes in political systems have also opened new markets, most notably in Asia and Latin America. For instance, Hong Kong, with its sophisticated fiber-optic–based telecommunications infrastructure and multinational banks, has become a center for organizations focusing on internet-enabled business. Many Latin American countries have also liberalized and expanded their global trade, most notably Brazil, which is home to more than half of the internet users in Latin America. Likewise, China has been rapidly evolving, though market entry for international players remains severely limited, and intellectual property issues and censorship continue to be a challenge. In sum, the globalization of the world's markets is another important factor contributing to the growth of global information-systems project teams.

Increased Outsourcing

The advances in telecommunications and increased globalization have enabled organizations to seek partners with inexpensive yet high-quality labor. Much like a firm would outsource the manufacturing of some component of a physical product, firms are also now outsourcing information system development, support, and management. In 2015, the global market of outsourcing services was almost US$90 billion (Statista, 2017). Companies are choosing to outsource some or all of their information systems development, support, or management for a variety of reasons, including (King, 2003)

- To reduce or control costs
- To free up internal resources

- To gain access to world-class capabilities
- To increase revenue potential of the organization
- To reduce time to market
- To increase process efficiencies
- To outsource noncore activities
- To compensate for a lack of specific capabilities or skills

In addition to these factors, a "buy-versus-build" mentality is becoming more pervasive with increases in cloud computing. Additionally, with better low-level support and more programming tasks being outsourced, organizational IT groups increasingly are being used to integrate off-the-shelf modules with applications developed by outsourcing partners. Increased system integration and the use of global outsourcing providers make effective project planning and management extremely important. Next, we will examine some of the challenges associated with managing global information systems project teams.

Ethical Dilemma: Implications of Global Outsourcing

From software development to call centers, many companies have used outsourcing to gain access to highly skilled but inexpensive labor in foreign countries, mainly India and China. Often, companies choose to outsource certain jobs because they have a hard time finding the right workers in the United States; in many cases, however, outsourcing is done to decrease costs, which increases a company's bottom line.

Although outsourcing can be beneficial for companies, it often results in domestic job cuts. For the displaced worker, the outsourcing is not beneficial. However, recent studies claim that offshore outsourcing is not a zero-sum game; companies often use the cost reductions from outsourcing to move into new business segments or to invest in new products, thereby creating new jobs domestically.

More importantly, global outsourcing can come at a cost for the overseas workers. In many developed countries, workers have fought for decades over their working conditions and, as a result, are treated well and are paid fair wages. For the overseas workers, this is often not the case. While global outsourcing creates jobs and provides additional ways of generating income, factors such as equitable pay, workplace safety, or respectful treatment are often lacking. As a project manager, you may find yourself in a quandary. On the one hand, you may struggle to find qualified team members domestically or you may be forced to reduce labor costs. On the other hand, you may not be sure if the overseas team members are treated as they would be in your home country.

Discussion Questions

1. Although you suspect that the overseas team members might not be treated as well as your domestic team members, you know that their work ultimately helps them provide for their families. Should this consideration outweigh other ethical issues? Why or why not?

2. As a project manager, how can you ensure the ethical treatment of overseas team members? Explain.

Based on: Welinder (2017).

Challenges for Managing Global Information Systems Project Teams

Whether or not a firm is trying to integrate information systems across countries, develop a system in one country for use in another, or outsource parts of its systems development abroad, it faces many challenges when it seeks to operate across national boundaries. Challenges for managing global information systems project teams can be categorized into four broad categories (see Figure 3.15):

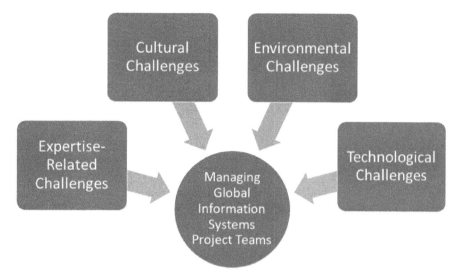

Figure 3.15 Challenges of managing global information systems project teams

1. Technology-related challenges
2. Cultural challenges
3. Human-resource challenges
4. Environmental challenges

Technology-Related Challenges

The primary technological challenge faced by organizations operating across national boundaries is related to the telecommunications infrastructure. The quality and speed of telecommunications can vary from country to country. For example, the quality of the telecommunications infrastructure can vary significantly, causing problems in data transfer and connectivity. Likewise, the sophistication and geographic coverage of a country's telecommunications infrastructure can also vary. In less developed countries, such as those in Asia or Africa, large areas can exist where no network access is available. Such gaps act as a significant barrier to developing global partnerships.

Cultural Challenges

Culture can be defined as the "collective programming of the mind that distinguishes the members of one group or category of people from another" (Hofstede, 2001, p. 9). According to Hofstede, cultures differ in a number of dimensions—namely, power distance, uncertainty avoidance, individualism/collectivism, masculinity/femininity, long-term orientation versus short term orientation, and indulgence versus restraint (see Table 3.6). As different nations have their own cultures and differ in these dimensions, it is essential to understand these differences when managing global project teams.

    The first dimension, **power distance**, describes that different societies have different views on hierarchies and power structures in organizations and teams. Whereas cultures high in power distance prefer hierarchical structures, cultures lower in power distance

Culture
The collective programming of the mind that distinguishes the members of one group or category of people from another.

Power distance
A cultural characteristic that describes how different societies handle the issue of human inequality.

Table 3.6 Critical Cultural Dimensions for Various Countries

Critical Cultural Dimensions	Countries				
	Group 1: United States, Canada, Australia	Group 2: Germany, Austria, Switzerland	Group 3: Mexico, Venezuela, Peru	Group 4: Japan	Group 5: China, Hong Kong, Singapore
Power Distance	Moderately low	Moderately low	Moderately high	Moderately high	High
Individualism/Collectivism	Highly individualistic	Moderately individualistic	Moderately to highly collectivistic	Moderately collectivistic	Moderately to highly collectivistic
Masculinity/Femininity	Moderately masculine	Moderately masculine	Moderately to highly masculine	Highly masculine	Moderately masculine
Uncertainty Avoidance	Moderately weak	Moderately strong	Moderately strong	Strong	Moderately weak
Long-Term Orientation versus Short-Term Orientation	Short term / normative	Long term / pragmatic	Short term / normative	Long term / pragmatic	Long term / pragmatic
Indulgence versus Restraint	Indulgence	Indulgence	Indulgence	Restraint	More on restraint

Based on: Hofstede (2018).

view individuals as equals. As a result, this is likely to influence leadership styles and collaborative behavior.

For instance, an information systems development project was undertaken by a Jamaican insurance company to improve its claims processing (Walsham, 2001). For this project, Indian software developers were hired to jointly develop the new information system with their Jamaican counterparts. In the initial project stages, the group worked effectively together. Over time, however, there was significant and ongoing conflict between the two groups. One of the major causes of this conflict related to differences in power distance between the Indian and Jamaican cultures. The Indian software developers, originating from a country with a relatively high power-distance culture, were viewed as being highly autocratic and were not used to being contradicted or questioned. In contrast, the Jamaican developers came from a relatively low power-distance culture, believing in consensual and democratic management styles. For them, it was most natural to sit down as a group and talk through issues when making decisions. The difference in power distance for these teams led to extensive clashes, delaying the actual development process and hurting the overall project quality.

Cultures also differ in terms or **uncertainty avoidance,** or people's willingness to take risks. Whereas team members from cultures high in uncertainty avoidance tend to be more cautious, people from cultures low in uncertainty avoidance are more willing to try new techniques or technologies. Relatedly, **individualism/collectivism** describes whether a culture values the individual over groups or vice versa. Whereas in individualistic societies, people tend to value personal achievement, the focus in collectivist cultures is on group goals. Consequently, this can cause conflicts within global project teams. The **masculinity/femininity** dimension explains in how much a culture values masculine qualities such as strength or dominance, or is characterized by feminine qualities such as modesty. As the other dimensions, this can have important consequences for not only user preferences, but also for team collaboration.

Uncertainty avoidance
A cultural characteristic that helps in understanding the risk-taking nature of a culture.

Individualism/ collectivism
A cultural characteristic that reflects the extent to which a society values the position of an individual versus the position of a group.

Masculinity/femininity
A cultural characteristic that refers to the degree to which a society is characterized by masculine or feminine qualities.

Long-term orientation versus short-term orientation
A cultural characteristic that reflects the extent to which a culture has a longer- or shorter-term orientation.

Indulgence versus restraint
A cultural characteristic that contrasts the extent to which a culture focuses on quantity of life versus quality of life.

In addition, cultures can have a longer-term orientation or a short-term orientation, as implied by a culture's **long-term orientation versus short-term orientation**. In particular, cultures with a long-term orientation are willing to forego short-term gratifications (such as material or social success) for the promise of future rewards. Finally, cultures can differ in **indulgence versus restraint,** or their focus on quantity of life versus quality of life. Whereas in cultures with a focus on quantity of life, the acquisition of material goods and competition is valued highly, cultures focusing on quality of life tend to value relationships and concern for others. In sum, global project teams composed of people with differing cultural values will be much more difficult to manage. Effective project teams will require members who are sensitive and respectful to the differences of others; it is crucial that project managers employ differing and flexible management techniques in order to help a team reach its optimal performance.

Other factors influencing global project team interaction include the following:

- Language, including accents, regional idioms, or colloquialisms
- Work culture, including habits and attitudes about work
- Aesthetics, such as different views about visual design
- Education, including literacy and attitudes about formal versus informal education
- Religion, beliefs, and attitudes about the role of spirituality in society as well as moral values
- Social organizations, such as the role of the family in society
- Political life and stability

As outlined in Table 3.7, these different factors can have tremendous effects on team interaction and performance. For instance, differences in language proficiency can lead to misunderstandings, which can have grave consequences when communicating crucial project information, such as technical specifications. Further, team members of global project teams have to adjust to different work cultures; for example, whereas Americans tend to first focus on a project's outcome, Europeans tend to use a more linear, incremental approach (Heichler, 2000). Clearly, managers of global project teams need to take a number of factors into account, so as to build a well-functioning team and achieve a successful project outcome.

Expertise Related Challenges

Apart from the cultural issues, the nature of the IS workforce can also pose significant challenges for global project teams. The level of workers' education and skills often widely varies, as does the cost for employing workers. Whereas companies operating in developed nations can draw on a large pool of skilled information systems personnel, these employees tend to be paid higher than in developing countries. In addition, different countries have historically focused on different industries, leading to different types of skills prevalent in different countries.

For instance, a cross-cultural software development project involving analysts and developers from both Norway and the United States led to conflict regarding the preferred development methodology and programming environment (Sarker and Sahay, 2004). This conflict hindered workload sharing and team cohesiveness.

Table 3.7 How Various Cultural Elements Can Affect Project Team Interaction and Performance

Cultural Element	How It Can Impact the Project
Language	Communication problems can influence project team efficiency, understanding, and performance.
Work Culture	Different skills, work habits, and attitudes can influence project performance and manpower constraints.
Aesthetics	Art, music, and dance reflect nonwork interests that can be used to enrich team communication and cohesiveness.
Education	Education levels limit skill levels, technological sophistication, and infrastructure.
Religion, Beliefs, and Attitudes	Basic values and beliefs can influence attitudes toward work, promptness, punctuality, mutual trust, respect, and cooperation.
Social Organization	Social norms can influence formal and informal communication, including negotiations and job assignments.
Political Life	Differing political systems can influence the delivery of supplies and equipment, human rights, the legal system, and overall stability.

Adapted from: Verma (1997).

Regulatory and Geoeconomic Challenges

Regulatory and geoeconomic issues can also pose significant challenges for managing global IS projects and teams due to differing rules and regulations. One example is the European Union General Data Protection Regulation of 2018, which regulates various ways in which data can be collected, stored, or transferred. For example, personal data collected in Europe can only be used for the purposes for which it was collected and cannot be easily transferred across national borders. This has caused significant challenges for U.S. organizations that employ European project team members.

Legal policies can also differ, which is often an outgrowth of the inherent culture of the country. For example, the copyright laws in China are fairly relaxed because copying is seen as a compliment to the originator of the work. The concept of ownership of intellectual property goes against the Chinese notion that the value of the society is greater than the value of the individual. The political environment can also play an important role in global project team management. A stable, political government that is keen on investing in information systems infrastructure is always more attractive to potential partners. Likewise, currency fluctuations can have significant implications for global operations and teams where changes in the exchange rate can quickly transform a low-cost geographical area to a high-cost area and vice versa.

In sum, various challenges can influence the difficulty of managing global project teams. In addition to these challenges, relatively minor issues such as differences in time zones or how intellectual property is viewed can pose formidable challenges to global project teams.

Developing Global Information Systems Project Teams

One of the keys to creating successful global project teams is to have members who can work together effectively. This means that effective project team members will not only have strong technical skills but will also be effective at working in cross-cultural teams. Unfortunately, people with good cross-cultural team training are in short supply. Nevertheless, there are several effective strategies for developing stronger global project teams, and these are discussed next (see Figure 3.16).

Figure 3.16   Strategies for developing global information systems project teams

Hire Individuals Experienced in Working across Cultures

The first strategy is very straightforward. Simply put, hiring individuals who are experienced in working on cross-cultural project teams and possess the necessary cultural sensitivity to empathize with other cultures will greatly enhance global project team performance. Pat Zilvitis, the CIO of Gillette, has repeatedly found that people who have "technical astuteness, business understanding, cultural sensitivity, and ability to communicate well" are perfect candidates for global project team assignments (Heichler, 2000). Given that it is often difficult to find people with global project team experience, another strategy is to develop the skills of existing employees. For example, many companies are rotating staff into global project teams or assigning staff to locations throughout the world.

Hire Individuals Who Can Speak Multiple Languages

A second strategy is to hire individuals who can speak different languages. Language problems within global project teams are often hidden beneath the surface. Many people are embarrassed to admit when they don't completely understand a foreign colleague. Unfortunately, the miscommunication of important design information can have disastrous effects on a project. Having at least one person at each remote location who is fluent in the host country's language can help alleviate this problem.

Make the Organizational Culture More Flexible

A third strategy is to design a flexible organizational culture that best reflects the cultural values of the local employees. For example, Fujitsu has been making strong gains in its international markets, especially in internet and multimedia products, after years of overseas failure. To gain flexibility, Fujitsu changed its culture significantly to fit the needs of local environments, such as the relaxation of strict Japanese standards of dress and the introduction of flexible working hours. This flexibility has led to enhanced organizational and project team performance.

Sensitize Teams to Global Cultural and Political Issues

A fourth strategy focuses on the development of mechanisms to help global project teams be more sensitive to the various cultural and political differences of their members. Such sensitivity and awareness can be developed through careful and in-depth training and by having a diverse mix of employees representing different cultures within the organization and team. Project team members who understand current events and the political climate of a global project team member's country will enhance project communication, team cohesiveness, and performance.

Globalization is a reality within the information systems departments of most large organizations. In the not too distant future, it will be a reality in virtually all organizations, both large and small. For better or worse, it appears that global outsourcing is here to stay. Thus, to be an effective project manager in this increasingly global environment, you must become skilled in understanding and working with cross-cultural teams.

Global Implications: Managing International Projects

Project managers who are successful in managing projects within their home countries are not always successful when assigned to manage a project in an international location. To increase your chances of success, prior to your assignment do the following:

1. Inform yourself about the country from books, newspapers, magazines, and websites.

2. Learn from others who've already experienced the country and culture.

3. Never assume that literal translations convey the spirit of a text.

4. Stay on top of current events by watching locally produced television and monitoring the local news.

5. Familiarize yourself with your host country by touring local parks, monuments, museums, entertainment locations, and other cultural venues.

6. Share meals and breaks with local workers and discuss more than just work-related issues, such as current local events and topics.

7. Know which sensitive topics to avoid during conversations.

8. Learn several words and phrases in the local language.

9. Download a translation app.

To create a successful project team environment, you need to build trust. Trust is built by showing sensitivity to and awareness of local issues, language, and culture. By following these steps, you will not only increase the project's likelihood of success; you will also make your project experience much more enjoyable.

Based on: Treitel (2000); Valacich and Schneider (2018).

Managing Project Teams and PMBOK

In this chapter, we have focused on an important part of Knowledge Area 9, *Project Resource Management*, of the *Project Management Institute Body of Knowledge* (*PMBOK*, 2017; see Figure 3.17). Specifically, we have discussed topics related to the processes *Develop Team* and *Manage Team*. Additionally, we have discussed issues related to Knowledge Area 2, the *Project Management Context*, by examining various organizational influences on projects and project managers, as well as several key general management skills for project managers. Together, this information provides a solid foundation for managing project teams.

Figure 3.17 Chapter 3 and *PMBOK* coverage

Key: ○ where the material is covered in the textbook; ● current chapter coverage

	Textbook Chapters ⟶	1	2	3	4	5	6	7	8	9	10	11	12
	PMBOK Knowledge Area												
1	Introduction												
1.2	Foundational Elements	○	○										
2	The Environment in Which Projects Operate												
2.2	Enterprise Environmental Factors		○										
2.2	Organizational Process Assets		○										
2.3	Organizational Systems		○										
3	The Role of the Project Manager												
3.2	Definition of a Project Manager	○											
3.3	The Project Manager's Sphere of Influence		○										
3.4	Project Manager Competences	○	○	●									
3.5	Performing Integration		○										
4	Project Integration Management												
4.1	Develop Project Charter					○							
4.2	Develop Project Management Plan					○							
4.3	Direct and Manage Project Work											○	
4.4	Manage Project Knowledge											○	
4.5	Monitor and Control Project Work											○	○
4.6	Perform Integrated Change Control												○
4.7	Close Project or Phase										○		○
5	Project Scope Management												
5.1	Plan Scope Management					○							
5.2	Collect Requirements					○							
5.3	Define Scope					○							
5.4	Create WBS					○	○						
5.5	Validate Scope					○							
5.6	Control Scope					○							○
6	Project Schedule Management												
6.1	Plan Schedule Management						○						
6.2	Define Activities						○						
6.3	Sequence Activities						○						
6.4	Estimate Activity Durations							○					
6.5	Develop Schedule							○					
6.6	Control Schedule							○					○
7	Project Cost Management												
7.1	Plan Cost Management								○				

		1	2	3	4	5	6	7	8	9	10	11	12
7.2	Estimate Costs								O				
7.3	Determine Budget								O				
7.4	Control Costs								O				O
8	**Project Quality Management**												
8.1	Plan Quality Management								O				
8.2	Manage Quality								O				
8.3	Control Quality								O				O
9	**Project Resource Management**												
9.1	Plan Resource Management							O					
9.2	Estimate Activity Resources						O	O					
9.3	Acquire Resources							O				O	
9.4	Develop Team			●									
9.5	Manage Team			●									
9.6	Control Resources							O					O
10	**Project Communications Management**												
10.1	Plan Communications Management				O								
10.2	Manage Communications				O							O	
10.3	Monitor Communications				O								O
11	**Project Risk Management**												
11.1	Plan Risk Management									O			
11.2	Identify Risks									O		O	
11.3	Perform Qualitative Risk Analysis									O			
11.4	Perform Quantitative Risk Analysis									O			
11.5	Plan Risk Responses									O			
11.6	Implement Risk Responses									O		O	
11.7	Monitor Risks									O			O
12	**Project Procurement Management**												
12.1	Plan Procurement Management										O		
12.2	Conduct Procurements										O	O	
12.3	Control Procurements										O		O
13	**Project Stakeholder Management**												
12.1	Identify Stakeholders				O								
12.2	Plan Stakeholder Engagement				O								
12.3	Manage Stakeholder Engagement				O							O	
12.4	Monitor Stakeholder Engagement				O								O

Running Case: Managing Project Teams

James Cheung, the assistant director of information technology at Jackie's, a Bay Area–based electronics retail store chain, walked into his building's conference room. It was early in the morning for James, but the meeting was important to him. He was going to put together his team for the customer-relationship project he had just been named to manage. It was James's first big project to manage at Jackie's, and he was excited about getting started.

"Hi, James," said Sarah Codey, the chief operations officer. Sarah sat next to a guy James did not know. "This is Trey Lyman, James. I've asked that he be on your project team to represent me."

James and Trey shook hands. "Nice to meet you, James. I'm looking forward to working with you on this project."

"Trey knows how important this project is to me," Sarah said, "so I expect him to keep me informed about your progress." She smiled.

Great, James thought, *more pressure. That's all I need.* Just then, Nick Baldwin, the head of marketing, walked into the conference room. With him was a young woman James recognized, but he wasn't sure where he had seen her.

"James," Nick said, "let me introduce you to Cindy Kobayashi. She is the assistant director of marketing. She will be representing marketing and me on your No Customer Escapes project."

"Hi, James," Cindy said. "I have a lot of ideas about what we can do. Even though I still have my regular job to worry about, I'm excited about working on this project."

"Who else will be on your team?" Sarah asked.

"I am bringing Kevin Woodfield from IT," James said. "He is in charge of systems integration in the IT department and reports to me. In addition to me and Kevin and Cindy and Trey, we will also have a store manager on the team. I'm trying to get Maria Gutierrez, the manager of the store in Riverside. Like the rest of us, she is really busy, but I think we have to have a store manager on the team."

"Riverside?" Sarah asked. "That's one of our top stores. Maria should have a lot of insight into the issues related to keeping customers if she is managing the Riverside store. And you are right, she is going to be very busy."

"So," Nick asked, "when is your first meeting?"

Adapted from: Valacich and George (2017).

Chapter Summary

Describe the characteristics of a project team and the factors that influence team performance. A project team consists of two or more people who are mutually accountable to the organization and to each member of the team; they are also highly interdependent, having both shared goals and complementary skills. Project teams do not automatically become highly interdependent and productive but must develop and evolve through various stages as they work together over time. When teams develop, they pass through five stages: forming, storming, norming, performing, and adjourning. Work design, composition, context, and process factors are just some of the many factors that influence team performance. The tools and techniques of two key processes, *Develop Team* and *Manage Team*, can help managers and their teams achieve successful projects.

Explain how to motivate team members. Motivation refers to an individual's intensity, direction, and persistence of effort toward attaining a goal. There have been contrasting views of how, why, and when people are motivated. Need theories of motivation deal with factors within a person that act to energize, direct, or stop various behaviors. For example, good working conditions may energize a person to work hard on a project. Process theories of motivation attempt to understand a person's behavior based on intrinsic or personal factors that are used to motivate specific behavior. In general, this perspective suggests that project managers need to create a proper environment, work processes, and rewards to inspire the greatest levels of motivation in people.

Explain the sources and effects of leadership, power, and conflict in a project team. Leadership is the ability to influence people toward the achievement of goals. There are three primary schools of thought regarding why certain people are great leaders. First, trait theories of leadership posit that personality, appearance, competency, and other personal characteristics differentiate leaders from nonleaders. Second, behavioral theories of leadership propose that people's actions, rather than personal traits, determine their potential to be successful leaders. Third, contingency theories of leadership propose that the situation is the most critical element for successful leadership. Power refers to the absolute capacity of a person to influence the behavior or attitudes of one or more target persons at a given point in time. Researchers have identified two general types of power that can be used to influence the behavior and attitudes of others: positional power and personal power. Positional power is based on an individual's position in an organization and can be one of five types: legitimate, reward, coercive, informational, and ecological. Personal power is based on an individual's unique characteristics and can be one of three types: expert, referent, and charismatic. Conflict is the opposition of people in an organization arising from incompatible or opposing needs, drives, wishes, or external or internal demands. There are two general types of conflict within project teams: functional and dysfunctional. Functional conflict helps support the goals of the team and improve its performance, whereas dysfunctional conflict hinders group performance and is destructive to team performance.

Explain why global project teams are increasing and describe the challenges of managing these teams. The use of global teams for information systems projects has become increasingly popular due to three primary factors: (1) advances in telecommunications, (2) increased globalization, and (3) increased outsourcing. Although global project teams have become widespread, there are many challenges for managing these teams, including (1) technology-related challenges, (2) cultural challenges, (3) human-resource challenges, and (4) regulatory and geoeconomic challenges. Because of this, you must become skilled in understanding and working with cross-cultural teams to be an effective project manager.

Key Terms Review

A. Absenteeism
B. Behavioral theories of leadership
C. Conflict
D. Conflict management
E. Contingency theories of leadership
F. Culture
G. Dysfunctional conflict
H. Equity theory
I. ERG theory
J. Expectancy theory
K. Functional conflict
L. Global project team
M. Globalization
N. Goal-setting theory
O. Hierarchy of needs
P. Individualism/collectivism
Q. Indulgence versus restraint
R. Job satisfaction
S. Leader
T. Leadership

U. Long-term orientation versus short-term orientation
V. Manager
W. Masculinity/femininity
X. Motivation
Y. Myers-Briggs Type Indicator (MBTI)
Z. Personal power
AA. Positional power
BB. Power
CC. Power distance
DD. Project team
EE. Reinforcement theory
FF. Theory of needs
GG. Theory X
HH. Theory Y
II. Theory Z
JJ. Trait theories of leadership
KK. Turnover
LL. Two-factor theory
MM. Uncertainty avoidance

Match each of the key terms with the definition that best fits it.

1. A cultural characteristic that contrasts the extent to which a culture focuses on quantity of life versus quality of life.
2. A cultural characteristic that describes how different societies handle the issue of human inequality.

3. A cultural characteristic that helps in understanding the risk-taking nature of a culture.

4. A cultural characteristic that refers to the degree to which a society is characterized by masculine or feminine qualities.

5. A cultural characteristic that reflects the extent to which a culture has a longer- or shorter-term orientation.

6. A cultural characteristic that reflects the extent to which a society values the position of an individual versus the position of a group.

7. A formal position of authority in an organization that is responsible for planning, organizing, directing, monitoring, and controlling the activities of others.

8. A hierarchy of needs—physiological, safety, social, esteem, and self-actualization—where as each need is met, the next higher-level need becomes the motivating focus.

9. A motivation theory that argues that both positive and negative feedback condition behavior.

10. A person, who, by virtue of his or her personal attributes, can exert influence on others.

11. A project team whose members are located throughout the world.

12. A set of leadership theories that argue people's actions determine their potential to be successful leaders.

13. A set of leadership theories that suggest personality, appearance, competency, and other personal characteristics differentiate leaders from nonleaders.

14. A set of leadership theories that suggest that the situation is most critical for identifying leadership success.

15. A widely used personality test.

16. An individual's intensity, direction, and persistence of effort toward attaining a goal.

17. Conflict that hinders group performance and interferes with team performance.

18. Conflict that supports the goals of the team and improves its performance.

19. Individuals compare their work inputs and outcomes with those of others and then respond to eliminate any inequities.

20. Individuals' motivation can be explained by their need for achievement, power, and affiliation.

21. Intrinsic factors (*motivational factors*) are related to job satisfaction, whereas extrinsic factors (*hygiene factors*) are associated with dissatisfaction.

22. Motivational theory reflecting the Japanese work philosophy that includes a belief in lifetime employment, strong company loyalty, and group consensus.

23. Motivational theory that assumes people dislike work, are lazy, dislike responsibilities, and must be coerced to work hard.

24. Motivational theory that assumes people like work, are creative, like autonomy, and seek responsibility.

25. People exert a high level of effort when they believe that (1) effort will lead to a good performance appraisal, (2) a good appraisal will lead to rewards, and (3) these rewards will satisfy their needs.

26. Power derived from an individual's position in an organization.

27. Power derived from an individual's unique characteristics.

28. Specific and difficult goals, with clear feedback on how well a person is meeting the goals, can enhance a person's work productivity.

29. The ability to influence people toward the achievement of goals.

30. The absolute capacity of a person to influence the behavior or attitudes of one or more target persons at a given point in time.

31. The collective programming of the mind that distinguishes the members of one group or category of people from another.

32. The failure to report to work.

33. The general attitude a person has toward his or her job.

34. The integration of economies throughout the world, enabled by innovation and technological progress.

35. The opposition of people in an organization arising from incompatible or opposing needs, drives, wishes, or external or internal demands.

36. The rate at which people voluntarily or involuntarily leave an organization.

37. The use of resolution and stimulation techniques to achieve a desired level of team conflict.

38. Three core needs—existence, relatedness, and growth—of which more than one need may be operative at the same time; if the fulfillment of a higher-level need is unrealized, the desire to satisfy a lower-level need becomes the motivating focus.

39. Two or more people who share the same goals, are interdependent, have complementary skills, and are mutually accountable to the organization and to each member of the team.

Review Questions

1. How is a project team different from a group?

2. Describe the five stages of project team development.

3. Discuss how work design, composition, context, and process influence project team performance.

4. What is motivation, and why is it important for project managers to understand why and how people are motivated?

5. Describe and contrast the hierarchy of needs, the ERG theory, and the two-factor theory.

6. What are process theories of motivation?

7. Contrast what is meant by hygiene factors versus motivational factors in the two-factor theory of motivation. Which is more important? Why?

8. Describe how leadership and power can be used to influence project team members.

9. Explain and contrast trait, behavioral, and contingency theories of leadership.

10. Describe various types of positional power and personal power.

11. Describe and contrast functional versus dysfunctional conflict and how conflict management techniques can be used to manage conflict within a team.

12. What factors have led to the increased use of global project teams?

13. Explain and contrast various technological, cultural, human-resource, and geoeconomic challenges of managing global project teams.

Chapter Exercises

1. Do you prefer to work as part of a team or alone? Why? How do you think your answer compares with others in your class? Does this preference depend on what type of task you are working on?

2. What types of problems might occur at each stage in the five-stage team development model?

3. Can a person be too motivated? Why or why not?

4. What motivates professional employees? What motivates hourly workers?

5. Do you think you have the traits and skills to be a leader? Why or why not?

6. Distinguish between leadership and management. Do you think you would be a better leader or a better manager? Why?

7. Which type of power—positional or personal—has the greatest influence on other team members within an information systems project team? Why?

8. Some conflict is good for a project team, whereas other types of conflict are bad. Which type of conflict causes the greatest problems in project teams? Why?

9. Global outsourcing appears to be here to stay. Use the web to identify a company that is providing low-cost labor from some less-developed part of the world. Provide a short report that explains who they are, where they are located, who their customers are, what services and capabilities they provide, how long they have been in business, and any other interesting information you can find in your research.

10. Examine Table 3.6 and rate yourself for each of the critical cultural dimensions. Do your ratings match those of your country in every instance? If they do, why do you think this is so? If not, why not?

11. Contrast the pros and cons of managing diverse project teams.

12. What are the implications of new forms of technology-mediated communication for managing project teams?

13. Leaders can come from all backgrounds, genders, and races. Meet with a team of three to five students and identify what makes the following individuals more effective (or less effective) leaders: Mark Zuckerberg, Harry Welch, Elon Musk, Bill Gates, and Oprah Winfrey. Write a one-page summary of your results.

14. Throughout your life—at school, work, or socially—you have undoubtedly participated on a team. Meet with a team of three to five students and identify, without naming names, the "worst team member I have ever worked with." During this discussion, identify the key factors as to why each nominated worst team member was chosen, and summarize this in a one-page report to your instructor.

Chapter Case: Sedona Management Group and Managing Project Teams

The Sedona Management Group (SMG) recognizes the importance of teamwork in the successful completion of projects. Tim Turnpaugh also believes in building a project team based on both the skills and diversity in background of the project team members. To Turnpaugh, diversity in background adds fresh ideas that can enhance the quality of SMG's products. As an example, the chief programmer at SMG not only has the expected skills in PHP, Ajax, and MySQL, but he is also a professional jazz musician. Another member of SMG's team, a graphic designer, was a physical therapist and an artist prior to joining the team. Turnpaugh believes that such diverse backgrounds allow people to approach problems differently, see issues from different perspectives, and in many ways, enhance the quality of the work environment. All these factors not only result in enhanced project quality but also help the team learn to "think outside the box" and build new products and services that enhance customer satisfaction and loyalty.

What does it take to be an employee at SMG? The Sedona team looks for intrinsically motivated individuals, people who enjoy their work, whether it be building applications or interacting with SMG's diverse client base.

While these individuals should have the necessary technical expertise, such as skills in PHP, Ajax, and MySQL, their ability to work as members of the Sedona team and create a fun work environment are also highly valued. SMG looks for people who strive for perfection in what they do. Turnpaugh believes that these characteristics—while they can be developed to some extent—are highly dependent on the person's basic personality and attitudes. Individuals who enjoy their work and pay attention to details make great employees for a self-managed work team environment, such as that at SMG. While compensation and other forms of extrinsic motivation are always important for any work environment, Turnpaugh seeks employees who are self-motivated to succeed and have fun while working.

In several situations, Turnpaugh has trained unskilled employees—what he calls *rookies*. He emphasizes that if an individual comes from a different background, the focus is not on stripping the employee's knowledge and starting over again but rather on finding ways to complement that existing knowledge with the knowledge that will be gained working with the team. In the case of the graphic designer turned web interface designer, the employee's knowledge as an artist augments her ability in designing the interface for the system. As these skills are merged, Turnpaugh calls these people *Ninjas*, in that they become experts in their areas—beyond the normal black belt. He adds that he would rather have a few Ninjas on his team than a bunch of non-Ninjas. Central to SMG's personnel philosophy is that recruitment is key. A smart, personable, hard-working individual can, in many instances, acquire the appropriate skills for his position. The reverse, however, is not true. While skilled, a person who isn't motivated to work hard and cannot enjoy the work environment may never acquire these attributes.

SMG's reward and recognition system is set up to reward both individual behavior and teamwork. While Turnpaugh recognizes individual members of the Sedona team who have done something extra to ensure customer satisfaction, rewards are also given for group-level performance to ensure people are pulling together as a team. To further enhance the social fabric and teamwork aspects of his organization, social events are frequently planned after the team has successfully completed a project. Many members of the Sedona team genuinely like each other and share common hobbies and time together after work.

Finally, Turnpaugh stresses the importance of smaller teams with three to seven members. Larger teams frequently suffer from problems associated with managing schedules and interteam communication. The Sedona team has found that communication is vital to the management and success of any project and that members of a smaller team tend to be in constant communication with each other. Consequently, these smaller teams can work more effectively toward fulfilling the customer's needs.

Chapter 3 Project Assignment

As you have learned from this chapter, it takes teamwork to successfully complete most projects. The members of your entertainment website development team must work together to achieve the project objectives. For this assignment, you will find out what you need to work as a successful team.

1. As an individual-level assignment, determine at least five things that really work well, and five that do not, when managing teams.

2. Get together with your team members and discuss what each of you has written in response to Question 1.

3. Establish a set of ground rules that you will use during the project to manage team interactions.

4. Also determine a responsibility assignment matrix that defines who will perform what work at a very general level.

5. Identify the skills that are most important for the project manager.

References

Adams, J. S. (1965). Inequity in Social Exchanges. In L. Berkowitz (ed.), *Advances in Experimental Social Psychology*. New York: Academic Press, pp. 267–300.

Alderfer, C. P. (1969). An Empirical Test of a New Theory of Human Needs. *Organizational Behavior and Human Performance*, May, 142–175.

Blanchard, K., Fowler, S., and Hawkins, L. (2005). *Self-Leadership and the One Minute Manager: Increasing Effectiveness through Situational Self Leadership*. New York: William Morrow.

Canadian Space Agency (2016, February). Evaluation of the Canadian Space Agency's International Space Station Assembly and Maintenance Operations Program. *Canadian Space Agency*. Retrieved July 4, 2018, from http://www.asc-csa.gc.ca/eng/publications/er-1415-0201.asp

Canadian Space Agency (2016, November 28). Dextre, the International Space Station's Robotic Handyman. *Canadian Space Agency*. Retrieved July 4, 2018, from http://www.asc-csa.gc.ca/eng/iss/dextre/default.asp

Carey, B. (2005, May 4). Remote Access: Canadarm 2 Gets a Hand from Ground Control. *Space.com*. Retrieved July 4, 2018, from http://www.space.com/1033-remote-access-canadarm-2-hand-ground-control.html

Choo, G. (2003, January 13). The Politics of Projects. *ProjectManagement.com*. Retrieved July 4, 2018, from https://www.projectmanagement.com/articles/157963/The-Politics-of-Projects

Fiedler, F. E. (1968). *A Theory of Leadership Effectiveness*. New York: McGraw-Hill.

Fisher, A. (2012, November 30). Super-Talented Employee Driving You Crazy? How to Deal. *Fortune*. Retrieved July 4, 2018, from http://fortune.com/2012/11/30/super-talented-employee-driving-you-crazy-how-to-deal

French, J. R. P., Jr., and Raven, B. (1959). The Bases of Social Power. In D. Cartwright (ed.), *Studies in Social Power*. Ann Arbor: University of Michigan, Institute for Social Research, pp. 150–167.

Heichler, E. (2000, June 15). A Head for the Business. *ComputerWorld*. Retrieved July 4, 2018, from http://www.computerworld.com.au/article/34819/head_business

Herzberg, F., Mausner, B, and Snyderman, B. (1959). *The Motivation to Work*. New York: Wiley.

Hofstede, G. (2001). *Cultures Consequences: Comparing Values, Behaviors, Institutions, and Organizations across Nations* (2nd ed.). Thousand Oaks, CA: Sage Publications.

Hofstede, G. (2018). Compare Countries. *Hofstede Insights*. Retrieved July 9, 2018, from https://www.hofstede-insights.com/product/compare-countries

Howard, A. (2001). Software Engineering Project Management. *Communications of the ACM* 44 (5): 23–24.

Ivancevich, J. M., and Duening, T. N. (2002). *Managing Einsteins: Leading High-Tech Workers in the Digital Age*. New York: McGraw Hill.

Jones, T. (2017, December 20). Six Tips for Choosing Effective Project Team Members. *BrightWork*. Retrieved July 4, 2018, from https://www.brightwork.com/blog/6-tips-choosing-effective-project-team-members

Jung, J. J. H., Schneider, C., and Valacich, J. (2010). Enhancing the Motivational Affordance of Information Systems: The Effects of Real-Time Performance Feedback and Goal Setting in Group Collaboration Environments. *Management Science* 56 (4): 724–742.

Kerr, J. (2014, July 25). Six Ways to Manage a Team of Superstars. *FastCompany*. Retrieved July 4, 2018, from https://www.fastcompany.com/3033481/6-ways-to-manage-a-team-of-superstars

King, J. (2003, September 15). IT's Global Itinerary: Offshore Outsourcing is Inevitable. *ComputerWorld*. Retrieved July 4, 2018, from http://www.computerworld.com/article/2572756/it-outsourcing/it-s-global-itinerary--offshore-outsourcing-is-inevitable.html

Komaki, J. L., Coombs, T., and Schepman, S. (1996). Motivational Implications of Reinforcement Theory. In R. M. Steers, L. W. Porter, and G. Bigley (eds.), *Motivation and Work Behavior* (6th ed.). New York: McGraw-Hill, pp. 87–107.

Locke, E. A. (1968). Towards a Theory of Task Motivation and Incentives. *Organizational Behavior and Human Performance*, May, pp. 157–189.

Maslow, A. (1954). *Motivation and Personality*. New York: Harper & Row.

McClelland, D. C. (1961). *The Achieving Society*. New York: Van Nostrand Reinhold.

McGregor, D. (1960). *The Human Side of Enterprise*. New York: McGraw-Hill.

Melymuka, K. (2004, April 12). How to Pick a Project Team. *ComputerWorld*. Retrieved July 4, 2018, from http://www.computerworld.com/article/2563667/it-management/how-to-pick-a-project-team.html

Ouchi, W. G. (1981). *Theory Z: How American Business Can Meet the Japanese Challenge*. Reading, MA: Addison-Wesley.

Owens, S. D., and McLaurin, J. R. (1993). Cultural Diversity and Projects: What the Project Manager Needs to Know. *Proceedings of the 1993 Seminars and Symposium*. Upper Darby, PA: Project Management Institute.

Project Management Institute (2017). *Agile Practice Guide*. Newton Square, PA: Author.

Project Management Institute (2017). *PMBOK: A Guide to the Project Management Body of Knowledge* (6th ed.). Newtown Square, PA: Author.

Robertson, R. (1992). *Globalization: Social Theory and Global Culture*. London: Sage.

Robbins, S. P., and Judge, T. A. (2017). *Organizational Behavior* (17th ed.). Boston: Pearson.

Ryan, L. (2018, January 25). The "Curse of Competence": Why Top Performers Quit Their Jobs. *Forbes.* Retrieved July 4, 2018, from https://www.forbes.com/sites/lizryan/2018/01/25/the-curse-of-competence-why-top-performers-quit-their-jobs

Sarker, S., and Sahay, S. (2004). Implications of Space and Time for Distributed Work: An Interpretive Study of US-Norwegian Systems Development Teams. *European Journal of Information Systems* 13 (1): 3–20.

Statista, 2017. Global Market Size of Outsourced Services from 2000 to 2015 (in Billion U.S. Dollars). *Statista.com.* Retrieved July 4, 2018, from https://www.statista.com/statistics/189788/global-outsourcing-market-size

Thamhain, H., and Wilemon, D. L. (1975). Conflict Management in Project Life Cycles. *Sloan Management Review* 17 (3): 21–50.

Treitel, R. (2000, October 9). Global Success. *ProjectManagement.com.* Retrieved July 4, 2018, from https://www.projectmanagement.com/articles/12706/Global-Success

Tucker, M. L., McCarthy, A. M., and Benton, D. A. (2002). *The Human Challenge: Managing Yourself and Others in Organizations* (7th ed.). Upper Saddle River, NJ: Prentice Hall.

Tuckman, B. (1965). Developmental Sequence in Small Groups. *Psychological Bulletin* 63 (6): 384–399.

Valacich, J., and Schneider, C. (2018). *Information Systems Today: Managing in the Digital World* (8th ed.). Boston: Pearson.

Verma, V. K. (1996). *Human Resource Skills for the Project Manager*. Newton Square, PA: Project Management Institute.

Verma, V. K. (1997). *Managing the Project Team*. Newton Square, PA: Project Management Institute.

Von Briel, F., Schneider, C., and Lowry, P. (2018). Absorbing Knowledge from and with External Partners: The Role of Social Integration Mechanisms. *Decision Sciences Journal.* https://doi.org/10.1111/deci.12314

Vroom, V. H. (1964). *Work and Motivation*. New York: Wiley.

Walsham, G. (2001). *Making a World of Difference: IS in a Global Context*. Chichester, UK: John Wiley & Sons.

Welinder, S. (2017, March 29). Outsourcing for Change: Building Ethics in a Global Economy. *Home Business.* Retrieved July 4, 2018, from https://homebusinessmag.com/growing-a-business/diversifying-a-biz/outsourcing-change-building-ethics-global-economy

Yukl, G. (2006). *Leadership in Organizations* (6th ed.). Upper Saddle River, NJ: Prentice Hall.

CHAPTER 4

Managing Project Stakeholders and Communication

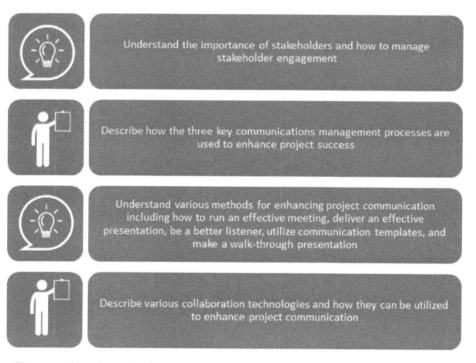

Figure 4.1 Chapter 4 learning objectives

For any company, communicating and interacting with the larger stakeholder community is essential. In an attempt to improve communication with its developer community, Microsoft launched Channel 9, a website promoting dialogue between internal software evangelists (Microsoft programming and application experts) and its external developer community (see Figure 4.2). Channel 9 provides up-to-date collections of video interviews with members of various Microsoft product groups so

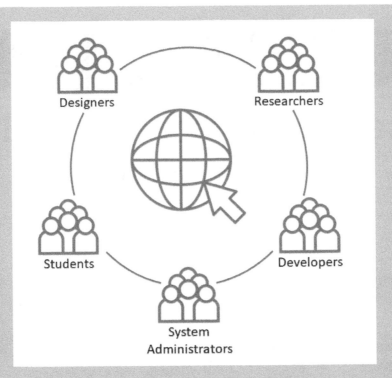

Figure 4.2 Channel 9 is improving Microsoft's communication with its developer community.

that the developer community can be the first to learn about changing plans, new developments, or potential problems. The site provides an online forum, allowing developers to create profiles for themselves and to post comments and questions about videos and other content. Channel 9 also incorporates blogs, wikis, and user-editable web pages to better reach out to the Microsoft developer community.

Visitors can gain an insider's view of current and future developments. The site was named after the United Airlines in-flight audio channel that broadcasts cockpit communications. Similarly, Microsoft envisions enhanced communication that will enable the organization to learn how to best serve its developer community by allowing developers to listen in on internal Microsoft communication. The welcome page on the site makes this point by stating, "We think developers need their own Channel 9, a way to listen in to the cockpit at Microsoft, an opportunity to learn how we fly, a chance to get to know our pilots." Microsoft is convinced that better communication is fundamental to better serving its customers through dialogue and learning.

Based on: Evers (2004); Microsoft (2016, 2018).

Introduction

In the previous chapter, we discussed how critical people are to the success of a project. We examined various aspects of project team composition and management, including motivation, leadership, power, conflict, and a variety of other issues. In addition, a project's stakeholders can positively or negatively affect a project. Thus effective communication within a project team as well as with a project's stakeholders is essential to project success. In information systems project teams, effective communication is particularly important because there is often a broad communication gap between technical development team members and nontechnical individuals, both inside and outside the team. This gap is the result of at least three factors: First, some individuals with technical training might not have adequate communication skills. Second, the nature of information technology is constantly changing, with new devices and jargon. Third, nontechnical stakeholders may not be able to effectively communicate their needs to the technical development team members. Together these factors can create formidable communication barriers between technical and nontechnical people. Likewise, identifying and effectively engaging stakeholders can help shape their expectations and align them with the project's objectives. In this chapter, therefore, we focus on managing stakeholders and project team communication. In the next section, we examine the key processes of project stakeholder management: *Identify Stakeholders*, *Plan Stakeholder Engagement*, *Manage Stakeholder Engagement*, and *Monitor Stakeholder Engagement*. We then examine three key communication processes for project teams: *Plan Communications Management*, *Manage Communications*, and *Monitor Communications*. We conclude by discussing several methods or techniques for enhancing project communication and describe various collaboration technologies that project teams can utilize to enhance communication.

Project Stakeholder Management

As defined in Chapter 1, stakeholders are individuals, groups, and organizations that are actively involved in the project, who have a vested interest in its success, and/or who have influence over the project and its results. As their influence can be positive or negative, the project management team must identify the project stakeholders in order to manage their expectations. If stakeholders expect too much from a project or if their expectations are not realistic, then they are unlikely to be satisfied with the project's progress or its end product. Failure to identify a key stakeholder can cause major problems for a project. Many different individuals can be stakeholders for a particular project. Key stakeholders include

- Project manager
- Customer
- Performing organization—those doing the work of the project
- Project team members
- Influencers—those who may not buy or use the project's product but who can have a positive or negative influence on the project
- Project management office
- Sponsor

The sponsor is the individual in the organization who has ultimate responsibility for the project and its success, and who may also have financial responsibility for it. Many others both inside and outside the project organization may be stakeholders. These include sellers, owners, government agencies, media, lobbying organizations, and so on. For example, stakeholders of a data center project that uses the water of a nearby river for cooling purposes include not only project team members and the performing organization, but also entities external to the organization, such as the data center's customers, neighbors, or even anglers who regularly fish downstream from the new data center. While the latter may not seem to be important at first, they may be highly concerned about the project's impact on recreational (or commercial) activities and may have a strong voice in the local community. As you can see, the types of stakeholders, their level of interest, and their potential influence are quite diverse, and it is critical to continuously engage stakeholders so as to resolve potential issues and steer their expectations into the intended direction. Many different individuals and groups with a stake in a project can contribute to different and conflicting expectations. The more expectations there are, and the more they contradict each other, the more difficult it will be to manage them. How does a project manager decide whom to try to keep happy? This is a big challenge. One rule of thumb is to try to meet the customer's requirements, but that does not mean everyone else can be safely ignored. Project stakeholder management thus includes four key processes (*PMBOK*, 2017):

1. *Identify Stakeholders.* The process involved in identifying stakeholders and analyzing and classifying their levels of interest, expectations, and potential influence
2. *Plan Stakeholder Engagement.* The processes for developing a stakeholder management plan, which specifies how to engage stakeholders at various phases of the project and how to maintain relationships with key stakeholders
3. *Manage Stakeholder Engagement.* The processes of communicating with stakeholders to increase support and/or minimize resistance
4. *Monitor Stakeholder Engagement.* The processes of monitoring the effectiveness of the stakeholder engagement processes and adjusting processes to maximize effectiveness

Next, we will discuss each of these processes individually.

Identify Stakeholders

The *Identify Stakeholders* process is critical to successful stakeholder engagement, as it helps managers understand the nature of the stakeholders, their interests, and potential influence they may have on project success. Consequently, identifying and classifying stakeholders helps guide the communication efforts throughout the different stages of a project. A key technique in the *Identify Stakeholders* process is stakeholder analysis, which involves identifying the different stakeholders, assessing their potential impact, as well as assessing possible stakeholder responses. Importantly, as the interest and influence of stakeholders may change, the project manager should conduct this analysis not only at the beginning of a project but also over the different stages of a project. In addition to having an interest in the project or its outcomes, stakeholders may have rights or ownership, or promote the project through the contribution of resources or knowledge. To help with the classification of stakeholders, project managers use tools such as power/interest grids, power/influence grids, or influence/impact grids, which are used to classify stakeholders based on their interest, influence, level of authority, or potential impact on a project's outcome (see Figure 4.3). Similarly, a salience model (typically in the form of a Venn diagram) classifies stakeholders based on the three dimensions: power, legitimacy, and urgency. A stakeholder's position in the diagram determines the level of needed engagement, based on the ability to influence the project outcome (power), legitimacy of their involvement, and urgency of communication needs (see Figure 4.4). The stakeholder register is created as an output of the *Identify Stakeholders* process. The stakeholder register contains not only names, addresses, and other pertinent information about stakeholders, but also assessments of their expectations of and influence on the various phases, as well as each stakeholder's classification.

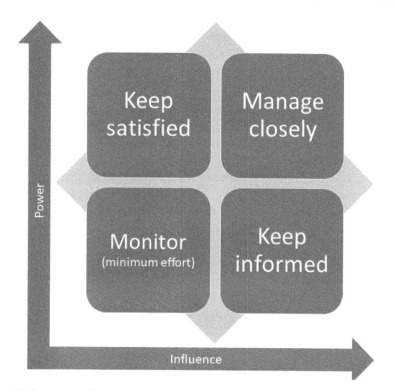

Figure 4.3 Power/influence grid

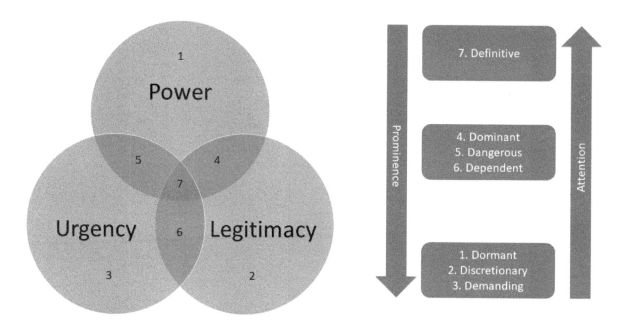

Figure 4.4 Salience model

Plan Stakeholder Engagement

Once the stakeholders and their interests, influence, and expectations have been iden-tified, the next step is to plan how to effectively maintain relationships with the various stakeholders, so as to harness positive influences and minimize any potential negative impacts. Typically, this process includes classifying stakeholders based on their level of support and their level of awareness of the project and its impacts (see Figure 4.5). A stakeholder engagement assessment matrix is used to indicate current and desired engagement levels for each stakeholder (see Figure 4.6). This matrix can be shared easily among team members and stakeholders outside the project team, to ensure that the right people are getting the right information in the right format at the right time.

The stakeholder engagement plan details the outputs of the stakeholder classifica-tion, as well as the methods of how and when information needs to be distributed, so as maximize the effectiveness of stakeholder engagement. Needless to say, analysis and assessment of stakeholders may contain sensitive information, and project managers should ensure that only information should be included or distributed that would not hurt the project if it were made public.

Manage Stakeholder Engagement

The *Manage Stakeholder Engagement* process puts the previous process in motion; during this ongoing process, communication activities are conducted to engage stakeholders, manage their expectations, and address concerns and resolve issues that may arise as the project progresses through the different phases. Typical outputs are the communications (such as reports or presentations), but also change requests arising from interactions with stakeholders, updates to other project documents (such as the stakeholder register), or lessons learned for future projects.

Figure 4.5 Project stakeholders can range from being unaware of the project and its impact to being actively engaged in ensuring the success of a project.

	Unaware	Resistant	Neutral	Supportive	Leading
Stakeholder 1	C		D		
Stakeholder 2			C,D		
Stakeholder 3			C	D	
...					
Stakeholder x		C	D		

Figure 4.6. A stakeholder engagement assessment matrix is used to indicate the current ("C") and desired ("D") level of each stakeholder's engagement.

Monitor Stakeholder Engagement

Just as the *Monitor Communications* process involves continuously assessing the effectiveness of communication processes, the *Monitor Stakeholder Engagement* process entails assessing the effectiveness of the strategies for engaging stakeholders and managing their relationships. For example, if the activities performed in the *Manage Stakeholder Engagement* process are ineffective in bringing a particular stakeholder from the current to the desired engagement level, communication activities may have to be adjusted, or changes to the project will need to be made to account for this.

Project Communications Management

Communication
A process by which information is exchanged between individuals through a common system of symbols, signs, or behavior.

Feedback
The response process by a receiver to a sender within the communication process.

Noise
Audio, visual, or environmental interference within the communication process.

Interactive communication
A form of communication in which two or more parties exchange information.

Push communication
A form of communication where information is distributed by the sender to specific recipients or general audiences, but receipt of the information is not ensured.

Pull communication
A form of communication where the receiver must retrieve the information.

Communication—a process by which information is exchanged between individuals through a common system of symbols, signs, or behavior (Verma, 1997)—is the lifeblood of a project team. Without effective communication, a team cannot be successful. Likewise, communication is key to engaging the project's stakeholders. In order for communication to be successful, the communication receiver must understand the message that the communication sender intended to send, and both the sender and receiver must agree that the receiver has understood the message (see Figure 4.7). After the sender encodes and transmits a message, the receiver decodes the message, acknowledges receipt, and sends **feedback** to ensure that the message was understood and provides a response. Within the communication process, **noise** can affect the transmission and reception of the message, either consciously or unconsciously, through audio, visual, or environmental interference. Communication noise can be as simple as an open window with a warm breeze, the smell of food when hungry, or the sight or sounds of people outside an open office door. The aforementioned example is an example of **interactive communication**, in which two or more parties exchange information. Another form of communication is **push communication**, such as emails or letters, where information is distributed by the sender to specific recipients or general audiences, but receipt of the information is not ensured, and the recipient may or may not acknowledge receipt or provide feedback. In contrast, **pull communication** takes place when the receiver accesses or retrieves information, such as from books or online repositories. Given the importance of communication for project success, the Project Management Institute has identified three key project communication processes (*PMBOK*, 2017):

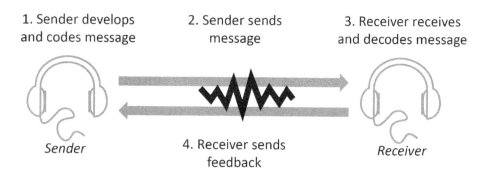

1. Sender develops and codes message   2. Sender sends message   3. Receiver receives and decodes message

Sender   4. Receiver sends feedback   *Receiver*

Figure 4.7 Successful communication requires that both the sender and receiver agree that the receiver has understood the message.

1. *Plan Communications Management.* A process for developing a comprehensive communications management that describes how project information will be communicated to meet stakeholders' information needs

2. *Manage Communications.* The processes involved in providing project information to all relevant stakeholders in a timely manner

3. *Monitor Communications.* The processes of monitoring the effectiveness of the communication processes and, if needed, adjusting processes to maximize effectiveness

In the remainder of this section, we examine each of these three key communication processes.

Tips from the Pros: Defining a Secure Communications Policy

Misuse of corporate email, instant messaging, and other communication resources has become a source of substantial liability in many organizations. Because of this, organizations are defining policies to better ensure that government regulations are met, sensitive data are secure, and customer privacy is protected.

Ken Beer, product line manager of Tumbleweed Communications, outlined ten steps to establishing a secure email policy.

1. *Clearly outline all personal use restrictions.* Make sure employees understand whether personal use is permitted and, if so, what types of correspondence and content are acceptable and unacceptable.

2. *Strictly prohibit unauthorized transmission of company trade secrets, confidential information, or privileged communication.* Because the majority of a company's intellectual capital is now stored digitally, it is crucial that employees do not transmit these valuable assets without consent.

3. *Be aware of industry-specific government regulations.* Various industries such as health care and financial services have differing standards for privacy of information; policies should reflect each industry's unique restrictions.

4. *Inform employees that their email and other computing activities may be monitored.* It is the organization's right to monitor electronic transmission, but employees should be notified and asked to sign a waiver acknowledging the acceptance of this policy.

5. *Implement tools to enforce polices.* Firewalls, spam filters, virtual private networks (VPNs), and other emerging tools should be utilized by the organization to better implement the policy.

6. *Carefully define what content can and cannot enter or leave your organization.* To limit corporate liability, firewall filters should look for profane, sexually explicit, racist, or other potentially litigious content, as well as for keywords that might refer to confidential product or customer information.

7. *Employ "intelligent" policy enforcement.* Not everyone in the organization should be treated equally. Different job functions and seniority may require different levels of restrictiveness.

8. *Protect sensitive business data from the vulnerability of plain-text email.* Use VPN, encryption, passwords, and other data securing technologies when transmitting sensitive information on public networks.

9. *Establish a secure public network.* Use capabilities of the existing messaging infrastructure to create secure and trusted communications channels between key members of the organization (e.g., CEO and CFO).

10. *Ensure the privacy of your customers' data.* Secure customer data as if it were critical organizational intellectual property.

Especially as the use of mobile devices has increased dramatically over the past years, email policies and standards should not be restricted to users' desktops. Rather, companies need to ensure that any devices used to access company-related emails need to be encrypted, password protected, and secured using company-approved security apps. This can be achieved using dedicated mobile device management (MDM) software, or by using MDM tools provide by services such as Office 365.

Based on: Beer (2003); Microsoft Office (2018).

Plan Communications Management

For a project to run smoothly, all project stakeholders need various types of information throughout the life of the project. **Plan Communications Management** is the process of developing a comprehensive plan for informing project stakeholders of all relevant information on a timely basis, so as to ensure effective and efficient communication. In short, this process focuses on identifying how information will be communicated; the resulting **communications management plan** should include how project information is stored, retrieved, and discarded at the end of the project.

Part of determining the communication requirements is not only analyzing who needs what information, but also how much effort should be expended to communicate particular information, so as to avoid wasting effort on unnecessary communication. Other considerations include the choice of communication medium, which include how urgently the information needs to be communicated, whether or not technology is available and sufficiently easy to use, whether the communication technology is sufficiently secure to guarantee the confidentiality of information, as well as other factors, such as team culture or dispersion across time and space. Because effective communication is fundamental to project success, planning communications is done very early in the life of the project. Normally, a communications management plan includes answers to various questions, including

- Who are the project's stakeholders / stakeholder groups?
- What are the information needs of each stakeholder or stakeholder group?
- When does this information need to be produced, and at what intervals?
- Where will this information be generated from?
- Who will be responsible for collecting, storing, and verifying the accuracy of this information?
- Who will be responsible for organizing, packaging, and disseminating this information?
- Who will be the contact person for each stakeholder or stakeholder group?
- In what format will this information be packaged and disseminated?
- What communication medium will be preferred for each stakeholder or stakeholder group?
- What resources (in terms of time and budget) are available for communication?

Once these questions are answered for each stakeholder, a comprehensive communications management plan can be developed. Typically, project teams use the project management plan, the stakeholder register, enterprise environmental factors, and organizational process assets as inputs to developing this plan. This plan will outline a summary of communication documents, work assignments, schedules, and distribution methods.

Manage Communications

Manage Communications focuses on getting needed project information to project stakeholders in a timely manner. In other words, the ongoing *Manage Communications* process is the execution of the *Plan Communications Management* process and includes responding to any ad hoc information requests by stakeholders. Thus *Manage Communications* is concerned with ensuring that project information is properly created, collected, stored, retrieved, distributed, monitored, and discarded. Normally, information can be distributed using a broad variety of methods, each with its own strengths and weaknesses. Some methods are easier for the information sender but more difficult or less convenient for the receiver. Apart from face-to-face meetings, most information today is exchanged digitally. One key purpose of many communication activities—especially within teams, but also between the project team and external stakeholders—is *performance reporting*. Project teams communicate in a variety of ways: written versus oral versus nonverbal, informal versus formal, vertical versus horizontal, or internal versus external to the team. Next, we briefly review the strengths and weaknesses of these various communication options. Given the importance of managing communications, we will devote the following section to different topics related to effective communication.

Common Problems: Communication in a Crisis

Internet of Things (IoT) devices such as the Nest Thermostat (by a company owned by Google) are becoming increasingly popular. Made possible by advances in hardware and software, IoT devices, as other digital devices, need continuous maintenance to improve performance, add features, or fix bugs in the software. In December 2015, Nest released a software update, which, unfortunately, introduced a new bug. This software bug caused the battery to drain, such that in an unusually cold night in mid-January 2016, many users woke up in the cold, leading Nest to scramble to fix the bug. In addition to fixing the bug, key to handling such incidents is communication, with the users, the general public, as well as Google's shareholders. As the Nest software update, any IS project carries risks that may necessitate emergency communication.

While not every issue results in widespread public attention, such issues can result in negative publicity, lack of consumer confidence, as well as have negative effects on share prices. Consequently, companies need to be prepared to deal with such crises, and an important step is to manage communication with the different stakeholders. Members of the Forbes Agency Council have proposed various rules to handle communication in such crises. Some of the most pertinent rules include

1. Take responsibility, rather than trying to cover up.
2. Be proactive, transparent, and accountable.
3. Be fast; don't wait until the situation spins out of control.
4. Be prepared for what might happen on social media.
5. Respond like a human, not like a lawyer.
6. Monitor social media and react fast.
7. Try to get an understanding of the situation.
8. Engage your PR team.
9. Put yourself in the affected stakeholders' shoes.
10. Be prepared and have a good communications plan.

Based on: Bilton (2016); Forbes Agency Council (2018).

Performance Reporting

Performance reporting
The collection and distribution of project performance information to stakeholders so that they understand the status of the project at any given time.

Performance reporting involves the collection and distribution of project performance information to stakeholders so that they understand the status of the project at any given time. Performance reporting involves three general types of reports: status, progress, and forecasting. **Status reports** describe current information about the project, such as project schedule or budget information. **Progress reports** describe what the project team has accomplished. Finally, **forecasting reports** make predictions about future status and progress. In general, performance reporting analyzes baseline versus actual data on project scope, schedule, cost, risk, and quality (*PMBOK*, 2017). Numerous standard tools and techniques for performance reporting will be described throughout the remainder of this book, including variance analysis, trend analysis, and earned value analysis.

Written, Oral, and Nonverbal Communication

Written communication—the exchange of memos, reports, letters, email, instant messaging, and so on through the use of standard symbols—provides a record of the communication and is particularly useful for formal and complex communication. Of course, written communication is relatively time-consuming to produce, and no matter what medium is chosen, key to effective communication is using the appropriate writing style for the audience. **Oral communication**—the exchange of spoken words—is fast, requires little effort to produce, and is less formal than written communication. One major drawback of oral communication is the ease with which messages can be distorted as they are passed along to others. Oral communication, especially presentations, can often be enhanced, however, through the use of visual aids, such as flip charts, handouts, or computer-based presentations (we will examine the factors that influence the quality of a presentation later in the chapter).

Nonverbal communication—information that is conveyed by body language through our posture, hands, facial expressions, eye contact, and personal space—can play an important role in transmitting and decoding oral communication. Research studies have found that up to 70 percent of what is really being communicated between individuals is done nonverbally (Barnum and Wolniansky, 1989). Table 4.1 summarizes whether oral or written communication is more effective for different types of project-related communication (see also Robbins and Judge, 2017; Verma, 1996).

Informal versus Formal Communication

Informal communication grows out of people's social interactions and is bound by convention, custom, and culture (Tucker, McCarthy, and Benton, 2003). Every project team has one or more informal communication methods, whether it is hallway conversations or instant messaging using technology such as WhatsApp, Google Hangouts, or Skype for Business. Different people with different relationships will have different ways of exchanging informal information. Sometimes informal information is very accurate, and sometimes it is not. It is often used to exchange rumors or gossip, but also serves some important uses for a project team. For example, informal communication

Status reports
Reports designed to disseminate current information about the project.

Progress reports
Reports designed to disseminate what the project team has accomplished.

Forecasting reports
Reports designed to disseminate predictions about future status and progress.

Written communication
The exchange of memos, reports, letters, email, instant messaging, and so on through the use of standard symbols.

Oral communication
The exchange of spoken words.

Nonverbal communication
The exchange of communication through body language, posture, hands, facial expressions, eye contact, and personal space.

Informal communication
The exchange of ad hoc, casual communications, usually taking place outside official communication channels.

Table 4.1 How and When to Use Oral and Written Communication

Purpose of Communication	Communication Method (Level of Effectiveness)		
	Oral	Written	Oral + Written
General overview	Medium	Medium	High
Immediate action required	Medium	Low	High
Future action required	Low	High	Medium
Directive, order, or policy change	Low	Medium	High
Progress report to supervisor	Low	Medium	High
Awareness campaign	Low	Low	High
Commendation for quality work	Low	Low	High
Reprimand a team member	High	Low	Medium
Settle a dispute	High	Low	Medium

Adapted from: Verma (1996).

is useful for having personal and collegial conversations, and it can be used to quickly exchange information when clarifying communications related to work activities.

In contrast, **formal communication** comprises the routine methods for communicating official information within organizations. Formal communication often follows customs and norms with regard to authority, rank, and the type of information. Formal communication is typically in writing and often follows a standard format so that formal documents can be easily identified and stored. Project teams use a variety of settings and communication technologies when exchanging formal versus informal communication, as shown in Figure 4.8.

Formal communication
The exchange of official information communicated through formal channels within organizations.

Vertical versus Horizontal Communication.

Vertical communication refers to communication that flows between higher and lower levels within an organization. Upward communication typically flows to a single individual such as a superior, while downward communication can flow to one or many individuals. Of course, there are exceptions, but vertical communication tends to be more formal.

Vertical communication
The exchange of information between higher and lower levels within an organization.

In contrast, **horizontal communication** refers to communication that flows among team members or across functional areas within the same level of an organization. Within-team communication is typically viewed as horizontal communication—even when cross-functional—and is typically less formal. External team communication is often viewed as being vertical and is more formal (see Figure 4.9).

Horizontal communication
The exchange of information among team members or across functional areas within the same level of an organization.

There are a broad range of options to choose from, with each communication method having strengths and weaknesses for exchanging different types of information. In the past, the general rule for communication was that formal communication was written and informal communication was oral. However, in addition to the actual information being distributed and updates to the project management plan, an important output of the *Manage Communications* process is ensuring that the communication and lessons learned will be available for future projects. Thus, given the need for having an effective team memory and the capability of modern web-based project management solutions, more and more information is being distributed digitally. In Chapter 5 we discuss the project management information system, a repository that contains all project-related documents, both paper and electronic.

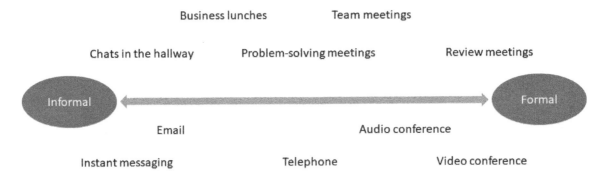

Figure 4.8 How project teams exchange formal and informal communication

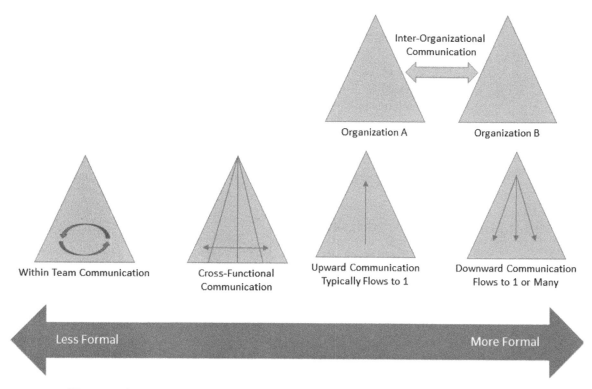

Figure 4.9 Horizontal communication is typically less formal than vertical communication.

Internal versus External Communication

Teams can draw on a variety of communication and collaboration tools—ranging from email to electronic meeting systems—to exchange information or to communicate with internal stakeholders (discussed later). However, for projects involving external stakeholders, a variety of tools suited for push communication are needed. Given the pervasiveness of social media, organizations communicate with external stakeholders and the general public not only via press releases but are using a wide variety of social media tools, ranging from Facebook to Twitter. These tools are especially useful when urgent information needs to be disseminated. While push communication is generally used to distribute project-related information, social media users are increasingly engaging in conversations with companies. Thus, especially for projects of wider public concern, the project manager needs to ensure that posts, tweets, and conversations are monitored and social media users' messages and concerns are responded to.

Monitor Communications

Given the importance of communications, it is necessary to monitor the effectiveness of the communication activities. Consequently, the *Monitor Communications* process involves assessing how well the communication reached the intended audiences, whether the communication had the intended impact, and what actions need to be taken to resolve any issues that may arise. Likewise, social media monitoring can help assess public sentiment on social media toward particular issues surrounding a project and can enable the project manager to formulate appropriate responses. Consequently, the *Monitor Communications* process may lead to renewed activities related to the *Plan Communications Management* and *Manage Communications* processes, so as to maintain the effectiveness of communication-related activities.

In this section, we discussed a variety of processes and techniques for better managing communication with project stakeholders. By actively managing the communication with stakeholders, you will more likely keep the project on track and head off problems due to ineffective communication. Making sure that all stakeholders clearly understand the project status as well as all outstanding issues that might impact the project is fundamental to success. Next, we examine several ways to enhance project communication.

Enhancing Project Communication

Although many people are natural communicators, nearly everyone can improve their communication skills. Being an effective communicator is likely the single biggest factor in determining how successful you will become in your career. In other words, if you cannot effectively use oral and written communication, the likelihood of great career success is quite low. Fortunately, there are many options for helping you improve your communication skills. For example, some organizations provide training seminars within the human resource management department to help employees develop these valuable skills. Another option that many students pursue is to join Toastmasters International (www.toastmasters.org), a worldwide organization dedicated to helping people become better communicators. Likewise, software tools such as Grammarly can be used to instantly provide feedback on grammatical errors in written communication, helping improve clarity and reduce the potential for misunderstandings. In the remainder of this section, we examine several techniques for improving your project communication skills.

Running Effective Project Meetings

Meetings are an important part of project team interaction. They are used for a broad variety of purposes, including planning actions, reviewing status, providing briefings and presentations, solving problems, and negotiating contracts. Unfortunately, most meetings are not as effective as they could be. Researchers have identified numerous potential problems that make meetings less effective than they could be. Among the most important problems are the following:

- Lack of adequate notification and preparation
- No agenda
- Wrong people or too many people in attendance
- Lack of control
- Political pressure and hidden agendas
- No conclusions or follow-up

Nonetheless, meetings need to occur and can provide many benefits to the team. Meetings that are well planned and executed can have a big positive impact on the team's performance. For example, well-planned meetings can help (Verma, 1996)

- Define the project, team members, and key stakeholders.
- Provide a forum for revising, updating, modifying, and clarifying key aspects of the project.
- Provide an opportunity for team members to better understand how their contribution fits within the scope of the overall project.
- Increase team member commitment to the project and the team through shared decision-making and collaboration.
- Increase work productivity and job satisfaction by clarifying task assignments and other project details.
- Provide an opportunity for the project manager to demonstrate leadership and vision.
- Provide an opportunity for project members to demonstrate their creativity, skills, and commitment to the project and team.

To run an effective meeting, you need to conduct several activities before, during, and after the meeting. For instance, prior to the meeting, you must carefully plan what should be accomplished; during the meeting, you must carefully control the agenda; and after the meeting, you must carefully document its outcomes and communicate them to all relevant parties. Figure 4.10 provides clear pre-, during, and post-meeting guidelines. Given that meetings are so valuable and important to project success, all project managers need to be skilled at running an effective meeting. In fact, to enable more effective meetings, many organizations develop a set of ground rules that are widely distributed to and agreed on by all organizational members (see Figure 4.11).

Making Effective Presentations

Presentations are used throughout the duration of the project for briefing team members and external stakeholders. Like meetings, presentations can provide many benefits to the team. Also, like meetings, presentations are often not well prepared or executed. Today, almost every presenter uses computer-based presentation software, such as Microsoft PowerPoint, Apple Keynote, or the online presentation software Prezi. One of the key benefits of such software is its ease of use—anyone can easily create a well-designed presentation and incorporate a variety of professional-looking animations, transitions, or other visual effects. Unfortunately, however, many tend to overuse these features, which distracts from the content of the presentation.

Thus any presentation needs to be well planned and designed. The planning and design of a presentation also includes organizing the content and ensuring a consistent design and readable fonts. In addition, effective delivery is a skill that is crucial in getting one's message across. As an effective presenter, you should help the audience focus on the content, rather than on the delivery, by making use of a clear voice, body language, eye contact, and so on. In sum, planning, design, and delivery are essential for an effective presentation, as highlighted in Table 4.2.

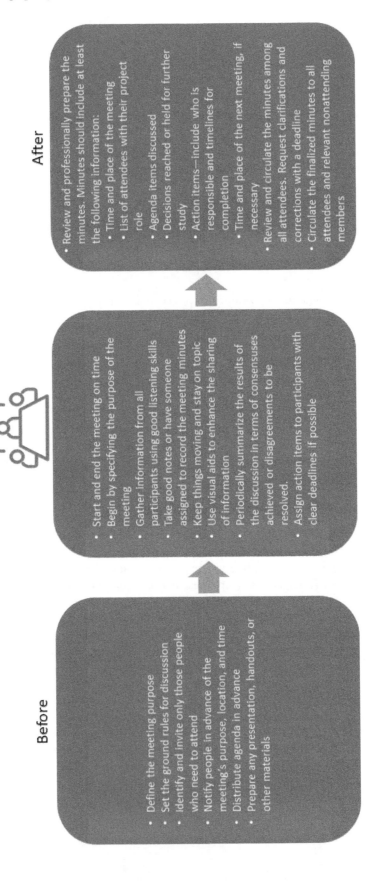

Before

- Define the meeting purpose
- Set the ground rules for discussion
- Identify and invite only those people who need to attend
- Notify people in advance of the meeting's purpose, location, and time
- Distribute agenda in advance
- Prepare any presentation, handouts, or other materials

- Start and end the meeting on time
- Begin by specifying the purpose of the meeting
- Gather information from all participants using good listening skills
- Take good notes or have someone assigned to record the meeting minutes
- Keep things moving and stay on topic
- Use visual aids to enhance the sharing of information
- Periodically summarize the results of the discussion in terms of consensuses achieved or disagreements to be resolved.
- Assign action items to participants with clear deadlines if possible

After

- Review and professionally prepare the minutes. Minutes should include at least the following information:
  - Time and place of the meeting
  - List of attendees with their project role
  - Agenda items discussed
  - Decisions reached or held for further study
  - Action items—include who is responsible and timelines for completion
  - Time and place of the next meeting, if necessary
- Review and circulate the minutes among all attendees. Request clarifications and corrections with a deadline
- Circulate the finalized minutes to all attendees and relevant nonattending members

Figure 4.10 Guidelines for running an effective project meeting. *Source:* Adapted from Verma (1996).

MEETING GROUND RULES

1. All team meetings will start and end on time.
2. All team members will arrive on time and be prepared to actively participate.
3. All team meetings will have an agenda, and team members will respect the agenda unless a majority of the members choose to deviate.
4. Any team members who have a meeting conflict will notify the meeting leader prior to the meeting if they will be absent, late, or have to leave early.
5. All team members will actively participate, listen carefully, and respect the opinions of others.
6. No one-to-one or side meetings will occur during a team meeting.
7. Team members will work hard to reach consensus on decisions using agreed upon methods for resolving disagreements (e.g., majority vote).
8. All team members are responsible for keeping the team on the agenda.
9. Breaks will be included in all meetings that last longer than one hour or when a member requests a short break.

Figure 4.11 Meeting ground rules.

Being a Better Listener

Listening
An active activity that consists of hearing, understanding, remembering, and acting.

Most people believe that they are good listeners; however, research has repeatedly shown that most people are relatively poor listeners (Kramer, 2001). **Listening** is an *active* activity that consists of hearing, understanding, remembering, and acting. Most people speak at a rate of around 120–140 words per minute, whereas people can listen to up to 600 words per minute. This gap between the speeds at which people talk and listen will sometimes allow our minds to wander to a point where we fail to *listen*—hear, understand, remember, and act on what is being said. The difference between a good and bad listener is usually easy to spot (see Table 4.3). Fortunately, a few simple rules can help you be a better listener (Tucker, McCarthy, and Benton, 2002):

1. *Listen without evaluating.* Don't judge or guess what is being said.
2. *Do not anticipate.* Don't assume you know what someone is going to say.
3. *Note taking.* Take detailed notes because we forget one-third to one half of what we hear within eight hours.
4. *Listen for themes and facts.* Try to organize what is being said into larger concepts.
5. *Do not fake attention.* Really paying attention is actually easier than faking it.
6. *Review.* Review what is being said and restate it back to the speaker as you understand it.

Table 4.2   Guidelines for Making an Effective Presentation

Presentation Planning	
Consider the audience	To design the most effective presentation, you need to consider the audience (e.g., What do they know about your topic? What is their education level?).
Focus on the message	Your presentation should be designed with a particular objective in mind.
Consider the presentation environment	Knowledge of the room size, shape, and lighting is valuable for designing an optimal presentation.
Presentation Design	
Organize the sequence	Organize your presentation so that like elements or topics are found in one place instead of randomly scattered throughout the material.
Keep it simple	Make sure that you don't pack too much information onto a slide so that it is difficult to read. Also, work to have as few slides as possible; in other words, only include information that you absolutely need.
Be consistent	Make sure that you use consistent types of fonts, font sizes, colors, design approach, and backgrounds.
Use variety	Use both textual and graphical slides to convey information in the most meaningful format.
Don't rely on the spellchecker alone	Make sure you carefully review your presentation for typographical and wording errors.
Use bells and whistles sparingly	Make sure that you use familiar graphical icons to guide and enhance slides; don't lose sight of your message as you add bells and whistles. Also, take great care when making transitions between slides and elements so that special effects don't take away from your message.
Handle supplemental materials carefully	Take care when using supplemental materials so that they don't distract the audience. For example, don't provide handouts until you want the audience to actually read them.
Have a clear beginning and end	At the beginning, introduce yourself and your teammates (if any), thank your audience for being there, and provide a clear outline of what will be covered during the presentation. At the conclusion, have an ending slide so that the audience clearly sees that the presentation is over.
Presentation Delivery	
Practice the presentation	Make sure that you thoroughly test your completed work on yourself and others to be certain it covers your points and presents them in an effective manner within the time allowed.
Arrive early and cue up your presentation	It is good practice when feasible to have your presentation ready to go before the arrival of the audience.
Learn to use the special software keys	Using special keys to navigate the presentation will allow you to focus on your message and not on the software.
Have a backup plan	Have a backup plan in case technology fails or your presentation is lost when traveling.
Speak confidently	To make an effective presentation, you must become an effective public speaker through practice.
Pay attention to your personal appearance	Your appearance and demeanor can greatly enhance how the audience receives your presentation.

Adapted from: Valacich and George (2017); Verma (1996).

Table 4.3   What Makes a Good Listener?

The Poor Listener . . .	The Good Listener . . .
Always interrupts	Does not interrupt
Is impatient	Waits until the end, then asks questions
Makes hasty judgments	Asks for clarification
Pays close attention	Shows disinterest (poor posture, wandering eyes)
Doesn't try to understand	Verifies understanding by repeating what was said
Doesn't respond	Gives feedback: smiles, nods, or frowns
Mentally prepares an argument to "win"	Avoids arguing and its negative effects on a relationship
Reacts to people and loses temper	Responds to the idea, not to the person
Fidgets with pen, paper clips	Gets rid of distractions
Goes off-subject	Concentrates on both the words and feelings behind them; stays on track

Adapted from: Verma (1996).

Being a better listener can pay numerous dividends when working with stakeholders and your team members. You will not only have better job performance; you will also improve your personal relationships with others.

Using Communication Templates and Glossaries

Communication templates
Specifications that enforce standards for the appearance and content of formal project documents.

Virtually all successful organizations have standard templates for most formal communications. **Communication templates** ensure that all formal documents follow a standard layout and contain all required information. Communication templates are used for both internal and external communication. Many organizations also prepare templates for crisis communication, so as to be able to react quickly and effectively in case a crisis arises. With the use of the web, communication templates can be further enhanced. For example, using the project management information system (discussed in Chapter 1), organizations can quickly create online templates for most project-related documents in which project members only have to fill in the blanks to create a report; once the report is created, other team members can be automatically notified, or online documents can be automatically routed to other team members or stakeholders. Thus, not only does the use of templates enhance team productivity, it also ensures that all related documents follow a standard format and include all required information. Given these benefits, there are countless possibilities for using predefined templates within project teams (see Figure 4.12). Further, as discussed throughout this book, communication among team members and with stakeholders external to the team is of crucial to project success. However, communication between technical and nontechnical people is often challenging due to differences in background knowledge, vocabularies, and so on. Often, one term means different things to different people, or different terms are used to mean the same thing. Consequently, having a project glossary that provides explanations for project-specific terms and acronyms can help establish a common vocabulary and can help avoid miscommunication.

Change Request		
To be completed by the requestor.		
CHANGE REQUEST NUMBER:	DATE SUBMITTED:	PRIORITY (H/M/L):
Requestor Name:		Project/Application Name:
Description of Request:		
Reason for Request		
To be completed by the project manager.		
Assigned To:		Date Assigned:
Skills Needed for Task:		
Estimated Effort Hours, Cost, and Duration:		
Comments:		
Customer Section		
Approval to Begin Work:		DATE:
Approval to Move Work to Production Status:		DATE:
Approval That Work Has Been Successfully Completed:		DATE:

Figure 4.12 A project template for requesting a design change

Making a Walk-Through Presentation

Walk-through
A peer-group review of any product created during the systems development process.

Users, management, developers, and other stakeholders attend numerous formal meetings to review various aspects of the project throughout its life. These meetings are called **walk-throughs** and are widely used by most professional development organizations. Walk-throughs have two primary objectives (Hoffer, George, and Valacich, 2007): First, they are used to ensure that a deliverable being reviewed at the meeting conforms to organizational standards and project specifications. Second, they are used to ensure that all relevant stakeholders understand and agree with the correctness and completeness of the deliverable. Experience has shown that walk-throughs are a very effective way to ensure the quality of an information system, and they have become a common day-to-day activity for many project managers. Walk-throughs have been used to review virtually all aspects of projects, including

- Project scope statements
- Budget and schedule reviews
- System specifications
- Logical and physical designs
- Code or program segments
- Test procedures and results
- Documentation and user training materials

Walk-throughs typically do not have to be overly formal or exceedingly long. However, to be most effective, it is important for all participants to understand the goals of the walk-through and when it should be completed. Typically, a walk-through should include participants with the following roles (Yourdon, 1989):

- *Coordinator.* Often the project leader or key analyst. Responsible for planning and facilitating the meeting. This person plans the meeting and facilitates a smooth meeting process.
- *Presenter.* Typically an analyst involved in the work being reviewed. Responsible for presenting the work product to the other participants.
- *User.* Participant(s) external from the project team. Responsible for ensuring that the work product evaluated meets the customers' requirements.
- *Secretary.* Usually a clerk assigned to the project team, or an analyst. Responsible for taking minutes and recording decisions or recommendations made during the walk-through.
- *Standards bearer.* Person from an organizational group that is responsible for establishing standard procedures, methods, and documentation formats. Responsible for adherence to technical standards established by the organization and for validating the work product.
- *Maintenance oracle.* Responsible for ensuring that the work product will be easy to maintain.

Typically, a walk-through review form (see Figure 4.13) is used to inform the attendees of the agenda, date, time, and place of the meeting, as well as to ensure that each role (outlined previously) is filled by a qualified individual. During the walk-through, the focus should be on reviewing various aspects of a project and finding defects, rather than finding solutions to any problems identified. As with any meeting, the focus should be on the work product, rather than the person or group responsible for creating the work product. Once the participants agree that the major weaknesses or defects have been identified, the coordinator polls the participants for their recommendations, which can include validation, validation pending specific changes, or the request for major changes. In case major changes are needed, these are recorded by the secretary in a walk-through action list (see Figure 4.14), and another walkthrough is scheduled to review the revised work product.

One of the key advantages to using a structured review process like a walkthrough is to ensure that formal review points occur during the project. At each subsequent phase of the project, a formal review should be conducted (and shown on the project schedule) to make sure that all aspects of the project are satisfactorily accomplished before assigning additional resources to it. This conservative approach of reviewing each major project activity with continuation contingent on successful completion of the prior phase is called *incremental commitment*. It is much easier to stop or redirect a project at any point when using this approach.

Using Collaboration Technologies to Enhance Project Communication

To successfully complete a project, team members need to exchange various types of information, using a variety of communication technologies. Traditionally, the communication tools of choice were the telephone and fax machines. However, especially for global project teams (which are separated by geographical boundaries and time zones), these tools are not well suited. Likewise, these tools are not well suited for multiperson communication and collaboration. Email, in contrast, can be used for exchanging documents and other content, but can quickly become unmanageable, especially in large project teams. Next, we discuss communication tools frequently used by project teams.

Walk-Through Review Form

Project/Segment:		Date:
Review Coordinator:		

Role	Name	Signature
Coordinator		
Presenter		
User		
Standards Bearer		
Secretary		
Maintenance Oracle		

Meeting Format and Length:

Issues Raised

ID	Reviewer	Description
1		
2		
3		
4		
5		

Group Decision:
_____ Accept product as-is
_____ Revise (no further walk-throughs)
_____ Review and schedule another walk-through

Figure 4.13 Walk-through review form

Ethical Dilemma: Is Big Brother Watching You?

If you think you are the only one reading your private email, we have some bad news for you. Ever since the inception of employer-employee relationships, employers have been trying to determine whether employees are doing their jobs effectively—if at all. Traditionally, offices have been equipped with surveillance equipment, which was mostly used for security purposes. Information technology, however, has taken employee monitoring to a whole new level. Using the right software, your employer can read your emails, monitor your web surfing, and even log the keystrokes on your computer.

In addition to this, technologies like radio-frequency identification (RFID) tags can be used to track employee movements throughout the company's buildings. Global positioning system (GPS)

Walk-Through Action List

Project/Segment:		Date and Time of Walk-Through:
Review Coordinator:		

Issues Raised in Review

ID	Issue	Fixed?	Comment
1			
2			
3			
4			
5			

Figure 4.14 Walk-through action list

technology could track your location virtually anywhere in the world if you are using a company vehicle or a company-issued mobile device. In the current legal environment, your company has the right to collect almost any information about what you do. Often, companies use this freedom to collect sensitive data under the disguise of attempting to safeguard their data or equipment. The Boston-based startup Humanize even introduced ID badges that are able to record biometric information, which can be analyzed to provide a plethora of information about each particular employee—for example, voice data can be analyzed to detect emotional states or communication behavior in team meetings. Likewise, companies have started to distribute fitness monitors such as Fitbit to track employees' behavior and adherence to wellness plans. Clearly, all these technologies are intrusions on the employees' privacy.

You might think that you are not affected by this. But if you are using a computer in your university's library for private activities that are not directly related to your studies, you might already be violating your university's appropriate use policies. Moreover, because you are using your university's (organization's) resources, they have complete rights to monitor what you are doing.

Discussion Questions

1. Do you believe that organizations have the right to monitor employees? Explain.
2. What communication monitoring policy should organizations use to best manage project teams?

Based on: Derousseau (2017), James (2004).

How Communication Methods Differ

All communication methods have strengths and weaknesses for supporting different types of project team communication (see Table 4.4). In addition, communication methods can differ in factors such as ease of use, urgency, and confidentiality. Likewise, collaboration technologies vary in their ability to structure the team-communication and problem-solving process. Electronic meeting software (discussed later) provides rigid communication and voting templates that highly structure the team's interaction (see Figure 4.15). Some technologies allow simultaneous, **synchronous communication**, whereas others support **asynchronous communication**. For example, videoconferencing supports synchronous communication, and voicemail and email are examples of asynchronous technologies (see Figure 4.16).

Communication technologies also vary in their ability to exchange rich information. **Information richness** is the extent to which a communication environment allows the exchange of verbal and nonverbal cues, supports interaction and feedback, and can be personalized to the communicator (Daft and Lengel, 1986). *Rich* environments support the exchange of verbal and nonverbal cues and rapid feedback; they are highly personal. Face-to-face communication is considered the richest environment. *Lean* environments allow a limited range of cues to be exchanged and limited or delayed feedback and are relatively impersonal. Because of their potential for information richness, various types of collaboration technologies are more appropriate for some communication than for others (see Figure 4.17). For example, when your communication is complex, difficult to accept, or involves a nonroutine problem, it may need a richer environment that provides a broad variety of cues, rapid feedback, and a personal orientation. However, for simple, routine, or impersonal communication, a relatively lean environment may be adequate.

Communication methods also differ in the number of people who can effectively participate in a specific communication event. For example, telephone communication is most effective with a low number of participants, whereas email can be used to communicate effectively with a large number of participants. As the quality, variety, and sophistication of communication methods have greatly improved, the role of these technologies within project teams, especially within information systems project teams, has continued to expand. To be a more effective communicator, you need to understand

Synchronous communication
A form of communication where all parties involved are present at the same time but not necessarily in the same place.

Asynchronous communication
A form of communication where all parties involved need not be available or present at the same time or the same place.

Information richness
The extent to which a communication environment allows the exchange of verbal and nonverbal cues, supports interaction and feedback, and can be personalized to the communicator.

Table 4.4 Different Communication Methods and Technologies Can Be Configured to a Situation and Have Strengths and Weakness for Different Types of Information

Communication Method	Structure	Interaction	Richness	Number of People
Face-to-face	Low-high	Synchronous	High	Low-high
Video conference	Medium-high	Synchronous	Medium-high	Low-medium
Telephone	Low-medium	Synchronous	Medium	Low
Instant Messenger	Low	Synchronous	Medium	Low
Synchronous groupware	Medium-high	Synchronous	Medium	Low-medium
Asynchronous groupware	Low-high	Asynchronous	Low-medium	Low-high
Email	Low-medium	Asynchronous	Low-medium	Low-high
Written mail	Medium-high	Asynchronous	Low	Low-high

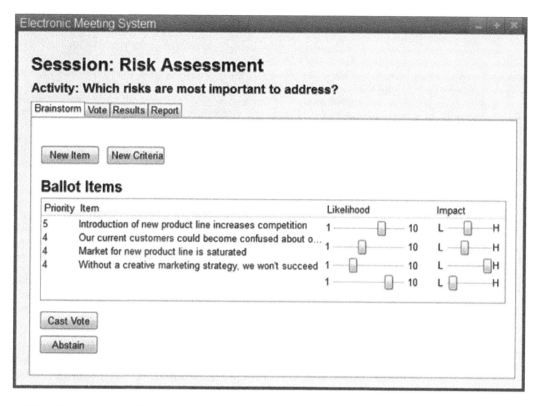

Figure 4.15   Electronic meeting software provides highly structured communication and voting templates.

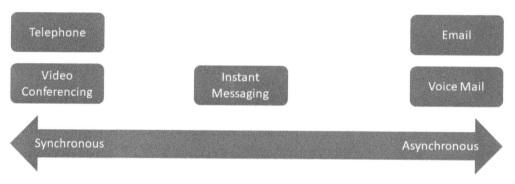

Figure 4.16   Videoconferencing supports synchronous communication, and voicemail and email are examples of asynchronous technologies.

the strengths and weaknesses of the various methods available, and select those that are most appropriate for the message and the audience. Next we examine various collaboration technologies that are being utilized by project teams and conclude with a description of enterprise-wide project management environments.

Collaboration Technologies

To build the best project teams, organizations constantly need to bring together the right combinations of people who as a group have the appropriate set of knowledge,

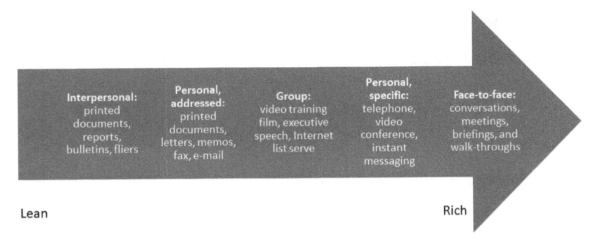

Lean   Rich

Figure 4.17   Communication can range from relatively lean to relatively rich. *Adapted from:* Kramer (2001).

skills, information, and authority to solve problems quickly and easily. Often, teams can consist of members from different locations or from around the world. Consequently, organizations need technologies that enable team members to interact either at the same place and time or at different times and in different locations, with structure to aid in interactive problem solving and access to software tools and information. Various technologies can fit the bill, as described in the following sections.

Videoconferencing

Videoconferencing
The use of integrated telephone, video recording, and playback technologies by two or more people to interact with each other from remote sites.

Videoconferencing has become an essential tool for person-to-person as well as multi-person team collaboration. Desktop videoconferencing, enabled by high-speed internet connections and applications such as Skype, Apple FaceTime, or Cisco WebEx, can facilitate various collaborative activities (see Figure 4.18). Likewise, people can use their mobile devices to conduct videoconferences on the go. In addition to enabling video calls, some videoconferencing applications (such as Skype for Business) also offer the possibility to share a participant's desktop, programs, or presentations with others during online meetings (see Figure 4.19). Whereas desktop videoconferencing is frequently used by smaller groups, large organizations use dedicated videoconferencing systems that can cost thousands of dollars.

Global Implications: Managing Effective Global Development Teams

Many high-technology organizations have home locations near other technology firms in order to leverage the local talent pool and other resources; within the United States, for example, such cities include Austin, Cambridge, San Jose, and Seattle. Being located near other related firms can provide many advantages but can also make hiring the best developers extremely competitive. Given this competitive hiring environment, the possibility of adding a second or third development shift is not likely (not to mention the fact that many talented developers only want "normal" working hours). To address this problem, many organizations have moved to global development teams with members throughout the world. These global teams can provide a clear strategic advantage to organizations by enabling them to work on mission-critical applications literally around the clock.

Although there are cost advantages to moving toward global development teams, these savings are often offset at least somewhat by additional travel and communication costs. For example, Colum Joyce, a global e-business strategy manager for the shipping giant DHL Worldwide Express Inc., stresses the importance of effective team communication. "A mastery of English is a key skill set, as it is the operating language of all cross-group communication for all development, whether it be verbal, hard copy, or electronic communication." Likewise, Stacy Kenworthy, president of ApplianceWare of Fremont, California, states that "you need to make substantial investments in communications . . . there is no getting away from face-to-face contact, so there's airfare, investments in process creation, investments in learning curve, and other frontend work. You're basically changing your organizational structure."

Some recommendations for managing global development teams include having a face-to-face kickoff meetings to conduct team-building activities, training team members on intercultural issues, and building trust by encouraging informal communication, in addition to establishing a communications management plan that accommodates for cultural, temporal, and spatial separation of team members.

It is clear that global teams can be an effective strategy for handling labor shortages, reducing costs, and shortening the development cycle for mission-critical applications. However, it is also clear that effective team communication processes are paramount to realizing the benefits of this strategy.

Based on: Gilhooly (2001); Wagner (2017).

Figure 4.18   Desktop videoconferencing is used for various collaborative activities.

Figure 4.19   Skype for Business offers the possibility to share a participant's screen with others.

Groupware

Groupware refers to a variety of different tools that aim to facilitate group collaboration. Group interactions can be distinguished based on time and space:

1. Time: Synchronous (coordinated in time) versus asynchronous (not coordinated in time)
2. Space: Face-to-face/collocated versus distributed

Different groupware tools offer different support for the resulting four types of interactions, as shown in Figure 4.20. Given the increasing use of global project teams, choosing the right groupware system can significantly increase team productivity, ultimately contributing to project success. Table 4.5 highlights the benefits of using groupware systems.

Asynchronous Groupware

While real-time (synchronous) communication (as enabled by conference calls or video conferences) is important for team collaboration, asynchronous collaboration tools are widely used when no immediate response from the communication partner is needed. Likewise, in globally distributed project teams, asynchronous collaboration is typically the norm, as the team members are distributed over different time zones.

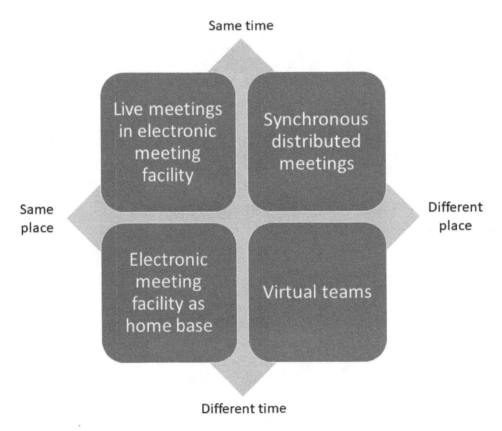

Figure 4.20 Groupware supports same and different time, as well as same and different place group interaction.

Table 4.5 The Benefits of Groupware

Benefits	Examples
Process structuring	Keeps teams on track and helps them avoid costly diversions (e.g., doesn't allow people to get off topic or the agenda)
Parallelism	Enables many people to speak and listen at the same time (e.g., everyone has an equal opportunity to participate)
Group size	Enables members in larger teams to participate (e.g., brings together broader perspectives, expertise, and participation)
Group memory	Automatically records member ideas, comments, votes (e.g., allows members to focus on content of discussions rather than on recording comments)
Access to external information	Can easily incorporate external electronic data and files (e.g., plans and proposal documents can be collected and easily distributed to all members)
Spanning time and space	Enables members to collaborate from different places at different times (e.g., reduces travel costs or allows people from remote locations to participate)
Anonymity	Member ideas, comments, and votes not identified to others (if desired) (e.g., can make it easier to discuss controversial or sensitive topics without fear of identification or retribution)

The internet has enabled a variety of asynchronous groupware systems, the most common being email. Other asynchronous tools commonly used in organizations include newsgroups and mailing lists for disseminating project information, workflow management systems to reduce paperwork and set up and monitor tasks, group calendars to facilitate scheduling, or collaborative writing tools to enable joint editing of documents. Wikis, made famous by the online encyclopedia Wikipedia, are one widely used class of collaborative writing tools. A wiki site consists of a web-based document that is linked to a database that records all edits made to that document. As all edits are recorded, any changes made to a document can be viewed and, if needed, easily reverted (see Figure 4.21).

Various solutions incorporate different functionalities of stand-alone tools. This integration can be traced back to the release of Lotus Notes in 1989. Today, the successor of Lotus Notes, IBM Notes, continues to be one of the most widely used group collaboration environments that facilitates various communication and collaboration needs. For the needs of smaller projects or organizations, there are various free web-based communication and project management tools (such as Asana).

Synchronous Groupware

In contrast to asynchronous groupware, which supports interactions taking place that are not coordinated in time, synchronous groupware enables real-time interaction. Commonly used tools enable not only videoconferencing, but also online chat, collaboration using shared whiteboards or shared computer screens, or electronic meetings. Tools focusing on facilitating electronic meetings are referred to as **electronic meeting systems (EMSs)**. Traditionally, EMSs were designed to support co-located meetings in dedicated facilities by providing a variety of advanced features to support group decision-making, ranging from idea generation to evaluation and voting, either identified or anonymous. Thus EMSs are useful for a variety of scenarios, such as brainstorming system requirements, conducting strategic planning sessions, or even board meetings. Today, EMSs are increasingly used to support real-time interactions of distributed teams. Most electronic meeting systems, such as the Microsoft Surface Hub, facilitate real-time communication by offering a virtual conference room; EMSs such as Cisco

Electronic meeting system
A collection of personal computers networked with sophisticated software tools to help group members solve problems and make decisions through interactive electronic idea generation, evaluation, and voting.

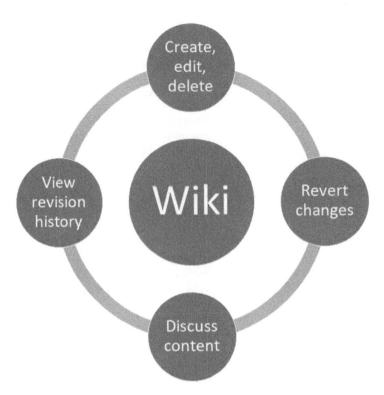

Figure 4.21   A wiki site consists of a web-based document that is linked to a database that records all edits made to that document.

WebEx enable virtual conferences that anyone can join using their own preferred videoconferencing software, from Skype to Polycom (see Figure 4.22). Likewise, Skype for business enables conference calls for up to 250 participants; other tools such as Convene support managing and electronically signing meeting documents or voting on resolutions. As a result, these tools are now commonplace in most global project teams.

Enterprise Social Networks

Enabled by the internet, many tools are converging, so that it becomes increasingly difficult to clearly differentiate synchronous and asynchronous groupware tools. Another class of tools that has gained popularity is enterprise social networks. Social networks such as Facebook offer a variety of tools that support communication and collaboration. For example, users can post status updates, share pictures or videos, or use online chat. Enterprise social networks such as Yammer are designed to offer similar functionality, but in a private, secure network that only authorized team members can access. Using such tools, team members can post updates on the completion of milestones or deliverables, can post documents and manage version control, or communicate and make group decisions.

Many large organizations set up enterprise social networks that are only accessible to authorized individuals (such as members of the organization, or key stakeholders). Within such networks, project teams can set up a private group to discuss technical specifications or other project-related issues or share key documents. Enterprise social networks such as Yammer enable team members to edit documents and view document changes made by other team members (see Figure 4.23). Often, the private group can

Figure 4.22 EMSs provide virtual conference rooms that anyone can access using their own preferred videoconferencing software.

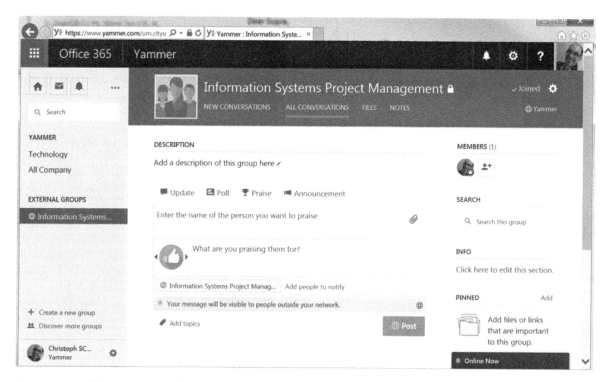

Figure 4.23 Enterprise social networks such as Microsoft Yammer offer a private, secure network that only authorized team members can access.

be extended to external stakeholders, such as customers, freelancers, or contractors, and different permissions can be assigned to different people or groups. Today's enterprise social networks can be integrated with a variety of other platforms, such as the SAP enterprise resource planning system, the Salesforce customer relationship system, or Microsoft SharePoint, a platform for team collaboration (Kelly, 2013).

Enterprise Project Management Environments

In addition to utilizing collaboration technologies to improve project team communication, many organizations are deploying enterprise-wide project management environments. These environments, such as Microsoft's Enterprise Project Management, provide a variety of capabilities to enhance the management of a portfolio of projects, especially when project teams are composed of members who are geographically dispersed. These environments provide a web-based interface for accessing all relevant project information and provide numerous capabilities, enabling an organization to

- Manage multiple projects as an overall portfolio for better decision-making in regard to resource assignment, problem identification, and trend and risk analysis
- More closely track resource usage and workload as well as plan better for short- and long-term resource assignments
- Manage stakeholders' expectations by effectively reporting project status in regard to time and resources
- Enforce organizational best practices of project methodologies and processes
- Support improved participation by enabling team members to easily manage, track, and report project updates
- Better manage project-related deliverables through the use of a central document repository with versioning and editing control

Given these capabilities, enterprise project management environments have become a powerful tool for enhancing project team communication and collaboration, especially for complex project environments where members are dispersed (potentially across the globe) and multiple projects are utilizing shared resources.

Managing Project Stakeholders and Communication and the PMBOK

In this chapter, we have focused primarily on Knowledge Area 10, *Project Communications Management*, and Knowledge Area 13, *Project Stakeholder Management*, within *PMBOK* (2017; see Figure 4.24). Specifically, three key processes of stakeholder management—*Identify Stakeholders*, *Plan Stakeholder Engagement*, *Manage Stakeholder Engagement*, and *Monitor Stakeholder Engagement*—and four key processes of communications management—*Plan Communications Management*, *Manage Communications*, and *Monitor Communications*—have been discussed. Together, this information provides a solid foundation for managing project stakeholders and communication.

Figure 4.24 Chapter 4 and *PMBOK* coverage

Key: ○ where the material is covered in the textbook; ● current chapter coverage

	Textbook Chapters ⟶	1	2	3	4	5	6	7	8	9	10	11	12
	PMBOK Knowledge Area												
1	Introduction												
1.2	Foundational Elements	○	○										
2	The Environment in Which Projects Operate												
2.2	Enterprise Environmental Factors		○										
2.2	Organizational Process Assets		○										
2.3	Organizational Systems		○										
3	The Role of the Project Manager												
3.2	Definition of a Project Manager	○											
3.3	The Project Manager's Sphere of Influence		○										
3.4	Project Manager Competences	○	○	○									
3.5	Performing Integration		○										
4	Project Integration Management												
4.1	Develop Project Charter					○							
4.2	Develop Project Management Plan					○							
4.3	Direct and Manage Project Work											○	
4.4	Manage Project Knowledge											○	
4.5	Monitor and Control Project Work											○	○
4.6	Perform Integrated Change Control												○
4.7	Close Project or Phase										○		○
5	Project Scope Management												
5.1	Plan Scope Management					○							
5.2	Collect Requirements					○							
5.3	Define Scope					○							
5.4	Create WBS					○	○						
5.5	Validate Scope					○							
5.6	Control Scope					○							○
6	Project Schedule Management												
6.1	Plan Schedule Management						○						
6.2	Define Activities						○						
6.3	Sequence Activities						○						
6.4	Estimate Activity Durations							○					
6.5	Develop Schedule							○					
6.6	Control Schedule							○					○
7	Project Cost Management												
7.1	Plan Cost Management								○				

#	Process	1	2	3	4	5	6	7	8	9	10	11
7.2	Estimate Costs								O			
7.3	Determine Budget								O			
7.4	Control Costs								O			O
8	**Project Quality Management**											
8.1	Plan Quality Management								O			
8.2	Manage Quality								O			
8.3	Control Quality								O			O
9	**Project Resource Management**											
9.1	Plan Resource Management							O				
9.2	Estimate Activity Resources						O	O				
9.3	Acquire Resources							O			O	
9.4	Develop Team			O							O	
9.5	Manage Team			O							O	
9.6	Control Resources							O				O
10	**Project Communications Management**											
10.1	Plan Communications Management				●							
10.2	Manage Communications				●						O	
10.3	Monitor Communications				●							O
11	**Project Risk Management**											
11.1	Plan Risk Management								O			
11.2	Identify Risks								O	O		
11.3	Perform Qualitative Risk Analysis								O			
11.4	Perform Quantitative Risk Analysis								O			
11.5	Plan Risk Responses								O			
11.6	Implement Risk Responses								O	O		
11.7	Monitor Risks								O			O
12	**Project Procurement Management**											
12.1	Plan Procurement Management									O		
12.2	Conduct Procurements									O	O	
12.3	Control Procurements									O		O
13	**Project Stakeholder Management**											
12.1	Identify Stakeholders				●							
12.2	Plan Stakeholder Engagement				●							
12.3	Manage Stakeholder Engagement				●						O	
12.4	Monitor Stakeholder Engagement				●							O

Running Case: Managing Stakeholders and Project Communication

It was the big project kickoff meeting. James and three other members of his team—Kevin, Trey, and Cindy—were all in the conference room down the hall from James's office in IT. Also meeting with them was Sarah Codey, Jackie's COO. Sarah was now the official executive sponsor of the project. She would not meet with the team on a regular basis—in fact, she would hardly meet with them at all—but she would be a key stakeholder for the project, and she would be their main link to the executive team at Jackie's. She had already convinced Nick Baldwin, the head of marketing, to free up Cindy from many of her daily duties as assistant director of marketing so Cindy could concentrate on the project. Sarah would be able to help the team in other ways as the project progressed. Sarah had just finished her "official" kickoff remarks to the team.

James had been successful in getting Maria Gutierrez, the manager of the Riverside store, to be on the team. Due to work pressures, though, Maria was not able to be in San Francisco for the meeting, and she was also late joining the meeting by speakerphone.

Just then, Maria called into the meeting. "Hello? This is Maria."

"Maria," James said, "I just wanted to say how glad I am that you can join us today and that you can be on the team."

"Can you hear me okay?" Maria asked. "Is that good? I can hear you, Jim."

"I can hear you fine," James replied

"This is Cindy."

"And this is Trey."

"Kevin here."

"And this is Sarah, Maria. Can you hear us all okay?"

"Trey, you might want to move closer to the microphone," Maria said. "Well, I'm glad to be on the team. I think this is going to be a really fun project. I just hope I have the time that I want to devote to it. Oh, and for future reference, Monday afternoon is a really bad time for me to meet."

"Why's that?" James asked.

"Tuesday is the release day for most new movies. Monday is the day we get most of the movies in, and

we have to get ready to set up the new displays for what we expect to be the big sellers. Moreover, we have to move lots of other stuff around to get ready."

"Of course," Cindy said. "I should have known that."

"Me too," James said. "I'll try to be better about that kind of thing. Which brings up a new topic—when can we meet? I need everyone to make sure I have access to their calendars, so I can set up a regular weekly meeting. That is part of the agenda I have for today's meeting—communication planning, which includes meetings, and information distribution."

"I need to leave," Sarah said, getting up from the conference table. "Once again, I wish you all a lot of success with this." Sarah walked toward the door.

"Thanks, Sarah," James said. "And now about communication."

"I think we should set up a SharePoint site for the project," Kevin said.

"Using SharePoint for the team is a great idea," Maria said, "since I am out here in Riverside and you guys are all in San Francisco."

"I'm going to be traveling a lot this quarter," Trey said, "so that works for me."

"And distribution?" James asked.

"Let's figure out who outside the team needs to know about what we are doing, and what they need to know and when," Kevin suggested.

"Good plan," Cindy said.

"Well, we know that Sarah is first on that list," James said. "But we also know that Trey will keep her informed." Everyone laughed. "But seriously . . ."

The team worked together through the rest of the meeting to list the project's key stakeholders and to prepare a stakeholder engagement plan.

Adapted from: Valacich and George (2017).

Chapter Summary

Understand the importance of stakeholders and how to manage stakeholder engagement. Stakeholders are individuals, groups, and organizations that are actively involved in the project, who have a vested interest in its success, and/or who have influence over the project and its results. As their influence can be positive or negative, the project management team must identify the project stakeholders in order to manage their expectations. The *Identify Stakeholders* process helps us understand the nature of the stakeholders, their interests, and potential influence they may have on project success. The stakeholder register contains assessments of each stakeholder's

expectations and influence in the various phases. Once the stakeholders and their interest, influence, and expectations have been identified, the next step is to plan how to effectively maintain relationships, so as to harness positive influences and minimize any potential negative impacts. A stakeholder engagement assessment matrix is used to indicate current and desired engagement levels for each stakeholder. The stakeholder engagement plan details the outputs of the stakeholder classification, as well as the methods of how and when information needs to be distributed. In the *Manage Stakeholder Engagement* process, communication activities are conducted to engage stakeholders, manage their expectations, and address concerns and resolve issues that may arise as the project progresses through the different phases. The *Monitor Stakeholder Engagement* process entails assessing the effectiveness of the strategies for engaging stakeholders and managing their relationships.

Describe how the three key communications management processes are used to enhance project success. Communication is the process by which information is exchanged between individuals through a common system of symbols, signs, or behavior. Effective communication is fundamental to project team success. Throughout a project, three key communications management processes are performed: *Plan Communications Management, Manage Communications*, and *Monitor Communications*. *Plan Communications Management* refers to the process of developing a comprehensive communications management plan that identifies the information needs of the stakeholders, when they need it, and in what format it should be delivered. *Manage Communications* includes the processes involved in providing project information to all relevant stakeholders in a timely manner. In other words, it is the execution of the communications management plan. The *Monitor Communications* process involves assessing in how far the communication reached the intended audiences, whether the communication had the intended impact, and what actions need to be taken to resolve any issues that may arise.

Describe various methods for enhancing team communication including how to run an effective meeting, deliver an effective presentation, be a better listener, utilize communication templates, and make a walk-through presentation. There are a variety of methods for enhancing project team communication. Meetings can be more effective if they are carefully planned and executed. Additionally, to get the most out of a meeting, you must carefully document the meeting outcomes and communicate them to all relevant parties. Like meetings, presentations are much more effective if they are carefully planned, designed, and delivered. Because most people are relatively poor listeners, improving team members' listening skills can enhance project team communication and overall project performance. Project team communication can also be enhanced through the use of communication templates by helping ensure that many important documents follow a standard layout and contain all required information. Walk-throughs are a special type of team meeting that utilizes both presentations and templates to assess a broad variety of project team deliverables. During walk-throughs, team members play various important roles to ensure project quality and meeting effectiveness.

Describe various collaboration technologies and how they can be utilized to enhance team communication. With the advent of the internet and other advanced communication technologies, project teams have many options to choose from when deciding how to communicate. All communication methods have strengths and weaknesses; not all methods are effective for all types of communication. Communication methods differ in how much structure they impose on the communication, in how far rich information can be conveyed, whether they allow synchronous or asynchronous exchanges, and how many team members can effectively communicate. A variety of collaboration technologies has become commonplace in organizations for supporting project teams, including videoconferencing, asynchronous groupware, synchronous groupware, and enterprise social networks.

Key Terms Review

A. Asynchronous communication
B. Communication
C. Communication templates
D. Communications management plan
E. Electronic meeting system (EMS)
F. Feedback
G. Forecasting reports
H. Formal communication
I. Groupware
J. Horizontal communication
K. Informal communication
L. Information richness
M. Interactive communication
N. Listening
O. Manage Communications
P. Noise

Q. Nonverbal communication
R. Oral communication
S. Performance reporting
T. Plan Communications Management
U. Progress reports
V. Pull communication
W. Push communication

X. Status reports
Y. Synchronous communication
Z. Vertical communication
AA. Videoconferencing
BB. Walk-through
CC. Written communication

Match each of the key terms with the definition that best fits it.

1. A collection of personal computers networked with sophisticated software tools to help group members solve problems and make decisions through interactive electronic idea generation, evaluation, and voting.
2. A form of communication in which two or more parties exchange information.
3. A form of communication where all parties involved are present at the same time but not necessarily at the same place.
4. A form of communication where all parties involved need not be available or present at the same time or the same place.
5. A form of communication where information is distributed by the sender to specific recipients or general audiences, but receipt of the information is not ensured.
6. A form of communication where the receiver must retrieve the information.
7. A peer-group review of any product created during the systems development process.
8. A process by which information is exchanged between individuals through a common system of symbols, signs, or behavior.
9. An *active* activity that consists of hearing, understanding, remembering, and acting.
10. Audio, visual, or environmental interference within the communication process.
11. Reports designed to disseminate current information about the project.
12. Reports designed to disseminate predictions about future status and progress.
13. Reports designed to disseminate what the project team has accomplished.
14. Software that enables people to work together more effectively.
15. Specifications that enforce standards for the appearance and content of formal project documents.
16. The collection and distribution of project performance information to stakeholders so that they understand the status of the project at any given time.
17. The exchange of ad hoc, casual communications, usually taking place outside official communication channels.
18. The exchange of communication through body language, posture, hands, facial expressions, eye contact, and personal space.
19. The exchange of information among team members or across functional areas within the same level of an organization.
20. The exchange of information between higher and lower levels within an organization.
21. The exchange of memos, reports, letters, email, instant messaging, and so on through the use of standard symbols.
22. The exchange of official information communicated through formal channels within organizations.
23. The exchange of spoken words.

24. The process of ensuring that project information is properly created, collected, stored, retrieved, distributed, monitored, and discarded.

25. The extent to which a communication environment allows the exchange of verbal and nonverbal cues, supports interaction and feedback, and can be personalized to the communicator.

26. The plan for informing project stakeholders of all relevant information on a timely basis, including how project information is stored, retrieved, and discarded at the end of the project

27. The process of developing a comprehensive plan for informing project stakeholders of all relevant information on a timely basis.

28. The response process by a receiver to a sender within the communication process.

29. The use of integrated telephone, video recording, and playback technologies by two or more people to interact with each other from remote sites.

Review Questions

1. What are the major processes involved in managing project communication?
2. Describe a stakeholder engagement matrix.
3. What are the major processes involved in managing project stakeholders?
4. What information do you need in order to develop a communications management plan?
5. Describe and contrast written versus oral versus nonverbal, informal versus formal, and vertical versus horizontal communication in a project team setting.
6. What is project performance reporting, and what reports are typically contained in a performance report?
7. Why are many project meetings less effective than they could be?
8. What benefits can meetings bring to project teams?
9. Describe how to run an effective meeting.
10. Describe how to make an effective presentation.
11. What steps can you take to be a better listener?
12. What is a communication template, and why does it enhance project team communication?
13. Describe the walk-through process. What roles need to be performed during a walk-through?
14. Describe various communication methods and how they differ.

Chapter Exercises

1. Find a project (IS-related or non–IS-related) on campus. Identify the stakeholders, classify the stakeholders using one of the techniques discussed, and prepare a three-minute briefing for your class to present your findings.
2. "Ineffective communication is the fault of the sender." Do you agree or disagree? Why?
3. Construct a communication matrix for a project you have previously worked on or are currently working on.
4. What is nonverbal communication? Does it help or hinder verbal communication?
5. Why do project teams need a broad variety of methods for distributing information?
6. Plan a project team meeting and write a memo that clearly defines the purpose of the meeting, identifies participants, and outlines the meeting agenda.
7. What problems can occur if a project team's members fail to effectively listen to one another?

8. Design a project communication template for sharing some type of project information with a project team.

9. Using the concept of information richness, give examples of project-related messages best conveyed face-to-face or using telephone, instant messaging, and email.

10. In what project situations would the richness of face-to-face communication be a drawback rather than an advantage? Which communication method would be preferable in those situations, and why?

11. Design a template that allows you to collect answers to at least ten different questions regarding a particular type of collaboration technology (e.g., email, instant messaging, videoconferencing, and so on) from family members, friends, or work colleagues who are not in your class and are regular users of this technology. Your goal is to find out how they use the technology, what they feel it is useful for, their likes, dislikes, and so on. Using email, send your template to these people and have them reply via email. Once you have your results, write a memo to your instructor reporting your findings; make sure you include your survey template.

12. Collect the same type of information requested in Exercise 11 from at least six people using interviews rather than an email survey. Once you have your results, write a memo reporting them to your instructor; make sure you include your interview questions.

13. Using the findings from your survey or interviews on collaboration technologies from Exercise 11 or 12, prepare a three-minute briefing for your class. Make sure you follow the guidelines presented in the chapter on making effective presentations.

14. Attend a staff meeting of an organization on your campus. Obtain permission first if the meeting is not open to the public, explaining that your purpose for attending the meeting is to study meeting dynamics for a class project. Evaluate the meeting according to the guidelines presented in the chapter. Specifically, identify any problems that made the meeting less effective than it could have been; also identify things that were done well. Prepare an evaluation of the meeting in the form of a memo to your instructor.

15. Most organizations, including universities, have policies concerning acceptable computer/network use (see https://it.eller.arizona.edu/acceptable-use-policy for an example). Assume you work for a for-profit organization and are assigned by your boss to develop a policy statement regarding acceptable use of instant messaging. Make sure your policy differentiates between internal and external use, work-related and personal use, and so on.

Chapter Case: Sedona Management Group and Managing Project Communication

Communication is one of the more important factors for success in project management, and the team at Sedona Management Group (SMG) recognizes this. Traditionally, computer professionals have been viewed as people who like to work in isolation. Communication between these IT professionals and the users for whom systems are being developed has typically been difficult. IT professionals have been viewed as individuals who can only communicate things in technical terms, frequently beyond the understanding of the everyday system user. Fortunately, this state of affairs has changed over the years, and now computer professionals need a combination of both strong technical and "soft" skills. These soft skills include interpersonal abilities—such as those required to lead teams, understand user needs, and educate users—and overall the ability to communicate effectively with all project stakeholders.

Two-way communication is critical to the Sedona team's business model. At the start of any project at SMG, communication between the customer and the team is very crucial. Tim Turnpaugh indicates that most of the time the customers do not have a clear idea of what they want in the initiating phase of a project. Therefore, it is important for the team to spend time with customers to determine their needs. For such meetings, the Sedona team usually favors face-to-face meetings, not only because of the importance and sensitivity of the information being shared, but also because face-to-face meetings often provide a richer context for interactions when people are unfamiliar with each other. These early meetings are important for helping develop and nurture the relationship between the customer and the Sedona team.

Over the life of the project, the predominant form of communication the Sedona team uses to communicate with the customer is verbal communication. This does not necessarily mean that face-to-face meetings are used all of the time. Instead, phone conversations are used occasionally for updates and any inquiries that the Sedona team or the customer may have when working on the project. Interestingly, Turnpaugh prefers that members of his team do not use voicemail for communication because he believes it creates a bad impression of inaccessibility to the customer. Answering the phone and being accessible during business hours are critical components of SMG's customer service and image management.

The company also makes extensive use of email to communicate with customers. Turnpaugh was a codeveloper of Continental Bank's initial email system and has been an advocate of email use for more than thirty-three years. Although it may not be a good medium for early meetings employed to assess user needs, email, according to Turnpaugh, is very helpful for disseminating status reports to the customer, as well as to other uses. Over time, the Sedona team has become sensitive to the communication preferences of their regular customers. For example, no one on the project team has ever personally seen one of SMG's long-term customers, but instead phone conversations and email have been the predominant modes of communicating with her.

In addition to SMG's need to communicate effectively with customers and other external stakeholders, the members of the Sedona team also must communicate with each other. Several forms of communication are used for this purpose. During a typical working day, Turnpaugh has formal and informal face-to-face meetings with coworkers to determine progress on various projects. For example, team members may update each other on the status of a project during a coffee break. In addition, it is typical for a project status meeting to occur at the start of every business day. During the planning phase of the projects undertaken at SMG, milestones are established, and through frequent informal and formal meetings, Turnpaugh and his team members can ensure that these milestones are being met. SMG strives to complete projects in a timely fashion—in many instances around three to six weeks—and frequent team communication is essential to keep projects on track and decrease the risk of project failure. In addition to these face-to-face meetings, SMG also uses email and instant messaging to facilitate team communication. The popularity of instant messaging as a form of communication has rapidly been increasing, and the Sedona team considers it a great way to keep each other updated on the status of a project and to collaborate. While such online communication is useful, Turnpaugh recognizes that it is not a replacement for face-to-face meetings or phone conversations.

Chapter 4 Project Assignment

During the life cycle of the entertainment website development project, you will need to communicate with other project team members as well as various other stakeholders. The purpose of this assignment is to create a communications management plan. You will need to determine who the project stakeholders are, what type of communications they need to receive and how often, and the most effective media necessary for those communications.

1. Identify the stakeholders of your project.

2. Create a stakeholder register that documents information such as key stakeholders' names and organizations, their roles on the project, and their influence on the project.

3. Identify the different types of information needed by stakeholders throughout the project.

4. Indicate when you will use each type of communication.

5. Create a communications management plan, which is a document that guides communication throughout the life of the project. This communications management plan will be a table with columns identifying stakeholders, type of information to provide to stakeholders, communication frequency, and communication media.

References

Barnum, C., and Wolniansky, N. (1989). Taking Cues from Body Language. *Management Review*, June 1, 1989, 59–60.

Beer, K. (2003, January 22). Top 10 Tips for Setting a Secure Communications Policy. *Computerworld*. Retrieved July 4, 2018, from http://www.computerworld.com/article/2580186/security0/top-10-tips-for-setting-a-secure-communications-policy.html

Bilton, N. (2016, January 13). Nest Thermostat Glitch Leaves Users in the Cold. *The New York Times*. Retrieved July 5, 2018, from https://www.nytimes.com/2016/01/14/fashion/nest-thermostat-glitch-battery-dies-software-freeze.html

Daft, R. L., and Lengel, R. H. (1986). Organizational Information Requirements, Media Richness, and Structural Design. *Management Science* 32, 554–571.

Derousseau, R. (2017, June 14). The Tech that Tracks Your Movements at Work. *BBC.com*. Retrieved July 4, 2018, from http://www.bbc.com/capital/story/20170613-the-tech-that-tracks-your-movements-at-work

Evers, J. (2004, April 6). Microsoft's Channel 9 Gets Social with Developers. *Computerworld*. Retrieved July 9, 2018, from https://www.computerworld.com/article/2563646/app-development/microsoft-s-channel-9-gets-social-with-developers.html

Forbes Agency Council (2017, June 23). Thirteen Golden Rules of PR Crisis Management. *Forbes.com*. Retrieved July 5, 2018, from https://www.forbes.com/sites/forbesagencycouncil/2017/06/20/13-golden-rules-of-pr-crisis-management

Gilhooly, K. (2001, June 25). The Staff That Never Sleeps. *ComputerWorld*. Retrieved July 4, 2018, from http://www.computerworld.com/article/2582004/it-skills-training/the-staff-that-never-sleeps.html

Hoffer, J. A., George, J. F., and Valacich, J. (2007). *Modern Systems Analysis and Design* (5th ed.). Upper Saddle River, NJ: Prentice Hall.

James, G. (2004, March 1). Can't Hide Your Prying Eyes. *Computerworld*. Retrieved July 4, 2018, from http://www.computerworld.com/article/2574708/data-privacy/can-t-hide-your-prying-eyes.html

Kelly, W. (2013, August 14). Six Reasons to Use Yammer for IT Project Management. *TechRepublic*. Retrieved July 4, 2018, from http://www.techrepublic.com/blog/it-consultant/six-reasons-to-use-yammer-for-it-project-management

Kramer, M. (2001). *Business Communication in Context*. Upper Saddle River, NJ: Prentice Hall.

Microsoft (2016, January 18). Check Out the New MVP Channel 9 Page! *Microsoft.com*. Retrieved July 4, 2018, from https://blogs.msdn.microsoft.com/mvpawardprogram/2016/01/18/check-out-the-new-mvp-channel-9-page

Microsoft (2018). About. *MSDN.com*. Retrieved July 4, 2018, from https://channel9.msdn.com/about

Microsoft Office (2018). The Small Business's Guide to Secure Email. *Office.com*. Retrieved July 5, 2018, from https://products.office.com/en-us/business/articles/the-small-business-guide-to-secure-email

Project Management Institute (2017). *Agile Practice Guide*. Newton Square, PA: Author.

Project Management Institute (2017). *PMBOK: A Guide to the Project Management Body of Knowledge* (6th ed.). Newtown Square, PA: Author.

Robbins, S. P., and Judge, T. A. (2017). *Organizational Behavior* (17th ed.). Boston: Pearson.

Tucker, M. L., McCarthy, A. M., and Benton, D. A. (2002). *The Human Challenge: Managing Yourself and Others in Organizations* (7th ed.). Upper Saddle River, NJ: Prentice Hall.

Valacich, J., and George, J. F., (2017). *Modern Systems Analysis and Design* (8th ed.). Boston: Pearson.

Verma, V. K. (1996). *Managing the Project Team*. Newton Square, PA: Project Management Institute.

Verma, V. K. (1997). *Human Resource Skills for the Project Manager*. Newton Square, PA: Project Management Institute.

Wagner, R. (2017, June 12). Good Practices for Distributed Project Teams. *International Project Management Association*. Retrieved July 4, 2018, from http://blog.ipma.world/good-practices-distributed-project-teams

Yourdon, E. (1989). *Structured Walkthroughs* (4th ed.). Upper Saddle River, NJ: Prentice Hall.

Agile Project Management Foundations

Agile Project Management Introduction

As highlighted in Chapter 1, ever more dynamic competitive environments, the increasing pace of technological change, and increasing uncertainty necessitate organizations to be highly adaptive. Instead of competing with well-known, predictable competitors, large and small organizations are facing competition from startups and small, nimble companies. Further, the requirements of many systems are not easily definable upfront and can change quickly.

Traditional organizations and project management approaches are not well suited for operating in such environments. In particular, approaches where most of the work is determined upfront and plans are difficult to adjust do not work well with unclear and frequently changing requirements. In contrast, agile approaches allow for such flexibility by incorporating frequent iterations and obtaining rapid and frequent feedback from customers. Above all, the agile mind-set places the customer at the center and aims to deliver valuable products.

Traditional approaches emphasize processes and tools, comprehensive documentation, contract negotiation, and following plans. In contrast, the *Manifesto for Agile Software Development* (often simply referred to as the **agile manifesto**), proposed in the early 2000s, emphasizes a focus on individuals and interactions, working software, customer collaboration, and responding to change (see Figure A1.1). Often seen as a subset of lean methods, agile methodologies focus on value, attempt to eliminate waste, and use small batch sizes. Note that agile itself is a philosophy, rather than a methodology that puts forth a set of principles; various methodologies (such as Crystal, Kanban, Scrum, and eXtreme Programming) implement the principles set out in the agile manifesto. Further, organizations are increasingly managing IS projects by using a **DevOps** approach, where, based on agile principles, engineers from both development and operations collaborate throughout the system's life cycle from design to development to operations and support. By using DevOps teams, organizations can optimize the reliability of the software as well as productivity, helping the organization gain the agility needed for innovation.

The signatories to the agile manifesto further agreed on the following principles (presented verbatim from Beck et al., 2001):

Agile manifesto
Declaration specifying the aims of agile approaches, emphasizing a focus on individuals and interactions, working software, customer collaboration, and responding to change, over processes and tools, comprehensive documentation, contract negotiation, and following plans.

DevOps
Approach to managing IS projects, where, based on agile principles, engineers from both development and operations collaborate throughout the system's life cycle.

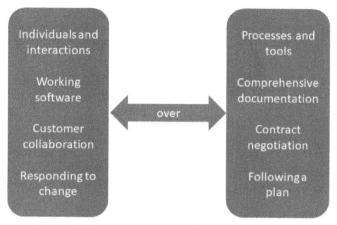

We are uncovering better ways of developing software by doing it and helping others do it. Through this work we have come to value:

Individuals and interactions	over	Processes and tools
Working software		Comprehensive documentation
Customer collaboration		Contract negotiation
Responding to change		Following a plan

That is, while there is value in the items on the right, we value the items on the left more.

Figure A1.1   The agile manifesto. *Source:* Beck et al. (2001).

1. Our highest priority is to satisfy the customer through early and continuous delivery of valuable software.
2. Welcome changing requirements, even late in development. Agile processes harness change for the customer's competitive advantage.
3. Deliver working software frequently, from a couple of weeks to a couple of months, with a preference to the shorter timescale.
4. Business people and developers must work together daily throughout the project.
5. Build projects around motivated individuals. Give them the environment and support they need, and trust them to get the job done.
6. The most efficient and effective method of conveying information to and within a development team is face-to-face conversation.
7. Working software is the primary measure of progress.
8. Agile processes promote sustainable development. The sponsors, developers, and users should be able to maintain a constant pace indefinitely.
9. Continuous attention to technical excellence and good design enhances agility.
10. Simplicity—the art of maximizing the amount of work not done—is essential.
11. The best architectures, requirements, and designs emerge from self-organizing teams.
12. At regular intervals, the team reflects on how to become more effective, then tunes and adjusts its behavior accordingly.

The Agile Project Life Cycle

Any project needs to balance time, costs, and scope to deliver a product with a specified performance or quality. In predictive life cycles, requirements are fixed at the start of the project, and the project team then moves through the different stages of analyzing, designing, building, testing, and deploying the system based on the requirements. As a result of defining the scope early in the project, the requirements drive time and costs, as well as the resulting quality. In contrast, agile approaches focus on quality, which delivers value to the customer; thus time, schedule, and scope are seen as mere constrains overshadowed by this larger goal of quality. Further, in agile approaches, requirements are assumed to vary or change. In other words, agile life cycles focus on delivering valuable products early and continuous delivery. Typically, the intended features of the finished product are prioritized; the team then starts working on the most important feature; once the work on this feature is finished, the team begins working on the second most important feature, and so on. Thus, in each **iteration**, the team performs processes related to planning, executing, and controlling: the team gathers the requirements, performs the necessary analyses, and designs, builds, tests, and deploys the feature, before moving onto the item with the next highest priority (see Figure A1.2). Typically, the iterations take the form of timeboxes of equal duration (such as thirty days), with the goal of each iteration being the delivery of a working feature.

Iteration
Development phase (typically timeboxed) in which all work pertaining to a specific deliverable is performed.

Depending on the project, hybrid approaches may be used. For example, some teams may choose to use agile approaches for building the software, but then use predictive approaches for later phases. At other times, agile approaches may be incorporated into predictive approaches, such as when new components or technologies are introduced into a well-known project. Conversely, some projects may necessitate incorporating external components, and an overall agile approach may include components that are built using predictive approaches. In any case, the choice of life cycle should depend on the needs of the particular project, such as the size or scope of the IS project, the timeline or duration of the project, and the number of people involved in the project. Likewise, there are a variety of sets of processes under the agile umbrella, including Crystal, Kanban, Scrum, and eXtreme Programming; thus the specific methodology chosen will depend on the nature of the project, the team composition, and so on. In the following,

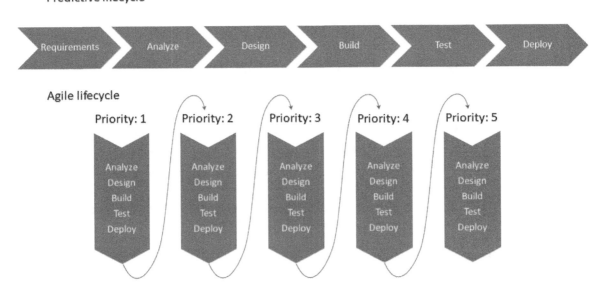

Figure A1.2 Predictive versus agile life cycles

Scrum
Widely used agile methodology that uses short sprints to deliver software at regular intervals.

Sprint
Iteration that lasts for one to two weeks and consists of a sprint planning meeting, daily stand-ups, a sprint demo, and a sprint retrospective.

Sprint planning meeting
Meeting during which the team jointly decides on which feature to implement during the sprint.

Daily stand-ups
Fifteen-minute stand-up meetings used to discuss issues faced during the previous day and goals for the current day.

Sprint review
Meeting during which the team presents the work completed during the sprint.

Sprint retrospective
Meeting during which the team discusses the sprint, identifies positive and negative aspects of the process, and agrees on changes to the process for the next sprint.

Product owner
The key stakeholder of the project who conveys the vision of the end product to the team and guides the team on the priority of features to deliver.

Scrum master
Facilitator aiding the Scrum team in being effective.

Scrum team
Team of five to seven cross-functional members who are jointly responsible for delivering the product on time and at the expected quality at the end of each sprint.

we will provide a high-level overview of Scrum, a widely used agile methodology, as an illustration to guide later discussions of topics related to agile methodologies.

Scrum

Scrum uses so-called **sprints**—iterations that last for one or two weeks—to deliver software at regular intervals. Each sprint consists of a **sprint planning meeting**, **daily stand-ups**, a **sprint review**, and a **sprint retrospective**. During the sprint planning meeting, the team jointly decides on which features to implement during the sprint; daily stand-ups (or Scrum meetings) are 15-minute stand-up meetings used to discuss issues faced during the previous day and goals for the current day; in the sprint review (sometimes called sprint demo), the team presents the work completed during the sprint; finally, the sprint retrospective is used to discuss the sprint, identify positive and negative aspects of the process, and agree on changes to the process for the next sprint.

Managing Agile Project Teams

Key to successfully managing agile projects is not only the use of agile methodologies, but also having a team with an agile mind-set. In particular, the focus on early and continuous delivery and the use of timeboxing requires minimizing distracting tasks and focusing on the items that currently have the highest priority. Further, agile teams—depending on the methodology comprised of three to nine collocated members dedicated to the project—are self-organizing teams that manage their own process and work together toward successful delivery. Also key to successful agile teams is having team members dedicated to the team. Given productivity losses associated with multitasking, agile team members should ideally be 100 percent dedicated to the team (which, apparently, is often infeasible in real-world projects). Agile teams normally have cross-functional team members who possess the skills needed to produce the finished product (such as designers, developers, and testers), without having to draw on outside people. An important role in agile teams is that of the product owner. Typically with a business background, the product owner is responsible for providing directions, interacting with stakeholders, and deciding on the feature to be delivered in the next iteration. Finally, agile teams have a team facilitator (see Figure A1.3).

In Scrum, these three specific roles are the **product owner**, the **Scrum master**, and the **Scrum team**. The product owner is the key stakeholder of the project, who conveys the vision of the end product to the team and guides the team on the priority of features to deliver. The Scrum master does not have authority over the team, but acts as a facilitator, helping remove challenges and aiding the team in being effective. The Scrum team, typically consisting of five to seven cross-functional members, is jointly responsible for delivering the product on time and at the expected quality at the end of each sprint. Taken together, using sprints of short durations, with specific meetings that structure each sprint, and having well-defined roles, Scrum is an example of an effective agile methodology.

Rather than controlling, leaders of agile teams need to empower their team members and facilitate the team's work. In agile teams, the leader's role shifts toward that of a facilitator, in that the leader practices servant leadership. Coined by Robert K. Greenleaf in 1970, the term **servant leader** refers to leaders who focus on serving the team and helping the team members succeed by listening, coaching, and facilitating collaboration within the team, between teams, and across the organization. While every organization can benefit from leaders adopting a servant leadership style, this style of leadership is key to successful agile projects, as the servant leader is critical in enabling

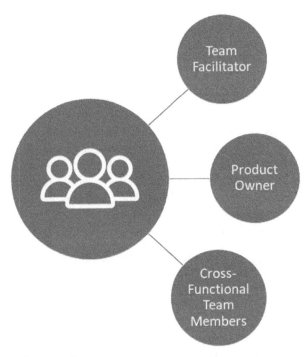

Figure A1.3   Three distinct roles in agile teams

Servant leader
A leader who focuses on serving the team and helping the team members succeed by listening, coaching, and facilitating collaboration within the team, between teams, and across the organization.

self-organizing teams to focus on feature delivery. The servant leader can interact with different organizational stakeholders and align their needs so as to remove organizational obstacles or provide support for activities that are beyond the skill set of the agile team members.

Managing Communication in Agile Projects

In agile teams, close collaboration, daily standups, and the focus on delivering features require a space where the team can interact, as well as spaces where the individual team members can complete their tasks with minimal interruption. Such a setup can be relatively easily established for collocated team members, and collocation is typically regarded as essential for teams using agile approaches. Nevertheless, various organizations have started using agile approaches with distributed teams. In these cases, it is essential to use communication technology to create shared spaces for team interactions. Commonly used tools such as videoconferencing or repositories for sharing documents are often used together with tools that enable spontaneous interactions. One such technique is an always-on videoconference, sometimes referred to as fishbowl window, which is live during the workday, enabling team members to meet and interact without having to set up dedicated meetings. Using such technologies enables distributed team members to collaborate as if they were collocated; however, these technologies cannot solve any issues associated with differences in time zones.

Key Terms Review

A. Agile manifesto

B. Daily stand-ups

C. DevOps

D. Iteration

E. Product owner

F. Scrum

G. Scrum master

H. Scrum team

I. Servant leader

J. Sprint

K. Sprint review

L. Sprint planning meeting

M. Sprint retrospective

Match each of the key terms with the definition that best fits it.

1. Meeting during which the team discusses the sprint, identifies positive and negative aspects of the process, and agrees on changes to the process for the next sprint.

2. Widely used agile methodology that uses short sprints to deliver software at regular intervals.

3. The key stakeholder of the project who conveys the vision of the end product to the team and guides the team on the priority of features to deliver.

4. A leader who focuses on serving the team and helping the team members succeed by listening, coaching, and facilitating collaboration within the team, between teams, and across the organization.

5. Meeting during which the team jointly decides on which feature to implement during the sprint.

6. Declaration specifying the aims of agile approaches, emphasizing a focus on individuals and interactions, working software, customer collaboration, and responding to change, over processes and tools, comprehensive documentation, contract negotiation, and following plans.

7. Approach to managing IS projects, where, based on agile principles, engineers from both development and operations collaborate throughout the system's life cycle.

8. Facilitator aiding the Scrum team in being effective.

9. Fifteen-minute stand-up meetings used to discuss issues faced during the previous day and goals for the current day.

10. Team of five to seven cross-functional members who are jointly responsible for delivering the product on time and at the expected quality at the end of each sprint.

11. Meeting during which the team presents the work completed during the sprint.

12. Iteration that lasts for one to two weeks and consists of a sprint planning meeting, daily stand-ups, a sprint demo, and a sprint retrospective.

13. Development phase (typically timeboxed) in which all work pertaining to a specific deliverable is performed.

Review Questions

1. What is the agile manifesto?

2. How do agile life cycles differ from traditional life cycles?

3. What is a sprint and what are the key features of a sprint?

4. Explain the three roles in a Scrum project.

5. What is a servant leader?

6. How can communication technology be used to facilitate distributed teams in agile projects?

Chapter Exercises

1. Interview an IS practitioner about her experiences with agile methodologies. What were the benefits? What were the drawbacks?

2. Using the web, find information about different agile methodologies. Choose two methodologies and compare and contrast their key aspects.

3. Research information about servant leadership. In what contexts is servant leadership used? Find an example where servant leadership has been helpful in the successful completion of a project.

4. In a team of three to five people, brainstorm about innovative technologies that can help bridge differences in time and space to enable distributed teams to collaborate on agile projects.

References

Beck, K., Beedle, M., van Bennekum, A., Cockburn, A., Cunningham, W., Fowler, M., Grenning, J., Highsmith, J., Hunt, A., Jeffries, R., Kern, J., Marick, B., Martin, R.C., Mellor, S., Schwaber, K., Sutherland, J., and Thomas, D. (2001). Manifesto for Agile Software Development. Retrieved July 4, 2018, from http://agile-manifesto.org

Mueller, E. (2017, July 24). What Is DevOps? *The Agile Admin*. Retrieved July 4, 2018, from https://theagileadmin.com/what-is-devops

Palmquist, M. S., Lapham, M. A., Miller, S., Chick, T., and Ozkaya, I. (2013). Parallel Worlds: Agile and Waterfall Differences and Similarities. *CMU Software Engineering Institute*. Retrieved July 4, 2018, from https://resources.sei.cmu.edu/asset_files/TechnicalNote/2013_004_001_62918.pdf

Project Management Institute (2017). *Agile Practice Guide*. Newton Square, PA: Author.

Project Management Institute (2017). *PMBOK: A Guide to the Project Management Body of Knowledge* (6th ed.). Newtown Square, PA: Author.

Smartsheet (2017). What's the Difference? Agile vs. Scrum vs. Waterfall vs. Kanban. *Smartsheet.com*. Retrieved July 4, 2018, from https://www.smartsheet.com/agile-vs-scrum-vs-waterfall-vs-kanban

PART II

Starting, Organizing, and Preparing the Project

CHAPTER 5

Managing Project Scope

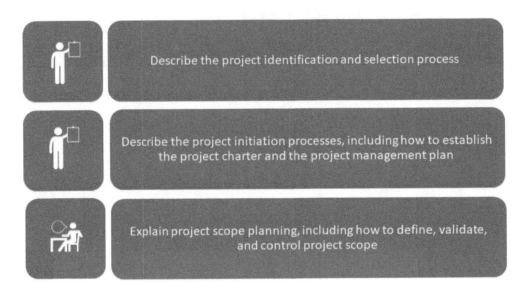

Describe the project identification and selection process

Describe the project initiation processes, including how to establish the project charter and the project management plan

Explain project scope planning, including how to define, validate, and control project scope

Figure 5.1 Chapter 5 learning objectives

Opening Case: Betting on the Value of Information Systems at Harrah's

Founded in 1937, Harrah's Entertainment Inc. is one of the largest casinos in the United States, with nearly thirty locations that operate under the brand names of Harrah's, Rio, Showboat, Horseshoe, and Harveys. Harrah's objective is to provide great customer service and build customer loyalty in the very competitive world of casino entertainment. Information systems and technology investments have become a cornerstone of Harrah's strategy for improved customer service and loyalty. To get the most from its technology-related investments, Harrah's has developed very robust financial projection monitoring, measuring, and tracking capabilities for accurately estimating the cost and benefits of all information systems and technology projects. As projects progress, all costs and benefits are carefully tracked and updated so that executives can "raise the bets" on promising projects and revamp or "fold" those that are underperforming (see Figure 5.2).

Evidence that Harrah's is on a "winning streak" in managing its technology investment portfolio is its number-one ranking (of 130 Fortune 1,000 companies) in best practices for technology portfolio management, as determined by researchers at Northwestern University. The "payout" for its improved portfolio management has been substantial; in the early 2000s project throughput had nearly tripled from 112 projects in 2001 to 324 in 2003, and more than 77 percent of all projects had been completed on time, on budget, and on target. Through careful planning and management, information

Figure 5.2 Harrah's uses a variety of sophisticated technologies to enhance gambling operations.

systems and technology have become a "sure thing" at Harrah's. However, just like any casino operator, Harrah's cannot rest on its laurels: casinos have always been a target of fraudsters trying to cheat the casinos in various ways, and are increasingly using innovative ways to improve their odds. In a recent case, fraudulent gamblers used laser scanning technology to predict the winning segment of a roulette wheel. For casino companies, this means that a range of sophisticated technologies—ranging from license plate readers to RFID chips to biometric face recognition—is needed to stay ahead of the game, so information systems project management continues to be a hot topic.

Based on: Chacos (2011); Joshi (2017); Melymuka (2004).

Introduction

Acquiring, developing, and maintaining information systems consume substantial resources for most organizations. Thus organizations can benefit from following a formal process for identifying and selecting projects. Project identification and selection focuses on the activities during which the need for a new or enhanced system is recognized. This activity does not deal with a specific project but, rather, identifies the portfolio of projects to be undertaken by the organization. Thus project identification and selection is often thought of as a preproject step to an overall project. This recognition of potential projects may come as part of a larger IS planning process, or from requests from managers and business units. Once a project has been identified and selected, the next step is to conduct a more detailed assessment during project initiation. This assessment does not focus on how the proposed system will operate but, rather, on understanding the scope of a proposed project and the feasibility of its completion, given the available resources. It is crucial that organizations understand whether resources should be devoted to a project, as mistakes can be very expensive (DeGiglio, 2002). Therefore, the focus of this chapter is on those processes necessary for better managing project identification and selection.

In the next section, we describe these processes. You will learn about a general method for identifying and selecting projects, and the deliverables and outcomes from this process. We will describe two activities that are important for the project identification and selection process—namely, corporate strategic planning and information systems planning. In addition, we present numerous techniques for assessing project feasibility. We then discuss processes associated with project initiation, such as developing the project charter and the project management plan, project scope planning, as well as scope definition, verification, and change control processes. Together, these topics will provide you with a clear understanding of how projects are identified, selected, and documented so that all stakeholders have a clear understanding of the project's scope.

Project Identification and Selection

Any organization faces resource limitations, and organizations have to carefully evaluate and prioritize the many potential projects before giving the go-ahead for any particular project. Typically, organizations assemble a portfolio of different programs and projects to achieve different objectives. The activities in identifying and selecting projects typically include:

1. Identifying information systems projects
2. Assessing project feasibility
3. Comparing alternative projects

Next, we will briefly discuss each of these key activities.

Identifying Information Systems Projects

Organizations initiate information systems projects for a variety of reasons. As discussed in Chapter 2, information systems projects can result from (see Figure 5.3)

- Requests by stakeholders
- Strategic opportunities
- Needs for changing or improving business processes
- Changing regulatory, legal, or social requirements

Different organizational members can be responsible for identifying information systems projects; depending on who is responsible, the foci of identified projects differ (see Figure 5.4). Whereas top managers or senior executives tend to focus on strategic considerations, IS steering committees tend to focus on projects that have benefits across the different business functions represented in the steering committee. Projects identified by user departments typically reflect tactical or immediate operational needs of the departments. Finally, IS managers or members of the development group tend to focus on the ease of developing and implementing the system, as well as integrating the new system with the existing information systems infrastructure. Further, different organizational members place differing importance on factors such as cost, schedule, risk, or complexity. The different foci of IS projects reflect the different uses of information systems in running, growing, and transforming organizations. The run-grow-transform model describes the need to balance IT budgets between operating and maintaining systems to support business operations ("run"), enhancing and expanding systems to support business growth ("grow"), and to innovate and drive the business to new levels ("transform"; see Figure 5.5).

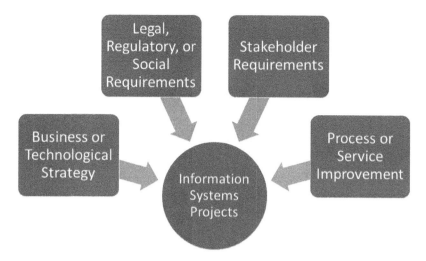

Figure 5.3   Sources for information systems projects

Figure 5.4   Different foci of IS development projects

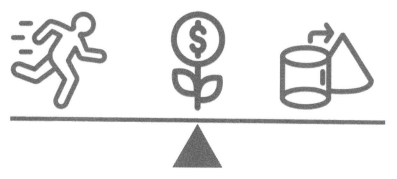

Figure 5.5   Companies need to balance IT budgets to run, grow, and transform the organization.

Traditionally, organizations used information systems to solve organizational problems or improve individual processes. In other words, organizations focused on developing particular systems that would help address an issue currently faced by the organization. However, organizations operate in increasingly uncertain environments; likewise, the speed of technological advances has increased tremendously. While business processes and information systems that support these processes may have to be adapted, the data and information needs underlying the processes are likely to remain relatively stable. Thus organizations are increasingly trying to first build a solid underlying data model. Based on the identified information needs, the organization can then select projects that are integrated across the organization, enabling the organization to quickly respond to changes in business strategy or business processes.

Key to identifying information systems projects is the alignment between the information systems and business objectives (often referred to as business-IT alignment). Consequently, we will briefly describe the relationship between corporate strategic planning and information systems planning, which drive project identification decisions.

Corporate Strategic Planning

In order to gain and sustain competitive advantage, organizations need to analyze their current state, envision their desired future state, and develop a plan to achieve that future state, as shown in Figure 5.6. Based on the understanding of the current state and the envisioned future state, top management can develop a strategic plan to achieve the vision. The process of determining goals and defining a strategy to achieve these goals is often referred to as **corporate strategic planning**.

Corporate strategic planning
An ongoing process of determining goals and defining a strategy to achieve these goals.

Mission statement
A statement that defines a company's purpose

Objective statements
A series of statements that express an organization's qualitative and quantitative goals for reaching a desired future position.

Competitive strategy
The plan of action and organization pursues to achieve its mission and objectives.

During these strategic planning processes, executives typically develop and refine the company's mission statement, statements of corporate objectives, as well as strategies designed to help the organization reach its objectives. The **mission statement** of a company typically states in very simple terms the purpose of a company. For instance, the mission statement for Microsoft is "to empower every person and every organization on the planet to achieve more" (see Figure 5.7). Closely linked to their mission, organizations also define several **objective statements** that refer to broad and timeless goals for the organization. These objectives reflect an organization's core values, and thus typically do not change substantially over time. Most objectives relate to some aspect of the organizational mission.

A **competitive strategy** is the plan of action an organization pursues to achieve its mission and objectives and gain or sustain a competitive advantage. Organizations' competitive strategies can be broadly classified as belonging to one of three types (Porter, 1980)—low-cost producer, product differentiation, and product focus or niche (see Table 5.1). Often, these generic strategies are used to compare the approaches of different companies within an industry. However, the generic strategies also influence information systems planning and investment decisions. For example, The Ritz-Carlton hotel group differentiates its hotels from the competition by offering superior quality and customer service. To achieve this strategy, The Ritz-Carlton invests significant resources in information systems that enable to company to integrate information about each individual guest, and make this information available at each point of contact. In contrast, many budget hotels and motels are implementing self-check-in kiosks that allow guests to get access to their rooms without the need for front office staff, thus substantially reducing costs.

Figure 5.6 Corporate strategic planning is a three-step process. *Adapted from*: Valacich and George (2017).

We believe in what people make possible.

Our mission is to empower every person and every organization on the planet to achieve more.

Figure 5.7 Microsoft's corporate mission statement. *Source:* www.microsoft.com.

Table 5.1 Generic Competitive Strategies

Strategy	Description
Low-cost producer	Focus on cost reductions to compete on price
Product differentiation	Focus on differentiating product offerings from the competitors (e.g., in terms of features, quality, design, or performance)
Product focus or niche	Focus on niche markets (while pursuing a low-cost or product differentiation strategy within that niche)

Based on: Porter (1985).

Value Chain Analysis

The organization's generic strategy can guide the overall objectives of information systems investment decisions (such as cost reduction). To understand *where* in the organization information systems can help achieve the organizational strategy, the organization's leadership uses value chain analysis (Porter, 1985; Shank and Govindarajan, 1993). **Value chain analysis** is the process of analyzing an organization's activities for making products and/or services to determine where value is added and costs are incurred. Having an understanding of the value chain can help determine where information systems can be most beneficial in reducing costs or helping differentiate the product or service.

Given the flexibility and ubiquitous nature of information systems, they can be used throughout the value chain to add business value. An organization's value chain can be regarded as a big input/output process (see Figure 5.8). The inputs—such as

Value chain analysis
The process of analyzing an organization's activities to determine where value is added to products and/or services and the costs incurred for doing so.

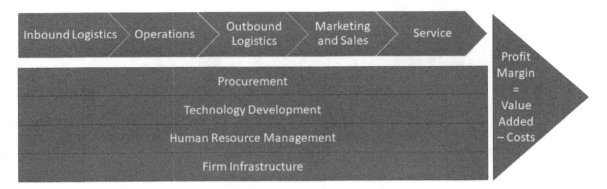

Figure 5.8 Organizational value chain. *Based on*: Porter (1985).

supplies and other resources—are processed to create the organization's products or services, which are marketed, sold, and then distributed to customers. In addition to the primary activities, a variety of supporting activities are used to create value. Once you understand in which activities, processes, or function value is added, you can determine the costs within each of the areas, as well as the major factors influencing costs. This will help you determine where processes could be improved or systems be implemented to create additional value or reduce costs. Further, you can compare your organization's value chain with other organizations, so as to identify other opportunities for adding value or reducing costs.

Understanding the mission, objectives, and strategy, as well as where in the value chain information systems can be used to support the strategy, will help an organization determine which activities are essential when trying to reach their objectives, effectively deploy resources, and build the information systems that add most value to their organization. In other words, *information systems development projects should be identified and selected through the clear understanding of the organizational mission, objectives, and strategies.* In the next section, we discuss how organizations conduct information systems planning to help them reach their objectives.

Information Systems Planning

Information systems planning
A structured process of assessing the information needs of an organization and defining the systems, databases, and technologies that will best satisfy those needs.

In addition to strategic planning, information systems planning helps an organization identify worthwhile information systems projects. **Information systems planning** is a structured process of assessing the information needs of an organization and defining the systems, databases, and technologies that will best satisfy those needs (Carlson, Gardner, and Ruth, 1989; Parker and Benson, 1989; Segars and Grover, 1999; Luftman, 2004). In other words, during information systems planning, you (or, more likely, senior information systems managers responsible for the planning) must understand the organization's current and future needs for data and information, and develop strategies for utilizing existing and future information systems and technologies to meet the organization's future needs. Information systems planning is a top-down process that takes into account external environmental factors—such as industry, relative organization size, competitors, region, and so on—that are likely to have an effect on the success of the firm. In short, the purpose of information systems planning is to determine the information systems and technologies that can help the organization achieve the objectives identified in the strategic planning processes.

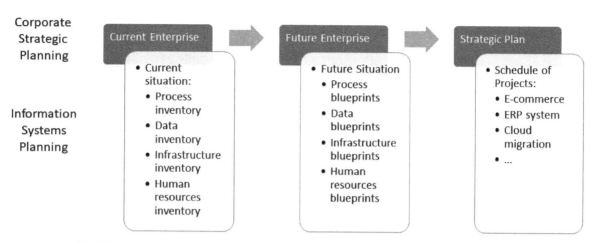

Figure 5.9 Parallel activities of corporate strategic planning and information systems planning. *Adapted from*: Valacich and George (2017).

The three information systems planning activities parallel those of corporate strategic planning, as shown in Figure 5.9. Like corporate strategic planning, information systems planning first considers the current situation in terms of processes, data, infrastructure, and human resources. Next, the organization develops target blueprints representing the desired future states of these assets to reach its objectives. Finally, the organization prioritizes and schedules the projects needed to achieve the future desired state.

Next, we will describe these three key activities:

1. *Describe the current situation.* Many organizations use a top-down approach for understanding the current organizational situation, where the organization's information needs are determined based on the organization's mission, objectives, and strategy. Thus a top-down approach takes a high-level organizational perspective; the advantages of top-down approaches are summarized in Table 5.2.

   In contrast to top-down approaches, planners using bottom-up approaches define projects based on problems and opportunities. Bottom-up approaches are often faster and less costly than top-down approaches, help identify pressing organizational problems, and help gain buy-in from all levels within the organization; however, projects identified using bottom-up approaches often neglect the informational needs of the *entire* organization and might result in disparate (and often redundant) information systems that are difficult to integrate.

Table 5.2 Advantages of the Top-Down Planning Approach

Advantage	Why It Is Important
Broader perspective	Top-down approaches help understand the business from general management's viewpoint.
Improved integration	Top-down approaches help focusing on evolving existing systems and integrating new system with the existing infrastructure.
Improved management support	Top-down approaches help gain management acceptance of the role of information systems to assist them in achieving business objectives.
Better understanding	Top-down approaches help gain the understanding necessary to implement information systems across the entire business rather than simply in individual operating units.

Adapted from: Couger et al. (1982).

Either approach on its own will result in a suboptimal portfolio of projects. For example, using top-down approaches alone will result in an incomplete portfolio that misses pressing operational needs. Thus most organizations use a combination of top-down and bottom-up approaches, to ensure strategic alignment while being able to address the most important operational and organizational needs. When using a combination of approaches, team members from all levels of the organization are involved in gathering project ideas, analyzing the ideas, and prioritizing the project s within the portfolio. Together, this can result in a project portfolio that represents the needs of the entire organization.

Describing the current situation involves analyzing not only the organization but also its competitive environment, so as to gain a detailed understanding of the organization, its different business functions, locations, as well as processes, data, and information systems (see Figure 5.10). As the planning progresses, this high-level information is then broken down to a more detailed level (see Figure 5.11). Matrices—such as a data entity-to-business function matrix—are used to capture which data entities are used by which part of the business (see Figure 5.12 for an example).

2. *Describe the target situation, trends, and constraints.* Next, the planning team defines the target situation, including the desired state of the business functions, units, locations, processes, data, and information systems (see Figure 5.5). As part of this process, the planning team updates the matrices to reflect these changes. In addition to organizational constraints, technological and business trends are likely to influence the target situation.

3. *Develop a transition strategy and plan.* Once the planning team has a thorough understanding of the current situation and has mapped out the target situation, the team can develop a comprehensive transition strategy and plan. Reflecting broad, long-range issues, this plan should provide sufficient information in regard to what needs to be done, how and when it needs to be done, and who in the organization will be responsible for doing it. Figure 5.13 shows the components of a typical information systems plan.

System service request
A formal request for correcting problems with an existing system, adding features to a system, or developing a new system.

The short- and long-term developmental needs identified in the information systems plan result in a series of projects (see Figure 5.14). The projects derived from the top-down planning process and bottom-up (or needs-driven) projects submitted as systems service requests (or change requests) together form the short-term systems development plan. A **system service request** (SSR; shown in Figure 5.15)—often arising from new data needs or changing business processes—is a formal request for correcting problems with an existing system, adding features to a system, or developing a new system. Collectively, the short- and long-term projects provide guidelines for selecting projects. Given the interrelationships between technologies, the projects need to take into account the enablers and constraints posed by other projects as well.

In this section, we discussed how organizations develop an information systems plan to decide how to use information systems to reach the overall strategic goals of the organization. Typically, the planning processes are conducted by senior executives and senior managers, and information systems project managers are normally not involved in these planning processes; yet the outcomes of the planning will play an important role in classifying and ranking potential projects.

Figure 5.10   Information systems planning information

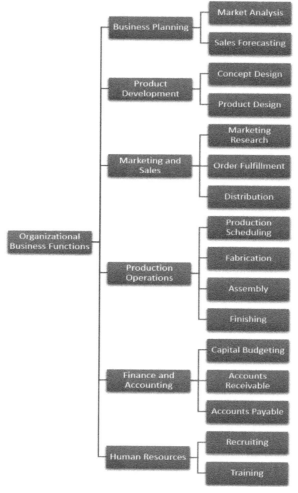

Figure 5.11   Functional decomposition of information systems planning information in Microsoft Word 2016

	Customer	Product	Vendor	Raw Material	Order	Work Center	Equipment	Employees	Invoice	Work Order	...
Marketing and Sales											
Marketing Research	X	X									
Order Fulfillment	X	X			X				X		
Distribution	X	X									
Production Operation											
Production Scheduling						X	X	X		X	
Fabrication						X	X	X		X	
Assembly						X	X	X		X	
Finishing						X	X	X		X	
Finance and Accounting											
Capital Budgeting					X	X	X				
Accounts Receivable	X	X	X	X	X				X		
Accounts Payable			X	X					X		
...											

Figure 5.12   Data entity-to-business function matrix. *Adapted from*: Valacich and George (2017).

I. Organizational Mission, Objectives, and Strategy
   Description of the mission, objectives, and strategy of the organization, as well as the current and future views of the company.
II. Informational Inventory
   Summary of the various business processes, functions, data entities, and information needs of the enterprise (in terms of both current and future needs).
III. Mission and Objectives of Information Systems
   Description of the primary role of information systems (e.g., a s a necessary cost, an investment, or a source of strategic advantage) in transforming the enterprise from its current to future state (representing the current best estimate of the overall role for IS within the organization).
IV. Constraints on IS Development
   Description of the limitations imposed by technology and current level of resources (financial, technological, and human resources) within the company.
V. Overall Systems Needs and Long-Term IS Strategies
   Summary of the overall systems needed within the company and the set of long-term (2–5 years) strategies chosen by the IS department to fill the needs.
VI. Short-Term Plan
   Detailed inventory of present projects and systems and a detailed plan of projects to be developed or advanced during the current year. These projects may be the result of the long-term IS strategies or of requests from managers that have already been approved and are in some stage of the life cycle.
VII. Conclusions
   Descriptions of likely but not-yet-certain events that may affect the plan, an inventory of business change elements as presently known, and a description of their estimated impact on the plan.

Figure 5.13   Outline of an information systems plan *Adapted from*: Valacich and George (2017).

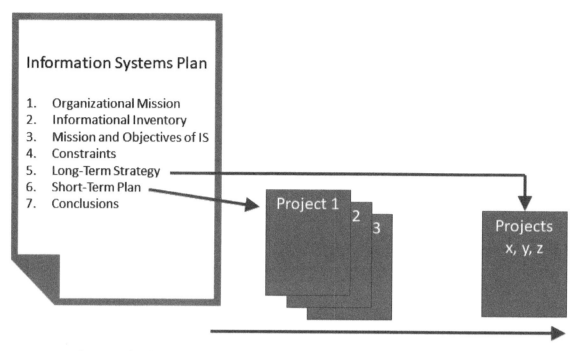

Figure 5.14 Systems development projects flow from the information systems plan. *Adapted from:* Valacich and George (2017).

Ethical Dilemma: Intelligent Disobedience for Bad Project Ideas

Intelligent disobedience often refers to the behavior of guide dogs when working with the blind. For instance, at a busy intersection, if the blind person initiates a movement to cross the street at an unsafe time, the guide dog will *intelligently* disobey this command. The blind person learns to trust the guide dog to their mutual benefit. Within organizations, experienced project managers are often the guide dogs who must resist doing what they are told to do by managers and customers with ineffective or unwise project ideas. Intelligent disobedience for project managers is, therefore, the ability to say no to the demands of powerful managers and customers that will put the project, and hence the organization, in harm's way. As with guide dogs, intelligent disobedience requires empowerment and trust. If a project manager does not feel that he or she will be supported when refusing an ill-conceived "command" by a powerful manager or customer, it is likely that many projects will be doomed to failure.

Discussion Questions

1. What steps can an organization take to encourage intelligent disobedience?
2. If you were a project manager facing a bad idea from a powerful customer or manager, how would you say no?

Based on: Kapur (2004); McGannon (2018).

Jackie's Electronics

System Service Request Form

REQUESTED BY   __Jackie Judson__   DATE: __August 1, 2019__

DEPARTMENT   __Marketing__

LOCATION   __Headquarters, 570c__

CONTACT   __Tel: 4-3290   FAX: 4-3270   e-mail: jjudson__

TYPE OF REQUEST
[x] New System
[ ] System Enhancement
[ ] System Error Correction

URGENCY
[ ] Immediate – Operations are impaired or opportunity lost
[ ] Problems exist, but can be worked around
[x] Business losses can be tolerated until new system installed

PROBLEM STATEMENT

Sales growth at Jackie's has caused a greater volume of work for the marketing department. This volume of work has greatly increased the volume and complexity of the data we need to deal with and understand. We are currently using manual methods and a complex PC-based electronic spreadsheet to track and forecast customer buying patterns. This method of analysis has many problems: (1) we are slow to catch buying trends as there is often a week or more delay before data can be taken from point of sales system and be manually entered it into our spreadsheet; (2) the process of manual data entry is prone to errors (which makes the results of our subsequent analysis suspect); and (3) the volume of data and the complexity of analyses conducted in the system seem to be overwhelming our current system—sometimes the program starts recalculating and never returns while for others it returns information that we know cannot be correct.

SERVICE REQUEST

I request a thorough analysis of our current method of tracking and analysis of customer purchasing activity with the intent to design and build a completely new information system. This system should handle all customer purchasing activity, support display and reporting of critical sales information, and assist marketing personnel in understanding the increasingly complex and competitive business environment. I feel that such a system will improve the competitiveness of Jackie's, particularly in our ability to better serve our customers.

IS LIAISON   __Jackie Cheung,   4-6207   FAX:4-6200   e- mail: jcheung__

SPONSOR   __Jackie Judson, Vice-President, Marketing__

. . . . TO BE COMPLETED BY SYSTEMS PRIORITY BOARD . . . .

[ ] Request approved   Assigned to _____
                              Start date _____
[ ] Recommend revision
[ ] Suggest user development
[ ] Reject for reason _____

Figure 5.15   System service request (SSR). *Adapted from*: Valacich and George (2017).

Assessing Project Feasibility

Once potential information systems projects have been identified, the next major activity focuses on classifying and ranking the identified projects based on their relative merits. This activity can be performed by top managers, a steering committee, business units, or the information systems development group. Depending on the organization's priorities and the project's initiators, different criteria (summarized in Table 5.3) are used for assessing the relative merit of a given project, and typically organizations base their assessment on multiple criteria. Once the relative ratings have been determined (for instance, by a steering committee), these ratings are used as inputs into the project selection process.

Given unlimited resources and infinite time, any project is feasible (Pressman, 2005). However, individuals and organizations must work within various constraints. As discussed in Chapter 2, the time, cost, and scope triangle outlines the boundaries of a given project. Therefore, the feasibility of any given project should be carefully assessed, so as to provide a sound basis for project selection. Assessing project feasibility involves evaluating a wide range of factors. While not all factors are of equal importance for all projects, assessing project feasibility typically involves evaluating the following feasibility factors:

- Economic feasibility
- Technical feasibility
- Operational feasibility
- Schedule feasibility
- Legal and contractual feasibility
- Political feasibility

Business case
The justification that presents the economic, technical, operational, schedule, legal and contractual, and political factors influencing a proposed project.

Together, the different feasibility factors are used to build the **business case** that is used to justify investing resources in the project. Next, we will examine various feasibility issues.

Assessing Economic Feasibility

Economic feasibility
The degree to which the benefits of a development project outweigh its costs.

Given tight budgets, it is crucial to examine a project's **economic feasibility**, or the degree to which the benefits of a development project outweigh its costs. In other words, economic feasibility assessment is based on a *cost-benefit analysis*—that is, an

Table 5.3 Possible Evaluation Criteria When Classifying and Ranking Projects

Evaluation Criterion	Description
Value chain analysis	Extent to which activities add value and costs when developing products and/or services
Strategic alignment	Extent to which the project is viewed as helping the organization achieve its strategic objectives and long-term goals
Potential benefits	Extent to which the project is viewed as improving profits, customer service, and so forth, and the duration of these benefits
Resource availability	Amount and type of resources the project requires and their availability
Project size/duration	Number of individuals and the length of time needed to complete the project
Technical difficulty/risks	Level of technical difficulty to successfully complete the project within given time and resource constraints

analysis of the predicted financial benefits and costs of the development project. While at this stage it is all but impossible to obtain exact estimates of all potential benefits and costs related to a particular project, the project manager should attempt to identify and quantify the costs and benefits as best as possible, so as to conduct an adequate economic feasibility assessment and make meaningful comparisons between competing projects. Once the potential benefits and costs are estimated, the project manager can draw on various techniques to determine in how far the benefits outweigh the costs. Typically, these analyses are conducted throughout the project's life to decide whether to continue, redirect, or kill it.

Determining Project Benefits. In organizational settings, information systems are built to obtain various benefits, such as automation, reduction of errors, or the provision of innovative services; likewise, systems can be built with the aim to improve speed, flexibility, efficiency, or employee morale. While some of these benefits are tangible, others are intangible.

Tangible benefit
A benefit that can be quantified with relative certainty.

Tangible benefits can quantified with relative certainty. For instance, cost reduction due to automatization can be measured with relative certainty. Likewise, reduction of errors can result in measurable cost savings. Most tangible benefits belong to one or more of the following categories:

- Cost reduction and avoidance
- Error reduction
- Increased flexibility
- Increased speed of activity
- Improvement of management planning and control
- Opening new markets and increasing sales opportunities

The tangible benefits for a proposed information system are summarized in a worksheet in Figure 5.16.

Intangible benefit
A benefit that cannot be easily quantified with relative certainty.

In contrast, **intangible benefits** *cannot* be easily quantified with relative certainty. Some intangible benefits, such as improved employee morale, may have direct benefits to an organization; other intangible benefits, such as improved accessibility of systems and services, may have broader societal implications. During project initiation, some tangible benefits are initially classified as intangible, as they cannot be assessed with certainty in the early stages of a project. Such intangible benefits can later be reclassified as the project manager gains a better understanding of the benefits; typically, this results in updates to the planning documents and budgets, to allow for monitoring and controlling the project's progress. Intangible benefits include

- Being able to stay on par with competitors
- Increased organizational flexibility
- Increased employee morale
- Promotion of organizational learning and understanding
- More timely information

In addition to determining project benefits, the project manager must identify the project costs.

Jackie's Electronics	
Project: No Customer Escapes	
Tangible Benefits Worksheet	
	Year 1 through 5
A. Cost reduction or avoidance	$ 5,000
B. Error reduction	$ 2,000
C. Increased flexibility	$ 7,500
D. Increased speed of activity	$ 10,500
E. Improvement in management planning or control	$ 25,000
F. Other	$ -
TOTAL tangible benefits	$ 50,000

Figure 5.16 Microsoft Excel 2016 spreadsheet showing the tangible benefits for a proposed system. *Adapted from*: Valacich and George (2017).

Tangible cost
A cost that can be quantified with relative certainty.

Intangible cost
A cost that cannot be easily quantified with relative certainty.

Determining Project Costs. Just as benefits can be tangible or intangible, so can costs. **Tangible costs** are those that can be quantified with relative certainty. In information systems development projects, tangible costs include items such as costs related to hardware, software, or development, or operational costs, such as employee training, energy, and network connectivity. In contrast, **intangible costs** are those items that cannot easily be quantified with relative certainty. Intangible costs can include reduced customer satisfaction during the implementation of the new system, or decreased employee morale due to increased restrictions or monitoring imposed by a new system. Table 5.4 provides a summary of common costs associated with the development and operation of an information system. Typically, predicting the costs associated with the development of an information system is difficult. As it is important to neither overestimate costs (to avoid overallocation of resources) nor underestimate costs (to reduce cost overruns), several guidelines have been developed to improve the process of estimating costs (Lederer and Prasad, 1992):

- Assign the initial estimating task to the final developers.
- Only finalize the initial estimate after a thorough study.
- Anticipate and control requirements changes.
- Monitor the progress of the proposed project.
- Evaluate proposed project progress by using independent auditors.
- Use the estimate to evaluate project personnel.
- Only approve cost estimates after careful analysis.
- Rely on documented facts, standards, and simple arithmetic formulas rather than guessing, intuition, personal memory, and complex formulas.
- Don't rely on cost-estimating software alone for an accurate estimate.

Table 5.4 Possible Information Systems Costs

Types of Costs	Examples
Procurement	• Consulting fees • Equipment purchase or lease • Equipment installation costs • Site preparation and modifications • Cost of capital • Management and staff time
Project-related	• Application software • Software modifications to fit local systems • Personnel, overhead, etc., for cloud development • Training users in application use • Collecting and analyzing data • Preparing documentation • Managing development
Start-up	• Operating system software • Networking equipment installation • Start-up personnel • Personnel searches and hiring activities • Disruption to the rest of the organization • API purchases
Operating	• System maintenance (hardware, software, and facilities) • Rental of space and equipment • Cloud rental • Management, operation, and planning personnel

Adapted from: King and Schrems (1978).

One-time cost
A cost associated with project start-up and development or system start-up.

Recurring cost
A cost resulting from the ongoing evolution and use of a system.

Another classification of costs is their recurrence (the same is true for benefits, although we do not discuss this difference for benefits). Costs associated with project initiation and development and startup of the system are only incurred once and are thus referred to as **one-time costs**; in addition to system development, such one-time costs comprise the acquisition of needed hard- and software, site preparation, data migration and system conversion, as well as user training (see Figure 5.17). These costs are captured in a worksheet. As for very large projects, one-time costs may be incurred over one or more years; separate one-time cost worksheets should be created for each year to facilitate present value calculations (as described later). Costs incurred from the ongoing evaluation and use of the system are referred to as **recurring costs**, and include

- Application software maintenance
- Incremental data storage expenses
- Incremental communications expenses
- New software and hardware leases
- Supplies and other expenses (e.g., paper, forms, data center personnel)

Recurring costs for a proposed information systems project are summarized in a worksheet in Figure 5.18.

Both one-time and recurring costs can consist of items that are fixed or variable. Whereas variable costs depend on usage (such as cloud storage or processing), fixed costs are independent of usage (such as the lease of a data center or the purchase of a new web server).

Jackie's Electronics Project: No Customer Escapes One-Time Costs Worksheet	Year 0
A. Development costs	$ 22,000
B. New hardware	$ 13,000
C. New (purchased) software, if any	
1. Packaged applications software	$ 5,000
2. Other	$ -
D. User training	$ 2,500
E. Site preparation	$ -
F. Other	$ -
TOTAL one-time costs	$ 42,500

Figure 5.17 Microsoft Excel 2016 spreadsheet showing the one-time costs for a proposed system. *Adapted from*: Valacich and George (2017).

Jackie's Electronics Project: No Customer Escapes Recurring Costs Worksheet	Year 1 through 5
A. Application software maintenance	$ 25,000
B. Incremental data storage required: 20 GB × $50 (estimated cost/GB = $50)	$ 1,000
C. Incremental communications expenses (lines, messages....)	$ 2,000
D. New software or hardware leases	$ -
E. Supplies	$ 500
F. Other	$ -
TOTAL one-time costs	$ 28,500

Figure 5.18 Microsoft Excel 2016 spreadsheet showing the recurring costs for a proposed system. *Adapted from* Valacich and George (2017).

Cost-benefit analysis
The use of a variety of analysis techniques for determining the financial feasibility of a project.

Cost-Benefit Analysis. Organizations use a variety of **cost-benefit analysis** techniques to compare the various costs and benefits for an information systems development project and determine its financial viability. Especially for projects of longer duration, these analyses should be based on present-day values in order to allow for meaningful comparisons of costs and benefits. This is especially important, as projects differ in duration, incur both one-time and recurring costs, and involve benefits that might only be realized in the future; likewise, it is important to base analyses on present-day values when comparing different projects with different life expectancies. Thus project managers use the concept of the *time value of money* (TVM) to compare present cash outlays and expected future returns.

The following simple example will help explain this concept. A friend of yours offers you her car, asking for three payments of $1,500 for three years, beginning next year, for a total of $4,500. If she would accept a single lump sum payment at the time of sale, should the single payment be more or less than $4,500? The answer to this question lies in the concept of the time value of money. As money can be invested, a dollar today is worth more than a dollar at a time in the future. Thus most of us would gladly accept $4,500 today rather than three payments of $1,500. The cost of capital (i.e., the rate at

Discount rate
The rate of return used to compute the present value of future cash flows.

which money can be borrowed or invested) is referred to as the **discount rate** in TVM calculations. Assuming the seller could invest the money received for the sale of the car for a 10 percent return, the **present value** of the three $1,500 payments could be calculated as follows:

Present value
The current value of a future cash flow.

$$PV_n = Y \times \frac{1}{(1 + i)^n}$$

where PV_n is the present value of Y dollars n years from now and i is the discount rate.

From our example, the present value of the three payments of $1,500 can be calculated as

$$PV_1 = 1,500 \times \frac{1}{(1 + .10)^1} = 1,500 \times .9091 = 1,363.65$$

$$PV_2 = 1,500 \times \frac{1}{(1 + .10)^2} = 1,500 \times .8264 = 1,239.60$$

$$PV_3 = 1,500 \times \frac{1}{(1 + .10)^3} = 1,500 \times .7513 = 1,126.95$$

where PV_1, PV_2, and PV_3 reflect the present value of each $1,500 payment in years 1, 2, and 3, respectively.

The *net present value (NPV)* of the three $1,500 payments is the sum of the present values calculated previously (*NPV = PV1 + PV2 + PV3* = $1,363.65 + $1,239.60 + $1,126.95 = $3,730.20). In other words, assuming a discount rate of 10 percent, the seller could accept a lump sum payment of $3,730.20 instead of three payments of $1,500.

When performing economic feasibility analyses, project managers first determine the costs and benefits, the expected life span of the project, as well as the cost of capital. Based on these factors, the project manager can then create a summary worksheet showing the present values of all benefits and costs, as well as all pertinent analyses (see Figure 5.19).

For example, to create the summary spreadsheet in Figure 5.18, the project manager assumed the project's useful life to be five years and the cost of capital to be 12 percent.

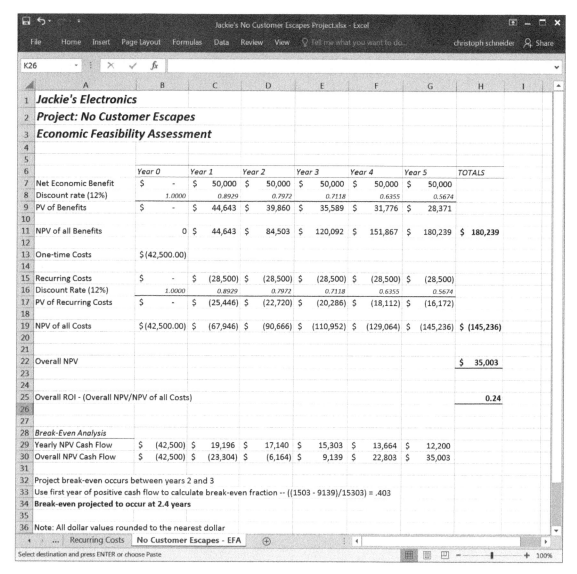

Figure 5.19 Microsoft Excel 2016 spreadsheet reflecting the present-value calculations of all benefits and costs for a proposed information systems project. *Adapted from*: Valacich and George (2017).

The NPV of the total tangible benefits is presented in cell H11; the NPV of the total costs is presented in cell H19. The overall NPV of $35,003 (shown in cell H22) indicates that the project has a positive return, as the overall benefits exceed the costs.

Cell H25 in the worksheet shows the overall return on investment (ROI; defined in Table 5.5). The overall ROI is useful in comparing projects that have different benefit and cost values and, possibly, different expected life-spans. While the ROI shown in the example is for the overall project, the ROI could be determined for each year of the project.

Break-even analysis
A type of cost-benefit analysis used to identify when (if ever) benefits will equal costs.

In addition to NPV and ROI, the example in Figure 5.16 shows a **break-even analysis**, which is used to determine when (if ever) the project will "break even" (i.e., when the benefits will equal costs). To determine the break-even point, the NPVs of the yearly cash flows are calculated by subtracting both the one-time costs and the present values of the recurring costs from the present value of the yearly benefits. The overall NPV of the cash flow (shown on line 30) reflects the total cash flows for all preceding years; as year 3 is the first in which the overall NPV cash-flow figure is nonnegative, breakeven occurs between years 2 and 3. The following formula can be used to determine the project's break-even point:

$$\text{Break-Even Ratio} = \frac{\text{Yearly NPV Cash Flow} - \text{Overall NPV Cash Flow}}{\text{Yearly NPV Cash Flow}}$$

Using data from Figure 5.16,

$$\text{Break-Even Ratio} = \frac{15{,}303 - 9{,}139}{15{,}303} = .403$$

Therefore, the project breaks even at approximately 2.4 years, or about 2 years and 5 months. Together, these different metrics can give a project review board a better understanding of the potential economic impact of a project and can help the review board make an informed decision about approving or rejecting a project. Given that most information systems projects have a usable life of more than one year, project managers typically use techniques using the concept of the TVM (see Table 5.5). You may consult an introductory finance or managerial accounting textbook for a more detailed discussion of TVM or other cost-benefit analysis techniques.

While the benefits and costs of many projects can be determined to a reasonable degree, a project manager often faces situations where costs or benefits cannot be easily determined during project initiation and planning, and it may not be possible to demonstrate that the project may break even or have an ROI above some organizational threshold. In such cases, the project manager includes a thorough analysis of intangible costs and benefits to justify the project. Further, a project manager may use optimistic, pessimistic, and expected cost and benefit estimates to produce a range of possible outcomes. Together with the list of intangible benefits and the support of the requesting business unit, the project manager can make a case for the project's economic feasibility. Likewise, a project manager can conduct some activities that would normally be done during the analysis phase, such as identifying shortcomings of an existing system and demonstrating how a new system will address these issues. In any case, especially when resources (such as capital) are scarce, the analysis of a project's economic feasibility must be as accurate as possible. Clearly, demonstrating a project's economic feasibility

Table 5.5 Commonly Used Economic Cost-Benefit Analysis Techniques

Analysis Technique	Description
Net present value (NPV)	NPV uses a discount rate determined from the company's cost of capital to establish the present value of the project. The discount rate is used to determine the present value of both cash receipts and outlays.
Return on investment (ROI)	ROI is the ratio of the net cash receipts of the project divided by the cash outlays of the project. Trade-off analysis can be made among projects competing for investment by comparing representative ROI ratios.
Break-even analysis (BEA)	BEA finds the amount of time required for the cumulative cash flows from a project to equal its initial and ongoing investment.

can be an open-ended activity; the extent and depth of these analyses depend on the particular project, stakeholders, and business conditions, but typically, assessing the economic feasibility for new types of information systems tends to be less clear-cut and more difficult.

Common Problems: Reducing Information Systems Development Costs

When performing economic feasibility analyses, project managers identify potential benefits and costs. For a project to be selected for development, its benefits typically need to exceed its costs. Therefore, one way to increase the potential value of a project to the organization is by reducing information systems development costs. Development costs can be controlled and reduced by following a few strategies, including

1. *Standardizing hardware platforms.* Standardizing server and storage platforms can significantly reduce recurring costs; quantity purchases can reduce one-time costs.

2. *Standardizing application infrastructure.* Common application environments reduce recurring costs by reducing system and data integration as well as ongoing maintenance costs.

3. *Improving security.* Standardizing on a single operating system and automating updates can reduce the need for individual desktop repair and upgrades, as well as increase overall system security and simplify administration; together, these steps reduce one-time and recurring system costs.

4. *Managing operations.* By carefully monitoring and proactively administering system updates and security repairs, operational problems can be dramatically reduced or eliminated, thus reducing recurring system costs.

As the amount of work reacting to system differences, security breaches, and update administration is reduced, organizational resources can be focused on providing organizational benefits. Looking for opportunities to better control one-time and recurring costs will enhance both project and organizational performance.

Based on: Burry (2003).

Assessing Technical Feasibility

Technical feasibility
The degree to which the development organization is able to construct a proposed system.

In addition to assessing a project's economic feasibility, a project manager needs to assess the project's **technical feasibility** to understand whether the organization will be able to construct the proposed system. This includes not only an assessment of the development group's expertise in the possible hardware, software, and operating environments to be used, but also of the size and complexity of the system and the group's experience with similar projects or systems. In this section, we will discuss a framework for assessing the technical feasibility of a project in which the level of technical project risk can be determined after answering a few fundamental questions.

As all projects have risks, the assessment of a project's technical feasibility should also include an assessment of the sources and types of the project's technical risks. Whereas risk is not necessarily something to avoid (see Chapter 9), riskier projects often tend to offer higher expected returns. Identifying the potential risks as early as possible in the project can help manage (and, if necessary, minimize) the risks. Not assessing and managing risks can result in the following consequences:

- Failure to attain expected benefits from the project
- Inaccurate project cost estimates
- Inaccurate project duration estimates
- Failure to achieve adequate system performance levels

- Failure to adequately integrate the new system with existing hardware, software, or organizational procedures

As you will learn in Chapter 9, approaches to managing risk include modifying the project management plan (described later) to avoid risk factors, carefully managing the risky aspects, and continuously monitoring whether potential risks are materializing.

As summarized in Table 5.6, how much technical risk is associated with a project depends on four major factors: project size, project structure, the development group's experience with the application and technology area, and the user group's experience with systems development projects and the application area (see also Kirsch, 2000). Based on these four factors, there are four general rules (see also Table 5.6):

1. *Large projects are riskier than small projects.* Typically, as the size of a project increases (relative to what the development group is familiar with), so does technical risk.

2. *Projects with structured and easily obtainable requirements are less risky than projects in which requirements are messy, ill-structured, ill-defined, or subject to the judgment of an individual.* For example, a human resources management system's requirements are relatively easy to determine due to legal reporting requirements and standard accounting procedures. In contrast, a new business analytics system may not have clear requirements, thus making its development more risky.

3. *Projects using standard technologies are less risky than projects using novel or nonstandard technologies.* If the development group lacks experience with a particular aspect of a project (such as novel technologies used), the project has a greater likelihood of experiencing difficulties; using standard tools, hardware, and software is typically less risky.

4. *A project is less risky when the user group is familiar with the systems development process and application area.* Users who are unfamiliar with the systems development process or the application area typically do not realize the effects of seemingly minor changes to the requirements for a system. Therefore, active involvement

Table 5.6 Technical Project Risk Assessment Factors

Factor	Examples
Project size	Number of members on the project team Project duration Number of organizational departments involved in the project Size of programming effort (e.g., hours, function points)
Project structure	New system or overhaul of existing system(s) Organizational, procedural, structural, or personnel changes resulting from system User perceptions and willingness to participate in effort Management commitment to system Amount of user information in system development effort
Development group	Familiarity with target hardware, software development environment, tools, and operating system Familiarity with proposed application area Familiarity with building similar systems of similar size
User group	Familiarity with information systems development process Familiarity with proposed application area Familiarity with using similar systems

Adapted from: Applegate, Austin, and McFarlan (2007).

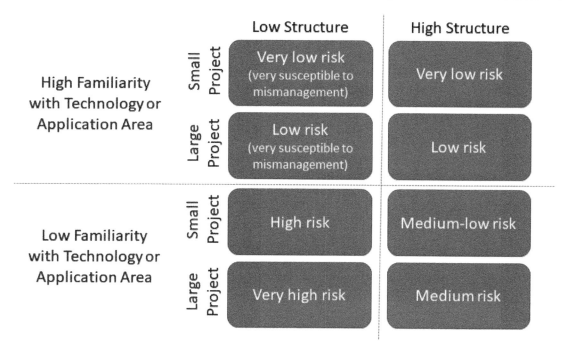

Figure 5.20   Effects of degree of project structure, project size, and familiarity with application area on project implementation risk. *Adapted from*: Applegate, Austin, and McFarlan, 2007

and cooperation between user and development groups can help reduce risks, as users familiar with the application area and the systems development process are more likely to understand how their involvement can influence project success.

Risk is typically seen as a portfolio issue, where organizations do not consider project risk in isolation, but have a mix of high-, medium-, and low-risk projects. As some high-risk projects may fail, an organization should not have too many of these projects. In contrast, avoiding high-risk projects altogether (and focusing on low-risk projects) prevents an organization from harnessing the opportunities of the latest innovative systems and technologies. Thus top management of an organization typically decides on the appropriate mix. Figure 5.20 shows the effects of degree of project structure, project size, and familiarity with application area on project implementation risk.

Global Implications: Deciding When to Offshore

Most economists and business leaders believe that offshore outsourcing is here to stay. As businesses work hard to remain competitive, most are examining what types of projects should or should not be sent offshore. To be successful, identifying the right projects is crucial. Unfortunately, there is no clear rule of thumb for selecting which projects to offshore. Nevertheless, organizations with long-term success in utilizing offshoring typically do not offshore the following types of projects:

- Complex projects that involve multiple coordinated teams

- Core-competency or core intellectual property related projects
- "Crash" projects to return another project back onto schedule
- New product development projects
- Projects initiated to produce immediate cost savings (because it typically takes time to realize project benefits)

In contrast, projects that have been identified as good candidates for offshoring include those for the maintenance, support, or extension of legacy systems, as well as non-mission-critical systems that do not involve key intellectual property or processes. Even though organizations may choose the "right" type of projects for offshoring, there is still a great risk of failure if the project is not carefully managed. Key management issues include having a local project manager who is experienced and skilled in managing an offshore team (and overcoming potential language barriers), good communication plans, and frequent milestones to ensure that problems are quickly identified. Organizations can realize many benefits from offshoring, however, as with all types of systems development projects, good project management is essential to realizing the optimal benefits.

Based on: Patil (2017); Printer (2004); Thibodeau (2004).

Assessing Other Feasibility Concerns

For any project, economic and technical feasibility are of paramount importance, but ignoring other types of feasibility, such as operational feasibility, schedule feasibility, legal and contractual feasibility, and political feasibility, can derail any project. Next, we will discuss these types of feasibility that should be considered when formulating the business case for a system during project initiation. First, **operational feasibility** is the degree to which a proposed system will solve business problems or take advantage of business opportunities, or the likelihood that the project will attain its desired objectives, as outlined in the systems service request (SSR) or project identification study. One part of assessing operational feasibility is to determine in how far the project is consistent with or necessary for accomplishing the information systems plan. In fact, the business case for any project can be strengthened by demonstrating that the project is aligned with to the business or information systems plan. In addition, assessing operational feasibility includes determining how the proposed system will affect organizational structures and procedures, as projects that have a large impact on an organization's structure or procedures are typically riskier. Thus understanding how the system will fit into the organization's current day-to-day operation will help determine the project's operational feasibility.

> **Operational feasibility**
> The degree to which a proposed system will solve business problems or take advantage of business opportunities.

Second, **schedule feasibility** is the degree to which the potential time frame and completion dates for all major activities within a project meet organizational deadlines and constraints for affecting change. The deadlines and constraints can depend on different factors. For example, a newly introduced regulation may necessitate an update of the organization's accounting system by a certain date, or a new e-commerce website may need to go live before the start of the busy holiday season. In addition, some resources may not be available at certain times, so completing certain project activities may not be possible during holiday or vacation periods, or during rushed business periods. Factors such as project team size, availability of key personnel, outsourcing activities, and changes in development environments may all be considered as having a possible impact on the eventual schedule; thus part of assessing schedule feasibility also includes evaluating scheduling trade-offs. As near-term activities can be planned with more certainty than long-term ones, assessing schedule feasibility during project initiation can only give a rough estimate of whether the system can be completed within the given constraints, and schedule feasibility should be reassessed as the project proceeds.

> **Schedule feasibility**
> The degree to which the potential time frame and completion dates for all major activities within a project meet organizational deadlines and constraints for affecting change.

In addition, any project is likely to have potential legal and contractual ramifications. Thus assessing **legal and contractual feasibility** issues is an important part of this stage. Depending on the system, legal considerations include copyright or intellectual property issues, nondisclosure agreements, as well as current or pending contractual obligations. Likewise, the development of a system may be constrained by current labor laws, antitrust legislation, foreign trade regulations or data protection directives, and financial reporting standards. Contractual obligations may involve ownership or

> **Legal and contractual feasibility**
> The degree to which potential legal and contractual ramifications due to the construction of a system influence project success.

licensing of software used in joint ventures, hardware or software licenses, or elements of a labor agreement (such as an agreement limiting the use of certain compensation mechanisms). Often, new systems may also require more or different licenses for third-party software. Finally, ownership of source code of systems that had initially been externally developed can have potential ramifications.

Finally, assessing **political feasibility** involves an evaluation of how key stakeholders within the organization view the proposed system. Many newly implemented information systems change the way information is distributed within organizations—and thus affect the distribution of power. Consequently, some of the affected stakeholders may not support the project, and may even attempt to block, disrupt, or change the intended focus of the project.

In sum, assessing the feasibility of a project includes the analysis of numerous issues, including economic, technical, operational, schedule, legal and contractual, and political issues related to the project. Yet project selection may be influenced by other factors. For example, if a project is seen as a strategic necessity and is regarded as being crucial for the organization's survival, it might be selected despite high costs or risk. On the other hand, projects may be selected due to low projected costs and risks. Likewise, the power of persuasiveness of key stakeholders may be determinants of project selection. Thus, while it is impossible to foresee all factors that influence project selection, it is nevertheless important to conduct a thorough examination of all factors that can be assessed, so as to allow the project review committee to make an informed decision when selecting projects for implementation. Next, we will discuss how alternative projects can be compared.

Comparing Alternative Projects

The third activity in the project initiation process is comparing alternative projects, so as to select projects for further development. Typically, this process considers a portfolio of short- and long-term projects, so as to select those that are most likely to help the organization achieve its business objectives. Additionally, as business conditions change over time, individual projects may become more or less important. Thus, identifying and selecting projects is a very important and ongoing activity.

As shown in Figure 5.21, project selection decisions must consider numerous factors such as the perceived needs of the organization, existing systems and ongoing projects, resource availability, evaluation criteria, current business conditions, and perspectives of the decision makers. Likewise, project selection decisions can have numerous outcomes. Of course, projects can be accepted or rejected. An accepted project typically receives funding to conduct the next project phase; a rejected project will no longer be considered for development. However, projects may also be accepted based on certain conditions, such as the approval or availability of needed resources, or dependent upon the successful development of a prototype or the demonstration that the development group will be able to develop a particularly difficult aspect of the system. Further, projects may be delayed until resources are available, or the requester may be asked to revise and resubmit their project proposal.

Multicriteria Analysis

A widely used method for deciding among different projects or among alternative designs for a given system is called *multicriteria analysis* (see Figure 5.22). **Multicriteria analysis** (sometimes called *multicriteria decision analysis*) uses a weighted scoring method for a variety of criteria to contrast alternative projects or system features. Let's

Political feasibility
The degree to which key stakeholders within the organization can affect project success.

Multicriteria analysis
A project selection method that uses weighted scoring for a variety of criteria to contrast alternative projects or system features.

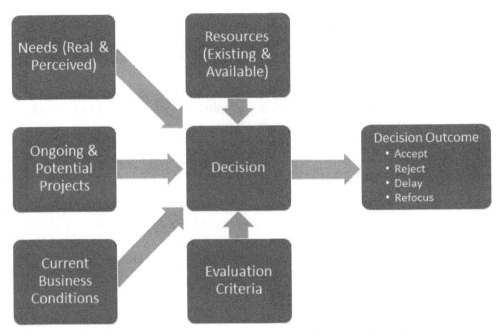

Figure 5.21 Project selection decisions must consider numerous factors and can have numerous outcomes. *Adapted from*: Valacich and George (2017).

Criteria	Weight	Alternative A Rating	Alternative A Score	Alternative B Rating	Alternative B Score	Alternative C Rating	Alternative C Score
Requirements							
Track purchases	15	5	75	5	75	5	75
Record reward point balances	15	1	15	5	75	5	75
Track reward redemptions	15	1	15	5	75	5	75
	45		105		225		225
Constraints							
Hardware requirements	15	4	60	5	75	3	45
Software requirements	15	4	60	4	60	3	45
Development costs	15	5	75	1	15	5	75
Operating costs	10	5	50	3	30	3	30
	55		245		180		195
Total	**100**		**350**		**405**		**420**

Figure 5.22 Alternative projects and system design decisions can benefit from the use of weighted multicriteria analysis. *Adapted from*: Valacich and George (2017).

suppose that three alternative designs—A, B, and C—are possible for a given system that has been identified and selected; during early planning meetings, three key system requirements and four key constraints (as shown in the left column of Figure 5.22) have been identified. Typically, the requirements and constraints differ in importance, and are thus weighted based on their relative importance. For example, it is possible that requirements might be more or less important than constraints. In any case, there are no hard and fast rules for the weights; thus the weights should be arrived at through a process of open discussions among the analysis team, users, and sometimes managers. To facilitate the analysis, the total of the weights for both the requirements and constraints should be 100 (percent).

In the next step, each alternative is rated on each requirement and constraint (e.g., on a scale of 0 to 5, with 5 being the highest rating). Just as the weights, ratings are subjective and should thus be determined through open discussion among users, analysts, and managers. Next, each requirement's and constraint's rating is multiplied by its weight to arrive at a score. These individual scores are then summed to arrive at an overall score for each alternative. As shown in Figure 5.21, each project has subtotals for requirements and constraints, as well as an overall score. The subtotals for the requirements suggest that alternatives B and C meet or exceed all requirements. However, only alternative A does not violate any constraints. The overall score suggests that alternative C might be the best option. However, decisions makers typically take all factors into account (rather than just the total score) in making their decision. For example, while alternative A does not meet two of the key requirements, it also has the lowest costs. Thus, while the decision of which project to implement will never be clear-cut, a thorough analysis will help in making the best decision for the organization.

Project Initiation

Project initiation
The process of authorizing a new project or continuing an existing project.

Once a project has been identified and selected based on strategic objectives of the organization, the project can be authorized. The process of authorizing the continuation of an existing project or the start of a new project is called **project initiation**. At this point, the project manager can develop the project charter, the project management plan, and the project management information system. Next, we will briefly discuss each of these key activities.

Developing the Project Charter

Project charter
A short document that serves as the foundation for the project, describes what the project will deliver, and authorizes the use of resources to complete the project.

Based on a solid business case, the **project charter** is a short document that serves as the foundation for the project, describes what the project will deliver, and authorizes the use of resources to complete the project. A project charter can vary in the amount of detail it contains but often includes high-level descriptions of the following elements:

- Project title and date of authorization
- Project manager name and contact information
- Customer name and contact information
- Project purpose
- Project objectives and description, as well as major deliverables
- Key requirements
- Project risk
- Projected start and completion dates and major milestones
- Approved financial resources
- Key stakeholders, project role, and responsibilities
- Key assumptions or approach
- Approval and exit criteria
- Signature section for key stakeholders

The project charter ensures that the project manager and the customer agree on a common understanding of the project. Further, the project charter helps communicate that a particular project has been chosen for development. In addition to developing the project charter, the project manager typically starts developing an **assumption log** to capture any project-related assumptions or constraints. A sample project charter is shown in Figure 5.23.

Assumption log
Document used to capture any project-related assumptions or constraints.

Jackie's Electronics
Project Charter

Project Name:	No Customer Escapes
Project Manager:	James Cheung (jcheung@jackies.com)
Customer:	Operations
Project Sponsor:	Sarah Codey (scodey@jackies.com)
Project Start/End (projected):	8/5/2019—11/29/2019
Prepared:	7/1/2019

Project Overview:
Project aim: design and implement a customer relationship management system in order to provide superior customer service by ... Specifically, the system will track customer purchases, assign points for cumulative purchases, and allow points to be redeemed for "rewards" ...

Objectives:
• Track customer purchases
• Accumulate redeemable points
• ...

Key Assumptions:
• System development will be outsourced
• Interface will be a Web browser
• ...

Stakeholders and Responsibilities:

Stakeholder	Role	Responsibility	Signature
Sarah Codey	Chief Operating Officer	Project Vision, Executive Sponsor	*Sarah Codey*
Bob Petroski	Senior Operations Manager	Monitoring, Resources	*Bob Petroski*
James Cheung	Project Manager	Plan, Monitor, Execute Project	*James Cheung*
Sally Fukuyama	Assistant Director, Marketing	System Functionality	*S. Fukuyama*
Sanjay Agarwal	Lead Analyst	Technical Architect	*Sanjay Agarwal*

Figure 5.23   A project charter for a proposed information systems project

Developing the Project Management Plan

Once the project is formally authorized, the next step is to develop the project management plan. The **project management plan** specifies *how* the project will be performed, and guides the execution, monitoring and controlling, and closing of a project (see Figure 5.24). The project management plan comprises a number of components that are developed during the various planning processes. These subcomponents typically depend on the nature of the project. Subcomponents you learned about earlier are the communications management plan and the stakeholder engagement plan. In this section of the book, you will learn about plans to manage scope, requirements, schedule, cost, quality, resources, risks, and procurement.

The project management plan is a living document, and many parts of the project management plan evolve as the project moves through its different phases. However, whereas various project management processes result in additions or changes to the project management plan, any changes to costs, schedule, or scope need to go through formal change management processes. In other words, once the scope has been defined, the schedule has been developed, and resources have been estimated, these are fixed as **baselines**; the scope, schedule, and cost baselines serve as a standard for measuring project progress and performance, and any changes to these baselines need to be formally approved. Finally, the project management plan may contain other subcomponents such as a description of the project life cycle, a description of the development approach, or plans for managing changes or measuring performance.

Establishing the Project Management Information System

The focus of this activity is to collect and organize the tools that you will use while managing the project and to develop the project management information system. Thus the

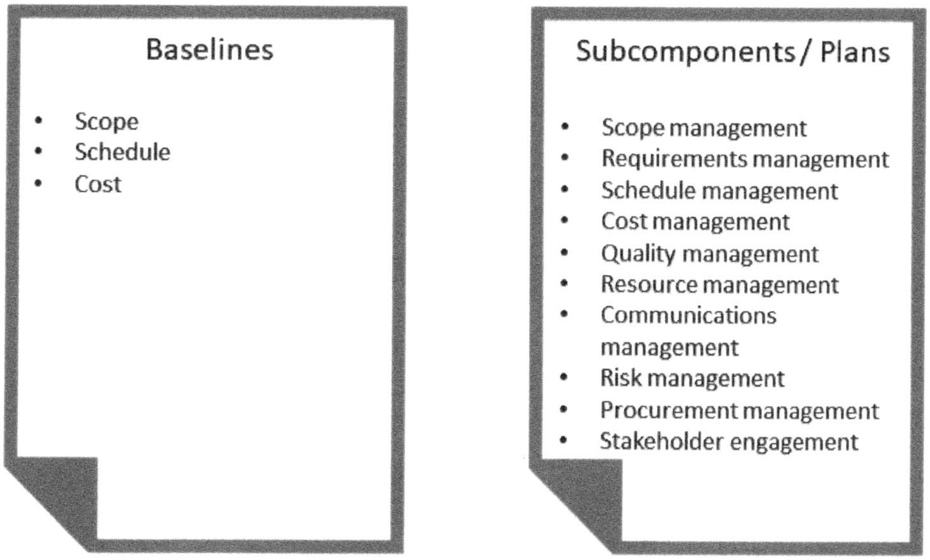

Project management plan
A plan specifying how the project will be performed, and guides the execution, monitoring and controlling, and closing of a project.

Baseline
Approved version of a project management plan component serving as a standard for measuring project progress and performance that can only be changed through formal change management processes.

Baselines
- Scope
- Schedule
- Cost

Subcomponents / Plans
- Scope management
- Requirements management
- Schedule management
- Cost management
- Quality management
- Resource management
- Communications management
- Risk management
- Procurement management
- Stakeholder engagement

Figure 5.24 Components of the project management plan

Project management information system
An online or hard-copy repository for all project correspondence, inputs, outputs, deliverables, procedures, and standards to support all aspects of a project.

project management information system serves as a central repository for all project correspondence, inputs, outputs, deliverables, procedures, and standards to support all aspects of a project. The project management information system contains both paper and electronic components. For example, hardcopies are filed in large three-ring binders, and electronic documents and communication are stored in electronic repositories or groupware systems (see Figure 5.25). The project management information system is used by all team members to guide orientation of new team members, communication with management and stakeholders, identifying future projects, and performing project audits and postproject reviews. Therefore diligently documenting all project information is one of the most important activities you will perform as project manager. Today, most project teams keep their project workbooks on the web. A website can be created so that all project members can easily access all project documents. This website can be a simple repository of documents or an elaborate site with password protection and security levels. The best feature of using a web-based repository is that it enables project members and customers to continually review a project's status and all related information.

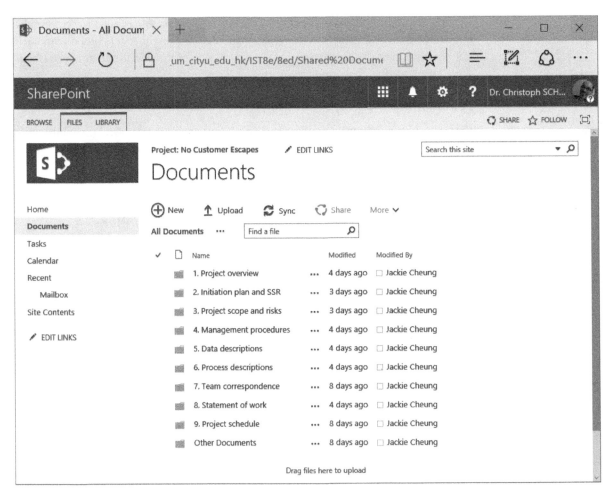

Figure 5.25 The project management information system can be a hard-copy or a groupware system such as Microsoft SharePoint Online.

Project Scope Planning, Verification, and Change Control

Once a project has been identified and formally selected, project scope planning can begin, to progressively elaborate and document the project management plan in order to effectively manage a project. During project scope planning, the project manager identifies requirements and develops the project scope statement. This document outlines all work that will be done, clearly describes what the project will deliver (including the criteria for acceptance), and helps make sure that you, the customer, and other project team members have a clear and common understanding of the project. The remaining activities of the project scope management process focus on scope validation and change control. Scope validation focuses on gaining formal acceptance of the project deliverables by the stakeholders—sponsor, customer, and other project team members. Scope change control focuses on formal procedures for managing proposed changes to the project scope. Each of these activities is briefly described next.

Plan Scope Management

The *Plan Scope Management* process lays out of the foundation for defining, validating, and controlling the project's scope. The project charter, as well as the project management plan (including the quality management plan, the project life cycle description, and the development approach) are used as inputs into this process, in addition to enterprise environmental factors (such as the organizational culture or infrastructure) and organizational process assets (such as policies and procedures and lessons learned). Using expert judgment, alternatives analysis, and meetings, the project manager creates the scope management plan, outlining the process used for preparing the scope statement, creating the work breakdown structure (WBS), approving the scope baseline, and accepting the deliverables, as well as the requirements management plan, which outlines the various processes and metrics used for planning, managing, and prioritizing requirements.

Collect Requirements

Based on the project charter and the business case, the project manager can start to collect the requirements from the key stakeholders, so as to ensure that the final product meets the stakeholders' needs. The *Collect Requirements* process is used to determine and document the various requirements and stakeholder needs. Using the business case, the project charter, and the project management plan and project documents (such as the stakeholder register) as major inputs, the project manager can begin the *Collect Requirements* process. Typically, the process of collecting requirements includes data gathering techniques such as interviewing or focus groups, analysis techniques (such as the analysis of existing documents or systems), and decision-making techniques such as voting or multicriteria analysis, in addition to prototyping to obtain early feedback. In collecting requirements, expert judgment is an important tool, as well as data gathering techniques such as brainstorming (also using the nominal group technique), interviews, focus groups, questionnaires, and benchmarking. Further, analyzing documents and existing systems can be valuable for determining requirements, and prototypes can be used to obtain feedback from the relevant stakeholders. During requirements meetings, skills such as observation and facilitation are important. Affinity diagrams and mind mapping help in further classifying and reviewing the requirements. The requirements specification as an output of the requirements collection process helps define the project's scope. Another important output of the *Collect Requirements* process is the requirements traceability matrix, which allows the project manager to link requirements with project objectives and also allows the project manager to track the different requirements and ensure their delivery.

Define Scope

Project scope
The work needed to deliver the final product based on the specifications.

Formally, the **project scope** refers to the work needed to deliver the final product, whereas the **product scope** refers to the actual features or functionalities of the product or services delivered.

The project scope statement provides a detailed description of the project and the outcomes. In the *Define Scope* process, the project manager will flesh out the project charter to address the following questions:

Product scope
The actual features or functionalities of the product or services delivered.

- What problem or opportunity does the project address?
- What quantifiable results are to be achieved?
- What needs to be done?
- How will success be measured?
- How will we know when we are finished?

Project scope statement
A document that describes in detail what the project will deliver and outlines generally all work required to complete the project.

This information serves to create the **project scope statement**. This document (as shown in Figure 5.26) will guide the entire project and ensures that both you and your customer reach a common understanding of project size, duration, and outcomes. Often, the project scope statement is quite formal and extensive, and can be used as the basis for a formal contractual agreement outlining firm deadlines, costs, and specifications.

Create WBS

Based on the project scope statement and the requirements documentation, the project manager can then develop a work breakdown structure (WBS). When major project deliverables are broken into smaller parts, accurate cost, task duration, and resource estimates can be made. As the project is divided into smaller and more manageable pieces, it becomes much easier to clearly assign tasks and responsibilities to various team members. The process of dividing the entire project into manageable tasks and then logically ordering them to ensure their smooth evolution is referred to as creating the work breakdown structure (WBS). This process is described in Chapter 6.

Validate Scope

Validate Scope
The process of obtaining the project stakeholders' formal acceptance of a project's deliverables.

Validate Scope is the process of obtaining the project stakeholders' formal acceptance of a project's deliverables. During this process, users, management, developers, and other project stakeholders perform inspections to ensure that the deliverables conform to organizational standards and to make sure that all relevant parties understand and agree on the acceptance (see Chapter 4, "Managing Project Communication," for more information on walk-throughs).

Control Scope

Control Scope
A formal process for ensuring that only agreed-upon changes are made to the project's scope.

A final project scope management activity is the project scope change control process. **Control Scope** is a formal process for assuring that only agreed-upon changes are made to the project's scope. Throughout the life of a project, various types of change requests can be made—from correcting minor or severe design defects to improving or extending system functionality and features. Requests are typically made using a system service request, as discussed previously and shown in Figure 5.15. Over the life of a project (or of a system), a log of all service requests is kept so that the status of any request can be immediately known. Many organizations have created web-based forms for submitting service requests and for keeping service logs (see Figure 5.27).

From a management perspective, as service requests are made, deciding which requests to accept and which to reject is a key issue. Because some requests will be more critical than others, a method of assessing and prioritizing the relative value of scope change requests must be established. In Chapter 12, we outline a formal process for managing the change control process.

Jackie's Electronics
Statement of Project Scope

Project Name:	No Customer Escapes
Project Manager:	James Cheung (jcheung@jackies.com)
Project Sponsor:	Sarah Codey (scodey@jackies.com)
Prepared:	7/1/2019

Problem/Opportunity Statement:

Sales growth has outpaced the marketing department's ability to accurately track and forecast customer buying trends. An improved method for performing this process must be found in order to reach company objectives

Project Objectives:

To enable the marketing departments to accurately track and forecast customer buying patterns in order to better serve customers with the best mix of products. This will also enable Jackie's to identify the proper application of production and material resources.

Project Description:

A new information system will be constructed that will collect all customer purchasing activity, support display and reporting of sales information, aggregate data, and show trends in order to assist marketing personnel in understanding dynamic market conditions. The project will follow Jackie's systems development life cycle.

Business Benefits:
- Improved understanding of customer buying patterns
- Improved utilization of marketing and sales personnel
- Improved utilization of production and materials

Project Deliverables:
- Customer tracking system analysis and design
- Customer tracking system programs
- Customer tracking documentation
- Training procedures

Estimated Duration:

4 months

Figure 5.26 A project scope statement for a proposed information systems project. *Adapted from*: Valacich and George (2017).

No.	Short Request Description	Requestor's Name	Request Date	Request Type	Urgency	Assigned To	Assigned Date	Status	Close Date
1									
2									
3									
4									
5									
6									
7									
8									
9									
10									

Figure 5.27 A system service request log

This controlled process should be applied when handling project scope change requests as well as any other relevant project change request items, including

- Project specifications
- Project schedules
- Budgets
- Resources

It is critical that the project scope change control process be completely integrated in the overall project control process so that any accepted changes are reflected in updated schedules, resource requirements, risk assessments, and other relevant items.

The primary reason that strict scope change control is necessary is that many projects suffer from **scope creep**—a progressive, uncontrolled increase in project scope. Scope creep is typically a result of a poorly designed scope change control process or a poorly defined project scope statement, or both. When either condition exists, small incremental features are often added to the system as it evolves, without careful evaluation or formal approval from all relevant stakeholders. As this continues, the project moves away from its original design, resulting in negative consequences for its schedule and budget. Consequently, without formal approval of scope changes, the project very likely will overrun its original budget and schedule because more is expected to be done without formal updating and approval. Left unchecked, scope creep can lead to a runaway project of constantly changing specifications, uncontrolled budgets, and abandoned schedules. Experienced project managers have found scope creep to be the single biggest reason for project failure or missed targets.

Scope creep
A progressive, uncontrolled increase in project scope.

Tips from the Pros: Outsmarting Scope Creep

Because scope creep—arising from lack of stakeholder involvement, different project visions, underestimated complexity, or lengthy duration—is the greatest threat to project success, all successful project managers should know how to manage it effectively. Mark Robinson, vice president for information technology at Saia Motor Freight, outlined ten steps for outsmarting scope creep:

1. *Educate your staff.* Make sure all project members understand the dangers of scope creep.
2. *Clearly define the project.* A poorly defined project is one of the leading causes of scope creep.
3. *Gather all relevant information.* Talk to all relevant parties to make sure the scope of the project is complete and is understood by all stakeholders very early in the life of the project.
4. *Define the objectives and deliverables.* Write a clear project scope statement that includes project objectives and deliverables.
5. *Assign a project sponsor.* Have a project sponsor at the beginning; changing team composition often leads to project scope changes.
6. *Create an approval process.* A clear project scope change control process is necessary to limit changes to only those that have been formally approved.
7. *Stay on track.* Use comprehensive project management techniques to keep the project on schedule, on budget, and on track.
8. *Create a good communication process.* Keep all project team members and stakeholders informed of project status and changes.
9. *Understand when change is necessary.* Sometimes it is necessary to make project changes; update all project materials—schedules, budgets, resources, and so on—when changes occur.
10. *Schedule regular meetings.* Regular meetings help keep everyone informed of the project's status and are useful for resolving any disagreements or misunderstandings.

Based on: Kurzawska (2018); Ruriani (2003).

Managing Project Scope and PMBOK

In this chapter, we have focused primarily on Knowledge Areas 4 and 5, *Project Integration Management* and *Project Scope Management*, respectively, within the Project Management Body of Knowledge (*PMBOK*, 2017) (see Figure 5.28). Specifically, eight key processes—*Develop Project Charter, Develop Preliminary Project Scope Statement, Develop Project Management Plan, Plan Scope Management, Define Scope, Create WBS, Validate Scope,* and *Control Scope*—have been discussed. Additionally, we have also reviewed issues related to Knowledge Area 3, *Project Management Processes,* as we've discussed how aspects of initiating projects and managing project scope fit within the broader context of project management. Together, this information provides a solid foundation for understanding project scope management.

Figure 5.28   Chapter 5 and *PMBOK* coverage

Key: O where the material is covered in the textbook; ● current chapter coverage

	Textbook Chapters ⟶	1	2	3	4	5	6	7	8	9	10	11	12
	PMBOK Knowledge Area												
1	Introduction												
1.2	Foundational Elements	O	O										
2	The Environment in Which Projects Operate												
2.2	Enterprise Environmental Factors		O										
2.2	Organizational Process Assets		O										
2.3	Organizational Systems		O										
3	The Role of the Project Manager												
3.2	Definition of a Project Manager	O											

3.3	The Project Manager's Sphere of Influence		O									
3.4	Project Manager Competences	O	O	O								
3.5	Performing Integration		O									
4	**Project Integration Management**											
4.1	Develop Project Charter					●						
4.2	Develop Project Management Plan					●						
4.3	Direct and Manage Project Work										O	
4.4	Manage Project Knowledge										O	
4.5	Monitor and Control Project Work										O	O
4.6	Perform Integrated Change Control											O
4.7	Close Project or Phase									O		O
5	**Project Scope Management**											
5.1	Plan Scope Management					●						
5.2	Collect Requirements					●						
5.3	Define Scope					●						
5.4	Create WBS					●	O					
5.5	Validate Scope					●						
5.6	Control Scope					●						O
6	**Project Schedule Management**											
6.1	Plan Schedule Management						O					
6.2	Define Activities						O					
6.3	Sequence Activities						O					
6.4	Estimate Activity Durations							O				
6.5	Develop Schedule							O				
6.6	Control Schedule							O				O
7	**Project Cost Management**											
7.1	Plan Cost Management								O			
7.2	Estimate Costs								O			
7.3	Determine Budget								O			
7.4	Control Costs								O			O
8	**Project Quality Management**											
8.1	Plan Quality Management								O			
8.2	Manage Quality								O			
8.3	Control Quality								O			O
9	**Project Resource Management**											
9.1	Plan Resource Management							O				
9.2	Estimate Activity Resources						O	O				
9.3	Acquire Resources							O			O	
9.4	Develop Team			O							O	
9.5	Manage Team			O							O	

		1	2	3	4	5	6	7	8	9	10	11	12
9.6	Control Resources								O				O
10	**Project Communications Management**												
10.1	Plan Communications Management				O								
10.2	Manage Communications				O							O	
10.3	Monitor Communications				O								O
11	**Project Risk Management**												
11.1	Plan Risk Management								O				
11.2	Identify Risks								O	O			
11.3	Perform Qualitative Risk Analysis								O				
11.4	Perform Quantitative Risk Analysis								O				
11.5	Plan Risk Responses								O				
11.6	Implement Risk Responses								O	O			
11.7	Monitor Risks								O				O
12	**Project Procurement Management**												
12.1	Plan Procurement Management										O		
12.2	Conduct Procurements										O	O	
12.3	Control Procurements										O		O
13	**Project Stakeholder Management**												
12.1	Identify Stakeholders				O								
12.2	Plan Stakeholder Engagement				O								
12.3	Manage Stakeholder Engagement				O							O	
12.4	Monitor Stakeholder Engagement				O								O

Running Case: Managing Project Scope

Now that the "No Customer Escapes" project team has been formed and a plan has been developed for distributing project information, James has begun working on the project charter, project management plan, project management information systems, and the project scope statement. He first drafted the project charter and posted it on the project's SharePoint site (see Figure 5.29). He then sent a short email message to all team members requesting feedback.

Minutes after James posted the project charter, his office phone rang.

"James, it's Cindy. I just looked over the project charter and have a few comments."

"Great," replied James. "It's just a draft. What do you think?"

"Well, I think that we need to explain more about how the system will work and why we think this new system will more than pay for itself."

"Those are good suggestions; I'm sure many others will also want to know that information. However,

the project charter is a pretty high-level document and doesn't get into too much detail. Basically, its purpose is to just formally announce the project, providing a very high-level description, as well as to briefly list the objectives, key assumptions, and stakeholders. The next document that I am working on, the project scope statement, is intended to provide more details on specific deliverables, costs, benefits, and so on. So, anyway, that type of more detailed information will be coming next."

"Oh, OK, that makes sense. I've never been on a project like this, so this is all new to me," said Cindy.

"Don't worry," replied James. "Getting that kind of feedback from you and the rest of the team will be key for us doing a thorough feasibility analysis. I'm going to need a lot of your help in identifying possible costs and benefits of the system. When we develop the project scope statement, we do a very thorough feasibility analysis—we examine financial, technical, operational, schedule, and legal and contractual

Jackie's Electronics
Project Charter

Project Name:	No Customer Escapes
Project Manager:	James Cheung (jcheung@jackies.com)
Customer:	Operations
Project Sponsor:	Sarah Codey (scodey@jackies.com)
Project Start/End (projected):	8/5/2019—11/29/2019
Prepared:	7/1/2019

Project Overview:
Project aim: design and implement a customer relationship management system in order to provide superior customer service by ... Specifically, the system will track customer purchases, assign points for cumulative purchases, and allow points to be redeemed for "rewards" ...

Objectives:
- Track customer purchases
- Accumulate redeemable points
- ...

Key Assumptions:
- System development will be outsourced
- Interface will be a Web browser
- ...

Stakeholders and Responsibilities:

Stakeholder	Role	Responsibility	Signature
Sarah Codey	Chief Operating Officer	Project Vision, Executive Sponsor	*Sarah Codey*
Bob Petroski	Senior Operations Manager	Monitoring, Resources	*Bob Petroski*
James Cheung	Project Manager	Plan, Monitor, Execute Project	*James Cheung*
Sally Fukuyama	Assistant Director, Marketing	System Functionality	*S. Fukuyama*
Sanjay Agarwal	Lead Analyst	Technical Architect	*Sanjay Agarwal*

Figure 5.29 A project charter for Jackie's customer relationship management system

feasibility, as well as potential political issues arising through the development of the system."

"Wow, we have to do all that? Why can't we just build the system? I think we all know what we want," replied Cindy.

"That is another great question," replied James. "I used to think exactly the same way, but what I learned in my last job was that there are great benefits to following a fairly formal project management process when designing a new system. By moving forward with care, we are much more likely to build the right system, on time and on budget."

"So," asked Cindy, "what's the next step?"

"Well, we need to do the feasibility analysis I just mentioned, which becomes part of the project scope statement. Once this is completed, we will have a walk-through presentation to management to make

sure they agree with and understand the scope, risks, and costs associated with making 'No Customer Escapes' a reality," said James.

"This is going to be a lot of work, but I am sure I am going to learn a lot," replied Cindy.

"So, let me get to work on the feasibility analysis," said James. "I will be sending requests out to all the team members to get their ideas. I should have this email ready within an hour or so."

"Great. I will look for it and will reply as soon as I can," answered Cindy.

"Thanks. The faster we get this background work done, the sooner we'll be able to move on to what the system will do," replied James.

"Sounds good. Talk to you later. Bye," Cindy said.

"Bye, Cindy, and thanks for your quick feedback," answered James.

Adapted from: Valacich and George (2017).

Chapter Summary

Describe the project initiation process, including how to identify, rank, and select information systems projects, as well as establish the project charter and the project management plan. Project initiation is the process of authorizing a new project or continuing an existing project. It generally includes four distinct activities: identifying, ranking, and selecting information systems projects, as well as establishing the project charter. This process can be performed by different organizational members or units, including top management, a steering committee, business units and functional managers, the development group, or the most senior information systems executive. Potential projects can be evaluated and selected using different methods, such as value chain analysis or multicriteria analysis. The quality of the process can be improved if decisions are guided by corporate strategic planning and information systems planning. Selected projects will be those considered most important in supporting the organizational strategy. A key activity in project initiation is the assessment of numerous feasibility issues associated with the project, including economic, technical, operational, schedule, legal and contractual, and political feasibility. All of these feasibility factors are influenced by the project size, the type of system proposed, and the collective experience of the development group and customers of the system. Once a project has been identified and selected, the project charter can be developed. The project charter is a short document

that serves as the foundation for the project, describes what the project will deliver, and authorizes the use of resources to complete the project. Its development helps assure that both you and your customer gain a common understanding of the project, and it also helps announce to the organization that a particular project has been chosen for development. The project management plan specifies how the project will be performed, and guides the execution, monitoring and controlling, and closing of a project. The scope, schedule, and cost baselines serve as a standard for measuring project progress and performance, and any changes to these baselines have to be formally approved. The project management information system serves as a central repository for all project correspondence, inputs, outputs, deliverables, procedures, and standards to support all aspects of a project.

Explain project scope planning, including how to define, validate, and control project scope. Project scope planning is the process of progressively elaborating and documenting the project management plan in order to effectively manage a project. Based on the project charter and the business case, the project manager can start to collect the requirements from the key stakeholders. The project scope statement describes in detail what the project will deliver and outlines generally all work required to complete the project. Developing a work breakdown structure (WBS) focuses on subdividing the major project deliverables into smaller, more manageable activities. Once it is completed, making accurate cost, task duration, and resource estimates is much easier. Scope validation refers to the process of reviewing and agreeing upon the project's scope definition by users, management, and the development group using a walkthrough.

Scope control refers to a formal process for assuring that only agreed-upon changes are made to the project's scope in order to reduce or eliminate scope creep and to assure that all scope changes are incorporated into all planning documents, as well as communicated to all project stakeholders.

Key Terms Review

A. Assumption log
B. Baseline
C. Break-even analysis
D. Business case
E. Competitive strategy
F. Control Scope
G. Corporate strategic planning
H. Cost-benefit analysis
I. Discount rate
J. Economic feasibility
K. Information systems planning
L. Intangible benefit
M. Intangible cost
N. Legal and contractual feasibility
O. Mission statement
P. Multicriteria analysis
Q. Objective statements
R. One-time cost
S. Operational feasibility

T. Political feasibility
U. Present value
V. Product scope
W. Project charter
X. Project initiation
Y. Project management information system
Z. Project management plan
AA. Project scope
BB. Project scope statement
CC. Recurring cost
DD. Schedule feasibility
EE. Scope creep
FF. System service request
GG. Tangible benefit
HH. Tangible cost
II. Technical feasibility
JJ. Validate Scope
KK. Value chain analysis

Match each of the key terms with the definition that best fits it.

1. A benefit that can be quantified with relative certainty.
2. A benefit that cannot be easily quantified with relative certainty.
3. A cost associated with project start-up and development or system startup.
4. A cost resulting from the ongoing evolution and use of a system.
5. A cost that can be quantified with relative certainty.
6. A cost that cannot be easily quantified with relative certainty.
7. A document that describes in detail what the project will deliver and outlines generally all work required to complete the project.
8. A formal process for assuring that only agreed-upon changes are made to the project's scope.
9. A formal request for correcting problems with an existing system, adding features to a system, or developing a new system.
10. A plan specifying how the project will be performed, and guides the execution, monitoring and controlling, and closing of a project.

11. A progressive, uncontrolled increase in project scope.

12. A project selection method that uses weighted scoring for a variety of criteria to contrast alternative projects or system features.

13. A series of statements that express an organization's qualitative and quantitative goals for reaching a desired future position.

14. A short document that serves as the foundation for the project, describes what the project will deliver, and authorizes the use of resources to complete the project.

15. A statement that defines a company's purpose.

16. A type of cost-benefit analysis used to identify when (if ever) benefits will equal costs.

17. An ongoing process of determining goals and defining a strategy to achieve the goals.

18. An online or hard-copy repository for all project correspondence, inputs, outputs, deliverables, procedures, and standards to support all aspects of a project.

19. A structured process of assessing the information needs of an organization and defining the systems, databases, and technologies that will best satisfy those needs.

20. Approved version of a project management plan component serving as a standard for measuring project progress and performance that can only be changed through formal change management processes.

21. Document used to capture any project-related assumptions or constraints.

22. The actual features or functionalities of the product or services delivered.

23. The current value of a future cash flow.

24. The degree to which a proposed system will solve business problems or take advantage of business opportunities.

25. The degree to which key stakeholders within the organization can affect project success.

26. The degree to which potential legal and contractual ramifications due to the construction of a system influence project success.

27. The degree to which the benefits of a development project outweigh its costs.

28. The degree to which the development organization is able to construct a proposed system.

29. The degree to which the potential time frame and completion dates for all major activities within a project meet organizational deadlines and constraints for affecting change.

30. The justification that presents the economic, technical, operational, schedule, legal and contractual, and political factors influencing a proposed project.

31. The plan of action and organization pursues to achieve its mission and objectives.

32. The process of analyzing an organization's activities to determine where value is added to products and/or services and the costs incurred for doing so.

33. The process of authorizing a new project or continuing an existing project.

34. The process of developing a more detailed description of the project and its outcomes.

35. The process of obtaining the project stakeholders' formal acceptance of a project's deliverables.

36. The rate of return used to compute the present value of future cash flows.

37. The use of a variety of analysis techniques for determining the financial feasibility of a project.

38. The work needed to deliver the final product based on the specifications.

Review Questions

1. Contrast the following terms:
   a. Mission, objective statements, competitive strategy
   b. Corporate strategic planning, information systems planning
   c. Top-down planning, bottom-up planning
   d. Low-cost producer, product differentiation, product focus or niche
   e. Break-even analysis, net present value, return on investment
   f. Economic feasibility, technical feasibility, legal and contractual feasibility, operational feasibility, political feasibility, schedule feasibility
   g. Intangible benefit, tangible benefit
   h. Intangible cost, tangible cost

2. Describe and contrast the characteristics of alternative methods for making information systems project identification decisions.

3. Describe the steps involved in corporate strategic planning.

4. What are three generic competitive strategies?

5. Describe what is meant by *information systems planning* and the steps involved in this process.

6. List and describe the advantages of top-down planning over other planning approaches.

7. Describe several project evaluation criteria.

8. What are the types, or categories, of benefits from an information systems project? What intangible benefits might an organization obtain from the development of an information systems project?

9. Describe three commonly used methods for performing economic cost-benefit analyses.

10. What are the potential consequences of not assessing the technical risks associated with an information systems development project? In what ways could you identify an information systems project that was technically riskier than another?

11. List and discuss the different types of project feasibility factors. Is any factor most important? Why or why not?

12. What is a project charter, and what information does it typically contain?

13. What is the project management information system, and what information does it contain?

14. What is the project scope statement, and what information does it contain?

15. What is contained in a project management plan?

16. What is a baseline? Why is it important to fix baselines?

17. Describe what occurs during *Validate Scope* and *Control Scope*.

18. What is scope creep, and why do organizations need to effectively manage changes to a project's scope?

Chapter Exercises

1. Write a mission statement for a business that you would like to start. State the area of business you will be in and which aspects of the business you value most highly. Once you have fleshed out your mission statement, describe the objectives and competitive strategy for achieving that mission.

2. Consider an organization that you believe does not conduct adequate strategic information systems planning. List at least six reasons why this type of planning is not done appropriately (or is not done at all). Are these reasons justifiable? What are the implications of this inadequate strategic information systems planning? What limits, problems, weaknesses, and barriers might this present?

3. Information systems planning, as depicted in this chapter, is highly related to corporate strategic planning. What might those responsible for information systems planning have to do if they operate in an organization without a formal corporate planning process?

4. The economic analysis carried out during the project initiation is rather cursory. Why is this? Consequently, what do you think are the most important factors for a potential project to survive this first phase of the life cycle?

5. In those organizations that do an excellent job of information systems planning, why might projects identified from a bottom-up process still find their way into the project initiation process?

6. Consider, as an example, buying a network of PCs for a department at your workplace, or alternatively, consider outfitting a laboratory of PCs for students at a university. For your example, estimate the one-time and recurring costs outlined in Table 5.4.

7. For the situation you chose in Exercise 6, either buying a network of PCs for a department at your workplace or outfitting a laboratory of PCs for students at a university, estimate the costs and benefits of your system. Then calculate the net present value (NPV) and return on investment (ROI) and present a break-even analysis (BEA). Assume a discount rate of 12 percent and a five-year time horizon.

8. Assuming monetary benefits of an information system at $85,000 per year, one-time costs of $75,000, recurring costs of $35,000 per year, a discount rate of 12 percent, and a 5-year time horizon, calculate the net present value (NPV) of the system's costs and benefits. Also calculate the overall return on investment (ROI) of the project and then present a break-even analysis (BEA). At what point does break-even occur?

9. Change the discount rate for Exercise 8 to 10 percent and redo the analysis.

10. Change the recurring costs in Exercise 8 to $40,000 and redo the analysis.

11. Change the time horizon in Exercise 8 to 3 years and redo the analysis.

12. For the situation you chose in Exercise 6, either buying a network of PCs for a department at your workplace or outfitting a laboratory of PCs for students at a university, conduct a multicriteria analysis that contrasts at least three alternative configurations with at least three different requirements and three different constraint criteria.

13. For the situation you chose in Exercise 6, either buying a network of PCs for a department at your workplace or outfitting a laboratory of PCs for students at a university, write a project charter. List your assumptions on a separate page.

14. For the situation you chose in Exercise 6, either buying a network of PCs for a department at your workplace or outfitting a laboratory of PCs for students at a university, write a project scope statement. List your assumptions on a separate page.

15. Different organizations use different formats for defining a project's charter. Search the web (e.g., search using the keywords *project charter template*) and contrast at least four different templates. What is similar? What is unique? Is there one best way to define a project's charter?

16. Using the information you gathered in Exercise 15, develop your own best-practices project charter template.

17. Different organizations use different formats for presenting a project scope statement. Search the web (e.g., search using the keywords *project scope statement template*) and contrast at least four different templates. What is similar? What is unique? Is there one best way to present a project scope statement?

18. Using the information you gathered in Exercise 17, develop your own best-practices project scope statement template.

19. In what ways is a request to change the scope of an information system handled differently from a request for a new information system? In what ways are they the same?

20. Describe a personal situation in which you experienced scope creep. Your example does not have to be a technology-oriented project.

Chapter Case: Sedona Management Group and Managing Project Scope

Over the last ten years, Sedona Management Group (SMG) has not missed an agreed-to deadline on any contract related to a development project they've undertaken. Given the statistics on project failures we have discussed so far in this book, this is rather astounding. Tim Turnpaugh attributes this success to the company's core competency—great project management. He recognizes that one of the most important and difficult aspects of project management is scope management, which involves defining and controlling what is or is not included in the project. For that reason, Turnpaugh dedicates a great deal of time to project initiation, which includes deciding what projects to pursue and then defining their scope.

At SMG, primary goals of scope management are to ensure that the project team and the customer have the same understanding of the project deliverables and that the deliverables are reasonable given budget and time constraints. The first step in managing scope is deciding which projects to pursue. What does the Sedona team look for in potential clients? Turnpaugh prefers to work for customers who come at a project with an aggressive attitude—where the company is willing to think outside the box and not be constrained by what has been accomplished in the past. In addition, over the last 10 years, SMG has built a solid reputation through word-of-mouth, and Turnpaugh avoids projects that might detract from that reputation. First, SMG stays away from projects in certain industries—for example, the adult entertainment industry. Second, the team prefers not to develop systems for customers who can't develop a clear vision of what they want to accomplish but rather want a system simply because everyone else has one. Third, Turnpaugh avoids customers that have low interest and motivation in the project because this may lead to downstream problems related to website maintenance— which ultimately may reflect poorly on the Sedona team. Finally, the team will not undertake a project for a customer who is not willing to be highly accessible during the various phases of the project life cycle because SMG feels such communication is critical to project success.

Turnpaugh states that in the project initiation phase, it is not uncommon for the customer to be somewhat vague in terms of what they're trying to achieve from the systems development effort. For this reason, it is essential to spend sufficient time with the customer on needs analysis. Using his personal knowledge and guided by a set of standard questions, Turnpaugh helped the Seattle Seahawks identify their needs, determine the market they are trying to tap, and in some cases, expand on that vision with new possibilities. One past client approached SMG with the idea of promoting a fitness chain. In the past, the target market for this industry may have involved males interested in weight training, but this firm wanted to target average individuals—particularly women—who wanted a place to exercise with a wide range of aerobic and strength-training options. Given this potential audience, the resultant website needed to include attributes that would appeal to women and entire families rather than just men. Not only does the content in such a site differ—for example, the website might need to include information on such amenities as daycare—but the physical design of the site also might need to be substantially different.

Another central aspect of project selection involves understanding the customer's budget for the project. Based on past experience, Turnpaugh knows how to price projects to be both profitable and attractive to the customer. In many cases, SMG likes to take a phased approach—that is, work on a simple website for a customer initially and then eventually make improvements to that existing website as the relationship with the customer develops over time. Turnpaugh refers to these kinds of projects as multiphase projects.

If necessary, the Sedona team will go through several iterations to make sure the customer's needs are understood. To accurately determine the duration and the cost of the project, Turnpaugh says that a tight scope is needed. In all instances, SMG likes to take projects one step at a time. Turnpaugh likens this to flying an airplane. A pilot can't worry about every event that might go wrong during a flight, but rather needs to focus on doing the current task correctly. Similarly, in the initiation phase of the project, the focus is on understanding the customer's needs.

Once a clear understanding of the project scope is gained, a project scope statement is developed. The scope statement forms part of the contract that will be drafted for the customer and ensures that both the Sedona team and the customer have a common understanding of project scope. The scope statement includes a detailed description of the project's product, a summary of all project deliverables (e.g., database and codes), and a statement of what determines project success. Anything beyond what is mentioned in the scope statement is a change request, which would entail longer project duration and an additional charge.

Through Sedona's interactions with the Seattle Seahawks, Turnpaugh determined that the organization met all of his requirements for potential clients. In interacting with Seahawks representative Mike Flood, Turnpaugh was immediately impressed with Flood's desire to not simply duplicate what other NFL teams were doing but to think about the purpose and opportunities that a website could provide. The Seahawks' website goes beyond providing simple information about the team but, rather, attempts to engage fans in a variety of interactive capabilities that continue to be enhanced. Despite this ongoing development, the original system was carefully scoped to meet the Seahawks organization's needs, as well as be achievable within Sedona's typical project life cycle.

Chapter 5 Project Assignment

An entertainment website should present value to fans through its contents and features. Therefore, these features must be developed properly to assure that the consumer is satisfied with the experience. The first step in the design process of your entertainment website is to examine several existing entertainers' websites. This is an important stage of this project to get a feel for the best practices. This analysis also shows common trends in entertainment sites. It can be used to determine the types of materials and features that users come to expect from sites such as the one to be designed.

This activity requires you to do an inventory of existing entertainment websites.

1. Find and examine four different entertainment websites (these could include sports personalities, musicians, actors/actresses, sports teams).

2. For each website, create a bulleted list of features or characteristics that it employs (e.g., biographical data, interaction with other users, media clips, merchandise access, access to entertainment, technologies used, etc.). Also include a short definition of the feature. Note: You should easily compile twenty or more features.

3. Indicate the relative importance of the criteria by assigning a weight to each. Please note that the weights should sum to 1.0 or 100 percent.

4. Determine how well each site used each of its features (i.e., through a critical examination of each site, decide what scores you give each entertainment/entertainer site on the features you came up with).

5. Following the example shown, create a weighted scoring table by multiplying each of the entertainment scores by the weight and determining an analysis score.

Criteria	Weight	Website 1	Website 2	. . .	Website n
Criteria 1 (e.g., ease of use)	0.20	5	2	. . .	2
Criteria 2 (e.g., merchandise availability)	0.10	1	4	. . .	4
Feature 3 (e.g., entertainer bio availability)	0.1	1	2	. . .	
. . . .	. . .	. . .	. . .	. . .	. . .
Feature n (e.g., interaction with entertainer)	0.5	5	5	. . .	5
Analysis score	Should add to 1.0	$(0.2 \times 5) + (0.1 \times 1)$ $+ (0.1 \times 1)$ $+ (0.5 \times 5)$ $= 3.6$	$(0.2 \times 2) + (0.1 \times 4)$ $+ (0.1 \times 2)$ $+ (0.5 \times 5)$ $= 3.3$	. . .	Ditto

6. Choose an entertainer for whom you would like to design a site. You can redesign a bad entertainment site you reviewed, or you can develop an entirely new site.

7. Develop your project charter. Typical parts of a project charter might include

   • Project name

   • Project sponsor

   • Assigned project manager

   • Project team members and their role in the project

   • Statement of purpose (i.e., overarching goals, including what entertainer you are focusing on)

- Statement of features, including
- What features seem to be important for entertainment websites?
- What features seem to be less important?
- Do certain features seem to be more appropriate for different types of celebrities?
- Are some features incompatible (e.g., if you do one thing, should you not do another)?
- Statement of objectives (i.e., specific high-level project deliverables)
- Stakeholders
- A basic statement of how the team will approach the work
- Authorized project resources (i.e., people, budget—for your case the budget may be based on hours, and you can assign a base rate to all of your work)
- Technology you are going to use for the website
- Site map, describing the various pages your site will contain and how they are related (this is a nested list showing the layout of the pages—that is, the main pages and subpages)
- Screen mock-ups (essentially, samples of what your screens will look like, easily done in Microsoft PowerPoint)
- Basic project timeline (which can be substantially refined in the project plan to follow)

References

Applegate, L. M., Austin, R. D., and McFarlan, F. W. (2007). *Corporate Information Strategy and Management: The Challenges of Managing in a Network Economy* (7th ed.). Boston: Irwin/McGraw-Hill.

Atkinson, R. A. (1990). The Motivations for Strategic Planning. *Journal of Information Systems Management* 7(4), 53–56.

Bell, S. (2013). *Run Grow Transform: Integrating Business and Lean IT*. Boca Raton, FL: CRC Press.

Burry, C. (2003, March 4). Increasing Value from Fixed IT Costs. *Computerworld*. Retrieved June 25, 2018, from http://www.computerworld.com/article/2579418/it-management/increasing-value-from-fixed-it-costs.html

Carlson, C. K., Gardner, E. P., and Ruth, S. R. (1989). Technology-Driven Long-Range Planning. *Journal of Information Systems Management* 6(3), 24–29.

Chacos, B. (2011, August 10). Seven Casino Technologies They Don't Want You to Know About. *Gizmodo*. Retrieved June 30, 2018, from https://www.gizmodo.com.au/2011/08/7-casino-technologies-they-dont-want-you-to-know-about

Couger, J. D., Colter, M. A., and Knapp, R. W. (1982). *Advanced System Development/Feasibility Techniques*. New York: Wiley.

DeGiglio, M. (2002, June 17). Measure for Measure: The Value of IT. *CSO Online*. Retrieved June 25, 2018, from http://www.csoonline.com/article/2113410/data-protection/measure-for-measure--the-value-of-it.html

Dewan, S., Michael, S. C., and Min, C. K. (1998). Firm Characteristics and Investments in Information Technology: Scale and Scope Effects. *Information Systems Research* 9(3), 219–232.

George, S. (2017, December 8). Align IT Functions with Business Strategy Using the Run-Grow-Transform Model. *Gartner*. Retrieved September 13, 2018, from https://www.gartner.com/smarterwithgartner/align-it-functions-with-business-strategy-using-the-run-grow-transform-model

Hoffer, J. A., George, J. F., and Valacich, J. (2007). *Modern Systems Analysis and Design* (5th ed.). Upper Saddle River, NJ: Prentice Hall.

IBM (2017). Self-Service Check-in at Hotels and Motels. *IBM.com*. Retrieved July 9, 2018, from http://www-03.ibm.com/services/ca/en/mobility/documents/FinalHotelGuideSelfServOnlineMag.pdf

Joshi, K. (2017, April 3). Cheating Roulette—The Technology Banned by Vegas. *Techportal.com*. Retrieved July 4, 2018, from https://thetechportal.com/2017/04/03/cheating-roulette-technology-banned-vegas

Kapur, G. K. (2004, August 30). Intelligent Disobedience. *Computerworld*. Retrieved June 25, 2018, from http://www.computerworld.com/article/2565647/it-project-management/intelligent-disobedience.html

King, J. L., and Schrems, E. (1978). Cost Benefit Analysis in Information Systems Development and Operation. *ACM Computing Surveys* 10(1), 19–34.

Kirsch, L. J. (2000). Software Project Management: An Integrated Perspective for an Emerging Paradigm. In *Framing the Domains of IT Management: Projecting the Future from the Past*, Zmud, R. W. (ed.). Cincinnati: Pinnaflex Educational Resources, pp. 285–304.

Kurzawska, K. (2018, February 23). What Is Scope Creep in Project Management? *Timecamp.com*. Retrieved July 5, 2018, form https://www.timecamp.com/blog/2018/02/scope-creep-project-management

Lederer, A. L., and Prasad, J. (1992). Nine Management Guidelines for Better Cost Estimating. *Communications of the ACM* 35(2), 51–59.

Luftman, J. N. (2004). *Managing the Information Technology Resource*. With Bullen, C. V., Liao, D., Nash, E., and Neumann, C. Upper Saddle River, NJ: Prentice Hall.

McGannon, B. (2018). *Intelligent Disobedience: The Difference Between Good and Great Leaders*. London: Routledge.

McKeen, J. D., Guimaraes, T., and Wetherbe, J. C. (1994). A Comparative Analysis of MIS Project Selection Mechanisms. *Data Base* 25 (February), 43–59.

Melymuka, K. (2004, May 3). Betting on IT Value. *ComputerWorld*. Retrieved June 25, 2017, from http://www.computerworld.com/article/2565259/it-management/betting-on-it-value.html

Parker, M. M., and Benson, R. J. (1989). Enterprisewide Information Management: State-of-the-Art Strategic Planning. *Journal of Information Systems Management* 6 (Summer), 14–23.

Patil, R. (2017, December 12). Five Factors to Consider While Hiring a Software Development Company. *Medium.com*. Retrieved July 5, 2018, from https://medium.com/@ritesh.patil732/5-factors-to-consider-while-hiring-a-software-development-company-139f57cba80e

Project Management Institute (2017). *Agile Practice Guide*. Newton Square, PA: Author.

Project Management Institute (2017). *PMBOK: A Guide to the Project Management Body of Knowledge* (6th ed.). Newtown Square, PA: Author.

Porter, M. (1980). *Competitive Strategy: Techniques for Analyzing Industries and Competitors*. New York: Free Press.

Porter, M. (1985). *Competitive Advantage*. New York: Free Press.

Pressman, R. S. (2005). *Software Engineering* (6th ed.). New York: McGraw-Hill.

Printer, H. (2004, November 8). When—and When Not—to Offshore. *ComputerWorld*. Retrieved June 25, 2018, from https://www.computerworld.com/article/2567152/it-outsourcing/when----and-when-not----to-offshore.html

Ross, J., and Feeny, D. (2000). The Evolving Role of the CIO. In *Framing the Domains of IT Management: Projecting the Future from the Past*, Zmud, R. W. (ed.). Cincinnati, OH: Pinnaflex Educational Resources, 385–402.

Ruriani, D. C. (2003, May). Outsmarting Scope Creep. *Inboundlogistics.com*. Retrieved June 25, 2018, from http://www.inboundlogistics.com/cms/article/outsmarting-scope-creep

Segars, A. H., and Grover, V. (1999). Profiles of Strategic Information Systems Planning. *Information Systems Research* 10(3), 199–232.

Shank, J. K., and Govindarajan, V. (1993). *Strategic Cost Management*. New York: Free Press.

Thibodeau, P. (2004, January 26). Internal Resistance Can Doom Offshore Projects. *ComputerWorld*. Retrieved January 25, 2018, from http://www.computerworld.com/article/2574652/it-outsourcing/internal-resistance-can-doom-offshore-projects.html

Valacich, J. and George, J. F., (2017). *Modern Systems Analysis and Design* (8th ed.). Boston: Pearson.

CHAPTER 6

Managing Project Scheduling

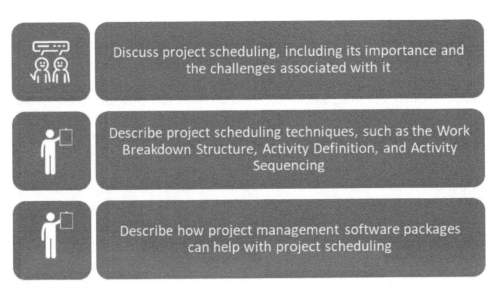

Discuss project scheduling, including its importance and the challenges associated with it

Describe project scheduling techniques, such as the Work Breakdown Structure, Activity Definition, and Activity Sequencing

Describe how project management software packages can help with project scheduling

Figure 6.1 Chapter 6 learning objectives

Opening Case: London's Oyster Card

Countless examples abound of projects being completed behind schedule, but the introduction of London's Oyster card is not one of them. For many projects, being completed on time is a critical success factor, and late completion is one of the main factors for a project being considered a failure. Consequently, project scheduling is a key aspect of project management.

Just like its digital cousins in cities from Hong Kong to Melbourne, London's Oyster card is a contactless payment card that allows commuters to pay for bus or subway rides by the touch of a card, without having to purchase a separate ticket for each individual journey. At the same time, the big data generated from passengers using the Oyster card allows London's transport department to optimize the

routing of buses and scheduling of different means of public transport. Given the magnitude of the project, Fujitsu, Cubic, EDS, and WS Atkins formed a consortium (named "TransSys") to build and implement the Oyster card system. Lessons learned from other mega-projects have shown that not only building but also implementing a system needs to be scheduled carefully. Consequently, TransSys decided to schedule a slow rollout, rather than a "big bang" implementation. Such a slow rollout allowed the consortium to thoroughly test all aspects of the system (even using mock-up subway stations) before going live. Having scheduled for such intensive testing phase greatly contributed to the project's success, with, as of 2018, close to three million cards being used for travel on a typical weekday.

Based on: Orton-Jones (2016); Transport for London (2018).

Figure 6.2 Oyster card readers at Canary Wharf. *Source*: CC-BY-SA-3.0, Kenneth Jorgensen.

Introduction

Project scheduling
The process of defining project activities, determining their sequence, and estimating their duration.

In the planning phase of any project, scheduling is a crucial activity. **Project scheduling** is the process of defining project activities, determining their sequence, and estimating their duration. To successfully complete a project, the project manager must be aware of all the activities the project entails. The project management team manages and tracks these activities through a process of decomposition, meaning that the entire project is broken down into more manageable and controllable parts. This decomposition is captured in the work breakdown structure (briefly introduced in the last chapter). Thus a project manager follows a "divide and conquer" strategy of breaking down a project into components that can be managed and controlled more easily than the project in its entirety.

Once the project's components are determined, the project management team establishes a sequence for carrying out the work associated with them. To help determine how to sequence these activities, the project manager considers technical constraints, safety or efficiency concerns, policies, the availability of resources, and the need to begin some tasks only after others are completed. Scheduling tools (such as network diagrams) help the project manager visualize the result of this planning process; project management software packages assist by offering powerful tools to create, maintain, and update these diagrams.

In addition to defining and sequencing activities, another important facet of project scheduling is assigning resources to those activities. In most cases, resource availability plays a significant role in determining the duration of a project. This chapter focuses on how to define and sequence project activities. The aspects of project schedule management involving resource estimation and allocation, as well as the management of those resources, are discussed in Chapter 7.

This chapter's opening section provides a brief overview of the importance and challenges associated with project scheduling. The subsequent section discusses specific techniques for breaking down a complex project into more manageable components. Once we have developed a list of manageable task components, they can be sequenced to most efficiently complete the project. The first step in this process is the creation of a work breakdown structure (WBS), a chart detailing the project's specific components. The second step is determining what activities are needed to complete those project components. The third step is to determine how to sequence these activities. Throughout this discussion we will highlight the different types of diagrams used to graphically represent project schedules, their benefits and drawbacks, and how project management software can help with the different project scheduling activities.

The Importance and Challenges of Project Scheduling

A project schedule is generally created early in the project, specifically during the initiation and planning phases. These schedules are used in the execution phase to offer guidance to the project team and are often updated to incorporate project changes. Schedules are also important in the monitoring and controlling processes, where they can be used for project tracking (see Figure 6.3). Although scheduling may seem mundane, its importance to the success of the project cannot be overstated. Without a clearly established project schedule, managers cannot accurately plan activities or, for that matter, track those activities to determine if the project is proceeding as planned—an aspect of project control. In a survey about the top challenges of project management (Stanleigh, 2005), the top five challenges were

1. Lack of clarity in scope of the project
2. Shifting organizational priorities
3. Project changes not well managed
4. A lack of project management skills
5. Training of project sponsors

The top challenge mentioned—lack of clarity about the scope of the project—is directly related to project scheduling. When project managers, in close cooperation with project team members and the project sponsor, create schedules that clearly characterize project activities, they are better prepared to accurately define the project's scope.

Schedules are rarely perfect because of the very difficult task of accounting for all potential problems. Project managers often find themselves in the unenviable position of having to modify project schedules on the fly to address circumstances that were unforeseen during the original schedule development. This is particularly problematic in organizations that compete in rapidly changing business environments. As business conditions or technology change, the project manager is frequently faced with new and unanticipated challenges. Although a project schedule should serve as the fundamental guide to successfully completing a project, project managers must also realize that these schedules may frequently need to be updated as the project progresses. For example, the

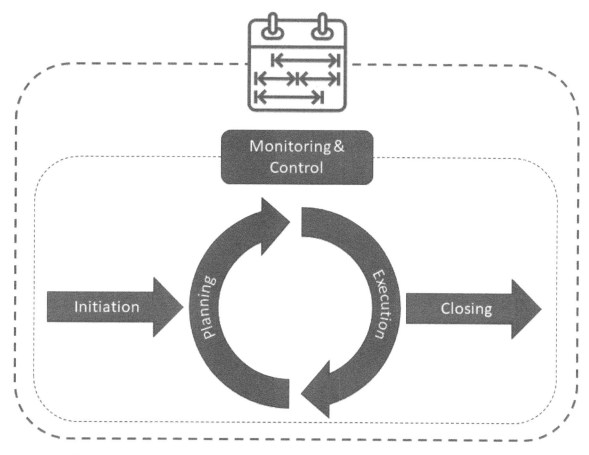

Figure 6.3 Project scheduling and the project management processes

loss of a talented systems developer after the project has already started may require an adjustment of the project schedule. It is also important to realize that project schedules may be created for different purposes, such as for internal management of project effort or for communicating with other stakeholders. Internal schedules may contain greater details on tasks and assignments. External schedules may be more general and may even have buffers built in to account for unexpected delays.

PMBOK highlights the importance of project scheduling as part of the Project Schedule Management knowledge area (see Figure 6.4), which includes the processes *Plan Schedule Management*, *Define Activities*, and *Sequence Activities* (which we discuss in this chapter), as well as *Estimate Activity Durations*, *Develop Schedule* (all discussed in Chapter 7), and *Control Schedule* (discussed in Chapter 12). Project Schedule Management is seen as a series of processes that interact not only with each other but also with other key knowledge areas and the overall project management life cycle.

As a project moves forward, estimations of the time needed to complete project components become progressively more accurate. Along with describing the WBS, which serves as the basis for Project Schedule Management processes, this chapter will focus on the processes of defining and sequencing activities.

This process of gradually moving toward more accurate estimates was originally reported by Barry Boehm (1981) and is referred to as a **cone of uncertainty** (see Figure 6.5). The cone of uncertainty graphically represents the uncertainty of early project time

Cone of uncertainty
A progressively more detailed and accurate projection of the project schedule and duration as the project manager or project team specifies project deliverables and activities in more detail.

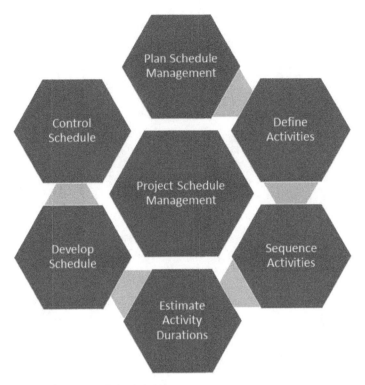

Figure 6.4   *PMBOK* (6th ed.) Project Schedule Management processes

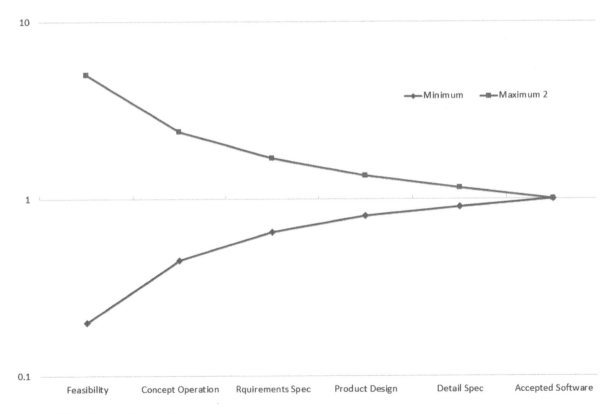

Figure 6.5   Cone of uncertainty

estimations, as well as the growing accuracy of these estimations as the project moves farther along. According to the PMI, projects progress through different estimation phases, including *rough order of magnitude (ROM) estimates*—important but inexact estimates occurring very early in a project's life cycle—that may be used to justify a project's consideration. These early estimates may vary by as much as +75 percent to −25 percent. *Budgetary estimates*, which occur later as the various project components are specified in greater detail, may vary only from +25 percent to −10 percent. Finally, *definitive estimates* for a project, developed when the project's resources and activities are highly detailed, may vary only from +10 percent to −5 percent. In both the cone of uncertainty and PMI's progressive estimates, greater knowledge about project costs and schedules is represented as project plans become more detailed.

Technological advances and specific types of scheduling software have had an enormous impact on the ability of managers to handle increasingly complex projects. For example, various project management apps facilitate managing schedules across time and space. Managers can post a cloud-based schedule that can be viewed by others involved in the project, and problem areas can quickly be identified and addressed. As remote activities are completed, remote managers can enter that information into the online schedule, providing a vehicle for almost real-time feedback to senior project managers. Likewise, using online tools can enhance transparency, enabling relevant stakeholders to stay abreast of the project's status. Further, scheduling software greatly increases the project managers' ability to manage complex projects.

Scheduling also involves the consideration of team resources, another major focus of this textbook. For instance, when developing project schedules and eventually determining project duration, the assignment of various types of resources (discussed further in Chapter 7) is critical to successful project management processes. An important resource is personnel, including both the project team and human resources external to the team. All of the team management techniques discussed in Chapter 3 are thus very important considerations during project scheduling.

Plan Schedule Management

Plan Schedule Management
The process associated with establishing the schedule management plan.

Schedule management plan
Component of the project management plan that provides guidance on *how* the schedule will be managed throughout the project.

Given the importance of scheduling, an essential process is **Plan Schedule Management**. The purpose of this process is to establish the **schedule management plan**, which provides guidance on *how* the schedule will be managed. In other words, during this process, the project manager defines various aspects related to scheduling, including what scheduling methodology will be used, the desired level of accuracy, the units used to measure resource usage (such as hours, days, weeks, or centimeters and grams versus inches and ounces), what thresholds are used for schedule control, and how schedule performance is measured. Often based on expert judgment and discussed in meetings, these criteria become part of the schedule management plan, which is an important component of the overall project management plan.

Tips from the Pros: Debunking Myths about Project Estimation

Estimating the time necessary to complete a project, despite being an imperfect science, is still an important aspect of project management. Project stakeholders are always concerned about whether the project will come in on time (and under budget), and usually have little use for answers such as "maybe" or "probably." Unfortunately, stakeholders usually demand accurate estimates precisely at the time (e.g., early in the project life cycle) when such estimates are likely to be the most inaccurate. After all, it would be nearly impossible to obtain support for a project without some sort of estimation as to time and budget, and useless to provide highly accurate estimates when all project deliverables have been completed.

Over time, the project management community has developed some assumptions believed to increase the quality of estimates. These project management practices were reconsidered by Phillip Armour (2002) in an article titled "Ten Unmyths of Project Estimation." Armour described an unmyth as a commonly held idea that is simply not true. Armour's ten unmyths of project estimation are:

1. *We can have accurate estimates.* The "accuracy" assumption should be tempered by what we know of the cone of uncertainty, but we should also be aware that an estimate is still an estimate, and therefore contains an assumption of possible error. Logically, this makes little sense because this would indicate that we are committing to a probability.

2. *The job of estimating is to come up with a date for completion.* The "end date" assumption assumes that when we estimate a time frame, we are estimating the date that the project will be finished. This is problematic because we are not predicting a specific time frame; we are predicting the *probability* that we will complete the project within a certain time frame.

3. *The estimate and the commitment are the same.* The "end date" assumption leads to the "commitment" assumption where people confuse the estimate of an end date and commitment to the estimate.

4. *A project estimate is dependent on the size of the final system.* The assumption that the estimate is dependent on the size of the final system is partly true: On average, larger systems take longer to complete than smaller ones. However, some large projects may not take very long if the system is similar to another that the project manager or organization has completed in the past.

5. *Historical data is an accurate indicator of productivity.* The historical data assumption is partly true in that previous experience from previous projects provides information about how long activities will take. However, the current project is not the same as the previous project no matter how much it appears to be so, and in fact, most companies hope past experience may speed things up for future projects.

6. *Productivity is an accurate indicator of project duration.* Productivity as an indicator of project duration is also problematic since in many cases productivity might be measured by the speed with which we can build something, without accounting for the quality or what we are building.

7. *Lines of code count is a good way to size a system.* Lines of code (LOC) may not provide a good metric for sizing a system because the number of lines may not represent the complexity of a system. For estimation purposes, the size of the system should be related to the amount of knowledge that must be obtained and the difficulty of obtaining such knowledge. We would not measure how much knowledge is in a book by weighing it, so why do we assume that several million lines of code *could not* be written to carry out simple tasks?

8. *Function points are a good way to size a system.* Similar to the logic used in LOC estimations, the use of function points—a popular method used to gauge the size and complexity of a system based on quantifying the functionality provided by a user—suffers similarly. This may be particularly true in modern development environments making greater use of code reuse from past applications. In this case, great functionality may exist but the application may be less complex to build.

9. *We can get the system faster by assigning more resources.* Adding people to hasten project completion is still one of the most common mistakes project teams make. While it would seem that the resources assigned to a project should have a direct bearing on the speed at which project tasks are completed, the relationship is actually more complicated than this. Different skill sets among participants, the ability to have a common understanding of both the problem and the solution, and the overhead of managing more resources may all contribute to delaying project completion rather than hastening it. This idea was concisely captured in *The Mythical Man-Month: Essays on Software Engineering*, in which author Fred Brooks posited that adding manpower to a late software project simply makes it later.

10. *Given enough time, we can create a defect-free system.* The assumption that we can create defect-free systems is also problematic. While we may strive for a defect-free end product, this may be an unreachable goal. Humans have a finite capacity for knowledge, and it is impossible for a project team to anticipate every conceivable variable that might affect the system.

Recognizing these assumptions is the first step toward overcoming them. Armour provides some tips regarding the issues raised previously:

- *Accuracy.* Strive for estimates that are accurate enough not to make bad decisions.
- *End date.* Define estimate outputs as a range of probabilities for given dates.
- *Commitment.* Establish processes with discrete estimate and commitment stages.
- *History.* Recognize that historical data may not be relevant. Think of it as an indicator, rather than as a predictor.
- *Productivity.* Recognize this assumption. Think of it as an indicator rather than a predictor.

- *Lines of code.* Recognize this assumption and try to find a better metric that represents knowledge.
- *Function points.* Recognize this assumption. As noted previously, try to determine a better method for measuring knowledge.
- *More people.* Be attentive to a critical mass of people and that adding more can hinder productivity.
- *Defect free.* Set goals for quality, and develop estimates that will allow achievement of quality goals realistically, realizing the goal is to satisfy the customer, not necessarily achieve perfection.

Based on: Armour (2002); Brooks (1995).

While the creation of the project schedule generally occurs early in the project—specifically during initiation and planning—schedules are used in project execution processes to offer guidance to the project team and are often updated to incorporate project changes. Schedules are also important in project control processes, where they are used for project tracking and managing project changes. They are further used to determine whether the project is progressing successfully. We now discuss some specific techniques for managing project schedules.

Techniques for Managing Project Schedules

Quite often, a complex task might seem overwhelming. A common analogy used in project management is, "How does one eat an elephant?" The answer is, "One bite at a time." Consider a home owner wanting to remodel her living room. The home owner might make this task less daunting by dividing it into smaller parts, such as researching options and deciding on a budget, hiring a professional designer, removing old furniture and carpets, painting walls, laying new carpets, and finally, setting up new furniture (see Figure 6.6). Each of those tasks is much more specific and easier to carry out than the overall project of remodeling the home.

Similarly, project managers will divide an entire project into discrete activities in order to set up a schedule. Representing a project as discrete activities allows the project manager to more easily allocate time and resources, and thus better estimate how long each of the activities will take. This process of breaking up work tasks or components to make them more easily manageable is termed **decomposition**. Decomposition is used at various stages of project scheduling. For example, decomposition is used to create the work breakdown structure (discussed later), which results in defining the various components that make up the entire project.

Decomposition
The process of subdividing tasks to make them more easily manageable.

Further, the decomposition process is also used to break down these components into the activities necessary to complete them. The next sections discuss the work breakdown structure, describing its inputs, tools and techniques, and outputs in detail.

Creating a Work Breakdown Structure (WBS)

A complex product, like almost anything else, can be divided into smaller, less complex parts. Consider a personal computer, which can be decomposed into many small, distinct components, such as a motherboard, a power supply and fans, the central processing

Figure 6.6 Breaking down a remodeling project

Product breakdown
structure (PBS)
The output from
the process of
dividing a product
into its individual
components.

unit, storage devices, and ports for plugging in peripheral devices. These major components can be further broken down into distinct subcomponents. The computer's hard drive can be further broken down into the case, the spindle, the platters, the read/write heads, actuator arms, a printed circuit board, the power connector, data connectors, and so on. Likewise, the computer's RAM can be broken down into the RAM chipsets that contain the individual memory cells holding the data, a printed circuit board, and so on. The list of components that make up a larger product is sometimes referred to as a **product breakdown structure** (PBS). A PBS shows a product's components in a hierarchical fashion, comparable to an organizational chart or a family tree (see Figure 6.7).

A work breakdown structure (WBS) is based on a similar concept. As the product breakdown structure describes the components of a product, a work breakdown structure describes the components needed to create the overall project (including the work involved in managing the project itself). As you can see from Figure 6.8, unlike the product breakdown structure, a work breakdown structure's purpose is not to provide a bill of materials but, rather, to serve as an aid in illustrating the project's scope and as a launching point for describing the activities necessary for creating the various subcomponents of the project (note that the WBS presented in Figure 6.8 is broken down by SDLC phases). To distinguish between a PBS and a WBS, the latter might include a system requirements analysis which documents the desired functionality of a system. This would fall outside the scope of a subcomponent of the product itself that might be documented in a PBS. The WBS is used in a variety of project activities that we will discuss in more detail in other chapters, including scope definition, costing, estimating, budgeting, and scheduling. The WBS plays a central role in the overall success of a project. Work breakdown structures can be presented in both hierarchical fashion and tabular form. This process of identifying all the deliverables necessary to complete the project is the first step in project scheduling. These deliverables are then decomposed into smaller and smaller deliverables. As an example, think for a moment about what it would take to build a custom home and its relationship to the concept of the WBS. There are many steps in building a home, including pouring the foundation, erecting

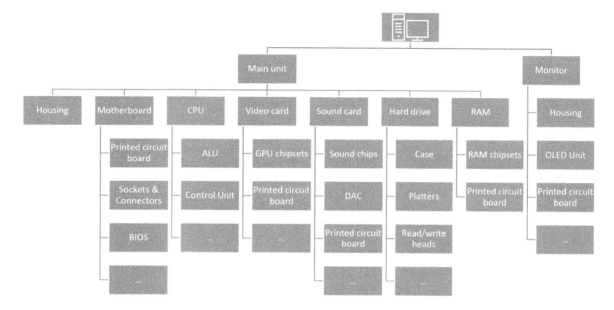

Figure 6.7 Product breakdown structure for a personal computer

and insulating the walls, installing electrical and plumbing components, putting on the roof, putting shingles on the roof, finishing all wall surfaces both inside and out, and inspecting the final product. A WBS representing the creation of a home (the overall project outcome or goal) would thus involve major deliverables such as the foundation, the walls, the plumbing and electrical systems, the roof, and so forth. Obviously, all of these major deliverables could also be further decomposed as well. For example, the foundation might include wood framing, smoothed cement, conduits for plumbing and electrical systems, and other components. The WBS is thus a technique for iteratively decomposing a project into subcomponents, which eventually (when at a sufficiently decomposed level) can be used to specify the individual activities necessary to produce the project outcome.

Many project managers regard a WBS as being oriented toward deliverables; as a result, they see all of the WBS components as objects (e.g., wood framing for a house's foundation). These objects are then created through activities, such as buying wood, measuring wood, cutting wood, laying out the frame, and the like (see this chapter's section on defining activities). Such activities usually have verb phrase labels (e.g., *cut wood for framing*), so they are often not considered to be part of the WBS. In contrast, other project managers view the WBS as composed not of objects, but of the activities themselves, always referring to the components of the WBS as tasks (e.g., creating a program module, as opposed to the program module itself). While opinions vary, one argument for separating the deliverables (as objects) from the activities needed to produce them is that such a method gives the "doers" more freedom about how to produce the deliverable (Berg and Colenso, 2000), which may have positive organizational effects. This book, therefore, treats the components of the WBS as deliverable-oriented and then examines the work necessary to create the deliverable in the *Define Activities* process. Keep in mind, however, that the WBS is a tool that should serve *you*; thus if your project (or organization) prefers a work-oriented WBS, then you should take that approach.

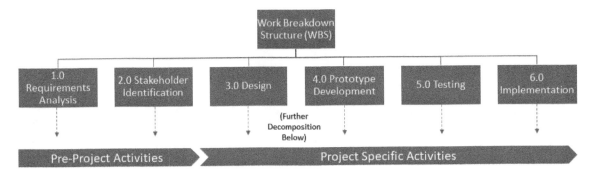

Figure 6.8 Work breakdown structure by SDLC phase

Create WBS—Inputs

Project managers creating a WBS rely on a variety of sources to determine how to decompose the entire project. In addition to the project management plan, the primary input of this process is the project scope statement, as well as the documented requirements (see Chapter 5). This statement covers the essence of the project by specifying the nature of the final deliverable as well as the broad steps necessary to complete the project. Other inputs can be the project manager's experiences with similar projects, organizational process assets (such as internal policies, procedures, or guidelines), or enterprise environmental factors.

Create WBS—Tools and Techniques

The primary technique for building a WBS is the process of decomposition. This decomposition process of breaking up a large project into smaller parts can proceed until the desired level of detail is reached. Typically, the entire project (level 0) is broken down into its major deliverables, which are then further decomposed until the work packages are reached at the lowest level of each branch of the WBS (again, note that a WBS focuses on verifiable products or results and thus does not include the activities needed to produce the results). Whereas some components need to be decomposed only into one or two levels, others might need more levels; thus, depending on the complexity of the major objectives, there might be several levels before the work package level (discussed later) is reached. During the planning stage, especially in projects of longer duration, a project management team might not be able to decompose some of the project's later components. In this case, the team defers breaking down these components until the components are further clarified and the decomposition takes place as the project progresses, a process called **rolling wave planning**. Usually, the project team and the customer are involved in creating the WBS to arrive at a clear understanding of what must be done to finish the project. Further, it often helps to use the expertise of the "doers"—that is, the people executing the different activities because these people have a good understanding of what needs to be done at a more detailed level. During decomposition, an owner should be assigned to each component of the WBS; the owner will be ultimately responsible for completing the deliverable.

After the major deliverables are identified, they should be structured and organized in the WBS. Following that, these major deliverables (which correspond to the higher levels of the WBS) need to be further decomposed into lower-level deliverables. Once the individual components have been assigned unique codes (usually in an outline

Rolling wave planning
A scheduling technique in which the team defers breaking down components until they are further clarified and the decomposition takes place as the project progresses.

number format, which clearly shows the component's level and which branch of the "tree" it belongs to), the project manager has to assess whether or not the components have been sufficiently broken down to provide enough detail at the lower levels. Care has to be taken that each higher-level deliverable is the sum of all the lower-level deliverables on the same branch so that each higher-level component contains only the lower-level components needed to complete it—nothing more and nothing less (sometimes referred to as the 100 percent rule). The following paragraphs describe decomposing a project in more detail.

Different strategies for determining the higher-level deliverables in the WBS can be employed. For example, the entire project can be broken down according to the major deliverables, phases of the project life cycle, functional areas, or a combination of these. As an example, Figure 6.9 can be used to represent the WBS for an enterprise resource planning (ERP) system, where the entire project is represented at level 0. Level 1 would then represent the different modules (such as accounting, finance, human resources, and so on) in the ERP. These level 1 modules could then be further broken down to include the subdeliverables needed for their completion.

Another method is to use the phases of the systems development life cycle (SDLC) or project life cycle as level 1 deliverables. This method has the advantage of assisting in sequencing the different activities in later phases of the planning stage. Refer back to Figure 6.8 for an example of a WBS oriented around the SDLC. Once the major deliverables have been identified, they should be represented in the WBS in a logical order to make interpreting the final WBS easier.

At the next level, the deliverables identified in the previous step would be decomposed into individual components, which are "verifiable products, services, or results" (*PMBOK*, p. 160). The level of detail needed here depends on the complexity of the major deliverables. As mentioned earlier, depending on the complexity of the first level, several levels of decomposition might be needed to reach the lowest level of each branch.

Work packages
The lowest-level units illustrated in the WBS, used to estimate project schedule and budget.

The lowest-level deliverables, **work packages**, are used to estimate the project's schedule and budget. Although the work packages should be detailed enough to allow for planning, managing, and control, too much detail can actually hinder the progress of the project by leading to micromanagement. What is a sufficient level of detail? Deciding on the size of a work package comes down to a tradeoff: if the work packages

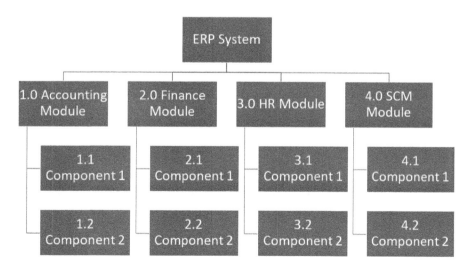

Figure 6.9 Sample work breakdown structure for an ERP system

are too detailed, the project will have to be micromanaged, but if the work packages are too complex and have too long a duration, the project manager can lose control over the progress of the project. In general, and dependent upon the size of the project, a work package should be relatively short in duration—that is, the deliverable should be finishable within one or two weeks. Project managers often follow the 8/80 rule: a work package should take no less than eight hours, but no more than 80 hours to complete. Another recommendation for the size of the work packages is that they should all be about the same size or should require about the same effort to produce. Finally, a work package should be specific enough to be completed by one person or a small, well-defined group.

Assigning numeric codes to the different deliverables, summary tasks, and activities will help to develop the activity list from the finished WBS. Again, these numeric codes should follow a simple outline number format that represents both the level of the deliverable and the branch it belongs to. As a final step in creating the WBS, the project management team should further verify that the decomposition is at the right level of detail for each branch.

The most common process of decomposing a project into different components normally follows a top-down approach, from higher-level to lower-level components. Sometimes, especially for particular types of projects, a bottom-up approach might be useful; in this approach, all team members try to determine as many of the tasks necessary to complete the project as possible. Then, they group those different tasks in some logical way to finally plan the entire project. This way of building a WBS can be useful for novel projects; further, it helps to get the buy-in of all project team members. A bottom-up approach, however, can be time-consuming.

Templates
Lists of activities from previous projects.

Another method of determining the deliverables and individual work packages needed to complete the project is the use of **templates**. Templates are lists of activities established during earlier projects. A project manager working on similar projects does not have to reinvent the wheel every time a new project is planned but, rather, can adapt and use the WBSs generated for earlier projects. Oftentimes, project managers have a repository of standard WBS templates to facilitate project planning. Experienced project managers can build a WBS based on their recollection of prior projects, but to avoid overlooking important deliverables, it is generally recommended to use documentation rather than to rely on recollection.

Most project scheduling processes, including the inputs, tools and techniques, and outputs already discussed, can be specified within Microsoft Project. Often, project managers create WBSs using diagramming tools such as Microsoft Visio. In Microsoft Visio, the WBS is represented in the form of an organizational chart. Alternatively, the objects or activities associated with the WBS can be entered in the Task Name column within the Gantt chart view of Microsoft Project (see Figure 6.10). As you will recall from Chapter 1, a Gantt chart is a bar chart showing the start and end dates for the activities of a project (recall that Gantt charts are now often referred to simply as bar charts). The Gantt chart lists activity names on the vertical axis and durations on the horizontal axis (Gantt charts are covered in more detail in Chapter 7). Although Figure 6.11 does not yet incorporate the time dimension of the various project tasks (note the absence of time illustrated on the horizontal axis), this Gantt chart view can be used early on to illustrate the WBS. As relationships and, later, task resource assignments and durations are defined (see Chapter 7), this task list depicting the WBS in Microsoft Project will start to look like a more formal Gantt chart.

If you have both Project and Visio installed on your computer, you can easily transform the tabular structure presented in Project into an organizational chart by using

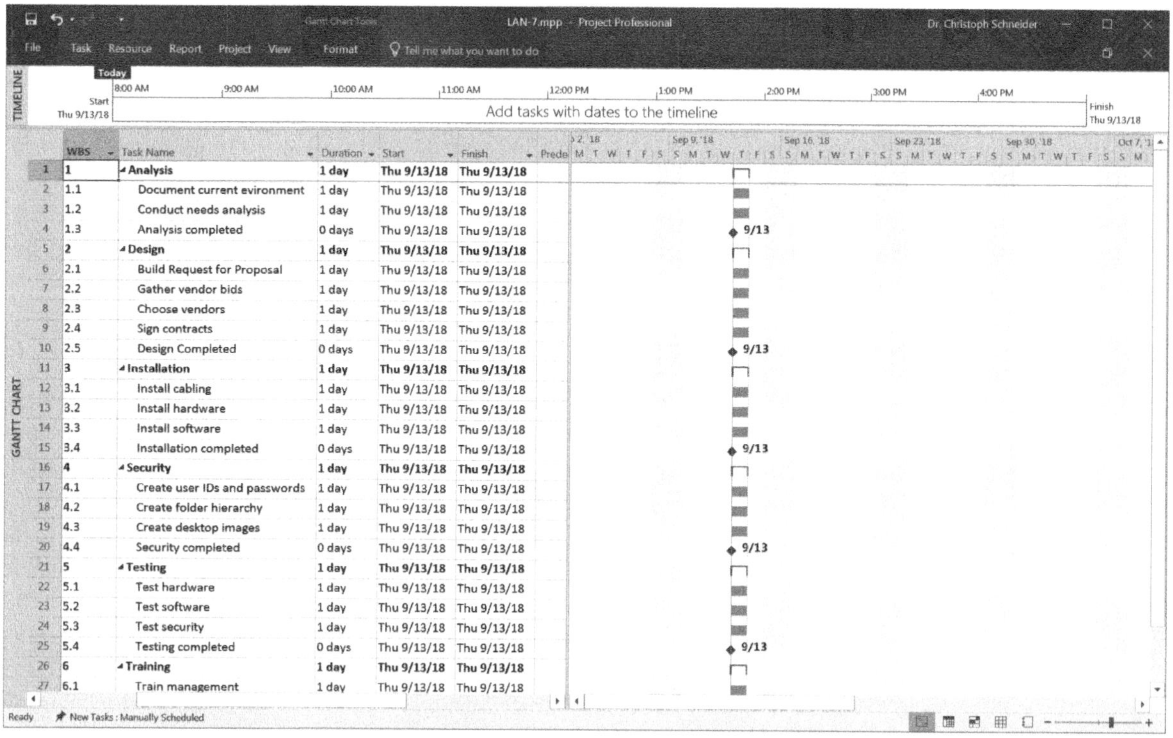

Figure 6.10   WBS in Microsoft Project 2016

the Visio WBS Chart Wizard in the analysis toolbar of Microsoft Project. Once you have entered the tasks, as well as additional information for each task, in Project, you can easily create a WBS dictionary by creating a report displaying the pertinent information for each task.

Create WBS—Outputs

The major output of this step is the **scope baseline**, which includes the project scope statement and the WBS, as well as a WBS dictionary. A **WBS dictionary** provides details about the individual components of the WBS, such as a description of each component, who is responsible for its completion, a statement of work, critical **milestones**, and preliminary estimates of costs or resources required.

When the WBS is first created, some of its components might not have been fully decomposed to the work package level, so they cannot yet be used for detailed estimation. These higher-level components are referred to as planning components, which are to be broken down at later stages. If the individual work packages have not been planned, a control account (or cost account) is established for future planning. These control accounts describe what work is to be performed in the future, who will perform it, and who will pay for it. Subcomponents of the control accounts are referred to as *planning packages*. These planning packages are at a higher level than the work packages; when using rolling wave planning, the planning packages are broken down into work packages and schedule activities some time before the execution of their corresponding components.

Scope baseline
A document containing the WBS and the WBS dictionary that specifies the deliverables and components of a project and serves to measure any deviations from that baseline during project execution.

WBS dictionary
A document that accompanies the WBS and provides additional information about the individual components of the WBS.

Milestones
Important dates within a project schedule that are meaningful in terms of the completion of specific sets of project events.

Defining the Activities

Define Activities is the next process in scheduling a project. In this stage, the different work packages of the WBS are broken down into discrete activities, and the attributes of these activities are defined, including a description, resource requirements, logical predecessor or successor activities, and the like. Clearly defining the different activities as well as their attributes greatly aids in determining the sequence of the activities. The inputs, tools and techniques, and outputs of this process will be discussed in the following sections.

Define Activities—Inputs

During the *Define Activities* process, the **activities** within a given project are identified. These activities are needed to produce the lowest-level deliverables of the WBS (namely, the work packages) and usually have verb labels (such as "pour cement"). Activities are used to guide the planning, scheduling, and execution of the project work, as well as to monitor and control progress. The scope baseline, the schedule management plan, organizational process assets (such as historical information, procedures, and policies), and enterprise environmental factors (such as availability of tools and resources and the project management information system) all serve as inputs during the *Define Activities* process. As defined earlier, the scope baseline is a document that contains the WBS and the WBS dictionary, as well as assumptions and constraints specified in the assumption log. The schedule management plan contains all pertinent information about how project scheduling is managed. Project managers may use historical information, specifically information about similar projects in the past, to develop a more accurate project schedule. Figure 6.11 summarizes the required inputs, the resulting outputs, and the tools and techniques used during activity definition.

Define Activities—Tools and Techniques

Defining project activities usually entails determining all the tasks needed to produce the WBS work packages. In other words, similar to using decomposition to arrive at the work packages, the project manager uses decomposition to break down the work packages into activities. Similar to our conversation about work packages, a central question in determining activities is, when is a sufficient level of detail reached? While there are no hard-and-fast rules for when to stop decomposition, there are a few guidelines. Typically, an activity

- Can be performed by one person or a well-defined group
- Has a single, clearly identifiable deliverable
- Has a known method or technique
- Has well-defined predecessor and successor steps
- Is measurable so that the level of completion can be determined

Another guideline for determining the level of detail needed is the duration of the activity. Usually, a project manager cannot oversee the task while it is being completed and will not be able to know the status of the activity during that time. Thus, if a task takes longer than a few days, a project manager will not know if everything is working out as planned while the person or group assigned to it is working on it. If something does not work according to plan, valuable time will be lost before the project manager

Define Activities
The process of identifying and defining activities that must be performed to produce project deliverables.

Activity
Small component used to plan, schedule, execute, monitor, and control the project.

	WBS	Task Name	Duration	Start	Finish	Predecessors	Resource Names
1	1	⊿ Analysis	1 day	Wed 1/2/19	Wed 1/2/19		
2	1.1	Document current evironment	1 day	Wed 1/2/19	Wed 1/2/19		
3	1.2	Conduct needs analysis	1 day	Wed 1/2/19	Wed 1/2/19		
4	1.3	Analysis completed	0 days	Wed 1/2/19	Wed 1/2/19		
5	2	⊿ Design					
6	2.1	Build Request for Proposal	1 day	Wed 1/2/19	Wed 1/2/19		
7	2.2	Gather vendor bids	1 day	Wed 1/2/19	Wed 1/2/19		
8	2.3	Choose vendors	1 day	Wed 1/2/19	Wed 1/2/19		
9	2.4	Sign contracts	1 day	Wed 1/2/19	Wed 1/2/19		
10	3	⊿ Installation					
11	3.1	Install cabling	1 day	Wed 1/2/19	Wed 1/2/19		
12	3.2	Install hardware	1 day	Wed 1/2/19	Wed 1/2/19		
13	3.3	Install software	1 day	Wed 1/2/19	Wed 1/2/19		
14	3.4	Installation completed	0 days	Wed 1/2/19	Wed 1/2/19		
15	4	⊿ Security					
16	4.1	Create user IDs and passwords	1 day	Wed 1/2/19	Wed 1/2/19		
17	4.2	Create folder hierarchy	1 day	Wed 1/2/19	Wed 1/2/19		
18	4.3	Create desktop images	1 day	Wed 1/2/19	Wed 1/2/19		
19	4.4	Security completed	0 days	Wed 1/2/19	Wed 1/2/19		
20	5	⊿ Testing					
21	5.1	Test hardware	1 day	Wed 1/2/19	Wed 1/2/19		
22	5.2	Test software	1 day	Wed 1/2/19	Wed 1/2/19		
23	5.3	Test security	1 day	Wed 1/2/19	Wed 1/2/19		
24	5.4	Testing completed	0 days	Wed 1/2/19	Wed 1/2/19		
25	6	⊿ Training					
26	6.1	Train management	1 day	Wed 1/2/19	Wed 1/2/19		
27	6.2	Train users	1 day	Wed 1/2/19	Wed 1/2/19		
28	6.3	Training completed	0 days	Wed 1/2/19	Wed 1/2/19		

Figure 6.11 The *PMBOK* (6th ed.) *Define Activities* process

will know about the problem. Limiting the duration of an activity to several hours or a few days, therefore, helps limit the negative impact of any potential delays.

Templates, as part of an organization's process assets that illustrate generic activity lists generated from information about similar projects in the past, can be used in scheduling other projects. For example, generating a report or a user interface almost always entails essentially the same activities, so information from prior projects can reliably be used to carry out this task.

Expert judgment may be used to better define project activities based on the recollection of a project expert. However, as the *PMBOK* guide acknowledges, this method may be less reliable than using documentation from prior projects. In addition to the experience of a project manager, the experience of "doers"—that is, the people carrying out the activities—is a valuable input in the activity definition phase. For instance, a database manager knows the detailed steps to be performed in setting up certain database queries.

Often, only the activities to be carried out in the project's next few steps can be planned at a sufficient level of detail. In this case, project managers use rolling wave planning, introduced earlier. Whereas the closest activities are planned at a detailed level, activities further in the future are planned only at a general level. During execution of the project, these activities are planned in more detail. Thus, as discussed earlier, there is a cone of uncertainty in which activities are planned in more detail as the project progresses. Because near-term activities are planned in great detail and future activities are planned in less detail, activities planned with different levels of detail can exist during any phase of the project life cycle (see Figure 6.12).

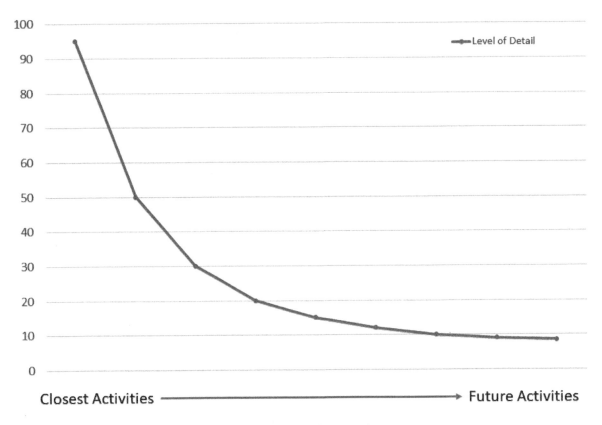

Figure 6.12   Rolling wave planning—level of detail for future tasks

Define Activities—Outputs

Outputs from the activity definition process include an activity list, supporting detail (such as activity attributes and milestones), and any requested changes to the project scope statement and the WBS. The activity list, an extension of the WBS, is a complete listing of all the schedule activities that make up the project. As an extension to the WBS, the activity list can be used to ensure that all project activities are also part of the current WBS. *Supporting detail* is a general term encompassing any information that can further define work packages. However, although the activity list is based on—and is an extension of—the WBS, the *PMBOK* does not consider the schedule activities as part of the WBS. Rather, it sees them as components of the project schedule (although, depending on your needs and your software's capabilities, you might choose to include the activities in the WBS).

The activity attributes include all pertinent attributes of a schedule activity, including description, constraints and assumptions, leads and lags (discussed later in this chapter), logical relationships, and predecessor and successor activities. These attributes help later in the activity sequencing process. Finally, during activity definition, a list of milestones is generated to aid in the execution of the project, as well as potential changes to the project management plan, such as to the schedule or cost baselines.

Sequencing the Activities

Sequence Activities
The process of determining relationships and logical sequence among activities.

Dependency
The logical relationship among activities.

Sequence Activities is the next process within the *PMBOK*'s Project Schedule Management knowledge area. The purpose of this process is to determine relationships and logical sequence among the activities and develop a network diagram. A network diagram is a schematic display that illustrates the various activities (or tasks) in a project as well as their sequential relationships.

The outputs of the *Sequence Activities* process guide this step in developing the project schedule, which involves determining the **dependencies** between the activities identified in the previous process and determining their necessary order. This is typically referred to as determining the precedence of the tasks. As noted earlier, often, one task is dependent on another. As an example, in home construction, putting a roof on the house is dependent on building the walls, which, in turn, is dependent on laying a cement foundation. Based on these logical relationships, a sequence of activities follows. This sequence of activities is no different from that which might occur in an information systems development project where, for example, the requirements for the system must be identified before system development can begin.

Based on the previous definition, project scheduling involves defining project activities, determining their sequence within a project schedule, estimating the resources needed, and estimating the activities' durations. Managers must clearly define project activities before the duration of each can be accurately estimated. Following the definition of each activity, project managers can begin to determine their dependencies and sequence and to estimate the resources and time needed to complete each specific activity. The estimation of each activity needs to be as accurate as possible because its length, in combination with the sequencing of all activities, leads to an overall estimation of the project's completion date. If the project must be completed to meet a specific date—say, to meet a government mandate—estimating the activities' time to completion can be especially crucial. The following sections discuss activity sequencing; Chapter 7 discusses estimating each activity's resources and duration.

When determining the sequencing of activities, it may be important in some instances for activities that can be performed in parallel to be scheduled simultaneously in order to speed project completion. This is particularly applicable when considering activities that affect the overall time required to complete the project (see the discussion of the critical path in Chapter 7). When determining the sequence of the project's activities, the project team should take into account certain constraints, which fall into one or more of these broad categories:

- Technical requirements and specifications
- Safety and efficiency
- Preferences and policies
- Resource availability

Technical requirements and specifications clearly dictate the sequence of some activities. It only makes sense that requirements collection must precede screen design in an information systems project. Sometimes, safety and efficiency should be considered. For example, important data should be backed up before installing new hardware or software; similarly, a system should be beta tested before the final version is launched. Whereas technical requirements, specifications, and safety concerns often require a certain sequence, efficiency concerns are not mandatory; in other words, a project manager can choose to use a different (and potentially suboptimal) sequence if other concerns (such as safety) override the efficiency criterion.

Company policies and preferences also influence the sequence of activities. In some companies, the marketing efforts start a long time before final product launch; for example, Microsoft typically announces new versions of its operating systems long before they are actually launched. When a project is behind schedule, these marketing efforts might have been more appropriately scheduled later in the project but were not because of corporate policies. Finally, the availability of resources can significantly influence the sequence of activities. If funding is tight at a certain stage of the project, some activities requiring more funds might have to be delayed until later stages while other activities take precedence. The various inputs, tools and techniques, and outputs of the *Sequence Activities* process are illustrated in Figure 6.13.

Global Implications: Managing Activities across the Globe

With the increasing tendency of organizations to conduct business across the globe—undertaking IS projects that involve team members from different company offices, possibly in different countries, and quite likely in different time zones—time is an important variable that cannot be overlooked. A project manager overseeing a globally distributed team must be aware of the impact of time on every aspect of the project from planning to closure. Some of these issues are noted in the following quote:

> Time is all-pervasive as it constantly helps to provide the organizing frame of reference for workgroups through agendas, meeting schedules, videoconference sessions, and *strategizing about "our time" and "their time" and about synchronizing activities.* Further, the success or failure of IS projects is heavily dependent on time. Project outcomes are often judged based on whether time deadlines are met, *which in turn depends on issues such as effective*

coordination of work. (Sarker and Sahay 2004, p. 5, emphasis added)

Sarker and Sahay studied virtual team formation in U.S. college students who had to complete an information systems development project with a group of team members from Norway. During the study, the authors uncovered four major time-related general principles with which globally distributed virtual teams must deal to effectively manage time over the course of a project.

1. Team members in different time zones likely have different cultural and social attitudes, and different physiological cycles with respect to time. These attitudes and cycles are difficult to change, and perceived lack of sympathy to these differences can cause problems in developing relationships.

2. With differences in time zones and possible differences with respect to daylight savings or standard time, seemingly simple clock-time

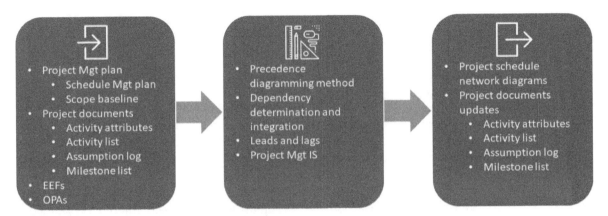

Figure 6.13 The *PMBOK* (6th ed.) *Sequence Activities* process

differences become increasingly difficult to accommodate. Mistakes regarding clock time can cause groups to miss important meetings and deadlines.

3. Being able to work simultaneously with team members who could be as many as twelve to sixteen hours behind or ahead becomes almost impossible. Because some tasks require responses from the distributed team members, groups can have long unproductive lapses while they wait for the other team members to respond.

4. Such lapses, even if only due to the time difference, can be interpreted by the waiting team members as incompetence or lack of commitment.

Given these issues, time management becomes increasingly critical, especially with globally distributed teams. A project manager must be aware of cultural differences with respect to the perception of time and different national holiday and vacation rules, and must actively manage the effects of time-related problems on team performance.

Based on: Mockaitis, Zander, and De Cieri (2018); Sarker and Sahay (2004).

Sequence Activities—Inputs

The activities defined in the previous stage are the most important input into the process of the *Sequence Activities* process. The activities' attributes (such as logical predecessor or successor activities) also serve to determine the project's best possible sequence. Further, the scope baseline, the schedule management plan, the milestone list, the assumption log (discussed in Chapter 5), as well as various organizational process assets (such as policies, templates, or lessons learned) and enterprise environmental factors (such as tools, systems, or standards) are used as inputs into this process. In many instances, the product description—which is simply a description of the product being constructed—or the product breakdown structure are also included as inputs to this process because developing the project schedule often depends on the product characteristics. In IS terms, the product description is the system being developed.

Sequence Activities—Tools and Techniques

A variety of tools and techniques can be used to illustrate the activity sequencing process. These include the precedence diagramming method, the arrow diagramming method, and conditional diagramming methods. The following paragraphs discuss the more commonly used methods of precedence diagramming and arrow diagramming.

Precedence diagramming method
A network diagramming technique that uses boxes connected by arrows to represent activities and their precedence relationships.

The **precedence diagramming method (PDM)** is a network diagramming technique that uses boxes connected by arrows to show the order and logical relationships (or dependencies) of activities within the project (see Figure 6.14). The boxes represent project activities, and the arrows represent the relationships among these activities or tasks. Key to PDM is its ability to illustrate four types of task dependencies among activities—that is, four ways that tasks exist in relation to other tasks. The first of these is finish-to-start, which is probably the most common of the task dependency types. Finish-to-start indicates that one activity cannot be started until another has been completed. For example, in an information systems development project, the programmer cannot begin actual programming until the programming language has been chosen. The second type of task dependency is start-to-start. In this situation, the start of the successor depends on the start of the predecessor. Again using our information systems example, programming cannot begin until some portion of the program design is decided on (e.g., 75 percent of the design activities might be completed). The third type of task dependency is finish-to-finish, meaning that the completion of the successor activity depends on the completion of the predecessor. In our information systems

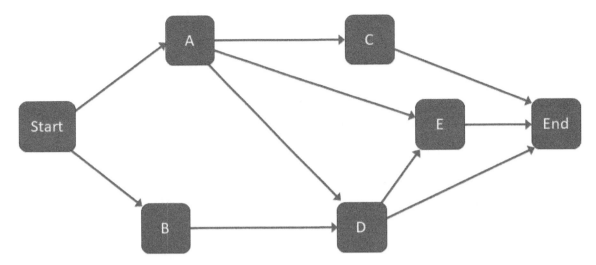

Figure 6.14 Precedence diagramming method

example, testing a system cannot be finished until the programming is completed. Finally, the fourth type of dependency is start-to-finish, in which the completion of the successor depends on the beginning of the predecessor. In our information systems example, a copy of the program—even if incomplete—cannot be saved until programming begins. Figure 6.15 illustrates all four of these types of dependencies.

A PDM diagram—which represents activities on nodes—is created based on the activity list as well as the activity attributes (specifically, the predecessor information) identified in the previous step (see Figure 6.15). First, a start node is created, indicating the beginning of the project. Then, based on the inputs, all activities with no predecessors are drawn as nodes (boxes) to the right of the start node (these will be the first activities of different sequences of activities because they have no predecessors) and connected with arrows to the start node. Then, the predecessor information is analyzed to determine what activities must follow, and these new activities are drawn to the right of those drawn in the previous step. Boxes are connected with arrows, taking into account the precedence relationships. This step is repeated until all activities are represented in the diagram. Finally, all nodes with no successor are connected to a dummy end node. Note that a dummy node—or **dummy activity**—is an activity of zero duration that is used to show a logical relationship or dependency in a network diagram.

As part of the project management information system, software such as Microsoft Project facilitates the creation of network diagrams. While creating the WBS and the activity definition, you have learned how to enter deliverables, activities, and predecessors in Microsoft Project's Gantt chart view. Switching to the Network diagram view renders the display of a PDM diagram. Note that Microsoft Project's network diagram presents information such as start and finish dates, as well as task durations. These are, strictly speaking, not part of a PDM diagram and will be discussed in Chapter 7.

The **arrow diagramming method (ADM)**—also called the activity on arrow (AOA) method—is a network diagramming technique that shows the project tasks or activities as the arrows in the diagram, as opposed to the nodes described in a PDM. The nodes in an ADM diagram can be conveniently used as milestones for the project (see Figure 6.16). Although this type of network diagramming method is sometimes easier to understand than a PDM diagram, one downside is that sometimes dummy nodes are needed to represent the different types of task dependencies mentioned previously. The

Dummy activity
An activity of zero duration that is used to show a logical relationship or dependency in a network diagram.

Arrow diagramming method
A network diagram consisting of arrows to represent activities and their precedence relationships and nodes to represent project milestones.

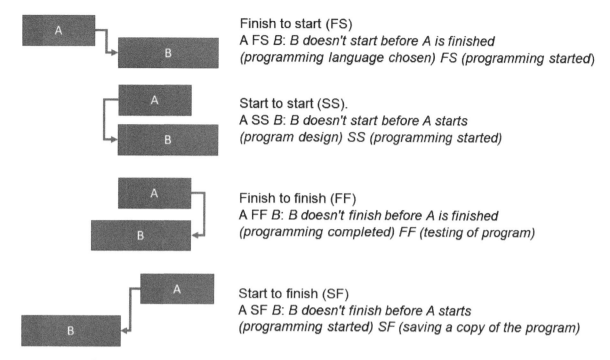

Finish to start (FS)
A FS *B*: *B doesn't start before A is finished*
(programming language chosen) FS (programming started)

Start to start (SS).
A SS *B*: *B doesn't start before A starts*
(program design) SS (programming started)

Finish to finish (FF)
A FF *B*: *B doesn't finish before A is finished*
(programming completed) FF (testing of program)

Start to finish (SF)
A SF *B*: *B doesn't finish before A starts*
(programming started) SF (saving a copy of the program)

Figure 6.15   Four types of task dependencies in order of decreasing frequency of occurrence

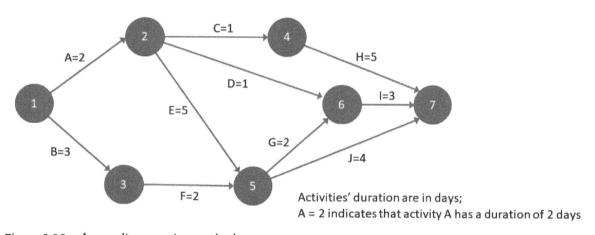

Activities' duration are in days;
A = 2 indicates that activity A has a duration of 2 days

Figure 6.16   Arrow diagramming method

widespread use of ADM diagrams has declined somewhat because most commercial software packages (including Microsoft Project) support PDM rather than ADM. This type of diagram is a useful tool, however, for teaching concepts such as the critical path, introduced in Chapter 2 and discussed in more detail in Chapter 7.

Mandatory dependencies
Relationships of activities that cannot be performed in parallel.

The relationships between different activities can take several forms. **Mandatory dependencies** represent the relationship between project activities that cannot be performed in parallel. In the construction example introduced earlier, the walls of a house cannot be erected before the foundation is built. In an information systems development project, a system cannot be built before the user requirements are determined.

Discretionary dependencies
Relationships of activities based on the preferences of project managers; often based on best-practices procedures.

Discretionary dependencies are those dependencies that are based on the preferences of project managers and are generally based on some type of best-practice procedure. An example might be the selection of a development language after doing a requirements analysis on what a system is supposed to do. Although it is certainly possible to choose the language first (for a variety of reasons, such as the skill set of those doing the development), it may make sense to make this choice after defining what the system is to do. Concerns for efficiency or decisions based on company policies or resource availability can result in the creation of discretionary dependencies.

External dependencies
Relationships of project activities and external events, such as the delivery of project components.

External dependencies represent the relationships between project activities and external events such as the delivery of an important project component. In an information systems development project, creating a new human resource intranet may require the installation of new hardware supplied by a vendor outside the control of the project team.

Internal dependencies
Relationships between project activities.

Finally, **internal dependencies** represent the relationships between project activities and are typically within the control of the project team. An example would be a dependency between installing a new operating system before installing the software.

Lead time
The amount of time by which a successor activity can be accelerated.

As the last step in activity sequencing, the leads and lags associated with the different activities should be determined. **Lead time** is the amount of time by which a successor activity can be accelerated, typically in a finish-to-start relationship. As an example, in a finish-to-start relationship, activity B may begin a certain amount of time before activity A has finished. As a specific information systems example, ongoing quality control inspections (activity B) may begin before the coding (activity A) has been completed. **Lag time** is a similar concept; it refers to the amount of time delay between the completion of one task and the start of the successor. A familiar example is the drying time for paint. While the task of painting a wall might take one hour, it might require an additional four hours of lag time before the next task—putting on the second coat of paint—can begin. An information systems example might include the time required to compile a program before testing it for errors.

Lag time
The time delay between the completion of one task and the start of the successor.

Sequence Activities—Outputs

Outputs from *Sequence Activities* process include project schedule network diagrams and updates to the activity list, the activity attributes discussed earlier, the milestone list, and the assumption log. Project schedule network diagrams can be any of the previously mentioned types, as well as others not listed here. Regardless of the type, the importance of a network diagram lies in its ability to graphically render the sequence of activities in the project schedule. Microsoft Project includes a built-in tool that automatically renders network diagrams based on the WBS entered by the user (see Figure 6.17). Updates to the project activity list are another important output and are generally used to identify any problems among the previously defined activities. Figure 6.13, discussed earlier, provides a summary of the required inputs, the resulting outputs, and the tools and techniques used during activity sequencing.

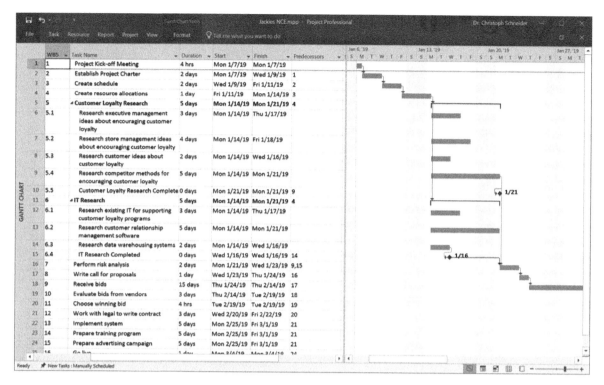

Figure 6.17   Network diagram in Microsoft Project 2016

Ethical Dilemma: Adherence to the WBS at All Costs

Work breakdown structures (WBS) have been used by organizations for some time. Consider the case of a large computer manufacturer (hereafter known as "the Company"). In the mid-1980s, because of several factors, including changes in upper management, the Company began using WBSs to streamline its various projects. On the surface, this seemed like an excellent idea because projects now had specific deliverables that were sufficiently decomposed to be manageable by one person or a small group of people. This ideally allowed managers to concentrate less on micromanaging every task. All the advantages of using WBS that we have presented were realized, but problems arose as well.

The Company had support for using WBSs—in fact, a directive from the highest-level executives that they were important and needed. However, at the same time, the CEO was experimenting with round-the-clock staffing and flextime, causing some unintended scheduling problems. Because of these experiments, mid- and lower-level managers failed to consider the non-work-related consequences of

strictly adhering to the new WBS-driven schedule. For example, if the start of Task C depended on the completion of Task B and had a four-hour duration and Task B was scheduled to be completed at 10:00 p.m. on a Tuesday, managers would schedule Task C to begin at 10:00 p.m. Tuesday and Task D to begin at 2:00 a.m. Wednesday. Given the differential skills of the project team members, in many cases employees were working different, and sometimes consecutive, shifts.

While seemingly efficient on the surface, employee feedback indicated the system occasionally failed because factors like family or personal obligations—for example, after-school events—made adhering to such a schedule difficult, if not impossible. The resultant conflict caused a breach between employees and management. In response, some managers started to use the WBS as a tool for punishment, justifying scheduling people to work at unreasonable times.

Although WBSs and the diagramming tools presented here have clear advantages, sometimes such systems can also have unintended consequences. The Company rectified these situations by setting up specific schedules for all team members, then assigning people to tasks, then going back to fill in the gaps. This resulted in projects' lasting longer than they might have, but now they place more reasonable requirements on team members' time. Unfortunately, these countermeasures were not instituted in time to keep several talented people from leaving the Company or to keep some managers from using the WBS as leverage to make life unpleasant for certain employees.

Despite the vast array of project management tools and techniques available to control project schedules, it is important to realize that (a) schedules are not set in stone, (b) rigid adherence to a schedule may have significant organizational consequences outside of the project itself, and (c) almost any tool can be misused. Organizations and managers need to constantly monitor for these unintended effects.

Discussion Questions

1. What steps can an organization take to diminish the misuse of project management tools, as in the provided example?
2. If you were a project manager in charge of employees affected by the situation provided, what approach might you use to discuss the issue with upper management?

Managing Project Scheduling and PMBOK

This chapter has discussed the fundamentals, characteristics, and challenges of developing a project schedule, focusing primarily on Knowledge Areas 5 and 6, *Project Scope Management* and *Project Schedule Management*. Continuing our conversation of project scope from Chapter 5, in this chapter we discussed the development of the WBS, which outlines the major deliverables associated with a project. After the development of the WBS, we then turned our attention to two processes associated with Project Schedule Management, *Define Activities* and *Sequence Activities*. These two processes involve, respectively, the identification of activities needed to produce the WBS deliverables, and then the sequencing of these activities. We also discussed the various tools and techniques available to address common project scheduling problems. Figure 6.18 summarizes this coverage and illustrates what will be discussed in upcoming chapters as well.

Figure 6.18   Chapter 6 and *PMBOK* coverage

Key: O where the material is covered in the textbook; ● current chapter coverage

	Textbook Chapters ⟶	1	2	3	4	5	6	7	8	9	10	11	12
	PMBOK Knowledge Area												
1	Introduction												
1.2	Foundational Elements	O	O										
2	The Environment in Which Projects Operate												
2.2	Enterprise Environmental Factors		O										
2.2	Organizational Process Assets		O										
2.3	Organizational Systems		O										
3	The Role of the Project Manager												
3.2	Definition of a Project Manager	O											
3.3	The Project Manager's Sphere of Influence		O										

No.	Process	1	2	3	4	5	6	7	8	9	10	11
3.4	Project Manager Competences	O	O	O								
3.5	Performing Integration		O									
4	**Project Integration Management**											
4.1	Develop Project Charter					O						
4.2	Develop Project Management Plan					O						
4.3	Direct and Manage Project Work										O	
4.4	Manage Project Knowledge										O	
4.5	Monitor and Control Project Work										O	O
4.6	Perform Integrated Change Control											O
4.7	Close Project or Phase									O		O
5	**Project Scope Management**											
5.1	Plan Scope Management					O						
5.2	Collect Requirements					O						
5.3	Define Scope					O						
5.4	Create WBS					O	●					
5.5	Validate Scope					O						
5.6	Control Scope					O						O
6	**Project Schedule Management**											
6.1	Plan Schedule Management						●					
6.2	Define Activities						●					
6.3	Sequence Activities						●					
6.4	Estimate Activity Durations							O				
6.5	Develop Schedule							O				
6.6	Control Schedule							O				O
7	**Project Cost Management**											
7.1	Plan Cost Management								O			
7.2	Estimate Costs								O			
7.3	Determine Budget								O			
7.4	Control Costs								O			O
8	**Project Quality Management**											
8.1	Plan Quality Management								O			
8.2	Manage Quality								O			
8.3	Control Quality								O			O
9	**Project Resource Management**											
9.1	Plan Resource Management							O				
9.2	Estimate Activity Resources						●	O				
9.3	Acquire Resources							O			O	
9.4	Develop Team			O							O	
9.5	Manage Team			O							O	
9.6	Control Resources							O				O

10	**Project Communications Management**													
10.1	Plan Communications Management				O									
10.2	Manage Communications				O								O	
10.3	Monitor Communications				O									O
11	**Project Risk Management**													
11.1	Plan Risk Management								O					
11.2	Identify Risks								O				O	
11.3	Perform Qualitative Risk Analysis								O					
11.4	Perform Quantitative Risk Analysis								O					
11.5	Plan Risk Responses								O					
11.6	Implement Risk Responses								O				O	
11.7	Monitor Risks								O					O
12	**Project Procurement Management**													
12.1	Plan Procurement Management									O				
12.2	Conduct Procurements									O	O			
12.3	Control Procurements									O				O
13	**Project Stakeholder Management**													
12.1	Identify Stakeholders				O									
12.2	Plan Stakeholder Engagement				O									
12.3	Manage Stakeholder Engagement				O								O	
12.4	Monitor Stakeholder Engagement				O									O

Running Case: Managing Project Scheduling

James Cheung walked into the conference room to find everyone on his team in their seats, sharing the scheduling information they had developed for the project. As usual, Maria was on speakerphone from Riverside. She had emailed over a couple of pages of information. James had stopped by the printer nearest his desk on his way to the meeting to pick up a printout of the information.

James plugged the projector into his laptop and adjusted the setting so that he could display the work on his laptop on the screen (see Table 6.1). "Here is the list of tasks that I have compiled, based on what you guys sent me. You'll see it is pretty high-level stuff at this point. I tried to order these in some kind of temporal sequence, but it's only an approximation at this point. As of right now, I have twenty-one different tasks."

"You're right," Kevin said. "These are pretty high level. Each one of these tasks is going to have to be broken down into subtasks."

"That's OK," Trey said. "I think this gives us a good place to start. Moreover, we can get a good first approximation of how long the entire project will take, and whether we can finish what needs to be done in the time given to us by Sarah and the rest of the executive team."

"Like we have a choice," Cindy replied.

"Clearly the kickoff meeting and going live are the bookends of the project," Maria added. "What can be done in parallel? Let's set up the basic schedule structure first, and then we can come back and refine the duration of each task."

"Sounds good," James said, switching to Microsoft Project (see Figure 6.19). "I've already given that some thought. Here is what I came up with."

"You can see that, for simplicity, I have collapsed all four of the customer loyalty research tasks into one and all three of the IT research tasks into one. But all seven of these tasks can be done in parallel," James explained.

"And implementation, preparation of the training program, and preparation of the advertising program can all be done in parallel too," Cindy pointed out.

"But some of these really depend on the others," Trey said.

Table 6.1 Running Case: Key High-Level Project Tasks

Project kickoff meeting
Establish project charter, objectives, etc.
Create schedule
Create resource allocations
Research executive management ideas about encouraging customer loyalty
Research store management ideas about encouraging customer loyalty
Research customer ideas about customer loyalty
Research competitor methods for encouraging customer loyalty
Research existing IT for supporting customer loyalty programs
Research customer relationship management software
Research data warehousing systems
Perform risk analysis
Write call for proposals
Receive bids
Evaluate bids from vendors
Choose winning bid
Work with Legal to write contract
Implement system
Prepare training program
Prepare advertising campaign
Go live

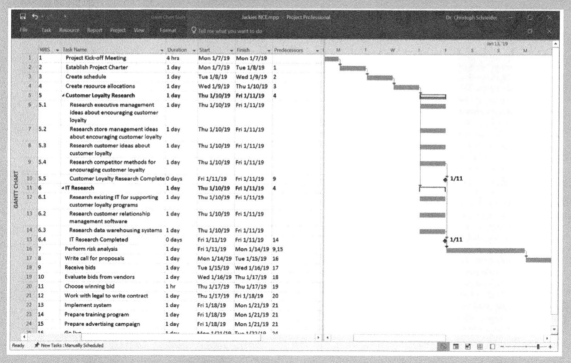

Figure 6.19   Microsoft Project 2016 initial Gantt chart for the "No Customer Escapes" project

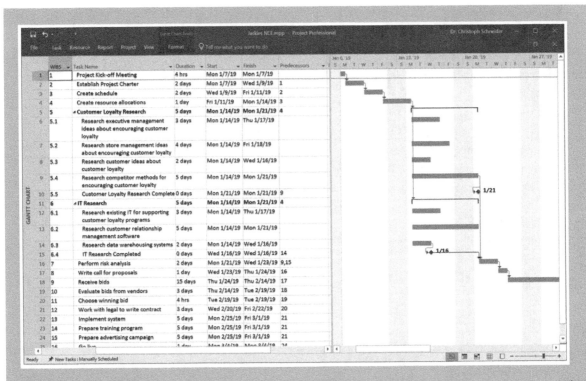

Figure 6.20 Microsoft Project 2016 Gantt chart for the "No Customer Escapes" project, with the team's revised estimated durations

The team spent the next hour trying to determine their best estimates for how the various tasks should be sequenced and making some rough estimates of their duration. The results of this discussion are shown in Figure 6.20.

"This is pretty good," James said, "but it's going to need some refining. Let me work on it. One thing I can see right now, though, is that we are going to need some additional resources to pull this off. We all need to think about what it is going to take to finish this project in the time we have and just how much each of us can contribute."

"You know," Kevin offered, "this is a pretty ambitious project."

Adapted from: Valacich and George (2017).

Chapter Summary

Discuss project scheduling, including its importance and the challenges associated with it. Managing project schedules are a critical aspect of project management. When developing a project schedule, the project manager together with relevant team members and other stakeholders develops an accurate and acceptable schedule. Schedules are hardly ever perfect because rarely is everything about a project known in advance. In addition, information systems related projects may introduce additional issues, such as technology upgrades, which create additional complications. Schedules are frequently refined as the project moves forward, consistent with the cone of uncertainty discussed in the chapter.

Describe project scheduling techniques, such as the work breakdown structure, activity definition, and activity sequencing. When developing a project schedule, the project manager together with relevant team members develops a work breakdown structure (WBS) by decomposing the entire project into smaller, more manageable parts, which in turn can be further decomposed. Mapping out this decomposition process results in a WBS that allows project managers to determine smaller specific deliverables that, when aggregated over the lifespan of the project, will result in the completion of the macro-level project deliverable. Once the initial WBS has been developed, project managers then define the activities outlined in the WBS to a level of detail fine enough to allow specific activities to be assigned to one person or to a small, well-defined group but still general enough to keep micromanagement from becoming an issue. Taking the output from the *Define Activities* process, project managers sequence the activities to optimize efficiency given a set of constraints. These constraints include technical requirements and specifications, safety and efficiency, preferences and policies, and resource availability. Precedence relationships as well as lead and lag times need to be considered in the *Schedule Activities* process.

Describe how project management software packages can help with project scheduling. Several project scheduling tools have been presented in this chapter. These software tools can assist in the *Create WBS, Define Activities,* and *Schedule Activities* processes. In many cases, these tools have the advantage of transferring information from one type of schematic to another. For example, Microsoft Project allows the creation of a WBS, which (after additional information is added) allows the user to display the same information in Gantt charts or precedence diagrams. Further, successful project managers use templates, which may come from previous projects they have worked on or from documentation from previous projects within the organization.

Key Terms Review

A. Activity
B. Arrow diagramming method
C. Cone of uncertainty
D. Decomposition
E. Define Activities
F. Dependency
G. Discretionary dependencies
H. Dummy activity
I. External dependencies
J. Internal dependencies
K. Lag time
L. Lead time
M. Mandatory dependencies

N. Milestones
O. Plan Schedule Management
P. Precedence diagramming method
Q. Product breakdown structure
R. Project scheduling
S. Rolling wave planning
T. Schedule management plan
U. Scope baseline
V. Sequence Activities
W. Templates
X. WBS dictionary
Y. Work packages

Match each of the key terms with the definition that best fits it.

1. A document containing the WBS and the WBS dictionary that specifies the deliverables and components of a project and serves to measure any deviations from that baseline during project execution.

2. A document that accompanies the WBS and provides additional information about the individual components of the WBS.

3. A network diagram consisting of arrows to represent activities and their precedence relationships and nodes to represent project milestones.

4. A network diagramming technique that uses boxes connected by arrows to represent activities and their precedence relationships.

5. A progressively more detailed and accurate projection of the project schedule and duration, as the project manager or project team specifies project deliverables and activities in more detail.

6. A scheduling technique in which the team defers breaking down components until they are further clarified and the decomposition takes place as the project progresses.

7. An activity of zero duration that is used to show a logical relationship or dependency in a network diagram.

8. Component of the project management plan that provides guidance on *how* the schedule will be managed throughout the project.

9. Important dates within a project schedule that are meaningful in terms of the completion of specific sets of project events.

10. Lists of activities from previous projects.

11. Relationships between project activities.

12. Relationships of activities based on the preferences of project managers; often based on best-practices procedures.

13. Relationships of activities that cannot be performed in parallel.

14. Relationships of project activities and external events, such as the delivery of project components.

15. Small component used to plan, schedule, execute, monitor, and control the project.

16. The amount of time by which a successor activity can be accelerated.

17. The logical relationship among activities.

18. The lowest-level units illustrated in the WBS, used to estimate project schedule and budget.

19. The output from the process of dividing a product into its individual components.

20. The process associated with establishing the schedule management plan.

21. The process of defining project activities, determining their sequence, and estimating their duration.

22. The process of determining relationships and logical sequence among activities.

23. The process of identifying and defining activities that must be performed to produce project deliverables.

24. The process of subdividing tasks to make them more easily manageable.

25. The time delay between the completion of one task and the start of the successor.

Review Questions

1. Compare and contrast a product breakdown structure (PBS) and a work breakdown structure (WBS).

2. Define decomposition.

3. Discuss why a WBS has different levels and what each level represents.

4. What is the difference between decomposing levels using a top-down approach and a bottom-up approach, and what types of projects are best suited to each approach?

5. Why are templates useful for developing project schedules?

6. What is a scope baseline, what are its components, and why is it important?

7. To what level of detail should activities be decomposed? Why?

8. Define a work package and describe its characteristics.

9. Describe strategies that project managers might use to define activities.

10. Describe the differences and similarities between the cone of uncertainty and rolling wave planning.

11. List and briefly describe the classes of constraints on determining the activity sequence. Do any constraints override others?

12. Give an example of each class of constraint on determining the activity sequence.

13. From a precedence diagramming method perspective, list and briefly discuss each type of task dependency.

14. From an arrow diagramming method perspective, list and briefly discuss each type of task dependency.

Chapter Exercises

1. You and your team members are tasked with developing a mobile app for managing your schedules and keeping track of exams and important events and deadlines. Fully decompose this project and discuss the level of detail where you stopped decomposing and explain why.

2. Create a WBS based on the decomposition you carried out for the previous question.

3. You have just been selected as the manager for a project to automate the distribution center at XYZ Co. This project has significant executive support and an engaged executive sponsor. The executive you report to asks you if you will be able to complete the project in less than six months. Describe to the executive sponsor what you must do from a project scheduling perspective before you can give her an answer. Based on what has been presented in this chapter, can you give her an answer? Why or why not?

4. After determining that there is a relatively high probability that the project can be completed within six months, the executive you report to wonders if she can trust your determination. After all, she has heard all the reports about IS projects going over budget and past their deadlines. Address these concerns. In other words, how would you assure her that your estimation is accurate?

5. Working in a small group, pick a project (it could be anything, such as planning a party, writing a group term paper, developing a mobile app, etc.) and then write the various tasks that need to be done to complete the project on Post-its (one task per Post-it). Then, use the Post-its to create the WBS from the project. Was it complete? Add missing tasks if necessary. Were some tasks at a lower level in the WBS than others? What was the most difficult part of doing this?

6. Create a precedence diagram based on the following information:
   - There are ten total tasks, named A–J.
   - Tasks A, B, and H have durations of two days.
   - Tasks C, E, I, and J have durations of three days.
   - Tasks D, F, and G have durations of one day.
   - Tasks A, B, and D can be conducted in parallel.
   - Task C must precede task B.
   - Tasks A and F must precede Task E.
   - Task E must precede Task G.
   - Tasks B and D must precede Tasks H and I, respectively.
   - Tasks G, H, and I may be conducted in parallel.
   - Tasks G, H, and I precede Task J.

7. Create an arrow diagram with the information from Exercise 6.

8. Create a precedence diagram for your project from Exercise 2.

9. Which diagramming method do you prefer? Why?

Chapter Case: Sedona Management Group and Managing Project Scheduling

Time is the least flexible factor during the life cycle of a project. No matter what else happens during the project, time continues to pass. Tim Turnpaugh recognizes that managing time through good project scheduling is integral to project success. As mentioned earlier, project schedules are managed so well at SMG that the team has not missed a deadline in the last ten years, and this includes SMG's projects for the Seattle Seahawks.

For any project, and in particular for the Seattle Seahawks' website, SMG's first step—as mentioned in Chapter 5—is to determine customer needs and project scope with a great deal of certainty. Once these two elements are established, it is much easier to determine the end date of a project. If customers are uncertain about their needs, the Sedona team understands that more time should be spent on needs analysis. Usually, the project team will start working on the project the next business day after the customer signs the contract with SMG. In the case of the initial Seattle Seahawks project, the primary focus was to provide information to customers interested in learning about the Seahawks organization. This included information about upcoming events, information about the team, and information about the overall organization. Given SMG's past experiences and leveraging the newest technologies to enhance development speed, Turnpaugh was able to provide very accurate estimates regarding the time required for the Seahawks project.

The first step in time management is activity definition, which involves identifying the various activities that need to be performed for project completion. Turnpaugh indicates that most projects SMG takes on have some fundamental reoccurring components. These include designing the database, working on the website content, working on the website presentation, connecting the presentation layer to the database, implementing the system, training users, and if necessary, maintaining the system. These components serve as the top level of the project work breakdown structure (WBS) and help define the various work packages associated with the project.

After establishing the WBS and subtasks, the focus is on developing the project schedule. Project scheduling, as discussed in this chapter, is concerned with establishing the order and duration of the tasks required to complete the project. Although

some mandatory dependencies certainly occur when designing the project, in many cases, tasks in a project schedule can occur in parallel rather than in a strict sequence. This was exactly the case with the Seahawks project, where the database design and website presentation-layer development occurred in parallel. In other instances, a sequence of activities is required, as with the tasks related to connecting the database to the presentation layer (what Turnpaugh refers to as *wiring up*). In this instance, wiring up cannot be performed until the first three activities have been completed.

The next step in managing the project schedule involves estimating the duration of each activity—that is, estimating the time it will take to complete the different activities. Through experience, Turnpaugh and other members of his team have become very good estimators of the time and resources it takes to complete various project tasks. In an iterative process, project resources, time estimates, and task sequencing requirements are manipulated until a completed project schedule is developed.

The Sedona team also takes several steps to control changes to the project schedule. To begin with, the project team always tries to develop a very realistic project schedule that is based on past experiences with other customers. The project team also has regular progress meetings, where they update each other on the status of their assigned work and adjust the schedule if needed. Through these meetings, activities that are not on track can be identified, and any actions needed (e.g., assigning more resources to a project task or, perhaps, doing the task in parallel with some other task) can be taken to ensure the timely completion of the project.

Chapter 6 Project Assignment

In this assignment, you will work on developing a schedule for your entertainment website project. The project end date needs to be consistent with the course duration. The project schedule will be developed using a Gantt chart in Microsoft Project.

1. Create a work breakdown structure (WBS) for your project. This involves developing a detailed list of tasks and subtasks that should be carried out to complete the project.

2. Create the schedule by assigning durations to the tasks identified, as well as sequencing them.

3. Add milestones to show the completion of each major deliverable.

4. Identify some challenges that you and your team members will face in following this schedule.

5. Identify and explain different techniques you will use during the life cycle of the project to manage project time.

References

Armour, P. (2002). Ten Unmyths of Project Estimation: Reconsidering Some Commonly Accepted Project Management Practices. *Communications of the ACM* 45(11), 15–18.

Berg, C., and Colenso, K. (2000). Work Breakdown Structure Practice Standard Project: WBS vs. Activities. *PM Network* 14(4), 69–71.

Boehm, B. W. (1981). *Software Engineering Economics*. Upper Saddle River, NJ: Prentice Hall.

Brooks, F. P. (1995). *The Mythical Man-Month: Essays on Software Engineering* (2nd ed.). Reading, MA: Addison-Wesley.

Mockaitis, A. I., Zander, L., and De Cieri, H. (2018). The Benefits of Global Teams for International Organizations: HR Implications. *The International Journal of Human Resource Management*, DOI: 10.1080/09585192.2018.1428722

Orton-Jones, C. (2016, May 22). Eight Lessons from Digital Megaprojects. *Raconteur*. Retrieved July 5, 2018, from https://www.raconteur.net/business/8-lessons-from-digital-megaprojects

Project Management Institute (2017). *Agile Practice Guide*. Newton Square, PA: Author.

Project Management Institute (2017). *PMBOK: A Guide to the Project Management Body of Knowledge* (6th ed.). Newtown Square, PA: Author.

Sarker, S., and Sahay, S. (2004). Implications of Space and Time for Distributed Work: An Interpretive Study of U.S.-Norwegian Systems Development Teams. *European Journal of Information Systems* 13(1), 3–20.

Stanleigh, M. (2005). The Top Project Management Challenges (2005). *Business Improvement Architects*. Retrieved January 31, 2017, from https://bia.ca/the-top-project-management-challenges-2005

Transport for London (2018). Daily Breakdown of Oyster Card Usage up to 31 March 2018. *TFL.gov.uk*. Retrieved July 5, 2018, from http://content.tfl.gov.uk/daily-breakdown-of-oyster-card-usage-data.pdf

Valacich, J., and George, J. F. (2017). *Modern Systems Analysis and Design* (8th ed.). Boston: Pearson.

CHAPTER 7

Managing Project Resources

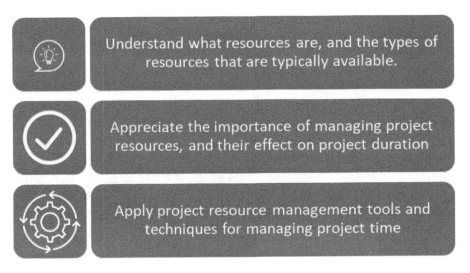

Understand what resources are, and the types of resources that are typically available.

Appreciate the importance of managing project resources, and their effect on project duration

Apply project resource management tools and techniques for managing project time

Figure 7.1 Chapter 7 learning objectives

Opening Case: London's "Digital Games"

Mega sports events such as the Olympic Games continue to capture tremendous public interest, and broadcasters are trying to use the newest technologies to offer their audiences a superior viewing experience. For the 2012 Olympic Games in London, the British Broadcasting Corporation (BBC) envisioned transforming the games into "digital games"—for the first time broadcasting the events in 4K ultra-high-definition video; delivering content in 3D; and enabling viewers using TVs, computers, and mobile devices to tune in on the action. Together, more than 2,500 hours of high-definition content needed to be delivered over seventeen days, using two dozen TV channels that were also accessible as online streams.

This project relied on a delicate interplay of different resources. First, transmitting the tremendous amounts of data needed for 4K video necessitated laying four miles of fiber optic cables between London's Olympic Park and BBC's TV center. Likewise, a studio capable of producing 4K content was needed. More than thirty 3D cameras were needed to capture content in 3D. Remote-controllable robotic cameras allowed photographers to get pictures from vantage points that would have been inaccessible. Given the expected viewership for major events with British athletes, BBC needed to double its streaming capacity. Further, BBC introduced a live interactive video player on its website, allowing viewers to not only watch the event but also rewind the stream and access additional content about the event. The BBC

Figure 7.2 London's Olympic Park. *Source*: CC-BY-ND-2.0, Kevin Neagle.

Olympics app was created to provide optimal experiences on Apple and Android devices, and the BBC Sport app allowed TiVo and smart TV users to view the events. The different streaming options were powered by Adobe Primetime, with BBC being the first public user.

Clearly, planning for, acquiring, and managing these vastly different resources was a tremendous undertaking. In the end, London's digital games turned out to be a success for Great Britain, the British athletes, and the British Broadcasting Corporation.

Based on: Orton-Jones (2016); Rubens (2012).

Introduction

Like any well-run organization—or even a well-run household—a project needs to use resources efficiently. Chapter 6 discussed the first part of Project Schedule Management, which we termed *project scheduling*. This included developing the WBS, the *Define Activities* process, and the *Sequence Activities* process. Chapter 6 thus included discussions on how a project can be divided into deliverables and activities, and how these activities are ordered. However, an additional aspect of Project Schedule Management is an understanding of how project task durations are determined. This also involves assessing the resources needed for each task, a process associated with Project Resource Management. This chapter explores the concepts of estimating activity resources, estimating activity durations, and developing the schedule. We will also discuss what resources are, why it is important to manage them, and what techniques and tools project managers have at their disposal to manage resources, to develop project schedules based on resources, and to avoid resource related problems that may influence project completion. As highlighted in earlier chapters, when managing resources, the project manager needs to keep in mind the triple constraint of scope, budget, and schedule, as changes in resource availability are likely to influence those critical aspects of any project.

What Are Resources?

Resource
A source of supply or support, such as money, people, materials, technology, and space.

Resources are commonly thought of as "sources of supply or support," a description that holds true in the case of project management resources, which include money, people, materials, technology, and space (see Figure 7.3). For information systems projects, a more specific listing of resources might include systems developers, project managers, systems analysts, stakeholders, development environments, facilities, and information architectures for both the development team and the final implementation of the system. We will discuss these various types of resources in more detail later in this chapter. As an example, a project manager may be charged with leading a project designed to integrate all of the existing software in different functional areas (financial, human resources, etc.) within a company. To succeed, the project manager must manage many different types of project resources, including people, hardware and software, funds, and office equipment, among others.

Types of Resources

Effectively managing human resources, equipment, space, and money is critical to project success. For information systems projects, human resources include not only the project team itself but possibly other stakeholders in the process. Equipment-related resources might include the various technologies—hardware, software, and infrastructure—needed for both the development of the information systems and for its testing and final implementation. Space also has to be considered because people interact with the organization for which the system is being designed and the development team occupies workspaces. Finally, and related to all of these, financial resources must be available to support the project. This section discusses in greater detail two of the primary types of project resources used in information systems projects, namely human resources and capital resources.

Human Resources

Human resources
All personnel involved in a project, including project team members and support staff.

Developing an information system involves using people with different skills. The project manager plays a key role in determining the human resources necessary for a project. As discussed extensively in Chapter 3, **Human resources** include all personnel involved in a project, including project team members and support staff. The job of systems analysts, for example, may be to elicit requirements from the customer, then determine

Figure 7.3   Some examples of project resources

the design of the system. Typically, these analysts not only understand the intricacies of systems development but are also knowledgeable about business processes. Their role is to elicit customer needs and convey them in a meaningful way to the personnel doing the actual systems development.

The systems developers, in contrast, depend less on business knowledge and more on in-depth technical knowledge of the hardware and software platforms necessary to optimize system performance. Other technology workers involved in a project include system architects or QA (quality assurance) testers. Certain project personnel may also be involved in acquiring both new personnel and necessary materials and technologies. Often, human resources to be managed during a project may also include stakeholders from the client's organization as well as stakeholders (such as upper management) from the firm undertaking the systems development project (such as top-level management). The project manager, therefore, must have skills in a variety of areas, including the project's technical domain and the business context, as well as excellent leadership, planning, and communication skills (see Chapters 3 and 4).

Effectively managing these resources is critical to the success of any project. Neglecting to properly manage human resources dramatically increases the likelihood of project failure. Project personnel must be monitored to ensure that necessary tasks are completed on time and on budget. Relationships with the customer must also be properly managed to ensure open and honest communication. Relationships with end users, who are often also the customer, must be managed to ensure an easy transition once the project is complete and ready to implement. Managing relationships with suppliers is also critical in ensuring that the necessary resources are available for use when needed. For all of these reasons, it is imperative that project managers develop and maintain good communication networks among all project stakeholders.

To estimate the human resources needed for a project, the tasks associated with the project are first defined as explained in Chapter 6; then the personnel needs for each task are evaluated. The selection of personnel may be influenced by the availability, cost, and skills of the project manager's resource pool. After determining the appropriate human resources to carry out a given activity as well as other resource requirements, the project manager can begin to estimate the duration of project tasks and develop the project schedule.

Global Implications: Human Resource Management as an Advantage to Offshoring

The types of projects that are most likely to be offshored were discussed in Chapter 5's "Global Implications: Deciding When to Offshore." With respect to managing human resources on a project, one other reason companies might choose to offshore is to "follow the sun" in an attempt to maintain a twenty-four-hour software development cycle. As a global player, Motorola has extensive experience with distributed teams. Based on its lessons learned over the years, Motorola revealed several techniques that it used to manage human resources across the globe during a critical project. Anticipating potential problems with globally distributed teams, the Motorola team identified ten problems likely to emerge and developed twelve techniques to alleviate them (see Figure 7.4).

As can be seen in Figure 7.4, many of these problems are resource management issues, including how to manage capital resources (e.g., choosing and managing the types of technology used by the project team to communicate, coordinate, and execute project activities across time and space) as well as human resources (developing a sense of "teamness" and managing cultural differences). Motorola's example shows that global resources can be used to the project's advantage if properly managed.

Based on: Battin, Crocker, Kreidler, and Subramanian (2001); Gordon (2018).

Global Development Issues and Solution Strategies

Category	Issue	Team liaisons	Continuous communication	Architectural principles	Incremental integration	Rational task assignment	Common tools and repositories	Common work products	Internat'l support contracts	Centralized bug reporting	Use of lessons learned	Don't impose process	Complete life cycle
Loss of communication richness	Geographical distance	X	X			X	X						
	Time zone differences	X	X	X	X	X	X						
	Domain expertise	X	X	X		X					X		
	Emergent technology	X	X	X	X	X							X
Coordination breakdown	Software integration	X	X	X	X	X							X
	Software conf. mngt.						X	X					
Geographical dispersion	Vendor support		X						X	X	X		
	Governmental issues										X		
Loss of "teamness"	Development process	X	X		X		X	X			X	X	X
Cultural differences	Local impression of remote teams	X	X								X		

Figure 7.4 Global project teams: problems and solutions. *Adapted from:* Battin, Crocker, Kreidler, and Subramanian (2001).

Capital Resources

Capital resources can be thought of as the tools and infrastructure used to produce other goods and services. Therefore, for the purposes of this section, we will group infrastructure and materials into the broader category of capital resources. In information systems development projects, both the development software and the technological platform on which the software resides are capital resources. As an example, if a big data project required the IBM SPSS analytics software, that software would be considered a capital resource. Similarly, if that software resided on an HP high performance computing server, the server also would be a capital resource. Even the software specifically used to organize project activities—such as Microsoft Project—might be regarded as a capital resource. Notably, in some instances, technology-related capital resources might be located outside the company itself, supplied through third-party providers. Acquiring necessary project materials or services from outside the company is the focus of Chapter 10, which deals with managing project procurement. Other types of capital resources more traditionally associated with non-IS projects, such as team meeting facilities, could also be part of the IS project environment.

Of specific interest for project teams is the growing use of a formal project management office (PMO). As defined in Chapter 2, a PMO is a dedicated part of the organization—frequently consisting of support personnel and a physical facility—whose purpose is to focus on various aspects of project management. The PMO serves as a center of excellence that fosters good project management practices. The PMO may provide a variety of benefits to project teams working on projects at any one time in the organization, including help with methodologies for planning or controlling project activities. In some instances, project managers are members of the PMO and are then assigned to new projects as they are launched.

The management of capital resources is particularly important when considering opportunity costs. **Opportunity costs** are a measure of the alternative opportunities forgone in the choice of one good or activity over others. Because organizations are typically involved in multiple projects and because buildings, technology, and other available infrastructure may sometimes be used by only one project at a time, organizations must decide how to use these limited available capital resources (see Figure 7.5). During project initiation—and specifically the selection process—project managers must clearly identify their capital resource needs to facilitate project selection decisions.

So far this discussion of capital resources has focused on how best to *use* capital resources to facilitate project completion and on the role of capital resource needs during project selection. However, capital resources can also be the goal of projects. Questions about the organization's focus must be carefully considered for projects designed to update technology. Potential questions include: How best can we improve our technology to support our business objectives? What changes to our existing infrastructure will we need to make in order to install the new technology? How much risk will the organization be taking in changing the capital resources? The organization and its leadership need to consider these questions and many others before making changes to the existing infrastructure.

An Overview of Managing Project Resources

The efficient and effective use of resources can often make or break a project. Because resources are limited, some might be hard to obtain (such as a systems analyst with specialized knowledge about a particular industry), expensive (such as a supercomputer with customized processors necessary for studying genetic diseases), or both (such as

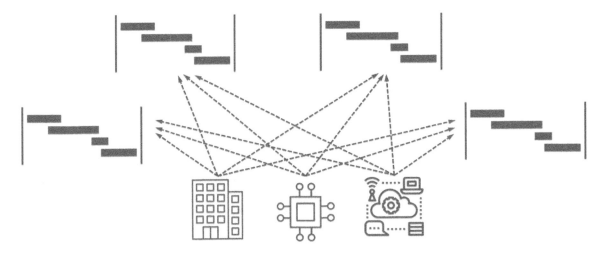

Figure 7.5 Managing information systems capital resources

highly skilled programmers). Consequently, managing project resources is an important part of the planning and execution stages of any project. In the following sections, you will learn more about the importance of managing resources, as well as the implications of failures and successes.

The Importance of Managing Resources

The efficient use of project resources should be a primary goal for every project manager because the allocation of resources can have a major influence on project schedules. Of specific concern are scarce resources because their allocation can easily scuttle the project schedule. For example, if a scarce resource, such as a limited number of experienced programmers, is not carefully allocated, critical project activities might be delayed.

Project resources can influence many of the key knowledge areas, such as project time, cost, quality, and risk management. In terms of Project Schedule Management, discussed both in Chapter 6 and the current chapter, resource allocation plays a large role in determining activity duration. For example, a particular task in a project—say, requirements gathering—could have a number of different durations, depending on the number of people allocated to the task and their skills. Project resources also influence Project Cost Management, discussed in Chapter 8. Resources obviously have costs, and how they are allocated impacts the project's budget. The resources used to complete tasks may also influence the quality of project deliverables. Finally, if specific resources to be used during the project are new, project risk may be increased.

Resources affect both the time to complete a project and its cost. If, because of poor planning, any necessary resources are unavailable for a task on a project's critical path, the entire project may be delayed. To correct the error, the project manager may assign additional resources to a task to try to get back on schedule; this is known as *crashing* and will be discussed later. However, even if the project's schedule gets back on track, crashing may well result in higher costs because the project manager must now cover the expenses of recruiting more people or paying overtime. Because poor resource planning is seldom an isolated incident, the likely result is a project that will run over budget and take longer than anticipated to complete.

In contrast, successful projects are usually defined by the fact that they come in at or under budget, meet their deadlines, and provide the needed functionality for the stakeholders (i.e., the benefits are delivered).

Managing Resources and the Project Life Cycle

When planning a project, project managers first decide on the deliverables of the project and the activities needed to produce them. Once they have determined the best sequence for the activities, they estimate the resources needed. The combination of resource needs and resource availability helps determine the time needed to complete the individual activities, as well as the entire project. Although the sequence of activities can be determined without considering the resources, the time needed to complete these activities, as well as the entire project, depends on the resources' availability. To address this need, project management software can be used to track and allocate resources.

Managing resources should be considered during the initiation, planning, execution, control, and close-out phases of the project's life cycle. Some examples of activities in each of these phases follow. During initiation, for instance, resources critical to the project should be considered when deciding which type of project to pursue. One selection criterion might be the availability of new technologies. During the planning phase, schedules should be developed with specific resources in mind, and scarce resources must be carefully allocated. During a project's execution phase, resource reallocation may become necessary as the project unfolds to protect the project schedule. During project control, managers need to constantly monitor the allocation and use of resources to facilitate any approved project changes. Finally, during project close-out, purchased resources and any outstanding contracts must be settled. Any discrepancies between purchased materials and delivered materials must be identified, and steps must be taken to settle those discrepancies.

Duration versus Effort

Effort
Actual time spent working on an activity.

Before jumping into the discussion of techniques for resource and duration estimating, we need to clarify the distinction between duration and effort. When completing an activity, the "doers" expend a certain amount of effort. **Effort** is the actual time required to perform an activity, not accounting for any breaks, meetings, and the like. For example, designing an interface might take eight hours of effort, so a programmer could finish the activity in one day. If, however, the programmer has to attend meetings during the day, she might need two or three days to complete the task. Although the effort would still be eight hours, the duration from start to finish for that task would be two

Duration
Elapsed time between the start and finish of an activity.

or three days. Thus **duration** is the time that elapses between the start and the finish of an activity, including any interruptions. When planning a project, managers have to take into account the number of people working on a task, potential interruptions, and the like to estimate the duration for each individual activity. In the next section, we examine several specific techniques for managing project resources.

Tips from the Pros: Managing Successful Big Data Projects

With the increasing ability to capture and analyze massive amounts of data, companies have been looking for ways to harness these data to gain and sustain competitive advantage. As other IS projects, big data projects are not without challenge, and many big data projects are not as successful as they could be. Professor Tom Davenport has examined some of the reasons that make big data projects successful.

1. *Technology.* As the handling and analysis of big data is often challenging when using traditional technologies, many big data projects circle around big-data specific technologies, including Python, Hadoop, or Hive. Yet surprisingly, the newest technologies are not necessarily what makes a big data project successful. Instead, many established companies can draw on valuable legacy technologies and skills for successfully implementing big data projects: Tom Davenport found that companies that leverage existing technologies and skills—ranging from data warehouse environments to SPSS, SAS, or R—are quicker in creating value through big data projects.

2. *People.* Whereas the market for talents possessing expertise in the newest big data technologies is red hot, Davenport found that forming teams from diverse backgrounds (and training employees on necessary skills) can matter more than hiring entirely new staff.

3. *Change management.* By nature, many big data projects have a tremendous impact on how people conduct their work; at times, work processes are being increasingly monitored,
and at other times, frontline workers have to learn entirely new processes. To get the most benefits from big data projects, it is thus essential to focus on human issues and to get the buy-in from those who are most affected by the new systems.

4. *Business objectives.* Many companies have data and are looking for a problem to solve with it. Those projects tend to be doomed to failure, often resulting in unsuccessful "fishing expeditions." As with any IS project, clear business objectives should drive any big data project.

5. *Project management.* Finally, big data projects need to focus on sound project management practices, ranging from getting executive sponsorship to engaging stakeholders throughout the process.

Finally, Davenport reminds us that we often hear about successful big data projects, but many big data projects fail. As our understanding of big data technologies is still evolving, failure is often an inevitable part of embarking on big data projects, and often successful big data projects depend on a final component—luck.

Based on: Davenport (2014).

Techniques for Managing Resources and Project Duration

When scheduling a project, managers can employ a wide variety of tools and techniques to facilitate resource management. These techniques are primarily used to estimate the resource needs associated with project activities, estimate the duration of the activities, and finally, develop the schedule. In Chapter 3, you learned how to develop and manage project teams; in Chapter 6, you learned how to define the project's deliverables and the associated activities, as well as how to define the sequence of these activities. Now you will learn how to estimate the resources and time needed, as well as how to tie everything together to create the project schedule. In Chapter 12, we will discuss the last aspect of project resource management—namely, how to control the resources.

Plan Resource Management

Before the project manager can begin estimating resources, it is important to develop a sound plan on how resources will be managed throughout the project life cycle. In other words, the project team needs to have a plan on how human and other resources will be estimated, acquired, and managed throughout the project. The *Plan Resource Management* process uses as inputs the project plan, the quality management plan (discussed in Chapter 8), the scope baseline, project documents (such as the project schedule, the requirements documentation, and the risk and stakeholder registers, while considering various enterprise environmental factors and organizational process assets. Using expert judgment, meetings, and various data representation formats, the project manager can create the resource management plan, which details how physical and human resources will be identified and acquired, as well as how human resources will be managed, including the roles and responsibilities, training, team development, and so on; further, this process will lead to the development of the team charter, as well as updates to the project's assumption log and resource-related components of the risk register (a formal listing of identified risks).

Estimate Activity Resources

The goal of the *Estimate Activity Resources* process, an aspect of the *PMBOK*'s Project Resource Management knowledge area, is to estimate the resources needed for each activity so they can be deployed in the most effective manner. In some instances, assigning more resources can speed the completion of activities, but in others, assigning more resources will actually hinder progress because of increased communication and coordination efforts. The following sections discuss how to estimate the resources needed and how to estimate the project's duration based on these estimates.

Estimate Activity Resources—Inputs

As Figure 7.6 shows, project managers rely on a wide variety of different inputs for the *Estimate Activity Resources* process. First, the resource management plan and the scope baseline give overall guidelines for managing resources and for identifying resource needs. In addition, they use outputs from prior stages of project planning. For example, the activity list and activity attributes identified during the activity definition phase help estimate the resources needed. Likewise, the project manager draws on the assumption log, cost estimates, and the risk register. As Figure 7.7 shows, the resource calendar enables the project manager to match resource needs with resource availability. In other words, a project manager has to know which resources she can draw upon before deciding on which resources to use. Finally, as in most processes, managers use enterprise environmental factors (such as resource location and availability) and organizational process assets (such as historical information from prior projects) to establish initial activity sequences and assign and manage resources. The different tools and techniques used for resource estimating, as well as the outputs, will be covered in the following sections.

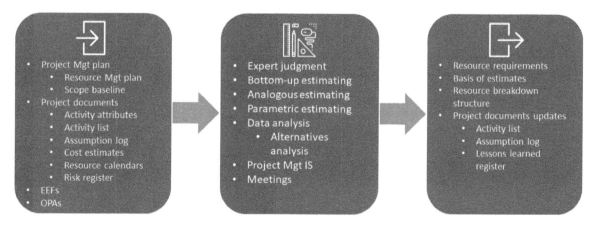

Figure 7.6   The *PMBOK* (6th ed.) *Estimate Activity Resources* process

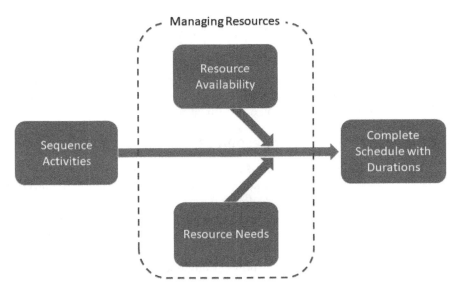

Figure 7.7 Project scheduling and managing resources

Estimate Activity Resources—Tools and Techniques

Although project managers can choose from among a variety of tools and techniques, they should never depend solely on the results of just one technique for estimating project resources. Rather, they should use a combination of estimation techniques (see Figure 7.8). If the results of these techniques converge, the project manager can be fairly confident about the accuracy of the resource estimates. Whether using one or several techniques to estimate resource needs, the project manager should avoid having to give quick estimates based on a gut feeling. Because such estimates will most likely be inaccurate, the project manager should always employ the techniques described as follows before providing any estimate.

Expert judgment
Estimation based on the experience of one or more experts on the particular activity or project.

One of the primary tools of project resource estimating is **expert judgment**. Usually, experts can give valuable inputs into estimating resource needs. In most cases, the "doers" can give very precise estimates about the resources needed. In an information systems project, the database administrator can give good estimates about how long it takes to create certain database queries, and a programmer can give good estimates about how long it takes to code common modules. However, the estimates should not be based solely on recollections of prior projects or activities, which will most likely lead to biased estimates because people often have a hard time remembering exact details. Rather, a combination of expert judgment and data (e.g., historical data recorded from prior projects) is preferable.

Published estimating data
Publicly available data from specific activities carried out on previous projects that may be used to more accurately estimate resource needs.

Another source of data about resource needs is **published estimating data** available from market research companies, a form of benchmarking. These companies gather and analyze research needs for a variety of projects in a variety of industries. When planning to implement a new cloud-based ERP system, for example, you can obtain benchmarking data both from ERP vendors and from independent organizations to help prepare estimates of resources needed. Usually these data are based on a number of different companies, so you can get a good overview of average, minimum, or maximum resource needs. These data also help benchmark one's resource needs against those of direct competitors or industry leaders.

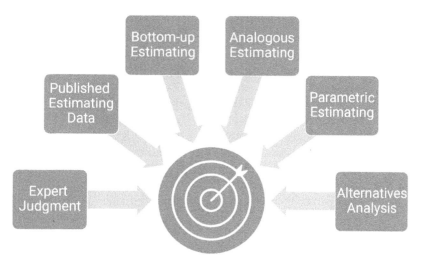

Figure 7.8   Increasing accuracy of resource estimates

Bottom-up estimating
An estimating technique in which estimates are made at the activity level, and then aggregated to arrive at an overall estimate.

Bottom-up estimating is a technique applied when the resource needs of a component cannot be easily estimated. This is often the case if the component itself is fairly complex. In this instance, the component should be decomposed further until the activity level is reached where reasonable estimates can be provided. If a component for an ERP system consists of, say, the user interface for the payroll module, it might be hard to estimate the resources needed to complete this deliverable; if so, the deliverable can be further decomposed into developing the individual screens, for which it is easier to estimate the resources needed. These lower-level estimates can then be combined into an estimate for the deliverable itself.

Analogous estimating
The estimation of activities' costs, durations, or resource requirements based on historical data of similar activities.

Analogous estimating is simply using the resource needs of a similar activity as a basis for estimating the current activity. For information systems development projects, analogous estimating can be used for standard tasks such as building interfaces. Historical data or expert judgment can be used to estimate the resource requirements of these activities because components like these are often fairly standardized and thus take the same amounts of time to complete. In addition to company historical data, published data (from past projects done in the company) about durations of similar activities can be used.

Parametric estimating
The estimation of activities' costs, durations, or resource requirements based on known relationships and project parameters.

Parametric estimating is a quantitatively based estimation technique that calculates durations, costs, or resource requirements based on based on known relationships and project parameters. In some cases, the number of lines of code a programmer generates in a normal workday can be used in conjunction with the number of lines of code estimated for a given activity to determine how many coders are needed to finish the activity within given time constraints. Note that given the increasing complexity of software projects, estimating lines of code is typically not used anymore, and project managers prefer other ways of estimating resource needs.

Alternatives analysis
An estimating technique in which trade-offs between the time needed, the resources invested, and the desired quality of the final deliverable are examined.

When estimating activity resources, the results of these methods should be carefully analyzed, typically using some form of **alternatives analysis**. Almost any activity requires a trade-off between the time needed, the resources invested, and the desired quality of the final deliverable. For example, assigning more human resources to a project might speed completion time but at tremendously higher costs; further, quality might be inconsistent across the people working on the activity. On the other hand, fewer people might still be able to complete the activity within the desired time frame but might introduce more errors because of time pressure. Other times, a project manager might realize that outsourcing the activity is the most efficient solution. Carefully analyzing alternatives helps a project manager make optimal choices, given the available resources and desired outcomes.

It should be noted that companies will use a variety of techniques to arrive at their estimations. Benchmarking against competitors is a common practice. For example, competing automakers might benchmark their time from conception to market. Techniques utilizing project team members, such as brainstorming sessions or mind mapping, might also be useful in gathering valuable information about expected project resource requirements.

As part of the project management information system, project management software such as Microsoft Project can facilitate estimating resource needs and matching those needs with resource availability and costs. One tool included in Microsoft Project is a resource calendar that can be used to assign resources or resource groups to specific activities. These calendars help the project manager by displaying whether a resource is available or might be tied up by a different activity. Further, costs can be assigned to the different resources, which helps in conducting alternatives analyses. To specify the details about the different resources, a Resource Sheet view lets you specify a name for each resource, as well as attributes such as type, standard and overtime rate, cost/use, and the like. Other views such as Resource Usage display the resource allocation in an easy-to-use way.

All of these techniques, however, are only as good as the inputs into the resource estimating process. In other words, if the activities are not clearly defined, the resource estimates will most likely be inaccurate, leading to frustrated clients and project managers. There has to be a clear, mutual understanding of project scope, the work packages that make up that scope, and the activities that are required for each work package before an accurate estimate can be made.

Estimate Activity Resources—Outputs

The primary output of the *Estimate Activity Resources* process (see Figure 7.6) is a detailed listing of the resource requirements (both types and quantities needed) for the individual activities. Often, the resource needs for different activities are combined to represent the resource needs for each WBS work package. The **activity resource requirements** can be very detailed and should include any assumptions made during the estimation process. In other words, the basis of the estimates should be carefully captured, including how the estimates were derived, any assumptions made, confidence levels, and so on. That way, if a certain assumption does not hold, the project manager immediately knows that the schedule has to be adjusted accordingly. These resource requirements will be an important input into the *Develop Schedule* process discussed later.

Activity resource requirements
A very detailed listing of the resource requirements for the individual activities.

Resource breakdown structure
A hierarchical, graphical representation of all needed resources ordered by type or category.

To represent the resources in an easy-to-use format, a **resource breakdown structure** (RBS) is created. Analogous to a product breakdown structure or a work breakdown structure, an RBS presents all needed resources hierarchically, usually ordered by type or category. An RBS helps visualize the different types of resources needed for a project. The RBS is useful in roll-up reporting, for instance, where the project manager wants to show all of the resources (both human and capital) necessary for completing various components of a project. As an example, level 0 of a WBS represents the entire scope of a project. The equivalent level in an RBS would then list all resources necessary for the entire project. At a lower level of the WBS, the corresponding RBS might illustrate those resources necessary to complete the particular work package(s) associated with a major component of the project (e.g., development of the user interface for a new system).

Finally, the *Define Activities* process (remember, that means defining all the activities necessary to create a particular project deliverable) has resulted in preliminary activity attributes, such as predecessors, successors, and constraints. Correspondingly, the *Estimate Activity Resources* process results in updates to project documents. The resources needed to carry out the activities estimated in the present stage also become part of a more refined set of activity attributes that can now be used to create more accurate schedules. Further, in case the process of estimating resources yields additional changes to the activities (e.g., the realization that additional resources may be necessary to carry out an activity), such changes will be incorporated into updated activity attributes. Needless to say, all changes must be approved following the project's change control guidelines.

Acquire Resources

In order to successfully complete the project, an important process is *Acquire Resources*. While we have covered human resources-related aspects in Chapter 3, and will cover project procurement in Chapter 10, acquiring human and physical resources takes place throughout the different phases of the project. When acquiring resources, the project manager typically has to balance factors such as availability and costs of resources, as well as factors such as ability or attitude for team resources. An important output of this process is the **resource calendar**, which displays the availability of the different resources. For human resources, a resource calendar specifies working and nonworking days, such as weekends or holidays. A project manager can use resource calendars to quickly identify whether specific resources are idle (and available) or occupied by another task. Every work resource should have its own calendar, which can be specified in many types of project management software.

Estimate Activity Durations

Another aspect of the activities that needs to be estimated is the activity durations. The **Estimate Activity Durations** process (see Figure 7.9) generally involves using both project scope and resource information to estimate the duration of the project activities. The people with the greatest knowledge of the specific activity are most often called on to approve the estimation. The duration estimates will then be combined with the activity sequencing to determine the duration of the entire project, as well as to identify the critical path. As with all project planning activities, activity duration estimations become more precise as the project progresses (recall the cone of uncertainty discussed in Chapter 6) because more detailed information is usually available during later stages of the project.

As Figure 7.9 shows, inputs for this phase include the scope baseline and schedule management plan, the activity list, attributes, team assignments, the resource breakdown structure, resource requirements, and the resource calendar, in addition to the risk register (a formal listing of identified risks). Finally, enterprise environmental factors (such as upcoming laws or regulations) and organizational process assets (such as historical information) serve as inputs to the activity duration estimation. Some of the inputs for the activity duration estimation were also inputs for or outputs from other processes. In those cases, we will only briefly mention their characteristics.

Resource calendar
A specific type of project calendar that is used to track the hours when certain resources are available.

Estimate Activity Durations
The process of estimating the duration of the project activities using both project scope and resource information.

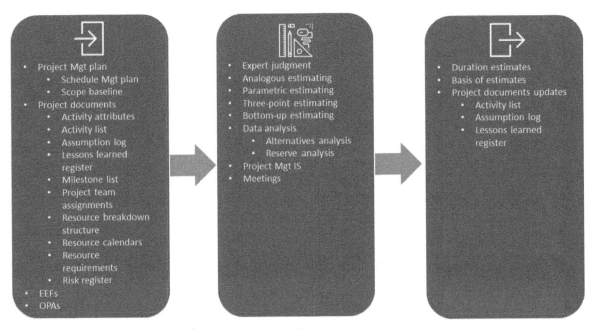

Figure 7.9 The *PMBOK* (6th ed.) *Estimate Activity Durations* process

Estimate Activity Durations—Inputs

The primary inputs of this process, then, are the activity list, associated attributes, and activity resource requirements. An initial estimate of these resource requirements has been determined during the *Estimate Activity Resources* process. The resource calendar (produced during the *Acquire Resources* process) specifies the availability of the different resources—that is, it specifies the times when the resources are available for a certain task. The scope of the project is captured in the scope baseline and is used as an input to keep the focus on the project's activities. Organizational process assets (such as templates, lessons learned, or past project files) can assist in the *Estimate Activity Durations* process. These can be used to better estimate activity durations and may consist of company historical documents as well as project team members' knowledge gained during previous projects. The risk register (described in Chapter 9) captures the different activities' risks, taking into consideration those that have a high probability of impacting the project schedule.

Reassessments related to calculating activity duration can also occur at this point. For instance, if it appears that an activity's duration is going to be too long, more resources could be assigned. As an example, the time needed to code an initial prototype can be greatly reduced by the number of programmers assigned to the task. This might require adding new resources to the project, the creation of a new resource calendar, or some similar measure. The caveat, of course, is that at some point, merely adding programmers will not shorten the task duration because the number of programming assignments is limited. The point is clear, however, that the amount of resources allocated to a given task will surely influence its duration.

Estimate Activity Durations—Tools and Techniques

Tools and techniques used during the *Estimate Activity Durations* process include expert judgment, analogous estimating, quantitatively based duration estimating (such

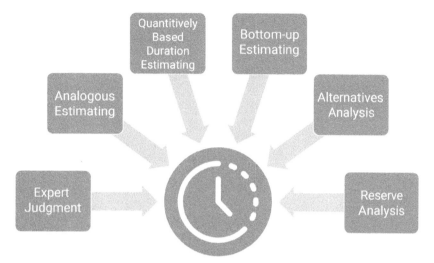

Figure 7.10 *Estimate Activity Durations* techniques

as parametric estimating or three-point estimating), bottom-up estimating, alternatives analysis, and reserve analysis (see Figure 7.10). As with resource estimating, using several techniques to estimate activity duration, as opposed to relying on only one, can increase the overall accuracy of any estimates. Next, each of these techniques is discussed in more detail.

Expert judgment, previously mentioned under the activity definition process, can be used as a means to better estimate activities' durations and their need for specific resources. As with its use during activity definition, care should be taken, for expert judgment can rely on the subjective opinion of project participants. While programmers might be able to give a fairly accurate estimate of how long it takes to write a certain number of lines of code, they might not be able to give accurate estimates of less common tasks.

As discussed earlier, bottom-up estimating is used when estimating durations for activities associated with complex components, where durations are difficult to estimate. Analogous estimating is simply using the duration of a similar activity as a basis for estimating the current activity. Further, the duration of an activity can be estimated using certain parameters, such as the amount of time it takes to program a certain number of lines of code. **Three-point estimates** can increase accuracy by accounting for optimistic, pessimistic, and most likely estimates. To arrive at an accurate estimate, these three estimates are averaged (i.e., using a triangular distribution), taking into consideration the risk involved in completing the activities.

If a high risk is associated with the activity, the estimate will lean toward the pessimistic end. **PERT** analysis is a specific form of three-point estimation, where probabilistic time estimates are applied to the optimistic, pessimistic, and most likely estimates. In contrast to using equal weights for optimistic, pessimistic, and most likely estimates, PERT uses a weighted average method. As shown in Figure 7.11, the most likely estimate is weighted by a factor of four, with the optimistic and pessimistic estimates having a weighting of one. People frequently mistakenly refer to something called a PERT chart, which in reality is an activity on node network diagram (discussed in Chapter 6). However, PERT is not a chart, but rather a mathematical technique used

Three-point estimates
The estimation of activities' durations by averaging the optimistic, pessimistic, and most likely estimates.

PERT
A specific form of three-point estimation that uses weighted average method to estimate activity durations.

$$PERT\ Weighted\ Average = \frac{optimistic\ time + 4 \times most\ likely\ time + pessimistic\ time}{6}$$

Example:
Optimistic time: 8 days
Most likely time: 10 days
Pessimistic time: 24 days

$$PERT\ Weighted\ Average = \frac{8\ days + 4 \times 10\ days + 24\ days}{6} = 12\ days$$

Figure 7.11 PERT analysis

to estimate task or project duration. Nonetheless, in many organizations the use of the term *PERT chart* to refer to an activity on node network diagram is common.

Reserve analysis
Technique used to establish contingency reserves during a project to guard against potential risk.

Reserve analysis considers the different activities to establish reserve times (basically, time set aside as a reserve in case activity durations don't match the plan) within a project schedule for the purpose of guarding against potential risks to the schedule. In the case of reserve time, any buffer in the project schedule should be documented and accounted for.

Typically, project managers use meetings and various decision-making techniques to arrive at better estimates of activity durations. For example, a widely used technique is brainstorming, where participants are charged with generating ideas without fear of group censure. A brainstorming session on estimating a project's duration, or possible problems that might be encountered, can serve as valuable input in the final estimation. Using mind mapping, visual representation of tasks and problems may help the project team come up with more accurate project representations and associated durations.

Estimate Activity Durations—Outputs

The outputs of the *Estimate Activity Durations* process are activity duration estimates (as part of updates to the activity attributes; refer back to Figure 7.9). Duration estimates associated with activities can be either fixed-point or range estimates. Often, customers desire a very precise, fixed-point estimate of the time needed to complete an activity. However, especially during the early stages of a project, it is frequently very difficult to give precise estimates unless the project team has done very similar projects in the past. The prudent project manager should try to provide range rather than point estimates. Further, the estimates should be precise only to the degree possible. In other words, if a project manager can give an estimate only within ±50 percent, she should not try to provide a ±10 percent estimate because this will lead to dissatisfaction (as well as other complications) if the actual time falls outside the range of the estimate (especially at the upper end). Usually, range estimates are expressed as time periods needed to complete the task, such as 6 months ±2 weeks.

Providing optimistic, pessimistic, and most likely estimates will give the customer a good picture of the different scenarios. These different estimates can be further supported by the likelihood of finishing the activity in the different times; for example, the project manager can say that there is a 50 percent chance of finishing the activity in ten days, a 30 percent chance of finishing in eight days, and a 20 percent chance of finishing in twelve days. As estimates become more precise during the course of the project (recall the cone of uncertainty), the customer can be provided with updated information. No matter how precise the estimates are, the project manager should take great care to continually provide the customer with the refined estimates; this way, the customer is in the loop and aware of any possible changes to the project's schedule.

As with other estimating processes, it is important to carefully record the basis of the estimates, including how the estimates were derived, what assumptions were made, or what constraints were considered. This will allow the project manager to revisit the estimates if necessary when developing the project schedule.

Develop Schedule

Develop Schedule
The process of determining start and finish dates for project activities.

Develop Schedule is an iterative process designed to determine start and finish dates for project activities. Just as activity sequencing (discussed in Chapter 6), activity durations are necessary to determine the final project schedule. During the process of schedule development, the activity duration estimates, in combination with the activity sequences, are used to establish the final project schedule, a critical component of the schedule baseline used to track the project's progress.

Develop Schedule—Inputs

Inputs to the *Develop Schedule* process include the schedule management plan, the scope baseline, project network diagrams, the activity list, activity attributes, activity duration estimates, resource requirements, resource calendars, the risk register, agreements from procurement, as well as enterprise environmental factors and organizational process assets (see Figure 7.12). Most of these inputs have been discussed in prior sections and will thus be mentioned only briefly.

As important input, the schedule management plan specifies policies such as working and nonworking days, or what hours and time periods are available for work scheduling. For example, is the project based on an eight-hour-a-day, forty-hour workweek

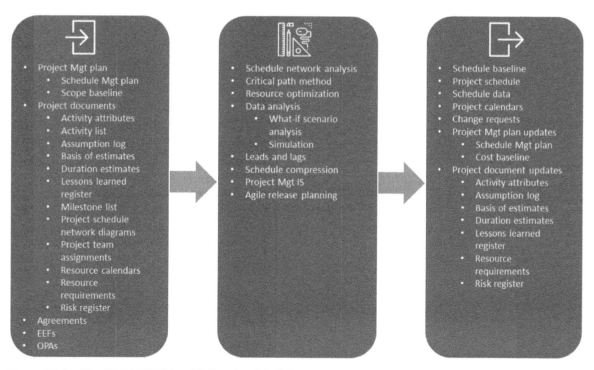

Figure 7.12 The *PMBOK* (6th ed.) *Develop Schedule* process

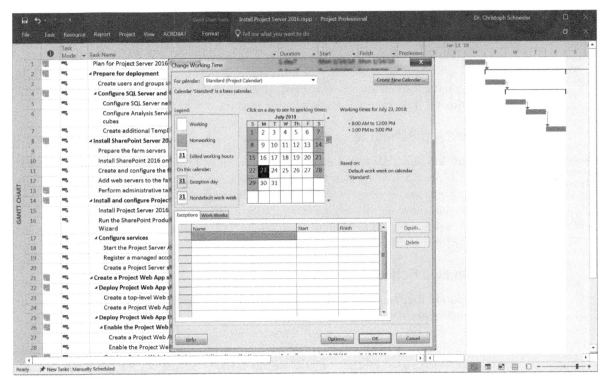

Figure 7.13 Changing working time in Microsoft Project 2016

or on a ten-hour-a-day, four-day workweek? Is overtime available, and if so, how much and how will it be allocated? Most software makes these working-time decisions easy to implement by allowing broad-level changes to organizational asset availability (i.e., put in holidays, personal time off, overtime, standard working time, and specified work weeks). Software such as Microsoft Project can be used to record and display resource availability information (see Figure 7.13).

The scope baseline presents the scope of the entire project and the assumption log details any constraints or assumptions that can affect the project's schedule. In terms of schedule development, constraints are usually of two types—imposed dates and milestones. **Imposed dates** are dates that are imposed to meet some type of development deadline. For example, a new information systems rollout may need to be in effect by a certain date for the company to keep its first-mover strategic advantage. Another example would be a date imposed by an environmental agency that the company must meet in order to remain in business. The most common types of such constraints are "start no earlier than" and "finish no later than" (see precedence relationships in Chapter 6 for a more comprehensive explanation). These and other constraint types are available in Microsoft Project (see Figure 7.14), which has a dropdown box containing all available constraint types. As defined in Chapter 6, milestones are dates in the schedule that are meaningful for the completion of specific sets of project events. Milestones are often set by senior management and usually cannot be changed. In many types of project management software, a milestone is represented by entering a task with a duration of zero.

The next inputs, including the activity list (which also includes activity attributes), activity duration estimates, project schedule network diagrams, activity resource requirements, and the resource calendar, were discussed previously. The risk register (as part

Imposed dates
Dates imposed to meet some type of development deadline.

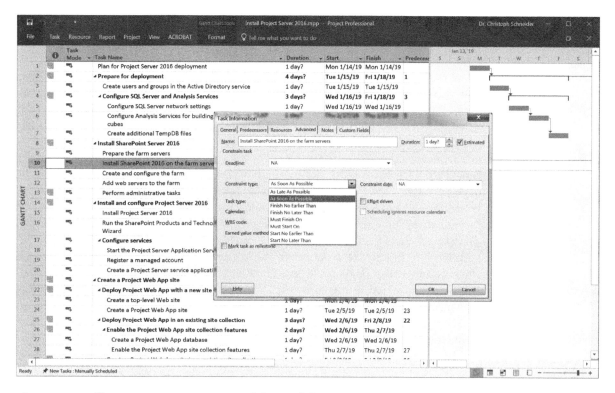

Figure 7.14   Choosing constraint types in Microsoft Project 2016

of the project management plan) specifies how control measures will be implemented to identify potential risks to the project schedule. For example, if the risk is high that a new mainframe computer will not be installed on time, this might influence the project schedule, and more contingency reserve (discussed earlier in this chapter) should be planned for this activity.

Develop Schedule—Tools and Techniques

Schedule network analysis
The process of calculating expected, early, and late start and finish dates of a project.

Dealing with the time component of project scheduling—calculating the expected start and finish dates, as well as early or late start and finish dates of project activities—is referred to as **schedule network analysis** (refer back to Figure 7.13). Schedule network analysis techniques aid managers in determining when activities can be performed, given resources and constraints. Some techniques require certain adjustments to the network diagrams. Specifically, the network diagrams have to be analyzed for any errors in the network, such as network loops (paths that follow through the same node more than once) or open ends (activities that do not have a successor). The following sections discuss the different techniques, as well as the use of project management software for schedule development.

One often-used technique is the critical path method (CPM), a network analysis technique that determines the sequence of task activities that directly affect the completion of a project. Introduced in Chapter 2, a project's critical path is the longest path through a network diagram that illustrates the shortest amount of time in which a project can be completed. While this definition may sound confusing, just remember that the purpose of the critical path is to establish how quickly a project can be completed given the tasks, durations, and dependencies illustrated in the schedule network diagram.

Figure 7.15 illustrates the concept of the critical path. In the figure, the critical path includes the activities A, E, G, and I. Therefore, if any of these activities (termed **critical activities**) is delayed, the completion of the entire project will be delayed because the overall time of the critical path increases. Activities not on the critical path can be delayed (to some extent) without affecting the duration of the entire project. Accordingly, these activities contain slack time (while Microsoft Project uses the term *slack*, others, such as the PMI, use the term *float*). In this figure, Path 4 has one day's slack time; Path 5 has two days' slack time, Path 6 has three days' slack time; Path 1 has four days' slack time; and Path 2 has six days' slack time; thus the activities on Path 2 can be delayed by a maximum of six days before the overall project schedule is affected (note that this only relates to the overall paths, rather than the individual activities). To determine a project's critical path, the durations of all activities on each individual path have to be added; the path with the longest overall duration is the critical path (note that there can be multiple critical paths). In Microsoft Project, the critical path is highlighted in red in the Network Diagram view (see Figure 7.16). Using project management software, the project team members do not have to do tedious calculations to determine the critical path, but it is critical that they understand the concept. Any changes in durations of critical activities will be reflected in the critical path.

The critical path method uses the concepts of **free float** (free slack) and **total float** (total slack) to determine the late and early completion times of a project. Described briefly in Chapter 2, free float is the time an activity can be delayed without affecting the immediately following activity; total float, in contrast, is the time an activity can be delayed without affecting the overall completion date of a project. Free float is only found in noncritical paths because any increase in duration of the activities in the critical path directly affects a project's schedule. The critical path is thus a path that has zero or negative total float. If a network path is not a critical path, it can have positive float; a delay in completion of one activity does not necessarily affect the completion date of the entire project. The existence of positive total float implies that somewhere in the

Critical activity
Any activity on the critical path.

Free float (free slack)
The time an activity can be delayed without affecting the immediately following activity.

Total float (total slack)
The time an activity can be delayed without affecting the overall completion date of a project.

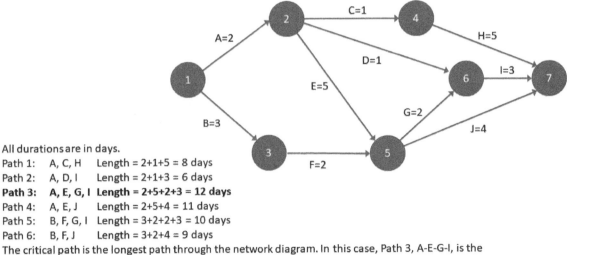

All durations are in days.
Path 1: A, C, H   Length = 2+1+5 = 8 days
Path 2: A, D, I   Length = 2+1+3 = 6 days
Path 3: A, E, G, I Length = 2+5+2+3 = 12 days
Path 4: A, E, J   Length = 2+5+4 = 11 days
Path 5: B, F, G, I Length = 3+2+2+3 = 10 days
Path 6: B, F, J   Length = 3+2+4 = 9 days
The critical path is the longest path through the network diagram. In this case, Path 3, A-E-G-I, is the longest path so it is the critical path for this project.

Figure 7.15   Concept of the critical path

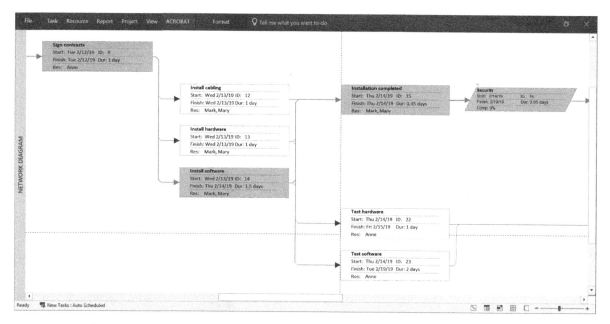

Figure 7.16 Critical path displayed in Microsoft Project 2016

project there is free float—that is, at least one activity can be delayed without affecting the early start date of its immediate successor.

Although the slack times can be calculated by doing a forward pass (to determine the early start and early finish dates) and a backward pass (to determine the late start and late finish dates) through a network diagram, doing so is tedious. Consequently, most project managers use project management software such as Microsoft Project for this process; in addition to greater ease of use, the software can provide real-time updates to any changes in the project schedule. In the Gantt chart view of Microsoft Project, slack can be presented, including task names, early and late start and finish dates, and free and total slack for the individual activities (see Figure 7.17). An update to the duration of any activity immediately updates the start and finish dates, as well as the slack times.

Another factor to consider during schedule network analysis is the use of leads and lags. In the activity sequencing stage, the leads and lags of the different activities have been established. To review, a lead is the time between the start of one activity and the start of an overlapping activity; a lag is the time between the finish of one activity and the start of a succeeding activity. As these leads and lags can significantly influence the schedule, their use should be carefully double-checked to minimize potential delays.

Facing resource constraints, project managers employ resource optimization techniques such as resource leveling or resource smoothing. **Resource leveling** is any form of network analysis where resource management issues drive scheduling decisions. This process involves rescheduling activities so that resource requirements for any particular phase of a project do not exceed the availability of those resources. As an example, in a particular software development environment, there may be only one person who has the skill set or knowledge needed to complete particular aspects of the development process. If multiple activities requiring that particular developer's skills were originally scheduled at the same time, resource leveling would be used to change the schedule so

Resource leveling
Any form of network analysis where resource management issues drive scheduling decisions.

WBS	Task Name	Duration	Start	Finish	Predecessors	Resource Names	Free Slack	Total Slack
1	⊿ Analysis	9 days	Mon 1/14/19	Thu 1/24/19			0 days	0 days
1.1	Document current evironment	4 days	Mon 1/14/19	Thu 1/17/19		Anne	0 days	0 days
1.2	Conduct needs analysis	1 wk	Fri 1/18/19	Thu 1/24/19	2	Joe	0 wks	0 wks
1.3	Analysis completed	0 days	Thu 1/24/19	Thu 1/24/19	3	Mark	0 days	0 days
2	⊿ Design	12 days	Fri 1/25/19	Mon 2/11/19			0 days	0 days
2.1	Build Request for Proposal	4 days	Fri 1/25/19	Wed 1/30/19	3	Mary	0 days	0 days
2.2	Gather vendor bids	1 wk	Thu 1/31/19	Wed 2/6/19	6	Anne	0 wks	0 wks
2.3	Choose vendors	2 days	Thu 2/7/19	Fri 2/8/19	7	Kit	0 days	0 days
2.4	Sign contracts	1 day	Mon 2/11/19	Mon 2/11/19	8	Anne	0 days	0 days
3	⊿ Installation	1.5 days	Tue 2/12/19	Wed 2/13/19	5		0 days	0 days
3.1	Install cabling	1 day	Tue 2/12/19	Tue 2/12/19	9	Mark,Mary	0.5 days	0.5 days
3.2	Install hardware	1 day	Tue 2/12/19	Tue 2/12/19	9	Mark,Mary	0.5 days	0.5 days
3.3	Install software	1.5 days	Tue 2/12/19	Wed 2/13/19	9	Mark,Mary	0 days	0 days
3.4	Installation completed	0 days	Wed 2/13/19	Wed 2/13/19	11,12,13	Mark,Mary	0 days	0 days
4	⊿ Security	3.23 days	Wed 2/13/19	Mon 2/18/19	14		0 days	0 days
4.1	Create user IDs and passwords	1 day	Wed 2/13/19	Thu 2/14/19	14	Joe	0 days	0 days
4.2	Create folder hierarchy	1 day	Thu 2/14/19	Fri 2/15/19	16	Mary	0 days	0 days
4.3	Create desktop images	1 day	Fri 2/15/19	Mon 2/18/19	17	Kit	0 days	0 days
4.4	Security completed	0 days	Mon 2/18/19	Mon 2/18/19	18	Mary	0 days	0 days
5	⊿ Testing	4.22 days	Wed 2/13/19	Tue 2/19/19	10		0 days	0 days
5.1	Test hardware	1 day	Wed 2/13/19	Thu 2/14/19	12	Anne	3.23 days	3.23 days
5.2	Test software	2 days	Wed 2/13/19	Fri 2/15/19	13	Anne	1.73 days	1.73 days
5.3	Test security	1 day	Mon 2/18/19	Tue 2/19/19	19	Mary	0 days	0 days
5.4	Testing completed	0 days	Tue 2/19/19	Tue 2/19/19	21,22,23	Mary	0 days	0 days
6	⊿ Training	6 days	Tue 2/19/19	Wed 2/27/19	20		0 days	0 days
6.1	Train management	3 days	Tue 2/19/19	Fri 2/22/19	24	Anne,Joe	0 days	0 days
6.2	Train users	3 days	Fri 2/22/19	Wed 2/27/19	26	Anne,Joe	0 days	0 days
6.3	Training completed	0 days	Wed 2/27/19	Wed 2/27/19	27	Anne,Joe	0 days	0 days

Figure 7.17   Free slack and total slack displayed in Microsoft Project 2016

Resource leveling heuristics
Rules of thumb used to allocate resources to project activities.

that they could be carried out at different times. **Resource leveling heuristics** are rules of thumb used to allocate limited resources during a project. For example, if conflicting needs for certain resources during the project must be resolved, the project manager might decide to allocate scarce resources to the activities most critical to the project or to delay noncritical activities. Such heuristics (or rules) can be entered into project management software, which automatically adjusts the project schedule and resource requirements. Resource leveling resulting from these types of resource constraints might lead to a suboptimal project schedule because one or more tasks might have to be delayed based on the availability of resources, delaying the entire schedule. Schedules based on resource leveling are referred to as resource-limited (or resource-constrained) schedules. Typically, resource leveling makes use of available float, so that the critical path may change due to resource leveling. In contrast, resource smoothing avoids changing the critical path (and project completion date) by only delaying activities within their free and total float

Critical chain method
A technique to develop a critical path using resource availability to determine activity sequences.

Critical chain
The longest path through a network diagram, considering both task dependencies and resource dependencies.

Similar to resource leveling, the **critical chain method** is used if activities contend for limited resources. When using the critical chain method, the critical path is first identified, independent of resource availability. Entering resource availability might then reveal conflicting activities, which were planned to be completed in parallel but draw upon the same (limited) resource. Based on resource availability, an alternative critical path is created. This new path, based on both task dependencies and resource dependencies, is referred to as a **critical chain**. If resources were unlimited, the critical path and the critical chain would be equal. So far, this process to some extent resembles resource leveling techniques. However, another advantage of the critical chain method is that it helps minimize uncertainty in a project's schedule, therefore leading to a shorter overall completion time. The following paragraphs explain how critical chain scheduling can be used to influence a project's completion date.

People assigned to multiple concurrent tasks often resort to multitasking—that is, working a bit on one task, going on to the next, working a bit on a third task, and so on, before restarting work on task one. Unfortunately, this approach often wastes time because it requires repeated setup for the individual tasks. Critical chain scheduling prohibits multitasking with the goal of arriving at a shorter overall completion time. Another factor often leading to long project durations is the uncertainty inherent in any project. To cope with this uncertainty, a project's activities often contain duration buffers (i.e., additional time allocated to an activity to account for any unforeseen circumstances). Because this buffer is added to every activity, the entire project contains more reserve time than is usually needed. Further, there is often a tendency to fill the allotted time; in other words, if a certain amount of time is allotted for an activity, people tend to use it (this is known as Parkinson's law). If a buffer is added to an activity, people tend to use this buffer as well, no matter whether the additional time is needed or not. CCM thus suggests following aggressive target duration schedules to reduce overallocation of time, placing buffers at more strategic locations in the project timeline, avoiding multitasking because of the associated switching costs, emphasizing resources and the contention for resources when planning, and finally tracking the status of buffers and managing both their depletion and replenishment.

Critical chain scheduling eliminates any buffers from individual activities; instead, a general project buffer is created. Eliminating individual buffers helps decrease the entire duration of the project, whereas the project buffer protects the final due date. The removal of individual buffers serves the additional purpose of discouraging people from engaging in multitasking or other distractions. Because the duration estimates (without the individual buffers) are very aggressive, people focus on the task at hand in order to finish it in the allotted time.

In addition to the project buffer, critical chain scheduling uses feeding buffers to protect the activities on the critical path. Usually in complex projects, many noncritical activities feed into critical activities. Because critical chain scheduling eliminates the individual safety buffers, a change in duration of a noncritical activity feeding into a critical activity would influence the critical path and thus the duration of the entire project. To prevent this, a feeding buffer (i.e., additional time) is added to any noncritical activity feeding into a critical activity. The project manager can easily monitor the use of the feeding buffers and the project buffer to determine whether the project is on schedule. Project management software frequently employs third-party add-ons for critical chain scheduling.

An additional tool for project schedule development is using data analytical techniques to assess the outcome of various scenarios on the overall project schedule. **Simulation** is the process of calculating project and activity durations using different assumptions, constraints, and resource allocations. Two commonly used types of simulation are Monte Carlo simulations and **what-if analyses**. You may recognize these two terms from your introductory statistics classes. Monte Carlo simulations are probabilistic analyses used to calculate a distribution of likely results (in our case likely project or task durations). What-if analyses take advantage of logic networks by simulating various scenarios, such as asking "What if a major component for a system is delayed?" Both these techniques allow additional insight into the duration of projects and project activities.

Often, project managers need to shorten project schedules to meet certain imposed dates or constraints. In such cases, the project manager can employ various

Simulation
A process of evaluating different scenarios and their effects on the project.

What-if analyses
A process of evaluating alternative strategies by observing how changes to selected factors affect other factors and outcomes.

schedule compression techniques, which are techniques used to shorten the project schedule while adhering to the overall project scope. These techniques are known as **crashing**, which looks at cost–schedule trade-offs, and **fast-tracking** (see Figure 7.18), which looks at the possibility of performing activities in parallel that would normally be done in sequence. An example of crashing might involve adding resources so that a data entry task scheduled to take two weeks could be completed in one week by hiring additional data entry personnel. Other types of crashing might involve the use of additional nonhuman resources, such as computer time, in order to shorten the time necessary to complete a task. Fast-tracking involves doing project tasks at the same time rather than in sequence. Fast-tracking requires, by necessity, that the task dependencies allow such parallel work. Sometimes, fast-tracking may increase project risk. For example, starting to code before all requirements are gathered may carry the risk of rework at later stages.

What else can be done to shorten the critical path (and the duration of the project)? Here, you might need some creativity. You might want to see if some activities might be further broken down to allow fast-tracking. If dependencies between activities originally did not allow fast-tracking, breaking up these activities might open new possibilities to complete tasks in parallel. Maybe some activities do not have to be completely finished before a successor activity can be started. Thinking creatively about the different activities on the critical path can help possibly take them off the critical path, which helps shorten the overall project schedule.

Another way to shorten the duration of the project might be to check the duration estimates of the critical activities—in other words, carefully examine the basis for the

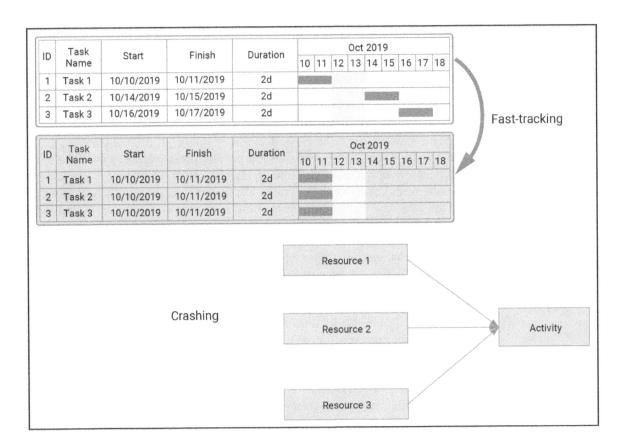

Figure 7.18   Fast-tracking and crashing

estimates (e.g., in Microsoft Project a simple double-click on the task duration will open a Task Information dialog box; see Figure 7.19). Oftentimes, duration estimates are based on rules of thumb or include fudge factors. Breaking down the critical activities to a more detailed level lets you obtain more precise estimates because it can remove "noise" from the estimates. Doing so can often lead to a shorter critical path. Sometimes, such a detailed breakdown might adjust the durations upward. Although this does not help shorten the critical path, it can save you from any surprises during the execution of the project, which can also be beneficial.

When using any of these techniques, a project manager should always monitor the project calendars and resource calendars. In a large software development project of a multinational corporation, virtual teams located in different regions of the world might be working on completing a certain task; thus teams could work in three continuous shifts. The resource calendar would specify these working times. On the other hand, the client organization might be available only during certain times, so that, for example, during requirements generation, the project team members cannot contact it. Such times would be specified in the project calendar.

While we present several software supported options for accomplishing the concepts in this chapter, the ease of doing so may be misleading, especially as the sophisticated form in which information is presented in software may give this information an aura of accuracy. However, the presentation does not guarantee accuracy. If any of the data entered into the system is unreliable or incorrect, the project manager's decision-making may be adversely affected. Thus sometimes it is also useful to perform the necessary calculations and adjustments by hand. Doing so is frequently educational because it will reveal what is going on behind the scenes in software, and any results can be easily entered into a Microsoft Project file for further analysis and collaboration.

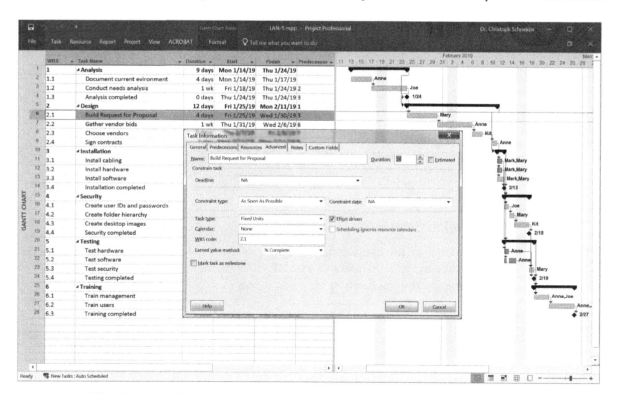

Figure 7.19 Task duration adjustments in Microsoft Project 2016

Schedule model
Data and information that are compiled and used in conjunction with manual methods or project management software to perform schedule network analysis to generate the project schedule.

Ultimately, all of the information that is generated through whatever schedule development techniques are used will be collected together and serve as the **schedule model**. The schedule model contains all of the logic, constraints, resources, and algorithms to perform scheduling calculations (Wilkens, 2004), and may contain various electronic files, such as diagrams or documents generated during the estimating tasks. Microsoft Project contains many of these elements (see Figures 7.13, 7.14, 7.16, and 7.17) and can be thought of as a schedule modeling tool. By running the model, we generate an output, the project schedule. The next section describes the outputs of the schedule development process in further detail.

Common Problems: Falling Prey to Critical Chain Assumptions

Consider two critical chain method assumptions regarding task duration estimation. The first is that when asked to estimate the duration of an activity, the activity owner's estimate includes a "safety factor" that serves as a personal buffer. The second is that people will tend to use such buffers if they are available (Parkinson's law). Both of these assumptions are plausible. After all, haven't we all taken the entire semester to complete a term paper even though we knew it would take only a week or two to complete it? The ultimate goal of CCM is to minimize or eliminate individual task-level buffers by incorporating them into feeding and project buffers (see the text for feeding and project buffers). One difficulty that arises with these assumptions is that some preliminary evidence suggests that Parkinson's law is not *always* in effect. According to Hill, Thomas, and Allen's 2000 study of more than five hundred tasks undertaken by the IS department in an international financial services organization, 60 percent were completed in less time than their estimated duration and 8 percent were completed within the original time estimate. Only 32 percent ran longer than their original estimates.

Some possible problems arise when a project manager using CCM blindly makes these assumptions, regardless of the conflicting evidence on Parkinson's law. How does a project manager estimate the safety factor that the task owner has incorporated into his or her estimate to arrive at more aggressive but appropriate estimates? One popular method is to reduce the original estimate by 33 percent. However, how can you be sure that the percentage you've chosen is appropriate? Do all task owners estimate the same safety factor? Furthermore, if you could accurately estimate the safety factors task owners have incorporated, can you expect that those task owners will agree to shorten their estimates?

According to Raz et al., if task owners know that the project manager is likely to shorten their duration estimates, they may add more of a safety factor. Finally, task owners who have shortened estimates imposed on them are likely to reduce their commitment to those estimates.

As powerful a tool as CCM can be, these issues need to be considered when using it. In this book, we have provided several techniques for estimating resources and task durations to provide you with a range of techniques to help minimize the disadvantages of any one technique.

Based on: Hill, Thomas, and Allen (2000); Raz, Barnes, and Dvir (2003).

Develop Schedule—Outputs

Outputs from the schedule development process include a preliminary project schedule, schedule model data, and the schedule baseline. In addition, outputs should include updates to the resource requirements, activity attributes, the project calendar, or the schedule management plan and the cost baseline, supporting detail, and resource requirement updates (refer back to Figure 7.12). The preliminary project schedule, at a minimum, should clearly show the start and finish dates of each activity. Additionally, the preliminary project schedule should contain schedule network diagrams with date information added, bar charts, and milestone charts.

This sort of information can be displayed in project management software. In the network diagram view of Microsoft Project, the individual activities are displayed, together with the duration and the start and finish dates, as well as the critical path (see Figure 7.17). In Microsoft Project, a Gantt chart view is the default type of bar chart; activities are shown as a task list oriented vertically, with the durations of the tasks represented by horizontal bars. This same chart may also show dependencies of the different activities (Figure 7.20). Finally, project milestones are displayed as diamonds (see, e.g., task 3.4 in Figure 7.20). A Gantt chart traditionally doesn't capture all aspects of a network diagram (such as the precedence relationships discussed in Chapter 6), but it does convey information about the duration of the various activities, and by capturing the various anticipated start and end dates of those activities, it also illustrates the duration of the overall project. Interestingly, project management software has evolved, combining both network diagram and bar chart functionality in Gantt chart representations. The arrows connecting the various duration bars associated with tasks in Figure 7.20 capture the relationship information that used to be more commonly available only in network diagrams.

Schedule model data provide managers with additional information about resource requirements, alternative schedules (e.g., best-case or worst-case), and contingency plans. Once the schedule has been finalized and approved, it becomes the **schedule baseline**. This baseline, which shows the set of original start and finish dates, activity durations, as well as work and cost estimates, serves as a basis for comparison during project execution. In Microsoft Project, you can save a schedule baseline. While project baseline data can be shown in many views within Microsoft Project, the Gantt chart view will show a black bar for the baseline and a colored bar for the actual progress of the project.

Resource leveling techniques might require changes to resource requirements, which then have to be updated accordingly. Further, schedule development processes

Schedule baseline
A document that contains the set of original start and finish dates, activity durations, as well as work and cost estimates, and serves as a basis for comparison during project execution.

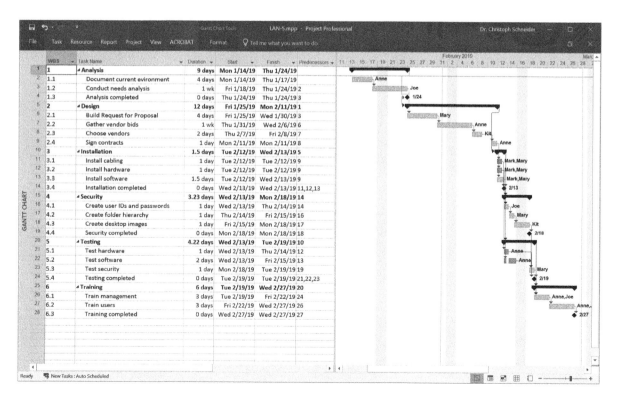

Figure 7.20   Components of the project schedule in Microsoft Project 2016

might necessitate updates to the activity attributes or the project calendar. Obviously, all changes have to follow the project's change control process. The schedule management plan, used to develop procedures for dealing with changes to the schedule as the project progresses, might have to be updated as well. If the schedule development process leads to the identification of any changes to these procedures, the schedule management plan has to be updated accordingly.

Control Schedule

Control Schedule
The process of monitoring project progress as compared to the schedule baseline.

The last process within the Project Schedule Management knowledge area is **Control Schedule**, which includes monitoring project progress as compared to the schedule baseline. Although control processes are covered in greater detail in the final chapter of this book, we will deal briefly with this topic here as it relates to Project Schedule Management. Inputs to the schedule control process include the schedule management plan, schedule baseline, scope baseline, and performance measurement baseline of the project management plan, as well as documents such as the project schedule, project calendars, or resource calendars, in addition to work performance data and organizational process assets (see Figure 7.21). The project schedule is the current version of the schedule, which shows the progress of the project activities up to the current date. Work performance data are used to track the project at the activity level, such as tracking which activities have or have not been finished on time.

Tools and techniques used during the *Control Schedule* process are primarily data analysis techniques. In addition, the project manager uses resource optimization and schedule compression techniques to analyze the critical path and leads and lags, as discussed earlier. Data analysis techniques used during schedule control include earned value analysis, iteration burndown charts, trend analysis, variance analysis, and what-if scenario analysis (discussed earlier). You will learn more about the different techniques in Chapter 12.

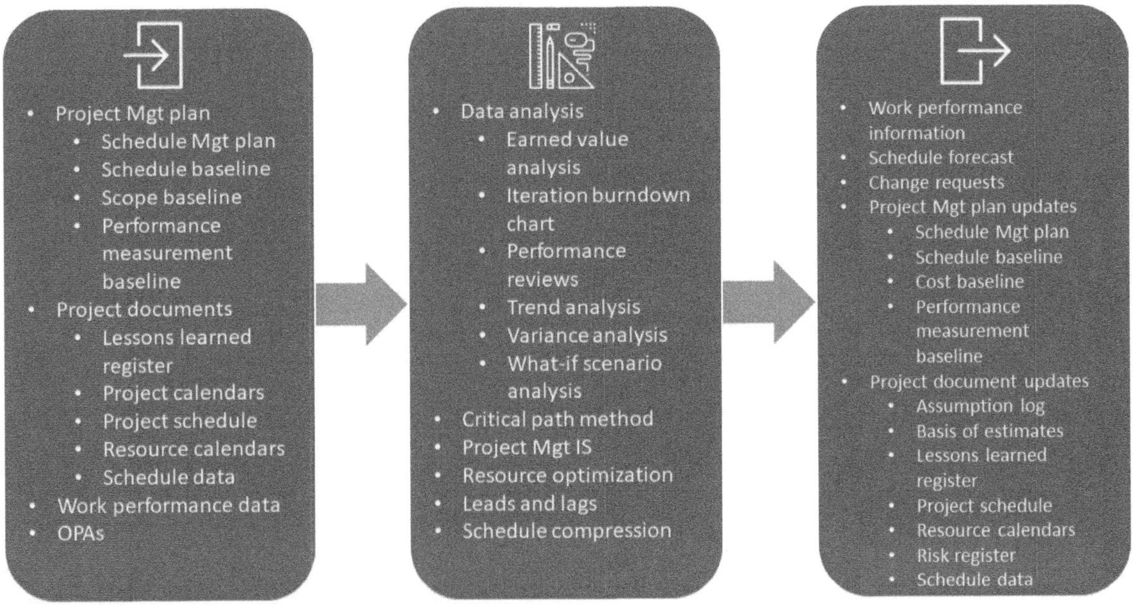

Figure 7.21 The *PMBOK* (6th ed.) *Control Schedule* process

Outputs from the schedule control process include work performance information, which highlights the project's progress as compared with the schedule baseline, as well as with the schedule forecasts and change requests, as needed. In addition, various sections of the project management plan might be updated, including the schedule management plan, the schedule baseline, the cost baseline, and the performance measurement plan. Finally, various project documents are updated, including the schedule and schedule data, resource calendars, assumptions, and the risk register, in addition to the lessons learned, which include documentation of the causes of variance from the project schedule. Documenting lessons learned can prevent these problems from occurring in similar future projects. This documentation becomes part of the organizational process assets.

Managing Project Resources and PMBOK

In this chapter, we have discussed the fundamentals, characteristics, and challenges related to allocating resources, estimating activity and project durations, and developing the final schedule with specific start and end dates. This information relates to *PMBOK* Knowledge Area 6, Project Schedule Management. In addition, we also identified types of resources and how they influence the estimation of task durations, which relates to Knowledge Area 9, Project Resource Management. Figure 7.22 identifies this coverage and illustrates the coverage of upcoming chapters.

Figure 7.22   Chapter 7 and *PMBOK* coverage

Key: O where the material is covered in the textbook; ● current chapter coverage

	Textbook Chapters ⟶	1	2	3	4	5	6	7	8	9	10	11	12
	PMBOK Knowledge Area												
1	Introduction												
1.2	Foundational Elements	O	O										
2	The Environment in Which Projects Operate												
2.2	Enterprise Environmental Factors		O										
2.2	Organizational Process Assets		O										
2.3	Organizational Systems		O										
3	The Role of the Project Manager												
3.2	Definition of a Project Manager	O											
3.3	The Project Manager's Sphere of Influence		O										
3.4	Project Manager Competences	O	O	O									
3.5	Performing Integration		O										
4	Project Integration Management												
4.1	Develop Project Charter					O							
4.2	Develop Project Management Plan					O							
4.3	Direct and Manage Project Work											O	
4.4	Manage Project Knowledge											O	

4.5	Monitor and Control Project Work												O	O
4.6	Perform Integrated Change Control													O
4.7	Close Project or Phase											O		O
5	**Project Scope Management**													
5.1	Plan Scope Management						O							
5.2	Collect Requirements						O							
5.3	Define Scope						O							
5.4	Create WBS						O	O						
5.5	Validate Scope						O							
5.6	Control Scope						O							O
6	**Project Schedule Management**													
6.1	Plan Schedule Management							O						
6.2	Define Activities							O						
6.3	Sequence Activities							O						
6.4	Estimate Activity Durations							●						
6.5	Develop Schedule							●						
6.6	Control Schedule							●						O
7	**Project Cost Management**													
7.1	Plan Cost Management								O					
7.2	Estimate Costs								O					
7.3	Determine Budget								O					
7.4	Control Costs								O					O
8	**Project Quality Management**													
8.1	Plan Quality Management								O					
8.2	Manage Quality								O					
8.3	Control Quality								O					O
9	**Project Resource Management**													
9.1	Plan Resource Management								●					
9.2	Estimate Activity Resources							O	●					
9.3	Acquire Resources								●			O		
9.4	Develop Team			O										
9.5	Manage Team			O										
9.6	Control Resources								●					O
10	**Project Communications Management**													
10.1	Plan Communications Management				O									
10.2	Manage Communications				O							O		
10.3	Monitor Communications				O									O
11	**Project Risk Management**													
11.1	Plan Risk Management									O				
11.2	Identify Risks									O		O		
11.3	Perform Qualitative Risk Analysis									O				

11.4	Perform Quantitative Risk Analysis									○			
11.5	Plan Risk Responses									○			
11.6	Implement Risk Responses									○		○	
11.7	Monitor Risks									○			○
12	**Project Procurement Management**												
12.1	Plan Procurement Management										○		
12.2	Conduct Procurements										○	○	
12.3	Control Procurements										○		○
13	**Project Stakeholder Management**												
12.1	Identify Stakeholders				○								
12.2	Plan Stakeholder Engagement				○								
12.3	Manage Stakeholder Engagement				○							○	
12.4	Monitor Stakeholder Engagement				○								○

Running Case: Managing Project Resources

Because it was Friday, James thought that most of his team members would be restless, so he started the meeting with a few minutes of informal chatting.

"Maria, does Friday mean a lot more customers at the store?" James asked.

"It depends, James. Customer volume is based on the deals we have, and as soon as these deals are over, customer volume drops drastically. I think that's why this project is so important for this company."

"I do most of my shopping on weekends," Kevin said, "unless the store has an online presence."

"Yes, time is a constraint. I was thinking about what other resources we might need to get this project completed," James said, trying to steer the conversation toward the main agenda of resource planning.

"Since the very first step is to understand different techniques to increase customer loyalty, we need to look at customer relations in depth," said Cindy.

"Do we have anyone who has customer relations expertise?" Trey asked.

"I think there's a new grad working for the store who specializes in customer relations. It would be great if you could get that person on our team, James," Cindy mentioned.

"OK, I'll talk to Nick as soon as possible about this," replied James.

"From the IT side, I think that smaller projects will have to be started. This would require a few more people for systems development and integration," Kevin said.

"Hold on, now. Before we get into IT, I suggest we understand how much money we have at our disposal, so that we can understand the extent of this project," Trey replied.

"But since this is an important project for the company, I'm sure Sarah will allocate as much as we want," James said, smiling. "To get an estimate of how much we should ask for, we need to know the extent of the project."

"That might require us to do a few iterations to get a good estimate. Would you guys excuse me for a moment? I have some new interns who need to be briefed before they start on Monday," said Maria.

Over the next couple of hours, working individually and, at times, together, each team member determined the different resources that they would require from their area of expertise and how much they would cost. They revised their estimates a few times for each of their resources and aggregated the costs to obtain the overall project cost. The final resource allocations would be presented to Sarah on Monday.

"This looks good. I think the cost would be fine with Sarah. Now let's see how the resources are spread out from the resource graph," said James (see Figure 7.23).

"Oh, with this resource allocation, the new marketing expert will have to work 120 hours for 3 weeks in a row!" said Kevin.

"I think we should share her a little more frugally," said Cindy with a grin.

After a few more adjustments the team managed to keep everyone's workload under forty-five hours a week, but it meant extending the overall project

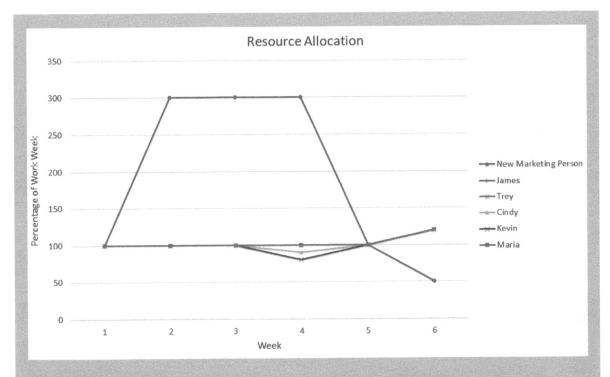

Figure 7.23 James's resource allocation

duration by three weeks. James looked slightly worried, seeing this figure.

"I'm sure Sarah would understand, with the 3-week extension. It's not like we've started the project. This is definitely a more realistic estimate of how quickly we can do this," said Trey, seeing James's apprehension.

Adapted from: Valacich and George (2017).

"Yes, I think this is a frank estimate of the time required given the resources we have," said James. It was well past 6:00 p.m. by then. James closed the projector and his laptop and said, "Thanks, everyone, for staying on late to complete the resource allocation and scheduling. See you guys on Monday!" He felt rather happy that he had a dedicated team to work with.

Chapter Summary

Understand what resources are, and the types of resources that are typically available. As project managers transition from activity definition and activity sequencing into full-blown project schedule development, the main determinant in estimating activity and project duration is the availability of appropriate resources. While the resources needed to complete a given task may be clear, those resources may not be available at the most opportune time or for the length of time required. Considering this, activity duration estimating becomes much more complex than just assigning resources and assuming they will be available. Identifying the appropriate human and capital

resources needed to complete the required project tasks, understanding their availability, and effectively managing these interactions can increase the project's likelihood of success immensely.

Appreciate the importance of managing project resources, and their effect on project duration. The efficient use of project resources should be a primary goal for every project manager because the allocation of resources can have a major influence on project schedules. Of specific concern are scarce resources, because their allocation can easily scuttle the project schedule. Poor management of project resources can have a negative influence on things like project time, cost, quality, and risk. As described in the chapter, project durations can vary, depending on the number of people assigned to the task and their respective skill levels. Project resources also influence project cost management. Resources obviously have costs, and how they are allocated impacts the project's budget. The resources used to complete tasks may also influence the quality of project deliverables. Finally, if specific resources to be used during the project are new, project risk may be increased.

Apply project resource management tools and techniques for managing project time. When estimating the resources and duration needed to complete an activity, project managers rely on several tools and techniques. For estimating resources, these include expert judgment, alternatives analysis, published estimating data, and bottom-up estimating. For estimating activity durations, they include expert judgment, parametric estimating, reserve analysis, three-point

estimating, and analogous estimating. Through the use of several estimating techniques for both resource and duration estimates, successful project managers are able to more accurately estimate resources and durations. After resources and durations have been estimated, the project manager is then ready to develop a full project schedule. By using several techniques, the successful project manager can develop an accurate schedule that can be used as a baseline to measure the progress of the project. Furthermore, the project manager can identify areas in the schedule with slack (float), should any unforeseen issues arise. These techniques include PERT analyses, the critical path method, and the critical chain method. By identifying areas of the schedule with slack, the project manager can use feeding buffers and project buffers to provide some insurance that the project can be completed in the allotted time. If these buffers are used up, the project manager may choose to fast-track or crash various activities in an attempt to complete some tasks faster than originally planned.

Key Terms Review

A. Activity resource requirements
B. Alternatives analysis
C. Analogous estimating
D. Bottom-up estimating
E. Capital resources
F. Control Schedule
G. Crashing
H. Critical activity
I. Critical chain
J. Critical chain method
K. Develop Schedule
L. Duration
M. Effort
N. Estimate Activity Durations
O. Expert judgment
P. Fast tracking
Q. Free float
R. Human resources
S. Imposed dates

T. Opportunity cost
U. Parametric estimating
V. PERT
W. Published estimating data
X. Reserve analysis
Y. Resource
Z. Resource breakdown structure
AA. Resource calendar
BB. Resource leveling
CC. Resource leveling heuristics
DD. Schedule baseline
EE. Schedule compression techniques
FF. Schedule model
GG. Schedule network analysis
HH. Simulation
II. Three-point estimates
JJ. Total float
KK. What-if analyses

Match each of the key terms with the definition that best fits it.

1. A document that contains the set of original start and finish dates, activity durations, as well as work and cost estimates, and serves as a basis for comparison during project execution.

2. A hierarchical, graphical representation of all needed resources ordered by type or category.

3. A process of evaluating alternative strategies by observing how changes to selected factors affect other factors and outcomes.

4. A process of evaluating different scenarios and their effects on the project.

5. A source of supply or support, such as money, people, materials, technology, and space.

6. A specific form of three-point estimation that uses weighted average method to estimate activity durations.

7. A specific type of project calendar used to track the hours when certain resources are available.

8. A technique to develop a critical path using resource availability to determine activity sequences.

9. A very detailed listing of the resource requirements for the individual activities.

10. Actual time spent working on an activity.

11. All personnel involved in a project, including project team members and support staff.

12. An estimating technique in which estimates are made at the activity level, and then aggregated to arrive at an overall estimate.

13. An estimating technique where trade-offs between the time needed, the resources invested, and the desired quality of the final deliverable are examined.

14. Any activity on the critical path.

15. Any form of network analysis where resource management issues drive scheduling decisions.

16. Data and information that are compiled and used in conjunction with manual methods or project management software to perform schedule network analysis to generate the project schedule.

17. Dates imposed to meet some type of development deadline.

18. Dedicating extra resources to a particular activity in an attempt to finish the activity sooner than the scheduled completion date.

19. Elapsed time between the start and finish of an activity.

20. Estimation based on the experience of one or more experts on the particular activity or project.

21. Performing activities in parallel that would normally be performed in sequence, in an attempt to shorten the duration of a project.

22. Publicly available data from specific activities carried out on previous projects that may be used to more accurately estimate resource needs.

23. Rules of thumb used to allocate resources to project activities.

24. Technique used to establish contingency reserves during a project to guard against potential risk.

25. Techniques used to shorten the project schedule while adhering to the overall project scope.

26. The estimation of activities' costs, durations, or resource requirements based on historical data of similar activities.

27. The estimation of activities' costs, durations, or resource requirements based on known relationships and project parameters.

28. The estimation of activities' durations by averaging the optimistic, pessimistic, and most likely estimates.

29. The longest path through a network diagram, considering both task dependencies and resource dependencies.

30. The measure of the alternative opportunities forgone in the choice of one good or activity over others.

31. The process of calculating expected, early, and late start and finish dates of a project.

32. The process of determining start and finish dates for project activities.

33. The process of estimating the duration of project activities using both project scope and resource information.

34. The process of monitoring project progress as compared to the schedule baseline.

35. The time an activity can be delayed without affecting the immediately following activity.

36. The time an activity can be delayed without affecting the overall completion date of a project.

37. The tools and infrastructure used to produce other goods and services.

Review Questions

1. Define *resources*. Discuss the differences between human and capital resources, and give three examples of each.

2. Discuss the differences between duration and effort with respect to estimating resources.

3. Should a project manager rely on only one technique for estimating resources? Why or why not?

4. Compare and contrast four techniques for estimating resources.

5. List and briefly discuss the outputs of resource estimating.

6. Choose four activity duration estimating techniques and compare and contrast them.

7. What is a critical path? What is the difference between the critical path method and the critical chain method?

8. Which activities on a network diagram can have free float or total float? Which activities can't have free or total float, and why not?

9. Define *schedule compression*. Describe the two methods for compressing a schedule.

10. What are buffers? Define and discuss the differences between the two types of buffers presented.

11. List the various techniques to exert schedule control.

Chapter Exercises

1. You have been chosen as the project manager for a project to develop an e-commerce presence for your company, which has, until now, been primarily a brick-and-mortar business. Upper management has arbitrarily chosen a launch date six months from now. You and your team have determined, through following the techniques described in this chapter, that completing the project in six months is possible, but unlikely. The project sponsor has asked you to tell him what day you expect the project to be complete. Explain why predicting the finish date down to the specific day is problematic. How might you explain this to reassure him that he has chosen the right project manager for the job?

2. Consider a situation where you have enough money either to purchase textbooks for the term *or* to purchase a desktop PC (assuming you need one). Which purchase would you choose? Discuss your decision with respect to opportunity costs.

3. Consider a paper you need to complete for a current class or consider some project you're working on or anticipate working on. Identify four tasks needed to complete the paper or project, estimate the durations of each task, and discuss how effort relates to the task duration you've determined.

4. Discuss a situation you've experienced when you made an inaccurate estimation for the duration of some activity. It doesn't necessarily need to be during a project, but discuss your reasoning for estimating the duration of the activity the way you did and the factors that caused your estimate to be inaccurate.

5. Describe a situation you've experienced where you had more time than needed to complete some task but took the entire time to complete it. Discuss the factors that influenced your filling up of the allotted time.

6. For the project described in Exercise 1, consider this situation. Your team has really performed well. The six-month launch date is rapidly approaching, and you have figured out a way to meet the deadline. To meet the deadline, you will have to either fast-track or crash four activities of the testing phase (system testing, integration testing, security testing, and acceptance testing) before you can go into deployment, training, and documentation. What method would you choose? Why?

7. Now, based on Exercises 1 and 7, you discover that the four activities of the testing phase mentioned in Exercise 7 have competing needs for the same resource. Discuss how this might change or reinforce your decision in Exercise 8, considering the concepts of resource leveling, free slack, and total slack.

8. Develop a three-point estimate for completing your degree. Discuss your reasoning for each of the three points.

9. Using the following weighting factors, conduct a PERT analysis on your estimate from Exercise 9. Optimistic × 1, most likely × 3, and pessimistic × 2.

Chapter Case: Sedona Management Group and Managing Project Resources

Resource management is a fundamental part of project management and involves the allocation of resources to the different activities that need to be performed for the successful and timely completion of any project. These resources include human resources, equipment, space, and money. Each of them may be scarce, and for that reason, they have to be used effectively.

Poor resource allocation can have an adverse effect on project duration, cost, quality, and risk. In terms of project duration, if the required resources are not available when needed, it will be difficult to finish the project as targeted. Moreover, the time it takes to complete an activity depends on the number of people allocated to that activity. Resources also have associated costs, and consequently, resource allocation will impact the project's budget. Similarly, the quality of the resources used during a project affects the quality of the project deliverables. Finally, if the resources being used are new to a project, project risk will be affected. Consequently, it is very important to manage project resources effectively.

One important resource that has to be considered in any information systems project is human resources—that is, the trained professionals who assess users' needs, develop systems, and implement those systems. The success or failure of projects largely depends on the people who are working on them. At Sedona Management Group (SMG), given the small size of the organization, team composition remains largely the same as the company takes on

new projects, such as the Seattle Seahawks' website development project. In addition, all members of the Sedona team typically have well-defined roles, which they repeat across projects, making efficient use of their individual skill sets (e.g., graphic design, database development, client communications, etc.). This approach may be different from other larger organizations, such as an IT consulting firm, where individuals are reassigned to new teams and roles as they take on new projects.

One challenge any project team takes on is multitasking (i.e., how to simultaneously manage a variety of different tasks). These diverse tasks may be related to one project (e.g., the interface designer may not only need to be working on continually gathering customer feedback but also may be involved in developing the interface itself), or in some instances on multiple projects, where a project member may be assigned to two or more projects (e.g., one project for the Seattle Seahawks and another for a small Seattle coffee shop). It is the job of Tim Turnpaugh to efficiently assign resources (in terms of personnel, equipment, etc.) so that the various projects the team is working on at a certain point in time are completed in a timely manner. He needs to watch for issues like committing a team member to too many tasks at one time or not having sufficient resources to carry out a task when needed. To prevent such problems, SMG practices project techniques like resource leveling, which essentially involves spreading the work in a more balanced fashion.

Chapter 7 Project Assignment

You will need different resources to complete the entertainment website development project. In this assignment, you will identify the needed resources as well as update the Gantt chart you developed as part of the assignment for the previous chapter with this information.

1. Determine the types of resources you will need to complete this project. These resources should include human resources as well as any equipment, in terms of software, technology, and so on.
2. Discuss how the allocation of these different resources will affect project time, cost, quality, and risk.
3. In the previous chapter, you developed a work breakdown structure (WBS). Allocate the resources you determined in Exercise 1 to the different tasks in the WBS, and update the Gantt chart you developed in the previous chapter with this information.
4. Determine how the allocation of project resources can affect the critical path of your project.
5. Discuss some ways in which you and your team members will handle any overallocation of resources in the project.

References

Battin, R. D., Crocker, R., Kreidler, J., and Subramanian, K. (2001). Leveraging Resources in Global Software Development. *IEEE Software* 18(2), 70–77.

Davenport, T. H. (2014, March 26). What Makes Big Data Projects Succeed. *HBR.org*. Retrieved July 13, 2018, from https://hbr.org/2014/03/what-makes-big-data-projects-succeed

Edwards, H. K., and Swidhar, V. (2005). Analysis of Software Requirements Engineering Exercises in a Global Virtual Team Setup. *Journal of Global Information Management* 13(2), 21–41.

Gordon, L. (2018, May 1). How to Leverage Offshore Developers for Devops. *InfoWorld*. Retrieved July 6, 2018, from https://www.infoworld.com/article/3269487/devops/how-to-leverage-offshore-developers-for-devops.html

Harreld, H. (2001). Moving onto the Web. *InfoWorld*, 23(21), 56.

Hill, J., Thomas, L. C., and Allen, D. E. (2000). Experts' Estimates of Task Durations in Software Development Projects. *International Journal of Project Management* 12(1), 13–24.

Leach, L. P. (2000). *Critical Chain Project Management*. Boston: Artech House.

Orton-Jones, C. (2016, May 22). Eight Lessons from Digital Megaprojects. *Raconteur*. Retrieved July 5, 2018, from https://www.raconteur.net/business/8-lessons-from-digital-megaprojects

Project Management Institute (2017). *Agile Practice Guide*. Newton Square, PA: Author.

Project Management Institute (2017). *PMBOK: A Guide to the Project Management Body of Knowledge* (6th ed.). Newtown Square, PA: Author.

Raz, T., Barnes, R., and Dvir, D. (2003). A Critical Look at Critical Chain Project Management. *Project Management Journal* 34(4), 24–32.

Rubens, P. (2012, June 17). Olympic Games Coverage: HD, Robotic Cameras and 3D. *BBC*. Retrieved July 6, 2018, from https://www.bbc.com/news/technology-18690822

Standish Group (2014). CHAOS Report: 21st Anniversary Edition. *Standish Group*. Retrieved July 4, 2018, from https://www.standishgroup.com/sample_research_files/CHAOSReport2014.pdf

Standish Group (2016). CHAOS Summary Report 2016. *Standish Group*. Retrieved July 4, 2018, from https://www.standishgroup.com

Valacich, J., and George, J. F. (2017). *Modern Systems Analysis and Design* (8th ed.). Boston: Pearson.

Wilkens, T. (2004). The Definition Conundrum. *Project Management Institute College of Scheduling*. Retrieved October 7, 2006, from http://www.pmicos.org/topics/jul2004.pdf

CHAPTER 8

Managing Project Costs and Quality

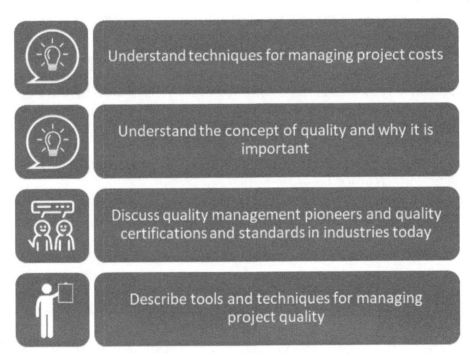

Figure 8.1   Chapter 8 learning objectives

In 2018, a number of companies found themselves in a race to develop self-driving (a.k.a. driverless or autonomous) cars. Among the contenders were automobile companies such as GM, Daimler, BMW, or Tesla; technology companies, such as Apple or Waymo (Google); or even ride-hailing companies, such as Uber. Self-driving cars use a combination of cameras, lidar sensors, GPS positioning technology, and various other sensors. At the heart of any self-driving car is complex software that helps detect other vehicles, road markings, pedestrians, or other objects, so as to safely get the car to the intended destination while not endangering other traffic participants. As such, any self-driving car project involves bringing together experts in a variety of areas, ranging from sensor technology to driving physics.

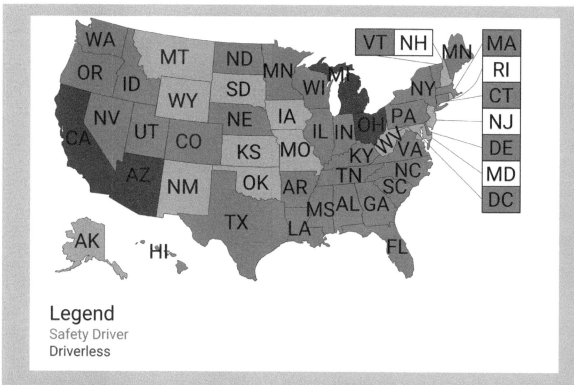

Figure 8.2 U.S. states allowing self-driving cars

For developers of self-driving vehicles, a goal is to ensure that the self-driving car is safe for the driver, the passengers, as well as for pedestrians and other traffic participants. Unfortunately, this is no easy feat. In early 2018, a prototype of Uber's self-driving cars, roaming the roads of Tempe, Arizona, collided with a pedestrian about to cross the street, resulting in her death. An investigation revealed that while the software had detected the pedestrian, the system labeled her as a "false positive," and thus did not slow down or brake the vehicle. Why did this happen? The "quality" of a self-driving car is a trade-off between various factors, and safety is only one of them. Another factor is driving comfort. Unfortunately, if the car is programmed to err on the safe side, comfort suffers, whereas when optimizing the system for the passengers' comfort, the system increasingly labels real objects as false positives. When developing a self-driving vehicle, what should determine "quality"?

Based on: Lee (2018).

Introduction

Completing a project within the agreed-upon scope and on time are key considerations of project success. Yet as organizational resources are limited, another key consideration is cost, as shown by frequent reports of projects running over budget. Thus the project manager has to carefully balance time, costs, and scope (see Figure 8.3), all while maintaining the desired quality. Project quality is often referred to as a fourth dimension of project management that must be considered along with the classic project constraints of cost, time, and scope. Project management experts argue that unless quality standards are realized, most projects should be considered failures, even if the other constraints of cost, time, and scope have been met. In this chapter, we will learn about the important areas of managing project costs and managing project quality as they pertain to information systems projects.

Figure 8.3   Time, cost, and scope triangle

Techniques for Managing Project Costs

In Chapter 4, you learned about different concepts used to estimate and compare the returns of different projects. In this section, you will learn about how costs are managed during a project. As with processes related to managing scope or resources, the first step is to plan how costs are managed throughout the project life cycle. Using the cost management plan as a basis, the project manager can estimate the costs, determine the budget, and—on an ongoing basis—control costs. You will recognize many inputs, tools and techniques, and outputs from the processes related to managing scope, resources, or duration, so we will only briefly cover these known concepts. Further, we will provide more detail about controlling costs in Chapter 12.

Plan Cost Management

As with managing other aspects of the project (as well as the project itself), the first step in managing costs is to develop a sound plan on how costs will be managed throughout the project life cycle, including estimation, budgeting, and monitoring and controlling. The *Plan Cost Management* process uses as inputs the project charter, the schedule management plan (discussed in Chapter 8), and the risk management plan (discussed in Chapter 9), while considering various enterprise environmental factors and organizational process assets. This process uses expert judgment, meetings, and various data analysis techniques (such as alternatives analyses) to create the cost management plan, which specifies units of measurements, level of precision, and levels of accuracy for planning and monitoring costs, control thresholds, control accounts, how performance will be measured, and how cost reports will be delivered.

Estimate Costs

The goal of this process is to estimate the financial resources needed to complete the project. Typically, costs are incurred for almost any aspect of the project, be it human resources, materials, outside services, equipment purchase or rental, and so on; further, especially for projects of longer duration, factors such as the rate of inflation and cost of capital need to be taken into account. As with any estimation processes, costs are typically difficult to estimate with high accuracy from the outset of the project. Rather, as the project manager is able to flesh out the details of different activities, more detailed estimates can be provided. Consequently, the *Estimate Costs* process is performed periodically throughout the project life cycle, so as to be able to provide more accurate cost estimates as the project progresses.

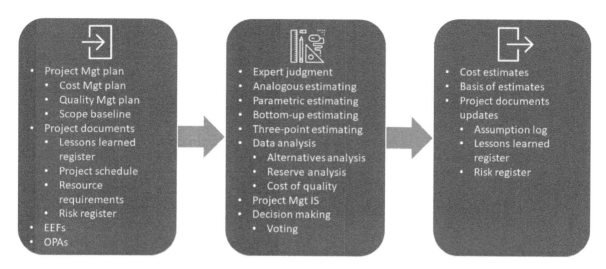

Figure 8.4 The *PMBOK* (6th ed.) *Estimate Costs* process

As Figure 8.4 shows, project managers rely on a wide variety of different inputs when estimating costs. First, the cost management plan, the quality management plan, and the scope baseline give overall guidelines for estimating costs. In addition, project managers use outputs from prior stages of project planning—for example, the lessons learned register, project schedule, resource requirements, and the risk register. Finally, as in most processes, managers use enterprise environmental factors (such as market conditions, available commercial information on standard cost rates, or exchange rates) and organizational process assets (such as historical information from prior projects) to establish cost estimates.

The tools and techniques used for the *Estimate Costs* process mirror those of resource or duration estimation. In particular, in addition to using expert judgment, project managers can use various types of software as part of the project management information system to assist with the estimating process. Commonly used tools and techniques include analogous estimating, parametric estimating, bottom-up estimating, and three-point estimating. Just as for estimating durations, the project manager can use a triangular distribution, or weight the most likely estimate more heavily; akin to PERT, a beta distribution weights the most likely estimate with the factor four. Further, the project manager can use various data analysis techniques such as alternatives analysis and reserve analysis, while taking into account the cost of quality (discussed later in this chapter).

The primary output of the cost estimating process (see Figure 8.4) is a detailed listing of the costs estimates (including contingency reserves to account for unforeseen or unplanned circumstances). As with resource or duration estimates, the basis of the estimates should be carefully captured, including how the estimates were derived, any assumptions made, confidence levels, and so on. Finally, outputs from the cost-estimating process includes updates to project documents such as the assumption log, the risk register, or lessons learned.

Determine Budget

Once all costs have been identified, the next step is to develop an overall project budget that serves as the cost baseline. In addition to the cost estimates (and the basis of the estimates), inputs to this process include the overall project scope baseline, as well as the cost and resource management plans and the risk register. Likewise, the project schedule is used to assign aggregated costs to calendar periods, especially for projects with longer duration. Finally, inputs to be used may include the business case and benefits management plan, external agreements for outside purchases, as well as enterprise environmental factors (such as exchange rates) and organizational process assets (such as historical information or policies and procedures).

Based on expert judgment, the project manager can then aggregate the costs by work packages; often, this includes reviewing historical information to develop analogous or parametric estimates (described in Chapter 7). In addition to estimating overall project costs, the project manager uses techniques such as reserve analysis to establish the management reserve (funding that is part of the overall budget, but not included in the costs baseline, to be used to account for unforeseen work). Given resource limitations and external constraints, the project manager may have to readjust the schedule to reconcile the budget with externally imposed funding limits (e.g., if funding for a multiyear project is only released on a yearly basis). Finally, the process of determining the budget might include acquiring financing for the project.

Cost baseline
A document that contains the approved project budget for all schedule activities and serves as a basis for comparison during project execution.

The output of this process is the **cost baseline**, which contains the approved project budget for all schedule activities and serves as a basis for comparison during project execution. The overall project budget is an aggregation of different components (see Figure 8.5): first, for each work package, estimates are derived by aggregating the activity cost estimates, together with a contingency reserve; the aggregated work packages, together with contingency reserves, make up the control accounts, which are then aggregated to form the cost baseline; the final project budget consists of the cost baseline and the management reserve (to complete unplanned project work). The cost baseline also allows for deriving funding requirements (total and by period). Finally, outputs of this process might include updates to the cost estimates, the project schedule, or the risk register.

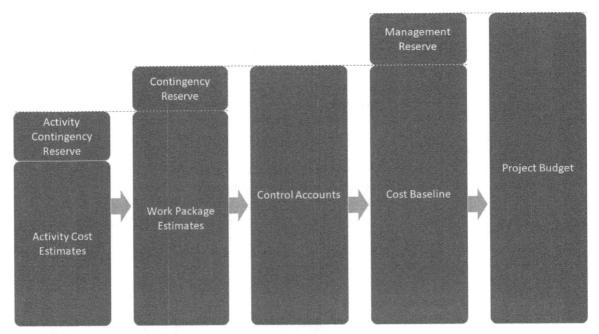

Figure 8.5   Components of the overall project budget

Control Costs

The last process within the Project Cost Management knowledge area is *Control Costs*, which includes monitoring project progress as compared to the cost baseline. Although we will cover control processes covered in greater detail in the final chapter of this book, we will briefly highlight this topic here. Using inputs such as the cost management plan, cost baseline, and performance measurement baseline of the project management plan, as well as funding requirements, work performance data, and other inputs, the project manager uses expert judgment, data analysis techniques such as earned value analysis, trend analysis, variance analysis, reserve analysis, and the to-complete performance index to produce work performance information, which highlights the project's progress as compared to the cost baseline. Further, important outputs of this process are cost forecasts and change requests, and updates to various sections of the project management plan, including the cost management plan, the cost baseline, and the performance measurement plan. Finally, various project documents are updated, including the cost estimates (and their basis), assumptions, and the risk register, in addition to the lessons learned, which include documentation of the causes of variance from the project cost baseline. This documentation becomes part of the organizational process assets.

What Is Quality?

Quality
The degree to which a set of inherent characteristics fulfill requirements.

Quality is about providing excellence in the products or services that an organization produces. The International Organization for Standardization defines **quality** as "the degree to which a set of inherent characteristics fulfill requirements" (ISO, 2015). Quality thus also depends somewhat on whom the quality issue affects; in other words, quality is to some extent determines by the customers' (and other stakeholders') expectations. For example, General Electric defines quality from different perspectives, including those of the customer, the process, and the employee (see Figure 8.6).

Why Is Project Quality Important?

Project quality is important because of its direct relationship to project success. Remember that project success can be defined as the degree to which project objectives have been achieved on time, within budget, and with the agreed upon quality and scope. Many examples of IS project success and failure can be attributed to project quality. In fact, many of the enterprise resource planning (ERP) systems implementation failures discussed earlier in the text can be attributed to inattention to project quality management.

Although quality is always an important concept, in some industries it can be critical. As an example, in the production of semiconductors, quality tolerances need to be quite tight to ensure that the products work as expected. As a consequence, a vast infrastructure of quality planning, monitoring, and control surrounds the process of semiconductor production. As one part of this quality system, semiconductor manufacturers use clean rooms—sealed, highly sterile environments where semiconductor manufacturing occurs—in the manufacturing process (see Figure 8.7). In addition to monitoring air filtration, temperature, and humidity, workers in a clean room also follow strict procedures to avoid contaminating the workplace. The importance of such processes and the monitoring of the resulting manufactured product can be critical, considering where such semiconductors are used. As an example, they may be used in the health care industry in medical equipment, or in an industry like aerospace where

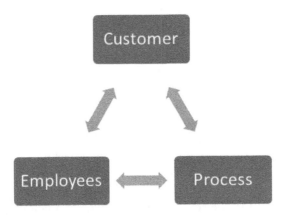

Figure 8.6 General Electric defines *quality* from different perspectives.

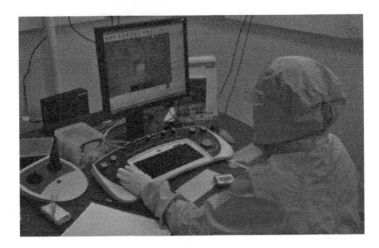

Figure 8.7 A clean room. *Source*: CC-BY-2.0, O. Usher (UCL MAPS).

they may be used to control flight functions of aircraft. Product quality in either environment can be a life or death matter.

While quality processes may be slightly different for developing information systems, quality planning, management, and control are just as important in the software industry. As discussed earlier, systems may be used in contexts where there is little or no tolerance for error. One such example might include a program designed to support air traffic controllers—a system that controls the regulation and scheduling of incoming and outgoing flights at a major airport (see Figure 8.8). In such a situation, a glitch in the software might result in anything from a disruption of normal services to more disastrous results. Such was the case in 2017 when on multiple occasions, computers of Hong Kong's new air traffic management system had to be rebooted to restore full functionality (Hong Kong Free Press, 2017). The quality errors resulted in a disruption to normal schedules, but more widespread system failure could have had much more serious consequences.

Frederick Reichheld, author of *The Loyalty Effect: The Hidden Force Behind Growth, Profits, and Lasting Value*, was quoted in *PM Network* regarding the importance of quality. Reichheld states that a simple 5 percent reduction in a company's customer defection rate can lead to a 25 to 85 percent increase in profits (Dimov and Alexandrova, 2003).

Figure 8.8 Air traffic control tower. *Source:* CC-BY-2.0, U.S. Army Corps of Engineers Savannah District.

Within the same article, Dimov and Alexandrova reference the results of research conducted by Xerox Corporation to determine the effect of customer satisfaction (one measure of quality) on purchase behavior. Xerox researchers found that customers who were "very satisfied" were 18 times more likely to repurchase from the company. Managing quality, therefore, is vital to a company's future success.

Companies have realized that quality issues detected by customers tend to have the highest costs, both in terms of rework or warranty issues and reputation. Therefore, organizations typically implement quality control processes to prevent defective product from reaching the customer. Even more effective in ensuring quality is to use quality assurance, so as to correct not only the deliverables, but to changes processes that led to substandard products in the first place, and to plan and design for quality. Finally, having a culture of commitment to quality throughout the organization is often seen as most effective in quality management (see Figure 8.9).

Managing Quality and the Project Life Cycle

Quality management processes are often considered during all phases of a project's life cycle, including initiation, planning, execution, control, and closeout. As teams initiate and choose projects, they need to understand what quality standards they must achieve. Quality perspectives also have to be practiced during the project planning phase as project teams develop the quality control mechanisms they'll use throughout the project life cycle. During execution and control, quality control mechanisms are put into place, giving the project team constant feedback on their performance. Finally, quality management is also practiced in project closure when the team documents its experiences for future organizational projects.

There is an important relationship between project teams and quality. Teams are often used to help establish the development of company quality standards for future projects (in many instances, these are former project teams). These quality standards can serve as a benchmark for future project efforts. In addition, once established, quality standards can be applied to how a team functions, what types of processes it uses to control quality, and how it can measure the success of its project management efforts.

Technology, as part of the project management information system, can facilitate the tracking and control of quality during IS projects. For instance, cost-benefit analyses are often performed using spreadsheet software. Project management software such as

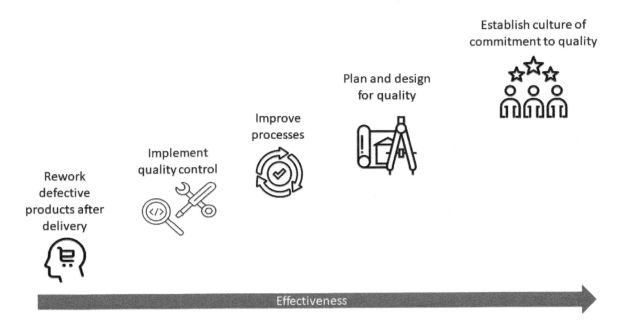

Figure 8.9 Five levels of quality management

Microsoft Project can also help project teams manage project quality. Microsoft Project's Enterprise edition, in fact, includes common repositories for project documents. Using a repository allows for more consistent documentation because project team members share and reuse common documents. Further, project tracking features within Microsoft Project enable managers to quickly identify problem areas and take steps to eliminate them, ultimately resulting in improved quality.

Ethical Dilemma: Finding the Right Balance between Speed and Quality

The mantra in many companies today is "do more with less." This expression is taking on a new meaning for IS project managers. Organizations are always focusing on costs. Consequently, IS projects, which used to take months, may have to be completed within weeks, while at the same time, the project deliverables are expected to be of the highest quality. Project managers are pressured to apply agile principles and also maintain quality. The struggle for project managers is to find the right balance between quality and speed.

Kevin Heard, a project manager at Clarkston Consulting, says that this battle is hard. According to Mr. Heard, whereas sacrificing quality today can lead to additional expenses in the future, ensuring quality may likely result in longer project life cycles. The situation worsens because staff resources are typically limited. As a result, the project manager needs to be adept at identifying available skills and making good use of limited resources.

Moreover, project managers are increasingly facing pressure from executives to take shortcuts on IS projects. For example, an IT manager at a midwestern manufacturer says that senior business leaders have been pressuring him to rush an enterprise resource planning (ERP) system by bypassing critical business processes. Ken McLennan, the senior vice president of business solutions at Fujitsu Consulting, says that project managers not only must resist this pressure but also should inform executives of the risks associated with cutting corners during IS projects. One risk that should be communicated to executives is that if project failures are publicized, the share price of the company will often be adversely affected.

Quality Pioneers and Standards

The concept of quality has evolved over the years. In this section we briefly discuss some quality pioneers who have influenced how today's businesses think of quality. In addition, as a result of the concept's evolution, quality processes have become so important to modern corporations that many industries have adopted standards for quality to signal their attention to a company's quality processes, as well as to the quality of their product or service. We will also briefly discuss some of today's more common quality standards and certifications before transitioning to our discussion of specific quality management techniques.

Quality Management Pioneers

There have been many quality management pioneers throughout history. This section discusses some of the most well-known quality proponents.

W. Edwards Deming

The statistician and quality expert W. Edwards Deming, who received a PhD in mathematics from Yale University in 1928, played a significant role in the economic resurgence of Japan following World War II, where he served as a consultant to Japanese industry. This role is particularly noteworthy because Deming's management philosophies had a significant impact on Japanese business thinking and, as a result, on global trade as corporations competed on quality. Based on his work, he achieved worldwide prominence and became known as the "prophet of quality." Today, he is probably best known for his fourteen points of quality (see Figure 8.10), stated in his popular publication *Out of Crisis.*

Joseph Juran

Born in 1904, Dr. Joseph Juran worked as an engineer until deciding to devote the remainder of his life to the study of quality management in 1945. Juran is often credited with adding the human element to what was previously a statistical view of project quality. Dr. Juran is further credited with the Pareto Principle, or the 80/20 rule. The Pareto Principle is a rule of thumb used to indicate that a small number of issues typically create the most work in projects. This rule of thumb can be applied in a variety of ways. For example, 80 percent of a project's problems are likely caused by 20 percent of the defects, or 80 percent of a project manager's time is consumed by 20 percent of the problems in a project. The 80/20 rule is typically used for project quality control, which we briefly introduce later in this chapter (see Figure 8.20) and then cover in more detail in Chapter 12. Juran was so influential that the American Society for Quality proposed changing the name of the Pareto Principle to the Juran Principle in 2003. Juran authored the *Quality Control Handbook* (first released in 1951), the standard reference

1. Create constancy of purpose for the improvement of product and service with the aim to become competitive, stay in business, and provide jobs.
2. Adopt the new philosophy of cooperation (win-win) in which everybody wins. Put it into practice and teach it to employees, customers, and suppliers.
3. Cease dependence on mass inspection to achieve quality. Improve the process and build quality into the product in the first place.
4. End the practice of awarding business on the basis of price tag alone. Instead, minimize total cost in the long run. Move toward a single supplier for any one item, on a long-term relationship of loyalty and trust.
5. Improve constantly and forever the system of production, service, planning, or any activity. This will improve quality and productivity and thus, constantly decrease costs.
6. Institute training for skills.
7. Adopt and institute leadership for the management of people, recognizing their different abilities, capabilities, and aspiration. The aim of leadership should be to help people, machines, and gadgets do a better job. Leadership of management is in need of overhaul, as well as leadership of production workers.
8. Drive out fear and build trust so that everyone can work effectively.
9. Break down barriers between departments. Abolish competition and build a win-win system of cooperation within the organization. People in research, design, sales, and production must work as a team to foresee problems of production and in use that might be encountered with the product or service.
10. Eliminate slogans, exhortations, and targets asking for zero defects or new levels of productivity. Such exhortations only create adversarial relationships, as the bulk of the causes of low quality and low productivity belong to the system and thus, lie beyond the power of the work force.
11. Eliminate numerical goals, numerical quotas, and management by objectives. Substitute leadership.
12. Remove barriers that rob people of joy in their work. This will mean abolishing the annual rating or merit system that ranks people and creates competition and conflict.
13. Institute a vigorous program of education and self-improvement.
14. Put everybody in the company to work to accomplish the transformation. The transformation is everybody's job.

Figure 8.10 W. E. Deming's fourteen points of quality

work in this domain, and developed the *Juran Trilogy*. With its focus on the three areas of quality planning, quality improvement, and quality control, the *Juran Trilogy* has been accepted worldwide as a model for quality management (see Figure 8.11).

Philip B. Crosby

Philip B. Crosby (1926–2001), founder of Philip Crosby Associates, dedicated his career to convincing managers that preventing problems was cheaper than fixing them. Crosby published fourteen best-selling books, the most recognized of which was *Quality Is Free* (1979). In his groundbreaking work, Crosby defined quality in an absolute way so that companies could readily see whether or not quality existed in the workplace.

Kaoru Ishikawa

Fishbone diagram A diagramming technique used to explore potential and real causes of problems.

Kaoru Ishikawa (1915–1989) is best known for his cause-and-effect diagram, also called Ishikawa or **fishbone diagram** (see Figure 8.23 later in this chapter), a diagramming technique used to explore potential and real causes of problems. The fishbone diagram typically organizes problems into categories relevant to the industry. This diagramming technique will also be mentioned in Chapter 9's consideration of project risk and discussed more extensively in Chapter 12's treatment of project control. Ishikawa is also known for his insistence that quality could always be taken one step further. Ishikawa

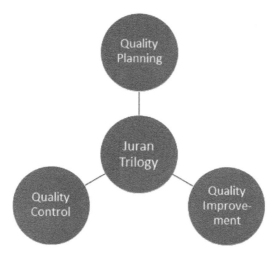

Figure 8.11 The Juran Trilogy focused on quality planning, quality improvement, and quality control.

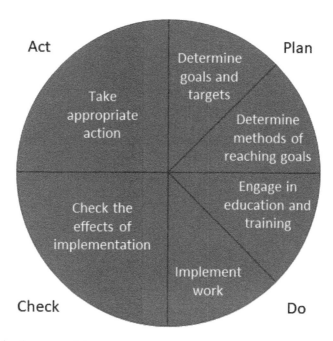

Figure 8.12 Plan-do-check-act model

expanded on Deming's plan-do-check-act model to create an actionable list of six items (see Figure 8.12):

1. Determine goals and target.
2. Determine methods of reaching goals.
3. Engage in education and training.
4. Implement work.
5. Check the effects of implementation.
6. Take appropriate action.

Robert Kaplan and David Norton

A new approach for managing and measuring business performance (including management and measurement related to quality) was developed in the early 1990s by Drs. Robert Kaplan and David Norton. They created a system named the **balanced scorecard**, which recognized some of the potential problems of previous management approaches. The balanced scorecard approach gives advice about what factors (or perspectives) companies should assess in addition to the traditional financial metrics that are typically used (Kaplan and Norton, 1992).

Balanced scorecard
A tool for assessing organizational activity from perspectives beyond the typical financial analysis.

The balanced scorecard is a management system (as opposed to simply being a measurement system) that helps firms clarify and accomplish their corporate vision and strategy. It is described as follows:

> The balanced scorecard retains traditional financial measures. But financial measures tell the story of past events, an adequate story for industrial age companies for which investments in long-term capabilities and customer relationships were not critical for success. These financial measures are inadequate, however, for guiding and evaluating the journey that information age companies must make to create future value through investment in customers, suppliers, employees, processes, technology, and innovation. (Kaplan and Norton, 1996, p. 7)

The balanced scorecard suggests viewing organizational activity from four perspectives: the learning and growth perspective, the business process perspective, the customer perspective, and the financial perspective. To use this method, metrics are developed and data are collected and analyzed to assess project performance relative to each of these perspectives. While the balanced scorecard was originally designed as a general management tool, it has been adapted to a wide variety of sectors and contexts, including the assessment of technology-focused projects. Given the inclusion of customer, business process, and learning perspective in this approach, this system has obvious implications for managing quality in organizations.

While many scholars and practitioners alike have focused on quality processes, these individuals have certainly played a large role establishing the quality standards used in industry today. Table 8.1 lists these project management pioneers and their achievements. In many cases, quality guidelines and metrics have been codified in quality standards, quality certifications, and quality awards. Among the more noteworthy are the ISO 9000 quality standard, the Six Sigma certification, and the Malcolm Baldrige Quality Award.

Quality Standards, Certifications, and Awards

In today's business environment, companies pursue several quality management standards or goals not only to improve organizational quality but also to send competitive signals to the marketplace for the purpose of product or service differentiation. In many instances, organizations that have achieved certain levels of quality certification may require business partners and suppliers to achieve that same level of certification. This section provides an overview of several well-known quality certifications.

ISO 9000
A set of quality management systems standards that provide guidance on management and improvement of quality.

ISO 9000 Certification

In 1987, the International Organization for Standardization instituted the voluntary ISO 9000 standard. **ISO 9000** is a set of quality management systems standards, which signifies that it is applicable to any industry or organization, including information

Table 8.1 Well-Known Quality Management Pioneers and Their Achievements

Quality Proponents	Achievements
W. Edwards Deming	Best known for his fourteen points of quality
Joseph Juran	Added the human element to project quality Credited with the Pareto Principle, or the 80/20 rule Wrote a model for quality management based on quality planning, quality improvement, and quality control
Philip B. Crosby	Convinced managers that preventing problems was cheaper than fixing them Defined quality in an absolute way
Kaoru Ishikawa	Best known for his cause-and-effect or fishbone diagram Also known for his insistence that quality could always be taken a step further Proposed an actionable list of six items to achieve quality
Robert Kaplan and David Norton	Balanced scorecard

systems focused enterprises. ISO 9000 is one of the most popular quality standards in the world. Thousands of organizations have adopted it, and more continue to do so on a regular basis.

The ISO 9000 family of standards is primarily concerned with quality management, specifically the processes that the organization performs to satisfy customer quality requirements, to satisfy regulatory requirements, to enhance customer satisfaction, and finally to provide for continual improvement in performance of these objectives. ISO 9000 is based on seven quality management principles that focus on different aspects of an organization's purpose (see Figure 8.13).

As a family of standards, ISO 9000 can be customized and applied to various industries. One example specific to information systems development is the problem of software configuration management. In the process of building computer software, change frequently occurs during the development stage. Despite the intention to control factors like scope creep, user requirements frequently evolve as a project moves forward. Software configuration management is a set of activities designed to help manage or control such changes by assisting developers or project managers in identifying those work products that are most likely to change, establishing relationships among work products so that the developer can anticipate any associated changes that will also need to be made, defining ways to manage different versions of work products, and reporting on changes that have been made. ISO 9000 can provide guidance to help a firm establish documented procedures for controlling such changes.

Six Sigma Certification

While the statistical usage of the term *Six Sigma* can be traced back much further in time, its application to quality management is attributed to a Motorola engineer named Bill Smith. In fact, Six Sigma is a registered trademark of the Motorola Company. The purpose of the Six Sigma quality methodology is to reduce variation and, therefore, the number of product or service defects. Six Sigma has been embraced as a management philosophy that relies on factors such as company culture to enhance quality.

Six Sigma certification requires a company to embrace and learn a body of knowledge related to quality, to pass proficiency tests on the subject matter, and then to demonstrate appropriate levels of competency in real environments. The body of knowledge associated with Six Sigma includes understanding the basics of what Six Sigma is, as well as the processes that help an organization define, measure, analyze, improve, and control its activities. Six Sigma certification testing is done at different levels of proficiency—for

Figure 8.13 ISO 9000 quality management principles

example, green belt, black belt, master black belt, and champion. In addition to the knowledge associated with each level of proficiency, certification also requires organizational personnel to exhibit the quality standards through hands-on activities.

Six Sigma standards, like the ISO 9000 standards discussed previously, may be applied to information systems projects. In fact, the overlap between the information systems project management techniques discussed in this book and Six Sigma are evident if we compare the project life cycle of initiation, planning, execution, control, and closure discussed in this book to the objectives that companies try to meet in implementing the Six Sigma methodology:

- Defining the problem, the customers' requirements, and critical project goals
- Measuring core business processes
- Analyzing the data collected
- Improving target processes
- Controlling improvements to ensure the processes remain in line with any changes, Six Sigma helps a company illustrate that they are adhering to processes that will improve both their product and service quality.

Baldrige National Quality Program

The Baldrige National Quality Program and the associated Malcolm Baldrige National Quality Award are focused on recognizing excellence and quality achievement. The award, established in 1987 and named after the former secretary of commerce, recognizes outstanding achievements in seven areas: leadership, strategic planning, customer and market focus, information and analysis, human resource focus, process management, and results.

Secretary Malcolm Baldrige was a firm believer that both quality and performance were crucial to the nation's long-term prosperity and economic health. The Malcolm Baldrige Quality Award program was established not only to recognize organizations operating in an exemplary fashion but also to provide a benchmark that can encourage other American companies to aggressively pursue a world-class commitment to excellence. While the award can be given to any type of firm, past award recipients have included technology-focused firms such as Xerox, AT&T, and IBM. Award recipients are assessed by third-party examiners across a number of dimensions, with performance rated on both customer satisfaction and business processes. The award also overlaps with the concepts discussed in this book. Information systems project management is concerned with following rigorous process and procedures to enhance customer satisfaction as it relates to the information system being designed.

Total Quality Management

Total quality management (TQM) is a systematic approach to managing quality that originated in the 1950s and has grown in popularity since that time. *Total quality* describes the culture, organization, and attitude of a company that works toward providing customers with products and services that truly satisfy their needs. Adopting such a culture necessitates quality in all aspects of a firm's operations. Processes are supposed to be done right the first time, with the goal of eliminating defects and waste from operations. TQM requires management and employees to become involved in the continuous improvement of the firm's goods and services. Companies that have implemented TQM include Ford Motor Company, Phillips Semiconductor, SGL Carbon, Motorola, and Toyota Motor Company.

Techniques for Managing Project Quality

The Project Management Institute outlines three Project Quality Management processes within the *PMBOK* (*PMBOK* Guide, 2017). As shown in Figure 8.14, these processes are *Plan Quality Management*, *Manage Quality*, and *Control Quality*. The processes of planning quality management and managing quality will be detailed later in this chapter. Quality control will be summarized in this chapter and discussed more fully in Chapter 12, which focuses on control processes.

Tips from the Pros: The Difficult Task of Managing IS Quality

Information technologies (IT) and the information systems (IS) function have become very important to any organization. Organizations are taking advantage of IT to support business operations and increase the value of their products and services in an attempt to gain a competitive advantage in the marketplace. To attain these goals, it is essential for organizations to implement an IS quality system. Management of IS quality can be quite difficult because it includes many dimensions and is judged differently by different stakeholders involved in a particular project. Although project team members may be concerned about the daily operational details associated with controlling project quality, clients will typically be more concerned with the end product.

Several issues should be addressed when implementing an IS quality system. These include:

- *Customer focus.* The main goal of the IS department should be to provide products/services that add value and contribute to keeping customers satisfied.

- *Process approach.* Resources, activities, and outcomes of the IS function are interrelated, and therefore, these associations should be managed as processes. Viewing the IS function as a process makes the implementation of continuous improvement activities easier.

- *Leadership.* Most quality programs are successful because of strong leadership. Strong leaders are the ones who are willing to invest energy and resources to make the IS quality program a success.

- *Culture.* The cultural environment of an organization influences the success of a quality program. A culture where IS is treated as an important and integral function in organizational change should be promoted.

- *Broad participation.* IS quality management should be a joint effort, where all stakeholders participate in, and contribute to, the success of the quality program.

- *Motivating the troops.* For a quality program to succeed, committed and motivated personnel are very essential. IS personnel should be aware of the benefits of a quality program, in terms of work satisfaction and personal rewards.

- *Training.* Well-trained personnel are more likely to be leaders and will more vigorously work toward the success of a quality program.

- *Measurement and constructive feedback.* After the implementation of the IS quality program, results should be measured systematically in order to provide feedback for continuous improvement.

- *Accountability for results and rewarding achievements.* Teams and individual persons should be rewarded for their efforts in the success of the quality program.

- *Self-assessment.* The quality program should be evaluated continuously to provide critical feedback, which can be used to sustain it.

Based on: Leicher (2017); Stylianou and Kumar (2000).

Plan Quality Management

Plan Quality Management
The process of identifying relevant quality standards and developing a plan to ensure the project meets those standards.

Plan Quality Management is the process of identifying relevant quality standards and developing a plan to ensure the project meets those standards. Quality planning is usually performed at the same time that other project planning issues are addressed because many planning issues (e.g., scheduling, resource allocation, etc.) have quality dimensions. Figure 8.15 lists the inputs, the tools and techniques used, and the resulting outputs of the *Plan Quality Management* process.

Figure 8.14   *PMBOK* (6th ed.) Project Quality Management processes

Figure 8.15 The *PMBOK* (6th ed.) *Plan Quality Management* process

Plan Quality Management—Inputs

Inputs to quality planning include the project charter and components of the project management plan, including the requirements management plan, the risk management plan, the stakeholder engagement plan, and the scope baseline. In addition, project documents such as the assumption log, the risk and stakeholder registers, the requirements documentation, and the requirements traceability matrix serve as inputs into the quality planning process. We have covered most of these inputs in other chapters (e.g., the project scope statement and project management plan). Further, the project manager draws on enterprise environmental factors, including the government regulations according to which the company must operate, as well as any rules standards or guidelines specific to the organization's products or services, organizational culture, working conditions, and so on.

Finally, organizational process assets include factors like the organization's quality policies, quality-related procedures and guidelines, and finally, any documented lessons learned from prior projects. An example of a **quality policy** is illustrated in Figure 8.16. As can be seen from Nestlé's quality policy, this particular firm places the customers at the center of all quality-related efforts.

Quality policy
The overall intentions and direction of an organization with regard to quality, as formally expressed by top management.

Plan Quality Management—Tools and Techniques

Some tools and techniques available during the planning quality management process include expert judgment; data gathering techniques such as brainstorming, interviews, or benchmarking; data analysis techniques such as cost-benefit analysis and cost of quality analysis; as well as test and inspection planning. Typically, the project manager uses flowcharts, logical data models, matrix diagrams, or mind mapping to present the data and facilitate decision-making.

In the *Plan Quality Management* process, experts in various areas of quality (such as assurance, control, measurement, improvement, or systems) can provide valuable input. You have learned about data gathering techniques like brainstorming and interviews in earlier chapters. **Benchmarking** is the study of a competitor's product or business practices for the purpose of improving a company's performance. In terms of IS project management, benchmarking may be used to compare a company's IS project management practices with those of other projects, both within or outside the organization. In this respect, benchmarking serves as an important tool for quality planning.

Benchmarking
The study of a competitor's product or business practices in order to improve the performance of one's own company.

Figure 8.16 Nestlé's quality policy. *Based on*: Nestlé (2014).

Capability maturity model
A technique used to determine a company's capabilities with respect to a set of procedures considered as best practices within a given industry.

Serving a function similar to benchmarking are **capability maturity models (CMMs).** Capability maturity models are used to determine a company's capabilities with respect to best practices within a given industry. More specifically, CMM is a methodology used to develop and refine how an organization approaches its software development process. CMMs were originally developed by the Software Engineering Institute (SEI), a research and development center sponsored by the U.S. Department of Defense. CMM is a five-level evolutionary model of increasingly organized and systematically more mature processes for systems development. These five maturity levels for software processes are shown in Figure 8.17. The CMM is similar to ISO 9001, one of the ISO 9000 series of standards discussed earlier in this chapter. ISO 9001 focuses specifically on the development and maintenance of software and specifies minimally acceptable quality levels for the processes used to develop software. CMM goes beyond ISO 9001 in establishing a framework for continuous process improvements surrounding software development, and in providing more detail on how to achieve these new quality standards.

Two important data analysis techniques used in the process are cost-benefit analysis and cost of quality analysis. As you have learned in Chapter 5, cost-benefit analyses originated as an analogy to investment decision-making, where "go" or "no-go" decisions were frequently made. However, the technique is flexible enough to allow decision makers to choose among a range of alternatives. Performing a cost-benefit analysis on alternative approaches to meeting project objectives might include calculating financial metrics, such as return on investment (ROI). In planning quality management, a cost-benefit analysis can be used to determine the trade-off between the benefits of higher quality and the costs incurred by ensuring a particular product meets those higher quality standards. For example, certain products may experience a "quality threshold." In other words, a product may be of very high quality, yet if it does not fill a customer need, it will not be purchased regardless of its quality. In this case, it would not make sense to incur additional costs to improve the product's quality. Likewise, meeting certain quality requirements incurs both costs and benefits, and the project manager has to evaluate how far the benefits of meeting the quality requirements (such as less rework or higher customer satisfaction) outweigh the costs (e.g., for using higher-skilled programmers, more testing, or using more expensive hardware).

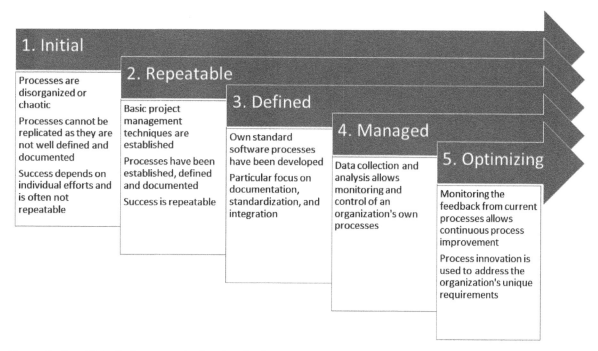

Figure 8.17 CMM's five maturity levels of software processes

Cost of quality
The cost to improve or ensure quality measures, as well as the cost associated with a lack of quality.

In assessing the costs and benefits of quality activities, an important concept is that of the **cost of quality (COQ)**. The cost of quality is composed of the cost of conformance (i.e., costs to prevent quality problems) and the cost of nonconformance (i.e., costs resulting from quality problems). The cost of conformance includes prevention costs (such as training or equipment) as well as appraisal costs (such as testing or inspections); the cost of nonconformance includes internal failure costs (such as rework or wastage) and external failure costs (such as loss of goodwill or business, warranty costs, or liability issues; see Figure 8.18). In other words, the cost of quality might represent the amount of money a business could lose from products or services not being done well the first time around, as well as the costs to do it well the first time around. Estimates are that the cost of quality may run from 15 to 30 percent of total costs for most businesses (see https://www.isixsigma.com/dictionary/cost-of-quality).

As an extreme example of the cost of quality, one need only think back to the Y2K programming issue, where dates were stored in two-digit representations to save storage space in early information systems (e.g., 98 instead of 1998). It was anticipated that once the year 2000 came to pass, systems with the two-digit date representation scheme would not able to distinguish between the year 1998 and 2098, resulting in systems errors in any calculation involving time (such as interest calculations). The Gartner Group estimated the worldwide costs for the Y2K issue to range from $300 to $600 billion dollars, including activities ranging from reprogramming efforts to the handling of lawsuits from angry clients. What was the cost of quality (i.e., the cost of not doing it right the first time) in this case? A high price tag indeed!

During the *Plan Quality Management* process, the project manager also plans the procedures for evaluating the deliverables. In information systems projects, this typically involves developing a master test plan that specifies how testing will be conducted (e.g.,

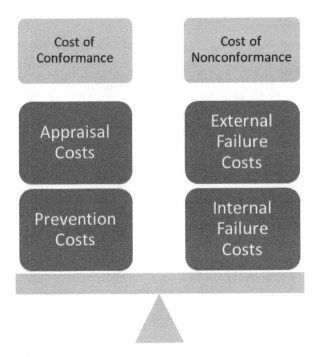

Figure 8.18 The cost of quality

code inspections, desk checking, unit testing, alpha and beta testing), who will do the testing, how tests will be executed, and what constitutes success or failure.

Typically, a series of diagrams can help in presenting data for meetings and decision-making. For example, project managers develop flowcharts (to represent the steps in a process), logical data models (to identify potential issues with data quality), matrix diagrams (to depict relationships between factors and objectives), or mind mapping (to organize ideas or concepts).

Plan Quality Management—Outputs

The outputs from the quality planning stage include a quality management plan (as part of the project management plan), quality metrics, and updates to the project management plan and documents. A **quality management plan** is a plan specifying how quality measures will be implemented during a project. Unlike the quality policy introduced previously, the quality management plan lays out the specifics, rather than a philosophy of how quality will be managed during the project. The components of a quality management plan (a rather substantial document) are shown in Figure 8.19. The quality management plan serves the additional purpose of being an input into the overall project management plan. **Quality metrics** are operational definitions of specific processes, events, or products, and include an explanation of how they will be measured in terms of quality.

As the quality planning stage is finalized, these quality planning outputs will serve as updates to the project management plan, in addition to potential changes to the scope baseline and the risk management plan. As with any process, this process is likely to result in updates to various project documents, including the lessons learned, risk, and stakeholder registers, and the requirements traceability matrix.

Quality management plan
A plan specifying how quality measures will be implemented during a project.

Quality metrics
Operational definitions of specific, processes, events, or products, as well as an explanation of how they will be measured in terms of quality.

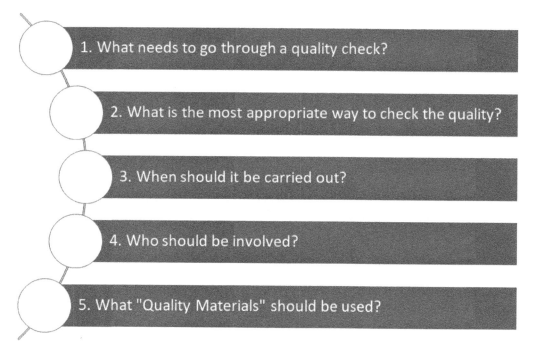

1. What needs to go through a quality check?

2. What is the most appropriate way to check the quality?

3. When should it be carried out?

4. Who should be involved?

5. What "Quality Materials" should be used?

Figure 8.19   Components of a quality management plan

Common Problems: The Costs of Software Quality

Worldwide costs of software failure in 2016 have been estimated to be as high as US$1.1 trillion, affecting 4.4 billion customers and amounting to over 315 years of lost time. To maintain a competitive edge in the marketplace, software firms must deliver products of high quality on time and within budget. However, software managers may avoid quality inspections in an attempt to bring their products to the market faster because they feel such quality mechanisms only delay the software development process.

The costs of quality are divided into two major categories: conformance and nonconformance. The cost of conformance is the amount spent on achieving high-quality products. This category of quality costs is further divided into prevention and appraisal costs. Prevention costs are those associated with preventing any defects before they happen, whereas appraisal costs are those incurred in assuring conformance to quality standards. The cost of nonconformance includes all the expenses that result when things go wrong. This category of quality costs is also further divided into two subcategories—internal failure costs and external failure costs. Internal failure costs occur before the product is sent to the customer, whereas external failure costs arise from product failure at the customer's location. Table 8.2 lists the different types of quality costs, along with examples of each.

How can organizations decrease the costs associated with software quality? The best strategy involves

- Avoiding any failure costs by driving defects to zero
- Investing in prevention activities to improve quality
- Reducing appraisal costs as quality improves
- Continuously evaluating and altering preventive efforts for more improvement

Quality improvements often result in cost savings that outweigh the money spent on quality efforts. Which of the provided strategies do you believe has the largest effect on controlling software quality?

Based on: McPeak (2017); Slaughter, Harter, and Krishnan (1998).

Table 8.2 Types of Quality Costs

Types of Cost	Example
Cost of Conformance	
Prevention costs	Costs of training staff in design methodologies
Appraisal costs	Code inspection and testing
Cost of Nonconformance	
Internal failure costs	Costs of rework in programming
External failure costs	Costs of support and maintenance

Manage Quality

Manage Quality
The process of ensuring that the project meets the quality standards outlined in the *Plan Quality Management* process.

The **Manage Quality** process is composed of all the activities and actions required to ensure that the project meets the quality standards outlined in the *Plan Quality Management* process. This ongoing process (sometimes referred to as quality assurance) focuses on the project processes, so that the project's final outcome meets stakeholder requirements. Thus the *Manage Quality* process uses inputs from the *Control Quality* process (discussed later) to improve processes as well as product design. For a list of the inputs required, the tools and techniques used, and the resulting outputs during the quality assurance process, see Figure 8.20.

Manage Quality—Inputs

As illustrated in Figure 8.20, the inputs to the quality assurance process include the quality management plan, quality metrics, quality control measurements, the lessons learned register, the risk report, as well as organizational process assets (such as quality templates, lessons learned from prior projects, or organizational quality management systems). The quality management plan and operational definitions were developed as part of the quality planning process outlined earlier. The quality management plan is used to outline the specifics of the quality measures that will be in place during the project. The results of the quality control measures are often based on quality testing procedures and should be formatted for further analyses.

Manage Quality—Tools and Techniques

The tools and techniques used as part of the *Plan Quality Management* process can also be used during the *Manage Quality* process. In particular, data gathering, representation, and analyses techniques can help implement the quality management plan. Three new tools are also used in the quality assurance process—specifically, quality audits, process analysis, and "design for X." **Quality audits** are activities designed to review other quality management procedures as well as to identify potential lessons learned. In a quality audit, the review is conducted in either scheduled or random fashion by trained personnel from within the organization or, in some cases, by qualified third-party auditors. Quality auditors typically examine a number of different project facets looking for ineffective or inefficient policies, processes, or procedures. Quality auditors may start with an established checklist and rate the various project facets evaluated. Such a checklist is shown in Figure 8.21.

Quality audit
Structured and independent review activities designed to review quality management procedures and to identify potential lessons learned.

Another tool used in the quality assurance process is a process analysis, which examines not what is done but how it is done. Likewise, root cause analysis aims to determine the causes for a particular quality problem. Once the root cause of a problem

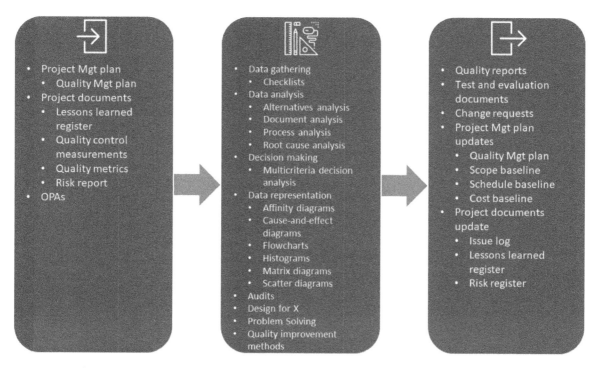

Figure 8.20 The *PMBOK* (6th ed.) *Manage Quality* process

QUALITY ASSURANCE FUNCTIONS	YES	NO
Does the quality assurance unit or qualified designee do the following?		
1. approve or reject devices processed by another company		
2. approve or reject devices packaged by another company		
3. approve or reject devices held under contract by another company		
4. help provide solutions for quality system problems		
5. verify implementation of solutions for quality system problems		
6. assure that all quality system checks are appropriate and adequate		
7. assure that all quality system checks are performed correctly		

Figure 8.21 Sample quality audit checklist from the FDA's Center for Devices and Radiological Health

is determined, steps can be taken to rectify the issue, so as to prevent the problem from reoccurring.

Any lessons learned and documented as part of the quality audit process are then used to improve performance during the current project or subsequent projects. Quality audits can be performed by in-house quality auditors or by outside auditors hired for a specific project.

The design of any product or service can have a number of objectives and involves trade-offs between various factors, such as quality, reliability, maintainability, service performance, and so on. Acknowledging these trade-offs, Design for X (DfX)—sometimes referred to as design for excellence—is a recent concept relating to a focus on particular aspects of a product or service, where the design efforts focus on maximizing quality or reliability, minimizing costs, and so on.

Manage Quality—Outputs

Finally, the outputs from the quality assurance process are quality reports, test and evaluation documents, and change requests. Often, such change requests affect different parts of the overall project management plan, such as the quality management plan, but also the scope, cost, and schedule baselines. Likewise, any identified issues and risks, as well as lessons learned, will be recorded in the issues log, the risk register, and the lessons learned register.

Control Quality

Control Quality The process of monitoring results to determine if the quality standards of the project are being met.

Control Quality involves monitoring results to determine if the quality standards of the project are being met. The *PMBOK* inputs, tools and techniques, and outputs are briefly presented here; Chapter 12 will cover them in much more depth.

The *Control Quality* process is interrelated with both the *Plan Quality Management* and the *Manage Quality* processes, in that outputs of these processes serve as inputs into the *Control Quality* process, and outputs from the *Control Quality* process serve as inputs into the *Manage Quality* process; as the *Manage Quality* process, *Control Quality* is an ongoing process. Figure 8.22 shows the *PMBOK* inputs, tools, and outputs for the *Control Quality* process. Inputs discussed earlier include the quality management plan, quality metrics, test and evaluation documents, organizational process assets and enterprise environmental factors, work performance data, approved change requests, and importantly, the deliverables to be tested or evaluated. As defined in Chapter 2, work performance data include data about the outputs of activities, or about the activities themselves.

Control chart Graphical, time-based chart used to display process results.

Pareto chart Histogram (or bar chart) where the values being plotted are arranged in descending order.

The most prominent tools and techniques in the *Control Quality* process are inspection and testing of the deliverables. Typically, inspection and testing are supported by the use of checklists and checksheets. Statistical sampling is used to identify samples for inspection or testing purposes. Further, questionnaires and surveys can be used to obtain feedback about the quality from customers or other stakeholders. Project managers can then perform performance reviews and data analyses (such as root cause analysis) based the information presented in various diagrams, such as cause-and-effect (also called fishbone or Ishikawa) diagrams (Figure 8.23), **control charts** (Figure 8.24), **Pareto charts** (Figure 8.25), flowcharting (Figure 8.26), histograms, run charts, or scatter diagrams. Often, these activities are accompanied by meetings to review the extent to which approved change requests were implemented and to discuss possible lessons learned. We depict a few of these tools graphically in this chapter but leave their explanation to Chapter 12.

Once you have utilized the various quality control tools and techniques to control the quality of the project, you will have produced a series of quality control outputs. The most obvious output is the verified deliverables—that is, the deliverables that are deemed as being of acceptable quality. Further, any quality control measurements serve as input into the *Manage Quality* process, where they are used to determine if process improvements are necessary to maintain the desired quality levels. Likewise, work performance information serves as an input for various other processes. Further, updates include change requests and potential updates to the project management plan and project documents, such as the issue log, the risk and lessons learned registers, and the test and evaluation documents. As with the inputs, and the tools and techniques for quality control, these outputs will be covered in more detail in Chapter 12.

Table 8.3 lists some of the tools and techniques available for Project Quality Management, as well as a short explanation of what they are.

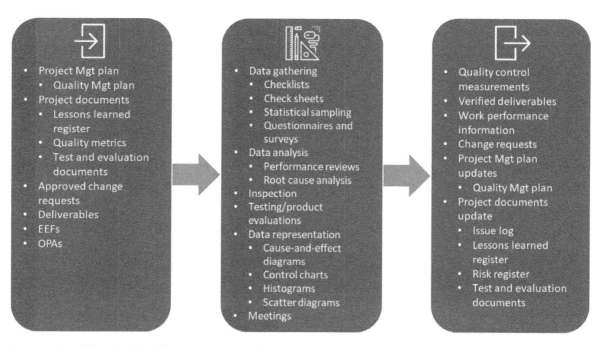

Figure 8.22 The *PMBOK* (6th ed.) *Control Quality* process

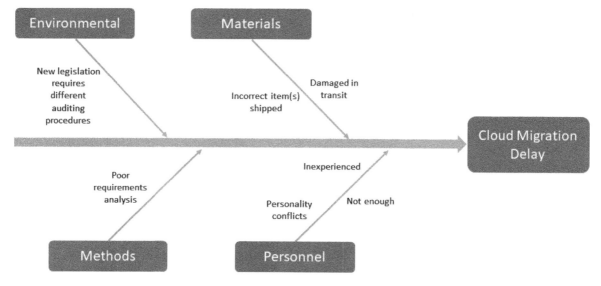

Figure 8.23 Cause-and-effect (fishbone) diagram

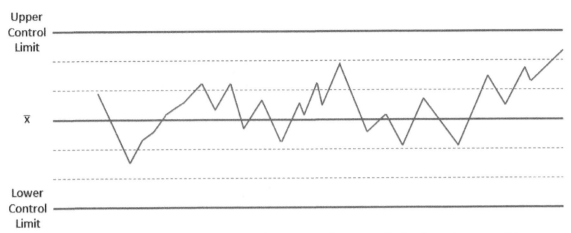

The x axis of all control charts consists of sample numbers (usually the time of the sample). Control charts have three common lines:

1. A center line, designated with an "x̄" which provides the average (x) of the process data.
2. An upper line designating the upper control limit (UCL), drawn at a distance representing three standard deviations above the average, showing the upper range of acceptable data.
3. The lower line designating the lower control limit (LCL), which shows the lower range of acceptable data.

Points outside of the UCL and LCL indicate that the process is out of control and/or unstable.

Figure 8.24   Control chart

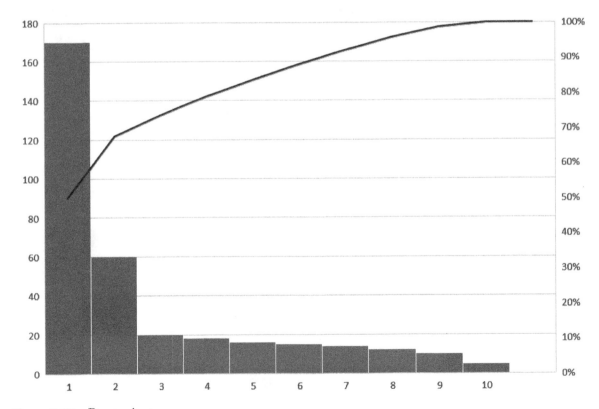

Figure 8.25   Pareto chart

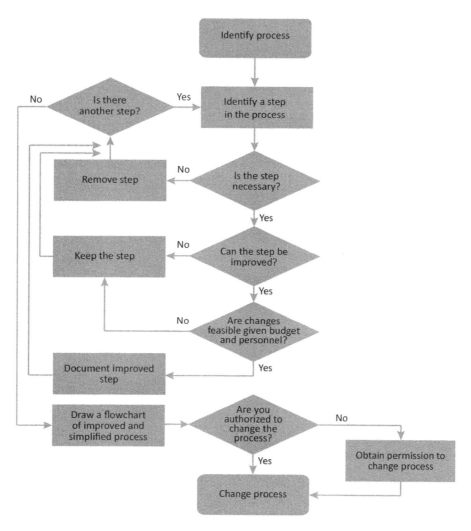

Figure 8.26   Quality control flowchart

Table 8.3   Tools and Techniques Available for Project Quality Management

Tools and Techniques	Short Explanation
Cost-benefit analysis	An evaluation of the costs and benefits of alternative approaches to a proposed activity to determine the best alternative.
Inspection	Measurement and testing procedures to determine whether results conform to the particular project standards.
Statistical sampling	The process of selecting a random sample from a population in order to infer characteristics about that population.
Control charts	Graphical, time-based charts used to display process results.
Cause-and-effect (fishbone) diagrams	A diagramming technique used to explore potential and real causes of problems. The fishbone diagram typically organizes problems into categories relevant to the industry.
Pareto diagrams	Histograms ordered in terms of the number of occurrences of project problems that have been identified.

Global Implications: Quality Assurance Works Better Than Quality Control for Offshore Projects

Assume both a client company and an offshore vendor assign a project manager to an outsourcing project. The main role of the project manager at the client company is to work closely with the development team to ensure that the milestones and the project requirements are being met; thus the home office project manager has to perform quality assurance rather than quality control. In an offshore project, managing quality is more difficult because by the time the project results are verified, correcting mistakes could be quite costly. In such cases, quality assurance is useful because it focuses on the processes required to produce the results and thus will help prevent problems before they occur. Here are some tips for managing project quality in offshore projects:

1. A set of clear and comprehensive requirements should be developed for the project.

2. The project deliverables must be clearly described, and all stakeholders should agree to and approve this definition.

3. Project success should be clearly defined by developing the criteria for assessing the project deliverables in terms of completeness and correctness.

4. The project plan should clearly describe how the development team will do the work.

5. Milestones should be set for the major deliverables, and there should be an approval and sign-off at each point to ensure quality.

6. All formal communication during the project life cycle should be addressed to the project managers. The project manager knows what is going on at every stage of the project and can, therefore, better manage everyone's expectations.

7. Any problems that arise during the life cycle of the project should be communicated and addressed as soon as possible.

Based on: Mochal (2002); Tardugno (2003); Tkach (2017).

Managing Project Costs and Quality and *PMBOK*

In this chapter, we have focused primarily on Knowledge Area 7, Project Cost Management, and Knowledge Area 8, Project Quality Management, within the Project Management Body of Knowledge (*PMBOK*, 2017). In addition to costs, Project Quality Management is often considered by some experts to be a fourth dimension that should be included in the cost-time-scope trade-off experienced during project management. Thus neither managing project costs nor managing project quality should be overlooked during any project and especially not during IS development. In this chapter, we have identified the various processes of Project Cost Management, including *Plan Cost Management*, *Estimate Costs*, *Determine Budget*, and *Control Costs*, as well as the processes associated with Project Quality Management, including *Plan Quality Management*, *Manage Quality*, and *Control Quality*. We have also identified the various tools and techniques that can be used in managing costs and quality. Figure 8.27 identifies this coverage and illustrates the coverage of upcoming chapters as well.

Figure 8.27 Chapter 8 and *PMBOK* coverage

Key: ○ where the material is covered in the textbook; ● current chapter coverage

	Textbook Chapters ⟶	1	2	3	4	5	6	7	8	9	10	11	12
	PMBOK Knowledge Area												
1	Introduction												
1.2	Foundational Elements	○	○										
2	The Environment in Which Projects Operate												
2.2	Enterprise Environmental Factors		○										
2.2	Organizational Process Assets		○										
2.3	Organizational Systems		○										
3	The Role of the Project Manager												
3.2	Definition of a Project Manager	○											
3.3	The Project Manager's Sphere of Influence		○										
3.4	Project Manager Competences	○	○	○									
3.5	Performing Integration		○										
4	Project Integration Management												
4.1	Develop Project Charter					○							
4.2	Develop Project Management Plan					○							
4.3	Direct and Manage Project Work											○	
4.4	Manage Project Knowledge											○	
4.5	Monitor and Control Project Work											○	○
4.6	Perform Integrated Change Control												○
4.7	Close Project or Phase										○		○
5	Project Scope Management												
5.1	Plan Scope Management					○							
5.2	Collect Requirements					○							
5.3	Define Scope					○							
5.4	Create WBS					○	○						
5.5	Validate Scope					○							
5.6	Control Scope					○							○
6	Project Schedule Management												
6.1	Plan Schedule Management						○						
6.2	Define Activities						○						
6.3	Sequence Activities						○						
6.4	Estimate Activity Durations							○					
6.5	Develop Schedule							○					
6.6	Control Schedule							○					○

#	Process												
7	**Project Cost Management**												
7.1	Plan Cost Management								●				
7.2	Estimate Costs								●				
7.3	Determine Budget								●				
7.4	Control Costs								●				○
8	**Project Quality Management**												
8.1	Plan Quality Management								●				
8.2	Manage Quality								●				
8.3	Control Quality								●				○
9	**Project Resource Management**												
9.1	Plan Resource Management							○					
9.2	Estimate Activity Resources						○	○					
9.3	Acquire Resources							○				○	
9.4	Develop Team			○								○	
9.5	Manage Team			○								○	
9.6	Control Resources							○					○
10	**Project Communications Management**												
10.1	Plan Communications Management				○								
10.2	Manage Communications				○							○	
10.3	Monitor Communications				○								○
11	**Project Risk Management**												
11.1	Plan Risk Management									○			
11.2	Identify Risks									○		○	
11.3	Perform Qualitative Risk Analysis									○			
11.4	Perform Quantitative Risk Analysis									○			
11.5	Plan Risk Responses									○			
11.6	Implement Risk Responses									○		○	
11.7	Monitor Risks									○			○
12	**Project Procurement Management**												
12.1	Plan Procurement Management										○		
12.2	Conduct Procurements										○	○	
12.3	Control Procurements										○		○
13	**Project Stakeholder Management**												
12.1	Identify Stakeholders				○								
12.2	Plan Stakeholder Engagement				○								
12.3	Manage Stakeholder Engagement				○							○	
12.4	Monitor Stakeholder Engagement				○								○

Running Case: Managing Project Costs and Quality

Cindy reviewed the project charter, looking at the objectives of the system: track customer purchases, create a point system for customers to use toward redeeming merchandise, reward customer loyalty, and improve management information. Cindy knew that the quality of this project needed to relate somehow to these objectives, but she wasn't quite sure how to approach the issue.

Certainly, a system to track customer purchases and then allocate points to those customers making purchases seemed to be rather straightforward. However, tracking whether they were adequately rewarding loyal customers and improving the information that management used—both being quality objectives—seemed a bit vaguer.

The next day after the initial updates on project status, Cindy presented her dilemma: "We need to figure out if this project is doing what management wants it to."

"Let's talk about customer loyalty for a second. Since we are measuring loyalty by the number of times a customer returns and makes a purchase, let's just track customer visits," said Trey.

"That's a good idea, but the problem is that we don't always know if they have visited. What if they pay cash?" said Kevin.

"Ah, good point. How about if we track their use of the points? That's really the key point of the new system anyway, isn't it?" asked Trey.

"Well, yeah, but remember, while we want to reward customers for their loyalty, I think the real goal is to see how this loyalty impacts the bottom line," said Kevin. "I think we need to somehow track the frequency of visits and maybe the size of the purchases. If these go up, the system is working. And then, let's not forget about the better information the system is supposed to provide to management. Is there a way to track information *quality*?"

"Wait," said Cindy. "All this is related to whether the system is doing what we want at the end. What about managing the quality during the development of the system? How do we handle that?"

The meeting went on for some time as the team looked through materials for quality project management techniques and considered how they could apply to this project.

Adapted from: Valacich and George (2017).

Chapter Summary

Understand techniques for managing project costs. Managing project costs involves a series of processes, ranging from planning cost management to estimating costs, determining the budget, and controlling costs. Just as with estimating resources or durations, when estimating the costs of completing an activity, project managers rely on several tools and techniques, such as expert judgment, alternatives analysis, parametric estimating, analogous estimating, three-point estimating, and reserve analysis. After costs have been estimated, the project manager is then ready to develop a full project budget. By using several techniques, the successful project manager can develop an accurate budget based on activity cost estimates, contingency reserves, and management reserves. Controlling costs involves evaluating the project's progress as compared to the approved cost baseline.

Understand the concept of quality and why it is important. Quality is defined by the International Organization for Standardization as "the degree to which a set of inherent characteristics fulfill requirements." Project quality is often defined by companies as both conformance to manufacturer specifications and fitness for use by the customer. Project quality is important because it has a direct relationship to project success. Many examples of information system project success and failure can be attributed to project quality. In many instances, information systems are used in contexts that have little or no tolerance for error. An example highlighted in the chapter was that of an air traffic control system—a system that controls the regulation and scheduling of incoming and outgoing flights at a major airport. A glitch in the software, caused by poor quality in designing or building such a system, could have disastrous results.

Discuss quality management pioneers and quality certifications and standards in industries today. There have been many quality management pioneers throughout history, including Deming, Juran, Crosby, and Ishikawa. Further, the need to manage quality has spurred the development of standards and systems supporting quality management, including ISO 9000 and Six Sigma, as well as awards for quality, such as the Baldrige Award. Adopting the procedures associated with quality certification programs may help improve the organization's bottom line.

Describe tools and techniques for managing project quality. Managing project quality can be accomplished by following the major processes of *Plan Quality Management*, *Manage Quality*, and *Control Quality*, as specified by *PMBOK*. Several tools and techniques were discussed in this chapter, including inspection, statistical control, control charts, cause and effect diagrams, and Pareto analysis. Each of these has specific uses within Project Quality Management. Technology also plays a major role in Project Quality Management. Statistical analysis, document repositories, and project data tracking represent just a few of the ways in which technology can be used during quality management.

Key Terms Review

A. Balanced scorecard
B. Benchmarking
C. Capability maturity models
D. Control chart
E. Control Quality
F. Cost of quality
G. Cost baseline
H. Fishbone diagram
I. ISO 9000
J. Manage Quality
K. Pareto chart
L. Plan Quality Management
M. Quality
N. Quality audit
O. Quality management plan
P. Quality metrics
Q. Quality policy

Match each of the key terms with the definition that best fits it.

1. A diagramming technique used to explore potential and real causes of problems.
2. A document that contains the approved project budget for all schedule activities and serves as a basis for comparison during project execution.
3. A plan specifying how quality measures will be implemented during a project.
4. A set of quality management systems standards that provide guidance on management and improvement of quality.
5. A technique used to determine a company's capabilities with respect to a set of procedures considered as best practices within a given industry.
6. A tool for assessing organizational activity from perspectives beyond the typical financial analysis.
7. Graphical, time-based chart used to display process results.
8. Histogram (or bar chart) where the values being plotted are arranged in descending order.
9. Operational definitions of specific, processes, events, or products, as well as an explanation of how they will be measured in terms of quality.
10. Structured and independent review activities designed to review quality management procedures and to identify potential lessons learned.
11. The cost to improve or ensure quality measures, as well as the cost associated with a lack of quality.
12. The degree to which a set of inherent characteristics fulfill requirements.
13. The overall intentions and direction of an organization with regard to quality, as formally expressed by top management.
14. The process of ensuring that the project meets the quality standards outlined in the *Plan Quality Management* process.

15. The process of identifying relevant quality standards and developing a plan to ensure the project meets those standards.

16. The process of monitoring results to determine if the quality standards of the project are being met.

17. The study of a competitor's product or business practices in order to improve the performance of one's own company.

Review Questions

1. List the processes of Project Cost Management.
2. List two inputs for each of the Project Cost Management processes.
3. List two tools or techniques for each of the Project Cost Management processes.
4. List two outputs for each of the Project Cost Management processes.
5. Define project quality.
6. Give two examples of quality during an ISD project.
7. List the processes of Project Quality Management.
8. List two inputs for each of the Project Quality Management processes.
9. List two tools or techniques for each of the Project Quality Management processes.
10. List two outputs for each of the Project Quality Management processes.
11. Describe the cost-benefit analysis.
12. What role does inspection play during Project Quality Management?
13. Describe the cause and effect (fishbone) diagram.
14. Describe the Pareto analysis. What is the 80/20 rule?
15. Describe the two well-known quality certifications.
16. Explain how technology can be used to manage quality.

Chapter Exercises

1. Using the internet, find an example of an information systems development project that suffered from cost overruns. What was the primary reason for the overrun?

2. For the example from Exercise 1, were the initial estimates accurate? If the initial estimates were inaccurate, what were the difficulties encountered in estimating project costs?

3. Provide some examples of quality problems in information systems development projects and discuss how these quality problems can be avoided.

4. Using the internet, perform a search for benchmarking. Describe what it is and its usefulness. Also explain how this tool is important in managing quality.

5. Compare and contrast quality assurance and quality control.

6. Think of a recent project that you were involved in (or the project you are involved in as part of your current course). Identify a problem that you encountered. Next, determine potential categories for causes associated with the specific problem. Based on this information, develop a fishbone diagram.

7. Think of a recent project that you were involved in (or the project you are involved in as part of your current course). What were some of the problems you encountered? Were some of the causes of the problems more frequent than others? Using the 80/20 rule discussed in the chapter, construct a Pareto diagram illustrating the problems you encountered and the frequency of the causes.

8. Using the internet or any other source, write a two-page report on quality management certifications.

9. Using the internet, perform a search for ISO 9000. What is involved in earning this certification? Is it important to have this certification? Why or why not?

10. Using the internet, perform a search for ISO 14000. What is involved in earning this certification? Is it important to have this certification? Why or why not?

11. Using the internet or any other source, write a two-page report on other quality management pioneers not mentioned in the chapter.

12. Discuss how a project team can know if their project delivers good quality.

Chapter Case: Sedona Management Group and Managing Project Quality

Every project is affected in different ways by its scope, time, and cost goals. These three areas represent project management's triple constraint. However, lately there has been more and more agreement that quality should be included as a fourth dimension. Quality management is a very important topic in project management because it influences project success. The main goal of Project Quality Management is to ensure that the project satisfies the needs for which it was undertaken.

The Sedona Management Group (SMG) acknowledges the importance of managing project quality. Over the last ten years, the team has done a great job managing project quality by consistently delivering products that meet stakeholders' expectations in a timely manner.

At SMG, project quality is illustrated by the amount of new work that Sedona does for repeat customers. In addition, due to the high quality of its work related to both interface design and underlying web architecture, SMG has gained a reputation for being able to "clean up" websites built by other vendors. Satisfied customers spread the word about SMG's quality workmanship, so word-of-mouth advertising has been responsible for a substantial amount of Sedona's work over the last decades.

One of the first steps SMG follows in managing project quality is quality planning, which involves identifying the quality standards that are important to any given project, and then determining how to achieve these standards. In the case of the Seattle Seahawks project, it was important not only that the

information conveyed on the website be accurate and easy to access but also that the system be highly reliable and secure. All of these factors were part of SMG's quality plan, part of which involved establishing the criteria that the Sedona team needed to meet to ensure project success.

While establishing quality objectives is important, part of managing project quality also involves establishing the quality management processes the team will practice as they develop the system. Such quality assurance and control processes include establishing sufficient communication with the clients to ensure that their needs are being met; scheduling regular project meetings to discuss issues, such as project problems and causes; and documenting problems so these lessons learned can be applied to future projects. Through regular meetings with the members of the project team, Turnpaugh ensures that these quality standards are being met throughout the life cycle of the project. The Sedona team also ensures quality by reusing software code that has proven reliable in past projects.

Mike Flood, vice president of community relations with the Seattle Seahawks, recognizes SMG's efforts at ensuring quality. He has been so satisfied that he regularly recommends SMG to other potential clients, and he has employed SMG for other Seahawks IS projects. Overall, the Sedona team has undertaken at least one project per year for the Seattle Seahawks since their original development of the Seahawks' website.

Chapter 8 Project Assignment

An activity associated with Project Quality Management is problem identification during a project. There are several techniques for doing this, one of which is the Pareto analysis. In this assignment, you will develop a quality plan for your project and create a Pareto diagram that identifies problems you are encountering. You will have to

1. Define quality as it relates to your project.

2. Determine the requirements of the website you will be developing.

3. The purpose of a quality management plan is to define overall project quality guidelines that will be applied to the project. Develop a quality management plan for your project. This plan should contain information about

- How you will control changes to the project
- How you will ensure that the developed website meets the requirements
- How you will ensure that the website works properly
- How you will plan for and execute testing, both when the website is being developed and when design is completed
- How you will track and resolve defects

4. Identify and define the problems you are encountering during the project life cycle.

5. Determine the importance of these problems by assigning a weight to each of them. Note that the weights should sum to 1.0 or 100 percent. Generate a Pareto diagram based on these problems and write a small paragraph on what you learn from this diagram.

Special Case: Making It Work—Meeting Customer Expectations

Peter Dimov, a manager of software development at InterImage, and Petya Alexandrova, founder and president of Digital Enterprises Inc., recommend the following steps for meeting customer expectations—a critical component to quality.

Step 1: Build a communication channel and a trusting relationship. These managers recommend *using* a bilateral mode of communication to ensure that you understand the customer's needs. To earn trust, they state, managers must ensure the credibility of the information they provide to the client.

Step 2: Exchange relevant and meaningful information. Dimov and Alexandrova have found that to avoid

potential misunderstandings, managers must learn about clients' personalities, thought processes, background, and company lingo. Further, they state that both formal and informal lines of communication should be established.

Step 3: Establish a system to measure success. For this step, the authors recommend that managers and clients develop a mutual acceptance of what makes a project successful.

Step 4: Conduct status meetings. As a final step, Dimov and Alexandrova stress the importance of status meetings to discuss and remedy any potential misunderstandings of misconceptions.

Based on: Dimov and Alexandrova (2003).

References

Deming, W. E. (1986). *Out of Crisis*. Cambridge, MA: MIT Press.

Dimov, P., and Alexandrova, P. (2003). Return Customers. *PM Network*, July, 48.

Hoffman, T. (2004, February 16). Balancing Act. *ComputerWorld*. Retrieved July 6, 2018, from http://www.computerworld.com/article/2574985/it-management/balancing--act.html

Hong Kong Free Press (2017, November 9). Computer Crashes Persist for Hong Kong's New Air Traffic System amid Warning of Possible Disaster from India. *Hong Kong Free Press*. Retrieved July 2, 2018, from https://www.hongkongfp.com/2017/11/09/computer-crashes-persist-hong-kongs-new-air-traffic-system-amid-warning-of-possible-disaster-from-india

International Organization for Standardization (2015). ISO9000:2015(en). Retrieved July 2, 2018, from https://www.iso.org/obp/ui/#iso:std:iso:9000:ed-4:v1:en

Ishikawa. K. (1985). *What Is Total Quality Control?* (Lu, D. J., trans.). Upper Saddle River, NJ: Prentice Hall.

Kaplan, R. S., and Norton, D. P. (1992). The Balanced Scorecard: Measures That Drive Performance. *Harvard Business Review* 70(1), 71–80.

Lee, T. B. (2018, May 8). Report: Software Bug Led to Death in Uber's Self-Driving Crash. *Ars Technica*. Retrieved July 6, 2018, from https://arstechnica.com/tech-policy/2018/05/report-software-bug-led-to-death-in-ubers-self-driving-crash

Leicher (2017, August 10). The Perception of Software Quality. *Hackernoon*. Retrieved July 6, 2018, from https://hackernoon.com/the-perception-of-software-quality-6e0e598c5a73

Nestlé (2014). Quality and Safety. *Nestle.com*. Retrieved July 6, 2018, from http://www.nestle.com/aboutus/quality-and-safety

McPeak, A. (2017, August 8). What's the True Cost of a Software Bug? *CrossBrowserTesting*. Retrieved July 6, 2018, from https://crossbrowsertesting.com/blog/development/software-bug-cost

McPeak, A. (2017, September 24). Speed vs. Quality—Which Is Preferred? *DZone*. Retrieved July 6, 2018, from https://dzone.com/articles/speed-vs-quality-which-is-preferred-1

Mochal, T. (2002, October 22). Assume a Quality Assurance Role to "Manage" an Outsourced Project. *TechRepublic*. Retrieved July 6, 2018, from http://www.techrepublic.com/article/assume-a-quality-assurance-role-to-manage-an-outsourced-project

Project Management Institute (2017). *Agile Practice Guide*. Newton Square, PA: Author.

Project Management Institute (2017). *PMBOK: A Guide to the Project Management Body of Knowledge* (6th ed.). Newtown Square, PA: Author.

Reichheld, F. (1996). The Loyalty Effect: The Hidden Force behind Growth, Profits, and Lasting Value. Cambridge, MA: Harvard Business School Press.

Slaughter, S. A., Harter, D. E., and Krishnan, M. S. (1998). Evaluating the Cost of Software Quality. *Communications of the ACM* 41(8), 67–73.

Stylianou, A. C., and Kumar, R. L. (2000). An Integrative Framework for IS Quality Management. *Communications of the ACM* 43(9), 99–104.

Tardugno, A. (2003, April 2). Ten Keys to Successful Outsourcing. *TechRepublic*. Retrieved July 6, 2018, from http://www.techrepublic.com/article/ten-keys-to-successful-outsourcing

Tkach, I. (2017, November 17). Four Common Problems of Managing an Offshore Development Team (And How to Avoid Them). *Forbes*. Retrieved July 6, 2018, from https://www.forbes.com/sites/forbestechcouncil/2017/11/16/four-common-problems-of-managing-an-offshore-development-team-and-how-to-avoid-them

Valacich, J. and George, J. F., (2017). *Modern Systems Analysis and Design* (8th ed.). Boston: Pearson.

CHAPTER 9

Managing Project Risk

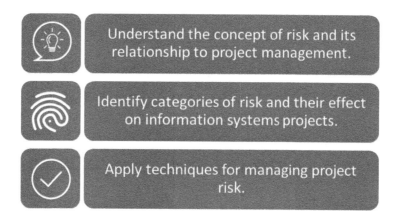

Figure 9.1 Chapter 9 learning objectives

Opening Case: Mobile App Development: Reducing the Risks

For customer-facing businesses, mobile apps are growing to become a strategic necessity. In the beginning, mobile apps would allow customers to view products or services or find store locations, but businesses have quickly added additional features. For example, restaurants from Domino's Pizza to the Cheesecake Factory have jumped on the digital bandwagon and now offer a range of services, from table reservations to online ordering and payment. To keep up with its competitors, the American casual restaurant chain Shake Shack developed a mobile app to allow customers to bypass long lines by placing orders via their mobile devices; once the order was ready at their chosen time and location, the customers would receive a text message notifying them that their order was ready for pickup.

Yet companies from Chipotle to Starbucks have experienced that while mobile ordering can boost online orders, it can also lead to delays and dissatisfaction from traditional customers. Making sure that both online and offline customers get the service they expect can be a challenge. Software flaws, customer acceptance, and changing in-store workflows could all negatively impact customer satisfaction and ultimately hurt business, and thus contribute to the overall risk of the project. Realizing such sources of negative risk, Shake Shack sought to find novel ways to reduce risks throughout the project. To ensure that the app was up to par right from the start, Shake Shack partnered with Applause, a crowdsourcing platform specializing on software testing and user experience (Figure 9.2). Hundreds of crowdsourced software testers were recruited to find bugs in the mobile app, as well as to suggest improvements to the app's usability. In the end, this risk mitigation technique helped make the app a success, with

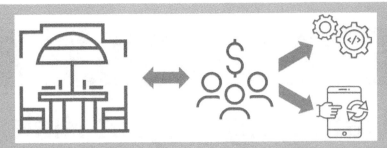

Figure 9.2   Shake Shack used crowdsourcing to mitigate risks.

more than 90 percent of actual users indicating that the app was visually appealing. Interestingly, the positive app experience even influenced the app users' perceptions of Shake Shack's food quality, with more than 85 percent indicating that the food quality surpassed that of their normal dine-in experiences.

Based on: Bouton (2017); Munarriz (2017).

Introduction

Organizations face risks virtually every day. Choices about which products to develop, which investments to make, which employees to hire, and which projects to undertake are all examples of organizational activities that involve risks. In this chapter, we will discuss the general concept of risk, its relationship to project management, identify categories of risk and their effect on information systems projects, and apply techniques for managing project risk; these techniques include risk management planning, risk identification, qualitative risk analysis, quantitative risk analysis, risk response planning, risk response implementation, and risk monitoring.

What Is Risk?

Commonly, risk is generally viewed as threatening. For example, the Merriam-Webster Online Dictionary (http://www.m-w.com/dictionary/risk) defines *risk* as (1) possibility of loss or injury; (2) someone or something that creates or suggests a hazard. A more accurate and sophisticated conceptualization of risk, however, involves an assessment of both the *probability* of a loss occurring and the *size* of the loss if it does occur. As an example, a company considering installing a new ERP will evaluate the risk associated with such an installation by assessing not just the likelihood of the system not doing what it is expected to do (i.e., the probability of failure), but also the resultant cost to the organization if such a failure occurs. Given that such ERPs are designed to affect a vast number of business functions, even if the likelihood of failure is small, the size of potential loss from such a failure may be quite large. As a result, such a system would normally be considered as highly risky. In contrast, a system focused on one functional area of a business or possibly on a less critical process (such as a parking permit system) may not be considered as risky, even if the probability of system failure is high. In such a case, the size of the business loss may be low, and thus the overall risk may be low.

Is risk always bad? PMI's definition of project risk would seem to indicate that risk might not always be something to be avoided: "**Risk** is an uncertain event or condition that, if it occurs, has a *positive* or a negative effect on one or more project objectives" (*PMBOK* 2017, p. 720). This is a slightly different view of risk and takes into consideration that some uncertain events may enhance the project, although others may create problems. Thus, as you will learn in this chapter, the goal of risk management is to

Risk
An uncertain event or condition that, if it occurs, has a positive or negative effect on one or more project objectives.

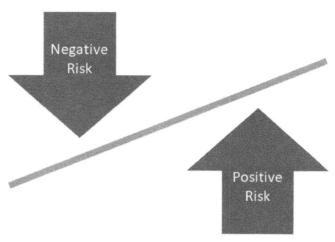

Figure 9.3 The goal of risk management is to minimize negative risks, while exploiting positive risks to maximize project outcomes.

Issue
An event or situation that has happened and has a negative effect on one or more project objectives.

minimize negative risks, while exploiting positive risks to maximize project outcomes (see Figure 9.3). In contrast to risks, which are uncertain future events or conditions, an **issue** is an event or situation that has already happened and has a negative impact on the project; thus specific actions or work-arounds are needed to address the issue and ensure that the project stays on track.

In managing risks, a project manager should not only focus on individual project risks, but also on the overall project risk. As you will see, carefully identifying and managing risks can help achieve successful project outcomes. Remember that while we have defined project success as the degree to which project objectives have been achieved on time, within budget, and with the agreed upon quality and scope, the project manager has to work with different stakeholders to decide what success means for a particular project.

Technology and Risk

Many (especially large) information systems projects are inherently riskier than other projects, with technology rapidly evolving and software being inherently complex. With the constant flux and ever-evolving nature of technology in today's business environment, the rate of change in information systems projects is higher than average. As new technologies are introduced, firms must quickly decide whether to invest in them or risk losing a potential competitive advantage or simply whether to match the capabilities of competitors who already have adopted a new technology. Likewise, in some cases, software updates may enable or necessitate changes in project scope, which can create special pressures in information systems projects. As an example, an enterprise system may be originally scoped to support multiple business units within a large corporation. In the middle of the development cycle for such an application, new capabilities may be released by the software vendor (e.g., SAP) that now enable better business-to-business integration, capabilities that are likely to be valued by the customer. Implementing these new capabilities, however, means that the project scope needs to be redefined. Similarly, it is possible that in the middle of a development project, new development tools will become available, such as a new platform for big data analytics. Should the project team adopt this new platform? How should the team respond if a software vendor is acquired, goes out of business, or support for an existing system is ended? The answers to such questions will depend on a large number of factors, including how far the project team has progressed, the project team's skill set, the estimated longevity of the project, and what sort of enhanced capabilities the change may provide for the development effort.

Further, information systems projects are inherently risky due to the complexity—and often unknown nature—of information systems. Many systems attempt to provide solutions that have never been tried before and are thus highly complex. With increasing functionality come exponential increases in code base and complexity, so that it is typically nearly impossible to test each logical path within the software's source code—even using automated tools—and almost no software can ever be free of errors or defects. In addition, information systems projects often suffer from unclear requirements and progressive, uncontrolled increases in project scope, but even small changes in a project's scope can pose large risks to a project. Adding to this complexity is the fact that information systems do not operate in a vacuum, and project success may not only depend on the system itself, but also on the firm's information systems architecture. Changes in hardware or in the networking infrastructure may introduce new complexities, provide new opportunities, and alter design needs—all of which influence project risk. Thus technological changes need to be constantly monitored and considered as the information systems project develops.

Other Sources of IS Project Risk

A source of risk specific to IS projects involves the complications associated with user acceptance. Many IS projects are very large in scope and may need to be replicated across different parts of the organization, possibly in different parts of the world. Because of this, project managers must be sure that any new system will meet the needs of a diverse set of users, adding risk to the project. Further, end users often think requests to change system requirements will be easier to implement than they really are. Small changes in scope—such as a request for an additional piece of data to be displayed on a customer support screen—may dramatically change the design of an underlying database, thus substantially changing project scope and potentially delaying system delivery. Project managers must constantly monitor and negotiate such project risks.

Another source of risk that is specific to the unique nature of IS projects relates to the acquisition and use of skilled personnel. Locating, hiring, and retaining competent IS personnel not only is a monumental task for human resource managers during projects but also represents a specific category of risk. Getting the right people on an IS project can mean the difference between success and failure. If an experienced programmer familiar with the project chooses to leave for a better job during the implementation of an IS, replacing him or her with someone who is less familiar with the project will almost certainly result in project delays. This is particularly problematic when dealing with IS personnel, because background and skill sets in different development environments can vary widely. Further, related to the potential technology changes, project team members' skills will also dictate whether newly introduced technologies can be used during the project.

Managing Risk and the Project Life Cycle

Risk may influence each of the project management process groups of initiation, planning, execution, monitoring and controlling, and closing. Even before project initiation, risk often occurs during project selection. During this process, top management must make project selection decisions based on the information provided to them. Project selection decisions are usually based on multiple criteria. One important criterion often considered is the project's synergy with the direction and goals of the initiating organization. Sometimes, this may be a difficult decision. Based on its industry position, what strategies (and thus what projects) is the company pursuing? If the company is following a diversification strategy, project risks may increase as it pursues projects outside its core competency. Take, for instance, a technology focused project from the global coffee vendor Starbucks. Facing the potential of a saturated retail coffee market, Starbucks has launched MyStarbucksIdea, a project for crowdsourcing ideas from its community (Schoultz, 2016). In pursuing such projects, Starbucks may need to build and manage various new technologies—an area where they may not have an adequate resource base, both in terms of skilled personnel and technology infrastructure. This serves to increase both corporate and project risks (see Figure 9.4). Next, during project initiation, risks may arise from lack of stakeholder support or problems with selecting or recruiting the right team members.

In the project planning processes, other types of project risk may also be encountered. Risk associated with procurement planning is one example of potential risk during an IS development project. The instability of new technologies used during an IS project may result in unreliable estimated delivery dates from vendors trying to win project contracts. Relying on these unrealistic delivery schedules can be very risky because the entire project can be delayed if the delivery of that technology is on the project's critical path.

Another risk during project planning is associated with developing the project schedule. Project schedules built around the work breakdown structure are generally based on previous project information or expert knowledge, as discussed in previous chapters. Neither of these techniques is completely foolproof. For example, if an IS development project schedule is based on archived project information, even slight differences between the previous and current projects can result in project delays. Further, basing schedule information on expert knowledge, although a valuable technique, nonetheless amounts to a risk taken by project managers because experts are only human, and humans make mistakes. In particular, people's rationality is limited not only by the information people have available, but also by cognitive or time limitations; this bounded rationality can lead to suboptimal decisions. Likewise, systematic errors in thinking (i.e., cognitive biases) influence judgments and decisions; Table 9.1 lists some cognitive biases commonly influencing project teams (note that there are dozens of possible cognitive biases; refer to any textbook on behavioral economics for a discussion on cognitive limitations and biases). Thus developing a project schedule and work breakdown structure during project planning inherently influences project risk.

During the execution, monitoring, and controlling of project activities, managers may find themselves faced with many decisions involving risk. For example, a vendor

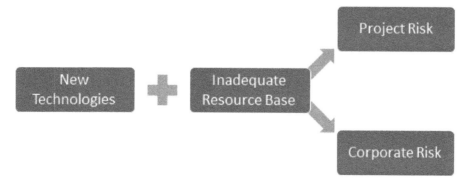

Figure 9.4 The use of new technologies can increase risk.

Table 9.1   Examples of Cognitive Biases Influencing Project Teams

Bias	Explanation
Anchoring bias	People's tendency to use even unrelated information as input into a judgment or decision
Availability heuristic	People's tendency to rely on examples or information that come to mind most easily
Confirmation bias	People's tendency to seek confirming evidence while discounting disconfirming evidence
False consensus effect	People's tendency to overestimate others' agreement
Functional fixedness	People's inability to see or realize other creative uses of an object (or skills of a person)
Optimism bias	People's tendency to believe that they are more successful than their peers

may inform a manager that a critical project component is in danger of not meeting the scheduled delivery date. A good project manager would have anticipated this risk and planned the appropriate response accordingly; if this has not been done, the project manager must decide whether to delay activities that are to be performed before and after the component's installation and focus on other project activities, or to proceed with the schedule as planned and take a risk that the component will be not delivered as scheduled. Another risk that may be taken by project managers involves technology upgrades, as discussed previously. Managers may find that an upgraded version of a technology has become available during execution. Even if the upgraded version comes at no additional cost, managers must still risk problems associated with the new version's functionality. Monitoring and controlling processes can also carry risk, such as when deciding how to test the individual modules and the entire system.

During project closing, managers may also face risk. One major risk involves the acceptance of a vendor's contract as finished. This can be especially risky if major contracts are involved because the acceptance of the project may trigger significant closing payments to project contractors. Once the contracts have been signed off as met, it may become more difficult to get vendors to return and fix any problems without additional charges. Finally, control processes are used to monitor and react to project risk, a topic discussed more thoroughly in Chapter 12.

Techniques for Managing Project Risk

Risk is natural during IS development projects and is often magnified because new technologies and methodologies are used. However, using established project management processes can help mitigate risk during IS projects. Specific risk management processes as identified by the *PMBOK* Guide (2017) include *Plan Risk Management*, *Identify Risks*, *Perform Qualitative Risk Analysis*, *Perform Quantitative Risk Analysis*, *Plan Risk Responses*, *Implement Risk Responses*, and *Monitor Risks*. Project managers can use various information systems during risk planning and risk identification, as well as in the analysis of risk. As an example, knowledge management systems may help project managers in the risk identification process. Similarly, statistical tools and big data analytics may also help the project manager conduct quantitative risk analysis. The project management processes related to risk are summarized in Figure 9.5. Each process, including specific examples applying the tools and techniques, is discussed in more detail in the following sections.

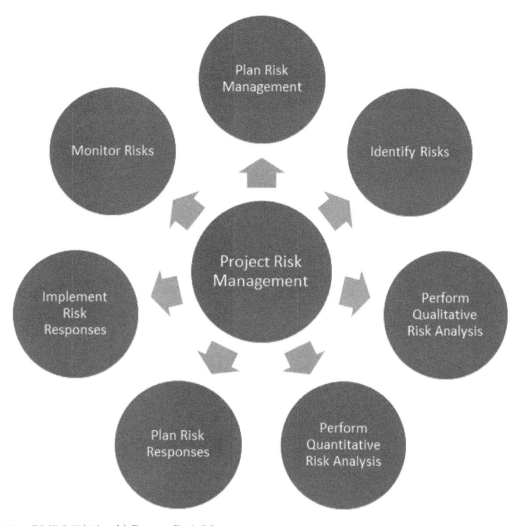

Figure 9.5 *PMBOK* (6th ed.) Project Risk Management processes

---

Common Problems: The Universal List of Software Project Risks

Software projects are notorious for being very difficult to manage, with many ending in failure. These problems are common not only among U.S. firms but also among organizations around the world. A survey of experienced software project managers from different countries (Finland, Hong Kong, and the United States) asked them to identify specific risk factors, and then rank and rate those risks in terms of their importance. The respondents considered nearly a dozen factors to be important. In order of their relative importance, they were

- Lack of top management commitment to the project

Based on: Keil et al. (1998); Wallace and Keil (2004).

- Failure to gain user commitment
- Misunderstanding the requirements
- Lack of adequate user involvement
- Failure to manage end user expectations
- Changing scope/objectives
- Lack of required knowledge/skills in the project personnel
- Lack of frozen requirements
- Introduction of new technology
- Insufficient/inappropriate staffing
- Conflict between user departments

Plan Risk Management

Plan Risk Management
A systematic approach to planning the risk management activities of a given project.

The **Plan Risk Management** process involves a systematic approach to planning the risk management activities for a given project. It is important to plan a risk management strategy that matches the types of risk that may be encountered during the project and the importance of the project to an organization. Consider the development of a small-scale stand-alone IS project; extensive project risk management planning may not be necessary in this case. On the other hand, even the upgrading of the operating systems for dozens of office PCs should involve risk management, as any problems can incapacitate large parts of the organization.

Plan Risk Management—Inputs

Figure 9.6 lists the inputs required, the tools and techniques used, and the resulting outputs of the *Plan Risk Management* process. The inputs of risk management planning are the project charter, the project management plan, project documents (such as the stakeholder register), enterprise environmental factors (attitudes toward risk and risk tolerance), and organizational process assets (such as lessons learned, templates, or the organizational processes put in place to handle risk).

Plan Risk Management—Tools and Techniques

Risk management planning meetings represent the main tool used in the *Plan Risk Management* process. These meetings should be attended by senior managers, project team leaders, stakeholders, project members who have decision-making responsibilities, as well as experts in the area of risk management. During such meetings, a variety of risk-related issues are discussed and decided, including determining the plans for conducting all risk management activities, as well as risk-related elements to be included in the budget and schedule. Further, responsibilities for dealing with risk are assigned. Likewise, data analysis techniques such as a stakeholder analysis can be helpful in determining the stakeholders' risk tolerance. All of these factors are assembled into the output of the risk management planning process, specifically the risk management plan.

Risk management plan
An overall plan used to outline risks and the strategies used to manage them.

Plan Risk Management—Outputs

The primary output from this process of risk management planning is a **risk management plan**. PMI lists the following potential components of a risk management plan:

- Project charter
- Project Mgt plan
  - All components
- Project documents
  - Stakeholder register
- EEFs
- OPAs

- Expert judgment
- Data analysis
  - Stakeholder analysis
- Meetings

- Risk Mgt plan

Figure 9.6 The *PMBOK* (6th ed.) *Plan Risk Management* process

- *Risk Strategy.* The risk strategy should provide a high-level outline of the approach to be followed in managing project risk.
- *Methodology.* The methodology should discuss the specific approaches to the management of risk during the project.
- *Roles and responsibilities.* This component of the risk management plan should establish project members' roles and responsibilities for the risk activities identified in the risk management plan.
- *Funding.* This is simply the preparation of a risk-management budget for the project, including various contingency and management reserves.
- *Timing.* This section of the risk management plan should outline how the risk management activities will fit within the project life cycle.
- *Risk categories.* A structured representation of risk categories, such as using a risk breakdown structure to represent risks as hierarchical categories (similar to a resource breakdown structure).
- *Stakeholder risk appetite.* This component of the risk management plan determines the criteria according to which risks will be acted upon, based on the risk appetite of the project stakeholders.
- *Definitions of risk probability and impacts.* Definitions of probability and impact levels (e.g., on a three-level scale as high, medium, or low, or on a five-level scale) and their expected impact, based on the nature of the project and the risk appetite of stakeholders.
- *Probability and impact matrix.* This section describes how risks are prioritized based on their probabilities and impacts, and provides templates for defining and categorizing risk impacts and probabilities.
- *Reporting formats.* This section outlines the format for the risk response plan and describes how risk management processes will be documented and communicated during the project.
- *Tracking.* Project risk planning activities should be tracked, documented, and archived for use during future projects.

Identify Risks

Identify Risks
The process of identifying and documenting a project's potential risks.

The **Identify Risks** process consists of identifying and documenting potential risks to the project. This process should be performed by project managers, project teams, the risk management team, experts, customers, end users, outside experts, and additional stakeholders.

Identify Risks—Inputs

Figure 9.7 illustrates the inputs, tools, and outputs of the *Identify Risks* process. The main inputs include various parts of the project management plan, including the requirements, schedule, cost, quality, and resource management plans, all of which are used to identify potential risks; likewise, the risk management plan specifies what is classified as risks, and how risks are classified and represented; the scope, schedule, and costs baselines are used to identify other areas that might lead to ambiguities or uncertainties. In addition to these components of the project management plan, various project documents serve as inputs, including the assumption and issue logs, cost and duration estimates, and requirements documentation and resource requirements; the stakeholder register helps identify stakeholders who may participate in risk identification activities

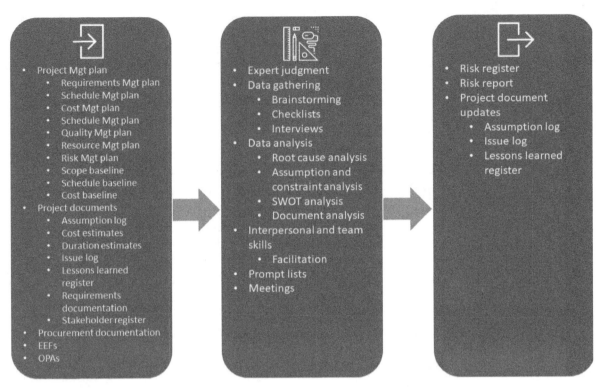

Figure 9.7 The *PMBOK* (6th ed.) *Identify Risks* process

or who may serve as risk owners, and the lessons learned register provides insights from prior projects. In addition, agreements and procurement documentation (discussed in Chapter 10) can be used to identify procurement-related risks. Finally, enterprise environment factors (such as publicly available risk-related information and benchmarks) and organizational process assets (such as organizational controls or checklists) are used in identifying project risks.

Identify Risks—Tools and Techniques

In addition to expert judgment, the project manager extensively uses data gathering and analysis techniques to identify risks. In prior sections, you have learned about the use of brainstorming and interviews to gather data to support various processes; in addition, checklists are valuable data gathering tools. In identifying risks, checklists enable risks for a project to be listed and checked off. They are especially useful for projects that are similar to past projects. Their limitation, however, is that it is often not feasible to develop a comprehensive list of potential project risks. You have also learned about various data analysis techniques, such as root cause analysis, or the analysis of assumptions and constraints. Another useful data analysis technique is a strengths, weaknesses, opportunities, and threats (SWOT) analysis. You may recognize this term from your management or marketing courses. A SWOT analysis can be used to increase the reach within which risks will be considered (see Figure 9.8). Finally, document analysis involves reviewing existing project documentation, which may include project plans and assumptions. Historical information is useful in developing the risk register and comprises any project risk management information collected during the course of previous projects. Specific sources of historical information may include

Figure 9.8 A SWOT analysis can be used to increase the reach within which risks will be considered.

- *Project files*, which include previous risk management plans, project reports, and lessons learned
- *Published information*, which is often contained in public databases, published reports, academic studies, and through published benchmarking information

Risk register
A formal record listing all project risks, explaining the nature of the risk and management of the risk.

Often, it is helpful to use prompt lists—which suggest risk categories—when developing the **risk register** (see Figure 9.9 for an example), the primary output from the risk identification process. Commonly used risk categories include technical, quality, or performance risks; project management risks; organizational risks; and external risks (see Table 9.2; PMI 2004).

The project manager may also use other commonly used strategic frameworks (such as PEST/PESTEL) to identify risk categories. Often, the different activities associated with identifying risks are conducted using meetings, where effective interpersonal and team skills are especially helpful in identifying a comprehensive list of risks.

Identify Risks—Outputs

The primary output of the risk identification process is the risk register, a key tool in managing project risk. The risk register includes a detailed list of identified risks

Table 9.2 Commonly Used Risk Categories (PMI 2004)

Risk Category	Examples
Technical risks	Reliance on new, unproven, or unreliable technology
Quality and performance risks	Performance goals that cannot be easily met Changing industry standards
Project management risks	Risks associated with poor project planning and poor use of recognized project management processes
Organizational risks	Inconsistent goals Lack of funding Conflicting priorities
External risks	Legal events Environmental concerns Natural disasters, such as earthquakes and floods

Risk Register

Ref	The Risk (What can happen and how it will it happen)	The risk of the event happening uncontrolled		Initial Risk score	Risk Control Plan (Strategies to eliminate or minimize risk)	The risk of the event happening with controls		Final Risk Score
		Consequence	Likelihood			Consequence	Likelihood	
1	Exposure to hazardous substances in various operations including cleaning, research, educational. Risk of injury includes: • Chemical burns to eyes, skin, body. • Inhalation of vapors and fumes. • Explosion from potential ignition sources.	Major	The event could occur at some time	High	Implementation of Hazardous Substance Guidelines including: 1. Elimination of hazardous substance where possible; 2. Substitution of hazardous substance with less hazardous; 3. Isolation of hazardous substance through engineering design; 4. Training requirements for users of hazardous substance; 5. Provision of personal protective equipment for users of hazardous substance.	Moderate	The event could occur, but only rarely	Medium

Figure 9.9 Sample risk register

Trigger
Event that serves as an early warning of risk.

and possible risk **triggers** (i.e., events that serve as early warnings of risk), potential responses to those risks, the root causes of the risk, and an updated list of risk categories (based on any new risks being identified that were not in the prior list of risk categories). A sample risk register is shown in Figure 9.9.

Ethical Dilemma: The Difficult Job of Managing Project Risk

Managers often face ethical dilemmas related to risk. Consider the following example of a project manager's ethical dilemma during software testing. Normally, alpha testing—testing conducted to ensure that bugs are being fixed before a beta version of the product is released to real customers—is performed using test scenarios and simulated test data. During alpha testing of a new module for an enterprise resource planning (ERP) system, you notice that the engineer responsible for the testing has not generated test data, but instead extracted live customer data from the existing system to use as test data set. Given that the module being tested is accessible to various unauthorized staff throughout the organization, there is the potential that confidential customer data may leak outside the organization. As the alpha testing is already nearing completion, you have to decide whether you should complete the test, risking that customer data may become exposed, or whether you should terminate the test and restart with simulated test data; under this circumstance, you risk a significant delay in completion of the project, and your organization may have to pay substantial contractual penalties to your client.

Discussion Questions

1. Under what situation(s) would it be permissible to use live data for system testing?
2. If you were a project manager facing pressure to reduce costs or project duration by cutting corners, what tactic would you use to try to convince the manager to follow your advice?

Perform Qualitative Risk Analysis

Perform Qualitative Risk Analysis
The evaluation of the potential impact and likelihood of specific risk occurrence.

The **Perform Qualitative Risk Analysis** process involves evaluating the potential impact and likelihood of specific risk occurrence, so as to prioritize risk responses. Throughout the life of the project, qualitative risk analysis tools are utilized to evaluate these dimensions. Figure 9.10 summarizes the required inputs, the tools and techniques used, and the resulting outputs for qualitative risk analysis.

Perform Qualitative Risk Analysis—Inputs

Inputs to the *Perform Qualitative Risk Analysis* process include the risk management plan, project documents (such as the risk register, the stakeholder register, and the assumption log), as well as enterprise environmental factors (such as commercial databases or industry studies) and organizational process assets (such as historical information from prior projects).

Perform Qualitative Risk Analysis—Tools and Techniques

A variety of tools and techniques specified by the *PMBOK* guide can be utilized in the *Perform Qualitative Risk Analysis* process. As with risk identification, expert judgment, data gathering techniques such as interviews, and meetings (using skilled facilitators) are commonly used to perform qualitative risk analysis; likewise, risk categorization, as previously discussed, can help determine which part of the project may be most susceptible to risk. For example, a risk breakdown structure (similar to a WBS) can be used to identify the risks organized by project component. During qualitative risk analysis, various data analysis techniques have proven helpful. In particular, these are risk data quality assessment, risk probability and impact assessment, as well as the assessment of

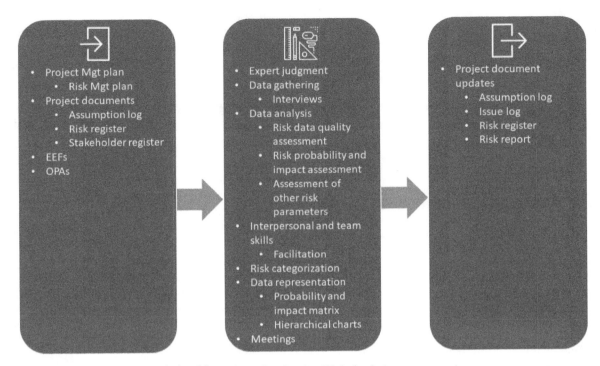

Figure 9.10 The *PMBOK* (6th ed.) *Perform Qualitative Risk Analysis* process

other risk parameters. As any outputs can only be as good as the inputs, assessing the quality of the risk data is an important first step in performing qualitative risk analyses; in other words, the project manager attempts to determine completeness, objectivity, relevance, timeliness, and other aspects of the quality of the risk data. This might include **project assumption testing**, a tool used to further test the assumptions embedded in risk identification. Data precision ranking can be used for risk data quality assessments. The following dimensions are considered in such a ranking:

Project assumption testing
A technique used during qualitative risk analysis to test the assumptions made during risk identification.

- The extent to which a risk is understood
- Available risk data
- Data quality
- Data integrity and reliability

Especially with ever-increasing availability of big data for project management, assessing the quality of these data becomes ever more important. Once the risk data has been determined to be of sufficient quality, the project manager determines risk probability and impact, which are important dimensions of qualitative risk analysis. Risk probability is concerned with the likelihood that a certain risk will occur and can be measured on a scale from very low to very high. Risk impact, or the consequences associated with the occurrence of a given risk, is concerned with the impact on project outcomes if the risk event occurs.

Probability/impact risk rating matrix
A technique used to analyze project risk in terms of its probability of occurrence and its impact on project outcomes.

During probability and impact assessment, a **probability/impact risk rating matrix** is used to graphically represent project risk in terms of its probability of occurring and its impact on project outcomes. Probability scales are generally measured on a 0 to 1 scale, where 0 represents no chance that the event will occur and 1 represents the certainty of its occurrence. Probability scores are most often determined through expert judgment and are thus susceptible to human error. Scores can be attributed on an ordinal scale, such as not at all likely to very likely, or by assigning specific values, such as 0.1, 0.2, 0.3, and so on. Impact scales represent the magnitude of the effect the risk occurrence may have on the project objective. Impact scores can be ratio scales, as for probability scales, or ordinal, in which specific values are assigned to potential impacts. Importantly, both measures and their associated scales should be developed independently by organizations to reflect their risk analysis preferences. An example of a probability/impact matrix is shown in Figure 9.11. Such a matrix can be applied to a particular project (which could help assess a project's overall risk relative to other projects), or to particular components or tasks within a single project (which might help a project team prepare for project risks).

In addition to assessing risk probability and impact, the assessment of various other characteristics can help prioritize risk responses (see Figure 9.12). In particular, important characteristics include the strategic impact, the detectability and manageability of the risk, and the controllability of the outcome; likewise, risks differ in urgency (i.e., how quickly risk response must be implemented before they become ineffective), proximity (i.e., how long it takes before a risk will have an impact), dormancy (i.e., when the risk occurrence can be detected), and connectivity (i.e., in how far a risk is interrelated with other risks); finally, risks differ in propinquity, or in how far they are considered to be significant by different stakeholders. Differences in these characteristics are typically represented using hierarchical charts, such as bubble charts, where different dimensions represent different characteristics. Further, the project manager uses data representation techniques such as probability and impact matrices and hierarchical charts to present the risks visually.

Perform Qualitative Risk Analysis—Outputs

The output from the qualitative risk analysis is updates to various project documents. Primarily, the project manager updates the risk register and the risk reports, in addition to updates to the assumption and issue logs, in case there have been changes to these items.

Perform Quantitative Risk Analysis

Perform Quantitative Risk Analysis
The analysis of the probability of occurrence and the impact of risk on project objectives using numerical techniques.

Similar to qualitative risk analysis, the **Perform Quantitative Risk Analysis** process is used to analyze the probability of occurrence and the impact of risk on project objectives. However, during quantitative risk analysis, more quantitative numerical analyses are conducted to determine the *extent* of the uncertainty. As quantitative risk analysis is effortful and requires high-quality data, it is typically only performed for large projects, or for projects with high strategic importance. However, big data analytics increasingly facilitates performing quantitative risk analysis even for smaller projects; further, project

	Very High	High	Medium	Low	Very Low
Catastrophic	High	High	Moderate	Moderate	Low
Critical	High	High	Moderate	Low	None
Marginal	Moderate	Moderate	Low	None	None
Negligible	Moderate	Low	Low	None	None

Figure 9.11   Probability/impact risk rating matrix

Figure 9.12 Other risk parameters include urgency, proximity, dormancy, manageability, controllability, detectability, connectivity, strategic impact, and propinquity.

managers can draw on ever more data to perform quantitative risk analyses, so as to arrive at more accurate estimates. As with performing qualitative risk analyses, this process is undertaken throughout the project.

Perform Quantitative Risk Analysis—Inputs

Figure 9.13 lists the required inputs, the tools and techniques used, and the resulting outputs of the *Perform Quantitative Risk Analysis* process. Decision techniques enable project managers to

- Assess the likelihood of realizing a specific project objective.
- Quantify risks in terms of additional scheduling and cost needs.
- Identify the most salient risks in terms of the project.
- Set realistic targets in terms of scope, cost, and schedule.

Quantitative risk analysis can be performed separately or with qualitative analysis. Decisions whether to use one or the other or both should be made on an individual project basis.

Inputs for this process comprise outputs from the previous risk management processes, including the risk management plan and the scope, schedule, and cost baselines,

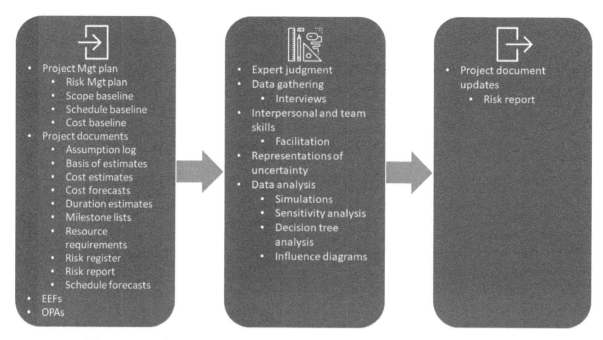

Figure 9.13 The *PMBOK* (6th ed.) *Perform Quantitative Risk Analysis* process

all of which can point to sources of risk. In addition, important inputs are cost and duration estimates, resource requirements, the milestone list, as well as cost and schedule forecasts, and the assumptions and bases of the estimates. The risk register and risk report provide input about individual and overall project risk. Other valuable input includes enterprise environmental factors (such as published reports or databases) and organizational process assets (such as lessons learned or risk-related information from prior projects).

Perform Quantitative Risk Analysis—Tools and Techniques

As with many other processes, important tools and techniques used in the *Perform Quantitative Risk Analysis* process include expert judgment and data gathering techniques such as interviewing. Interviewing techniques are instrumental during the *Perform Quantitative Risk Analysis* process because interviews with project experts and other stakeholders can assist in quantifying risk probabilities and consequences. A skilled facilitator can be valuable during interviews as well as risk workshops.

Probability distributions can be applied to represent risks or uncertain estimates. Such probability distributions can illustrate the probability of something's occurring or, in some cases, more general results such as optimistic, most likely, and pessimistic scenarios.

Quantitative risk analysis techniques include the use of *sensitivity analysis*, *decision tree analysis*, *expected monetary value analysis (EMV)*, and *simulation*. **Sensitivity analysis** is used to determine which risks have the largest potential impact on a project. One example of a sensitivity analysis is the **tornado analysis**, which graphically shows, in descending order, which risks can cause the greatest variability in some outcome. The risks at the top can cause the greatest variability, and the risks at the bottom cause the least variability. A tornado analysis is illustrated in Figure 9.14; it shows how different risks can cause variability in the base value of an information system. In this case,

Sensitivity analysis
A technique used to examine the potential impact of specific risks to a project.

Tornado analysis
A diagramming technique that graphically shows, in descending order, which risks can cause the greatest variability on some outcome.

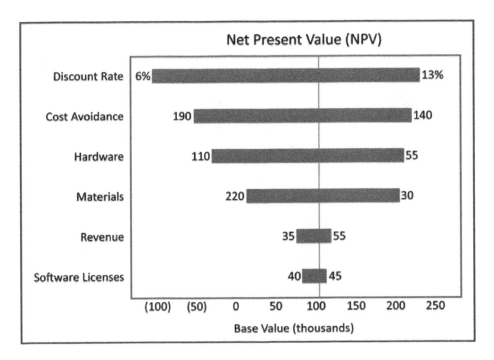

Figure 9.14 Tornado analysis

changes in the discount rate, the ability to avoid costs, and the changing nature of hardware costs are the top three risk factors and could have a very large effect on the base value of this system. Conversely, uncertainty about the system's ultimate revenue generating capability and about the costs associated with software licenses are likely to have much smaller effects on the base value. Another way of diagrammatically representing project risk is the use of influence diagrams, which represent the interrelationships among entities, outcomes, and influences in a project. Using such diagram can help identify which aspects may be uncertain; such uncertainties can then be associated with a certain probability distribution.

Expected monetary value analysis is a statistical technique that captures the average value of potential projects by analyzing the likelihood of possible project outcomes as well as each outcome's financial consequences. A graphical depiction of EMV can be captured in a decision tree analysis. A **decision tree analysis** is a diagramming technique used to evaluate a given course of action in terms of its costs and benefits relative to other courses of action. Figure 9.15 depicts a decision tree; the right-hand column shows the net path values. As illustrated in the figure, the choice to build a new plant or upgrade the existing plant was conducted using the EMV approach following these steps. First, the various *project options* are depicted (in this case, building a new plant or upgrading an existing plant). Next, the possible *project consequences* of pursuing those projects are illustrated (shown in the diagram as scenarios of strong and weak demand), along with their probability of occurrence and financial results. The *net path value* represents the value associated with a particular path (e.g., the first path in the diagram is valued at $200M) minus the costs of pursuing that option ($120M). To arrive at the EMV for each *project option*, you simply multiply the probability times the expected financial result for each *project consequence*, and then sum those values for each *project option*; finally, subtract the *initial estimated project cost* of each *project option*. Thus the EMV calculations as illustrated for Project 1 (new plant) would be

Expected monetary analysis (EMV)
A statistical technique that captures the average value of potential projects by analyzing the likelihood of possible project outcomes as well as each outcome's financial consequences.

Decision tree analysis
A diagramming technique used to evaluate courses of action in terms of their potential cost and benefits relative to other courses of action.

$$EMV = ((65\% \times \$200M) + (35\% \times \$90M)) - \$120M = \$41.5M$$

For Project 2 (upgrade), the EMV calculations would be

$$EMV = ((65\% \times \$120M) + (35\% \times \$60M)) - \$50M = \$49.0M$$

Using the EMV technique, a project selection committee would rate Project 2 as more desirable because of its higher EMV. In a decision tree diagram, the designation "True" indicates the selected project, whereas "False" indicates the rejected option. While this particular decision-making scenario focuses on a capital strategy (upgrading an existent plant or building a new plant), this technique could just as easily be applied to a *make, buy, or upgrade* decision related to an information system.

As defined in Chapter 7, simulation is a process of evaluating different scenarios and their effects on the project. Simulations typically refer to analytical methods that imitate some sort of real-life systems. Without using simulations, spreadsheet-based "what-if" models typically only examine the effect of changes in input variables to one outcome at a time. In contrast, simulations vary input variables and examine multiple possible outcomes.

Monte Carlo analysis is probably the most recognized form of simulation analysis. In the case of a Monte Carlo simulation, values for uncertain input variables (such as changes in resource availability or time to complete particular project tasks) are randomly generated over and over (typically several thousand times) to achieve a distribution of possible project outcomes. The results of such analysis are typically displayed as an S-curve, representing the cumulative probability distribution of likely outcomes.

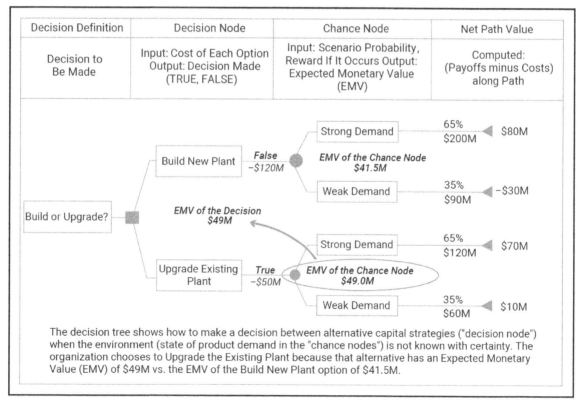

Decision Definition	Decision Node	Chance Node	Net Path Value
Decision to Be Made	Input: Cost of Each Option Output: Decision Made (TRUE, FALSE)	Input: Scenario Probability, Reward If It Occurs Output: Expected Monetary Value (EMV)	Computed: (Payoffs minus Costs) along Path

The decision tree shows how to make a decision between alternative capital strategies ("decision node") when the environment (state of product demand in the "chance nodes") is not known with certainty. The organization chooses to Upgrade the Existing Plant because that alternative has an Expected Monetary Value (EMV) of $49M vs. the EMV of the Build New Plant option of $41.5M.

Figure 9.15   Decision tree and EMV analysis

Perform Quantitative Risk Analysis—Outputs

Outputs from this stage again include updates to various project documents. Such updates include an overall assessment of the exposure to project risk (including the chances of project success and the degree of remaining variability), as well as a probabilistic analysis of the project; this helps with planning the contingency reserves needed, identifying individual project risks, as well as identifying the major drivers of overall project risk. In addition, outputs include prioritization of project risks and possible risk responses. Finally, as quantitative risk analysis is performed throughout the project, trends in risks may become visible, which can assist in prioritizing changing risks and planning appropriate response.

Tips from the Pros: Effective Risk Management

Identifying and assessing risks should be an ongoing activity, yet in many organizations, these activities do not produce the desired results. Steve Minsky, the CEO of risk management software provider LogicManager Inc., suggests a five-step approach to improve the effectiveness of risk assessment:

1. *Look for root causes.* Understanding the root causes of events is the first step in any risk assessment. Identifying the root cause as being related to issues with processes, systems, people, relationships, or external issues will suggest appropriate mitigation approaches.

2. *Remove subjectivity.* Subjectivity in risk assessments is one of their biggest impediments. Consequently, Minsky suggests standardizing scales and criteria used to evaluate risks across the organization to minimize duplicate work and increase the usefulness of the assessments for different departments and business units.

3. *Link risks to controls.* Without having clear linkages between the risk and potential controls or mitigation strategies, it will be impossible to assess the effectiveness of the controls. Therefore, it is crucial to have a formal approach to linking risks to controls, even if a control is used to address multiple risks.

4. *Link risks to strategic goals.* Making sure to identify the risks associated with the most important strategic goals will help prioritize risks and obtain resources for potential mitigation approaches.

5. *Make risk a part of everyone's job responsibility.* By making risk part of everyone's day-to-day activities and responsibilities, you can minimize the chance that you will wake up to surprises, ranging from missed deadlines to budget overruns.

It is clear that different contexts call for different strategies to mitigate risk, and each situation may present special challenges. By following a structured approach to assessing risks, project managers can effectively control risk and bring projects to successful completion.

Based on: Minsky (2016).

Plan Risk Responses

Plan Risk Responses
The process of developing methods for responding to project risks.

During the **Plan Risk Responses** process, methods for responding to project risks are developed. Responses are developed based on anticipated adverse effects of risk, as well as any opportunities that may be present as a result of a specific risk. Risk response planning should consider the severity of the risk, the type of project, and cost-benefit information. This process focuses on developing suitable risk management strategies as well as determining who is responsible for dealing with the risk. All project stakeholders should agree upon any risk planning actions to be implemented. In general, the responses should focus on minimizing individual threats and maximizing individual opportunities, so as to reduce the project's exposure to negative risks. Any response to be implemented should be appropriate, realistic, and cost-effective. Depending on the risks and their potential impacts, project managers may develop backup strategies, in case the originally planned risk responses may not be as effective as planned. Figure 9.16 shows the required inputs, tools, and techniques used, and resulting outputs of the *Plan Risk Responses* process.

Plan Risk Responses—Inputs

Inputs to the risk response planning process include the project management plan and, in particular, the resource management plan, the risk management plan, and the cost baseline; these help determine roles and responsibilities, as well as resources and contingency funds available for responding to risks. Further, various project documents serve as inputs to this process, including the project schedule, team assignments, resource calendars, and the stakeholder register (to help with scheduling resources for responding to risks and identifying risk owners). **Risk owners** (project members who are responsible for specific risk activity decisions) should be involved during risk response planning. Other project documents include the risk register and risk reports (to prioritize risk responses), as well as the lessons learned register, which points to successful or unsuccessful risk responses from earlier projects. Finally, enterprise environmental factors (such as risk thresholds) and organizational process assets (such as experts on response strategies) serve as inputs to this process.

Risk owner
Project member responsible for specific risk activity decisions.

Plan Risk Responses—Tools and Techniques

Many techniques and strategies are available for risk response planning. In planning risk responses, typical techniques include the use of expert judgment, data gathering and analysis skills, decision-making skills, as well as interpersonal and team skills. Particular strategies to deal with risks include escalation, avoidance/exploitation, transference/sharing, mitigation/enhancement, and acceptance.

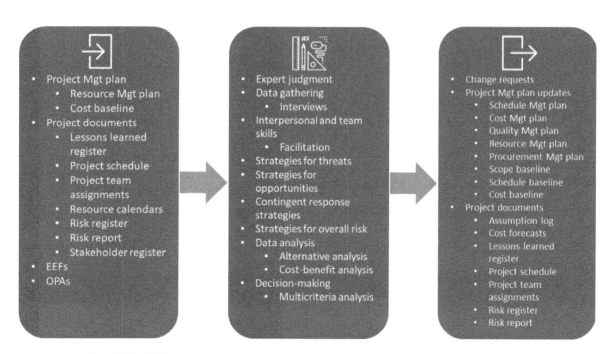

Figure 9.16 The *PMBOK* (6th ed.) *Plan Risk Responses* process

Risk escalation
A risk response strategy that involves assigning the response to a higher organizational level if the threat is beyond the authority of the project manager.

Risk avoidance
A risk response strategy designed to avoid potential project risks.

Risk transference
A risk response strategy designed to transfer risk to another party.

Risk mitigation
A risk response strategy in which steps are taken to mitigate project risk.

Risk acceptance
A risk response strategy in which risks are simply accepted and contingency strategies are planned.

Risk escalation involves assigning the response to a higher organizational level—for example, if the threat is beyond the authority of the project manager or has implications beyond the particular project.

Risk avoidance is designed to avoid any identified threats to the project. Within an IS development project, this may include avoiding the use of an untested technology or avoiding changes to the scope of the system. Analogously, the project manager may seek to exploit opportunities to reap the most benefits, such as by assigning capable staff or utilizing new technologies.

Risk transference involves the transfer of risk to another party. Risk transference is often facilitated through the use of contracts in which the risk associated with a given activity is transferred to another party. Depending on the type of contract being used, risk may be transferred from the seller to the buyer or from the buyer to the seller. For a detailed discussion of contracts, see Chapter 10, the procurement management chapter. A project manager may also share an opportunity and transfer it to a third party to share the benefits (as in joint ventures or teams).

Risk mitigation is used to reduce, eliminate, or transfer the chances of risk occurrence or to reduce the impact of the risk on project objectives. An example of risk mitigation during an IS development project is the use of a known technology provider rather than reliance on a less established vendor. Analogous to mitigating a threat, a project manager may enhance an opportunity, so as to increase the probability or impact. Having contingency plans can help identify the best risk mitigation strategies.

Risk acceptance occurs when managers simply decide that an effective response cannot be developed for a specific risk, or when the expected impact is minimal and any response would be costlier than taking no action. In such a circumstance, the project team may decide to not alter the project management plan to deal with this particular risk, given the lack of a suitable response strategy. For example, an IS development project team may accept the risk that a new version of a particular software released during the execution phase of a project may not function as intended.

On the overall project risk level, the same strategies can be used for opportunities and threats (although escalation is often not an option for overall project risk). Depending on the risks, some strategies may be contingent on certain events or conditions. In any case, the choice of strategy typically depends on the probabilities and impacts estimated during the *Perform Qualitative Risk Analysis* and *Perform Quantitative Risk Analysis* processes.

Plan Risk Responses—Outputs

Outputs from the risk response planning process include updates to the project management plan, including the schedule, cost, quality, resource, and procurement management plans, as well as to the scope, schedule, and cost baselines. Any of these changes have to go through formal approval procedures in the form of change requests. Other outputs include updates to the risk register and risk report, updates to the cost forecasts, project schedule, and project team assignments, as well as updates to the assumption log and lessons learned register. In the risk register, the responses are captured in a **risk response plan**, which includes some or all of the following components:

Risk response plan
A documented plan for risk response.

- Any risks that have been identified, along with a description and the areas and objectives the identified risk may affect
- The roles and responsibilities of any risk owners

- Qualitative and quantitative risk analysis results, as well as any trends identified during either of these processes
- A description of the risk response strategies, including escalation, avoidance/exploitation, transference/sharing, mitigation/enhancement, and acceptance, and the specific risks to which the various strategies will be applied
- An acknowledgment of any residual risk projected to remain after any risk response strategies have been applied
- A list of actions to be used to implement the risk response strategies
- Budget and schedule information for any risk response
- Any contingency plans used as part of an active response to accept risks

Residual risks
Any risks remaining after risk response strategies have been applied.

Secondary risks
Any risks resulting from the application of a risk response strategy.

Risk-related contractual agreements
Any contracts for the purpose of risk transference during the project.

Some other terms are also useful to understand in risk response planning. **Residual risks**, or those risks that remain after avoidance, transfer, or mitigation strategies have been applied, are identified during risk response planning. **Secondary risks** are those risks resulting from the application of a risk response strategy. **Risk-related contractual agreements** for the purpose of risk transference are another important output of risk response planning. During an IS development project, they could include a transfer of responsibility for systems implementation or some other phase of systems development. Contingency reserve (a provision held in reserve by the project sponsor to meet unanticipated changes in factors like project scope) amounts needed should be estimated based on risk information generated during risk management. Inputs to other processes, as with other risk management activities, represent another important output to be considered during response planning. For example, identified risks and their assigned response strategies may provide information for other project management processes. These risk response planning outputs serve as inputs to the project plan so that the risk response activities can be incorporated into the project schedule.

Global Implications: Outsourcing and Project Risk

There have been conflicting arguments for and against outsourcing. Advocates of the practice argue that it results in significant cost reduction, given that it provides access to advanced capabilities, cheaper labor, and reduced requirements to support an additional organizational function outside of one's core competency. Opponents argue that outsourcing involves major risks. While certainly outsourcing does provide many opportunities, it is also important—particularly given the focus of this chapter—to understand the relationship between outsourcing and project risk.

One type of risk associated with outsourcing software development projects concerns internal resistance. Managers, project managers, developers, and other personnel in a company may feel threatened because they fear that there will be shifts in responsibilities and power or possibly layoffs. For those reasons, affected individuals may act to sabotage an offshore project throughout the life cycle of the project, adversely affecting project success. According to Rick Pfeiffer, former head of Asia-Pacific IT and operations at General Electric Co., internal opposition plays a major role in 60 percent of failed offshore projects. Some of the ways to deal with internal resistance include ensuring strong support from upper management, picking the right people to be on the team, getting managers involved early in the outsourcing process, and appropriately reassuring employees regarding the goals of the outsourcing effort and how it will affect the company and project team members.

Another risk associated with outsourcing and offshoring is security and privacy. Some American companies fear that their data or proprietary processes might fall into the wrong hands. For example, recently, Jolly Technologies, which is a division of the U.S. company Jolly Inc., reported that portions of the source code and confidential design documents relating to one of its key products were stolen by an insider at its research and development center in Mumbai. Because of weak intellectual property laws and inefficient enforcement, the probability of intellectual property theft may be more pronounced in other countries. To ensure security and privacy, American companies have been demanding that outsourcing companies in these countries put security measures in place. These include physical security measures, such as electric fencing around buildings, the use of card keys and biometric authentication devices to gain access to facilities, and closed-circuit TVs for surveillance. Companies also want their data and information systems to be protected through the use of event logging and monitoring tools, intrusion-detection systems, firewalls, and encryption technologies.

Based on: Gnatyk (2018); Ribeiro (2004); Thibodeau (2004); Vijayan (2004).

Implement Risk Responses

Implement Risk Responses
The process of reacting to identified project risks so as to minimize threats and maximize opportunities, and manage overall project risk exposure.

The **Implement Risk Responses** process puts the *Plan Risk Responses* process into motion. Performed throughout the project, this process is designed to implement the risk response plan devised in the *Plan Risk Responses* process, so as to minimize threats and maximize opportunities and manage overall project risk exposure. We will discuss the inputs, tools and techniques, and outputs of this process in Chapter 11.

Monitor Risks

Monitor Risks
The process of monitoring identified risks for change and controlling those changes.

Project risk response audits
Audits designed to evaluate the effectiveness of risk response strategies and risk owners.

Periodic project risk reviews
Reviews designed to review existing risk activities and to monitor any changes to the project.

Technical performance measurement
A tool used to determine whether important technical milestones are being met.

Consistent with the process of project management control, identified risks must be monitored for change and controlled. Just as implementing risk responses, the **Monitor Risks** process generally takes place over the entire life of the project. Although risk monitoring will be covered in depth in Chapter 12, we introduce the topic here. The purpose of risk monitoring and control is to identify, analyze, and plan for newly arising risks; to watch existent risks (on the watch list); to monitor conditions that would trigger risk responses; and finally, to determine if such responses are working. Risk monitoring employs such tools as reserve analysis using performance data, **project risk response audits, technical performance analysis,** and others to update the risk register and project management plan and other outputs. Again, a more complete treatment of this topic is reserved for Chapter 12. Figure 9.17 shows a list of the required inputs, tools and techniques used, and resulting outputs of the *Monitor Risks* process.

Managing Project Risk and *PMBOK*

In this chapter, we have focused primarily on Knowledge Area 11, Project Risk Management, within the Project Management Body of Knowledge (*PMBOK*, 2017). In this chapter, we have identified the various processes of Project Risk Management, including *Plan Risk Management, Identify Risks, Perform Qualitative Risk Analysis, Perform Quantitative Risk Analysis, Plan Risk Responses, Implement Risk Responses,* and *Monitor Risks.* We have also identified the various tools and techniques that can be used in managing risk. Figure 9.18 identifies this coverage and illustrates the coverage of upcoming chapters as well.

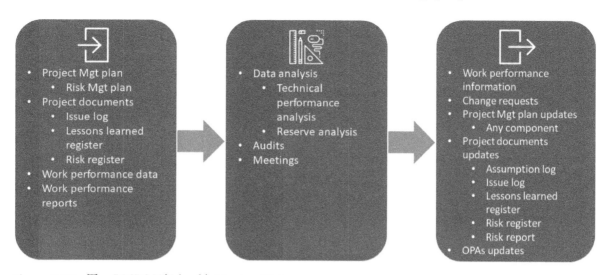

Figure 9.17 The *PMBOK* (6th ed.) *Monitor Risks* process

Figure 9.18 Chapter 9 and *PMBOK* (6th ed.) coverage

Key: ○ where the material is covered in the textbook; ● current chapter coverage

	Textbook Chapters ⟶	1	2	3	4	5	6	7	8	9	10	11	12
	PMBOK Knowledge Area												
1	Introduction												
1.2	Foundational Elements	○	○										
2	The Environment in Which Projects Operate												
2.2	Enterprise Environmental Factors		○										
2.2	Organizational Process Assets		○										
2.3	Organizational Systems		○										
3	The Role of the Project Manager												
3.2	Definition of a Project Manager	○											
3.3	The Project Manager's Sphere of Influence		○										
3.4	Project Manager Competences	○	○	○									
3.5	Performing Integration		○										
4	Project Integration Management												
4.1	Develop Project Charter					○							
4.2	Develop Project Management Plan					○							
4.3	Direct and Manage Project Work											○	
4.4	Manage Project Knowledge											○	
4.5	Monitor and Control Project Work											○	○
4.6	Perform Integrated Change Control												○
4.7	Close Project or Phase										○		○

#	Process	1	2	3	4	5	6	7	8	9	10	11	12	13
5	**Project Scope Management**													
5.1	Plan Scope Management					O								
5.2	Collect Requirements					O								
5.3	Define Scope					O								
5.4	Create WBS					O	O							
5.5	Validate Scope					O								
5.6	Control Scope					O								O
6	**Project Schedule Management**													
6.1	Plan Schedule Management						O							
6.2	Define Activities						O							
6.3	Sequence Activities						O							
6.4	Estimate Activity Durations							O						
6.5	Develop Schedule							O						
6.6	Control Schedule							O						O
7	**Project Cost Management**													
7.1	Plan Cost Management								O					
7.2	Estimate Costs								O					
7.3	Determine Budget								O					
7.4	Control Costs								O					O
8	**Project Quality Management**													
8.1	Plan Quality Management								O					
8.2	Manage Quality								O					
8.3	Control Quality								O					O
9	**Project Resource Management**													
9.1	Plan Resource Management							O						
9.2	Estimate Activity Resources						O	O						
9.3	Acquire Resources							O				O		
9.4	Develop Team			O								O		
9.5	Manage Team			O								O		
9.6	Control Resources							O						O
10	**Project Communications Management**													
10.1	Plan Communications Management				O									
10.2	Manage Communications				O							O		
10.3	Monitor Communications				O									O
11	**Project Risk Management**													
11.1	Plan Risk Management									●				
11.2	Identify Risks									●		O		
11.3	Perform Qualitative Risk Analysis									●				
11.4	Perform Quantitative Risk Analysis									●				
11.5	Plan Risk Responses									●				
11.6	Implement Risk Responses									●		O		

		1	2	3	4	5	6	7	8	9	10	11	12	13
11.7	Monitor Risks											●		○
12	**Project Procurement Management**													
12.1	Plan Procurement Management											○		
12.2	Conduct Procurements											○	○	
12.3	Control Procurements											○		○
13	**Project Stakeholder Management**													
12.1	Identify Stakeholders			○										
12.2	Plan Stakeholder Engagement			○										
12.3	Manage Stakeholder Engagement			○									○	
12.4	Monitor Stakeholder Engagement			○										○

Running Case: Managing Project Risk

"I received the official notice of Maria's promotion to Minneapolis. It's too bad that we lost our only contact on the floor," says James.

"I'm sure Maria will be willing to spend some time on the project from Minneapolis. At least for the transition phase while we find someone else to replace her on the project," said Cindy.

"I'm not sure," said James. "Trey has talked to her and said that she would require a few months to settle into her new environment before she can contribute to the project."

"Looks like we'll just have to work without her till the next person comes in!" Cindy exclaimed.

"That's fine," said James as he turned to Kevin and Trey. "Would you both find out the tasks that Maria was assigned and the resources that she had planned for those tasks? I'd like to see how much is done and how much is left. Depending on this, I'd like to see how much can be held off till the new person comes in."

"Sure," said Kevin, while Trey nodded his head. Both of them walked out of conference room chatting about Maria.

James took a brief call, and after getting off the phone said, "We got a new person from the store in Irvine, California! His name is Rick Piccoli. He should be on the phone with us in a few minutes."

Just then, Trey stormed into the room and said, "Angela McKenzie has given her two months' notice because she received an offer from BestBuy. I'm sure we've lost her, too."

"That's okay. Forget about Maria's part; I think we've got her replacement. Would you both see the status of Angela's part in the project? By the way, Maria's replacement is Rick Piccoli from the Irvine store," said James.

Trey nodded his head in his characteristic manner and left.

"One after the other!" James exclaimed. "This really had the potential to throw off the project. Managing project risk would not have been so easy without such explicit scheduling and resource allocation."

"I can take on most of Angela's work," offered Cindy. "I've done a little bit of customer relations quite some time back."

"Thanks. I'll need all the help I can get if I want to keep this project on schedule!"

Adapted from: Valacich and George (2017).

Chapter Summary

Understand the concept of risk and its relationship to project management. Risk is frequently defined in terms of potential losses, but as we have seen from this chapter, the Project Management Institute thinks of risk as "an uncertain event or condition that, if it occurs, has a *positive* or a negative effect on a project objective"; accordingly, risks can offer opportunities as well as threats. Further, risk should be considered to be a combination of both the probability of occurrence and the overall effect of the occurrence. Risk may be associated with the project management process groups of initiation, planning, execution, closing, and control. Teams may be formed to manage risk during projects, and the forming of teams may be risky as well.

Identify sources of risk and their effect on information systems projects. Risk is natural during IS development projects. Specific sources of risk were discussed as they pertain to the unique nature of IS projects. Among these were risks as a result of the rapid technological change associated with today's businesses, the difficulty of hiring and retaining key IS personnel, acceptance by diverse users, and the numerous systems development methodologies available. Using established project management processes can help mitigate risk during IS projects.

Apply techniques for managing project risk. Specific risk management processes include *Plan Risk Management*, *Identify Risks*, *Perform Qualitative Risk Analysis*, *Perform Quantitative Risk Analysis*, *Plan Risk Responses*, *Implement Risk Responses*, and *Monitor Risks*. Many tools and techniques used during risk management were discussed in this chapter. Among them were information gathering techniques such as brainstorming. Qualitative and quantitative analysis tools such as probability/impact matrices were discussed. Finally, risk response strategies such as escalation, avoidance, mitigation/exploitation, transference/sharing, and acceptance were also discussed.

Key Terms Review

A. Decision tree analysis
B. Expected monetary value analysis
C. Identify Risks
D. Implement Risk Responses
E. Issue
F. Monitor Risks
G. Perform Qualitative Risk Analysis
H. Perform Quantitative Risk Analysis
I. Periodic project risk reviews
J. Plan Risk Management
K. Plan Risk Responses
L. Probability/impact risk rating matrix
M. Project assumption testing
N. Project risk response audits
O. Residual risks
P. Risk

Q. Risk acceptance
R. Risk avoidance
S. Risk escalation
T. Risk management plan
U. Risk mitigation
V. Risk owner
W. Risk register
X. Risk response plan
Y. Risk transference
Z. Risk-related contractual agreements
AA. Secondary risks
BB. Sensitivity analysis
CC. Technical performance measurement
DD. Tornado analysis
EE. Trigger

Match each of the key terms with the definition that best fits it.

1. A diagramming technique that graphically shows, in descending order, which risks can cause the greatest variability on some outcome.

2. A diagramming technique used to evaluate courses of action in terms of their potential cost and benefits relative to other courses of action.

3. A documented plan for risk response.

4. A formal record listing all project risks, explaining the nature of the risk and management of the risk.

5. A risk response strategy designed to avoid potential project risks.

6. A risk response strategy designed to transfer risk to another party.

7. A risk response strategy in which risks are simply accepted and contingency strategies are planned.

8. A risk response strategy in which steps are taken to mitigate project risk.

9. A risk response strategy that involves assigning the response to a higher organizational level if the threat is beyond the authority of the project manager.

10. A statistical technique that captures the average value of potential projects by analyzing the likelihood of possible project outcomes as well as each outcome's financial consequence.

11. A systematic approach to planning the risk management activities of a given project.

12. A technique used during qualitative risk analysis to test the assumptions made during risk identification.

13. A technique used to analyze project risk in terms of its probability of occurrence and its impact on project outcomes.

14. A technique used to examine the potential impact of specific risks to a project.

15. An event or situation that has happened and has a negative effect on one or more project objectives.

16. A tool used to determine whether important technical milestones are being met.

17. An overall plan used to outline risks and the strategies used to manage them.

18. An uncertain event or condition that, if it occurs, has a positive or negative effect on one or more project objectives.

19. Any contracts for the purpose of risk transference during the project.

20. Any risks remaining after risk response strategies have been applied.

21. Any risks resulting from the application of a risk response strategy.

22. Audits designed to evaluate the effectiveness of risk response strategies and risk owners.

23. Event that serves as an early warning of risk.

24. Project member responsible for specific risk activity decisions.

25. Reviews designed to review existing risk activities and to monitor any changes to the project.

26. The analysis of the probability of occurrence and the impact of risk on project objectives using numerical techniques.

27. The evaluation of the potential impact and likelihood of specific risk occurrence.

28. The process of developing methods for responding to project risks.

29. The process of identifying and documenting a project's potential risk.

30. The process of monitoring identified risks for change and controlling those changes.

31. The process of reacting to identified project risks so as to minimize threats and maximize opportunities and manage overall project risk exposure.

Review Questions

1. Define risk.

2. Explain how project risk can have both a positive and a negative effect on a project objective.

3. Describe how risk can affect each stage of the project life cycle.

4. What are the different risk management processes? Provide a brief description of each.

5. Give two examples of risk during an information systems development project.

6. List two inputs for each of the Project Risk Management processes *(note that the Implement Risk Responses process is not discussed in this chapter)*.

7. List two outputs for each of the Project Risk Management processes *(note that the Implement Risk Responses process is not discussed in this chapter)*.

8. List two tools or techniques for each of the Project Risk Management processes *(note that the Implement Risk Responses process is not discussed in this chapter)*.

9. Describe probability/impact risk analysis.

10. Discuss qualitative risk analysis.

11. Discuss the various techniques for quantitative risk analysis.

12. List the common elements of a risk response plan.

13. Compare and contrast risk avoidance, risk transference, risk mitigation, and risk acceptance.

14. Explain the different categories of risk pertaining to the uniqueness of IS projects.

Chapter Exercises

1. Identify the common sources of risks in information systems projects. Provide suggestions for managing them.

2. Find an example of a risk management plan on the internet or any other source. What are the elements of this plan?

3. Using the internet or any other source, write a two-page report on information gathering techniques. Be sure to discuss the information gathering techniques discussed in the chapter.

4. Think of a recent project that you were involved in (or the project you are involved in as part of your current course). What were some of the risks you faced? Were some of the risks more likely to occur than others? What was the potential impact of the risks you faced? Using this information, construct a probability/impact matrix as outlined in this chapter.

5. Using the internet or any other source, write a two-page report on qualitative and quantitative risk analysis. Be sure to discuss the analyses discussed in the chapter.

Chapter Case: Sedona Management Group and Managing Project Risk

All projects involve a certain level of risk. Project risk is any uncertain event that may have a positive or negative effect on a project objective. Project Risk Management, therefore, involves understanding the possible problems that might occur during the project life cycle and how they will affect the success of the project. Significant improvements in project outcomes result from effectively managing project risk. Organizations need to understand that Project Risk Management processes are an investment—these processes cost money but can also yield benefits.

Sedona Management Group (SMG) typically associates different categories of risks with the information systems projects they pursue. The first category includes risks associated with the constant flux of technology in today's business environment. The team at SMG has mitigated—or reduced—this type of risk by constantly scanning for new technologies that will reduce development time, reduce the costs of maintenance, and stimulate the reuse of code in an efficient manner for new projects. The second category includes risks associated with locating, hiring, and retaining competent personnel. As mentioned in an earlier case, SMG strives to provide a work environment that has a fun organizational culture and that is also professionally and financially rewarding. Providing such a work environment has been a critical element in SMG's ability to hire and retain valued employees and in its success in today's high-technology business environment. The third category involves risks associated with the user's acceptance of the system. The Sedona team mitigates this type of risk by keeping the customer constantly involved throughout the life cycle of the project. Consequently, SMG's customers know what to expect, and there are no surprises.

Risk occurs at every stage of the project life cycle. In the initiation phase, risk occurs in the project selection process. In any company, the selection of the wrong project, whether in terms of profitability or complexity, may harm the company. In the case of SMG's commercial website development business, the result might be that the company could no longer sustain itself. As a result, SMG employs a detailed process for selecting projects, and as mentioned earlier, projects that don't meet SMG's criteria are rejected.

In the planning stage, other types of risks may be encountered. Tim Turnpaugh recognizes that the probability of project success increases with good planning. The company's experience with successful projects over the last ten years helps the Sedona team define the scope, time, and cost of any project quite accurately. By using processes that accurately identify project scope, the team can determine the budget and time it would take to complete the project. All of these standardized processes are used to manage project risk. The contract that SMG uses for its clients also minimizes the risks associated with the development process by explicitly describing the customers' expectations, the technology used in the development of the system, the capabilities of the final system, the customer's availability for project related communication, and finally the costs associated with any changes in project scope.

In the execution phase, other types of risks will be encountered. Despite a thorough plan developed with the client, there is still the risk that the project somehow won't meet client expectations. To mitigate this risk, SMG involves the customer throughout the development process, so that any potential issues can be identified early. In the case of the Seattle Seahawks, the Sedona team produced several different potential designs based on the initial requirements set forth by the Seahawks. Mike Flood, the Seahawks' manager in charge of the development effort, was able to assess these prototypes in connection with potential website users and chose

to continue the development process with the version that seemed to best meet their needs.

Another area where risk can be managed is in project control and closure. Project control involves measuring the progress of the project in terms of the project objectives, monitoring any deviation from the project plan, and taking any corrective action required to match the progress with the plan. Turnpaugh has rigid rules about change requests. If the customer requests any substantial changes during the project life cycle, these change requests will result in a modified project budget and schedule. The purpose of project closure involves ensuring that the project deliverables have been completed and delivering the final product to the customer. The Sedona team ensures that the customer understands how to adequately maintain the delivered system, which prevents downstream maintenance risks, as well as risks to Sedona's reputation. At the closure stage, SMG also documents any lessons learned during the project to reduce the risks of future efforts.

Chapter 9 Project Assignment

During the life cycle of a project, it is important to manage risk because it can have an impact on the project scope, schedule, and budget. In this exercise, you will have to identify the potential risks that might occur when you are developing the entertainment website.

1. Define *risk* as it relates to your project.

2. Identify sources of risks that will occur at different stages of your project.

3. Referring to Chapter 8 (which discusses quality management), develop a cause-and-effect, or fishbone, diagram to trace the root causes of the risks you identified for Question 2.

4. Discuss the different techniques (e.g., risk escalation, avoidance/exploitation, transference/sharing, mitigation/enhancement, and acceptance) that you will use to address these risks.

5. Develop a risk response plan, which is a documented plan for risk response. The document should contain

   - The identified risks
   - The project areas or objectives the risk may affect
   - The roles and responsibilities of any risk owners
   - A description of the risk response strategies, including escalation, avoidance/exploitation, transference/sharing, mitigation/enhancement, and acceptance that will be used to address the identified risks
   - An acknowledgement of any residual risks projected to remain after any risk response strategies have been applied
   - A list of actions to be used to implement the risk response strategies

References

Boulton, C. (2017, June 20). Shake Shack's Secret Sauce for Getting Mobile Apps Right. *CIO.com*. Retrieved July 13, 2018, from https://www.cio.com/article/3202025/mobile/shake-shacks-secret-sauce-for-getting-mobile-apps-right.html

Essex, D. (2003). A Matter of Public Record. *PM Network*, August, 22–26.

Gnatyk, R. (2018, April 29). How to Minimize Risks in Software Development Offshoring. *N-iX*. Retrieved July 6, 2018, from https://www.n-ix.com/how-to-minimize-risks-software-development-offshoring

Hall, P. (2003). Make Haste Slowly. *PM Network*, August, 32–35.

Harpham, B. (2016, August 8). How to Improve Risk Management with Big Data Analytics. *Project Management.com.* Retrieved March 9, 2018, from https://www.projectmanagement.com/articles/339344/How-to-Improve-Risk-Management-with-Big-Data-Analytics

Keil, M., Cule, P. E., Lyytinen, K., and Schmidt, R. (1998). A Framework for Identifying Software Project Risks. *Communications of the ACM* 41(11), 76–83.

Knutson, J. (2003). A Project Management Renaissance: The Future Is Already Here. *PM Network*, July, 60–61.

Mezak, S. (2018, February 6). Fifteen Risk Areas for Software Development Outsourcing. *CIO.com.* Retrieved July 6, 2018, from https://www.cio.com/article/3253947/outsourcing/15-risk-areas-for-software-development-outsourcing.html

Minsky, S. (2016, March 4). Manage Tomorrow's Surprises Today. *ebizQ.* Retrieved September 20, 2018, from http://www.ebizq.net/blogs/chief_risk_officer/2016/03/5_tips_for_more_effective_risk.php

Munarriz, R. (2017, January 30). Your Smartphone May Be Destroying Starbucks and Chipotle. *The Motley Fool.* Retrieved July 13, 2018, from https://www.fool.com/investing/2017/01/30/your-smartphone-may-be-destroying-starbucks-and-ch.aspx

Project Management Institute (2017). *Agile Practice Guide.* Newton Square, PA: Author.

Project Management Institute (2017). *PMBOK: A Guide to the Project Management Body of Knowledge* (6th ed.). Newtown Square, PA: Author.

Rao, H. R., Nam, K., and Chaudhury, A. (1996). Information Systems Outsourcing. *Communications of the ACM* 39(7), 27–28.

Ribeiro, J. (2004, August 5). Source Code Stolen from U.S. Software Company in India. *ComputerWorld.* Retrieved July 9, 2018, from http://www.computerworld.com/article/2566652/technology-law-regulation/source-code-stolen-from-u-s--software-company-in-india.html

Schoultz, M. (2016, February 28). My Starbucks Idea: How Starbucks Used IT for Business Crowdsourcing. *Digital Spark Marketing.* Retrieved May 24, 2018, from https://digitalsparkmarketing.com/my-starbucks-idea

Thibodeau, P. (2004, January 26). Internal Resistance can Doom Offshore Projects. *ComputerWorld.* Retrieved July 9, 2018, from http://www.computerworld.com/article/2574652/it-outsourcing/internal-resistance-can-doom-offshore-projects.html

Valacich, J., and George, J. F. (2017). *Modern Systems Analysis and Design* (8th ed.). Boston: Pearson.

Vijayan, J. (2004, August 30). Security Expectations, Response Rise in India. *ComputerWorld.* Retrieved July 9, 2018, from https://www.computerworld.com/article/2566635/it-outsourcing/security-expectations--response-rise-in-india.html

Wallace, L., and Keil, M. (2004). Software Project Risks and Their Effect on Outcomes. *Communications of the ACM* 47(4), 68–73.

Managing Project Procurement

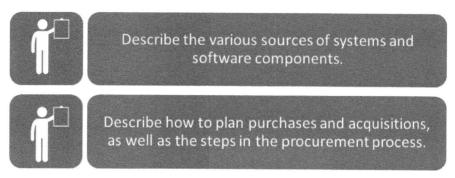

Describe the various sources of systems and software components.

Describe how to plan purchases and acquisitions, as well as the steps in the procurement process.

Figure 10.1   Chapter 10 learning objectives

Opening Case: Outsourcing Is Big Business

Outsourcing is big business. Research and consulting firm Gartner estimated that worldwide spending on information technology (IT) services would surpass US$1 trillion in 2017. When an organization decides to outsource its IT development and management, it typically looks to a few familiar firms. IBM, one of the best-known names in IT, is the leader in the global managed IT services market. Together, IBM, DXC Technology, and Fujitsu are controlling more than 50 percent of that market.

IT outsourcing varies in scope and range of services provided, but outsourcing contracts typically involve a company's handing over such major tasks as data center management, software development, call center operations, and desktop and network support to an IT service provider.

Known for its many widely recognized brands, such as Cuervo tequila (Figure 10.2), Guinness beer, and Smirnoff vodka, beverage maker Diageo

extensively used IT outsourcing and had a long-term agreement with HP for the management of its IT infrastructure. In 2003, Diageo signed over management of its worldwide IT infrastructure to IBM. Analysts estimated the deal to be worth $400–500 million over seven years. As Diageo was formed through the merger of beverage makers Guinness and Grand Met, along with subsequent acquisitions, another part of the outsourcing agreement involved the integration of several disparate systems the company had acquired through that mergers and acquisition process. In 2014, Diageo signed an agreement with the Indian outsourcing company Tata Consulting Services to manage its IT infrastructure. Clearly, companies are always looking for IT services provides that best meet their needs. Diageo's switch to Tata is a sign that other players beyond the traditional giants continue to gain market share.

Based on: BCC (2018); Flinders (2014); Hines (2003); Van der Meulen and Pettey (2018).

Figure 10.2   Tequila is distilled from the blue agave. *Source*: CC-BY-SA-4.0, Faguilal.

Introduction

As the opening case illustrates, outsourcing the management of a company's information technology infrastructure is big business, and procurement of information technology and information systems has become a major part of most projects. Almost no serious systems development is done from scratch by in-house information systems personnel anymore. Instead, entire systems or various system components are purchased from outside the organization and then integrated with existing systems. In some cases, development and management of systems is completely handed over to another company, as is the case with the outsourcing example in the opening case. As in the opening case, companies tend to attempt to reduce costs for systems that do not add strategic value—that is, if the system is used to run the business and considered a cost center (see the "run, grow, transform" model introduced in Chapter 5). Whether a company is procuring an entire information systems infrastructure and its management or simply the software components needed for its internal systems development efforts, procurement, the subject of this chapter, becomes a key project management activity.

This chapter has two main parts. The first part is about the many current choices available today for systems development. This section of the chapter is organized according to the types of organizations from which software or its components can be procured. These include packaged software providers, open source software, Software-as-a-Service (SaaS) providers, vendors of enterprise-wide solution software, and information technology services firms. The second part of the chapter is about the procurement process and the various steps that are a part of it. These project procurement processes include *Plan Procurement Management*, *Conduct Procurements*, and *Control Procurements*.

Alternatives to Internal Systems Development

In the early days of computer-based organizational information systems, companies typically had to develop systems from scratch to support their individual business processes. Few experienced systems developers existed, and systems development methodologies were often only loosely followed. As a result, documentation was often lacking, and systems maintenance tended to be a daunting task. Addressing these issues, systems developers increasingly attempted to take a more engineering-oriented approach to systems development, with a stronger focus on highly structured methodologies and well-documented development processes. This was increasingly possible due to the emergence of computer-assisted software engineering (CASE) tools, which not only helped develop systems, but also helped create useful documentation. However, this focus on highly structured methodologies led to relatively rigid and inflexible systems, which could not easily be adapted to changing business needs. For in-house development, organizations now increasingly turn to agile methodologies, which allow for an expedited approach to systems development focusing on iterative development, incremental delivery, and frequent feedback, so as to be able to quickly react to changing business conditions or user needs.

In the first wave of developing computer-based information systems, organizations were forced to develop their own systems internally, as the off-the-shelf software industry only took off in the late 1960s, and organizations did not have the possibility to purchase packaged software for even generic business functions such as accounting or human resources. As the packaged software industry took off, many developers continued to believe that high quality software that would meet the organization's needs could only be built in-house and rejected off-the-shelf software—often referred to as the "not built here" syndrome. While more rigorous development methodologies helped improve the quality of the software and the documentation, systems development continued to be a relatively slow process. With the widespread diffusion of the internet in the mid-1990s, organizations' business needs tended change more rapidly, making slow and inflexible in-house development processes increasingly impractical. Thus, especially for generic business processes, obtaining software from outside providers has become the norm.

Therefore, information systems development today typically involves the procurement of individual systems components or even entire systems. Consequently, internal IT departments now focus less on developing systems, but spend increasing efforts integrating externally obtained components and systems. The question is, how and where can organizations obtain components or entire systems? In this chapter, we will discuss the various sources of software. Given the various options, understanding **external acquisition** (i.e., the procurement of products and/or services from an outside vendor) and the associated procurement processes become increasingly important; we will discuss these processes in the latter part of this chapter.

External acquisition
The procurement of products and/or services from an outside vendor.

External Acquisition

Broadly categorized, there are five sources of externally developed information systems or application software: (1) packaged software providers, (2) open source software, (3) Software-as-a-Service providers, (4) vendors of enterprise-wide solution software, and (5) information technology services firms (Figure 10.3). Whereas some of the organizations focus on generic software for common business processes, others provide custom-made systems or solutions for their clients' particular needs. When deciding on how to externally acquire systems, organizations need to consider the lifetime costs of a system, which not only include the initial costs for purchasing and installing the system, but also the ongoing costs for system maintenance, which tend to be lower for commercial off-the-shelf software (often referred to as COTS) than for custom-built systems.

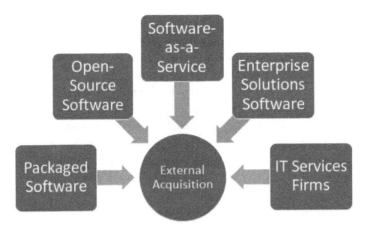

Figure 10.3   Sources of externally developed information systems or application software

Packaged Software Producers

Since the 1960s, the software industry has seen tremendous growth. Today, several of the largest computer companies are primarily focusing on software development. For example, whereas Microsoft at times has ventured into developing hardware, such as the Surface family of devices, more than 63 percent of the company's revenue comes from selling software, such as the Windows operating system, the Office productivity suite, or the CRM and ERP application Dynamics 365. Likewise, Oracle almost entirely focuses on database software and enterprise systems, as does SAP, which is one of the largest developers of enterprise-wide information systems.

Various companies focus on developing prepackaged software geared toward generic tasks or business processes. For example, Intuit's Quicken, QuickPay, and QuickBooks can be used for relatively standardized accounting tasks in almost all industries. These systems, developed by **packaged software producers**, are normally sold as is, and are thus often referred to as off-the-shelf or shrink-wrapped systems; this type of software is typically distributed as executables, so the source code cannot be accessed. While large software companies typically offer broad-based packages targeted at mass markets, other companies focus on very specific needs of niche markets, such as software for running a day care center. Packaged software producers may focus on one particular platform or may develop software for different platforms (such as Microsoft Office, which is offered as PC and as Mac versions). Typically, packaged software producers consult with key customers in the early stages of development, so as to define market needs and test and improve the system.

A distinguishing aspect of off-the-shelf software systems is that they are generic and can typically not be customized to account for the needs of individual organizations. As they cannot be customized, such applications are sometimes referred to as **turnkey systems.** However, producers of turnkey systems typically take user feedback into account when developing future releases of their applications. Other of-the-shelf systems can be modified to a certain degree, allowing organizations to adapt the system to their particular needs. Yet those modifications are typically limited, and organizations are unlikely to find shrink-wrapped software that meets the exact needs of the organization. Based on published estimates, at most 70 percent of any given off-the-shelf application meets the of an organization, with up to 30 percent of the features going unused.

Packaged software producer
Company in the business of developing and selling off-the-shelf software.

Turnkey system
Off-the-shelf software that cannot be modified to meet the specific, individual needs of an organization.

Open Source Software

Open source software
Systems software,
applications, and
programming
languages of which
the source code is
freely available for use
and/or modification.

In contrast to proprietary off-the-shelf software, the source code of **open source software** can be accessed and modified as needed. Rather than being developed by commercial entities, open source software is developed by (sometimes very large) communities of interested people (these can be independent individuals or employees of software firms). Open source software alternatives now exist for most types of systems, ranging from operating systems (e.g., Linux and Android), database systems (MySQL), web browsers (Firefox), to email software (Thunderbird). While open source software is often freely available, various companies have developed business models around providing service or maintenance for open source software, or by selling enterprise versions with higher levels of reliability security, or scalability, so as to reduce risks for organizations.

Software-as-a-Service Providers

On-demand computing
Provision of computing
resources on the basis
of users' needs.

Utility computing
A service provisioning
model where
resources (such as
processing, data
storage, or networking)
are provided as
needed, and the
organization only pays
for the services used.

Both off-the-shelf and open source software are typically designed to be installed and run in-house, on an organization's computers. In contrast, Software-as-a-Service (SaaS) providers offer software that is hosted "in the cloud" (i.e., on the provider's infrastructure). In other words, this software is typically accessed remotely via a web browser, and the software itself (as well as the data in some cases) is stored on the providers' systems. In other words, SaaS can be seen as a form of **on-demand computing**, where computing resources are provided on an as-needed basis. Typically, SaaS providers use a **utility computing model**, such that the organization only pays for the resources (processing, data storage, or data traffic) that are being used (Dignan, 2002), and resources can be adjusted based on demand, making such systems highly scalable. Given that the provider is responsible for the purchase, installation, and maintenance of the underlying infrastructure, using SaaS is a form of risk transference.

Just as open source software has seen rapid increases in popularity, increases in bandwidth have contributed to increasing popularity of SaaS. SaaS providers offer a variety of software, ranging from office automation tools (such as Microsoft Office Online) to enterprise resource planning systems, often geared toward small and medium enterprises. For example, Salesforce.com offers customer relationship management systems, and SAP even offers enterprise resource planning systems (SAP Business ByDesign) on a SaaS basis. In addition to software being hosted in the cloud, organizations can use Platform-as-a-Service (PaaS) and Infrastructure-as-a-Service (IaaS). For example, providers such as Rackspace.com, Amazon.com, and Microsoft Azure provide platforms that allow customers to run their own applications (PaaS), or offer basic computing infrastructure (such as processing, storage, or networking) on an as-needed basis (IaaS), giving the customer maximum control over what is being implemented.

Enterprise Solutions Software

**Enterprise resource planning (ERP)
system**
A system that
integrates individual
traditional business
functions into a
series of modules
so that a single
transaction occurs
seamlessly within a
single information
system rather than
over several separate
systems.

As organizations have grown to be more complex, they have attempted to move away from disparate legacy systems toward integrated systems for managing business processes. Such integrated solutions, called **enterprise resource planning systems (ERP)**, provide modules supporting individual business functions, such as accounting, distribution, manufacturing, and human resources. However, rather than purely focusing on business functions, these modules are integrated in a way to allow for seamless integration of business processes, such that a process can be completed without having to move data between separate systems. Likewise, such systems increase data quality and availability throughout an organization, allowing the organization to have more up-to-date and complete information about business processes, customers, and the like. For example, the handling of an order, including the order entry, inventory management, shipping, billing, and after-sales-service processes are integrated in a unified system, such that all aspects of a transaction can be completed within the same system using the same underlying data. ERP systems are typically developed by very large software companies, the most well-known being SAP and Oracle; recently, these behemoths have seen increased completion from ERP solutions targeted at small and medium enterprises, often provided on an SaaS basis.

Using an integrated system helps increase the consistency and accuracy of the data and helps speed up business processes. Further, ERP systems are often somewhat flexible, in that they allow adding modules and configuring processes based on a company's particular needs. However, given the very nature of these systems, they tend to be very large and highly complex, so that implementing ERP systems is typically a lengthy, costly, and risky project. In fact, examples abound where ERP installation projects have run far over budget or time or have been abandoned before the system has been implemented. In addition, implementing ERP systems requires standardizing data and processes across the organization, and many large-scale ERP systems (notably SAP) necessitate modifications to a company's business processes to match the software. Both of these aspects greatly contribute to the risk of implementing such systems, especially if stakeholders do not sign off on the objective of standardization. Given the complexity and risk of going with one single ERP solution, some companies have moved toward a **best-of-breed strategy**, integrating different modules from different ERP vendors (e.g., SAP's order entry modules and Oracle's financial and human resources modules) to maximize the benefits. Yet this approach introduces new difficulties, such as integrating the systems, data, and user interfaces, and sacrifices the benefits offered by having a unified single system.

Best-of-breed strategy
A strategy of using different software products from different sources (including in house development) to capitalize on the strengths of different products.

Information Technology Services Firms

As you have seen, options for obtaining information systems abound. However, off-the-shelf software, open source software, and enterprise systems are to a large extent designed in a one-size-fits-all approach. Designed to appeal to the greatest market, such systems may not suit the exact needs of an organization. Likewise, an organization may need a very particular system to gain or sustain competitive advantage, or may need to integrate disparate systems from various sources. Yet, developing systems is not the core competency of most organizations, and organizations often lack the expertise or resources to develop custom systems in-house. Filling this void, various **IT services firms** focus on developing custom information systems for organizations' internal use or on hosting systems; in addition, IT services firms provide other consultancy or systems maintenance services. As you can see from the list of the top ten global software firms presented in Table 10.1, several of the top ten firms offer IT services. In addition to having extensive expertise in systems development, they also understand specific business areas and industry sectors, such as banking, manufacturing, retail, and so on. Whereas companies such as IBM or HP have initially focused primarily on hardware, they have now transitioned their business models to focus on consulting; Hewlett Packard Enterprise—which was formed after HP acquired EDS—merged its enterprise services business with Computer Sciences Corp. and is now known as DXC.technology. In addition to the companies listed in Table 10.1, other notable IT services include Accenture, Wipro, and Capgemini.

IT services firm
A firm that helps companies develop custom information systems for internal use or develop, host, and run applications for customers.

Table 10.2 compares the five different sources for systems and software components. Choosing the most suitable supplier will be determined by your needs, not by

Table 10.1 The Top Ten Global Software Companies

Rank	Company	2017 Software/Services Revenue (Million USD)	Software Business Sector
1	IBM	$70,224	Middleware / application server / web server / systems integration services / IT consulting
2	Microsoft	$51,5298	Operating systems / application software
3	HP	$48,238	Business solutions
4	Hewlett Packard Enterprises	$47,023	Systems integration services / IT consulting
5	Accenture	$32,882	Systems integration services / IT consulting
6	Oracle	$32,379	Database / business process management
7	Ericsson	$26,016	Telecommunication services
8	SAP	$24,414	Business process management
9	Apple	$24,348	Operating systems / application software
10	Tata	$16,596	Systems integration services

Adapted from: Software Magazine (2018).

Table 10.2 Comparison of Five Different Sources of Software Components

Producers	When to Go to This Type of Organization for Software	Internal Staffing Requirements
Packaged software producers	When supported task is generic	Some IS and user staff to define requirements and evaluate packages
Open source	When the supported task is generic but cost is an issue, as well as when companies want to have the flexibility to view and modify the source code	Some IS and user staff to define software requirements and evaluate packages
Software-as-a-Service providers	When the company already invests heavily in IT and has standard business processes	Ideally, none
Enterprise-wide solutions	For complete systems that cross functional boundaries	Some internal staff necessary, but mostly consultants
IT services firms	When task requires custom support and the system can't be built internally	Internal staff may be needed, depending on application

what the supplier has to sell. The results of your procurement planning analysis will define the type of product you want to buy and will make working with an external supplier much easier, productive, and worthwhile.

Tips from the Pros: Ensuring Offshore Project Success

As you have read, procurement many times reaches offshore. Although offshore providers are often sought for their lower costs, they frequently do not have the necessary management and organizational skills to deliver all of the anticipated business benefits. Here are some tips on how to ensure that offshore procurement is successful, from Craig Rintoul, a consultant who specializes in outsourcing and IT management and who works with PA Consulting Group in Cambridge, Massachusetts.

1. *Onshore team*: The onshore business leadership team must take a hands-on approach. They must ensure that the offshore team delivers business benefits. The onshore team has to ensure that the offshore team delivers both technical and business benefits.

2. *Program management*: Offshore projects are very susceptible to changes in budget, timing, and deliverables. The program management team needs to be able to redeploy resources as needed and to anticipate change before it happens.

3. *Delivery of benefits*: Early benefit delivery from offshore projects is very important in proving feasibility and sustainability of service. Specific benefits need to be aligned with each requirement and linked to implementation milestones. It is important to plainly map dependencies so that it is clear what needs to be done to deliver a particular milestone.

4. *Change and project management*: The geographic separation and mix of cultures inherent in an offshore project increase risk, worsen problems that arise, and lengthen time to resolution. A back-to-basics approach in project and change management will increase the chances of success. The offshore vendor's and the client's responsibilities need to be clearly defined and understood by both parties.

5. *Geographic and cultural differences*. One of the greatest challenges is overcoming differences in language, culture, and geography. While good communication is important to any project, it is crucial to offshore projects. The onshore company has to be aware of cultural differences and their effect on how directions are received, how problems are resolved, and how responsibilities are delegated. When agreeing on schedules or reviewing specifications, onshore project managers should ensure that everyone correctly understands the details. Scheduling is also made difficult by differences in the number and timing of local holidays and vacation practices across countries. In some countries, for example, workers may typically get four to six weeks of paid vacation per year.

Based on: De Marco (2017); Rintoul (2004).

Steps in the Procurement Process

Once the decision has been made to externally acquire systems or services (or both), the project team begins the project procurement process. According to the *PMBOK* (2017), there are three major processes in the Project Procurement Management knowledge area. These are *Plan Procurement Management*, *Conduct Procurements*, and *Control Procurements* (see Figure 10.4). As with all other management processes in the *PMBOK*, each of the procurement processes can be understood in terms of its inputs, internal tools and techniques, and outputs.

A quick look at Table 2.2 (in Chapter 2) will show which process group each of the three procurement processes belongs in. *Plan Procurement Management* is part of planning; *Conduct Procurements* belongs to the executing process group; and *Control Procurements* is part of the monitoring and controlling process group. There are no procurement processes in the initiating and closing process groups.

The *Plan Procurement Management* process helps determine which of your projects needs can best be met by obtaining services or products from outside the project organization. Typically, this implies vendors from outside of the overall organization, although it is possible for some services and products to be obtained from other units within the organization. Once the decision has been made to procure externally, a cost estimate for budgeting purposes is created, before the documents needed to support the processes of requesting seller responses and selecting sellers are created. These documents are used to seek proposals from prospective vendors. They describe what is to be purchased and ask for offers from vendors who are interested in providing it. Common names for these documents include invitation for bid, request for proposal (RFP), request for quotation, tender notice, or invitation for negotiation. In this chapter, we will refer to these procurement documents primarily as RFPs, which are typically issued to a list of qualified sellers. The main task of requesting seller responses is to obtain bids that respond to the RFP. Once these documents have been created, the *Conduct Procurements* process

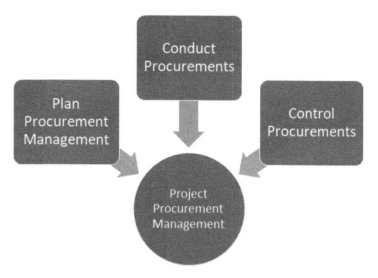

Figure 10.4 *PMBOK* (6th ed.) Project Procurement Management processes

begins. Here, seller responses are obtained and the bids are compared and judged by the selection criteria that the project organization has established; typically, this involves separately evaluating quality and cost, before performing a combined evaluation to determine the proposal that best meets the organization's needs. A vendor is chosen, and a contract is negotiated and signed. *Control Procurements* is the process through which the project organization works with the vendor for the duration of the contract, including managing relationships and monitoring performance, and, once the terms of the contract have been satisfactorily met, close the contract. Both sides of the agreement accept the work performed, and the contract is completed. In the next sections, you will read more about each of these three processes.

Plan Procurement Management

Plan Procurement Management involves determining which project needs can best be met by external acquisition, and how procurement is performed. In other words, the purpose of this process is to develop make-or-buy decisions, a procurement management plan, a procurement strategy, cost estimates, bid documents, a statement of work, and source selection criteria.

Plan Procurement Management—Inputs

As detailed in Figure 10.5, the inputs for the *Plan Procurement Management* process are the project charter, business documents (such as the business case and the benefits management plan), the project management plan (and, in particular, the scope baseline as well as the scope, quality, and resource management plans), project documents (including the milestone list, resource requirements, project team assignments, the stakeholder and risk registers, and the requirements documentation and traceability matrix). Finally, inputs include enterprise environmental factors and organizational process assets. The project charter provides the current boundaries of the project, including requirements, constraints, and assumptions. The most common constraint is limited funding. The project management plan provides the overall plan for managing the project and includes subsidiary plans that can provide guidance for procurement (see Chapter 5); various

Plan Procurement Management
The process of determining which project needs can best be met by external acquisition and planning how procurement activities are performed.

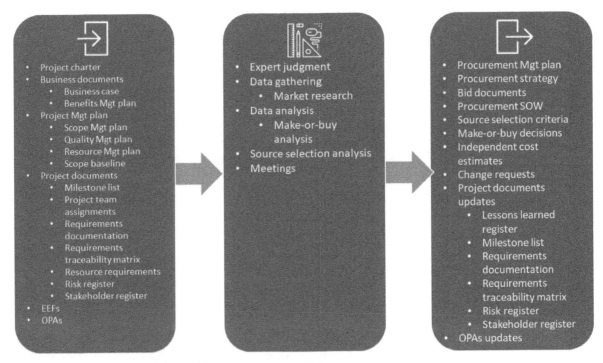

Figure 10.5 The *PMBOK* (6th ed.) *Plan Procurement Management* process

project documents inform about milestones, resource availability, potential risks, or stakeholder needs. Enterprise environmental factors include the services and products available in the marketplace, the key providers, typical terms and conditions, legal procurement advice, and the circumstances under which the services or products are available. Organizational process assets are the existing formal and informal policies, procedures, guidelines, and management systems that are considered in developing the procurement management plan. Some organizational process assets include lists of preapproved vendors, which limit the number of direct sellers to the organization. Further, organizational process assets include the different types of contracts used by the procuring organization. Three types of possible contracts are fixed-price, cost-reimbursable, and time-and-material contracts. In addition, depending on the project, the customer and vendor may agree on yet other terms to fit the specific needs of the project.

For a **fixed price contract**, the project requirements have been sufficiently detailed for suppliers to feel comfortable in establishing a fixed price. The supplier or vendor is bound to the price provided in the contract. A fixed-price contract is less problematic when the product or service is well-defined. Often fixed price contracts include incentives for performance (in terms of cost, schedule, or technical performance); especially for contracts with longer durations, fixed price contracts can allow for economic price

A **cost-reimbursable contract** (sometimes referred to as *cost-plus contract*) involves the reimbursement of the vendor's actual costs in providing the product or service plus—typically, a fixed fee that represents the vendor's profits. Costs are considered to be either direct or indirect. Direct costs are those incurred by the vendor in providing the product or service. Indirect costs, also called *overhead costs*, are part of the vendor's cost of doing business and involve such things as the salaries of managing executives. Indirect costs are typically billed as a percentage of direct costs. For example, many sponsored research contracts between universities and government sources involve

Fixed-price contract
A type of contract specifying a fixed price for a product/service.

Cost-reimbursable contract
A type of contract that involves payment for the actual cost of the product plus a fee that represents the vendor's profits.

cost-reimbursable contracts, and indirect cost rates set by universities are as high as 50 percent or more. As with fixed-price contracts, cost-reimbursable contracts may include an incentive for performance, or additional funds (beyond the vendor's costs) are awarded if certain performance objectives are met.

Time-and-material contract
A type of contract where vendors provide an hourly rate and estimate the amount of time and materials required.

Under **time and materials (T&M) contracts,** vendors state an hourly rate and estimate the amount of time and materials required. It is possible to cap a T&M contract by asking the vendor to provide a not-to-exceed price. Otherwise, the price is open. For a T&M contract, it is often recommended that contract requirements specify review points and progress assessments. The contractor may also want to tie payment to deliverables (Porter-Roth, 2002).

Global Implications of Outsourcing: Managing Security

The key motivation for procuring development services offshore is to save money and improve productivity. In the process, however, security may suffer. The issue is not so much that firms in India and China do not observe standard security measures such as firewalls and data backup—they do. The real issue is that differences in culture result in differences in how corporate data are treated. In close-knit cultures such as India, the attitude toward personal privacy is more relaxed than in the United States and Europe. Workers may not think twice about sharing what could be sensitive corporate and client data, according to Gartner India research vice president Partha Iyengar.

What can a company do to ensure that security is not overlooked in the procurement of services offshore? Suggestions from Iyengar and others include

- Document corporate processes and get vendors to sign off on them.
- Have vendors perform background checks on their staff.
- In some countries, such as India, ask vendors to hire only applicants who have Indian passports, which can be acquired only after passing vigorous security checks by Indian law enforcement.
- Have vendors increase security awareness through employee training.
- Write security and regulatory compliance concerns into the procurement contract.
- Visit offshore outsourcing facilities and check them out personally.
- Investigate and understand local laws regarding internet access and restrictions.

Based on: De Marco (2017); Pruitt (2004).

Plan Procurement Management—Tools and Techniques

As with most project management processes, expert judgement and meetings are used in the *Plan Procurement Management* process. Further, data about sellers, services, and products are gathered during market research, at industry conferences, or from online sources. The project team can also develop a list of qualified vendors from the internet, relevant local sources, or library directories. The key data analysis technique used in procurement planning is a **make-or-buy analysis.** For information systems projects, "make" used to be the routine determination, but now the routine decision is often more likely to be "buy."

Make-or-buy analysis
A technique determine whether a product or service should be produced in-house or procured from an outside vendor.

Evaluation criteria
Criteria used to rate proposals that are received in response to a request for proposals.

In addition, **evaluation criteria** (sometimes referred to as source selection criteria) used to rate proposals that are received in response to a request for proposals are developed. The criteria can be objective or subjective, and they are often included in the RFP. Typically, the vendors can be selected based on cost, quality, or a combination of the two factors; similar to a cost-based method, a fixed budget can be used, which sellers have to meet. Other criteria include how well the vendor understands the problem, whether or not the vendor has the technical ability to perform appropriately, and whether the vendor has or can obtain the resources necessary to deliver what is promised in the proposal. Buyers may also want to consider how long the vendor has been in business, how many employees the vendor has, whether an established vendor may be about to change business lines or emphases, and the number of other comparable projects the vendor has completed or is currently engaged in. In exceptional cases (such as for highly specific systems or services), only a sole provider may be asked to provide a proposal. Sometimes the organization issuing the RFP may prepare its own **independent estimates** for the price for whatever is being procured. These estimates act as a check against the prices offered in the proposals; likewise, independent estimates help provide realistic cost ceilings. Major differences in these estimates and the prices in the proposals obtained indicate the vendor did not adequately understand what was being asked for or did not respond fully. Sometimes these independent estimates are called should-cost estimates.

Plan Procurement Management—Outputs

As with all types of planning, *Plan Procurement Management* attempts to anticipate all of the resources and processes necessary to make the overall effort a success. One of the key outputs for this process, then, is a **procurement management plan**. The plan addresses such issues as how multiple vendors will be managed, where standardized procurement documents can be obtained, and how procurement will be coordinated with other project tasks. Further aspects covered in the procurement management plan include a timetable, performance metrics for procurement contracts, responsibilities of stakeholders, and so on. In addition to the procurement management plan, an important output of this process is "make-or-buy decisions," which list which project products and services the project team will purchase and which it will develop. This includes products and services needed to do the work of the project, as well as for operating the project's ultimate product. For those products or services that will be acquired externally, a procurement strategy specifies how the product/service will be delivered, which contract type will be used, and what different phases and milestones are used in the procurement process. Especially for large projects, independent cost estimates may be obtained, so as to achieve realistic cost estimates.

Another key output is a statement of work. The **statement of work (SOW)** is a document prepared for potential vendors that describes the service or product being sought in enough detail that potential vendors can determine if they can supply it. The SOW helps ensure a common understanding of the project needs and is a very useful communication tool. Figure 10.6 shows a sample outline for an SOW. This outline gives you an idea of the scope of information required in a typical SOW. Statements of work are not necessarily static documents. Instead, they tend to be revised and refined as they move through the procurement process. For example, an SOW may change after a prospective vendor has suggested a cheaper or more efficient way to provide the desired product or service. In addition to the statement of work, the *Plan Procurement Management* process results in the agreed upon evaluation criteria.

Based on the procurement strategy, the statement of work, cost estimates, and the evaluation criteria, **procurement documents** to solicit proposals from vendors can be developed. The most common procurement document is the **request for proposal (RFP)**. According to Porter-Roth (2002), an RFP is "a standard tool used by governments and businesses to purchase equipment and services by promoting competitive proposals among suppliers." An RFP allows buyers and suppliers to communicate using the same rules, requirements, schedule, and information. It is more than just a presentation of a problem that needs a solution: once a vendor responds to the request, the RFP becomes a foundation for the future working relationship between the buyer and the

Independent estimates Estimates prepared independently of proposals which act as a check against the prices offered in proposals.

Procurement management plan A plan that addresses such issues as how multiple vendors will be managed, where standardized procurement documents can be obtained, and how procurement will be coordinated with other project tasks.

Statement of work (SOW) Document prepared for potential vendors that describes the service or product being sought.

Procurement documents Documents used to solicit proposals from vendors.

Request for proposal (RFP) A document provided to vendors to ask them to propose a solution to a specific problem related to your project.

```
1. Introduction and Overview
   1.1 Background
   1.2 Scope of Work
   1.3 Objectives
2. Requirements
   2.1 Tasks
        • Desired Methodology
        • Illustrations/Drawings/Diagrams, if any
        • Specifications
        • Data/Property/Facilities
        • Level-of-Effort
        • Place/Travel
   2.2 End Results/Deliverables
        2.2.1 List of Deliverables by Task
   2.3 Schedules/Milestones
        2.3.1 Who Does What When Report
   2.4 Other Considerations
3. Progress/Quality Control
   The following is required to monitor progress:
   • Weekly Status Report
   • Weekly Meetings
   • Monthly Progress Report
   • Project Management Team Meetings
   • Program Reviews
   • Outlines and Drafts
4. Transmittal/Delivery/Accessibility
5. Notes
6. References
```

Figure 10.6 Sample outline of a statement of work

vendor (or supplier). In fact, the proposal prepared by the vendor often becomes a part of the final contract, as an addendum or exhibit, between the supplier and the vendor.

Although the format and content of RFPs differ by industry, individual company, and the product or service sought, the basic parts of an RFP include

1. Project overview and administrative information
2. Project details
   2.1. Scope of work
   2.2. Outcome and performance standards
   2.3. Deliverables
   2.4. Project timeline
3. Supplier qualifications and references
4. Pricing
5. Bidding process and procedure for evaluation of bids
   5.1. Proposal preparation requirements
   5.2. Evaluation and award
6. Contract and license agreement
   6.1. Project terms and conditions

The project overview and administrative information section contains an overview of the company and a statement of the problem the RFP is designed to solve. The administrative information part of this section lists all of the requirements for an acceptable proposal. These include where and when to submit the proposal, if and when a bidders' conference will be held, the relevant dates for procurement, specific requirements for preparing proposals, how proposals will be evaluated, RFP staff contact names and addresses, and other information required for a supplier to be judged responsive. The project details section includes an overview of the relevant technical information and the SOW so that potential vendors can determine if they can provide the solution that is being sought. This section will include technical factors critical to the success of the project, functional specifications, performance specifications, and so on. This section also contains information about the project's needs for implementation, installation, training, maintenance, and related matters, such as staffing requirements, installation schedule, and acceptance test requirements.

The third part of the RFP, the supplier qualifications and references section, is a request for information about the potential vendor. Its purpose is to help the buyer determine if the vendor is really qualified to supply the needed product or service. Information requested includes the vendor's financial status, the number of its currently installed systems or components, and the names of customers who can provide references for the vendor. The fourth section, the pricing section, provides a detailed format for vendors to follow to prepare their price proposals. Pricing can be broken down into separate items for such things as maintenance, licensing, and documentation. If the RFP is for a complete system, then the price proposal should include separate items for software, hardware, installation, systems integration, and so on. In any proposal, the vendor should also distinguish between one-time and recurring costs. The fifth section specifies how proposals should be prepared and how bids will be evaluated. The last section, the contract and license agreement section, provides guidance to potential vendors on how to respond to contracts and agreements, and also provides contracts used by the buyer so suppliers can study them.

Creating and evaluating an RFP is often a project in itself and can take up to six months or longer. Often an RFP team is created to manage the process, and the RFP team has a project leader. Like any other project, creating and evaluating an RFP requires following many different steps, typically in a specific order. A sample list of activities to be followed for an RFP is presented in Figure 10.7. Note that many activities occur before the main work on the RFP begins and that many other activities take place after the RFP has been written and sent to potential vendors. Most of the activities listed in Figure 10.7 under post-RFP activities are covered when discussing solicitation and source selection.

Typically, the *Plan Procurement Management* process also results in updates to various project documents, including the milestone list, requirements documentation and traceability matrix, as well as the risk, stakeholder, and lessons-learned registers. Likewise, information on qualified sellers is updated in the organizational process assets.

A final output is requested changes. Requested changes to the project management plan could result from the *Plan Procurement Management* process, and these changes are processed through the *Perform Integrated Change Control* process (see Chapter 12).

Pre-RFP Activities:
- Identify need
- Perform preliminary study
- Write project justification
- Estimate budget for external acquisition
- Approve RFP project

RFP Activities:
- Identify RFP team members
- Identify key milestones and create preliminary project schedule
- Identify high-level requirements
- Start preliminary research (vendors and technology)
- Identify users and determine user requirements
- Develop technical requirements
  - Review technical requirements with users
  - Review technical requirements against corporate standards & constraints
  - Finalize technical requirements
- Develop management requirements
  - Review management requirements with users
  - Review management against corporate standards
  - Finalize management requirements
- Write RFP
- Specify evaluation criteria
- Publish RFP

Post-RFP Activities:
- Reply to suppliers' questions
- Receive and evaluate proposals
- Follow up with suppliers (as needed)
- Hold supplier presentations, site visits, demonstrations & reference checks
- Select winning proposal
- Negotiate contract
- Debrief suppliers of losing proposals
- Archive losing proposals
- Implement project

Figure 10.7 Sample Project Schedule for a Request for Proposal

---

Common Problems: Choosing the Right Support Contract

A big part of procuring IT services is obtaining product support for your organization from the vendor of the services. Two key types of service contracts are available: incident-based support models and subscription-oriented models. Incident-based (i.e., pay-as-you-go) models provide for the vendor to charge the client organization for each support related call the vendor handles. A subscription-oriented (sometimes called fixed price) model involves unlimited support from the vendor for a monthly fee.

According to Billy Marshall, vice president of enterprise sales at Red Hat, the Linux provider, incident-based support contracts are a bad idea for any organization. He cites two main reasons. The first is that a contract based on payment per support call provides an incentive for the vendor to sell bad or broken technology to clients. If the amount of revenue a vendor receives is tied to the volume of service calls received, then the natural result, according to Marshall, is "poor technology, poor documentation, and poor service such that the customer is required to call repeatedly." The second reason that incident-based support contracts are a bad idea is that

they promote "incident hoarding." Given that they are penalized for each call they make (i.e., they have to pay for each call with real money), customers search for other ways to take care of their problems rather than waste a support call. They may try to solve the problems themselves or engage in extensive searches on the internet for solutions. Such behavior may in the long run be even more expensive than support calls because customers waste time looking for solutions instead of doing the jobs they are paid to do and because the solutions they find may actually cost the organization additional money if they are so bad that they cause their own costly problems.

Marshall recommends subscription-based support contracts that give customers the opportunity for unlimited contact with the vendor's technical support staff. The emphasis in such contracts is on maximizing the value the customer derives from the technology the vendor delivers. Marshall says such contracts "allow customers to build better infrastructures by building more worthwhile customer–vendor relationships. Customers are allowed—even encouraged—to freely collaborate with their chosen vendors to create better technology and solutions."

Based on: M3 (2018); Marshall (2004).

Conduct Procurements

The goal of the *Conduct Procurements* process is a contract with a vendor to supply the desired product or service. Thus this process involves all activities associated with requesting seller responses, selecting sellers, and negotiating and awarding the contract. **Requesting seller responses** involves obtaining responses to the procurement documents produced during *Plan Procurement Management*. Based on the evaluation criteria established in the *Plan Procurement Management* process, the project manager can then select the winning seller and begin contract negotiations. A contract is a legal relationship between parties, and it is subject to remedy in the court system. Most organizations have policies governing who can sign a procurement contract on behalf of the organization. Because contracts are legal documents, they are typically subject to lengthy internal reviews by an organization's legal representatives.

Requesting seller responses
The process of obtaining responses to the procurement documents produced during *Plan Procurement Management*.

Conduct Procurements—Inputs

Procurement documentation (such as bid documents, SOW, cost estimates, and source selection criteria), established in the *Plan Procurement Management* process, as well as the actual seller responses form the basis for selecting sellers. Further, as with the *Plan Procurement Management* process, inputs include components of the project management plan, such as the cost baselines, as well as the scope, requirements, risk, communications, configuration, and procurement management plans. Further, project documents such as the project schedule, the requirements documentation, as well as the risk, stakeholder, and lessons-learned registers can serve as inputs into the process conduct procurement. Finally, enterprise environmental factors (such as marketplace conditions, historical information on relationships with particular sellers, or laws and regulations governing procurement processes) and organizational process assets (such as organizational policies or lists of preapproved sellers) are all used in selecting sellers.

Conduct Procurements—Tools and Techniques

Tools and techniques include advertising, bidder conferences, data analysis, expert judgment, and interpersonal and team skills. We will discuss each of these next. First, procurement documents can be sent to preapproved vendors and any others that the project team has identified as potential bidders. Potential vendors can also be identified through advertising in newspapers or trade magazines or professional journals. Another way to attract potential bidders is through vendor conferences (also called contractor or bidder conferences), where members of the project team can meet with prospective bidders. At these conferences, project team members can explain the procurement process and goals, and potential bidders can ask questions. The answers to some of the questions asked at these conferences may even become part of the revised procurement document. The main activity of this process is to evaluate the proposals received, based on the procurement documents developed in the *Plan Procurement Management* process.

The process of selecting sellers follows the approach of a multicriteria analysis, as introduced in Chapter 5. A **weighting system** is a method to quantitatively compare the proposals that are received from prospective vendors. Each of the proposals is seen as an alternative solution, and each of the evaluation criteria are converted to attributes. A value is assigned to each attribute of each alternative. The attributes themselves are then weighted to reflect their relative importance. Attribute values are then multiplied by the weights to generate scores, and the scores are totaled across attributes to give sum totals for each alternative. The alternative with the highest score should then be

Weighting system
A method used to quantitatively compare proposals that are received from potential vendors.

Table 10.3 Weighted Evaluation of Three Proposals

	Weight	Company Alpha		Company Beta		Company Gamma	
		Rating	Score	Rating	Score	Rating	Score
Price	40	3	120	3	120	2	80
Vendor Technical Ability	10	4	40	4	40	4	40
Solution Functionality	15	4	60	3	45	2	30
Vendor Experience	10	3	30	3	30	4	40
Vendor Financial Resources	15	4	60	3	45	4	60
PMI Certified Project Manager	10	5	50	1	10	1	10
Total	100		360		290		260

the best one, and as such, it should be the best alternative in the set. The vendor with the best alternative should be chosen for the contract.

An example of how this technique works is included in Table 10.3. On the left, we have listed six different evaluation criteria. These criteria were all derived during the *Plan Procurement Management* process, and for simplicity, we have kept them at a fairly high level. The criteria are weighted in terms of what is most important to the project team. In this case, price is considered the most important criterion, with 40 percent of the total weight. Solution functionality and the vendor's financial resources carry the most weight after price, with 15 percent each. The remaining three criteria, vendor technical ability, vendor experience, and whether the vendor team has a PMI certified project manager, all carry 10 percent of the total weight. Notice that all of the weights add up to 100. Weights are arrived at in discussions among the project team and others who possess key knowledge or have a stake in the effort. Weights tend to be fairly subjective; thus open discussions can reveal underlying assumptions before attempting to reach consensus.

In this example, we have received three proposals in response to our RFP. Each one is listed across the top of Table 10.3. We have simply named the potential suppliers Company Alpha, Company Beta, and Company Gamma. Under each company name, there are two columns. The first is for the ratings given to each evaluation criterion for that proposal. The second is for the score for each criterion for that proposal. Scores are computed by multiplying the weight for a criterion by the proposal's rating for that criterion. The ratings are on a scale of 1 to 5. A rating of 1 indicates that the proposal does not meet the evaluation criterion very well. A rating of 5 indicates that the proposal meets or exceeds the criterion. Ratings are even more subjective than weights and should also be determined through ample open discussion among the members of the evaluation team. The final step is to add the weighted scores for each proposal. We have included totals for the weights and for each proposal. Note that the proposal from Company Alpha is the best because it scored a total of 360 points. The proposal from Company Beta is second best with 290 points, and the proposal from Company Gamma, with 260 points, is last. The proposal from Company Alpha should win.

Screening system
A system using minimum values for one or more performance criteria to eliminate proposals that do not meet the minimum values.

A different way to select a winning proposal is to use a **screening system.** Under a screening system, the project team establishes minimum values for one or more of the performance criteria. Any proposal that does not meet the minimum values is eliminated. To see how this works, look again at Table 10.3. Let's assume that the project team has decided that any proposal that did not score at least a 3 on price would be eliminated. Because 1 is the worst rating for a criterion, a 1 on price would mean that the proposal's price was very high and out of range. A rating of 5 would mean that the proposal's price would be considered good. A 3 would be in the middle—neither too high nor too low—and, therefore, a 3 would be a reasonable minimum. Looking at Table 10.3, the proposal from Company Gamma has been given a rating of 2 on price, so it would be eliminated from further consideration. That still leaves the proposals from Companies Alpha and Beta, both of which have ratings of 3 on price. We would then move to another criterion to distinguish between the two remaining proposals. Let's choose whether or not the proposal features a PMI certified project manager. The proposal from Company Alpha has a rating of 5 on this criterion, meaning it does have a PMI certified project manager. The proposal from Company Beta has a rating of 1, meaning the proposal does not mention a PMI certified project manager. The proposal from Company Beta would be eliminated, and in this case, the proposal from Company Alpha would once again be chosen as the winner.

Seller rating systems have been developed by some companies as an additional way to select vendors. These systems use information about vendors, such as their past performance, quality ratings, delivery performance, and contractual compliance. Companies may have such information on vendors because they have dealt with them before and collected this information as part of the procurement process.

As noted previously, expert judgment can be called upon to develop the criteria used to evaluate proposals, and it can also be used to evaluate proposals directly. Proposals can be circulated to domain experts from universities or the government or other organizations, and these experts can provide their own evaluations and rankings of the proposals, independent of the procuring organization. The expertise can also come from within the organization but from outside the project team, and can include legal, financial, accounting, manufacturing, engineering, and other experts.

Expert judgment is useful not only in evaluating the proposals, but also during contract negotiations, which result in a signed contract. Likewise, interpersonal and team skills help achieve a successful outcome of any contract negotiations. In **contract negotiation**, representatives from the buyer and the vendor chosen for the contract engage in discussions to clarify and reach agreement on the structure and the requirements of the contract prior to its being signed. All agreements reached to date should be reflected in the contract. Topics to be covered include responsibilities, authority, applicable terms and laws, contracting financing, and price. Typically, the buying organization will have personnel who are in charge of negotiating contracts. If this is the case, it is very important that the people in charge of contracts have access to any documents that were generated during the proposal process, as well as to the individuals who were involved. Personnel from purchasing also may play a role in contract negotiations.

Conduct Procurements—Outputs

The key output from the *Conduct Procurements* process is the contract. As a legally binding agreement, a contract should not only specify the deliverables, milestones, and pricing and payment terms, but also specify what is considered acceptable quality, outline any incentives or penalties, and discuss how changes are handled and performance is reported, how the contract may be terminated, how subcontractors are approved, what future product support may be provided, and other general terms and conditions. Further, this process may result in updates to the scope, schedule, and cost baselines, as well as to the requirements, quality, communications, risk, and procurement management plans; as with any updates to the project management plan, these updates have to go through formal change control processes. In addition, other project documents, such as the requirements documentation, requirements traceability matrix, resource calendar,

Seller rating system
A system used to select vendors based on factors such as past performance, quality ratings, delivery performance, and contractual compliance.

Contract negotiation
Discussions between the buyer and seller to clarify and reach agreement on the structure and the requirements of the contract.

and stakeholder and risk registers, are updated, in addition to the lessons-learned register. In case of multiple sellers, another output is a list of the selected sellers for further approval by senior management. Finally, updates to the organizational process assets are seller lists, as well as any information on positive or negative experiences with sellers.

Ethical Dilemma: When Relations between Procurement Managers and Vendors Are Too Close

A big part of procurement is working with vendors. Procurement officials work with vendors to get the best deal for their companies. The relationship between procurement and outside vendors is supposed to be neutral, with each side out to get the best deal for the organizations they represent. Sometimes, however, the relationship turns cozy. Procurement managers and vendors become too close, especially in industries where few vendors can supply what a company needs. In these situations, vendors have considerable power over procurement and over the managers who are in charge of buying. Vendors in such situations have more influence over the terms of the deal than would be the case if lots of vendors were available, a situation that favors the buying organization. Where there are few vendors, the buying organization is at a disadvantage. To make it easier for a procurement manager to go along with a deal that is disadvantageous to his or her company, a powerful vendor may offer kickbacks or other inducements, such as a job at the vendor's at some point down the road or other personal favors.

The ethical issues involved in procurement are well illustrated by a case that involved the airplane manufacturer Boeing Co. and the U.S. Air Force. For more than a decade as the air force's second-highest contracting officer, Darleen Druyun systematically steered various contracts to Boeing, as she admitted during her trial in October 2004. She left the air force and went to work as a vice president for Boeing in December 2002, but she was fired in 2003 when it

was revealed that she had negotiated her $250,000 per year job at Boeing while overseeing the company's contracts with the air force. She was found guilty of conspiracy to violate conflict-of-interest laws and was sentenced to nine months in prison.

Among the things she admitted to doing, Ms. Druyun confessed to handing Boeing a $4 billion project to upgrade C-130 transport planes, even though Boeing rival Lockheed Martin Corp. had manufactured the planes and was in a better position to modernize them. One of the reasons Ms. Druyun gave for awarding the contract to Boeing was that the company had hired and retained her daughter and son-in-law as employees. During her trial, Ms. Druyun also confessed to negotiating "sweetheart" deals with Boeing for two other aircraft programs: (1) maintenance of C-17 cargo planes, and (2) a restructuring of plans to buy early-warning aircraft for the North Atlantic Treaty Organization. Ms. Druyun admitted at trial that both deals were overpriced in Boeing's favor. Her biggest deal favoring Boeing, however, was a proposed $23 billion deal to lease aerial-tankers for refueling aircraft from Boeing as a way to provide "a parting gift to Boeing" before leaving the air force.

On its part, after the trial, Boeing issued a statement pledging to "work with any and all government agencies that have concerns about the actions of Ms. Druyun." Chief Executive Officer Harry Stonecipher said Ms. Druyun's admissions of wrongdoing during her trial came "as a total surprise."

Discussion Questions

1. What is the proper role for a procurement officer in relation to his or her company's major vendors? Justify your answer.

2. How might a procurement officer resist the temptations offered by a powerful vendor to steer business their way? What are the ethical implications of such a situation? What do you think Ms. Druyun should have done in her role in U.S. Air Force procurement?

Based on: Pacztor (2004); Perlo-Freeman (2017).

Control Procurements

The final procurement process is *Control Procurements*, which is primarily concerned with ensuring that the product or service procured meets the agreed upon performance standards. In this ongoing process, the project manager monitors the performance of the seller, implements needed changes, and closes the contract. In addition to monitoring the performance of the seller, this process also includes the payment of invoices. Typically, this process involves inspections and audits to compare what was contracted for with what has been done or delivered. If the contracted work meets the requirements, the procurement is closed after all outstanding invoices have been paid. Any disputes are handled through a claims administration process. We will discuss the *Control Procurements* process in more detail in Chapter 12.

Managing Project Procurement and PMBOK

As Figure 10.8 demonstrates, you have covered almost all of the *Project Management Body of Knowledge* after reading this chapter. We have only two chapters left in the book—Chapters 11 and 12. The primary topic of Chapter 10 is project procurement, and as you can see from Figure 10.8, this material corresponds to Chapter 12 in *PMBOK*, which covers Project Procurement Management. All three areas of the *PMBOK* that relate to procurement were covered over the course of this chapter.

Figure 10.8 Chapter 10 and *PMBOK* coverage

Key: O where the material is covered in the textbook; ● current chapter coverage

	Textbook Chapters →	1	2	3	4	5	6	7	8	9	10	11	12
	PMBOK Knowledge Area												
1	Introduction												
1.2	Foundational Elements	O	O										
2	The Environment in Which Projects Operate												
2.2	Enterprise Environmental Factors		O										
2.2	Organizational Process Assets		O										
2.3	Organizational Systems		O										
3	The Role of the Project Manager												
3.2	Definition of a Project Manager	O											
3.3	The Project Manager's Sphere of Influence		O										
3.4	Project Manager Competences	O	O	O									
3.5	Performing Integration		O										
4	Project Integration Management												
4.1	Develop Project Charter					O							
4.2	Develop Project Management Plan					O							
4.3	Direct and Manage Project Work											O	
4.4	Manage Project Knowledge											O	
4.5	Monitor and Control Project Work											O	O
4.6	Perform Integrated Change Control												O
4.7	Close Project or Phase										O		O

#	Process											
5	**Project Scope Management**											
5.1	Plan Scope Management					O						
5.2	Collect Requirements					O						
5.3	Define Scope					O						
5.4	Create WBS					O	O					
5.5	Validate Scope					O						
5.6	Control Scope					O						O
6	**Project Schedule Management**											
6.1	Plan Schedule Management						O					
6.2	Define Activities						O					
6.3	Sequence Activities						O					
6.4	Estimate Activity Durations							O				
6.5	Develop Schedule							O				
6.6	Control Schedule							O				O
7	**Project Cost Management**											
7.1	Plan Cost Management								O			
7.2	Estimate Costs								O			
7.3	Determine Budget								O			
7.4	Control Costs								O			O
8	**Project Quality Management**											
8.1	Plan Quality Management								O			
8.2	Manage Quality								O			
8.3	Control Quality								O			O
9	**Project Resource Management**											
9.1	Plan Resource Management							O				
9.2	Estimate Activity Resources						O	O				
9.3	Acquire Resources							O			O	
9.4	Develop Team			O							O	
9.5	Manage Team			O							O	
9.6	Control Resources							O				O
10	**Project Communications Management**											
10.1	Plan Communications Management				O							
10.2	Manage Communications				O						O	
10.3	Monitor Communications				O							O
11	**Project Risk Management**											
11.1	Plan Risk Management									O		
11.2	Identify Risks									O	O	
11.3	Perform Qualitative Risk Analysis									O		
11.4	Perform Quantitative Risk Analysis									O		
11.5	Plan Risk Responses									O		

11.6	Implement Risk Responses												○		○	
11.7	Monitor Risks												○			○
12	**Project Procurement Management**															
12.1	Plan Procurement Management													●		
12.2	Conduct Procurements													●	○	
12.3	Control Procurements													●		○
13	**Project Stakeholder Management**															
12.1	Identify Stakeholders			○												
12.2	Plan Stakeholder Engagement			○												
12.3	Manage Stakeholder Engagement			○											○	
12.4	Monitor Stakeholder Engagement			○												○

Running Case: Managing Project Procurement

Although the customer loyalty project at Jackie's Electronics went slowly at first, the past few weeks were fast-paced and busy, project manager James Cheung thought to himself. The weeks it took to finish the request for proposals (RFP), to line up potential vendors to submit bids, and to receive the bids all seemed to have zipped right by. James was on his way to meet with Sarah Codey, the company's COO, to discuss the remaining bids and the one he thought should win.

"Hi, Sarah," James said, as he walked into her office and sat down at her desk.

"Hi, James," Sarah said. "I'll be right with you." Sarah finished replying to an email message and then turned around and faced James. "I have been reviewing the three remaining bids. Even though I opposed it originally, I think your strategy of having a panel of IT and marketing professionals rate the bids and eliminate the inappropriate ones turned out to be a good one. I think we can succeed with any one of these proposals. Do you have a favorite?"

"Well, actually, I have already compared the remaining proposals, and I do have one that I think we should choose," James replied. "Just for review, here is a copy of the memo I sent you, with the requirements and constraints, and with the three competing systems summarized" (Table 10.4).

"Thanks," Sarah said. "This keeps me from having to dig through all my stuff to find my copy. Did you also bring me a copy of your evaluation matrix?"

Adapted from: Valacich and George (2017).

"Yes, here it is." (See Table 10.5.)

"So, your matrix favors the XCT CRM system," Sarah noticed. "Looks like their proposal meets our requirements the best, but the Nova group's proposal does the best job with the constraints."

"Yes, but just barely. There is only a five-point difference between XCT and Nova, so they are pretty comparable when it comes to constraints. But I think the XCT system has a pretty clear advantage in meeting our requirements."

"We've never worked with XCT, but they seem to be pretty highly rated in your matrix in terms of all of the requirements. You have them ranked better than the other two proposals for implementation, scalability, and vendor support. The 5 you gave them for proven performance is one of the few 5s you have in your whole matrix."

"They are one of the best companies in the industry to work with," James responded. "Their reputation is stellar."

"OK, then," Sarah said. "Your numbers convince me. But I don't have the authority to approve this choice alone. Let me get started on the approval process. Meanwhile, I think you better set up a meeting with the legal team to get started on a contract." Sarah smiled.

"Will do," James said, and he sighed with relief.

Table 10.4 Requirements, Constraints, and Alternatives for Jackie's Customer Loyalty Project

Requirements:
Effective customer incentives—System should be able to effectively store customer activity and convert to rewards and other incentives.
Easy for customers to use—Interface should be intuitive for customer use.
Proven performance—System as proposed should have been used successfully by other clients.
Easy to implement—Implementation should not require outside consultants or extraordinary skills on the part of our staff or require specialized hardware.
Scalable—System should be easily expandable as number of participating customers grows.
Vendor support—Vendor should have proven track record of reliable support and infrastructure in place to provide it.
Constraints:
Cost to buy—Licenses for one year should be less than US$500,000.
Cost to operate—Total operating costs should be no more than US$1 million per year. Time to implement—Duration of implementation should not exceed three months.
Staff to implement—Implementation should be successful with the staff we have and with the skills they already possess.
Alternatives:
Alternative A: Data warehousing—centered system designed and licensed by Standard Basic Systems Inc. (SBSI). The data warehousing tools at the heart of the system were designed and developed by SBSI, and work with standard relational DBMS and relational/OO hybrid DBMS. The SBSI tools and approach have been used for many years and are well-known in the industry, but SBSI-certified staff are essential for implementation, operation, and maintenance. The license is relatively expensive. The customer loyalty application using the SBSI data warehousing tools is an established application, used by many retail businesses in other industries.
Alternative B: Customer relationship management—centered system designed and licensed by XRA Corporation. XRA is a pioneer in CRM systems, so its CRM is widely recognized as an industry leader. The system includes tools that support customer loyalty programs. The CRM system itself is large and complex, but pricing in this proposal is based only on modules used for the customer loyalty application.
Alternative C: Proprietary system designed and licensed by Nova Innovation Group Inc. The system is relatively new and leading edge, so it has only been implemented in a few sites. The vendor is truly innovative but small and inexperienced. The customer interface, designed for a standard web browser, is stunning in its design and is extremely easy for customers to use to check on their loyalty program status.

Table 10.5 Evaluation Matrix for Customer Loyalty Proposals

	Weight	SBSI Rating	SBSI Score	XRI Rating	XRI Score	Nova Rating	Nova Score
Requirements							
Effective customer incentives	15	5	75	4	60	4	60
Easy for customers to use	10	3	30	4	40	5	50
Proven performance	10	4	40	5	50	3	30
Easy to implement	5	3	15	4	20	3	15
Scalable	10	3	30	4	40	3	30
Vendor support	10	3	30	4	40	3	30
	60		220		250		
Constraints							
Purchase cost	15	3	45	4	60	5	75
Operating costs	10	3	30	4	40	4	40
Time needed for implementation	5	3	15	3	15	3	15
Staff needed for implementation	10	3	30	4	40	3	30
	40		120		155		160
Total	100		340		405		375

Chapter Summary

Describe the various sources of systems and software components. Systems are hardly ever developed from scratch in-house these days. Instead, systems, software, and software components are procured from various other organizations. These organizations include packaged software providers, open source software, Software-as-a-Service (SaaS) providers, vendors of enterprise-wide solution software, and information technology services firms. Each different source of systems and software has its own advantages and disadvantages, and making the proper choice among them depends on knowing their strengths and weaknesses.

Describe how to plan purchases and acquisitions, as well as the steps in the procurement process. Project Procurement Management is the part of a project that covers the acquisition of resources, whether products or services or both, from outside the project's home organization. Project Procurement Management, according to *PMBOK*, has three processes: *Plan Procurement Management*, *Conduct Procurements*, and *Control Procurements*. *Plan Procurement Management* is the process of determining which project needs can best be met by external acquisition and planning how procurement activities are performed. One of the

key processes at the heart of planning purchases and acquisitions is the make-or-buy decision. Major outputs of the process are a procurement strategy, a statement of work (a document that describes the product or service being sought), as well as bid documents that describe what is to be procured and ask for offers from vendors who are interested in providing it. Such a document has many names but is referred to here primarily as a *request for proposal*, or *RFP*. Another important output of planning contracting is the set of evaluation criteria used to judge the proposals that vendors write in response to the RFP. Another important part of this process is an attempt to find the potential vendors who are the best equipped to respond to the RFP. Once responses or bids are in hand, the *Conduct Procurements* process begins. Here the bids are compared with each other and are judged by the selection criteria that the project organization has established. One vendor is chosen, and a contract is prepared. One way to help determine the best proposal is the use of a weighted system; another way is the use of a screening system. Finally, *Control Procurements* is the process through which the project organization works with the vendor for the duration of the contract. Once the terms of the contract have been satisfactorily met, contract closure begins. Both sides of the agreement accept the work performed, and the contract is completed.

Key Terms Review

A. Best-of-breed strategy
B. Contract negotiation
C. Cost-reimbursable contract
D. Enterprise resource planning (ERP) system
E. Evaluation criteria
F. External acquisition
G. Fixed-price contract
H. Independent estimates
I. IT services firm
J. Make-or-buy analysis
K. On-demand computing
L. Open source software
M. Packaged software producer

N. Plan Procurement Management
O. Procurement documents
P. Procurement management plan
Q. Request for proposal (RFP)
R. Requesting seller responses
S. Screening system
T. Seller rating system
U. Statement of work (SOW)
V. Time-and-materials contract
W. Turnkey system
X. Utility computing
Y. Weighting system

Match each of the key terms with the definition that best fits it.

1. A document provided to vendors to ask them to propose a solution to a specific problem related to your project.

2. A method used to quantitatively compare proposals that are received from potential vendors.

3. A plan that addresses such issues as who will prepare the evaluation criteria, how multiple vendors will be managed, where standardized procurement documents can be obtained, and how procurement will be coordinated with other project tasks.

4. A service provisioning model where resources (such as processing, data storage, or networking) are provided as needed, and the organization only pays for the services used.

5. A strategy of using different software products from different sources (including in house development) to capitalize on the strengths of different products.

6. A system that integrates individual traditional business functions into a series of modules so that a single transaction occurs seamlessly within a single information system rather than over several separate systems.

7. A system used to select vendors based on factors such as past performance, quality ratings, delivery performance, and contractual compliance.

8. A system using minimum values for one or more performance criteria to eliminate proposals that do not meet the minimum values.

9. A technique to determine whether a product or service should be produced in-house or procured from an outside vendor.

10. A type of contract specifying a fixed price for a product/service.

11. A type of contract that involves payment for the actual cost of the product plus a fee that represents the vendor's profits.

12. A type of contract where vendors provide an hourly rate and estimate the amount of time and materials required.

13. Company in the business of developing and selling off-the-shelf software.

14. Criteria used to rate proposals that are received in response to a request for proposals.

15. Discussions between the buyer and seller to clarify and reach agreements on the structure and the requirements of the contract.

16. Document prepared for potential vendors that describes the service or product being sought.

17. Documents used to solicit proposals from vendors.

18. Estimates prepared independently of proposals which act as a check against the prices offered in proposals.

19. Firm that helps companies develop custom information systems for internal use or develop, host, and run applications for customers.

20. Off-the-shelf software that cannot be modified to meet the specific, individual needs of an organization.

21. Provision of computing resources on the basis of users' needs.

22. Systems software, applications, and programming languages of which the source code is freely available for use and/or modification.

23. The process of determining which project needs can best be met by external acquisition and planning how procurement activities are performed.

24. The process of obtaining responses to the procurement documents produced during *Plan Procurement Management*.

25. The procurement of products and/or services from an outside vendor.

Review Questions

1. Describe the types of software and systems that IT services firms produce.

2. What is an ERP system?

3. What is Software-as-a-Service?

4. What is open source software, and what are its benefits?

5. Explain the *Plan Procurement Management* process, including its inputs, processes, and outputs.

6. What is a statement of work? Why is it so important to procurement?

7. Explain how to conduct procurement, including its inputs, processes, and outputs.

8. What is an RFP? What is it good for?

9. What are the basic contents recommended for any RFP?

10. Explain how seller responses are requested.

11. Explain how sellers are selected.

12. Explain how a weighting system is used for comparing proposals from an RFP.

13. Explain how a screening system is used for comparing proposals from an RFP.

14. Why is a contract a special document? How is it treated differently from other documents?

Chapter Exercises

1. Compare and contrast the various organizations that supply systems and systems components. What are their relative strengths and weaknesses? For each source, describe a situation where that particular source would be the best choice.

2. Create a statement for work for a job that you know well.

3. Locate an RFP from someone you know (e.g., a parent, an employer, a professor). Analyze it carefully, comparing its structure and content to the guidelines provided in the chapter, and write a two-page essay about what you find.

4. Explain how project procurement fits within the larger picture of project management. When would you ever be involved in a project that did not involve procurement of products and services from outside your organization?

5. Bob's project team is working on developing a webstore. As part of their project, the team has decided it makes little sense to develop their own shopping cart system, given that so many complete shopping cart systems are available on the market. Bob's team needs to write an RFP for a shopping cart system. Do some research on shopping cart systems for webstores, and using the outline in this chapter for the contents of an RFP, write a short version of the RFP Bob's group would need.

6. Bob's team, described in Exercise 5, has issued its RFP and has received three responses. The team has developed the following evaluation criteria. Price is the most important criterion; the second most important is the extent to which the shopping cart system can be modified; the third most important is the number of features available in the system; fourth is the number of years the vendor has been in business; and fifth is the number of employees the vendor has. For price, the lowest price is best. For modification, more is better, and the same is true of the number of features. The longer the vendor has been in business, and the more people the vendor employs, the better. The first proposal, from Three Guys Who Are Programmers Inc. had a licensing cost of US$1,500 per year with unlimited clients and charged US$400 per year for technical assistance. Bob's team judged the system from Three Guys to be moderately modifiable, but it had very few features. Three Guys has been in business for two years and currently employs twelve people. The second proposal, from Global Domination Software Inc. (GDSI), cost US$5,000 per year for a license with unlimited clients, and technical assistance was offered for free as long as there were fewer than twelve requests for assistance. After that, each request cost US$100. Bob's team found the software to be very limited in terms of the number of modifications that could be made, but it had an incredibly high number of features. GDSI has been in business for twenty-five years and has twenty thousand employees worldwide. The last proposal was from E-Commerce Associates Inc. (ECA). A one-year license for unlimited clients with free technical assistance cost US$3,000. The software was moderately modifiable and had an average number of e-commerce features. ECA has been in business for ten years and currently has fifty employees. Which proposal should Bob's team choose? Which proposal should win? Create a weighting system like the one described in this chapter (use a spreadsheet if you want), and demonstrate which proposal should be chosen.

7. Using the information supplied in Exercise 6, develop a screening system that will help you choose among the alternative proposals. First, use price as your filter. Next, try aspects of the software, such as the number of features. Which proposal wins under these schemes? Is it the same as the proposal that won in Exercise 7? If you had a different winner, explain why.

Chapter Case: Sedona Management Group and Managing Project Procurement

Many companies do not have the required personnel or expertise to develop the systems that they need. Consequently, when these companies need new systems, they elect to outsource such projects to other companies that specialize in systems development. This process is known as *procurement* and involves the acquisition of goods or services from an outside source. The advantages associated with outsourcing include the availability of knowledge and expertise that might not be available internally, an increase in the revenue potential of the acquiring organization, and a reduction of time to market the final product.

The Seattle Seahawks' core competency is running a professional sports organization, not website development. When they realized they needed a website for the reasons mentioned in previous chapter cases, they decided to outsource the project. To make sure that it was completed successfully, the Seahawks went through several of the processes related to Project Procurement Management, including the processes *Plan Procurement Management*, *Conduct Procurements*, and *Control Procurements*. The main purpose of Project Procurement Management is to manage the acquisition of resources from an outside source.

One of the first steps the Seattle Seahawks followed in managing procurement was to plan how to procure the website. During this process, the Seahawks focused on identifying project needs and which of those needs would be best met by using services outside the organization. The Seattle Seahawks wanted a reliable and secure website that conveyed accurate information and was easy to access. An initial statement of work (SOW) was developed, which allowed prospective outsourcing partners to determine whether they were capable of providing the service or the product required, as well as to determine an appropriate price for the project.

Next, the focus is on identifying the evaluation criteria that will be used to determine which vendor will be awarded the contract. Writing a request for proposal (RFP) is typically a part of the solicitation planning phase. The RFP is a document that is used to solicit proposals from prospective sellers. The RFP issued by the Seattle Seahawks contained, among other features, a statement of purpose of the RFP, background information on the company, the statement of work, and schedule constraints. Once the RFP was available, it was issued to the prospective sellers.

After receiving proposals from the prospective sellers, the Seattle Seahawks went through the process of selecting sellers, where they evaluated the bidders' proposals to choose the best one. The evaluation criteria identified earlier were used to make this choice. During this stage of procurement management, the Seattle Seahawks chose Sedona Management Group (SMG) to work on their website development project. The Seahawks' key criteria were project quality and the ability of the outsourcing partner to deliver its products on time and on budget. SMG excelled in both dimensions.

Once the Sedona team was informed that they would be working on the website development project, Mike Flood from the Seattle Seahawks met with the project team several times to further communicate the project needs. After the project requirements were clearly determined, the next step was to work on the contract. SMG uses a fixed price contract, which involves a fixed total price for a well-defined product or service. In such a contract, the Seattle Seahawks were exposed to a low level of risk because the risk associated with cost overruns was assumed by the developer—in this case SMG. However, given SMG's well delineated project management processes, the Sedona team was confident that they could deliver the project on time and within budget.

The Seahawks–SMG contract consisted of several sections. The first section laid out the assumptions the team used to develop the contract. These assumptions included information about the technology to be used to develop the system and which server would be used to host the system, as well as the contact information of the individual from SMG who would be available for immediate information during business hours throughout the development process. The second section included the scope of work, which included a detailed description of all the activities the Sedona team would perform to complete the project. In the next section, the terms of the contract were explained regarding project cost and the delivery date. In a section entitled "Other Considerations," SMG explained that the Seattle Seahawks would own the final code, the database, and the website once the project was completed. The Sedona team began working on the project the next business day after both parties agreed to the clauses of the contract.

Chapter 10 Project Assignment

An important part of an entertainment website is the availability of a shopping cart for fans to buy the products being promoted by the entertainer. The success of your website requires this feature, but you realize that it is beyond your and your team members' expertise. So you decide to outsource this feature. In this exercise, you will work on the documents you require for the outsourcing process.

1. Conduct a make-or-buy analysis. This analysis involves identifying the pros and cons of developing this feature yourself or outsourcing.

2. Develop a statement of work (SOW) for the shopping cart development project. The SOW is a document prepared for the vendors that describes thoroughly the product being sought. The SOW should contain

- An introduction and overview section, which includes some background information about your project, the scope of work, and the objectives of the project being outsourced
- A requirements section for the shopping cart feature
- The list of deliverables
- A list of milestones
- Any other considerations

3. Develop a request for proposal (RFP) for this outsourcing project. The RFP is a document that will be submitted to potential vendors, asking them to propose a solution to the shopping cart problem. The RFP should contain

- A project overview
- An administrative section, which contains contact information
- Technical requirements
- Management requirements
- Suppliers' section
- Any appendices

4. Determine the evaluation criteria you and your team will use to rate the received proposals.

5. Compare and contrast the different types of contracts that are available. Indicate which one of these you will use for this outsourcing project. Provide justification for your answer.

References

Banker, R. D., Davis, G. B., and Slaughter, S. A. (1998). Software Development Practices, Software Complexity, and Software Maintenance Performance: A Field Study. *Management Science* 44(4), 433–450.

BCC (2018, January 24). Global Managed IT Services Market to Grow 11.5% Annually through 2021. *BCC Research*. Retrieved July 9, 2018, from https://globenewswire.com/news-release/2018/01/24/1304153/0/en/Global-Managed-IT-Services-Market-to-Grow-11-5-Annually-Through-2021.html

De Marco, N. (2017, September 14). Breaking Down the Most Common IT Outsourcing Concerns. *Baires-Dev*. Retrieved July 9, 2018, from https://www.bairesdev.com/breaking-down-the-most-common-it-outsourcing-concerns

Dignan, L. (2003, June 26). IT's Exercise in Utilities. *CNET News.com*. Retrieved July 9, 2018, from https://www.cnet.com/news/its-exercise-in-utilities

Flinders, K. (2014, February 20). Diageo Selects TCS for Global Services. *ComputerWeekly.com*. Retrieved July 9, 2018, from https://www.computerweekly.com/news/2240214760/Diageo-selects-TCS-for-global-services

Hamm, S. (2005, January 31). Linux Inc. *BusinessWeek*. Retrieved November 14, 2018, from https://www.bloomberg.com/news/articles/2005-01-30/linux-inc-dot

Hines, M. (2003, August 25). IBM Spirits Diageo Away from HP. *CNET News.com*. Retrieved July 9, 2018, from https://www.cnet.com/news/ibm-spirits-diageo-away-from-hp

Ketler, K., and Willems, J. R. (1999). A Study of the Outsourcing Decision: Preliminary Results. *Proceedings of SIGCPR '99*, New Orleans, LA, 182–189.

Kharpal, A. (2016, November 3). Google Android Hits Market Share Record with Nearly 9 in Every 10 Smartphones Using It. *CNBC*. Retrieved July 9, 2018, from http://www.cnbc.com/2016/11/03/google-android-hits-market-share-record-with-nearly-9-inevery-10-smartphones-using-it.html

King, J. (2003). IT's Global Itinerary: Offshore Outsourcing Is Inevitable. *ComputerWorld*. Retrieved October 12, 2006, from https://www.computerworld.com/article/2572756/it-outsourcing/it-s-global-itinerary--offshore-outsourcing-is-inevitable.html

King, J., and Cole-Gomolski, B. (1999). IT Doing Less Development, More Installation, Outsourcing. *ComputerWorld*, January 25, 4.

Marshall, B. (2004, June 1). Support Contracts Can Encourage Lousy Products. *ComputerWorld*. Retrieved July 9, 2018, from http://www.computerworld.com/article/2564630/it-management/support-contracts-can-encourage-lousy-products.html

M3 (2018, March 21). Five Benefits of Fixed IT Costs. *M3 Networks*. Retrieved July 9, 2018, from https://m3networks.co.uk/general/5-benefits-of-fixed-it-costs

Pacztor, A. (2004). Air Force Ex-Official's Dealings Put Pentagon under Spotlight. *Wall Street Journal*, October 4, A2.

Perlo-Freeman, S. (2017, May 5). The Boeing Tanker Case. *World Peace Foundation*. Retrieved July 9, 2018, from https://sites.tufts.edu/corruptarmsdeals/2017/05/05/the-boeing-tanker-case

Pettey, C., and van der Meulen, R. (2012, May 21). Gartner Says Worldwide IT Outsourcing Market Grew 7.8 Percent in 2011. *Gartner.com*. Retrieved July 9, 2018, from http://www.gartner.com/newsroom/id/2021215

Porter-Roth, B. (2002). *Request for Proposal: A Guide to Effective RFP Development*. Boston: Addison-Wesley.

Project Management Institute. (2000). *A Guide to the Project Management Body of Knowledge*. Newton Square, PA: Author.

Project Management Institute (2017). *Agile Practice Guide*. Newton Square, PA: Author.

Project Management Institute (2017). *PMBOK: A Guide to the Project Management Body of Knowledge* (6th ed.). Newtown Square, PA: Author.

Pruitt, S. (2004, September 21). When Outsourcing, Don't Forget Security, Experts Say. *ComputerWorld*. Retrieved July 9, 2018, from http://www.computerworld.com/article/2566094/it-outsourcing/when-outsourcing--don-t-forget-security--experts-say.html

Rintoul, C. (2004, February 2). Ten Tips for Assuring Offshore Project Success. *ComputerWorld*. Retrieved July 9, 2018, from http://www.computerworld.com/article/2574573/it-outsourcing/10-tips-for-assuring-offshore-project-success.html

Software Magazine (2018). Software 500. *Software Magazine*. Retrieved July 5, 2018, from http://www.rcpbuyersguide.com/top-companies.php

Statista, 2017. Global Market Size of Outsourced Services from 2000 to 2015 (in Billion U.S. Dollars). *Statista.com*. Retrieved July 9, 2018, from https://www.statista.com/statistics/189788/global-outsourcing-market-size

Top 500 (2017). Operating System Family/Linux. *Top500.org*. Retrieved February 20, 2017, from https://www.top500.org/statistics/details/osfam/1

Valacich, J., and George, J. F., (2017). *Modern Systems Analysis and Design* (8th ed.). Boston: Pearson.

Van der Meulen, R., and Pettey, C. (2018, January 16). Gartner Says Global IT Spending to Reach $3.7 Trillion in 2018. *Gartner.com*. Retrieved July 9, 2018, from https://www.gartner.com/newsroom/id/3845563

Woodie, A. (2005, June 16). ERP Market Grew Solidly in 2004, AMR Research Says. *The Windows Observer* 2(25). Retrieved July 9, 2018, from www.itjungle.com/breaking/bn061605-story01.html

Starting, Organizing, and Preparing Agile Projects

In contrast to predictive life cycles, agile projects use an iterative approach. Thus, rather than planning the project as best as possible before embarking on project execution, in agile projects, planning, execution, and monitoring and controlling go hand in hand. Consequently, not only the delivery but also the detailed planning is conducted by the project team.

Agile projects have a number of unique features when it comes to planning. First, project plans using predictive life cycles are organized around tasks—how long will the tasks take, the sequence of the tasks, what resources will be needed to complete the tasks, and so on. In contrast, project plans in agile approaches are feature-based—the focus is on what features will be delivered and when these features will be delivered. Second, whereas defining and fixing the project's scope in the beginning is of crucial importance in projects using predictive life cycles, the scope of agile projects can often not be known from the outset. In fact, agile approaches are often best suited for projects characterized by uncertainty and changing requirements. Thus, rather than focusing on nailing down the project's scope in the beginning, it is more important to have a sound *process* in place that allows for refining the scope as the project progresses. The prototypes developed during the iterations can then help narrow down the requirements and obtain a clearer picture of the project's scope. Third, predictive life cycles focus on planning the project schedule in detail, with different durations for different tasks. In contrast, agile projects focus on short cycles that allow for rapid feedback and adaptation of deliverables and processes. Fourth, the iterative nature and evolving scope make detailed cost planning impossible. Instead, agile projects use high-level forecasts derived from the team size, their hourly rate, and the expected number of iterations, plus estimates for materials and overhead. Fifth, rather than planning for overall project risk, agile project teams identify and manage risks for each iteration, enabling the team to flexibly adjust and prioritize requirements so as to balance risk exposure. Sixth, whereas traditionally the project manager creates and manages the project plan, in agile projects, the plan is created and managed by the agile project team, in close collaboration with the customer.

Preplanning

The first step of agile projects is preplanning. During this stage, the project team lays the foundations for the entire project. As in traditional projects, the business case drives the project. Likewise, a product vision statement is created, identifying the target customers, the need, the benefit of the product to be developed, and the key differentiation from the competition. In his book *Crossing the Chasm*, Geoffrey Moore provided a helpful model that can be applied to developing product vision statements. Following this model, a product vision statement should include the following aspects:

- FOR (whom? Who is the target customer?)
- WHO (wants to do what? What is their need or opportunity?)
- THE (product) IS A (type of product/product category)
- THAT (does what? What are the key benefits value propositions?)
- UNLIKE (what is delivered by the primary competitive alternative)
- OUR PRODUCT (offers differentiation by)

As an example, a new online learning platform could be described as follows:

> *FOR busy executives WHO LIKE TO achieve subject mastery rather than earn credits, [THE] mylearningplatform.com IS AN online learning platform THAT allows people to design their own learning experience. UNLIKE traditional online courses, OUR SERVICE allows creating a fully customized curriculum that can be completed on the learner's own pace.*

Product backlog
User-centric list of all work needed to complete the project.

User story
Simple description of a feature described from the user's point of view.

Based on such product vision statement, the **product backlog** including business and technical requirements can be created. The product backlog is typically user-centric, focusing on what adds value for the user. In other words, the product backlog often takes the form of **user stories**, which normally follow the structure: *As a < type of user >, I want < some goal > so that < some reason >*. For example, entries on the product backlog for *mylearningplatform.com* could be "As a beginner, I want to select learning modules" or "As an advanced learner, I want to assess my mastery of the subject matter so that I know the progress toward my study goal." As the product backlog contains all requirements of the final product, it can be used to derive high-level estimates for project cost and duration. Keep in mind that at this point, the estimates are at a very high level, and are likely to be refined due to the iterative nature of agile projects.

Once the project team has agreed on the duration of the iterations, the overall project duration can be estimated based on how many iterations are expected to complete the project, as the duration of each iteration is fixed in agile projects. Likewise, the number of iterations, the team size, and the team members' rate can be used to come up with a cost estimate for the project. The duration of the iterations is typically based on various factors. For example, if a higher degree of flexibility is desired or uncertainty is high, teams tend to choose shorter durations; in contrast, when more predictability is desired, durations tend to be longer. Likewise, if customers take longer to provide feedback, longer iterations are often used, as are used when there is a larger number of external systems interfacing with the system being developed. Overall, there is no one-size-fits-all "ideal" iteration length, and what works for one agile team may not work for another agile team.

Agile project charter
Project charter for agile projects, which includes the product vision, who benefits, the release criteria, and a team charter.

Together with these product-focused aspects of the preplanning process, the team can create the **agile project charter**. Unlike traditional project charters, the agile project charter not only includes the product vision and who benefits, but also specifies the release criteria (What is "done"?) and includes a team charter. In other words, the project team needs to agree on ground rules, working agreements, and group norms.

Planning

Release Planning

Following the preplanning phase, the agile project team needs to plan releases and iterations (see Figure A2.1). A release typically focuses on implementing one or more user stories from the product backlog. During release planning, the agile project team determines which user stories will be implemented for each release and will plan the dates for the releases to create a release backlog. The project team can then determine which programming tasks need to be completed during each iteration. Thus a release can consist of one or more iterations, and while iterations are timeboxed and happen at prespecified intervals, not every iteration results in release.

Iteration Planning

The incremental nature of agile projects suggests that detailed planning is only conducted for the next iteration. In other words, once an iteration has been completed, the agile project team holds an iteration planning meeting to plan the next iteration. The short, timeboxed nature of the iterations helps teams come up with relatively accurate estimates for what can be accomplished during the next iteration.

Iteration backlog
List of items to be completed during an iteration.

As shown in Figure A2.2, the iteration planning meeting focuses on developing the **iteration backlog** (i.e., determining the scope of the next iteration), taking into account the capacity of the team and the availability of the team members. First, the project team needs to achieve consensus on the priority of the features contained in the product backlog. Next, the team needs to decide which features can be completed within the next iteration, before identifying the necessary tasks needed to develop the feature; note that the project team needs to not only develop new features in an iteration, but also fix bugs or problems discovered during reviews of earlier iterations. This step includes assigning tasks to team members and estimating the time and costs to complete the task, taking into account complexity, technical challenges, relative difficulties, or other aspects that may influence the time needed for each task. If these estimates reveal that the time required is shorter or longer than the iteration, the team has to add or remove features (with removed features being added to the product backlog).

Especially early in the project, the project team might lack experience in working together and may not be calibrated well. Consequently, the team may have to complete this iteration planning process several times before agreement on the tasks to be completed for the next iteration is reached. At the same time, it is typically recommended that such iteration planning meeting should take no more than four hours. As teams

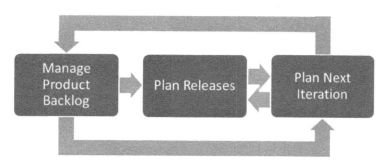

Figure A2.1   Agile project planning. *Based on:* Sliger and Broderick (2008).

Figure A2.2   Iteration planning. *Based on:* Koppensteiner and Udo (2009).

learn over time how much time is needed to implement certain features, estimates tend to become more precise and the time needed for planning the next iteration is reduced. Normally, teams base their estimates on historical data, such as the number of items completed during the last iteration—referred to as **velocity**—when estimating time to completion (a related approach is to use the average velocity of a number of iterations).

Velocity
The number of items completed during the last iteration.

One important component of iteration planning is planning and managing risks. Uncertain and dynamic requirements and environments inherently increase project risk, and it is impossible to manage risk for the entire project from the outset. On the other hand, the iterative and incremental nature of agile projects helps manage risks in such situations. In particular, agile project teams can analyze and manage risks for each iteration; likewise, reviews at the end of each iteration help improve the processes for managing risks. Further, as different requirements have different risk exposure, agile project teams can take this into consideration when deciding on the priority of the requirements. As a consequence, agile project teams need to identify, analyze, and manage risks for each iteration.

Backlog Refinement

The third major planning process in agile projects is managing the product backlog. As you will remember, one of the benefits of agile projects is that they are well suited for dynamic environments with high requirements uncertainty. As a result, the product backlog is likely to change throughout the project. On the one hand, features from the product backlog are implemented during an iteration, and are thus removed from the product backlog. On the other hand, features may be added to or removed from the backlog, or features may be reprioritized based on the delivered prototype. Consequently, the product backlog not only changes, but so does the number of iterations and/or releases, as well as the entire project duration. For example, if features are added for the next

Backlog refinement
The process of reviewing, adding, deleting, or reprioritizing product backlog items and generating user stories for the next iteration.

iteration, this will influence subsequent iterations as well; likewise, these changes would affect which iterations would be included in which releases. This **backlog refinement** typically happens in the middle or at the end of an iteration, to allow for the generation of user stories (together with the product owner) for the next iteration.

"Daily Standup" Meetings

Taking place during an iteration (i.e., execution), daily meetings are essential for the success of agile projects, as they allow for communicating the progress of each team member. Daily standups are used to communicate the status of the assigned tasks (i.e., have they been completed or not), the tasks to be completed before the next standup, and any problems the team member foresees in completing the upcoming tasks. Importantly, standups are used for communicating the status and potential problems but are not used for solving problems. This way the team facilitator (or scrum master) obtains an overview of the status, as well as an overview of any obstacles that may need to be removed to ensure productivity of the team members. Typically, daily standups are limited to fifteen minutes, with a maximum of one minute per team member for status reporting.

Key Terms Review

A. Agile project charter
B. Backlog refinement
C. Iteration backlog

D. Product backlog
E. User story
F. Velocity

Match each of the key terms with the definition that best fits it.

1. List of items to be completed during an iteration.
2. Project charter for agile projects, which includes the product vision, who benefits, the release criteria, and a team charter.
3. Simple description of a feature described from the user's point of view.
4. The number of items completed during the last iteration.
5. The process of reviewing, adding, deleting, or reprioritizing product backlog items and generating user stories for the next iteration.
6. User-centric list of all work needed to complete the project.

Review Questions

1. What are the unique features of agile project planning?
2. Explain what is meant by a product backlog.
3. What is the difference between release planning and iteration planning?
4. Why is backlog refinement an important activity?
5. Explain the purpose of daily standup meetings.

Chapter Exercises

1. Search the web for information about software to support agile project planning. What features do those programs offer?

2. Interview an IS project manager about her experiences with agile planning. What were the biggest issues in moving from traditional planning to agile planning? What worked better? What did not work so well?

3. In a team of three to five people, come up with a new app idea and develop a product vision statement.

4. Develop a product backlog for the app idea identified in Exercise 3.

References

Alexander, M. (2018, June 19). Agile Project Management: A Comprehensive Guide. *CIO.com*. Retrieved June 21, 2018, from https://www.cio.com/article/3156998/agile-development/agile-project-management-a-beginners-guide.html

Koppensteiner, S., and Udo, N. (2009). *An Agile Guide to the Planning Processes*. Paper presented at PMI Global Congress 2009—EMEA, Amsterdam, North Holland, The Netherlands. Newton Square, PA: Project Management Institute. Retrieved June 20, 2018, from https://www.pmi.org/learning/library/agile-guide-planning-agile-approach-6837

Losito, S. (2015, December 2). How to Plan in an Agile Environment. *Projectmanager.com*. Retrieved June 21, 2018, from https://www.projectmanager.com/blog/how-to-plan-in-an-agile-environment

Mightybytes (2012, April 26). Three Agile Exercises to Help Clients in the Discovery Process. Retrieved June 20, 2018, from https://www.mightybytes.com/blog/scrum_series_three_agile_discovery_exercises

Moore, G. (1991). *Crossing the Chasm*. New York: HarperCollins.

Project Management Institute (2017). *Agile Practice Guide*. Newton Square, PA: Author.

Project Management Institute (2017). *PMBOK: A Guide to the Project Management Body of Knowledge* (6th ed.). Newtown Square, PA: Author.

Sliger, M., and Broderick, S. (2008). *The Software Project Manager's Bridge to Agility*. New York: Addison-Wesley.

Yodiz.com (2017, September 17). Ten Tips for Effective Agile Sprint Planning. *Medium.com*. Retrieved June 21, 2018, from https://medium.com/

PART III

Executing, Controlling, and Ending the Project

Managing Project Execution

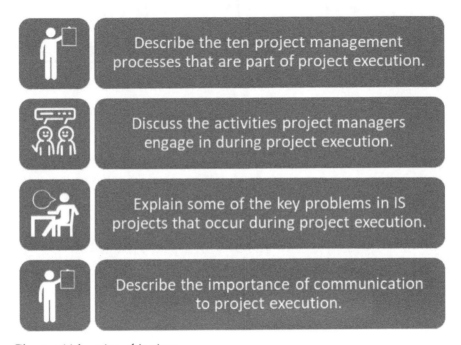

- Describe the ten project management processes that are part of project execution.
- Discuss the activities project managers engage in during project execution.
- Explain some of the key problems in IS projects that occur during project execution.
- Describe the importance of communication to project execution.

Figure 11.1 Chapter 11 learning objectives

Opening Case: REI

Good business ideas often start with a pressing need. In the case of Recreational Equipment Inc. (REI), this was a mountaineer's inability to purchase high-quality ice axes in the United States. Having imported ice axes from Austria in the mid-1930s, Mary and Lloyd Anderson formed REI as a consumer cooperative in 1938, with the aim of sharing climbing gear with other mountaineers and outdoor enthusiasts. In 1944, the co-op set up its first own retail store, and shortly thereafter started its still highly popular gear rental business.

Today, REI is one of the most well-known suppliers of outdoor products in the United States, selling outdoor gear in its over 130 stores, as well as through its website REI.com. REI not only carries high-quality products from various brand name suppliers; it also offers a diverse range of equipment and apparel under the REI brand name, as well as bicycles and gear under the Novara brand (Figure 11.2).

Having started with a six-person development team in 1988, the Gear and Apparel division now comprises more than sixty staff members, who develop, design, and source REI-branded products, working on more than six hundred projects annually. With the number of concurrent projects having increased tremendously, project managers at the

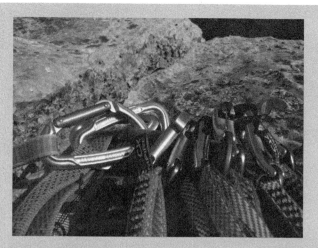

Figure 11.2 REI was founded in 1938 by a group of mountain climbers.

Gear and Apparel division soon realized that their traditional ways of collaborating posed serious limitations to the division's productivity. For instance, project documents were stored on various disparate systems, servers, or personal hard drives, so that managing planning tasks became a nightmare and managing the portfolio of products and projects was all but impossible.

Adding to this was the division's reliance on face-to-face meetings, conference calls, faxes, and email for collaboration, which often resulted in duplication of effort and wasted time during project execution. Often, resources—ranging from product designers to tools needed for developing prototypes—were assigned to multiple projects concurrently, and were not available when needed, leading to bottlenecks in the product development process.

Facing these issues, the Gear and Apparel division realized the need to improve the efficiency of existing processes. Rather than working off disparate documents, development processes needed be optimized using integrated project management solutions that would allow to integrate and align project management tools, processes, tasks, documents, and other data. As a first step in improving the efficiency of the division's processes, the Gear and Apparel division turned to an external solutions provider to model existing business processes, perform various what-if analyses, and finally develop and implement optimized processes.

The new, optimized processes, together with project management software, helped REI's project managers better handle project portfolios and balance resources across various projects within a product portfolio. This greatly facilitated project execution, resulting in faster development time, increased productivity, and higher quality and consistency of the products developed. For REI, this improvement of project execution processes has paid off: REI's own branded products have received various awards, ranging from Gear of the Year Awards from *Outside Magazine* to Editor's Choice Awards from *Backpacker Magazine*.

Based on: Microsoft (2006); REI (2018); SGB Media (2006).

Introduction

Project execution
The process of carrying out the project plan to accomplish the required work.

In Chapter 2, you read about the five different project management process groups: initiating, planning, executing, monitoring and controlling, and closing. Planning is easily the most extensive and involved process in project management. In Chapters 5 through 10, we discussed many different aspects of project planning, from planning for scope, schedule, resources, costs, quality, risk, and procurement. Once the planning phase is complete, it is time to carry out said plan in the real world. **Project execution** is where the project plan is carried out; it is where the product of the project is created. For information technology (IT) projects, execution is where the system is developed and released.

In Chapter 1, we discussed the large number of IS projects that fail because they are either late, over budget, or do not meet specifications. Such project failures waste thousands of work hours and millions of dollars each year. We also discussed the causes of project failure, including failed communication within the project, poor planning, poor quality control, poor project management, lack of attention to human and organizational factors, and so on. Some of these causes of project failure, most notably failed communication, poor management, and lack of attention to detail, occur as part of the project execution process. Learning about project execution involves learning how to compare actual results to the plan, so as to make adjustments as needed to avoid these problems and thus be better able to ensure a successful project outcome.

In *PMBOK*, some of the main processes of the executing and the closing process groups are part of Project Integration Management. Project Integration Management comprises seven major processes: (1) *Develop Project Charter*, (2) *Develop Project Management Plan*, (3) *Direct and Manage Project Work*, (4) *Manage Project Knowledge*, (5) *Monitor and Control Project Work*, (6) *Perform Integrated Change Control*, and (7) *Close Project or Phase*. The first two processes, dealing with planning, were featured in Chapter 5, while the last three processes are the focus of Chapter 12. This chapter is about directing and managing project work and managing project knowledge; in addition, this chapter covers monitoring progress, managing change, communication, and documentation.

The chapter is organized as follows: The next section introduces the different project management processes that make up project execution in *PMBOK*. The inputs, tools and techniques, and outputs of project execution are all discussed. Here we will discuss the various activities project managers engage in during execution, such as the kickoff meeting, as well as the problems that are common to the execution of IS projects. The section after that deals with key duties for project managers during execution—namely, monitoring progress and managing change. In the next section, we discuss an area that

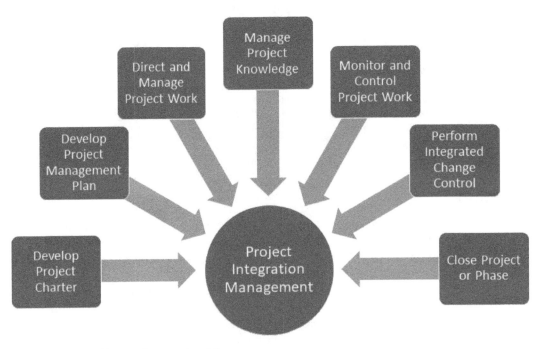

Figure 11.3 *PMBOK* Project Integration Management processes

is central to successful project execution: managing communication and documentation. The last section in the chapter focuses on project execution and *PMBOK*.

Project Plan Execution

According to *PMBOK*, ten project management processes are part of the executing process group (refer back to Figure 2.21). These ten processes are as follows: (1) *Direct and Manage Project Work*, (2) *Manage Project Knowledge*, (3) *Manage Quality*, (4) *Acquire Resources*, (5) *Develop Team*, (6) *Manage Team*, (7) *Manage Communications*, (8) *Implement Risk Responses*, (9) *Conduct Procurements*, and (10) *Manage Stakeholder Engagement*. The *Direct and Manage Project Work* process involves managing the technical and organizational processes and interfaces that are necessary for completing the project work identified in the project management plan. Completing the work envisioned in the plan results in producing the deliverables defined there. The next process, *Manage Project Knowledge*, involves all activities in using existing knowledge and creating and documenting new knowledge in working toward the project's objectives. The *Manage Quality* process is part of the Project Quality Management knowledge area discussed in Chapter 8, and, as you may recall, involves evaluating project progress on a regular basis in order to determine if the project will satisfy established quality standards. The next two processes, *Acquire Resources* and *Develop Team*, are part of the Project Resource Management knowledge area of *PMBOK* and were discussed in Chapters 3 and 7. Acquiring human and physical resources involves balancing factors such as availability and costs of resources, whereas team development involves improving project performance through improving individual and group competencies and interactions. *Manage Communications* is part of the Project Communications Management knowledge area and was introduced in Chapter 4. The *Manage Communications* process involves making needed information available to project stakeholders in a timely manner. The *Implement Risk Responses* process, part of the Project Risk Management knowledge area discussed in Chapter 9, puts the risk management plan in motion. The *Conduct Procurements* process is part of Project Procurement Management and was discussed in Chapter 10; remember that this process involves requesting seller responses to obtain bids and proposals for performing project plan activities, as well as selecting sellers from among the proposals that have been received. The *Manage Stakeholder Engagement* process entails assessing the effectiveness of the strategies for engaging stakeholders and managing their relationships.

Direct and Manage Project Work

Direct and Manage Project Work, like the other key processes in *PMBOK*, requires inputs, tools, and techniques to get the job done, and it produces outputs (Figure 11.4). *Direct and Manage Project Work* has five main inputs: the project management plan, project documentation, approved change requests, enterprise environmental factors, and organizational process assets. The most obvious input is the project management plan itself; the different components of the project management plan give guidance on how the project will be executed. Useful project documents during this process include the project schedule and milestone list, project communications (such as performance reports or status updates), the risk register and risk reports, as well as the change log and lessons-learned register. Approved change requests (discussed in more detail in Chapter 12) are documented and authorized changes to the project scope, either to reduce it or to enlarge it, and include approved corrective actions, approved preventive action, or approved defect repairs. Enterprise environmental factors influencing the *Direct and Manage Project Work* process include the organizational structure, infrastructure, or the risk thresholds of the stakeholders. Finally, organizational process assets include policies, process, and procedures related to managing the project, managing issues and defects, and controlling change and risk; further, organizational process assets used during this process include databases to capture the status of issues or defect and to capture performance measurement data, as well as information from previous projects that can guide the activities performed during this process.

Directing and managing project work frequently takes place in meetings with the relevant attendees; such meetings are conducted to kick of the project, discuss progress or problems, and so on. Recall from Chapter 9 that any issues arising during the project need to be carefully managed, so as to avoid or minimize negative effects on the project objectives. Typically, experts in the relevant areas are consulted. As discussed in Chapter 1, in addition to project management software, a project management information system includes configuration management systems, source code management systems, collaboration systems, knowledge bases containing historical project information, and other systems.

Direct and Manage Project Work has seven main outputs. These are deliverables, work performance data, issue log, change requests, project management plan updates, project documents updates, and organizational process assets updates. The deliverables are simply the verifiable products and services identified in the project plan that must be produced or provided in order to complete the project. The deliverables are the reason for the project in the first place. Especially for projects such as software, the unique deliverables are likely to evolve, resulting in multiple versions. Using configuration management systems and source code management systems (such as Github) can help apply proper change control activities. The second output, work performance data, reflects the status of project activities recorded in the project plan. When a project task has been completed, that data has to be communicated to the project manager and documented in the project management information system, along with the resources

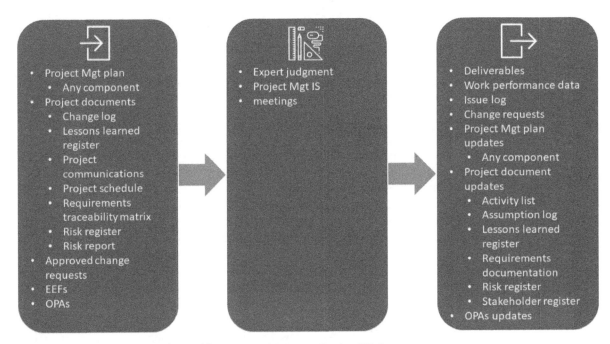

- Project Mgt plan
  - Any component
- Project documents
  - Change log
  - Lessons learned register
  - Project communications
  - Project schedule
  - Requirements traceability matrix
  - Risk register
  - Risk report
- Approved change requests
- EEFs
- OPAs

- Expert judgment
- Project Mgt IS
- meetings

- Deliverables
- Work performance data
- Issue log
- Change requests
- Project Mgt plan updates
  - Any component
- Project document updates
  - Activity list
  - Assumption log
  - Lessons learned register
  - Requirements documentation
  - Risk register
  - Stakeholder register
- OPAs updates

Figure 11.4 The *PMBOK* (6th ed.) *Direct and Manage Project Work* process

that were used to complete the task. The extent to which quality standards have been met must also be recorded. In addition to data about schedule, resources, and quality, work performance data also can include data about costs and the status of deliverables. You will recall reading in more detail about performance reporting in Chapter 4. It is important to remember that performance reporting also involves reporting on work that has not yet been completed, especially if that work is behind schedule. The issue log is used to capture, track, and manage any issues that may arise while directing and managing project work; this log contains the type of issue, a description, priority, who raised the issue, as well as a target date to resolve the issue, the current status, and the final solution. Change requests reflect the fact that projects are not static and that product requirements change even as the project plan is being executed. These changing requirements may involve resources and scheduling as well as functional requirements and features. Successfully tracking and managing change requests is an essential part of any project, but this is especially true for IS projects. Many of the problems encountered in IS projects are related to unsuccessful change management. Change requests can include corrective actions, preventive actions, defect repairs, and updates to the project management plan or project documents. Finally, the process direct and management project work can result in changes to organizational process assets, the project management plan, and various project documents, such as the requirements documentation (in case new requirements are discovered), the activity list (if new or different activities are needed), risk and stakeholder registers the assumption log, and the lessons-learned register.

Project Manager Activities during Execution

From the list of processes highlighted in the previous section, you can see that project managers do many different things during project execution. Here we will briefly describe three: holding the project kickoff meeting, establishing and managing channels for communication, and managing procurement activities.

Project kickoff meeting
A ceremonial meeting marking the beginning of a project in a very public and memorable way.

The **project kickoff meeting** is largely ceremonial. It is important because it marks the beginning of a project in a public and memorable way. The project team in the Jackie's Electronics case held their kickoff meeting at the end of Chapter 4. Sometimes a project kickoff can be quite an elaborate affair, with food, live music, gifts, and decorations. The kickoff does not always have to be a big party. Sometimes it is a simple meeting where the project team meets with the project sponsor, who explains what is involved and what is expected for the project. Who attends the kickoff sends a strong signal to the project team and the company as a whole as to how important the project is. For example, if the chief executive officer and the company president both attend the kickoff, everyone knows this project is important to the entire organization. Whatever form the kickoff takes, it should be something special and out of the ordinary that signifies the start of a dedicated group effort. Just how elaborate the kickoff is depends on the style of the project manager and the budget for the project.

Once the project has begun, it is vital to the project's success that the team establish open, two-way communication channels. Creating and monitoring these channels is also part of the project manager's role. There are many different ways for teams to communicate during project execution, including the project management information system, regular meetings, all types of electronic communication, written reports, and web-based systems that run on the organization's intranet. All of these communication channels will be explored in more detail later in the chapter.

As you saw in Chapter 10, procurement can be a prominent part of any project. Three key procurement activities occur during project execution. The first is soliciting bids and quotes and proposals from potential vendors; the second is deciding among vendors; and the third is administering the contract with the winning vendor (note that soliciting bids and selecting vendors could be separate from the actual project). For medium and large projects, many different procurement activities will be going on simultaneously, with more than one solicitation and with more than one contract to administer. Keeping on top of all of these simultaneous activities is another responsibility the project manager must manage successfully.

Manage Project Knowledge

In addition to managing and directing project work, managing knowledge is an important part of executing a project (see Figure 11.5). First, using existing knowledge will help improve project outcomes; second, documenting knowledge created during the project will help ensure the success of future projects. During this process, it is important to facilitate the exchange and capturing of both explicit and tacit knowledge. Whereas explicit knowledge can be easily codified, documented, and archived, tacit knowledge cannot be easily transferred from one person to another. Consequently, in addition to implementing technology-based knowledge management systems, it is important to foster an atmosphere that encourages knowledge sharing among the involved parties and to capture who has the knowledge needed. Inputs into this ongoing process include the project management plan, project documents, deliverables, enterprise environmental factors, and organizational process assets. Project documents such as the stakeholder register, project team assignments, and the resources breakdown structure help determine where knowledge resides and what knowledge may be missing; likewise, the lesson learned register helps determine best practices in managing knowledge. The deliverables from the *Direct and Manage Project Work* process can provide valuable sources of knowledge. Enterprise environmental factors that have an impact on the *Manage Project Knowledge* process include the culture of the organization, stakeholders, and customers, the existence of experts in the area of project management, the degree of geographic dispersion of team members, as well as legal and regulatory requirements, such as non-disclosure agreements or other confidentiality arrangements. Finally, organizational

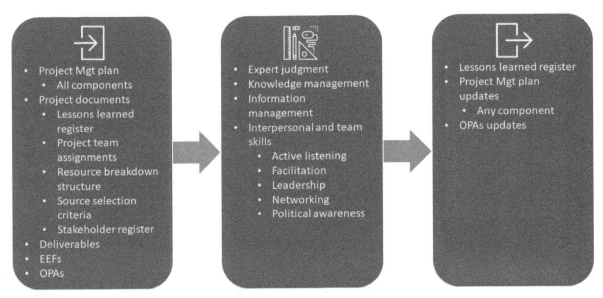

Figure 11.5 The *PMBOK* (6th ed.) *Manage Project Knowledge* process

process assets influencing the *Manage Project Knowledge* process are standards and procedures related to confidentiality, data protection, and the like, personnel development, communication requirements (formal vs. informal), as well as formal procedures related to sharing knowledge and information.

As with any process, expert judgement from experts in areas such as knowledge management or organizational learning can help ensure the success of the *Manage Project Knowledge* process. The foremost tools and techniques used are those designed for knowledge management and information management. Knowledge management tools such as communities of practice, workshops, knowledge fairs, or networking enable individuals to share tacit knowledge; as social integration mechanisms, they provide the resources that help group members interact, create positive feelings among group members, provide shared frames of reference, and set interrelated goals resulting in coordinated efforts. As such, these mechanisms facilitate knowledge sharing and are a critical factor in enabling the absorption of tacit knowledge (von Briel et al., 2018). Information management tools and techniques are primarily used to share and document codified knowledge; these tools can include the project management information system, the lessons-learned register, as well as the methods used for documenting explicit knowledge. Other tools and techniques are internal expert networks, enabling people to find others who may have relevant knowledge, and knowledge portals, enabling people to contact experts who may have the needed knowledge (Valacich and Schneider, 2018). The project manager uses interpersonal and team skills such as active listening, facilitation, networking, as well as leadership and political awareness to create an atmosphere that encourages knowledge sharing.

The outputs of this process include the lessons-learned register, where knowledge is captured as it is created; updates to the project management plan; as well as updates to organizational process assets, where newly created knowledge is codified and documented.

Monitoring Progress and Managing Change

Executing the project plan means that all the preparations are done, and now it is time to do the job. If the plan has been put together well, and if it is written at the necessary level of detail, then all the project manager has to do is follow directions. What could be simpler? Actually, execution is anything but simple. Things rarely go as planned. The assurance "Everything is going according to plan" may be common in the movies and on TV, but it's not one that most project managers use often. Instead, it sometimes seems that nothing goes according to plan. A big part of a project manager's job during execution is to monitor everything to understand what is not going according to plan and what the implications are for missing expectations. The next two subsections focus on monitoring progress and the activities a project manager engages in during execution. Then, we discuss managing change and the problems common to IS project execution.

Tips from the Pros: Tips for New Managers

New managers face a tough challenge. They have to manage the work of others while learning how to be a manager at the same time. Here are some guidelines for becoming a good manager when starting out. Although these tips apply to all aspects of managing a project, most of them are especially applicable to the execution phase.

1. *Don't make promises you can't or won't keep.* This is one of the worst things a new manager can do. Not keeping promises erodes trust and leads to a lack of respect on the part of the employee.

2. *Don't offer inappropriate awards.* Rewards should match performance. A coffee mug is

appropriate for cutting a couple of days off the schedule, not for saving the project millions of dollars.

3. *Reward ambitious workers with important tasks.*

4. *Set aside time to meet with workers* to talk about things from both your perspective and theirs.

5. *Ask workers about their career goals* and how you can help them achieve their objectives.

6. *Offer your top performers* opportunities for training.

7. *Ask workers about their outside interests* and offer them rewards that match those interests, such as gift certificates and event tickets.

Adapted from: McCarthy (2018); Solomon (2001).

8. *Comment on good or bad work right away.* Don't save feedback for regularly scheduled employee performance evaluations.

9. *Don't assume good workers know how much they are valued.* People don't always know how good they are and how much they are appreciated. Don't ignore good workers, as that is a sure way to get them to stop doing so well.

10. *Take your role as manager seriously.* Don't put off rewards and feedback, and don't downplay the importance of regularly scheduled performance evaluations.

Monitoring Progress

Monitoring progress The process of keeping track of all project tasks and the details surrounding each one.

Once the project plan has been approved, then all of the tasks have been identified, along with who is responsible for each task, the resources that are necessary to complete them, the deliverables for each task, the milestones for the deliverables to be delivered, and the relationship of each task to all of the other tasks. The project manager's job in **monitoring progress** is to keep track of all tasks and all of the details surrounding each one. The more well-defined the schedule and the deliverables, the easier it is to check progress. It is easier to compare reality to expectations when expectations are explicitly defined. To measure reality accurately, however, requires open, two-way communication. Even medium-sized projects would soon overwhelm managers if there were not ways to keep track of all the details. You have read about different techniques that have been developed to keep track of those details, such as PERT and Gantt charts. A more powerful method is project management software, but the basic idea of an organized system for project management is the same.

For an example of how a project manager might use project management software, refer to Figure 11.6. The figure shows two weeks in the life of a project. Five related activities are to be performed during this time: (1) write a request for proposals (RFP); (2) create a list of potential vendors to receive the RFP; (3) prepare an information presentation for the potential vendors; (4) invite the vendors to the presentation; and (5) hold the presentation. You can see from the calendar in Figure 11.6 that writing the RFP takes five days, creating the list of vendors to invite takes two days, and the other three tasks all take one day each. You can't really tell from the calendar how the activities are related; for that, you need to look at a network diagram that represents these two weeks of the project (Figure 11.7).

Figure 11.7 shows that writing the RFP is the starting activity in this network, and holding the presentation for vendors is the ending activity. The RFP must be completed before anything else can start, and all of the other activities have to be completed before the presentation can take place. The critical path for this network goes from writing the RFP, through creating the vendor list, through inviting the vendors, to the final presentation. The actual creation of the presentation is off the critical path, so whoever has that responsibility has two days of slack time.

Suppose at a regularly scheduled staff meeting, the person in charge of creating the presentation announces that she suddenly has to leave town immediately on family

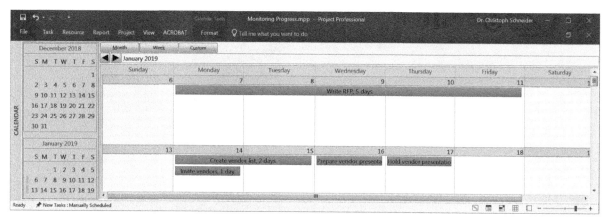

Figure 11.6   Two weeks in a project schedule in Microsoft Project 2016

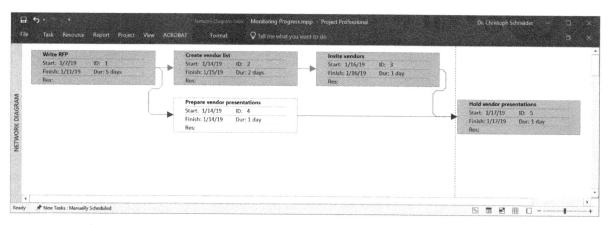

Figure 11.7   Original project network diagram in Microsoft Project 2016

business. Luckily there is a staff member available who can put together the presentation, but because he is new to the project and to the organization, it will take him three days instead of one to prepare the same quality presentation. With this change, there are now two critical paths through the network. Nothing can go wrong if the presentation is to be held on January 17, as planned, and the auditorium is already booked for that day. The booking can't be changed without losing a hefty deposit. Just as the project manager begins to think about the current situation and how she can't afford any more problems, another staff member says he has determined he can put together a complete list of potential vendors in only one day. He can save time by starting with another list of potential vendors that fits their needs and was used by another project team. Now the critical path changes again (Figure 11.8), going through the presentation preparation. Neither creating the vendor list nor inviting the vendors is on the critical path. The project manager has just won another day of slack.

This example has been kept simple to prove a point. Most project managers probably wish their lives were that easy. Just to give you an idea of how difficult and demanding project execution can be, here is a list of all the things project managers must do simultaneously for each project they manage:

• Allocate and distribute work to team members at the right time while also managing task dependencies

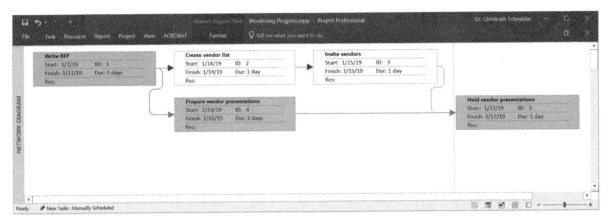

Figure 11.8 Microsoft Project 2016 network diagram after change in duration of two activities

- Update progress of each task
- Determine consequences and predict their effects on future tasks and milestones
- Manage changing team membership
- Manage roles of third parties, such as vendors and suppliers
- Enforce ownership of tasks

Notice that the first three activities in this list involve monitoring. Project managers can't allocate work during execution unless they know the status of all the tasks being worked on at a particular point in time and who is assigned to work on each task. The progress on a task can't be updated unless the project manager knows the status of the task. The effects of the present on the future can't be determined unless the project manager understands the present. In other words, you can't figure out where you want to go and how to get there until you know where you are. Project managers have to continually monitor project activities in order to get the needed information to manage the project effectively. Regular staff meetings are one way to get this information, but there are others, and we will have more to say about them later in the chapter. The last three activities in the list have more to do with managing personnel than with monitoring. Team membership is not static, and people leaving and joining a project can have significant impacts. Tasks left unfinished through a team member's departure have to be reassigned to someone else, and new people have to be brought up to speed on the project and how they can contribute. The project manager also has to deal with people outside the project team, such as vendors, who also contribute to the project. The more procurement a project involves, the more effort the project manager will have to expend on managing third-party relationships. Finally, the project manager has to make sure that the people assigned to different tasks, whether inside the project organization or working for a third party, continue to take responsibility for those tasks. In Chapter 12, we will discuss more formal techniques for monitoring and controlling the progress of projects.

Common Problems: Anticipating Problems during Execution

During execution, the project team is focused on the job at hand, which is successfully implementing the project plan. With the focus on execution, the project team often does not spend the time and energy it should on anticipating and finding problems. The State of California's Department of Finance has prepared a list of potential problems that may arise during project execution. They include

1. Lack of good data on activity progress
2. Inadequate requirements definition
3. Frequent and uncontrolled changes to the project baseline
4. Poor time and cost estimates

5. Difficulties in concluding the project because of ill-specified completion criteria
6. High personnel turnover
7. Inadequate monitoring and directing of project activities

Many of these problems will not arise if careful planning takes place. Planning, however, is not perfect, and one of the jobs of the project manager and project team is to make sure that inadequate planning is not translated into inadequate deliverables during execution. Once a problem is suspected, it is very important that the project team act immediately to take care of it, regardless of the cause.

Managing Change

Managing change
The process of dealing with change requests during project execution.

Given the pressure to change system requirements during project execution, it is almost certain that a project team will be **managing change** related to the project, dealing with change requests during project execution. Likewise, any problems that might arise during project execution might require changes that need to be carefully managed. So, how does a project manager deal with changes? First, it is important to note that every request for change does not result in a change to the requirements. Every request should be documented. Processes should be set up to review each request to determine if it can or should be accepted. Every change that is accepted will affect the project deliverables, the schedule, and the budget, so changes have to be considered very seriously. Each project organization will typically have in place organizational processes and procedures for change evaluation and implementation. We will discuss how to manage and control change in more detail in Chapter 12.

Common System Development Project Problems

People-related mistakes
System development mistakes arising from adding people too late to a project, lack of necessary skills, or unrealistic expectations.

Process-related mistakes
System development mistakes arising from insufficient planning, overly optimistic schedules, or planning to catch up later.

Product-related mistakes
System development mistakes arising from feature creep and requirements gold-plating.

Technology-related mistakes
System development mistakes arising from overestimating savings from new tools or methods, or the silver-bullet syndrome.

Despite the best efforts of the best project manager, things can still go wrong during project execution. IS projects are notorious for being problematic. Steve McConnell lists thirty-six different classic development mistakes in systems development projects, ten of which are included in Table 11.1. Most of the **people-related mistakes, process-related mistakes, product-related mistakes**, and **technology-related mistakes** listed in Table 11.1 are easily understood from their brief descriptions, such as unrealistic expectations, insufficient planning, and overestimated savings from new tools or methods. Some of the others warrant additional explanation.

In the realm of people-related mistakes, *weak personnel* refers to employees who are not adequately trained in the skills necessary to a particular project. Personnel who do not have the necessary technical skills for a specific project will struggle, and the project will suffer. The second type of mistake in this category, adding people late to a project, may not seem like a mistake. In fact, common sense would dictate that additional people should add to productivity because the remaining work can now be divided among more people, leaving each person with less to do in the same amount of time. But as Brooks (1995) convincingly argued, adding more people also adds more need for coordination among all the people on the project, new and old. Adding more people often actually ends up reducing productivity on a project. Brooks also identified the problem called the *silver-bullet syndrome*. The **silver-bullet syndrome** occurs when

Table 11.1   Ten of Steve McConnell's Thirty-Six Classic Development Mistakes

People-Related	Process-Related	Product-Related	Technology-Related
Weak personnel Adding people to a project late Unrealistic expectations	Insufficient planning Overly optimistic schedules Planning to catch up later	Feature creep Requirements gold-plating	Silver-bullet syndrome Overestimated savings from new tools or methods

Silver-bullet syndrome
A problem that occurs when developers believe a new and usually untried technology is all that is needed to cure the ills of any development project.

Feature creep
The tendency of systems requirements to change over the lifetime of the development project.

Requirements gold-plating
Adding more requirements than necessary to an application, even before the beginning of a project.

developers believe a new (and usually untried) technology is all that is needed to cure the ills of any development project. In application development, however, there is no silver bullet. No one technology can solve every problem, and those who believe there is are likely to be disappointed.

Two other mistakes from the list that need additional explanation are both product-related: feature creep and requirements gold-plating. **Feature creep** refers to the tendency of system requirements to change over the lifetime of the development project. It is called *feature creep* because more and more features that were not in the original specifications for the application "creep in" during the development process. The average project may see a 25 percent change in requirements, all of which can delay the project and add costs. Changes to an application typically cost fifty to two hundred times less if they are made during requirements determination rather than during the physical design process. **Requirements gold-plating** means an application may have more requirements than it needs, even before the development project begins. In addition to being unnecessary, many of these requirements can be extreme and complex.

Communication and Documentation

We have already mentioned the need for open, two-way communication in any successful project. Communication serves to facilitate the exchange of information and can take many forms. The staff of REI's Gear and Apparel Division relied on such traditional communication modes as meetings, conference calls, faxes, and email. Here we briefly discuss five methods to support team communication: meetings, presentations and written reports, the project management information system, electronic communication, and web-based solutions (Figure 11.9). We follow this discussion on communication with a discussion of documentation.

Meetings

Meetings have been around for a long time. If they are short, well-run, and focused, they can be a very effective means of exchanging information (see Chapter 4, especially Figure 4.10, for more about how to run a project meeting effectively.) If the purpose of a regularly scheduled staff meeting is for everyone to report on their progress and their problems and for the project manager to provide information on the larger project status, then meetings can work well. But we all know from learned experience that meetings do not always work well, sadly. Sometimes meetings are not well run, and the discussion is allowed to drift. Sometimes people seem unwilling or unable to exchange necessary information. Getting everyone involved to come to the same place at the same time on a given day, giving up time they would rather be using to do their "real work," can also be an issue. Although meetings are familiar and potentially useful, they have enough problems that project team communication can successfully occur in other

Figure 11.9 Communication for project management

ways. In addition to meetings about progress updates, meetings can be held to discuss technical issues, solve problems, or exchange retrospective thoughts about the project.

Written Reports

One of the other ways that project team communication can occur is the preparation and distribution of written reports about the project and its progress. The emphasis here is on written, rather than oral, and regular, rather than ad hoc. We should also emphasize that the reports need to be timely and accurate. Reports that do not reflect the current status of project tasks are practically worthless. The point of regular written reporting is to let the project manager know the status of all of the various tasks that are part of the project. Having regular written reports generates a discipline for providing up-to-date information that the project manager can use to put together an overall picture of the project's status.

Project Management Information Systems

Once project managers have status information, they can use it to update the status of the overall project and determine just where things are and how far things are from where they want them to be. As you have seen, the project management information systems and project management software (e.g., Microsoft Project) make the project manager's job in this regard much easier. A host of information systems are available to support project management, from shareware to commercial systems that run on every conceivable platform.

Electronic Communication

We have already discussed the topics of meetings and written reports as ways to communicate project information. The types of meetings we indicated in our discussions were traditional meetings where people come together in one place and time for a certain duration to accomplish their meeting goals. The types of reports we discussed were also traditional: written, printed on paper, and distributed manually to those concerned. Today, it is no longer necessary to hold every meeting in one place and at one time, and printed paper reports that are centrally distributed are becoming less and less common. Using online chat, audioconferencing, and videoconferencing, meeting participants can be geographically dispersed during a same-time meeting. People who are far away from the meeting place can still participate. Similarly, the meeting can be asynchronous, with people contributing over time, so that the meeting itself might span a week, giving people the opportunity to log in and contribute over that entire period. The reports can be transmitted in the body of email messages or they can be attachments. Alternatively, they can be posted to online collaboration platforms such as Microsoft SharePoint.

Global Implications: Project Execution after Outsourcing

Whether development project work is outsourced overseas or to another firm in the same country, in many instances this means that some employees within the company have lost their jobs. Project managers in an outsourcing situation have to manage everyone on the team, whether they are part of the outsourced work team or part of the local team. What project managers may not realize is that local survivors of the outsourcing effort may not all react in the same way. Determining how different individuals react and how their reactions affect the project execution effort is one more burden project managers have to bear.

Survivors of outsourcing can react in many different ways. While you would expect them all to be happy they have kept their jobs, basic reactions will vary. Some employees will be outraged that outsourcing occurred in the first place; others will be afraid they might be next. Some will work even harder to make sure they survive the next outsourcing efforts;

others may become incapacitated by guilt caused by their surviving while other employees they knew and worked with lost their jobs.

How can project managers deal with such a wide range of reactions? Ignoring the ways different employees react to outsourcing is the wrong thing to do, according to Eileen Strider, an organizational effectiveness consultant. One approach is to let employees vent their concerns and fears. It is also important for executives to be honest with employees about why outsourcing occurred and to provide them with some semblance of stability. In extreme cases, employees may be encouraged to seek counseling, or the company itself may need to bring in counselors if feelings of fear and betrayal are widespread. The important point is that employee reactions need to be recognized and dealt with because employee reactions to outsourcing affect their work, which in turn affects the entire project.

Based on: Hamblen (2004), Maertz et al. (2010).

Web-Based Solutions

One of the main objectives of communication during a project is the exchange of status information. Project managers need to be able to react to problems and to proactively prevent problems during project execution, but they can only do these things effectively if they know the current status of all of the constituent parts of the project. Instead of having each team member or each third-party vendor report progress and delays to the project manager, who then has to use that information to update the project, why not allow team members and third parties to update the project management information system directly? Such direct updating is supported with web-based access to the project management information system. Users can access the system through their web browsers and report on the status of their tasks. Web accessible project management tools range from project management software to knowledge management systems, document repositories, communication systems, and meeting systems (Figure 11.10). An example of a commercial system especially relevant to project execution is Microsoft's Project Online cloud-based solution.

Microsoft Project Online and other web-based tools like it offer many communication related capabilities. Team members and third parties can access the system from anywhere they have access to a web browser. All team members can update the status of their tasks, and the overall project software is immediately updated. Team members

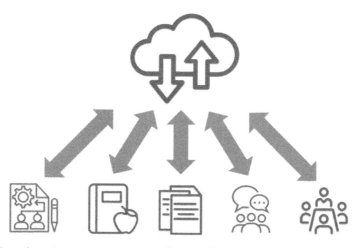

Figure 11.10 Web-based project management tools are offered on a Software-as-a-Service basis

can notify each other of when their tasks will be completed (which is useful for those who are downstream of and dependent on these tasks), and their availability for new work. Project managers will then be able to monitor the project in real time, provided team members and vendors update their task status in a timely and accurate manner. With current information, managers should be able to better anticipate and deal with problems as they arise.

Documentation

Communication is usually accompanied by documentation. Ordinarily someone takes minutes in a meeting. People often log phone calls and make notes about their contents. Electronic communication media, such as email, are their own documentation because electronic messages are stored on computer servers for later retrieval. Documentation, which creates a record of how the project proceeds over time, is important for many reasons. First, a record of the process is valuable for the project team in case they need to trace how a decision was made or how a product specification has changed during the project. Second, documentation provides a record that can be audited or that can be used as part of a legal defense in case of disputes between buyers and suppliers. Third, documentation from an outstandingly successful project may be used as the source of best practices to improve processes in other projects.

Ethical Dilemma: Relying on a Professional Code of Ethics

During project execution, you may run into ethical dilemmas and you may want to review a professional code of ethics from the project management profession for guidance. Where do you find a professional code of ethics for project management?

The Project Management Institute's ideas on projects and their management have become standards in the industry. PMI has established a detailed member code of ethics that is available on their website (http://www.pmi.org/about/ethics/code).

Although PMI is the predominant professional institute for project management, it is not the only one. The Association for Project Management (APM), the primary project management professional association in the United Kingdom, also has a code of ethics, which is available at https://www.apm.org.uk/about-us/how-apm-is-run/apm-code-of-professional-conduct. It is useful to visit the APM site and compare its code of ethics with the PMI code.

Discussion Questions
1. Compare the PMI and APM codes of ethics. What is contained in both codes?
2. What are the primary differences between the two codes? What may be the reasons for these differences?
3. What's the point of professional codes of ethics? Why are they needed?

Managing Project Execution and PMBOK

The primary topic of Chapter 11 has been project plan execution; as Figure 11.11 shows, we have covered topics from the knowledge areas of integration management, quality, resource, communications, risk, procurement, and stakeholder management.

Figure 11.11   Chapter 11 and *PMBOK* coverage

Key: ○ where the material is covered in the textbook; ● current chapter coverage

	Textbook Chapters ⟶	1	2	3	4	5	6	7	8	9	10	11	12
	PMBOK Knowledge Area												
1	Introduction												
1.2	Foundational Elements	○	○										
2	The Environment in Which Projects Operate												
2.2	Enterprise Environmental Factors		○										
2.2	Organizational Process Assets		○										
2.3	Organizational Systems		○										
3	The Role of the Project Manager												
3.2	Definition of a Project Manager	○											
3.3	The Project Manager's Sphere of Influence		○										
3.4	Project Manager Competences	○	○	○									
3.5	Performing Integration		○										
4	Project Integration Management												
4.1	Develop Project Charter					○							
4.2	Develop Project Management Plan					○							
4.3	Direct and Manage Project Work											●	
4.4	Manage Project Knowledge											●	
4.5	Monitor and Control Project Work											●	○
4.6	Perform Integrated Change Control												○
4.7	Close Project or Phase										○		○
5	Project Scope Management												
5.1	Plan Scope Management					○							
5.2	Collect Requirements					○							
5.3	Define Scope					○							
5.4	Create WBS					○	○						

No.	Process										
5.5	Validate Scope					○					
5.6	Control Scope					○					○
6	**Project Schedule Management**										
6.1	Plan Schedule Management							○			
6.2	Define Activities							○			
6.3	Sequence Activities							○			
6.4	Estimate Activity Durations							○			
6.5	Develop Schedule							○			
6.6	Control Schedule							○			○
7	**Project Cost Management**										
7.1	Plan Cost Management								○		
7.2	Estimate Costs								○		
7.3	Determine Budget								○		
7.4	Control Costs								○		○
8	**Project Quality Management**										
8.1	Plan Quality Management								○		
8.2	Manage Quality								○		
8.3	Control Quality								○		○
9	**Project Resource Management**										
9.1	Plan Resource Management							○			
9.2	Estimate Activity Resources						○	○			
9.3	Acquire Resources							○		●	
9.4	Develop Team			○						●	
9.5	Manage Team			○						●	
9.6	Control Resources							○			○
10	**Project Communications Management**										
10.1	Plan Communications Management				○						
10.2	Manage Communications				○					●	
10.3	Monitor Communications				○						○
11	**Project Risk Management**										
11.1	Plan Risk Management								○		
11.2	Identify Risks								○	●	
11.3	Perform Qualitative Risk Analysis								○		
11.4	Perform Quantitative Risk Analysis								○		
11.5	Plan Risk Responses								○		
11.6	Implement Risk Responses								○	●	
11.7	Monitor Risks								○		○
12	**Project Procurement Management**										
12.1	Plan Procurement Management									○	
12.2	Conduct Procurements									○	●
12.3	Control Procurements									○	○

13	Project Stakeholder Management													
12.1	Identify Stakeholders				○									
12.2	Plan Stakeholder Engagement				○									
12.3	Manage Stakeholder Engagement				○								●	
12.4	Monitor Stakeholder Engagement				○									○

Running Case: Managing Project Execution

As James was driving to work on June 20, he dreaded the day ahead of him.

The pilot implementation of Jackie's Electronics' new customer relationship management (CRM) system was originally scheduled for July 31. With the go-live date being less than six weeks away, it was close to impossible to meet that date. The team had decided on the XCT CRM system, but the installation had been much more complex than initially planned, so the implementation was way behind schedule. Kevin Woodfield, James's team member who was in charge of systems integration for Jackie's, asked James to hire external consultants with XCT experience to help with implementation. This was difficult decision to make, as employing external consultants would mean that the approved budget limit would be exceeded.

Nick Baldwin, the head of marketing, further added to the implementation problems by submitting various requests for changes to the system's original specifications. Initially, according to the project charter, the new system was supposed to track purchases, assign membership points, and allow these points to be redeemed for "rewards" (in the form of dollars-off coupons) at local stores. Enrolled customers could access Jackie's website to check their account activity and account balances. Once a customer had earned enough points, he or she would be rewarded with a coupon that they would have to print out and bring to a store to use. The decision to keep everything electronic was made to reduce the considerable costs associated with printing and mailing coupons to customers.

Although the decision had been made very early in the project, Nick Baldwin and his marketing team suddenly submitted a change request that would allow customers to choose between having coupons mailed to them once they had accumulated sufficient points or printing them at home. While this was convenient for the customers, it added significant complexity to the XCT system implementation, in addition to reducing the benefits from cost savings.

In addition, James had learned yesterday from Cindy Kobayashi, the marketing representative on his team, that Baldwin wanted yet another change. In addition to allowing customers to use printed coupons for in-store purchases, he wanted to enable customers to use eCoupons for online purchases at Jackie's website. In addition to adding another layer of complexity to the XCT system implementation, this also meant that Jackie's existing systems for ordering online would have to be changed to allow for the use of eCoupons.

Just when James thought these were enough problems for a day, Rick Piccoli, Maria's replacement at the Irvine store, informed James that his store would not be ready by the end of July to pilot the new system. James hoped that this problem would solve itself, given that they weren't going to be ready at the go-live date anyway, but Rick indicated that it would take several months before the store would be ready. Slowly it dawned on James that Rick was not overly keen on using his store for the pilot. But maybe he could talk Maria Gutierrez into letting them use her Minneapolis store as the pilot site. Maria used to be on their team before she was transferred to Minneapolis. James thought she would be willing to help.

James had almost reached his office, and he would have to call Sarah Codey and update her on the status of the project. He was not looking forward to telling her that they would not be able to make the go-live date; however, he thought that it didn't matter anyway, given that Rick wouldn't let the team use his store as a pilot location, and they would have to find another store. James would also have to tell Sarah that he was going to have to go over budget, too, as there was no way they would be ready for the pilot anywhere close to the originally scheduled go-live date without the help of consultants, as Kevin had requested. Further, he would have to freeze the requirements, and reject the latest change request filed by marketing. Luckily, Nick had not yet submitted the change request for the use of eCoupons, but

James would have to make sure that Nick would not submit this additional request.

There was a slight change that, if he could hire the consultants, fight off the change requests, and get Maria to let him use her store for the pilot, they might be ready to launch a pilot in Minneapolis on October 15. Yet this still only gave him four months to complete the project. He and his team would have to work hard to make that happen.

James realized he had missed his turn. *Great*, he thought. Things could only get better from here.

Adapted from: Valacich and George (2017).

Chapter Summary

Describe the ten project management processes that are part of project execution. According to *PMBOK*, ten project management processes are part of the executing process group: *Direct and Manage Project Work, Manage Project Knowledge, Manage Quality, Acquire Resources, Develop Team, Manage Team, Manage Communications, Implement Risk Responses, Conduct Procurements*, and *Manage Stakeholder Engagement*. The *Direct and Manage Project Work* process involves managing the technical and organizational processes and interfaces that are necessary for completing the project work identified. *Manage Project Knowledge* involves all activities in using existing knowledge and creating and documenting new knowledge. *Manage Quality* involves evaluating project progress on a regular basis in order to determine if the project will satisfy established quality standards. *Acquire Resources* involves balancing factors such as availability and costs of resources, whereas team development involves improving project performance through improving individual and group competencies and interactions. *Manage Communications* involves making needed information available to project stakeholders in a timely manner. The *Implement Risk Responses* process puts the risk management plan in motion. *Conduct Procurements* involves requesting seller responses to obtain bids and proposals for performing project plan activities, as well as selecting sellers from among the proposals that have been received. *Manage Stakeholder Engagement* entails assessing the effectiveness of the strategies for engaging stakeholders and managing their relationships.

Discuss the activities project managers engage in during project execution. A big part of a project manager's job during execution is to monitor everything in order to understand what is not going according to plan and what the implications are for missing expectations. Another big part of the job is managing change, in both project requirements and project personnel. Other activities a project manager engages in during execution include organizing the project kickoff meeting, establishing and managing channels for communication, and managing procurement activities.

Explain some of the key problems in IS projects that occur during project execution. Many different types of problems can occur during project execution. Some of the problems discussed in this chapter include having to deal with weak personnel, adding people late to a project, feature creep, and requirements gold-plating.

Describe the importance of communication to project execution. The quality of communication among project team members can be the difference between a successful and an unsuccessful project. Some useful channels for communication discussed in this chapter include regular team meetings, regular written reports, project management information systems, electronic communications, and web-based project plan execution systems.

Key Terms Review

A. Feature creep
B. Managing change
C. Monitoring progress
D. People-related mistakes
E. Process-related mistakes
F. Product-related mistakes

G. Project execution
H. Project kickoff meeting
I. Requirements gold-plating

J. Silver-bullet syndrome
K. Technology-related mistakes

Match each of the key terms with the definition that best fits it.

1. A ceremonial meeting marking the beginning of a project in a very public and memorable way.

2. A problem that occurs when developers believe a new and usually untried technology is all that is needed to cure the ills of any development project.

3. Adding more requirements than necessary to an application, even before the beginning of a project.

4. System development mistakes arising from adding people too late to a project, lack of necessary skills, or unrealistic expectations.

5. System development mistakes arising from feature creep and requirements gold-plating.

6. System development mistakes arising from insufficient planning, overly optimistic schedules, or planning to catch up later.

7. System development mistakes arising from overestimating savings from new tools or methods or the silver-bullet syndrome.

8. The process of carrying out the project plan to accomplish the required work.

9. The process of dealing with change requests during project execution.

10. The process of keeping track of all project tasks and the details surrounding each one.

11. The tendency of systems requirements to change over the lifetime of the development project.

Review Questions

1. What is project plan execution?

2. According to *PMBOK*, what are the ten management processes that make up the executing process group? Where else in the book have you studied some of them?

3. Explain the inputs to the *Direct and Manage Project Work* process.

4. Explain the tools and techniques that are used in the *Direct and Manage Project Work* process.

5. Explain the outputs from the *Direct and Manage Project Work* process.

6. Describe some of the activities that project managers perform during project execution.

7. What four problems are commonly encountered during project execution?

8. What are two types of change that project managers have to deal with during project execution?

9. Name and describe five different ways that project teams can communicate during the *Direct and Manage Project Work* process.

10. Explain how project execution can be documented.

Chapter Exercises

1. Note that one of the management processes in the executing process group is associated with procurement. Why is procurement such a major part of execution?

2. Why is managing project knowledge so important to project plan execution? What can project managers do to facilitate knowledge management?

3. Using the web and other resources, research information systems for project execution. Write a report that describes each system you found and that compares and contrasts the features of each system.

Task	Duration	Predecessor
1	1 day	—
2	3 days	1
3	2 days	1
4	3 days	2
5	5 days	3
6	3 days	4, 5
7	1 day	6

4. Suppose you are the project manager for the following project: First, draw a network diagram for the project. Determine the critical path and slack times for all of the tasks. This completes your plan for the project schedule. During project execution, you become aware of the need to change the duration of Task 4 to five days.

   Meanwhile, Task 3 has been finished one day early, so it only took one day to do. What, if any, effects do these changes have on your project? What would have happened if you had not been monitoring the status of the project?

5. Find and interview project managers about how they communicate with team members concerning their projects during project execution. Which methods work best for them? How do they incorporate communication into their execution activities? Write a report explaining what you found.

6. Everyone has managed projects, whether in the workplace, in school, or at home. Describe the activities you undertook during execution. What type of system did you use to manage the project (e.g., computer-based or manual)? How well did the system work for you? What kinds of problems did you encounter and how did you deal with them?

Chapter Case: Sedona Management Group and Managing Project Execution

Project execution is the phase of the project in which the activities necessary for project completion are undertaken. The execution processes include coordinating the project resources to carry out the project plans developed in the planning stage. The products or deliverables of the project are produced during the project execution phase. Ten project management processes form the executing process group, one of which is the core *Direct and Manage Project Work* process.

Project execution comprises several key activities, including providing project leadership, monitoring progress, assuring quality, managing change, and managing channels for communication. Positive leadership contributes to project success. A positive leader is one who is a good team builder and communicator, has high self-esteem, focuses on results, demonstrates trust and respect, and sets realistic goals. Tim Turnpaugh takes his role as Sedona Management Group's (SMG's) leader very seriously. Over the years, the practices that have worked best for him as a project leader include the establishment of clear goals, strict adherence to the project schedule, and keeping project team members motivated. For

any project, Turnpaugh has to ensure that he clearly understands the customer's needs and, at the same time, that every project team member has that same level of understanding.

Another best practice Turnpaugh employs as a project leader is to establish milestones for any project SMG takes on and then assess those milestones over the life cycle of the project. By doing detailed planning during earlier project phases—including identifying tasks, allocating resources for tasks, and identifying the outputs from each task—the Sedona team can create a good baseline for use in comparing their actual progress with the project's planned progress.

In the case of the Seattle Seahawks, Turnpaugh and his team created a detailed plan for building the Seahawks' website. Mike Flood of the Seahawks identified several key characteristics the Seahawks needed for their website. Flood wanted a website that was secure and reliable, conveyed accurate information, and was easy to access. Based on these requirements and through the experience gained with working for other clients, Turnpaugh determined the system that would work best for the

Seahawks, and a contract was drafted. The contract had a very detailed scope of work that stated clearly what the Sedona team would accomplish for the Seattle Seahawks. In the event that after signing the contract, the customer asked for some significant change to the project scope during project execution, Turnpaugh would only undertake the change if the project's budget and the delivery date for the final product were changed. Change control is essential for ensuring timely project execution.

Communication is also a key factor influencing successful project execution. In addition to the considerable amount of time SMG spends with each client during the initiation and planning stages, during the project execution phase SMG has regular meetings with the customer to ensure that the project is going according to the customer's expectations. As mentioned earlier, during the execution phase, Turnpaugh ensures that both someone from his team and from the customer's organization are always accessible for exchanging information.

Chapter 11 Project Assignment

In the execution phase, you will perform the activities necessary to ensure project completion. Some of the important activities include monitoring progress and managing change. In this exercise, you will learn about each of these different activities.

1. Describe project execution as it relates to your project. In other words, explain what you will do to ensure project completion.

2. You developed a Gantt chart for the project assignment in Chapter 6 and updated it with resource information in Chapter 7. Determine how many of the activities you have completed so far, and update the Gantt chart from Chapter 7 with this new information.

3. Describe any changes to the project plan that have been needed so far. Were all these change requests approved?

4. Develop a progress report that describes what you and your team members have accomplished so far for the entertainment website development project. The progress report should include:

   - Your accomplishments so far, related to the tracking Gantt chart you developed previously

   - Your plans, which include what remains to be accomplished for project completion

   - Any issues that have surfaced during the project life cycle

   - A list of any approved changes made to the project

5. Describe how you and your team members keep each other updated on the status of your project. In particular, indicate the different forms of communication you are using (e.g., email, face-to-face meetings, collaborative tools, and so on).

References

Brooks, F. P., Jr. (1995). *The Mythical Man-Month. Anniversary*. Reading, MA: Addison-Wesley.

Hamblen, M. (2004, November 8). Sidebar: After the Outsourcing. *ComputerWorld*. Retrieved July 9, 2018, from http://www.computerworld.com/article/2567426/it-outsourcing/sidebar--after-the-outsourcing.amp.html

Maertz, C. P., Wiley, J. W., LeRouge, C., and Campion, M. A. (2010). Downsizing Effects on Survivors: Layoffs, Offshoring, and Outsourcing. *Industrial Relations: A Journal of Economy and Society*, 49(2), 275–285.

McCarthy, D. (2018, February 13). Fifteen Tips for New Managers. *The Balance Careers*. Retrieved April 19, 2018, from https://www.thebalancecareers.com/tips-for-new-managers-part-1-2275957

McConnell, S. (1996). *Rapid Development*. Redmond, WA: Microsoft Press.

Microsoft (2006, October 12). REI Improves Its Product Development Processes by Integrating Process and Project Management Tasks. *Microsoft.com*. Retrieved July 9, 2018, from https://blogs.msdn.microsoft.com/shishirs/2006/10/12/rei-improves-its-product-development-processes-by-integrating-process-and-project-management-tasks

Project Management Institute (2000). *A Guide to the Project Management Body of Knowledge*. Newton Square, PA: Author.

Project Management Institute (2017). *Agile Practice Guide*. Newton Square, PA: Author.

Project Management Institute (2017). *PMBOK: A Guide to the Project Management Body of Knowledge* (6th ed.). Newton Square, PA: Author.

REI (2018). REI History. *REI.com*. Retrieved July 9, 2018, from http://reihistory.com

SGB Media (2006, March 24). Fromson Joins REI as VP of Gear and Apparel. *SGB Media*. Retrieved July 9, 2018, from https://sgb online.com/fromson-joins-rei-as-vp-of-gear-and-apparel

Solomon, M. (2001, October 29). Tips for New Managers. *ComputerWorld*. Retrieved July 9, 2018, from http://www.computerworld.com/article/2585028/it-skills-training/tips--for-new--managers.html

Valacich, J., and George, J. F., (2017). *Modern Systems Analysis and Design* (8th ed.). Boston: Pearson.

Valacich, J., and Schneider, C. (2018). *Information Systems Today: Managing in the Digital World* (8th ed.). Boston: Pearson.

von Briel, F., Schneider, C., and Lowry, P. B. (2018). Absorbing Knowledge from and with External Partners: The Role of Social Integration Mechanisms. *Decision Sciences Journal*. https://doi.org/10.1111/deci.12314

CHAPTER 12

Managing Project Control and Closure

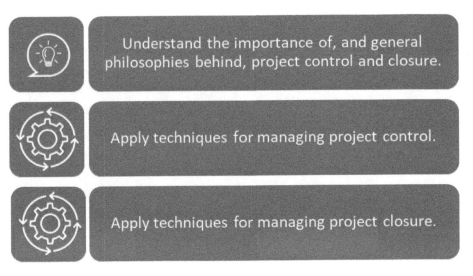

Figure 12.1 Chapter 12 learning objectives

Opening Case: Poor Project Control Derailing Projects

Today, citizens and companies in various countries and regions can use self-service portals to interact with government agencies, allowing them to save significant amounts of time and money. In Australia, apprentices and companies providing training were hoping to be able to use the "Australian apprentice management system" (AAMS), a new self-service portal that would replace the existing system that—after being in operation for sixteen years—had reached the end of its useful life. Not only was the new AUS$20 million system expected to make the lives of apprentices and training companies easier; it was also expected to save government departments close to AUS$50 million, as the need to handle

paper-based forms would be eliminated.

After the completion of a tender process in 2014, Australia's Department of Education and Training awarded the contract to NEC in May 2015, with a scheduled go-live date in July 2016. However, the system turned out to be highly complex due to the need to interface with various other governmental systems at the federal, state, and territory levels. After a series of significant delays, it was found that the new system would not meet current and future needs, and the Department of Education and Training decided to terminate the project in mid-2018.

What went wrong? One of the main reasons the AAMS project failed was the lack of control during

416

execution. An independent audit by consulting firm PwC revealed a number of problems related to project governance and control, contract management, and stakeholder management. First, from the outset, the project was doomed to fail, as there was no involvement of end users when the business case and request for tender were developed. This failure to review the requirements continued throughout the project, with project management failing to continuously review the objectives, the envisioned project benefits, and the end users' needs. Whereas these issues had been raised in early 2017, there had been no change in practices to effectively address the issues. Likewise, project management failed to thoroughly review the impacts of various scope changes, which—in total—amounted to more than AUS$1 million in extra costs as well as significant delays. Other problems included insufficient vendor management and a lack of clear performance milestones. Whereas almost all of the project budget had already been spent, the new system was deemed beyond repair, and the various unresolved problems eventually contributed to the cancellation of the project.

Based on: Hendry (2017; 2018).

Introduction

Throughout this textbook, we have discussed most of the concepts and techniques for initiating, planning, and executing a project successfully. Possibly the most important aspect to consider for ensuring project management success is project control, as indicated in the opening case. After all, how successful can a project be if once the planning is finished you sit back and wait for the tasks to be completed? What happens if a critical task takes two weeks longer to complete than planned? How do you know if costs are running unexpectedly high? Could issues arise that affect the quality of the product you are producing or the risks associated with the project? Are you even aware of these potential problems? Project control is an important element in the overall success of a project because it allows managers to identify and deal with issues that arise and promotes flexibility within the plan to allow for inevitable difficulties.

Given the overarching role that project control plays in project management, project control techniques span all preceding project life cycle phases and overlap many of the project management knowledge areas already discussed in this book. We will explore how control can be exerted over the various project phases and describe specific techniques and tools that successful project managers use to control projects and ensure their successful completion (see Figure 12.2).

In addition to project control, another important concept that successful project managers embrace is project closure. Think back to your freshman year. After completing your first classes, you undoubtedly had learned some lessons that you continue to use today in your academic career. Once your finals were over, that wasn't technically the end of your classes. Your instructors "signed off" on your completion of the courses by giving you a final grade. Just as you learned lessons and received confirmation that your efforts were sufficient to pass those classes, successful project managers seek verification from the project stakeholders that they have successfully completed all the deliverables. If problems arise, project managers document them to enable the project team to reflect on them and apply any lessons learned to reduce the likelihood of project failures in the future. We will present the elements and techniques of project closure that help ensure the success of the current project and provide valuable information for future projects.

What Is Project Control?

Project control is the process of monitoring and measuring project progress and influencing the project plan to account for any discrepancies between planned progress and actual progress. Project control allows a project manager to keep tabs on the progress

Project control
The process of monitoring and measuring project progress and influencing the plan to account for any discrepancies between planned progress and actual progress.

of the various tasks, identify problems, solve problems, and make changes to the plan based on any problems and their solutions.

For instance, consider a project manager who requires a series of weekly status reports from each project team member. In the course of reviewing these reports, the project manager realizes that one of the more critical project team members is repeatedly late with deliverables. Considering the importance of that team member's role in the project, the project manager now has valuable information for making decisions about this unproductive team member. Does the person need a different form of incentive or perhaps more task support? Should the person be replaced? Armed with sufficient information, the successful project manager can now make an appropriate decision. Sometimes, independent **project audits** are performed to provide independent assessment of the status of a project and its adherence to standards and plans.

Project audit
A systematic and formal inquiry into a project's expenditures, schedule, and quality of work.

What Is Project Closure?

Project closure involves the final implementation and training related to the project, getting acceptance and signoff on it, and finally archiving the results of the project and lessons learned. For instance, your client has commissioned a new customer relationship management (CRM) software package from you, and you have developed the package to meet your client's specifications. Now you must install the new package at your client's location and train their personnel to use it. Next, you must gain approval from the stakeholders and clients that the delivered product meets their requirements and fulfills the contract. Finally, you archive the materials generated over the course of the project and write an end report that summarizes the project management methods used. This report allows you to document any lessons learned over the course of the project and to record any unresolved issues.

Project closure
Final implementation and training related to the project, acceptance and signoff on the project, and archiving of the project's results and lessons learned.

Closure occurs at the termination of a project or project phase and consists of careful and detailed documentation of the project's results so that all related information reflects the most accurate account of the success or failure of the project. Projects and project activities can conclude with a natural or unnatural termination. A *natural termination* occurs when the requirements of the project or phase have been met—the project or phase has been completed and is a success. An *unnatural termination* occurs when the project is stopped before completion. Several events can cause unnatural termination of a project or phase. For instance, it may be learned that some assumptions that were used to guide the project proved false, that the performance of the system or the development team was somehow inadequate, that the project requirements are no longer relevant or valid in the current business environment, or that the legal environment has changed. The most likely reasons for unnatural termination of a project relate to running out of time or money, or both. In order for future teams to learn from past projects, accurate and complete documentation is required. It is important to note that project closure activities occur throughout the duration of the project. Failure to comprehensively close each phase as it concludes will likely result in the loss of important information; especially for projects that were terminated unnaturally, failure to document the knowledge gained and lessons learned would render the project a complete waste of time. In short, a project or project phase is not complete until it is closed.

Global Implications: Managing Project Control

One of the realities of offshoring is that you cannot just outsource a software development project. The company doing the outsourcing cannot assume that an offshore development team will do better work than its in-house programmers. Software development is a creative and dynamic process that requires constant attention. Throughout the project life cycle, growth plans, changing technology requirements, and differing customer requirements can alter project plans, and therefore, such changes must be managed and controlled properly. There has to be constant engagement between the outsourcing company and the offshore team.

Recently, far more tools have become available for managing offshore projects. The outsourcing company and the offshore company can use these tools for interpersonal collaboration and for sharing software artifacts. At the same time, these tools provide a measure of command and control to the outsourcing company. Most current groupware tools were designed primarily for in-house use, but now new tools are available to the open source software community that allow developers to coordinate and manage their disparate needs, making them particularly suitable for use in offshore software development projects. These tools can be web-based or can be hosted by one of the parties in the outsourcing relationship.

Software-configuration management tools are also very useful in managing offshore projects. These tools keep track of software assets, such as source code, compiled binaries, documentation, and test results. They are very suitable for offshore software development because members of the development team can be widely dispersed and still receive the information, which can be accessed over the web or hosted by either the onshore company or the offshore team. Such tools run on Windows, Mac OS, and Linux workstations.

The final category of tools that is particularly suitable for managing offshore projects includes quality assurance tools. These include static analysis, load testing, and runtime debugging tools that the onshore company can use to verify all externally developed code. Also, the offshore team can use new automated error prevention tools when developing code. Such tools allow error-free code by enforcing coding standards and building testing into the development process.

Based on: Contorer (2017); Zeichick (2004).

The Importance and Philosophies of Project Control and Closure

This section provides an overview of both project control and project closure. We first discuss the importance of project control and provide an example of project control issues. We follow this with a discussion of the philosophies of project control and the levers for exerting control over projects. We then discuss the importance of project closure and provide an example of successful project closure.

Why Is Project Control Important?

Controlling processes (*PMBOK*, 2017) are important factors in all project management knowledge areas: integration, scope, schedule, cost, quality, resource, communications, risk, procurement, and stakeholder management. Considering that control processes occur at every stage of a successful project's life cycle, it is easy to see how important project control is. Again, think back over your college career up to this point. Surely you or a classmate has run into a situation where a course required in your major was already full or unavailable when you tried to register. To keep the status of your project (your degree) on track, you didn't just allow the unavailability of that class to push back the attainment of your goals. Hopefully, you exerted control over your project by enrolling in an alternate class (to keep your number of credits above a certain level), or you approached the instructor of that course to arrange for enrollment under special circumstances, or you even made changes to your existing plan by deciding to take the class during the summer session. As you can see, successful outcomes of any project require control at every stage of the project.

Example of Project Control Problems

One specific example of a project that had problems as a result of ineffective control was the Denver International Airport (DIA) Computerized Baggage Handling System (CBHS). In 1989, the construction of DIA had been through almost a decade of planning and was finally transitioning into the execution stage. During the construction of the airport, each airline was responsible for developing and building its own baggage-handling system. United Airlines had planned on making DIA its major hub, so it commissioned construction of a complex, technologically advanced baggage-handling system. Recognizing the utility of such an advanced baggage-handling system, the DIA project managers decided to mirror this effort and develop an airport-wide system similar to United's. The problem was that when DIA made this decision, the other airlines had already begun to plan their own individual baggage-handling systems. In a sense, a change request had occurred at two levels: First, each airline was requested to change the specifics of its own baggage-handling project. In addition, DIA as a whole was now implementing a change for the baggage-handling capabilities of the entire airport. Both changes endangered the timely completion of the airport.

After developing specifications for an airport-wide CBHS and requesting bids from several companies for the new system, airport planners were surprised to find that only three bids were submitted and all three were insufficient. Even the company commissioned by United (BAE Automated Systems Inc.) decided not to bid on the new airport-wide CBHS. Following the unsuccessful request for bids, airport planners and management pressured BAE to develop the airport-wide CBHS despite overwhelming evidence of the difficulties involved. In essence, these new plans were a dramatic change in project scope, and DIA's change management and scope control processes were now threatening the potential success of the system.

Considering the difficulty of developing the system under such time pressure, BAE tried to implement its own scope-control processes. One of these was the use of freeze dates, meaning that changes could not be made to certain components of the baggage-handling system after a specified date. These control techniques, had they been followed, might have allowed BAE to complete the airport-wide CBHS, but several events over the next several months ensured the project's failure. The chief airport engineer and main champion for the airport-wide system, Walter Slinger, died six months after the contract to build the system had been awarded to BAE. Prior to Slinger's death, reasonably tight controls were being enforced to try to make the project a success. However, soon after Slinger's passing, airlines began requesting changes to the system design, and these changes, which were frequently approved, caused delays that mounted until the opening of the airport was delayed. Rather than opening in October 1993, as originally planned, the airport finally opened in late February 1995, a delay of sixteen months. Worse, the airport was close to US$2 billion over budget. While many other factors contributed to the DIA CBHS failure, lack of project control on the part of both DIA and BAE can be seen as a major contributor to the cost overruns and delays.

A graphic example of problems with this project happened in April 1994. The City of Denver invited the press to observe BAE's test of the system. The press watched as baggage was thrown from the telecars transporting it. Reporters saw clothing and personal items from some of the seven thousand bags lying on the ground under the telecar tracks. Clearly, initial tests conducted prior to the press event should have been part of the project control process.

BAE's original contract with United Airlines had been frozen to allow BAE to work for DIA rather than only for United. The failure of the airport-wide system meant that United's originally planned CBHS had been sacrificed as well, and United was forced to use a very scaled-down version of the CBHS and only for outgoing baggage. The remaining airlines went back to the labor-intensive motorized carts seen at most other airports (Mähring, Holmström, Keil, and Montealegre, 2004). All in all, changes to the DIA project were not managed effectively.

Philosophies of Controlling Projects

Just as management styles differ, project managers also subscribe to different philosophies of project control. A **philosophy of project control** refers, in a sense, to the management style the manager employs in following a plan and dealing with problems or changes that arise. Two distinctly different approaches are the **dogmatic philosophy** and the **laid-back philosophy**. As the names imply, a manager who subscribes to a dogmatic philosophy has little or no tolerance for deviation from the original plan and may manage autocratically to maintain adherence to the plan. At the other end of the spectrum, a manager who subscribes to the laid-back philosophy may simply embrace the multiple changes or problems that arise. A more likely scenario is for a manager to embrace a philosophy somewhere between these two extremes, which might be thought of as a **pragmatic philosophy**.

Each of these philosophies might be appropriate in a given situation. One common determinant for the most appropriate project control philosophy is the size of the project. At the extreme end, consider studying for a pop quiz. It is likely that you engage in little formalized planning; rather than developing a work breakdown structure, producing a network diagram that sequences the tasks, and the like, you probably will look over the course notes and skim through the textbook. You probably do not track and document deviations from this very informal plan, nor will you identify these as potential problem areas. Finally, you are unlikely to produce formal documents related to the closure of this project. This does not mean that this type of planning is inappropriate for this type of project. In this case, the team is small (one person), the project has very limited scope (reviewing one chapter), and the downside risks of not optimizing on the project may be limited (because the pop quiz is worth only a few points). For this relatively small project, the laid-back philosophy you have taken is more than adequate—in fact, preferred—because it allows you to focus on reviewing the material rather than *planning* how to review the material and so forth.

Contrast the student reviewing for the quiz with the DIA CBHS project. This was a very large project with high stakes, involving many large airlines and national stakeholders. From the beginning, the chief engineer adopted a dogmatic philosophy, and while he was sometimes controversial, he was also known as a project manager who ensured that projects were well controlled and successful. After his death, his replacement, Gail Edmond, managed using a more laid-back style. Whether a function of the authority vested in her by the City of Denver or of her personal style, following Slinger's death, the airlines began requesting significant changes to the system that, under the original plan, should not have been allowed after the specified freeze dates (Mähring et al., 2004).

Levers for Controlling Projects

In addition to the philosophy of project control employed, the project manager also needs to exert control. Before we discuss specific formalized project control techniques, let's first examine several levers that successful managers use to exert control over projects, including communication, participation, analysis and action, and commitment.

Philosophy of project control
The management style the manager employs in following a plan and dealing with problems or changes in the plan.

Dogmatic philosophy
A philosophy of project control that emphasizes strict adherence to the project plan, with little tolerance for deviations.

Laid-back philosophy
A philosophy of project control that allows for project problems or change issues to be dealt with as they arise, on an ad hoc basis.

Pragmatic philosophy
A compromise between the dogmatic and laid-back philosophies that sticks to a plan but is flexible enough to allow for changes.

Communication

Perhaps the most important aspect of successful project management is the efficient flow of information. In this respect, successful communication is *required* to successfully control a project. Consider the difficulty of controlling a project if you don't implement your control techniques because your ability to communicate with team members is hampered or nonexistent. How will your software engineers know that they need to crash a task if you don't have effective ways for communicating with them? Conversely, how will you know whether a task is on track or needs to be crashed if the team members responsible for that task do not communicate with you? Another communication issue is the quality of the communication. Even if project team members do communicate with you, what happens if their communications are ambiguous or are not focused on the appropriate issues? Communication for communication's sake is not effective. Project communication must be timely, focused, directed at the correct person, and thorough enough to effectively accomplish the goal.

Ethical Dilemma: To Blow the Whistle or Not?

Performance reporting is an important tool in project control. It involves collecting and reviewing information about project status to take any corrective actions that might be needed to bring the project in conformance to the plan. However, evidence suggests that both employees and outside contractors sometimes withhold unwelcome but important information concerning projects and their status. Consequently, information about problems may never reach the higher levels of the organizational hierarchy, and decision makers who have the necessary authority cannot take any corrective actions to change the direction of the project.

Communicating bad news up the hierarchy, or "blowing the whistle," can be extremely difficult in organizations. Employees often choose not to blow the whistle because of the personal risks involved. In most organizations, whistle blowing is seen as an "illegitimate" behavior, so these employees face the fear of being fired because they will be blamed for the negative consequences of unwelcome information.

Consequently, they withhold the information, a situation known as the mum effect. Sometimes when employees do choose to blow the whistle, upper management ignores the information. This is known as the deaf effect, where there is reluctance to hear the whistle.

The conditions for effective whistle blowing vary across different organizations. Organizations should strive to become "healthy" by creating an environment where employees are not afraid to communicate bad news. At the same time, the feedback gathered from these employees should be used effectively to change the direction of the project, if necessary. Large organizations with established and legitimate audit staffs typically have a healthy climate for whistle blowing. Another way to promote a healthy climate is to outsource project audits, essentially having a third-party from outside the organization responsible for reporting on a project's status—reducing the political consequences of whistle blowing.

Discussion Questions

1. What type of organizational culture might "inhibit" whistle blowing?
2. What should a project manager do to encourage his project team's willingness to report project problems?

Based on: Keil and Robey (2001); McLannahan (2017).

Participation

Obviously, you expect participation from your team members, and in some cases, you will encounter team members who excel and participate with energy and enthusiasm. However, you will also encounter team members who prefer to go with the flow and not offer suggestions or participate beyond the most basic requirements. These team members need to be encouraged to participate, to offer opinions, and to take responsibility when problems arise. The importance of project team participation, as well as the participation of all project stakeholders, is emphasized in the introductory chapters of this textbook, which are focused on managing project communications and managing project teams. Critical topics in these chapters related to the relationship between participation and project control include project team selection, motivation, and conflict management, to name a few.

Analysis and Action

The ability to analyze situations is also an important lever for exerting control. After all, how effective will your controlling process be if you haven't properly analyzed the problem you happen to be dealing with? Analysis is important for taking the most appropriate course of action to resolve the problem or, at the very least, for understanding the situation in such a way as to minimize further problems that may arise. If action is required, taking that action in a timely and decisive fashion is crucial. In fact, the longer a problem persists, the more costly and difficult it will be to resolve. For this reason, leadership—as well as the topics related to project-related decision-making—are also critically important. In a project where communication is encouraged and effective, participation is required and embraced, and analysis is conducted regularly and accurately, appropriate actions leading to project success should occur naturally.

Commitment

A final lever that project managers use to assist with project control relates to gaining commitment from project stakeholders, including other project team members. By encouraging commitment to the goals of the project, schedule, and project management concepts, team members will feel more responsible for meeting such goals, following and keeping up with the schedule, and following project management concepts. Team members who are committed should feel a greater responsibility and accountability for their role in the project. The project manager's ability to gain the commitment of team members and other stakeholders is related to leadership ability and communication style, and to the ability to influence project team members (topics covered in Chapters 3 and 4).

Now that we have discussed the importance of project control, project control philosophies, and levers for exerting project control, let us turn to the importance of project closure before we begin examining techniques for controlling and closing projects.

Why Is Project Closure Important?

Project closure may seem to be a noncritical step, but successful project managers fully embrace the closure process when finishing a project. It may seem obvious that the handover of the project needs to occur for the project to end, but what might happen if the handover is inadequate? Part of the handover procedure includes training the end users and other organizational members on the use of the new product. If that step is glossed over, all of the project team's hard work may be worthless. Hence, proper training and adequate installation and support for an appropriate period of time following the handover are required to ensure that the client organization can adequately implement its new system or product. In addition, formal signed-off closure helps prevent a project from going on and on without ever truly being finished. Another issue to consider during the closure process is the documentation and archiving of the project management methods used. As a project team member or manager, you can expect to take part in future projects. It is likely that in these future projects, you will encounter issues and problems similar to those you encountered during the current project. Two years from now, you might face a problem like one you faced on the current project, but after two years, it may be difficult to remember how you dealt with the problem originally. Furthermore, your approach to the problem might have been ineffective, and in this case, the lesson you learned was not to address that problem in the same manner if it came up again. While we all think that we will surely remember the details of such problems, the reality is that most project managers are constantly juggling many balls; thus keeping documentation on lessons learned helps prevent you from repeating mistakes, allows you to concentrate on other issues, and finally, provides your organization with knowledge transfer on how to approach such issues in the future. By not following through with these closure procedures, you set yourself up to repeat mistakes and produce products that are insufficient for the needs of the client. Further, good project closure activities allow you to better assess whether you met client needs and then document how to enhance your success with clients in the future.

In the next section, we present techniques that can be used to control projects with specific examples for implementing these techniques. Following this, the final section will conclude with techniques for managing project closure.

Techniques for Managing Project Control

Project control spans many of the knowledge areas of project management, and therefore, this section of the chapter is rather extensive in order to adequately address all of the control topics identified by *PMBOK*. First, we will introduce the use of standard operating procedures as an overarching project control technique that is applicable to the entire project life cycle. Then, we will briefly review those techniques listed in *PMBOK*'s Project Integration Management section under the titles *Monitor and Control Project Work* and *Perform Integrated Change Control*. Following this, we will turn to a more detailed discussion of control techniques associated with the different project management core areas of knowledge listed in the *PMBOK* Guide. These include *Validate Scope*, *Control Scope*, *Control Schedule*, *Control Costs*, *Control Quality*, *Control Resources*, *Monitor Communications*, *Monitor Risks*, *Control Procurements*, and *Monitor Stakeholder Engagement* (see Figure 12.2).

Standard Operating Procedures

Standard operating procedures
Activities and reporting methods instituted during the course of the project to monitor its progress and to provide reports for project managers and stakeholders.

Project log
A document used to record any items identified during the project.

Standard operating procedures are activities and reporting methods instituted during the course of the project to monitor its progress and to provide reports for project managers and stakeholders. These may include regularly scheduled meetings, logs that are maintained as records of the progress being made, and regularly distributed reports so that managers and stakeholders can keep track of the progress being made. Chapter 4 provided important concepts to keep in mind as you plan for meetings. In previous chapters, you have encountered various **project logs**; a project log is a document used to record any items identified during the project. Common project logs include the assumption log, used to record any assumptions made when estimating costs, resource needs, risks, and so on; the change log, used to document any changes submitted during the project, as well as to document the status of these requested changes; and the issue log, used to document any issues encountered during the project. Many successful project managers also keep personal project logs in the form of notes, voice recordings, or even a journal or diary. Figure 12.3 shows an example of a project log. Regular reporting

Monitoring and Controlling

- Monitor and Control Project Work
- Perform Integrated Change Control
- Validate Scope
- Control Scope
- Control Schedule
- Control Costs
- Control Quality
- Control Resources
- Monitor Communications
- Monitor Risks
- Control Procurements
- Monitor Stakeholder Engagement

Figure 12.2 *PMBOK* (6th ed.) monitoring and controlling processes

is another key technique for controlling a project. Stakeholders like to be kept informed on the status of various parts of the project, project managers like to stay well informed of any problems or issues that come along, and individual team members like to see how their contributions are influencing the status of the entire project. Figure 12.4 shows a progress report template. Likewise, project management software such as Microsoft Project provide various reports to present an overview of the project's current status (see Figure 12.5).

Monitor and Control Project Work

Monitor and Control Project Work
The process of collecting, measuring, and disseminating data related to performance, as well as assessing measurements and trends in order to make any improvements.

The **Monitor and Control Project Work** process includes techniques that project teams should use to monitor and control the various project processes, including initiation, planning, execution, and closure (note that the responsibility for monitoring and controlling can be shared between the project manager and the project management office). Understanding the current status of the project activities as well as forecast states allows one to diagnose the project and understand what corrective actions have been taken or need to be taken to bring the project back on track. As detailed in Figure 12.6, the inputs for this process include the project management plan, various project documents, work performance information, agreements, enterprise environmental factors, and organizational process assets. The project management plan defines how various aspects of the project will be executed, monitored and controlled, and closed. Potentially relevant project documents include cost and schedule forecasts, the milestone list, quality reports, the risk register and risk report, the basis of the various estimates, as well as the assumption and issue logs. Work performance information, derived by comparing work performance data with the relevant components of the project management plan or project documents, indicates the status of the different project activities that need to be completed. Agreements are used when comparing seller performance with the work delivered. Enterprise environmental factors used include the project management information system, the available infrastructure, risk thresholds of the stakeholders, as well as standards and regulations that may need to be met. Finally, organizational process assets include organizational standards and procedures, reporting methods, procedures for financial control, issue management, and defect management, as well as organizational knowledge related to process measurement and other lessons learned.

The primary techniques that can be used for monitoring and controlling project work are various data analysis tools, including alternatives analysis, cost-benefit analysis, earned value analysis, root cause analysis, trend analysis, and variance analysis. You have already encountered some of these techniques; we will discuss others in more detail in later sections. Further, expert judgment, which has been discussed in prior chapters, relies on skilled and experienced personnel to make recommendations related to monitoring and controlling project work. Finally, important techniques include meetings and decision-making, to update stakeholders on the status or agree on necessary adjustments.

Project Log: Human Resource Intranet Project

Table of contents

1.0 Statement of Purpose

The purpose of this document is to keep an ongoing record of the progress on the project. This document includes (a) the date when progress on the project was monitored and (b) a list of the different events that happened on that date.

2.0 Project Log

Date	Event(s)
<Enter date here>	<Enter events(s) here>
.....	
June 3, 2019	Meeting held between client (HR Department) and IS Department. An initial project scope statement was devised, which was to be expanded on by the project manager.
June 6, 2019	Project team members selected.
June 7, 2019	Project team members met and went over project scope, developing the scope statement in more detail for client approval.
June 14, 2019	Meeting between project manager and client on the amended scope statement.
June 15, 2019	Stakeholder list and communication plan generated
<Add rows as necessary>	

Figure 12.3 Sample project log

Forecasts
Estimates or predictions of conditions or events in the project's future.

Finally, the outputs from the *Monitor and Control Project Work* process include work performance reports (such as status reports of progress reports, discussed in Chapter 4), change requests, updates to the project management plan, or updates to project documents, such as cost and schedule forecasts, the issue log, the risk register, as well as the lessons-learned register. **Forecasts** are estimates or predictions of conditions or

---

Project Progress Report

Period: Start date thru end date (Week Number)
Project Manager: Project Manager's Name

Items Completed (this period)
· List items completed this period.

Scheduled Items Not Completed:
· List items/targets missed in this reporting period.

Activities Next Period:
· List scheduled activities for next period.

Issues:
· List any new issues identified this period from the Project Issues Log.
· List any resolved issues this period from the Project Issues Log.

Changes to Schedule:
· Identify any predicted slippage to the schedule.
· List causes of slippage.
· Specify corrective action.

Figure 12.4 Progress report template

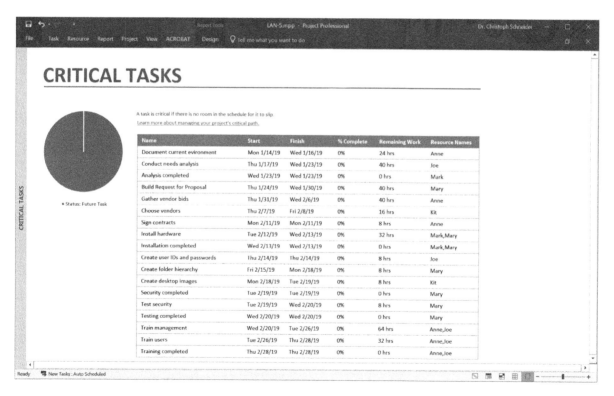

Figure 12.5 Report showing critical tasks in Microsoft Project 2016

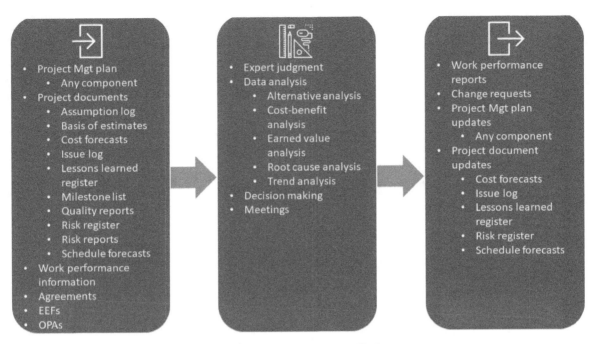

Figure 12.6 The *PMBOK* (6th ed.) *Monitor and Control Project Work* process

Recommended corrective actions Documented recommendations needed to bring future project performance into conformance with the project management plan.

Recommended preventive actions Documented recommendations that minimize the probability of negative consequences to the project.

events in the project's future; they are determined from information and knowledge available at the time of the forecast. While the project is being executed, changes may be requested to reduce the project scope, modify the project cost, revise the project schedule, and so on. Thus change requests, resulting from the need to bring the project back on track or adjust scope, quality, schedule, or cost baselines include recommended corrective actions, recommended preventive actions, and recommended defect repair, and requested changes. **Recommended corrective actions** are documented recommendations needed to bring future project performance into conformance with the project management plan. For example, corrective action will need to be taken when the project manager realizes that activities on the critical path will not be completed on time. **Recommended preventive actions** are documented recommendations that minimize the probability of negative consequences to the project. For example, Figure 12.7 shows the corrective actions recommended by the Government Accountability Office (GAO) to make sure an ERP project in the Department of Defense (DOD) stayed on target.

Tips from the Pros: Some Managerial and Financial Tools to Help with Project Control

Project control ensures that all stakeholders work together to achieve the project objectives and that the project progresses in line with the plan established in the planning stage. The steps in project control include setting performance standards, monitoring current performance, and taking any corrective actions necessary when there are any deviations. This is known as the *checks-and-balances approach*. Several managerial and financial tools are available to help with this process. Managerial tools include

1. *Feasibility analysis.* This analysis helps determine whether the project is feasible from organizational, financial, political, and technological perspectives. More importantly, it establishes how the project should be done.

2. *Schedule monitoring.* Activities can be classified as critical and noncritical. A critical activity must be completed on schedule, whereas a noncritical activity has some slack, which means that it can be delayed. During schedule

monitoring, the project manager ensures that the critical activities are completed as scheduled while still keeping an eye on the noncritical activities.

3. *The establishment of a steering committee.* This committee includes senior managers who represent users and general management, as well as the director of the IT function or the CIO. The purpose of this committee is to monitor the project's performance and ensure that the project deliverables are according to standard. In addition, this committee can also help resolve conflicts—for example, in disputes of resources or project scope.

4. *System development life cycle (SDLC) standards.* The project is broken into phases, with people assigned to document each phase and authorize transition to the next phase. The life cycle can, therefore, be used as a checklist, enabling top management to trace progress on a project at any given time.

5. *Quality assurance.* General management and the project steering committee should evaluate the project management process and the system being developed in terms of quality measurements.

6. *Project management tools.* These tools help in the scheduling, control, and communication of project activities.

7. *The liaison officer.* This person acts as the liaison between the users and the various functions in the IT department, coordinating all project-related activities, communicating requests from end users to IT, and reporting the project status to the end users. With the help of the liaison officer, the project manager can improve control over the project because the liaison officer gives a clear and reliable account of the project's status.

Financial tools include

1. *Continuous cost/benefit analysis.* The investments in the project should be financially justifiable. Performing a cost/benefit analysis periodically ensures that the benefits the project will produce outweigh its cost.

2. *Project budgeting.* A detailed project budget should be developed, including expenses for components such as human resources, hardware, and software at various stages.

3. *Budget deviation analysis.* By comparing the actual performance with the budget, general management and the project manager can detect any major deviations from the planned budget and correct them before such deviations lead to any major consequences.

Based on: Ahituv, Zviran, and Glezer (1999); Alexander (2017).

GAO's recommended corrective actions for the Navy's ERP implementation.

1. Develop and implement the quantitative metrics needed to evaluate project performance and risks and use the metrics to assess progress and compliance with disciplined processes.

2. Establish an independent verification and validation (IV & V) function and direct that all IV & V reports be provided to Navy management and the appropriate DOD investment review board.

3. Institute semiannual reviews of the program.

Figure 12.7 Recommended corrective actions for the U.S. Navy's ERP implementation. *Adapted from:* http://ww.gao.gov/new.items/d05858.pdf.

Perform Integrated Change Control

Perform Integrated Change Control The process of identifying, evaluating, and managing changes that occur from project initiation through project closure.

Perform Integrated Change Control involves the identification, evaluation, and management of changes that occur from project initiation through project closure. Figure 12.8 provides a summary of the inputs, tools and techniques, and outputs associated with integrated change control. As any changes may have far-reaching impacts on various aspects of the overall project, all requested changes need to be formally documented and reviewed, before making the decision to approve, defer, or reject the change request following the established change management procedures. Change requests can arise as outputs from the *Monitor and Control Project Work* process, as well as from various other processes. In addition to the change requests, important inputs to this process include the project management plan, different project documents, work performance reports, enterprise environmental factors, and organizational process assets. The project management plan (introduced in Chapter 5) outlines the change management plan and the configuration management plan and provides the cost, schedule, and scope baselines necessary to identify and control changes. Project documents used in this process include the basis of estimates, the requirements traceability matrix, as well as the risk report. As discussed previously, work performance data is an indication of the status of the different activities required to complete the project. Requested changes are often identified when the project is executed, and these need to be documented and managed. Recommended preventive actions, corrective actions, and defect repair have been discussed previously as the outputs of the *Monitor and Control Project Work* process. Enterprise environmental factors used include legal restrictions, various standards or regulatory requirements, as well as organizational governance frameworks and contracting and purchasing constraints. Finally, organizational process assets include the configuration management knowledge base, as well as procedures related to change control.

Change control system A formal, documented process that describes the procedures by which the project and product scope can be changed.

Among the tools used during this process, change control tools take a central role. Change management tools, manual or automated, are used to identify, document, decide on, and track changes. A **change control system** is a formal, documented process that describes the procedures for changing the project scope and product scope. Although we have introduced the concept of a change control system here in the scope control section, the term *change control system* is a generic term that includes a systematic process or system that the project team uses to handle changes to a variety of project aspects. Additional examples include change control systems focused on controlling schedules or costs. These change control systems can be implemented as flowcharts, as in Figure 12.9, or they can be a checklist of items that must be addressed or satisfied before the change can be instituted.

Configuration management system A scope control technique that ensures that the requested changes to the project and product scope are thoroughly considered and documented before being implemented.

Likewise, configuration management tools allow for identifying configuration items, recording the status of the configuration items, and allow for verifying and auditing the configuration. A **configuration management system** provides guidelines that ensure that the requested changes to the project and product scope are thoroughly considered and documented before being implemented. Similar to the change control system illustrated in Figure 12.9, a configuration management system can be represented in the form of a flowchart.

In software development, version control software such as the Concurrent Version System (CVS), Apache Subversion (SVN), or Git are frequently used for these purposes. In assessing the impact of changes and deciding on the appropriate action, expert judgment and meetings are used, along with techniques such as alternatives analysis and cost-benefit analysis. Decisions on the change requests can then be made using multicriteria decision analysis, voting, or autocratic decision-making.

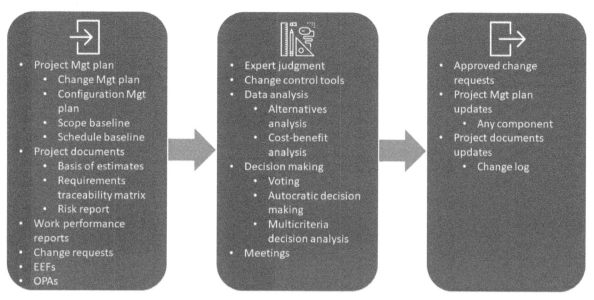

Figure 12.8 The *PMBOK* (6th ed.) *Perform Integrated Change Control* process

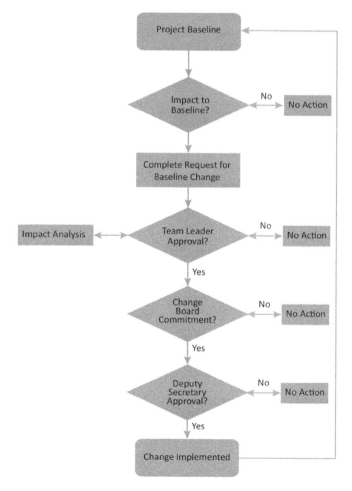

Figure 12.9 Change control system example

Approved change requests
Documented and authorized changes that are scheduled for implementation by the project team.

Approved corrective actions
Documented and authorized guidelines necessary to bring future project performance in conformance with the project management plan.

Approved preventive actions
Documented and authorized guidelines intended to reduce the probability of negative consequences to the project due to identified risks.

Approved defect repair
Documented and authorized actions that are necessary to correct defects in the project deliverables.

Rejected change requests
Requested changes that were not chosen for implementation.

Outputs from the integrated change control process are approved change requests, updates to the project management plan, and updates to the change log. **Approved change requests** are the documented and authorized changes that are scheduled for implementation by the project team (see Figure 12.10). These can take the form of **approved corrective actions**, which are documented and authorized guidelines necessary to bring future project performance in conformance to the project management plan, and **approved preventive actions**, which are those that are intended to reduce the probability of negative consequences to the project due to identified risks. An **approved defect repair** is any documented and authorized action that is needed to correct defects in project deliverables. Alternatively, changes can be deferred or rejected. **Rejected change requests** are those changes that have not been scheduled for implementation.

We now turn our attention to those project control techniques that are specific to the different project management core areas of knowledge. These processes include *Validate Scope, Control Scope, Control Schedule, Control Costs, Control Quality, Control Resources, Monitor Communications, Monitor Risks, Control Procurements,* and *Monitor Stakeholder Engagement.*

Validate Scope

Defined in Chapter 5, *Validate Scope* is the process of obtaining the project stakeholders' formal acceptance of a project's deliverables. The primary input into this process is the verified deliverables (i.e., deliverables that have passed the quality control process) and work performance data, in addition to the scope management plan, requirements management plan, and scope baseline; further, inputs include quality reports, the requirements documentation and traceability matrix, quality reports, and lessons-learned register. The deliverables are then inspected based on the requirements and specified acceptance criteria, before a decision is made (using voting, if needed) on the acceptance of the deliverable. The primary output is accepted deliverables, as well

---

2.0 Change Request Log: HR Intranet Project

No	Description	Requestor Name	Request Date	Request type	Urgency	Assigned To	Assigned Date	Status	Close Date
1	Change regarding project scope – additional linkages to employee salary information with appropriate levels of security	John Allen	8/15/19	Scope	High	Bob Doe	8/16/19	In-Progress	<pending>
2	New layout of homepage requested by client to include additional menu items on top of screen	Sue King	8/28/19	Scope	Moderate	Lynn Talbot	8/30/19	In-Progress	<pending>
	....								
	<add rows as necessary>								

Figure 12.10 Approved change request form

as work performance information, change requests, and update to project documents, including the requirements documentation, requirements traceability matrix, and the lessons-learned register.

Control Scope

As defined in Chapter 5, *Control Scope* is a formal process for assuring that only agreed-upon changes are made to the project's scope. Figure 12.11 depicts a summary of the inputs, tools and techniques, and outputs associated with scope control. Inputs to the *Control Scope* process include different parts of the project management plan, project documents, work performance data, and organizational process assets. Relevant parts of the project management plan include the scope baseline, scope management plan, the requirements management plan, change management plan, and configuration management plan, in addition to the performance measurement baseline. The scope management plan is a document that describes how the project scope is defined, documented, verified, managed, and controlled during the project life cycle. Project documents include the requirements documentation and the requirements traceability matrix, as well as the lessons-learned register. Work performance data includes data on change requests and deliverables, such as how many change requests were received and/or approved. Relevant organizational process assets are monitoring and reporting methods, as well as policies, procedures, and guidelines related to scope control.

Variance analysis
Techniques used to evaluate differences between planned baselines and actual performance.

To transform these inputs into outputs, project managers analyze data using variance and trend analysis. **Variance analysis** is an umbrella term referring to a set of techniques that can be used to determine the status of the various project management areas in order to evaluate the difference between the planned baselines and the actual results, and to identify and correct any problems causing unacceptable variances. Within each control process, a variety of techniques can be utilized to conduct variance analyses

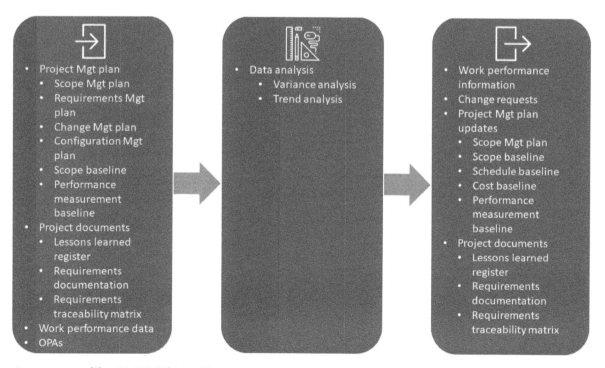

Figure 12.11 The *PMBOK* (6th ed.) *Control Scope* process

(see Figure 12.12). As an example, scope variance analysis involves identifying the cause of variance relative to the project baseline and determining whether any corrective action is needed. Scope variance analysis draws upon variance analyses done in other core project areas, such as project quality, costs, and schedule. Scope reporting specifically refers to the process of periodically ascertaining and documenting the status of cost, schedule, and technical (quality) performance. Trend analysis is used to monitor performance over time, so as to identify any trends that may signal potential problems. You will learn how features within Microsoft Project can be used to aid in variance analysis later in this chapter.

Outputs from the scope control process include change requests that will affect the project scope, as well as work performance information that demonstrates the performance of the project as compared with the scope baseline. In addition, outputs include updates to the project management plan—in particular, updates to the scope, schedule, cost, and performance measurement baselines and the scope management plan. Further, outputs include updates to the requirements documentation, the requirements traceability matrix, and the lessons-learned register. If the approved change requests have an effect on the project scope, the historical database of the organizational process assets must be updated with the causes of variances identified during variance analysis, the justification for any corrective action, and any lessons learned during the scope control process.

Many scope control processes can be executed using project management software. As discussed in Chapters 5 and 6, one of the deliverables of the scope management process that is extremely valuable for large projects with many tasks is the work breakdown structure (WBS), which can be created in products such as Microsoft Project (see Figure 12.13).

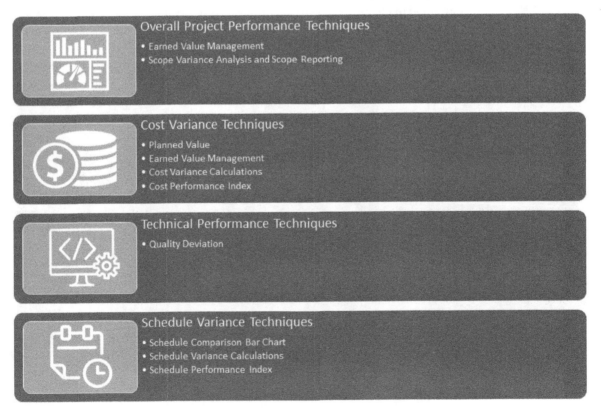

Overall Project Performance Techniques
- Earned Value Management
- Scope Variance Analysis and Scope Reporting

Cost Variance Techniques
- Planned Value
- Earned Value Management
- Cost Variance Calculations
- Cost Performance Index

Technical Performance Techniques
- Quality Deviation

Schedule Variance Techniques
- Schedule Comparison Bar Chart
- Schedule Variance Calculations
- Schedule Performance Index

Figure 12.12   Variance analysis techniques

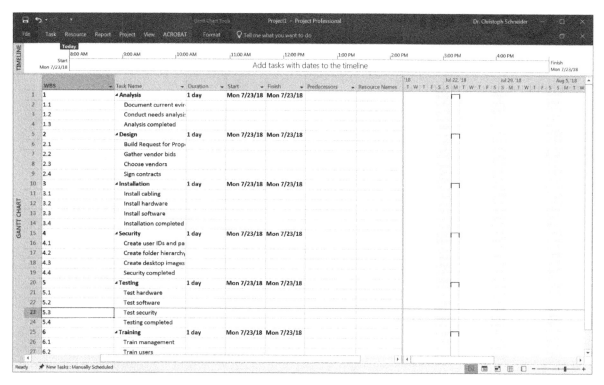

Figure 12.13   WBS created in Microsoft Project 2016

Further, if any of the change requests are approved through the scope control process, it is easy to modify the WBS because it only involves moving or copying and pasting tasks within the already created document.

Common Problems: Recovering Troubled Projects

Variances are likely to occur on any project. In a successful project, variances are acceptable. In contrast, a troubled project is one in which the variances are beyond acceptable tolerances. It is identified by poor performance in terms of time, cost, and quality. The task of the project team is to recover the troubled project and take corrective actions to bring it back in line with the plan.

The first step in the recovery process is to recognize that the project is in trouble. Fortunately, some warning signs assist in this process:

- None of the project team members know when the project will be completed.

- The project deliverables do not meet the set quality standards.

- Team members have to work overtime to complete their parts of the work.

- The project requirements are not stable.

- The stakeholders have lost interest in the project because they believe that it will never be completed.

- The morale of the team is low, and conflicts among team members are rampant.

- The customer is planning to sue the performing organization for not delivering the project.

The next step is to get a detailed assessment regarding the status of the project. The project manager should determine the status of each of the work packages in the work breakdown structure (WBS). This assessment can help the project manager determine whether the project can be recovered or should be terminated.

If the project can be recovered, the final step is to develop the recovery plan. The project manager should determine what corrective actions should be taken to regain control of the project. This involves identifying any repair work needed, any issues to be resolved, and any other outstanding items. Here are some general guidelines that can be used to recover troubled projects:

- When trying to resolve project issues, the project team should focus on analyzing the findings to develop the recovery plan instead of focusing on what happened or who is to blame.

- There are no ready-made recipes or silver-bullet solutions. The project team should work together to develop the recovery plan.

- The project should be recovered to bring it in conformance with the objectives.

- Any work activity listed as "done" or "completed" should only be so categorized if all aspects of the activity are fully completed.

- It is important to be realistic in determining what can or cannot be fixed, and to prioritize the issues to be addressed.

- The project team members should be open-minded and ready to accept any changes.

Based on: Alexander (2018); Sifri (2003).

Control Schedule

As defined in Chapter 7, *Control Schedule* is the process of monitoring project progress as compared to the schedule baseline. Inputs to the *Control Schedule* process include the schedule management plan, schedule baseline, scope baseline, and performance measurement baseline of the project management plan, as well as documents such as the project schedule, project calendars, or resource calendars, schedule data, and the lessons-learned register. Other inputs include work performance data and organizational process assets. Whereas the schedule management plan specifies how the project schedule will be managed and controlled, the different baselines serve as a basis for comparison to determine any deviations. The project schedule is the current version of the schedule, which shows the progress of the project activities up to the current date. Project and resource calendars are important inputs for making schedule forecasts. Work performance data are used to track the project at the activity level, such as tracking which activities have or have not been finished on time. Organizational process assets that can be useful include policies, procedures, guidelines, or tools related to schedule control, as well as methods used for monitoring and reporting progress and deviations.

As detailed in Figure 12.14, the tools and techniques that can be used to convert these inputs into outputs include different data analysis techniques, as well as evaluating the impact of any deviations on the critical path. In trying to bring the schedule back on track, project managers use techniques such as resource optimization, schedule compression, or adjust leads and lags (discussed in Chapter 7). These activities are greatly facilitated by the project management information system, and, in particular, software that is used for scheduling, such as Microsoft Project. Common data analysis techniques used during schedule control include performance reviews, earned value analysis, iteration burndown charts, trend analysis, variance analysis, as well as what-if scenario analysis (discussed earlier). Performance reviews involve describing what the project team has accomplished during a certain period of time and determining the magnitude and criticality of schedule variations. Variance analysis is used to evaluate potential and actual variance on the project schedule. We will discuss trend analysis and earned value analysis in the following section on cost control. You will learn more about iteration burndown charts in the Part III Appendix.

Outputs from the *Control Schedule* process include schedule forecasts, work performance information, change requests (including recommended corrective actions), and updates to the project management plan and project documents. Schedule forecasts are typically based on past performance and future performance, taking into consideration

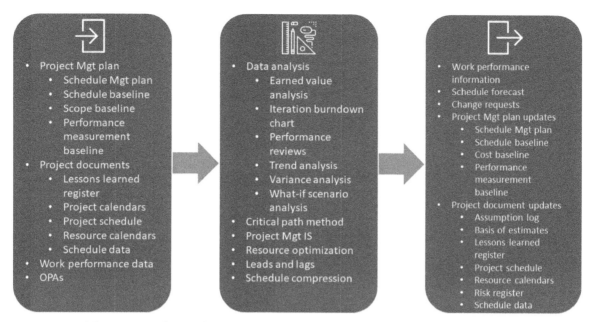

Figure 12.14   The *PMBOK* (6th ed.) *Control Schedule* process

effects of implemented corrective or preventive actions. Work performance information highlights the project's progress as compared to the schedule baseline. Further, various sections of the project management plan might be updated, including the schedule management plan, the schedule baseline, the cost baseline, and the performance measurement plan. The results of the different analyses can lead to new change requests. Recommended corrective actions are the procedures initiated to address schedule performance problems. If the approved change requests have an effect on the project schedule, the historical database of the organizational process assets must be updated with the causes of variances identified, the justification for any corrective action, and any lessons learned during the schedule control process. The approved change requests will impact the project schedule, and as a result, the schedule baseline, as well as cost and performance management baselines, may have to be updated; likewise, this process may result in changes to the schedule management plan. Finally, various project documents are updated, including the project schedule and schedule data, resource calendars, the assumption log, the basis of estimates, and the risk register, in addition to the lessons learned, which include documentation of the causes of variance from the project schedule. Documenting lessons learned can prevent these problems from occurring in similar future projects. This documentation becomes part of the organizational process assets.

A feature of Microsoft Project that is helpful in schedule control is the tracking Gantt chart. After the project schedule has been approved, a Gantt chart can be created based on the information in the approved schedule. As the project progresses, the Gantt chart can be updated with the actual schedule information. The tracking Gantt chart compares planned (the schedule baseline) and actual project schedule information (see Figure 12.15). This chart allows the project team to monitor the progress of individual tasks and the progress of the whole project. As can be seen in Figure 12.15 at the summary level, the analysis and design modules have been completed. The installation module is 52 percent complete, with varying percentages of completion for its individual tasks. If the actual date were, say, February 8, 2019, we might be feeling good about

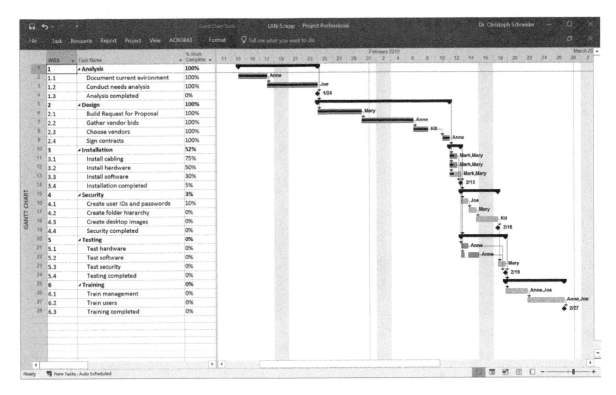

Figure 12.15   Tracking Gantt chart in Microsoft Project 2016

the progress on this project because we are getting portions of tasks done ahead of our baseline schedule. However, if the date were February 20, 2019, we might be concerned that we have yet to complete the installation phase of the project. We can see from the tracking Gantt chart that we are behind with respect to our approved schedule.

Control Costs

Control Costs is the process of monitoring cost performance to ensure that only appropriate changes are included in the modified cost baseline. As shown in Figure 12.16, the inputs to the *Control Costs* process include the project management plan (including the cost management plan, the cost baseline, and the performance measurement baseline), project funding requirements, work performance data, project documents (such as the lessons-learned register), and organizational process assets (such as cost control–related polities and guidelines, as well as tools for cost control and methods for monitoring and reporting). The project management plan components include plans for managing costs and performance. The cost baseline is a time-phased budget that is used to measure and monitor cost performance. An example is presented in Figure 12.17, where the cost baselines for possible alternatives to migrate applications currently hosted in-house to a cloud environment are presented. Funding requirements are determined from the cost baseline, but it is common for funding requirements to exceed the cost baseline by a margin to account for cost overruns. As discussed in Chapter 8, budgetary estimates for the cost baseline can be done top-down or bottom-up. In top-down budgeting, senior management sets spending limits, which allows for greater control over expenses. In bottom-up budgeting, expected costs have the potential to be more accurate, but less

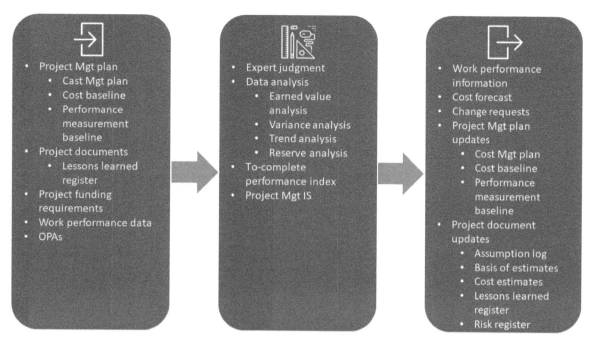

Figure 12.16 The *PMBOK* (6th ed.) *Control Costs* process

incentive is provided to economize. Work performance data is an indication of the status and cost of the different activities required to complete the project.

The *PMBOK* Guide recognizes several tools and techniques to assist in cost control. The primary tools are different data analysis techniques (such as earned value analysis, variance analysis, trend analysis, and reserve analysis); these techniques are assisted by expert judgment and different components of the project management information system. The different data analysis techniques help assess the current status and deviations from the forecast status, determine trends, or use reserve analysis to identify if contingency reserves may be needed, or if they can be freed up for other purposes.

The **earned value analysis (EVA)** technique is a very powerful cost-control method that provides estimates of the likelihood the project will meet schedule and budget requirements. It will be discussed in more detail later in this chapter as a specific technique associated with project cost control.

Using the concepts of earned value analysis, the project manager can perform variance analysis to determine cost and schedule variances, and can determine trends in performance over time, which allows for forecasting. Variance analysis helps the project team assess the magnitude of any variance that may occur during project execution. Large deviations from the planned cost performance should be carefully investigated, and corrective actions should be taken to bring the future cost performance in conformance to the budgeted project cost. Trend analysis is a cost control method for examining project cost performance over time to determine whether performance is improving or deteriorating. Figure 12.18 shows one method for evaluating cost performance over time by graphing the percentage over or under budget across time. Forecasts are estimates or predictions of conditions or events in the project's future that are determined from information and knowledge available at the time they are made. An example might include forecasted changes in pricing or availability of resources needed by the project team. In addition, project managers calculate the to-complete

Earned value analysis (EVA)
A technique that measures project performance over time, and provides a way to forecast future performance based on past performance.

Areas	Program's Optimal ("Desired State") Annual Cost Percentage	Current Costs (Non-Cloud Environment)	Current Percentages	Estimated Cloud Hosting Costs	Estimated Cloud Hosting Percentages	Projected Savings from Migrating to Cloud vs Current Hosting Environment (Includes One-Time Migration Costs)
Consulting Services	85%	$2,062,000	63.9%	$2,091,000	92.1%	($29,000)
Application Development	30%	$1,000,000	31.0%	$1,000,000	44.0%	
Project Management	10%	$250,000	7.7%	$250,000	11.0%	
Security Certification & Accreditation (e.g., Privacy Impact Assessment)	5%	$100,000	3.1%	$100,000	4.4%	
Application Maintenance	30%	$500,000	15.5%	$500,000	22.0%	
Systems Administration	10%	$200,000	6.2%	$75,000	3.3%	
Cloud Environment Management				$50,000	2.2%	
Migration (one-time)				$35,000	1.5%	
Customization (one-time)				$75,000	3.3%	
Travel		$7,000	0.2%	$5,000	0.2%	
Miscellaneous Costs		$5,000	0.2%	$1,000	0.04%	
Hosting Environment	15%	$1,165,000	36.1%	$180,000	7.9%	$985,000
Infrastructure	10%	$1,000,000	31.0%	$50,000	2.2%	
Software Licenses	1%	$100,000	3.1%	$35,000	1.5%	
Software Patches	1%	$25,000	0.8%	$7,000	0.3%	
System or Software Ugrades	1%	$25,000	0.8%	$5,000	0.2%	
Network or Infrastructure Customization (one-time)			0.0%	$75,000	3.3%	
Backup & Recovery	1%	$10,000	0.3%	$5,000	0.2%	
Miscellaneous Costs	1%	$5,000	0.2%	$3,000	0.1%	
Total	100%	$3,227,000	100%	$2,271,000	100%	$956,000

Figure 12.17 Cost baseline for cloud migration in Microsoft Excel 2016. *Based on*: GSA (2016).

performance index, providing an estimate of the required cost performance to complete the remaining work within budget.

As in many of the control techniques listed throughout this chapter, project management software can assist the project team in tracking actual performance against planned performance and in forecasting the effects of any changes on the planned project cost.

Finally, the outputs of the cost control process include work performance information (resulting from the different analysis techniques), cost forecasts, as well as updates to the project management plan, including the cost baseline, the performance management baseline, and the cost management plan; these change requests have to go through the regular change control processes. If any of the change requests are approved, they will affect the cost baseline. Consequently, the cost baseline (as part of the project management plan) needs to be updated to reflect the approved changes. Based on the earned value technique, the work performance information will be reported to the key stakeholders. Similarly, the earned value technique will provide a forecasted completion date as well as the cost at completion. The process of cost control itself can lead to the need for change requests.

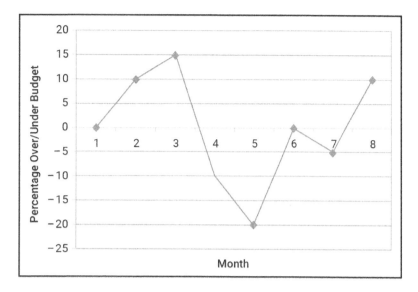

Figure 12.18 Cost performance over time

Earned Value Analysis, Variance Analysis, and Forecasting

The earned value analysis technique incorporates scope, time, and cost data to monitor project performance. Given a cost baseline, the project team can determine how well the project is meeting scope, time, and cost goals by entering actual information and then comparing it to the baseline.

The easiest way to get started with earned value analysis is to break the project into discrete time periods, usually by activities or summary activities from the WBS. Key values are then calculated for each activity. The key terms and their formulas are

- *Planned value* (PV) is the budgeted cost for the work scheduled to be completed on an activity up to a given point in time. Because it is part of the established budget, its value should be known. Planned value is also known as the *budgeted cost of work scheduled* (BCWS).

- *Earned value* (EV) involves the budgeted amount for the work actually completed on the activity during a given time period. This is the product of the planned value and the percentage of work completed on the activity during that time period (*EV = PV × % completed*). Earned value is also known as the *budgeted cost of work performed* (BCWP).

- *Actual cost* (AC) refers to the actual costs associated with work on an activity during a particular time period. It is not calculated but drawn from invoices and other financial records. Actual cost is also known as the *actual cost of work performed* (ACWP).

Table 12.1 provides an example of earned value calculations. Suppose a project included an activity A that took a week to be completed and cost a total of $10,000. The planned value of PV is $10,000. The percentage of work completed on activity A during week 1 is 100 percent. Therefore, the earned value (EV) is $10,000 (100% × $10,000). From Table 12.1 we can see that during week 1, $12,000 was spent on activity A, when the budget had allotted $10,000 for this activity. The actual cost (AC) is therefore $12,000.

Table 12.1 Earned Value Calculations for Activity A over Two Weeks

Activity A	Week 1	Week 2
Earned value (EV)	10,000	10,000
Planned value (PV)	10,000	10,000
Actual cost (AC)	12,000	8,000
Cost variance (CV)	−2,000	2,000
Schedule variance (SV)	0	0
Cost performance index (CPI)	83%	125%
Schedule performance index (SPI)	100%	100%

Using these values, we can now perform variance analysis to determine variances in cost or schedule. The key terms and their formulas are

- *Cost variance* (CV) is the difference between the earned value (EV) and the actual cost (AC), ($CV = EV - AC$). Cost variance is thus a monetary indicator of whether the project has cost more than it should have up to a particular point in time. If EV is greater than the AC, this means the organization has "earned" more value on the project than it has actually cost, and thus the project is currently coming in under budget. If EV is less than AC, the project is costing more than it should.

- *Schedule variance* (SV) is the difference between the scheduled completion of the activity and the actual completion. This is the difference between EV and PV ($SV = EV - PV$). Schedule variance is thus a monetary indicator of whether the project is on time. If EV (a monetary measure of the amount of work that has been completed at this point in the project) is greater than the PV (a monetary measure of the amount of work that *should* have been competed at this point in the project), then SV is positive, indicating that the project is ahead of schedule.

- *Cost performance index* (CPI) is the ratio of EV to AC and is expressed as a percentage $CPI = (EV \div AC) \times 100$. Similar to cost variance, CPI looks at EV and AC—but this time as a ratio—to calculate how efficiently the project is being accomplished from a cost standpoint. A CPI value of 100 percent means the project is progressing as expected in relation to project costs. A CPI value of less than 100 percent (e.g., 80 percent) means that the project is costing more than expected and has been only about 80 percent efficient from a cost perspective. A CPI of greater than 100 percent means the project team is being more efficient than anticipated in relationship to project costs.

- *Schedule performance index* (SPI) is the ratio of EV to PV and is also expressed as a percentage, $SPI = (EV \div PV) \times 100$. Similar to schedule variance, SPI looks at EV and PV—but this time as a ratio—to calculate how efficiently the project is being accomplished from a schedule standpoint. A SPI value of 100 percent means the project is progressing as expected in relation to the project schedule. If the SPI is below 100 percent (e.g., 80 percent), the indication is that the activity (or project as a whole) is behind schedule 20 percent. If the SPI is above 100 percent, the indication is that the activity is ahead of schedule.

In the example, the cost variance is the difference between the earned value (EV) and the actual cost (AC), or −$2,000. A negative CV means that it cost more than planned to perform the work. The schedule variance is the difference between the earned value (EV) and the planned value (PV), which is 0.

The cost performance index (CPI) is the ratio of the EV to the AC, expressed as a percentage, which is 83 percent. The CPI indicates that the activity is over budget. The schedule performance index is the ratio of the EV to the PV expressed as a percentage, which is 100 percent. This indicates that the activity is on schedule. Therefore, from a quick glance at Table 12.1, an experienced project manager could see that after the first week activity A was on track to meet its scheduled completion time (SPI) but was over budget for the first week (CPI). The key to understanding the variances and indexes described is that for variances, negative values indicate possible problems, while for indexes, values below 100 percent indicate possible problems.

To use earned value analysis to determine the status of the entire project (as opposed to just one activity), all project activities that have been fully or partially completed must be analyzed. Depending on the size and scope of the project, the time periods under examination may be days, weeks, or months. Performing a project-level EVM allows you to gauge the overall health of the entire project. Table 12.2 shows an EVM for a ten-week project. From this example, we can see that after six weeks, this particular project is over budget and behind schedule. Knowing that the project is currently behind schedule and over budget allows you to make changes or arrangements to the remaining activities to bring it back to the planned schedule and budget.

EV analysis can also be used for trend analysis and forecasts, allowing managers to determine how critical it is to make changes in an effort to bring schedules and budgets back under control. Estimate at completion (EAC) and estimate to complete (ETC; see Table 12.2) give estimates for how much the completed project will cost and how much money is needed to finish the remaining work. In other words, if no changes are made and the remaining tasks end up being similar to previous tasks in terms of budget and schedule, these two estimates will give you an idea of how much the project will cost.

To compute the estimated cost at completion, the additional piece of information required is the budget at completion (BAC), or the total budgeted cost of the project. To compute the estimate at completion (EAC), the budget at completion (BAC) is divided by the cost performance index (CPI) for the current project status ($EAC = BAC \div CPI$); other formulas may be needed, depending on the project. As an example, if the originally anticipated cost (BAC) is US$100,000 and the project CPI is .80, then the EAC is US$125,000 (i.e., the cost is running over budget). To compute the estimate to complete (ETC), the project manager simply deducts the actual cost (AC) from the EAC. Using this information, the project manager can compute the variance at completion (VAC) by subtracting the estimate at completion from the budget at completion ($VAC = BAC - EAC$) to obtain an estimate of the projected surplus or deficit when the project is completed.

Finally, the project manager can compute the to-complete performance index (TCPI). The TCPI is a measure of the required efficiency so that the project can be completed with the remaining available resources; it is calculated as follows: $TCPI = (BAC - EV) \div (BAC - AC)$. In other words, the TCPI is derived by dividing the remaining work by the remaining funds. If the remaining work is larger than the remaining funds (TCPI > 1), the project will be more difficult to finish; if the remaining funds are larger than the remaining work (TCPI < 1), the project will be easier to finish. The TCPI might be based on the estimate at completion (EAC), rather than the original budget; in this case, the formula is $TCPI = (BAC - EV) \div (EAC - AC)$.

Microsoft Project has built-in variance analysis tools that allow the project manager to determine whether there have been any deviations from the baseline. As the tasks are updated with the actual information as the project progresses, Microsoft Project automatically calculates the variance. The project manager can refer to this information

Table 12.2 Project Level EVM for a Ten-Week Project

	Week 1	Week 2	Week 3	Week 4	Week 5	Week 6	Week 7	Week 8	Week 9	Week 10	Plan	%	EV
Initial meeting with sponsor	16,000										16,000	100	16,000
Draft project requirements		24,000	8,000								32,000	100	32,000
Review with stakeholders			4,000	8,000							12,000	100	12,000
Develop and approve project charter				9,000							9,000	100	9,000
Develop WBS				12,000							12,000	100	12,000
Estimate durations					13,000						13,000	100	13,000
Assign resources					8,000	8,000					16,000	75	12,000
Determine task relationships					8,000						8,000	50	4,000
Enter cost information					16,000						16,000	25	4,000
Review plan with stakeholders							8,000				8,000		
Review off-the-shelf training materials								23,000			23,000		
Negotiate contract for materials								24,000	16,000		40,000		
Develop communications about new training									18,000		18,000		
Create survey to determine needs										24,000	24,000		
Administer survey										12,000	12,000		
Develop list of instructors										6,000	6,000		
Coordinate with facilities to setup classrooms							30,000	30,000			60,000		
Schedule courses										4,000	4,000		
Develop system for signing up for classes										16,000	16,000		

Develop course evaluation form												
Weekly PV	16,000	24,000	12,000	29,000	45,000	8,000	38,000	77,000	34,000	82,000	20,000	20,000
PV or cumulative plan	16,000	40,000	52,000	81,000	126,000	134,000	172,000	249,000	283,000	365,000	365,000	114,000
Weekly AC	17,000	25,000	13,000	30,000	46,000	9,000						
AC or cumulative actual	17,000	42,000	55,000	85,000	131,000	140,000						
Weekly EV	16,000	24,000	12,000	29,000	27,000	6,000						
EV or cumulative EV	16,000	40,000	52,000	81,000	108,000	114,000						
Project EV as of Week 6						114,000						
Project PV as of Week 6						134,000						
Project AC as of Week 6						140,000						
CV = EV – AC						–26,000						
SV = EV – PV						–20,000						
CPI = EV / AC						81.43%						
SVI = EV / PV						85.07%						
EAC						448,246						
ETC						308,246						
VAC						–83,246						
TCPI						1.115						

to determine whether there are any variances to budget or schedule so that corrective actions can be taken to bring the project in conformance to the plans. Figure 12.9 shows how this feature of Microsoft Project can be used to determine the variance in a project schedule.

Control Quality

Control Quality
The process of screening project results to determine whether they conform to relevant quality standards and then identifying means to eliminate causes of unsatisfactory results.

The **Control Quality** process involves screening project results to determine whether they conform to relevant quality standards and then identifying means to eliminate causes of unsatisfactory results. As discussed in Chapter 8 and shown in Figure 12.20, the inputs required for the *Control Quality* process include the quality management plan, quality metrics, test and evaluation documents, organizational process assets and enterprise environmental factors, work performance data, approved change requests, and the deliverables to be tested or evaluated. The quality management plan specifies how quality measures will be implemented during a project (see Figure 12.21). Quality metrics—such as response time for a software application—define specific processes, events, or products, and include an explanation of how their quality will be measured.

Test and evaluation documents, another input for the *Control Quality* process, produced as part of quality planning, are tools (such as quality checklists) used to ensure that a specific set of actions necessary for quality control has been correctly performed (see Figure 12.22 for an abbreviated example of items that might be found on a quality checklist). Organizational process assets include organizational standards, policies, templates, or procedures related to quality or issue reporting; relatedly, enterprise environmental factors include external rules, regulations, or standards, as well as the project management information system. Work performance data includes data about the

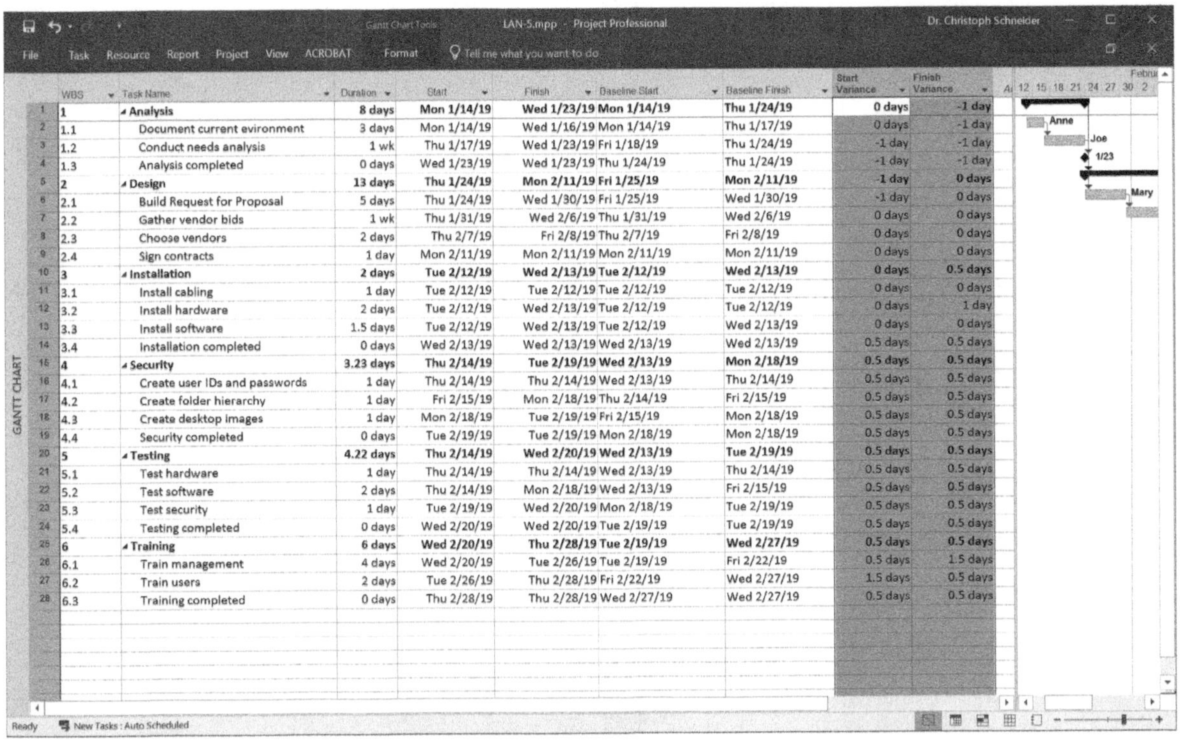

	WBS	Task Name	Duration	Start	Finish	Baseline Start	Baseline Finish	Start Variance	Finish Variance
1	1	**Analysis**	**8 days**	**Mon 1/14/19**	**Wed 1/23/19**	**Mon 1/14/19**	**Thu 1/24/19**	**0 days**	**-1 day**
2	1.1	Document current evironment	3 days	Mon 1/14/19	Wed 1/16/19	Mon 1/14/19	Thu 1/17/19	0 days	-1 day
3	1.2	Conduct needs analysis	1 wk	Thu 1/17/19	Wed 1/23/19	Fri 1/18/19	Thu 1/24/19	-1 day	-1 day
4	1.3	Analysis completed	0 days	Wed 1/23/19	Wed 1/23/19	Thu 1/24/19	Thu 1/24/19	-1 day	-1 day
5	2	**Design**	**13 days**	**Thu 1/24/19**	**Mon 2/11/19**	**Fri 1/25/19**	**Mon 2/11/19**	**-1 day**	**0 days**
6	2.1	Build Request for Proposal	5 days	Thu 1/24/19	Wed 1/30/19	Fri 1/25/19	Wed 1/30/19	-1 day	0 days
7	2.2	Gather vendor bids	1 wk	Thu 1/31/19	Wed 2/6/19	Thu 1/31/19	Wed 2/6/19	0 days	0 days
8	2.3	Choose vendors	2 days	Thu 2/7/19	Fri 2/8/19	Thu 2/7/19	Fri 2/8/19	0 days	0 days
9	2.4	Sign contracts	1 day	Mon 2/11/19	Mon 2/11/19	Mon 2/11/19	Mon 2/11/19	0 days	0 days
10	3	**Installation**	**2 days**	**Tue 2/12/19**	**Wed 2/13/19**	**Tue 2/12/19**	**Wed 2/13/19**	**0 days**	**0.5 days**
11	3.1	Install cabling	1 day	Tue 2/12/19	Tue 2/12/19	Tue 2/12/19	Tue 2/12/19	0 days	0 days
12	3.2	Install hardware	2 days	Tue 2/12/19	Wed 2/13/19	Tue 2/12/19	Tue 2/12/19	0 days	1 day
13	3.3	Install software	1.5 days	Tue 2/12/19	Wed 2/13/19	Tue 2/12/19	Wed 2/13/19	0 days	0 days
14	3.4	Installation completed	0 days	Wed 2/13/19	Wed 2/13/19	Wed 2/13/19	Wed 2/13/19	0.5 days	0.5 days
15	4	**Security**	**3.23 days**	**Thu 2/14/19**	**Tue 2/19/19**	**Wed 2/13/19**	**Mon 2/18/19**	**0.5 days**	**0.5 days**
16	4.1	Create user IDs and passwords	1 day	Thu 2/14/19	Thu 2/14/19	Wed 2/13/19	Thu 2/14/19	0.5 days	0.5 days
17	4.2	Create folder hierarchy	1 day	Fri 2/15/19	Mon 2/18/19	Thu 2/14/19	Fri 2/15/19	0.5 days	0.5 days
18	4.3	Create desktop images	1 day	Mon 2/18/19	Tue 2/19/19	Fri 2/15/19	Mon 2/18/19	0.5 days	0.5 days
19	4.4	Security completed	0 days	Tue 2/19/19	Tue 2/19/19	Mon 2/18/19	Mon 2/18/19	0.5 days	0.5 days
20	5	**Testing**	**4.22 days**	**Thu 2/14/19**	**Wed 2/20/19**	**Wed 2/13/19**	**Tue 2/19/19**	**0.5 days**	**0.5 days**
21	5.1	Test hardware	1 day	Thu 2/14/19	Thu 2/14/19	Wed 2/13/19	Thu 2/14/19	0.5 days	0.5 days
22	5.2	Test software	2 days	Thu 2/14/19	Mon 2/18/19	Wed 2/13/19	Fri 2/15/19	0.5 days	0.5 days
23	5.3	Test security	1 day	Tue 2/19/19	Wed 2/20/19	Mon 2/18/19	Tue 2/19/19	0.5 days	0.5 days
24	5.4	Testing completed	0 days	Wed 2/20/19	Wed 2/20/19	Tue 2/19/19	Tue 2/19/19	0.5 days	0.5 days
25	6	**Training**	**6 days**	**Wed 2/20/19**	**Thu 2/28/19**	**Tue 2/19/19**	**Wed 2/27/19**	**0.5 days**	**0.5 days**
26	6.1	Train management	4 days	Wed 2/20/19	Tue 2/26/19	Tue 2/19/19	Fri 2/22/19	0.5 days	1.5 days
27	6.2	Train users	2 days	Tue 2/26/19	Thu 2/28/19	Fri 2/22/19	Wed 2/27/19	1.5 days	0.5 days
28	6.3	Training completed	0 days	Thu 2/28/19	Thu 2/28/19	Wed 2/27/19	Wed 2/27/19	0.5 days	0.5 days

Figure 12.19 Variance analysis in Microsoft Project 2016

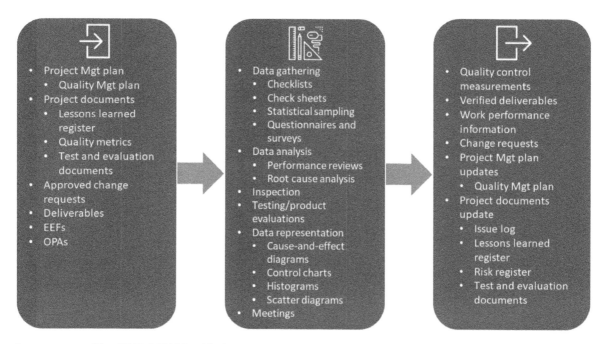

Figure 12.20 The *PMBOK* (6th ed.) *Control Quality* process

Figure 12.21 Quality management plan table of contents

Quality Checklist				
Requirement	Yes	No	N/A	Comments/Remarks
Is there a well-developed set of procedures and metrics that have been identified and agreed upon for the project?				
Is there is an established and accessible knowledge base for the acceptable procedures and metrics (for example, project plan, test plan and training plan)				
Have the project team members been trained (according to the training plan) so as to adhere to the quality requirements mentioned in the above knowledge base?				
Is there an individual who is entrusted with the authority of verifying and enforcing the project quality?				
Are the procedures and metrics mentioned in the plans being followed?				
Are proper measurement techniques being used to gauge the quality of the project?				
Do the deliverables meet the project requirements?				
Are any problems recognized in the testing phase being properly documented?				
Are corrective actions being taken for identified problems in the testing phase?				
Are any changes to the test plan and the project plan (as identified in the testing phase) being properly incorporated?				

Figure 12.22   Quality checklist example

outputs of activities, or about the activities themselves. An approved change request impacts project quality because it requires a modification of the quality management plan. A deliverable is any unique and verifiable product of a process that is defined in the project management plan.

The tools and techniques recommended for *PMBOK*'s *Control Quality* process include data gathering, analysis, and representation techniques, as well as inspection and testing and meetings.

Inspection is used to verify that a deliverable meets applicable standards, whereas testing is used to find defects; both inspection and testing are supported by the use of checklists and checksheets that allow for performing tests in a structured way. Inspection and testing should be performed throughout the project. Project managers can then perform performance reviews and data analyses (such as root cause analysis) based the information presented in various diagrams, such as cause-and-effect (also called *fishbone* or *Ishikawa*) diagrams, control charts, Pareto charts, flowcharts, histograms, run charts, or scatter diagrams. Typically, these activities are accompanied by meetings to review how far approved change requests were implemented and to discuss possible lessons learned. These tools and techniques were also introduced in Chapter 8, but we discuss them in some detail here as well.

In information systems projects, inspection and testing can be conducted with or without code execution. For example, the code can be manually compared to lists of frequent errors, or automated tools can be used for syntax checking. Likewise, the code can be executed and testers can perform walk-throughs or desk checking, or automated tools can be used for unit, integration, or system testing. Further, the final product will undergo alpha testing, where simulated data are used to test system recovery, security, performance, and behavior under stress, and beta testing, where real users test the system using live data. As it is often inefficient or infeasible to test every single deliverable, statistical sampling is used to identify samples for inspection or testing purposes. Statistical sampling involves selecting a random sample from a population in order to infer characteristics about that population. Further, questionnaires and surveys can be used to obtain feedback about the quality from customers or other stakeholders.

Cause-and-effect (fishbone) diagrams are a diagramming technique used to explore potential and real causes of problems. The fishbone diagram typically organizes problems into categories relevant to the industry and allows project team members to work backward from major problems (outputs) to identify potential causes (inputs) (see Figure 12.23). As illustrated in the figure, a delay in a cloud migration project could be traced back to a variety of potential problem areas, including personnel, materials, methods, and environmental factors. Each of these main factors could in turn be the result of several different issues. Personnel problems might include inexperienced programmers, too few people working on the project, or personality conflicts among those working on the project. Similarly, materials related issues causing project delays might include incorrect shipments or materials damaged in transit. Fishbone diagrams are a tool for structuring the project team's thinking about potential problem areas and then uncovering the specific causes of problems in those areas. While we discuss fishbone diagrams as a control technique in this chapter, it is also useful in managing project quality (see Chapter 8) and managing project risk (see Chapter 9) as a method to anticipate potential project problems and risk factors.

Control charts are graphical, time-based charts used to display process results. As shown in Figure 12.23, these charts can be used to determine whether process deviations are the result of random or systematic causes. Normally fluctuations around the mean, or target value, on such a chart will be random (see the solid line on Figure 12.24). Control charts provide a visual tool for the project team to examine these

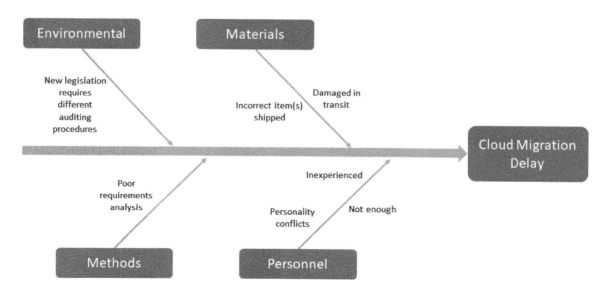

Figure 12.23 A Cause-and-effect diagram

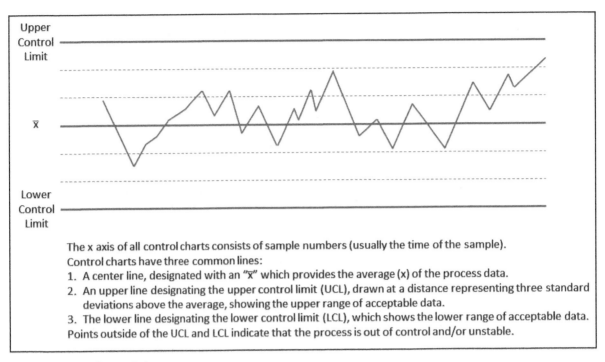

The x axis of all control charts consists of sample numbers (usually the time of the sample).
Control charts have three common lines:
1. A center line, designated with an "x̄" which provides the average (x) of the process data.
2. An upper line designating the upper control limit (UCL), drawn at a distance representing three standard deviations above the average, showing the upper range of acceptable data.
3. The lower line designating the lower control limit (LCL), which shows the lower range of acceptable data.
Points outside of the UCL and LCL indicate that the process is out of control and/or unstable.

Figure 12.24   Control chart

fluctuations. Sudden systematic results on one side of the target value might require an investigation by the project team. Likewise, any deviations beyond three standard deviations from the average (represented by the upper and lower control limits in Figure 12.24) indicate problems with a process, indicating the need for further investigation. A more concrete example in the information systems domain might be search time in a corporate intranet. If, during systems testing, search time suddenly and inexplicably started to take longer than expected (see the dashed line on Figure 12.24), an investigation might be launched to determine the cause and possible solutions (e.g., a larger server or better networking technology).

A flowchart is a graphical representation of a process (see Figure 12.25). Flowcharting helps analyze how problems occur so that approaches can be developed to deal with them. A histogram is a bar chart showing a distribution of variables, with the height of each column representing the relative frequency of a quality problem. As an example, a histogram could be used to show categories of objects along with the frequency of their occurrence. One such application of a histogram is a Pareto diagram, which shows the various types of problems being encountered in a project, along with each problem's frequency (see Figure 12.26). Pareto diagrams were named based on Pareto's law, or the 80/20 rule, which states that 80 percent of problems are the result of 20 percent of the causes. By helping identify those problems occurring most frequently, the Pareto diagram gives the project team guidance on what problems are most critical to solve.

Run charts show trends in a process over time, variation over time, or declines or improvements in a process over time. These charts are used for trend analysis. A scatter diagram (see Figure 12.27) represents the pattern of relationship between two variables. The quality team can use this tool to study and identify the possible relationship

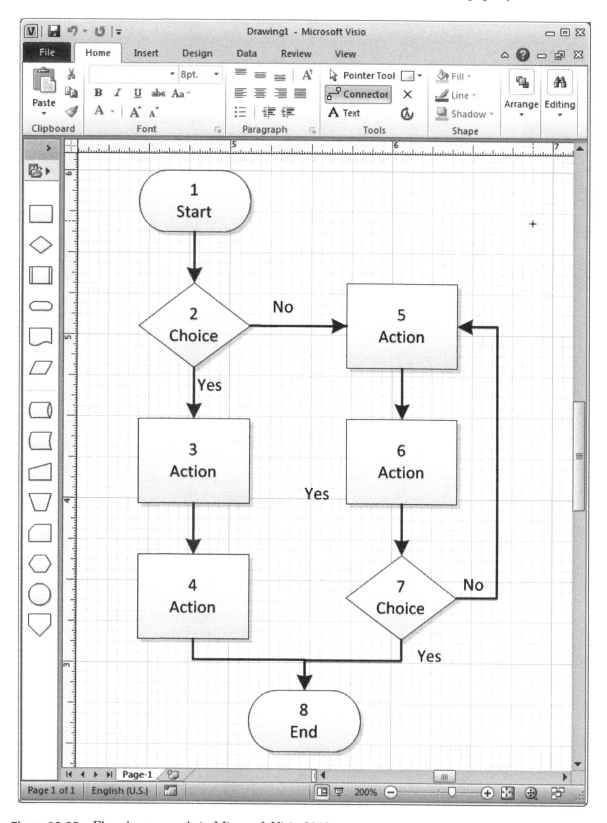

Figure 12.25 Flowchart example in Microsoft Visio 2010

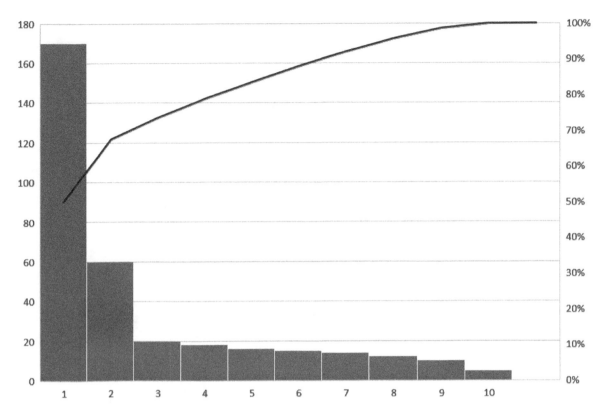

Figure 12.26 Pareto diagram

between changes observed in the variables. This particular figure illustrates an exponentially increasing number of errors as the program grows in complexity.

The outputs from the *Perform Quality Control* process include quality control measurements, verified deliverables, work performance information, change requests, as well as updates to the project management plan and project documents. As discussed in Chapter 8, quality control measurements serve as input into the *Manage Quality* process, where they are used to determine if process improvements are necessary to maintain the desired quality levels. Likewise, work performance information serves as input for various other processes. The quality of project deliverables is compared to the standards, and only those that conform to the standards are accepted; thus, the verified deliverables are those deliverables that are deemed as being of acceptable quality. Further, updates include change requests and potential updates to the project management plan (in particular, the quality management plan) and project documents, such as the issue log, the risk and lessons-learned registers, and the test and evaluation documents. For example, the lessons-learned register is updated with the causes of variances, the justification for any corrective action, and any other lessons learned during the process.

Control Resources

For any project, resources are crucial to successful completion. The ongoing *Control Resources* process involves making sure that any physical resources (such as facilities, equipment, servers, etc.) are available when needed, monitoring resources usage, and

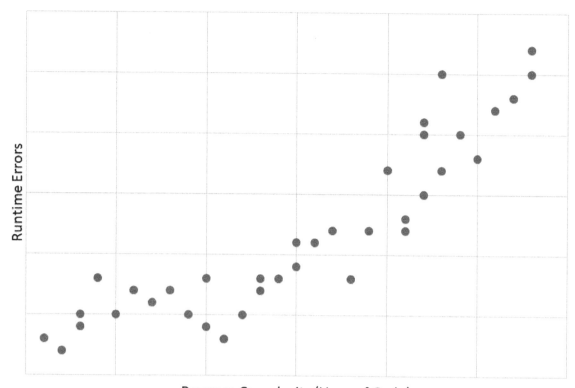

Figure 12.27 Scatter diagram showing software errors by system size

comparing the actual utilization to the planned utilization. If any resources are no longer needed, they can be released to free them up for other uses.

Inputs into this process include the project management plan, project documents, work performance data, agreements, and organizational process assets. One of the most important component of the project management plan is the resource management plan. Next, project documents include the issue log, the resource requirements, resource breakdown structure, and resource assignments, as well as the project schedule, the risk register, and the lessons-learned register. Together, these documents indicate which resources are used and which are needed, whether there are any issues associated with physical resources, which other resources may be available, and how resource issues could be addressed. Further, work performance data are used to monitor project status and resource usage, agreements are related to resources external to the organizations, and organizational process assets include any policies or procedures for handling issues, as well as lessons learned from earlier projects.

As with other monitoring and controlling processes, the project management information system supports the *Control Resources* process by helping track resource utilization. Likewise, data analysis tools (such as alternatives analysis, cost benefit analysis, performance reviews, and trend analysis) are used to identify problems or choose between potential alternatives. Likewise, the project manager should methodically approach any issues, starting from identifying and defining the problem, investigating and analyzing the issues, choosing a solution, and finally checking whether the issue has been resolved. Particularly when additional resources are needed, interpersonal and team skills such as negotiation or influencing can be useful.

Outputs of this process include change requests, work performance information (regarding resource utilization), as well as updates to the project management plan (in particular, the resources management plan and cost and schedule baseline). Further outputs are updates to project documents (such as the resource breakdown structure, physical resource assignments, the issue and assumption logs, as well as the risk and lessons-learned registers).

Monitor Risks

As defined in Chapter 9, the *Monitor Risks* process involves identifying, analyzing, and planning for new risks, keeping track of identified risks, reanalyzing existing risks, monitoring trigger conditions for contingency plans, monitoring residual risks, and reviewing the execution of risk responses (see Figure 12.28). The inputs to the *Monitor Risks* process include the risk management plan, risk register, approved change requests, work performance information, and performance reports. The risk management plan, developed during the risk management planning process, includes information such as the assignment of people (including the risk owners), time, and other resources to project risk management. The risk register (Figure 12.29) provides valuable information, including identified risks and risk owners, agreed-upon risk responses, specific implementation actions, warning signs of risk, residual and secondary risks, and the time and cost contingency reserves. An approved change request impacts project risk because it incurs a modification of the risk management plan developed in the risk management planning process. Work performance information includes project deliverables status, corrective actions, and performance reports. Performance reports provide information on work performance, such as an analysis that may influence the risk management processes.

To transform these inputs into outputs, the *PMBOK* Guide specifies certain tools and techniques that may be used during the *Monitor Risks* process; they include risk reassessment, risk audits, variance and trend analysis, technical performance measurement, reserve analysis, and status meetings. Risk reassessment involves evaluating new risks as the project progresses because new risks may emerge and additional response

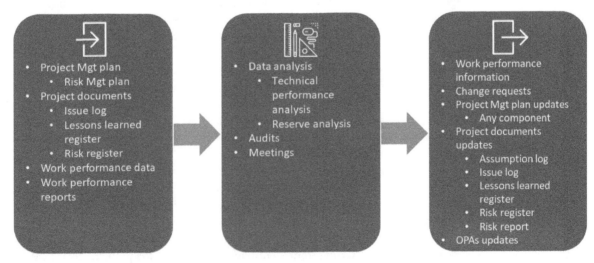

Figure 12.28 The *PMBOK* (6th ed.) *Monitor Risks* process

\<Project Name\>
Risk Register

\<Author\>

\<Date\>

1.0 Statement of Purpose

The purpose of this document is to document and track identified risks to ensure that appropriate personnel are assigned and strategies are applied to address the risks. This document contains: a) a description of the Project's scope, b) the risk rating scheme for \<project name\>, c) recommended response for each rating, and d) the register itself.

2.0 Project Scope

\<Describe \<project name\>'s scope here\>

3.0 Risk Rating Scheme

CONSEQUENCES		LIKELIHOOD	
Rating	Consequence	Rating	Likelihood
1	Major	A	Will occur in most cases.
2	Moderate	B	Could occur at some time.
3	Minor	C	Could occur, but rarely
4	Insignificant	D	May occur, but probably never will

		CONSEQUENCES			
		1	2	3	4
Likelihood	A	E	E	H	M
	B	E	H	M	M
	C	H	M	M	L
	D	M	M	L	N

Recommended Mitigation Actions

Grade	Description	Mitigation Action
E	Extreme Risk	Mitigation actions to reduce the likelihood and seriousness of risk to be identified and implemented as soon as the project commences.
H	High Risk	Mitigation actions to reduce the likelihood and seriousness of risk to be identified and appropriate actions implemented during project planning and/or during project execution
M	Medium Risk	Mitigation actions to reduce the likelihood and seriousness of risk to be identified and appropriate actions implemented during project execution.

(continued)

Figure 12.29   Sample risk register

| L | Low Risk | Mitigation actions to reduce the likelihood and seriousness of risk to be identified and evaluated for possible action if funds permit. |
| N | Negligible Risk | To be noted; no action is needed unless grading increases over time. |

CHANGE SINCE LAST ASSESSMENT	
New	New risk item
--	No Change
↓	Grade decrease
↑	Grade increase

4.0 Risk Register

ID#	Description of Risk	Likelihood	Consequence	Grade	Change	Actions Taken	Responsible Party	$
1.1	Inadequate Funding	B	2	H	New	Re-scope Project	Project Manager	n/a
1.2								
<Add more rows as necessary>								

Figure 12.29 Sample risk register (*continued*)

planning may be required to deal with them. Risk reassessment may be part of a regularly planned project team meeting, where team members are asked if existing risks have changed or if there are new risks that need to be dealt with. Designed to evaluate the effectiveness of risk strategies as well as risk owners, project risk response audits are often conducted during different phases of the project life cycle to examine and document the effectiveness of risk responses. Variance analysis, as discussed earlier, allows the project team to identify deviations from the baseline plan. Large deviations should be carefully investigated, and corrective actions should be taken to bring performance in conformance to the plan. Trend analysis is conducted by having the project team examine performance data over time to determine whether performance is ameliorating or deteriorating. Technical performance measurement is a particularly important tool in IS development projects. If performance metrics—such as the accuracy of inventory updates when implementing a new corporate-wide inventory system—do not meet the goals associated with a specific project milestone, risks to the schedule may be indicated. Reserve analysis is a comparison of the amount of contingency reserves remaining with the amount of risk remaining at any time in the project. As an example, a large information systems project done for a major petroleum company may literally have financial contingency reserves in the millions of dollars; however, if risk is high (which might be revealed through a tool such as trend analysis, discussed earlier), these contingency reserves may still not be sufficient.

Reserve analysis allows the project team to determine whether the remaining reserve is adequate. Status meetings are an important part of communicating, monitoring, and controlling projects. Project risk management should be discussed at these meetings because risk management becomes easier the more it is practiced and because talking more about risks becomes easier and more accurate with frequent discussions.

The outputs from the *Monitor Risks* process include updates to the risk register, requested changes, recommended corrective actions, recommended preventive actions, updates to the organizational process assets, and updates to the project management plan. The risk register—which details all project risks identified at the beginning and during the life of a project, an assessment of their likelihood of occurrence, the seriousness of their potential impact, and initial plans for mitigating the risks—must be updated with the outcomes of risk assessments, risk audits, and periodic risk reviews. This includes updating the probability, impact, priority, response plans, ownership, and other elements of the risk register (Figure 12.29).

The implementation of contingency plans or work-arounds leads to the need for changes to the risk management plan. Recommended corrective actions include contingency and work-around plans, which are both responses that were not initially planned but are needed to deal with emerging risks as the project progresses. Recommended preventive actions are necessary to bring the project into compliance with the project management plan. The historical database of organizational process assets is updated with the causes of variances, the justification for any corrective action, and any lessons learned during the risk monitoring and control process. If the approved change requests have an impact on the risk management processes, then the corresponding components of the project management plan related to risk management must be revised and reissued to reflect the approved changes.

Control Procurements

Control Procurements
The process of comparing what was contracted for with what is being done or has been done to ensure that both parties perform according to the contract, as well as closing the contract.

The **Control Procurements** process is primarily concerned with ensuring that the product or service procured meets the agreed upon performance standards. In this ongoing process, the project manager monitors the performance of the seller, implements needed changes, and closes the contract. In addition to monitoring the performance of the seller, this process also includes the payment of invoices. Typically, both the buyer and the seller control procurements to ensure that the other party meets the requirements and obligations.

The agreements (i.e., contracts) resulting from *Conduct Procurements* are the most obvious input into this process. Because *Control Procurements* involves comparing what was contracted for with what has been done, other key inputs are the procurement management plan and procurement documentation, approved change requests, and work performance data. Change requests may include changes to the terms of the contract or to descriptions of the work to be performed. In addition, other inputs include project management plan components, including the requirements management plan, risk management plan, and change management plan, as well as the schedule baseline. Further inputs into this process include project documents such as the requirements documentation and requirements traceability matrix, the risk and stakeholder registers, milestone lists and quality reports, as well as the assumption log and lessons-learned register. Finally, organizational process assets (such as procurement policies), as well as enterprise environmental factors such as the change control systems, financial management systems, and the code of ethics, are being used during this process.

Procurement audit
A review performed to examine the procurement process from the *Plan Procurement Management* process through the *Conduct Procurements* process.

As with most processes, expert judgment (in particular, expertise related to law, finance, claims administration, or to the functional areas involved) is one of the most valuable tools the project manager can draw from. Experts from the functional areas can be useful in performing inspections of the work performed; inspections are conducted by the procuring organization, with the assistance of the vendor, to determine if there are any weaknesses in the vendor's work processes or deliverables. Likewise, experts can provide useful input during audits of the procurement process. The **procurement audit** is performed to review the procurement process beginning with the *Plan Procurement Management* process through the *Conduct Procurements* process.

The project manager also uses different data analysis techniques to monitor the supplier's performance. In particular, **buyer-conducted performance reviews** are structured reviews of the vendor's progress in fulfilling the terms of the contract. They focus on how well the vendor has been able to adhere to the project's standards for quality and to the project's budget and schedule. Other data analysis techniques include trend analysis and earned value analysis. Finally, claims may arise if the buyer or the vendor contest whether required work was done or what the submitted work is worth. **Claims administration** refers to the process through which claims, or disputes, are managed, following the agreements established in the contract. **Contract closure** supports the process of closing the project (see Chapter 4) and involves verification that all products and services contracted for are acceptable. Its inputs are the procurement management plan, the contract management plan, contract documentation of work performed, and the contract closure procedure.

The primary outputs of the control procurement process are formally closed procurements, by which the buyer provides notice to the vendor that the contract has been completed. Further, outputs from the monitoring and control processes include work performance information and updates to the procurement documentation. This documentation is the result of buyer-conducted performance reviews, vendor performance reporting, and inspections and audits. Other updates include requests for changes to project management plan components, such as the risk and procurement management plans and the schedule and cost baselines. Further, this process typically results in updates to project documents, such as the resource requirements, requirements traceability matrix, risk and stakeholder registers, as well as the lessons-learned register. Finally, organizational process assets are updated, including updates to the lists of prequalified sellers, documentation of the seller's performance evaluation, payment schedules, the procurement file, as well as the lessons-learned repository, which can provide very useful information for future procurement planning. The procurement file contains all contract records to be included in the final project documentation.

Monitor Communications and Stakeholder Engagement

Just as the other monitoring and control processes, the *Monitor Communications* and *Monitor Stakeholder Engagement* processes are used to ensure that things go according to plan. Given the importance of engaging stakeholders for project success, it is crucial to ensure that their information needs are addressed and that the plans for engaging stakeholders are reviewed as the project progresses to maximize the effectiveness of stakeholder engagement. Thus *Monitor Communications* is important for ensuring that the right messages reach the right audiences and have the desired effects.

Both *Monitor Communications* and *Monitor Stakeholder Engagement* use similar inputs, including the project management plan, project documents, work performance data, enterprise environmental factors, and organizational process assets. Project management plan components include the resource management plan, which highlights the organization of the project; the stakeholder management plan, which identifies how stakeholders should be engaged; and the communications management plan, which specifies how information is communicated to the team members and other stakeholders. Next, important project documents to be considered are not only the communications themselves, but the issue log containing any communication breakdowns and the lessons-learned register, which can help identify what worked or did not work; the *Monitor Stakeholder Engagement* process also uses the risk register and stakeholder

Buyer-conducted performance reviews Structured reviews of the vendor's progress in fulfilling the terms of the contract.

Claims administration The management of claims or disputes related to whether required work was done or what the submitted work is worth.

Contract closure The process of verifying that all products and services contracted are acceptable.

register. The work performance data include metadata about the communications distributed and data about the project status. Enterprise environmental factors include the organizational culture, communication channels, changing trends or habits, or the location and distribution of resources or project facilities. Finally, organizational process assets include guidelines for developing, storing, retrieving, or disposing of information; social media policies and procedures; policies related to ethics and security; and/or communication requirements.

Tools and techniques used in the *Monitor Communications* process include first and foremost expert judgement; experts in communication systems and in different areas of communication can assess the effectiveness of communications and can recommend changes to the way communications are managed. Data representation tools such as the stakeholder engagement matrix can help assess if the right communications have reached the right audiences. During any communication within the team or with other stakeholders (such as during face-to-face or virtual meetings), interpersonal and team skills are useful for distributing information or resolving conflict. Finally, the project management information systems can help store or distribute information.

Tools and techniques used in the *Monitor Stakeholder Engagement* process include data analysis (supported by different data representation tools) and decision-making. For example, stakeholder analysis is used to examine if stakeholders or their positions have changed, root cause analysis can be used to determine why certain engagement strategies did not have the intended results, and alternatives analysis is then used to compare the effectiveness of other methods to engage stakeholders. These alternatives can be compared using multicriteria decision-making or voting. During this process, meetings can be valuable in uncovering any issues or monitoring engagement. Communication and interpersonal and team skills are used during meetings as well as when distributing information to or receiving feedback from stakeholders.

As with the inputs, *Monitor Communications* and *Monitor Stakeholder Engagement* have similar outputs. These include work performance information (about the communication activities), change requests (to adjust how communication is managed or stakeholders are engaged), updates to the communications management and stakeholder engagement plans, as well as updates to project documents, including the stakeholder register (in case new communication requirements arise), the risk register (pertaining to stakeholder risks), the issue log, and the lessons-learned register.

Microsoft Project has many built-in reports, views, and filters to assist in project control. For example, for schedule control, the project manager can quickly run a report to list all the tasks that have been completed (see Figure 12.30). Corrective actions can be taken to make sure that those tasks that have not yet been completed as planned are finished as soon as possible. This information can be included in the performance reports, too. These reports can also be used for cost control. Figure 12.31 shows a report

ID	Task Name	Duration	Start	Finish	% Comp.	Cost
2	Document current environmen	4 days	Mon 9/17/2018	Thu 9/20/2018	100%	$0.00
3	Conduct needs analysis	1 week	Thu 9/20/2018	Wed 9/26/2018	100%	$0.00
6	Build Request for Proposal	4 days	Wed 9/26/2018	Mon 10/1/2018	100%	$0.00
7	Gather vendor bids	1 week	Mon 10/1/2018	Fri 10/5/2018	100%	$0.00
8	Choose vendors	2 days	Fri 10/5/2018	Mon 10/8/2018	100%	$0.00
9	Sign contracts	1 day	Mon 10/8/2018	Mon 10/8/2018	100%	$0.00

Figure 12.30 Report of completed tasks

		Over-Budget Tasks as of Wed 10/16/19 LAN-4.mpp				
ID	Task Name	Fixed Cost	Fixed Cost Accrual	Total Cost	Baseline	Variance
2	Document current environment	$ 50,000.00	Prorated	$ 51,120.00	$ 46,000.00	$ 5,120.00
3	Conduct needs analysis	$ 2,000.00	Prorated	$ 2,000.00	$ 1,000.00	$ 3,000.00
4	Analysis completed	$ 2,000.00	Prorated	$ 2,000.00	$ 1,000.00	$ 1,000.00
		$ 54,000.00		$ 57,120.00	$ 48,000.00	$ 9,120.00

Figure 12.31   Report of overbudget tasks

of tasks that are over budget. After looking at this report, the project manager can determine the appropriate corrective actions to make sure these tasks are within budget.

Techniques for Managing Project Closure

Now that your project has been executed, you've exercised control to keep it on track, and its final deliverables are ready for implementation, what's next? In this section, we discuss techniques that successful project managers use to close a project.

While the size of the project may determine the intensity of the closure processes, project closure at any level is very important to clients, stakeholders, team members, and project managers for future projects. Three elements are critical to successful project closure: production of an end report, project handover, and a postimplementation review.

End Report

End report
Document that contains a record of the project management techniques employed over the course of the project, surveys, and outstanding items that still need to be resolved.

Two primary closure documents are created when a project is completed. The first is the **end report**, also called a *project closure report*, which addresses the project management methods and techniques followed over the project life cycle. Suggested content for the end report is shown in Figure 12.32.

Other items to include in the end report might be a list of outstanding items. Outstanding items are items or activities that remain to be addressed but, because of their nature, may have to be taken care of by the clients themselves or assigned to a team member to attend to after the official project handover. Finally, the end report can also document the lessons learned during the project.

Project closure typically involves the aforementioned end report and a second document entitled the postimplementation review. We will discuss the postimplementation review document following the next section on project handover.

Project Handover

Handover
The process of delivering the project to the client and training personnel to use it.

This is the step you've been waiting for. You now get to hand over your hard work to the client. The question is whether the client is actually prepared to take over the project you are ready to deliver. The **handover** is the process by which the appropriate personnel are brought up to speed on the new product or system. This includes training the client's personnel on the new artifact and debriefing project team members.

Postimplementation Review

Postimplementation review
A document that is usually completed six to twelve months after implementation as a check on whether the outcomes of the project were as expected, whether ongoing costs are as expected, and whether implementing the product yields net benefits.

Finally, you've completed your project (hopefully on time and on budget). How successful was it? While your project's performance with respect to the planned schedule and budget are important measuring sticks for the success of the project, how did the client organization perceive the success of its investment in you? Did the product meet the client's requirements? The **postimplementation review**—also sometimes called the *postproject review*—is a document that is usually completed six to twelve months after implementation as a check on whether the outcomes of the project were as expected, whether ongoing costs are as expected, and whether implementing the product yields net benefits (see Figure 12.33).

End Report Contents

1. Evaluation of the achievement of the project's objectives summarizing whether the project was successful or not
2. Evaluation of the project's performance against the planned target time and cost
3. Effects on the original project plan and business case of any approved changes
4. Final analysis of change issues received during the project
5. Total impact of approved changes
6. Analysis for all quality work carried out
7. Post-Project Review date and plan

Figure 12.32 Sample table of contents for an end report

<u>**Table of Contents**</u>

1. **EXECUTIVE SUMMARY.** **6**
2. **PROJECT HISTORY** **6**
    - 2.1. DETAILS 7
    - 2.2. OBJECTIVES 7
    - 2.3. SCOPE 7
    - 2.4. CURRENT STATUS 8
3. **REVIEW METHODOLOGY** **8**
    - 3.1. INTERVIEWS 9
    - 3.2. QUESTIONNAIRES AND SURVEYS 10
    - 3.3. HARDWARE & NETWORK PERFORMANCE 10
    - 3.4. SUPPORT ANALYSIS 11
    - 3.5. <OTHER> 11
4. **REVIEW OUTCOMES (FINDINGS).** **11**
    - 4.1. COST ASSESSMENT 12
    - 4.2. VENDOR ASSESSMENT 12
    - 4.3. BENEFITS ASSESSMENT 12
    - 4.4. SUPPORT ASSESSMENT 13
    - 4.5. COMPLIANCE WITH SERVICE LEVEL AGREEMENTS 14
    - 4.6. SOFTWARE EVALUATION 15
    - 4.7. <OTHER> 15
5. **RECOMMENDATIONS** **16**
    - 5.1. STRENGTHS & WEAKNESSES 16
        - 5.1.1. Strengths 17
        - 5.1.2. Weaknesses 18
        - 5.1.3. Opportunities. 18
        - 5.1.4. Threats 18
    - 5.2. LESSONS LEARNED 19
    - 5.3. FUTURE PROJECT OBJECTIVES 21

Figure 12.33 Sample postimplementation review table of contents

Project Control and Closure and PMBOK

This chapter has discussed the fundamentals, characteristics, and challenges of managing various controlling and closure processes over the course of a project. We have defined control, identified the major philosophies of control, and discussed how control can be achieved. We have also discussed how closure is important in the context of a project and discussed several documents that can help the closure process occur. Figure 12.34 details this coverage.

Figure 12.34 Chapter 12 and *PMBOK* coverage

Key: ○ where the material is covered in the textbook; ● current chapter coverage

	Textbook Chapters ⟶	1	2	3	4	5	6	7	8	9	10	11	12
	PMBOK Knowledge Area												
1	Introduction												
1.2	Foundational Elements	○	○										
2	The Environment in Which Projects Operate												
2.2	Enterprise Environmental Factors		○										
2.2	Organizational Process Assets		○										
2.3	Organizational Systems		○										
3	The Role of the Project Manager												
3.2	Definition of a Project Manager	○											
3.3	The Project Manager's Sphere of Influence		○										
3.4	Project Manager Competences	○	○	○									
3.5	Performing Integration		○										
4	Project Integration Management												
4.1	Develop Project Charter					○							
4.2	Develop Project Management Plan					○							
4.3	Direct and Manage Project Work											○	
4.4	Manage Project Knowledge											○	
4.5	Monitor and Control Project Work											○	●
4.6	Perform Integrated Change Control												●
4.7	Close Project or Phase										○		●
5	Project Scope Management												
5.1	Plan Scope Management					○							
5.2	Collect Requirements					○							
5.3	Define Scope					○							
5.4	Create WBS					○	○						
5.5	Validate Scope					○							
5.6	Control Scope					○							●
6	Project Schedule Management												
6.1	Plan Schedule Management						○						

#	Process	1	2	3	4	5	6	7	8	9	10	11	12
6.2	Define Activities						O						
6.3	Sequence Activities						O						
6.4	Estimate Activity Durations							O					
6.5	Develop Schedule							O					
6.6	Control Schedule							O					●
7	**Project Cost Management**												
7.1	Plan Cost Management								O				
7.2	Estimate Costs								O				
7.3	Determine Budget								O				
7.4	Control Costs								O				●
8	**Project Quality Management**												
8.1	Plan Quality Management								O				
8.2	Manage Quality								O				
8.3	Control Quality								O				●
9	**Project Resource Management**												
9.1	Plan Resource Management							O					
9.2	Estimate Activity Resources						O	O					
9.3	Acquire Resources							O				O	
9.4	Develop Team			O								O	
9.5	Manage Team			O								O	
9.6	Control Resources							O					●
10	**Project Communications Management**												
10.1	Plan Communications Management				O								
10.2	Manage Communications				O							O	
10.3	Monitor Communications				O								●
11	**Project Risk Management**												
11.1	Plan Risk Management									O			
11.2	Identify Risks									O		O	
11.3	Perform Qualitative Risk Analysis									O			
11.4	Perform Quantitative Risk Analysis									O			
11.5	Plan Risk Responses									O			
11.6	Implement Risk Responses									O		O	
11.7	Monitor Risks									O			●
12	**Project Procurement Management**												
12.1	Plan Procurement Management										O		
12.2	Conduct Procurements										O	O	
12.3	Control Procurements										O		●
13	**Project Stakeholder Management**												
12.1	Identify Stakeholders				O								
12.2	Plan Stakeholder Engagement				O								
12.3	Manage Stakeholder Engagement				O							O	
12.4	Monitor Stakeholder Engagement				O								●

Running Case: Managing Project Control and Closure

"How long did they say they'd give us on-site support at no extra cost?" asked James.

"Six months," Kevin answered.

"Are they on schedule for the last kiosks at Piccoli's store?"

"Yep!"

"Wow, that's great!"

"They also completed half of Maria's store too. I'm quite sure we are going to pull this project off well before schedule! I think the documentation is coming along well, too."

Cindy raised a thumbs-up.

"There is one last component that needs to be completed before we start winding down this project. We need to show the metrics for the pilots to Sarah," said James.

"I'll do that," said Trey. "I have nearly all the performance metrics that we ran last week at Piccoli's store. I'll just update it one more time before I send it in to Sarah."

"Well," said James, "I think, with that, we are at our last stage of the project. I've got T-shirts for all you guys!"

"Actually, James, I don't think we are done," said Cindy.

Oh? James wondered.

"Yeah, remember all that 'there are great benefits to following a fairly formal project management process when designing a new system' and 'moving forward with care' stuff you taught me at the beginning?"

"Ah, you're talking about lessons learned, aren't you?" James realized.

Adapted from: Valacich and George (2017).

Cindy replied, "Yes, and realizing that we were getting close to the end, I searched around and found some information about closing a project. The stuff I read talked about a document called lessons learned. I don't know about the rest of you, but I know I learned a lot that I'll need to know when I work on projects in the future. If I could refer back to some file that contains information about what went well, what didn't, and how we dealt with the stuff that didn't, it would make future projects go more smoothly."

"So, with all that extra time you had to search around to find information on finishing up the project, I don't suppose you wrote this lessons-learned document up, did you?" James asked hopefully.

"Well, no. But I didn't get the feeling it should be a one-person job. I found this template that I think we can modify a little to fit with the Jackie's structure and culture a little better." (See Figure 12.35.) "A big part of it is one last project meeting to discuss the particulars because each one of us probably learned something a little different than everyone else. By doing it together in a meeting, we'll make sure we don't leave anything out."

"All right," James said. "In addition to the T-shirt, Cindy gets the 'Keeping us all on track' award."

Everybody laughed while Cindy sighed and shook her head.

The team closed down the project by submitting the reports and documentation to Sarah and conducting a final meeting to compose the lessons-learned document.

Chapter Summary

Define project control and closure. Project control can be thought of as the processes that allow monitoring and measurement of project progress and directing influence over the plan to account for any discrepancies between the actual progress and the planned progress made up to that point. Project closure involves both the final implementation and training related to the project, getting acceptance and signoff on the project, and finally archiving the results of the project and lessons learned from the project.

Understand the importance of and general philosophies behind project control and closure. Project control is important because it allows a project

manager to keep tabs on the progress of the various tasks, identify problems, solve problems, and make changes to the plan based on any problems and their solutions. Project closure is important because it ensures that the handover of the project is successful and documentation occurs so that future projects can be improved from lessons learned from previous projects. Producing an end report, handover, and conducting a postimplementation review ensures proper project closure. General philosophies underlying project control include the dogmatic philosophy (where the established plan is followed to the letter, no ifs, ands, or buts) and the laid-back philosophy (where little or no control is exerted and the project can take

\<Project Name\>
Lessons Learned

\<Author\>

\<Date\>

1.0 Statement of Purpose
The purpose of this template is to provide a repository of knowledge gained from experience so that future projects and the organization may benefit. This document contains a) a project journal, b) the close-out discussion of lessons learned, and c) acknowledgement signatures from project team members.

2.0 Project Journal
At each project status meeting, discuss and record areas of success and areas that need improvement. Discuss the processes that led to success, and suggest ways to improve deficient areas.

AREAS OF SUCCESS

Meeting Date	Description
\<Enter Date Here\>	\<Enter Description Here\>
\<Add more rows as necessary\>	

AREAS FOR IMPROVEMENT

Meeting Date	Description
\<Enter Date Here\>	\<Enter Description Here\>
\<Add more rows as necessary	

CONCLUSIONS

\<Enter conclusions drawn from the above items here\>

3.0 Close-Out Discussion of Lessons Learned
Conduct a meeting with relevant stakeholders to fill out the following sections on Lessons Learned from \<Project Name\>.

LIST THIS PROJECT'S TOP THREE SUCCESSES

Description	Factors Influential in Success
\<Add rows as necessary\>	

LIST THIS PROJECT'S TOP THREE FAILURES.

Description	Factors Influential in Failure
\<Add rows as necessary\>	

(continued)

Figure 12.35   Sample lessons-learned document template

LIST AND DESCRIBE POTENTIAL STRATEGIES TO ADDRESS FAILURES OR AREAS NEEDING IMPROVEMENT

Description	Strategies to Improve
<Add rows as necessary>	

4.0 Acknowledgement Signatures
Project Manager:

As project manager on <project name>, I hereby acknowledge and agree with the information contained in this document

Name	Position	Signature	Date

The signatures above represent stakeholders' agreement and acknowledgement of the information contained in this document. Those signing this document agree that this is the formal Lessons Learned document for <project name> to be filed with <enter location of project documentation here>.

Figure 12.35 Sample lessons-learned document template (*continued*)

on a life of its own). A pragmatic philosophy is a compromise between the two; the plan is followed, but flexibility exists to deal with problems as they arise. Communication, participation, analysis, action, and commitment all give a project manager the necessary tools for exerting control over the project.

Apply techniques for managing project control and closure. There are many techniques for controlling projects. Typically, these techniques can be applied to the project as a whole—as in *PMBOK*'s topic of Project Integration Management—or in the individual areas of validate scope and control scope, schedule, costs, quality, resources, and procurements, as well as monitoring risks, communication, and stakeholder engagement control. This chapter discusses and provides examples of control exercised across all these areas. In addition, we discuss the importance of good project closure, as well as some techniques for accomplishing this. Organizations that embrace formalized processes related to control and closure can head off problems before they occur and more actively manage costs and schedules over the course of the project.

Key Terms Review

A. Approved change requests
B. Approved corrective actions
C. Approved defect repairs
D. Approved preventive actions
E. Buyer-conducted performance reviews
F. Change control system
G. Claims administration
H. Configuration management system
I. Contract closure
J. Control Costs

K. Control Procurements
L. Control Quality
M. Dogmatic philosophy
N. Earned value analysis
O. End report
P. Forecasts
Q. Handover
R. Laid-back philosophy
S. Monitor and Control Project Work
T. Perform Integrated Change Control

U. Philosophy of project control
V. Postimplementation review
W. Pragmatic philosophy
X. Procurement audit
Y. Project audit
Z. Project closure

AA. Project control
BB. Project log
CC. Recommended corrective actions
DD. Recommended preventive actions
EE. Rejected change request
FF. Standard operating procedures
GG. Variance analysis

Match each of the key terms with the definition that best fits it.

1. A compromise between the dogmatic and laid-back philosophies that sticks to a plan but is flexible enough to allow for changes.

2. A document that is usually completed six to twelve months after implementation as a check on whether the outcomes of the project were as expected, whether ongoing costs are as expected, and whether implementing the product yields net benefits.

3. A document used to record any items identified during the project.

4. A formal, documented process that describes the procedures by which the project scope and product scope can be changed.

5. A philosophy of project control that allows for project problems or change issues to be dealt with as they arise, on an ad hoc basis.

6. A philosophy of project control that emphasizes strict adherence to the project plan, with little tolerance for deviations.

7. A review performed to examine the procurement process from the *Plan Procurement Management* process through the *Conduct Procurements* process.

8. A scope control technique that ensures that the requested changes to the project and product scope are thoroughly considered and documented before being implemented.

9. A systematic and formal inquiry into a project's expenditures, schedule, and quality of work.

10. A technique that measures project performance over time, and provides a way to forecast future performance based on past performance.

11. Activities and reporting methods instituted during the course of the project to monitor the progress of the project and provide reports for project managers and for project stakeholders.

12. Document that contains a record of the project management techniques that were employed over the course of the project, surveys, and outstanding items that still need to be resolved.

13. Documented and authorized actions that are necessary to correct defects in the project deliverables.

14. Documented and authorized changes that are scheduled for implementation by the project team.

15. Documented and authorized guidelines intended to reduce the probability of negative consequences to the project due to identified risks.

16. Documented and authorized guidelines necessary to bring future project performance in conformance with the project management plan.

17. Documented recommendations needed to bring future project performance into conformance with the project management plan.

18. Documented recommendations that minimize the probability of negative consequences to the project.

19. Estimates or predictions of conditions or events in the project's future.

20. Final implementation and training related to the project, acceptance and signoff on the project, and archiving of the project's results and lessons learned.

21. Requested changes that were not chosen for implementation.

22. Structured reviews of the vendor's progress in fulfilling the terms of the contract.

23. Techniques used to evaluate differences between planned baselines and actual performance

24. The management of claims or disputes related to whether required work was done or what the submitted work is worth.

25. The management style that the manager employs with respect to following the plan and dealing with problems or changes in the plan.

26. The process of collecting, measuring, and disseminating data related to performance, as well as assessing measurements and trends in order to make any improvements.

27. The process of comparing what was contracted for with what is being done or has been done to ensure that both parties perform according to the contract, and closing the contract.

28. The process of delivering the project to the client and training personnel to use it.

29. The process of ensuring that only appropriate changes are included in the modified cost baseline.

30. The process of identifying, evaluating, and managing changes that occur from project initiation through project closure.

31. The process of monitoring and measuring project progress and influencing the plan to account for any discrepancies between planned progress and actual progress.

32. The process of screening the project results to determine whether they conform to relevant quality standards and identifying means to eliminate causes of unsatisfactory results.

33. The process of verifying that all products and services contracted are acceptable.

Review Questions

1. Define *project control*.

2. Explain what a project control philosophy is.

3. Discuss the different types of project control philosophies with respect to the kinds of projects that might be appropriate for each type.

4. Explain how controlling processes can affect project integration, scope, time, cost, quality, and risk.

5. List and briefly describe the various levers that can be used to exert control over a project.

6. List and briefly describe the various project control techniques.

7. Describe the components of standard operating procedures techniques.

8. List and provide the formulas (if required) for the components of an earned value management (EVM) analysis.

9. Explain how cost performance indexes and schedule performance indexes provide estimates on the budget and schedule performance of the project.

10. Define project closure.

11. Describe what is involved in project handover.

12. Compare and contrast an end report with a postimplementation review.

Chapter Exercises

1. Discuss how the computerized baggage handling system (CBHS) project at Denver International Airport (DIA) could have been a success with proper control.

2. For a class project for this (or another) course, compare and contrast the three different philosophies of controlling projects. Which one do you believe is the best?

3. For a class project for this (or another) course, list and explain the different levers that you can use to exert control over projects. Give an example of how you could use each lever to control your project.

4. The planned value for a project is US$17,800, the earned value is US$19,450, and the actual cost is US$21,870. Based on this information, calculate the cost performance index and the schedule performance index. What do these indices tell you about the status of the project in terms of cost and schedule?

5. The budget at completion of this project was estimated at US$20,000, and the estimated time to complete was thirteen months. Use the information from Exercise 4 to compute the estimated cost at completion and the estimated time to complete. Is the project on budget and schedule?

6. Use the internet or any other source to search "variance analysis." Define what it is and explain its usefulness in project control.

7. Review Chapter 8 for the different tools and techniques that can be used in performing quality control. For your own project, explain how you used different techniques to control quality. Which techniques were more or less effective? Why?

8. "Once a project is completed, the project team members should forget about it and move to the next project." Do you agree with this statement? Explain why.

9. Compare and contrast the different reports produced during project closure.

10. How can the performing organization assess whether the project is a success at the client's organization?

Chapter Case: Sedona Management Group and Managing Project Control and Closure

Project control is the process of ensuring that project objectives are being met. It is the project team's job to measure progress toward the project objectives, monitor any divergence from the plan developed in the initiation and planning phase, and take any corrective actions necessary to match progress to the plan. Controlling processes are performed at all of the other phases of the project life cycle. Once the project objectives have been met, the final phase in the project life cycle is project closure, which involves formalizing the acceptance of the project and bringing the project to an orderly end.

Tim Turnpaugh recognizes the importance of control during the life cycle of a project. There are many project control techniques, but at Sedona Management Group, two project control techniques have consistently helped ensure project success. The first technique is the use of standard operating procedures. SMG has established a well-defined process of assessing what the customer needs, and this type of project control occurs in both the initiation and planning phases of a project. By using standardized requirements-gathering techniques, as well as having established planning templates that have proven successful in the past, SMG reduces project risk as well as variance in the quality or timing of project outcomes.

A second control technique SMG employees rely on is prevention. Turnpaugh tells members of his team to "inspect what they expect." In other words, project team members are charged with preventing problems by ensuring that the various requirements of the project are met. In many cases, given the variety of projects that any project team might be concurrently managing, a team may become lax in ensuring that each feature of a system works as expected. This is particularly important in situations where an IS project team may be employing reusable code. Turnpaugh believes it is critical to never assume that the application will behave the same way it has in the past, and that the only way to ensure performance is through testing of all features during development.

During project closure, the team prepares to deliver the project to the customer by ensuring the project is functioning correctly, making sure the personnel responsible for managing the new system are appropriately trained, obtaining customer acceptance, and finally documenting—for the project team's own purposes—any problems or issues that they may want to attend to in future projects. Closing activities also include personnel transition, the discussion of lessons learned, and verifying and documenting the project results to formalize the stakeholders' acceptance of the project deliverables.

Chapter 12 Project Assignment

Throughout the project life cycle, control processes are important to ensure that the project objectives are being met. Once all these project objectives have been met, the project should be brought to formal closure. In this assignment, you will discuss the control and closing processes that will be used for your project.

1. "Prevention is better than the cure." Discuss this statement as it applies to your project. In other words, explain what preventive measures will be used to ensure project success.

2. Explain the importance of an earned value analysis. Also define BCWP, ACWP, BCWS, CPI, SPI, EAC, and ETC.

3. Conduct an earned value analysis, using BCWP, ACWP, and BCWS to calculate CPI, SPI, EAC, and ETC. You will need to estimate your own values for your project for the BCWP, ACWP, and BCWS in order to come up with your CPI, SPI, EAC, and ETC. Costs can be calculated by assuming that each individual on your team works for US$35/hour.

4. Create a project closure document, which includes:
   - A statement indicating whether the project objectives were met
   - What requirements of the project were not met
   - A tracking Gantt chart
   - An explanation of whether the project schedule and budget were met, based on the earned value analysis

5. Write a list of lessons learned in the project process. Explain what you did effectively, what you did ineffectively, and what you will do differently next time.

References

Ahituv, N., Zviran, M., and Glezer, C. (1999). Top Management Toolbox for Managing Corporate IT. *Communications of the ACM* 42(4), 93–99.

Alexander, M. (2017, August 18). Project Management: Five Tips for Managing Your Project Budget. *CIO.com*. Retrieved July 9, 2018, from https://www.cio.com/article/2406862/project-management/project-management-project-management-4-ways-to-manage-your-budget.html

Alexander, M. (2018, April 12). How to Get a Failing Project Back on Track. *CIO.com*. Retrieved July 9, 2018, from https://www.cio.com/article/3268414/project-management/how-to-get-a-failing-project-back-on-track.html

Contorer, A. (2017, December 6). Techniques for Success with Offshore Software Development. *FPComplete.com*. Retrieved July 9, 2018, from https://www.fpcomplete.com/blog/techniques-for-success-with-offshore-software-development

GSA (2016, December). Best Business Practices for USG Cloud Adoption. *Office of Information Technology, Category Federal Acquisition Service, General Services Administration*. Retrieved July 9, 2018, from https://www.gsa.gov/portal/mediaId/153806/fileName/GSACloudBestBusinessPractices.action

Hendry, J. (2017, July 6). Delays Plague National Apprenticeship System Rollout. *ITNews.com.au*. Retrieved July 9, 2018, from https://www.itnews.com.au/news/delays-plague-national-apprenticeship-system-rollout-467613

Hendry, J. (2018, May 18). Education Dumps Troubled $20M Apprentice IT System. *ITNews.com.au*. Retrieved July 9, 2018, from https://www.itnews.com.au/news/education-dumps-troubled-20m-apprentice-it-system-49126

Keil, M., and Robey, D. (2001). Blowing the Whistle on Troubled Software Projects. *Communications of the ACM* 44(4), 87–93.

Mähring, M, Holmström, J., Keil, M., and Montealegre, R. (2004). Trojan-Actor Networks and Swift Translation: Bringing Actor-Network Theory to IT Project Escalation Studies. *Information Technology and People* 17(2), 210–238.

McLannahan, B. (2017, November 7). The Whistleblowers. *FT.com*. Retrieved July 9, 2018, from https://ig.ft.com/special-reports/whistleblowers

Project Management Institute (2017). *Agile Practice Guide*. Newton Square, PA: Author.

Project Management Institute (2017). *PMBOK: A Guide to the Project Management Body of Knowledge* (6th ed.). Newtown Square, PA: Author.

Sifri, G. (2003, March 19). Getting Derailed Projects Back on Track. *TechRepublic*. Retrieved July 9, 2018, from http://www.techrepublic.com/article/getting-derailed-projects-back-on-track

Valacich, J., and George, J. F. (2017). *Modern Systems Analysis and Design* (8th ed.). Boston: Pearson.

Zeichick, A. (2004, March 5). Tools Foster Engagement with Offshore Developers. *InfoWorld*. Retrieved July 9, 2018, from http://www.infoworld.com/article/2665688/application-development/tools-foster-engagement-with-offshore-developers.html

Executing, Controlling, and Closing Projects in Agile Environments

In traditional projects using predictive life cycles, project execution starts when (at least part of) the planning has been completed. Project execution entails those processes associated with carrying out the actual project work, as well as monitoring and controlling various aspects of the project, including costs, scope, quality, or communications. Once the final deliverable has been created, the project is handed over to the (internal or external) client, an end report is created, and a postcompletion report is conducted. In contrast, in agile projects, planning and execution go hand in hand and prototypes are delivered frequently; these aspects contribute to the suitability of agile methodologies for uncertain environments and changing requirements.

As you may recall from the Part I Appendix, an iteration is a timeboxed development phase in which all work pertaining to a specific deliverable is performed. Typically, iterations last for two weeks, but can be as long as four weeks. As requirements are likely to change or evolve during the life of an agile project, it is important for an agile team to keep learning about the effectiveness of the approaches used, improve processes, or adapt to changing requirements. This learning is not only concerned with the actual work performed, but also with the processes used during the agile project. Thus, the agile team uses not only quantitative data about performance, but also takes into account qualitative data, such as team member's evaluations of the effectiveness of processes. As problems are identified, the agile team tries to isolate the root causes of these problems, so as to continuously improve. Consequently, a key aspect of iterations is that they typically end with a review and a retrospective, which also serve monitoring and controlling purposes.

Iterations and Increments

Following the agile manifesto, "working software is the primary measure of progress." Thus arguably the most important outcome of an iteration is completed work. But what does *completed work* mean? In the preplanning phase, the agile team has agreed on the "definition of done." In different teams and in different contexts, "done" can mean different things, but "done" typically means that the coding has been completed and the software is usable. Often, "done" also indicates that the product has been tested and is free of bugs.

By definition, agile approaches are incremental. Thus what is delivered at the end of an iteration is not just one or more completed product backlog items, but the combination of the product backlog items completed during the current iteration and the product backlog items completed during all previous iterations, together referred to as an **increment**. In other words, it is not sufficient to deliver a usable new feature, but the entire *increment* must be "done" and usable, so that it could be released by the product owner, if so decided.

Whereas agile approaches are highly flexible, monitoring the team's progress is nevertheless an important activity. Two useful tools to monitor progress and performance are velocity and iteration burndown charts. As discussed in the Part II Appendix, the velocity is the number of items completed during the iteration and can be used to estimate how much work the team can complete over a certain time period. Ideally, the velocity would remain relatively constant over time, or increase gradually (as the team optimizes processes or relationships). If the velocity is highly fluctuating, this may indicate problems in the iteration planning processes.

In addition to velocity, an **iteration burn-down chart** is used to track the team's progress within an iteration (see Figure A3.1). An iteration burn-down chart is used to visualize the progress over time, where the completion of features is plotted against days in the iteration, from the top left to the bottom right corner of the chart (a release burn-down chart plots features against iterations to examine progress of the overall project, as opposed to progress within an iteration). As features are completed and tested, the number of remaining features to be completed during the iteration decreases, and the "effort remaining" line moves downward. This way, the team (and the stakeholders) can get a quick overview of the progress during an iteration and the team's productivity. If the slope of the line approximates the "ideal effort," this indicates that the work has been broken down sufficiently; in contrast, if the line resembles stairs with intermittent steep drops, this indicates that the work has not been broken down sufficiently, or that

Increment
The combination of the product backlog items completed during the current iteration and the product backlog items completed during all previous iterations.

Iteration burn-down chart
Chart used to display the development team's progress during an iteration.

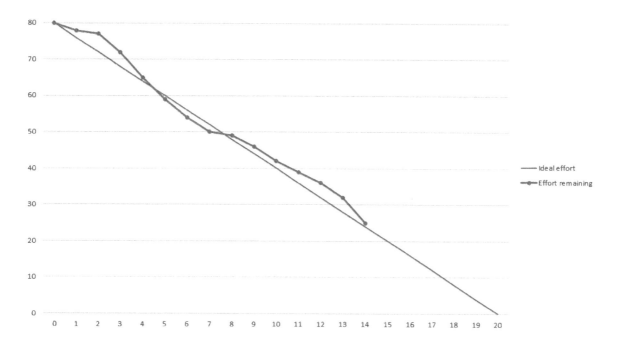

Figure A3.1   Iteration burn-down chart

unforeseen issues have arisen. In certain situations, such as when new features are added to the backlog, the line may actually slope upward; while there might be valid reasons for this, adding features during an iteration should normally be avoided.

Akin to an iteration burn-down chart, a release burn-up chart is used to display the increase in delivered functionality; to symbolize the increase in functionality, a burn-up chart has a positive slope. Thus it can be used to visualize a project's progress toward completion, as well as to calculate the magnitude of scope changes and the project's estimate at completion (EAC).

Coding and Integration in Agile Projects

Coding is the core of any information systems development project. As such, agile approaches emphasize ways to effectively and efficiently create high quality code. Just as in traditional approaches, following coding standards not only helps in finding and fixing bugs, but also helps in passing work between developers or discussing potential solutions to problems. One specific approach to increasing the quality of the code produced is **pair programming**, an agile coding technique that is based on the concept that two heads (or two pairs of eyes) are better than one. In pair programming, two programmers work together: one (the "driver") doing the actual coding work, and the other one (the "navigator") reviewing the code as it is being created. (Note that sometimes a pair consists of a programmer and a business user.) While pair programming can lead to increased productivity and code quality, it is not always easy to pair up programmers who function well together. Consequently, to still harness the advantages of having two pairs of eyes, it is advocated to (at least) have all code reviewed by another person. Likewise, manual code reviews and walk-throughs can help discover issues at an early stage. In order to keep the code easy to maintain, agile teams attempt to improve the structure of the code on an ongoing basis, a process referred to as *refactoring*. Examples of refactoring to improve ease of maintenance or code understanding include using clear naming conventions for methods or classes or removing unused or duplicate code where possible.

The short duration of the iterations, as well as the need to deliver functional increments necessitates not only that new code is continuously reviewed, but that it is continuously tested and integrated with the existing code. Often, agile teams perform nightly builds and conduct automated tests using software tools such as Apache Ant or NAnt, which compile the code into binaries, package the binaries, and sometimes include tools to perform automated tests. Nightly builds allow the team to fix any errors before continuing their work. Often, the build is started every time new code is committed to the version control system (such as CVS, SVN, or Git; see Chapter 12). This continuous integration (often referred to as *frequent integration*) allows teams to fix errors before they lead to further, potentially more serious, downstream issues. If a developer is working on more complex code that is only infrequently committed, it is still advisable to test the local copy of the code multiple times a day, to ensure full functionality of the code.

Testing in Agile Projects

In agile projects, different types of tests are conducted by different types of people at different times. These include unit tests, integration tests, regression tests, exploratory tests, and acceptance tests (see Figure A3.2). While agile focuses on automated tests, some tests are performed by the developers, and others are performed by the customers or the users. First, **unit tests** are used by the developers to test the functionality of single

Pair programming
An approach to increasing the quality of the code that uses two programmers working together, with one doing the actual coding work and the other one reviewing the code as it is being created.

Unit test
Test used to inspect the functionality of single methods or classes.

methods or classes. In simple terms, unit testing answers the question of whether the code works. Next, **integration tests** are used to test whether new code works together with already completed code, often taking into consideration dependencies with other systems. Such tests, intended to test the entire application, can be conducted using smaller sets of test data or using extensive live databases. Integration tests answer the question of if the code works together with the rest of the system. Once any bugs that have been found are fixed or new functionalities are introduced, **regression tests** are used to test if the bug has indeed been fixed, that the revised code does not contain any new bugs, and that the new or revised code does not break any existing functionality. Regression tests answer the question of if the system still works the way it used to or should. In other words, whereas integration tests are used to test whether individual modules work together, regression testing focuses on discovering whether new bugs have been introduced as a result of changes to the system.

Whereas automated tests can find known problems, a system might still behave in unexpected ways. Consequently, **exploratory testing** can be used to find new bugs. In other words, exploratory testing is aimed at trying to "break" the system. Typically performed in an unscripted fashion, exploratory testing tends to resemble the ways users interact with a live system.

In addition to these tests, an important component of agile projects is user acceptance. Consequently, an important test is the **acceptance test**. Typically created by the product owner, acceptance tests focus on assessing whether the new feature correctly addresses the associated user story. In other words, acceptance tests answer the question of whether the system delivers the expected business benefits or meets the requirements. Typically, acceptance tests are written in a GIVEN-WHEN-THEN format, such as *GIVEN fifteen available seats in a course WHEN a student wants to register for the course THEN add student to course and reduce the number of available seats to fourteen.*

Integration test
Test used to verify whether new code works together with already completed code.

Regression test
Test used to verify that a bug has indeed been fixed, that revised code does not contain any new bugs, or that new or revised code does not break any existing functionality.

Exploratory testing
Testing used to find unknown problems by using the system in an unscripted fashion.

Acceptance test
Test focused on assessing whether a new feature correctly addresses the associated user story.

Figure A3.2   Testing in agile projects

Likewise, it is important to obtain feedback from users of the system, such as feedback regarding usability, visual design, or accessibility. Such user testing should occur continuously during the project, but can start even before coding has begun (e.g., using high-fidelity prototypes that are developed using sophisticated software packages and that are very similar to the finished product).

Reviews and Retrospectives

A review (sometimes called "sprint demo") is a meeting at the end of an iteration in which the team presents the work completed during the iteration and the key stakeholders inspect the work and adapt the product backlog and/or release plan. Thus a review meeting is not only attended by the agile team but should also be open to all potential stakeholders. Normally, the product owner provides a high-level status overview of the iteration, highlighting what has been completed and what has not been completed, before the development team presents a demo of the completed features. This meeting is an opportunity to inspect the iteration itself, the increment, the product backlog, as well as other aspects, such as budget or timeline; it is also an opportunity to adapt the product backlog or release plan, if needed. As such, the review meeting is an opportunity for the team to learn. Sometimes it is recommended to demonstrate completed increments at least every two weeks, so that the agile team can make sufficient progress, but does not veer off track. Further, review meetings are important for engaging stakeholders. As agile projects inherently have a high degree of uncertainty, it is essential to keep stakeholders actively engaged throughout the project, which can help mitigate risks and build trust. Actively engaging stakeholders can thus help ensure project success. In addition to frequent demonstrations, posting artifacts in publicly accessible locations can be helpful in obtaining rapid feedback from stakeholders.

In contrast to a review, which focuses on the work completed, a retrospective (in Scrum referred to as "sprint retrospective") is a meeting during which the team discusses the iteration (sprint) itself; during a retrospective, the team identifies positive and negative aspects of the process and agrees on changes to the process for the next iteration. Thus, the focus of a retrospective is on learning from the last iteration and improving the processes for future iterations, so as to be more effective and increase quality. Any improvements identified during a retrospective can then be implemented at the next iteration. Further, a retrospective is an important part of managing quality in agile projects; as the comparatively small size of the iterations allow for discovering quality issues early on, it is during these meetings that the team can examine the quality issues and determine their root causes.

Normally conducted after the review meeting and before the next planning meeting, retrospectives can be conducted at other times as well, such as at the completion of an important milestone, a new release, or when the team gets stuck.

Closing Agile Projects

As with traditional project management methodologies, closing is an important aspect of a project. At this stage, the various lessons learned are archived, so as to be available for use in future projects. Further, any storyboards may be archived as part of project documentation. After the product has been handed over, lessons learned have been documented, and any loose end have been tied up, agile projects often end with a celebration to provide recognition to the people involved in the project.

Key Terms Review

A. Acceptance test

B. Exploratory testing

C. Increment

D. Integration test

E. Iteration burn-down chart

F. Pair programming

G. Regression test

H. Unit test

Match each of the key terms with the definition that best fits it.

1. An approach to increasing the quality of the code that uses two programmers working together, with one doing the actual coding work and the other one reviewing the code as it is being created.

2. Chart used to display the development team's progress during an iteration.

3. Test focused on assessing whether a new feature correctly addresses the associated user story.

4. Test used to inspect the functionality of single methods or classes.

5. Test used to verify that a bug has indeed been fixed, that revised code does not contain any new bugs, or that new or revised code does not break any existing functionality.

6. Test used to verify whether new code works together with already completed code.

7. Testing used to find unknown problems by using the system in an unscripted fashion.

8. The combination of the product backlog items completed during the current iteration and the product backlog items completed during all previous iterations.

Review Questions

1. Compare and contrast iterations and increments.

2. What is the difference between a burn-down and a burn-up chart?

3. What are the key benefits of pair programming?

4. Why is frequent integration an important aspect of agile projects?

5. What is the difference between unit testing and integration testing?

Chapter Exercises

1. In a team of three to five people, come up with a new app idea and develop five to seven user stories. Now discuss what "done" means and develop a "definition of done."

2. Compare and contrast the role of the business user in projects using agile and traditional approaches.

3. Interview an agile project manager about her experiences with pair programming. What were the biggest issues in implementing pair programming? How did she overcome these issues?

4. Search the web for software build tools. What functionalities do these tools offer? How can they help improve the quality of agile projects?

5. Develop acceptance tests for the user stories developed in Exercise 1.

References

Hayes, W. (2014, September 22). Agile Metrics: Seven Categories. *Carnegie Mellon Software Engineering Institute.* Retrieved June 27, 2018, from https://insights.sei.cmu.edu/sei_blog/2014/09/agile-metrics-seven-categories .html

Nee, N. Y. (2010). Metrics for Agile Projects: Finding the Right Tools for the Job. Paper presented at PMI Global Congress 2010—North America, Washington, DC. Newton Square, PA: Project Management Institute. Retrieved June 27, 2018, from https://www.pmi.org/learning/library/agile-metrics-progress-tracking-status-6564

Pavlichenko, I. (2017, June 5). Sprint Review: Much More Than Just a Demo. *Scrum.org*. Retrieved June 22, 2018, from https://www.scrum.org/resources/blog/sprint-review-much-more-just-demo

Project Management Institute (2017). *Agile Practice Guide*. Newton Square, PA: Author.

Project Management Institute (2017). *PMBOK: A Guide to the Project Management Body of Knowledge* (6th ed.). Newton Square, PA: Author.

Thomas, S. (2008, June 17). Agile Project Execution. *It's a Delivery Thing*. Retrieved June 22, 2018, from http://itsadeliverything.com/agile-project-execution

Index